T0212345

Lecture Notes in Artificial Intelligence 11156

Subseries of Lecture Notes in Computer Science

More information about this series at http://www.springer.com/series/1244

Michael T. Cox · Peter Funk
Shahina Begum (Eds.)

Case-Based Reasoning Research and Development

26th International Conference, ICCBR 2018
Stockholm, Sweden, July 9–12, 2018
Proceedings

 Springer

Editors
Michael T. Cox
Wright State University
Dayton, OH, USA

Shahina Begum ⓘ
Mälardalen University
Västeras, Sweden

Peter Funk ⓘ
Mälardalen University
Västeras, Sweden

ISSN 0302-9743   ISSN 1611-3349   (electronic)
Lecture Notes in Artificial Intelligence
ISBN 978-3-030-01080-5   ISBN 978-3-030-01081-2   (eBook)
https://doi.org/10.1007/978-3-030-01081-2

Library of Congress Control Number: 2018955569

LNCS Sublibrary: SL7 – Artificial Intelligence

This Springer imprint is published by the registered company Springer Nature Switzerland AG
The registered company address is: Gewerbestrasse 11, 6330 Cham, Switzerland

Preface

Inside this manuscript, you will discover the scientific papers from the 26th International Conference on Case-Based Reasoning (ICCBR 2018). The conference took place during July 9–12, in Stockholm, Sweden. The ICCBR conference is the premier annual meeting of the case-based reasoning (CBR) research community. The theme of ICCBR 2018 was "The Future of CBR" and was highlighted by several activities, including a lively panel discussion of the same moniker.

ICCBR 2018 was held at the beautiful Stockholmsmässan Conference Center in Stockholm, and it was co-located with the 27th International Joint Conference on Artificial Intelligence (IJCAI) and the 23rd European Conference on Artificial Intelligence (ECAI). Along with the other Federated AI Meeting (FAIM) conferences (i.e., AAMAS, ICML, and SoCS), immediately preceding IJCAI-ECAI-18, the ICCBR conference started with a day-long social gathering (Monday), followed by a workshop day and doctoral consortium (Tuesday), and concluded with two days (Wednesday and Thursday) of major technical presentations and invited talks.

Tuesday included a lively panel discussion focused on the conference theme. Moderated by Peter Funk (Mälardalen University, Sweden), the discussants (Kerstin Bach - NTNU, Norway; David Leake - Indiana University, USA; Antonio Sánchez Ruiz-Granados - Universidad Complutense de Madrid, Spain; Rosina Weber - Drexel, USA; and Nirmalie Wiratunga - Robert Gordon University, UK) explored the future of CBR and the vision it represents. In addition to the panel, the day included workshops, a doctoral consortium for senior PhD students in the community, and ICCBR's second video competition. The themes of the six workshops were "Case-Based Reasoning and the Explanation of Intelligent Systems," "Synergies Between CBR and Machine Learning," "Computation and CBR," "CBR and Deep Learning," "Knowledge-Based Systems in Computational Design and Media," and "Reasoning About Time and CBR." We thank the chairs of these workshops for their persistence, the hard work that produced the results, and their willingness to examine new topics related to the CBR field of artificial intelligence.

Both Wednesday and Thursday began with a plenary address by noted researchers. Professor Hector Munoz-Avila (Lehigh University, USA) described recent advances in CBR and a new area of research called goal-driven autonomy. Professor Barry Smyth (University College, Ireland) talked about how CBR is used in recommender systems to promote positive choices that bear on physical fitness. These proceedings contain a full-length invited paper for the first and an abstract of the second presentation.

During these two days, 39 papers were also presented as plenary oral or poster presentations; they were selected among 77 submissions. Included in the proceedings, these papers address many themes related to the theory and application of CBR and its future direction. Topics included multiple papers on textual CBR and a number of cognitive and human-oriented papers as well as hybrid research between CBR and machine learning.

Taking a cue from last year's invited talk on analogical reasoning by Henri Prade, the main technical presentations on Wednesday included a Special Track on Computational Analogy. Although a first for ICCBR, the idea of a special track for the conference is not new in the community; it represents an analogical adaptation of the 18 year string of CBR special tracks at FLAIRS (the yearly conference of the Florida Artificial Intelligence Research Society). Analogy and CBR are closely related research areas. Both employ prior cases to reason in complex situations with incomplete information. Organized by Irina Rabkina (Northwestern University, USA), Pierre-Alexandre Murena (Telecom ParisTech, France), and Fadi Badra (Université Paris, France), four technical papers had oral presentations in the special track, and four analogy posters received acceptance. In future years, we hope the special track concept enables us to publish maturing work that first appears in a workshop format or otherwise grow the community and its outreach.

Here we wish to acknowledge the essential support of the many people who were crucial to organizing ICCBR 2018. First, Mobyen Uddin Ahmed (Mälardalen University, Sweden) did a wonderful job arranging the many details as local chair. Second, Dustin Dannenhauer (Naval Research Lab, USA) performed the difficult task of publicity chair. Along with Mobyen Ahmed and Shamsul Alam (both of Mälardalen), Dustin managed the development and maintenance of the conference website and social media connections. Mirjam Minor (Goethe University, Germany) managed all six workshops, from the call for workshop proposals to their organization at the conference and the separate proceedings. Cindy Marling (Ohio University, USA) and Antonio A. Sánchez Ruiz Granados (Universidad Complutense de Madrid, Spain) were in charge of the doctoral consortium, an event that is critical to the future of CBR research and in line with this year's conference theme. Nirmalie Wiratunga (Robert Gordon) served as sponsorship chair, significantly increasing financial sponsorships. Finally, Michael Floyd (Knexus Research, USA) and Brian Schack (Indiana University, USA) organized the Video Competition (the second of a new ICCBR tradition).

We are also grateful to the members of the Advisory Committee, who provided invaluable guidance when called upon, and to the members of the ICCBR Program Committee (and additional reviewers), who carefully reviewed the paper submissions. We also give thanks to the local support group at Mälardalen University (Sweden) and students from Wright State University (USA) for their volunteer work before, during, and after the conference. Additionally, we would like to thank all the authors who submitted the interesting and technically detailed papers you see herein and therefore contributed to its success, as well as the conference attendees, who made these days memorable for everyone.

Most importantly, we are very grateful for the support of our many sponsors, including the National Science Foundation, Smart Information Flow Technologies, the journal *Artificial Intelligence*, Brains4AI, British Telecon, Knexus Research, Springer, and the Telenor-NTNU AI Laboratory. Given the extra expenses this year associated with a large commercial conference center, these sponsors made the difference between fiscal success and a financial deficit.

Finally, it was indeed a splendid experience to be in Stockholm. The last time IJCAI was in Stockholm, CBR had a significant presence. IJCAI 1999 had two sessions on CBR, an applications session where a CBR paper won distinguished paper award, and a day-long workshop entitled "Automating the Construction of Case-Based Reasoners." This year, ICCBR brought the CBR community to Stockholm as an equal partner with IJCAI and all of the other FAIM conferences. Who know what the lies open to us in the future? To be part of this future, be sure to attend ICCBR 2019 in Otzenhausen, Germany, and keep an eye on http://www.iccbr.org.

July 2018

Michael T. Cox
Peter Funk
Shahina Begum

Organization

Program Committee

Mobyen Uddin Ahmed	Mälardalen University, Sweden
Kerstin Bach	Norwegian University of Science and Technology, Norway
Fadi Badra	Université Paris 13, France
Shahina Begum	Mälardalen University, Sweden
Ralph Bergmann	University of Trier, Germany
Tarek Richard Besold	City, University of London, UK
Isabelle Bichindaritz	State University of New York at Oswego, USA
Derek Bridge	University College Cork, Ireland
Hernan Casakin	Ariel University, Israel
Sutanu Chakraborti	Indian Institute of Technology Madras, India
Alexandra Coman	Capital One
Antoine Cornuéjols	AgroParisTech, France
Michael Cox	Wright State Research Institute, USA
Dustin Dannenhauer	Naval Research Laboratory
Sarah Jane Delany	Dublin Institute of Technology, Ireland
Jean-Louis Dessalles	Telecom ParisTech, France
Belen Diaz-Agudo	Universidad Complutense de Madrid, Spain
Odd Erik	Norwegian University of Science and Technology, Norway
Thomas Eskridge	Florida Institute of Technology, USA
Mark Finlayson	Florida International University, USA
Tesca Fitzgerald	Georgia Institute of Technology, USA
Michael Floyd	Knexus Research
Kenneth Forbus	Northwestern University
Scott Friedman	SIFT
Peter Funk	Mälardalen University, Sweden
Ashok Goel	Georgia Institute of Technology, USA
Pedro González Calero	Universidad Politécnica de Madrid, Spain
Vahid Jalali	Indiana University Bloomington, USA
Stelios Kapetanakis	University of Brighton, UK
Mark Keane	UCD Dublin, Ireland
Joseph Kendall-Morwick	University of Central Missouri, USA
Kai-Uwe Kuehnberger	University of Osnabrück, Institute of Cognitive Science, Germany
Luc Lamontagne	Laval University, Canada
Philippe Langlais	University of Montreal, Canada
David Leake	Indiana University Bloomington, USA

Yves Lepage	Waseda University, Japan
Jean Lieber	LORIA, Inria Lorraine, France
Ramon Lopez De Mantaras	IIIA - CSIC
Abhijit Mahabal	Google
Cindy Marling	Ohio University, USA
Stewart Massie	Robert Gordon University, UK
Clifton McFate	QRG
Mirjam Minor	Goethe University Frankfurt, Germany
Stefania Montani	University of Piemonte Orientale, Italy
Hector Munoz-Avila	Lehigh University, USA
Pierre-Alexandre Murena	Telecom ParisTech, France
Emmanuel Nauer	LORIA, France
Santiago Ontañón	Drexel University, USA
Miltos Petridis	Middlesex University London, UK
Marc Pickett	Google
Enric Plaza	IIIA-CSIC
Luigi Portinale	University of Piemonte Orientale, Italy
Irina Rabkina	Northwestern University
Juan Recio-Garcia	Universidad Complutense de Madrid, Spain
Gilles Richard	IRIT Toulouse, France
Jonathan Rubin	PARC, A Xerox Company
Ute Schmid	University of Bamberg, Germany
Steven Schockaert	Cardiff University, UK
Barry Smyth	University College Dublin, Ireland
Frode Soermo	Verdande Technology
Antonio A. Sánchez-Ruiz	Universidad Politécnica de Madrid, Spain
Ian Watson	University of Auckland, New Zealand
Rosina Weber	Drexel University, USA
David Wilson	UNC Charlotte, USA
Nirmalie Wiratunga	Robert Gordon University, UK

Additional Reviewers

Ahmed, Mobyen Uddin	Kübler, Eric
Eyorokon, Vahid	Martin, Kyle
Fitzgerald, Tesca	Mathew, Ditty
Funk, Peter	Rugaber, Spencer
Grumbach, Lisa	Wijekoon, Anjana
Herold, Miriam	Zeyen, Christian
Klein, Patrick	

Contents

Special Track: Computational Analogy

Invited Paper

Adaptive Goal Driven Autonomy

Héctor Muñoz-Avila[(⊠)]

Computer Science and Engineering, Lehigh University, 19 Memorial Drive West,
Bethlehem, PA 18015-3084, USA
munoz@cse.lehigh.edu

Abstract. Goal-driven autonomy (GDA) is a reflective model of goal
reasoning combining deliberative planning and plan execution monitoring. GDA's is the focus of increasing interest due in part to the need to
ensure that autonomous agents behave as intended. However, to perform
well, comprehensive GDA agents require substantial domain knowledge.
In this paper I focus on our work to automatically learn knowledge used
by GDA agents. I also discuss future research directions.

1 Introduction

Goal-driven autonomy (GDA) is a reflective model of goal reasoning combining
deliberative planning and plan execution monitoring. The key aspect of GDA
is the intermix between the agent's observations (e.g., from sensors), goal reasoning, including formulating new goals, and acting according to the goals it is
pursuing. GDA is related to fields such as the actor's view of planning [15] (i.e.,
a framework for interleaving planning and execution), online planning [20] (i.e.,
refining a planning solution while executing it in the environment), cognitive
systems [21] (e.g., agents endowed with self-reflection capabilities) and general
agency [4]. The key distinctive feature of goal reasoning agents is their capability
to adjust their goals, including changing their goals altogether while acting in an
environment. This in contrast to approaches such as replanning [14,36] where
the plan generated is modified due to changes in the environment while still
aiming to achieve the same goals. For example, in [26], we use guiding principles
we called motivators to select which goals to achieve. As indicated in [2], there
is an increasing interest in goal reasoning, in part, because of applications such
as UUVs' control [29], air combat [13] and disaster response [33].

To perform well, comprehensive GDA agents require substantial domain
knowledge to determine expected states [24], identify and explain discrepancies
[22], formulate new goals [39], and manage pending goals [37]. This requires, for
example, the agent's programmers to anticipate what discrepancies can occur,
identify what goals can be formulated, and define their relative priority.

In this paper, I will focus on our work to automatically learn knowledge used
by GDA agents performed over the past years. This includes:

This work is supported in part under ONR N00014-18-1-2009 and NSF 1217888.

© Springer Nature Switzerland AG 2018
M. T. Cox et al. (Eds.): ICCBR 2018, LNAI 11156, pp. 3–12, 2018.
https://doi.org/10.1007/978-3-030-01081-2_1

- Using reinforcement Learning to acquire planning, explanation and goal formulation knowledge (Sect. 3).
- Using case-based reasoning techniques for learning expectations, and goals (Sect. 4).
- Formulating a taxonomy of automatically generated expectations using learned hierarchical task network representations (Sect. 5).

In Sect. 6, I will discuss ongoing research directions including computing expectations beyond a linear sequence of actions.

2   The Goal Driven Autonomy Model

GDA agents generate a plan π achieving some goals g using a planning domain Σ [5,24,25] (see Fig. 1). They continually monitor the environment to check if the agent's own expectations x are met in the state s. When a discrepancy D is found between the agent's expectations X and the environment s, the agent

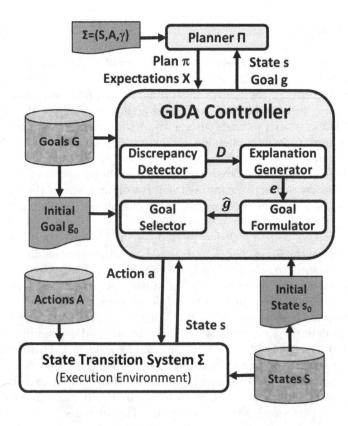

Fig. 1. The goal-driven autonomy model [24,25]

generate a plausible explanation e for d; as a result of this explanation, a new goal $\hat{g}$ is generated, thereby restarting the cycle with $g = \hat{g}$.

If A denotes all actions in the domain and S denotes all states, the following are the knowledge artifacts needed by GDA agents:

- Σ, which contains a function $\gamma : S \times A \to S$, indicating for each action $a \in A$, and every state $s \in S$, what is the resulting state $\gamma(s)$ when applying a in s.
- Π, a planning system. In addition to Σ, it may include additional knowledge to generate plans such as HTN planning knowledge.
- G, the collection of all goals that can be pursued by the agents.
- Given an action a in a plan π, what are the expectations of when executing a. This is dependent on where a occurs in π as well as the initial state from which π started its execution.
- The explanation knowledge. For example, explanation knowledge may consist of a collection of rules of the form $D \to e$, indicating for a discrepancy D what is its explanation e.
- Goal formulation knowledge. For example, goal formulation knowledge may consist of a collection of rules of the form $e \to \tilde{g}$, indicating for each explanation, what is the next goal to achieve.
- Goal selection knowledge. In its most simple form it always selects to last goal generated by Goal Formulator (i.e., $g = \tilde{g}$).

3 Learning Plan, Explanation and Goal Formulation Knowledge with Reinforcement Learning

We explored the use of reinforcement learning (RL) techniques [35] to learn planning knowledge for GDA. The assumptions are that the agent knows the plausible actions $A_s \subset A$ that can be taken in an state $s \in S$. But the problem is that the agent doesn't know, among those actions in A_s, which is the best or even a good action to take. Typical of RL, the agent aims at learning the value of each action $a \in A_s$ in such a way that it maximizes its rewards. The result of RL's learning process is a policy $\pi : S \to A$, indicating for every state, which action $\pi(s)$ to take [17].

We also took advantage of RL's capabilities to both select plausible explanations for a discrepancy [12] and to select possible goals for a given explanation [18]. In both cases we formulate the selection problem as a Markov Decision Problem (see Table 1). The aim is to choose the best explanation among the possible discrepancies. Thus we view each discrepancy as an state and each explanation as an action. All other aspects of the GDA process being equal, if the overall performance of the GDA agent improves, we will assign a positive reward to the explanation selected and a negative reward otherwise. This means that the agent could consider multiple plausible explanations for the same discrepancy and over time it learns the value of each explanation (i.e., higher value means more plausible explanation).

We did a similar approach to learn goal selection knowledge but this time modeling the possible explanations as the states and the choice of a goal as the

Table 1. Modeling explanation selection and goal formulation as an MDP

MDP	Actions	States
Explanation generation	All possible explanations	All possible discrepancies
Goal formulation	All possible goals	All possible explanations

action. These were separate works and we never tried to simultaneously learn explanation selection and goal formulation knowledge. We will retake this point in the future work section.

We tested our approach in adversarial games. Specifically real-time strategy (RTS) games. In these games players control armies to defeat an opponent. These games add elements that make game playing challenging: armies consists of different types of units. The outcome of unit versus unit combat follows a paper-rock-scissors design: archers can easily defeat gryphons but are themselves easily defeated by knights. In turn knights can be easily defeated by gryphons. Thus, the best players are those who maintain a well balanced army and know how to manage it during battle. Another aspect that makes RTS games even more challenging is the fact that players make their moves synchronously thereby rewarding players that can make decisions quickly.

In our experiments [12,17,18], the GDA agent is controlling a player that is competing against various opponents, one at the time in each game instance. These opponents used a variety of hard coded strategies. For testing we did the typical leave-one-out strategy: given N opponents, the GDA agent trained by playing against $N - 1$ opponents and was tested against the remaining opponent not used in training. The results were compelling showing a significant improvement by the learning GDA agent. The reward function was the difference in score between the GDA player and its opponent. Thus, a positive score means the GDA is defeating the opponent whereas a negative reward indicates that the opponent is winning.

4 Learning Expectations and Goals with Case-Based Reasoning

Case-based reasoning (CBR) is a problem solving method in which cases, instances of previous problem-solving episodes, are reused to solve new problems [1]. One of the situations when it is desirable to use CBR is when there are gaps in the knowledge preventing the formulation of a complete theory, one that can be reasoned by using first-principles. This is precisely the situation we encountered when computing the expectations after taking an action a in state s, the agent does not have any knowledge about the expected state. Furthermore, since the gaming domains are nondeterministic, meaning that after applying an action a to an state s there could be many possible resulting states a_s and the agent initially does not know which are those states and the probability that anyone of them will be reached after applying action a in s. To solve this problem we created a case base, CB_X of expectations [18]:

$$CB_X : S \times A \rightarrow 2^{S \times [0,1]}$$

This case base maps for each state-action pair (s, a) a probability distribution of pairs (q, p) indicating the probability p of reaching state q. In a typical CBR manner, each time the controller selects an action a from state s (i.e., as indicated by a policy π as described in the previous section), then one of the following two steps is performed:

- If q was never reached before when action a was selected from state s, then (q, p) is stored in the CB_X with $p = 1/N_{(s,a)}$, where $N_{(s,a)}$ is the number of times a has been selected when reaching state s.
- If q has been selected $N_{(s,a,q)}$ times then the value of p is updated to $p = (N_{(s,a,q)} + 1)/N_{(s,a)}$.

CBR is also used to learn to associate a goal state s_π to a policy π [18,19]. Following a policy from an starting state s_0 produces an execution trace $s_0 \, \pi(s_0) \, \cdots \, \pi(s_n) \, s_{n+1}$. If an state q appears with at least some predefined frequency f on the last k steps in the trace then q is assigned to be the goal of the policy (f and k are parameters set by the user). Otherwise s_{n+1} is assigned to be the goal. Since different chains may be generated for the same initial state and policy, we keep a probability distribution of goals akin to the way we kept a provability distribution of expectations described before. Although we only annotate the policy with the goal having the highest probability.

The goals are used as described in the previous section in the goal formulation procedure. When a goal g_π is selected, its associated policy π is executed. Since our agents perform on-line learning, π changes over time, which may result in g_π itself changing.

5   A Taxonomy of Expectations with HTN Planning

For this research thrust, we leverage on our previous work for automatically learning hierarchical task networks (HTN) [16,40]. The learning problem can be succinctly described as follows: given a collection of plans generated by some (possibly unknown) agent and a collection of tasks T, learn HTN planning knowledge in a manner that is consistent with the given collection of plans. The learned HTN indicate how to decompose a task $t \in T$ into subtasks $t_1 \, \cdots \, t_m$ in T and the applicability conditions (i.e., the preconditions) under which this task decomposition, $t \rightarrow t_1 \, \cdots \, t_m$, is valid. The learned HTNs can be used by the HTN planner SHOP [27] to generate plans. That is, we set $\Pi = SHOP$ and π is an HTN plan.

Under the premise of using HTN planning for plan generation, we examine the notion of expectations for GDA agents. Expectations play an important role in the performance of GDA agents [8]: if the expectations are too general,

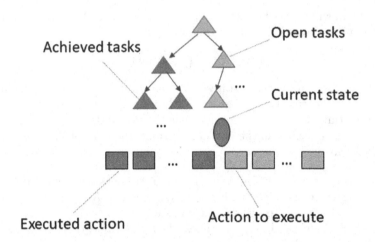

Fig. 2. Generic HTN; actions are divided between those already executed and those to execute; analogously, tasks are divided between those accomplished and those that remain open

many unnecessary discrepancies will be found triggering unnecessary and possible detrimental GDA process. An example of a detrimental situation is the following: suppose in an RTS game that the GDA is very close to destroying an opponent's town hall, thereby defeating the opponent. Suppose that at the same time the player unexpectedly detects a large opponent's force poised to take over the player's resource gathering operation (resources are needed to increase a player's army). This discrepancy may trigger a new goal to defend the resource gathering operation, which in turn may deviate part of the army from attacking the town hall and miss the chance of winning the game. If the expectations are too narrow, discrepancies can be missed in situations were formulating a goal would have been beneficial.

We studied the problem of eliciting expectations from plans [9] and from HTN plans [8]. The basic premise is to divide the plan into two portions: the actions already executed and the actions that remain to execute Fig. 2. SHOP propagates forward the state and the next action to execute is checked against the current state. Correspondingly, the task hierarchy can be divided between those tasks that have been achieved because their underlying portion of the plan is executed and those that are open (i.e., remain to be achieved) because some of its underlying actions have not been achieved.

We explored 5 forms of expectations used in by GDA agents and more generally in goal reasoning agents:

- **None.** It checks the preconditions of the next action to execute. That is, if the preconditions are applicable in the current state. This is useful, for example, in the early stages of an RTS game when the player is focusing on building its own economy. It typically focus on a predefined plan (this is called the build order [28]). As soon as the preconditions of the next action become applicable, it executes it. For example, building a peasant requires a certain amount of gold; the player needs to wait until that amount is reached before actually proceeding to build the peasant. All the following expectations check the preconditions of the next action plus some additional conditions.

- **Immediate.** It checks if the effects of the last executed action has been completed. This can be useful in highly reactive environments such as first-person shooter games were for example the agent is checking if after jumping it reaches the targeted platform.
- **State.** This is the most common form of expectations used in GDA. The agent checks if the conditions in the state obtained by projecting from the starting state after each action executed so far match the observations in the environment. This is a natural way for GDA agent using a variety of conditions in the state including symbolic [25], ontological [6] and numerical [38]. It ensures that the part of the plan that remains to be executed, it is still executable from the current state.
- **Informed.** This is a form we created [9]. Instead of projecting the whole state, it projects only the accumulated effects from the actions executed so far. The basic idea is that only the accumulated effects are the necessary conditions that should be checked against the actual state. There might be observations in the actual state that do not match the projected state, but if those observations are not propagated conditions, there is no need to trigger the GDA process. For example, if in an RTS game, the plan π calls for taking a resource area in the center of the map, and while executing this plan it detects some neutral units in a nearby location that pose no threat to the plan, they can simply ignore them, without triggering an unnecessary GDA cycle. In contrast, state expectations will trigger an iteration of the GDA cycle every time any observation doesn't match the expected state.
- **informed-k.** Informed-k expectations are informed expectations that are checked every k steps, where k is an input parameter to the agent. These expectations were created for situations when there are costs associated with sensing if a condition in the expectations matches an actual observation in the state [7]. For example, a vehicle might need to stop to turn the sensors, in which case the cost can be measured in terms of the time it needs to remain immobile.

Various experiments were made using variations of benchmark domains from the literature such as the Mudworld [23] and the Arsonist [30] domains. In these experiments all other components of the GDA agent were the same and the only change was the type of expectations they were computing [7–9]. The following observations were made: none and immediate expectations had no or very low sensing costs but GDA agents frequently failed to achieve the goals it expected to have achieved. GDA agents using state expectations achieved all goals that the agent expected to achieve but had the highest sensing costs compared to agents using other forms of expectations. Using informed expectations also achieve all goals but at a much lower costs than when using state expectations. Depending on the parameter k, Informed-k expectations also achieved all goals while having the lowest cost.

6   Current and Future Research Directions

We are currently exploring a variety of directions. First, existing work on expectations (ours and others) assume the plan π as a sequence of actions (possibly augmented with a hierarchy of tasks). When the solution π is a policy, existing research is looking at the execution trace from following the policy [17]; that is, a sequence of actions. We are currently exploring goal regression for policies, which unlike for the case of sequences of actions, cannot guarantee the minimal set of necessary conditions as opposed to the deterministic case [32]. We are exploring combining informed and goal regression expectations for the non-deterministic case [31].

Second, we also will like to explore the definitions of different forms of expectations for domains that include a combination of numeric and symbolic variables and outcomes are dictated by (a possible unknown) probability distribution. This includes situations when, for example, the agent's gasoline consumption is determined using a probability distribution while at the same time it is ascertaining if a message was sent or not.

Third, we will like to explore the interaction between the different components of the GDA process. For example, how the learned planning knowledge affects the expectations; in turn how discrepancies generated as a result of expectations elicited in this particular way affect the kinds of explanations generated and how this in turn determine the goals formulated. For this purpose we need a common plan representation formalism. We recently adopted the hierarchical goal networks (HGNs) formalism [34] instead of hierarchical task networks (HTN) for the planning formalism used by the planner Π. Unlike HTNs, HGNs represent goals, not tasks, at all echelons of the hierarchy. This has been shown to be useful to learn the hierarchies [3]; it also been shown to be particularly suitable for execution monitoring [10,11] as the agent can determine directly if a goal is achieved; unlike tasks in HTNs that do not have explicit semantics. In HTNs, the only way to fulfill tasks is by executing the underlying plan generated from the HTN planning process. HGNs have the same expressiveness as total-oder HTN planning [34].

Acknowledgements. This research is supported by ONR under grant N00014-18-1-2009 and by NSF under grant 1217888. No work of this scope can be done by a single person; I will like to thank the following external collaborators: David W. Aha and David Wilson (Naval Research Laboratory), Michael T. Cox and Matthew Molineaux (Wright State University); I will also like to thank the following (current and former) students: Dustin Dannenhauer, Chad Hogg, Sriram Gopalakrishnan, Morgan Fine-Morris, Noah Reifsnyder and Ulit Jaidee.

References

1. Aamodt, A., Plaza, E.: Case-based reasoning: foundational issues, methodological variations, and system approaches. AI Commun. **7**(1), 39–59 (1994)
2. Aha, D.W.: Goal reasoning: foundations emerging applications and prospects. AI Mag. Under review (2018)
3. Choi, D., Langley, P.: Learning teleoreactive logic programs from problem solving. In: Kramer, S., Pfahringer, B. (eds.) ILP 2005. LNCS (LNAI), vol. 3625, pp. 51–68. Springer, Heidelberg (2005). https://doi.org/10.1007/11536314_4
4. Coddington, A.M., Luck, M.: A motivation-based planning and execution framework. Int. J. Artif. Intell. Tools **13**(01), 5–25 (2004)
5. Cox, M.T.: Perpetual self-aware cognitive agents. AI Mag. **28**(1), 32 (2007)
6. Dannenhauer, D., Munoz-Avila, H.: LUIGi: a goal-driven autonomy agent reasoning with ontologies. In: Advances in Cognitive Systems (ACS 2013) (2013)
7. Dannenhauer, D.: Self monitoring goal driven autonomy agents. Ph.D. thesis, Lehigh University (2017)
8. Dannenhauer, D., Munoz-Avila, H.: Raising expectations in GDA agents acting in dynamic environments. In: IJCAI, pp. 2241–2247 (2015)
9. Dannenhauer, D., Munoz-Avila, H., Cox, M.T.: Informed expectations to guide GDA agents in partially observable environments. In: IJCAI, pp. 2493–2499 (2016)
10. Dvorak, D.D., Ingham, M.D., Morris, J.R., Gersh, J.: Goal-based operations: an overview. JACIC **6**(3), 123–141 (2009)
11. Dvorak, D.L., Amador, A.V., Starbird, T.W.: Comparison of goal-based operations and command sequencing. In: Proceedings of the 10th International Conference on Space Operations (2008)
12. Finestrali, G., Muñoz-Avila, H.: Case-based learning of applicability conditions for stochastic explanations. In: Delany, S.J., Ontañón, S. (eds.) ICCBR 2013. LNCS (LNAI), vol. 7969, pp. 89–103. Springer, Heidelberg (2013). https://doi.org/10.1007/978-3-642-39056-2_7
13. Floyd, M.W., Karneeb, J., Aha, D.W.: Case-based team recognition using learned opponent models. In: Aha, D.W., Lieber, J. (eds.) ICCBR 2017. LNCS (LNAI), vol. 10339, pp. 123–138. Springer, Cham (2017). https://doi.org/10.1007/978-3-319-61030-6_9
14. Fox, M., Gerevini, A., Long, D., Serina, I.: Plan stability: replanning versus plan repair. In: ICAPS, vol. 6, pp. 212–221 (2006)
15. Ghallab, M., Nau, D., Traverso, P.: The actor's view of automated planning and acting: a position paper. Artif. Intell. **208**, 1–17 (2014)
16. Hogg, C., Muñoz-Avila, H., Kuter, U.: HTN-MAKER: learning HTNs with minimal additional knowledge engineering required. In: Conference on Artificial Intelligence (AAAI), pp. 950–956. AAAI Press (2008)
17. Jaidee, U., Muñoz-Avila, H., Aha, D.W.: Learning and reusing goal-specific policies for goal-driven autonomy. In: Agudo, B.D., Watson, I. (eds.) ICCBR 2012. LNCS (LNAI), vol. 7466, pp. 182–195. Springer, Heidelberg (2012). https://doi.org/10.1007/978-3-642-32986-9_15
18. Jaidee, U., Muñoz-Avila, H., Aha, D.W.: Integrated learning for goal-driven autonomy. In: Proceedings of the Twenty-Second International Joint Conference on Artificial Intelligence-Volume Volume Three, pp. 2450–2455. AAAI Press (2011)
19. Jaidee, U., Muñoz-Avila, H., Aha, D.W.: Case-based goal-driven coordination of multiple learning agents. In: Delany, S.J., Ontañón, S. (eds.) ICCBR 2013. LNCS (LNAI), vol. 7969, pp. 164–178. Springer, Heidelberg (2013). https://doi.org/10.1007/978-3-642-39056-2_12

20. Keller, T., Eyerich, P.: PROST: probabilistic planning based on UCT. In: ICAPS (2012)
21. Langley, P.: The cognitive systems paradigm. Adv. Cogn. Syst. **1**, 3–13 (2012)
22. Molineaux, M.: Understanding What May Have Happened in Dynamic, Partially Observable Environments. Ph.D. thesis, George Mason University (2017)
23. Molineaux, M., Aha, D.W.: Learning unknown event models. In: AAAI, pp. 395–401 (2014)
24. Molineaux, M., Klenk, M., Aha, D.W.: Goal-driven autonomy in a navy strategy simulation. In: AAAI (2010)
25. Muñoz-Avila, H., Jaidee, U., Aha, D.W., Carter, E.: Goal-driven autonomy with case-based reasoning. In: Bichindaritz, I., Montani, S. (eds.) ICCBR 2010. LNCS (LNAI), vol. 6176, pp. 228–241. Springer, Heidelberg (2010). https://doi.org/10.1007/978-3-642-14274-1_18
26. Muñoz-Avila, H., Wilson, M.A., Aha, D.W.: Guiding the ass with goal motivation weights. In: Goal Reasoning: Papers from the ACS Workshop, pp. 133–145 (2015)
27. Nau, D.S., Cao, Y., Lotem, A., Muñoz-Avila, H.: SHOP: simple hierarchical ordered planner. In: Dean, T. (ed.) International Joint Conference on Artificial Intelligence (IJCAI), pp. 968–973. Morgan Kaufmann, August 1999
28. Ontanón, S., Synnaeve, G., Uriarte, A., Richoux, F., Churchill, D., Preuss, M.: A survey of real-time strategy game ai research and competition in starcraft. IEEE Trans. Comput. Intell. AI Games **5**(4), 293–311 (2013)
29. Oxenham, M., Green, R.: From direct tasking to goal-driven autonomy for autonomous underwater vehicles. In: 5th Goal Reasoning Workshop at IJCAI 2017 (2017)
30. Paisner, M., Maynord, M., Cox, M.T., Perlis, D.: Goal-driven autonomy in dynamic environments. In: Goal Reasoning: Papers from the ACS Workshop, p. 79 (2013)
31. Reifsnyder, N., Munoz-Avila, H.: Goal reasoning with goldilocks and regression expectations in nondeterministic domains. In: 6th Goal Reasoning Workshop at IJCAI/FAIM 2018 (2018)
32. Reiter, R.: The frame problem in the situation calculus: a simple solution (sometimes) and a completeness result for goal regression. In: Lifschitz, V. (ed.) Artificial Intelligence and Mathematical Theory of Computation: Papers in Honor of John McCarthy, (Ed.). Academic Press (1991)
33. Roberts, M., et al.: Goal reasoning to coordinate robotic teams for disaster relief. In: Proceedings of ICAPS-15 PlanRob Workshop, pp. 127–138. Citeseer (2015)
34. Shivashankar, V.: Hierarchical Goal Network Planning: Formalisms and Algorithms for Planning and Acting. Ph.D. thesis, Department of Computer Science, University of Maryland (2015)
35. Sutton, R.S., Barto, A.G.: Reinforcement Learning: An Introduction. MIT Press, Cambridge (1998)
36. Warfield, I., Hogg, C., Lee-Urban, S., Munoz-Avila, H.: Adaptation of hierarchical task network plans. In: FLAIRS Conference, pp. 429–434 (2007)
37. Weber, B.G., Mateas, M., Jhala, A.: Applying goal-driven autonomy to starcraft. In: AIIDE (2010)
38. Wilson, M.A., McMahon, J., Aha, D.W.: Bounded expectations for discrepancy detection in goal-driven autonomy. In: AI and Robotics: Papers from the AAAI Workshop (2014)
39. Wilson, M.A., Molineaux, M., Aha, D.W.: Domain-independent heuristics for goal formulation. In: FLAIRS Conference (2013)
40. Zhuo, H.H., Muñoz-Avila, H., Yang, Q.: Learning hierarchical task network domains from partially observed plan traces. Artif. Intell. **212**, 134–157 (2014)

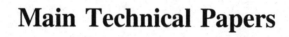

Main Technical Papers

Answering with Cases: A CBR Approach to Deep Learning

Kareem Amin[1,3]([✉]), Stelios Kapetanakis[4,5], Klaus-Dieter Althoff[1,2], Andreas Dengel[1,3], and Miltos Petridis[6]

[1] German Research Center for Artificial Intelligence, Smart Data and Knowledge Services, Trippstadter Strae 122, 67663 Kaiserslautern, Germany
{kareem.amin,klaus-dieter.althoff,andreas.dengel}@dfki.uni-kl.de
[2] Institute of Computer Science, Intelligent Information Systems Lab, University of Hildesheim, Hildesheim, Germany
[3] Kaiserslautern University, P.O. Box 3049, 67663 Kaiserslautern, Germany
[4] School of Computing Engineering and Mathematics, University of Brighton, Brighton, UK
s.kapetanakis@brighton.ac.uk
[5] Gluru Research, Gluru, London, UK
stelios@gluru.co
[6] Department of Computing, University of Middlesex, London, UK
m.petridis@mdx.ac.uk

Abstract. Every year tenths of thousands of customer support engineers around the world deal with, and proactively solve, complex help-desk tickets. Daily, almost every customer support expert will turn his/her attention to a prioritization strategy, to achieve the best possible result. To assist with this, in this paper we describe a novel case-based reasoning application to address the tasks of: high solution accuracy and shorter prediction resolution time. We describe how appropriate cases can be generated to assist engineers and how our solution can scale over time to produce domain-specific reusable cases for similar problems. Our work is evaluated using data from 5000 cases from the automotive industry.

Keywords: Case-based reasoning · Deep learning
Natural language processing

1 Introduction

Effective Customer Support can be a challenge. Both for a company and for a trained system engineer it depends on endless hours of case scanning, a large variety of complex factors and in cases obscure case definitions. To complete a series of tickets successfully a help-desk engineer needs an appropriate prioritization strategy for every working day. The engineer must select a suitable prioritization route, based on the problem description, complexity and historical evidence upon its possible solution. The aim of this work is to help support

M. T. Cox et al. (Eds.): ICCBR 2018, LNAI 11156, pp. 15–27, 2018.
https://doi.org/10.1007/978-3-030-01081-2_2

engineers to achieve the best possible outcome for a given ticket. We propose case-based reasoning (CBR) as the problem solver by increasing the solution accuracy and provide shorter prediction resolution time.

This work combines deep learning and big data with CBR to automate the acquisition of a domain specific knowledge. The growth of intensive data-driven decision-making has caused broad recognition [1], and the promise that Artificial Intelligence (AI) technologies can augment it even further. Within the Case-based Reasoning community there have been several examples of applying data-driven methods to fast changing work environments with several benefits from it. Recently, the customer experience industry has adopted a data-centric vision in an equivalent way, as companies embrace the power of data to optimise their business workflows and the quality of their services [1].

In this work we focus on large-scale ticket management support, helping help-desk managers to optimize their prioritization strategy and achieve superior performance. A key concept in that of timely ticket resolution, measured in resolved tickets per minute, which usually leads to high resolution vs. lower accuracy. Research on successful customer support ticket resolutions has identified several features that influence resolutions results. For example, the work of Maddern et al. [14] looks at the effect of grammatically incorrect sentences, abbreviations, mix between different languages and semantic challenges. Besides the knowledge containers domain vocabulary: how similarity measures are formulated and are able to identify the adaptation knowledge [7].

Deep Learning algorithms are effective when dealing with learning from large amounts of structured or unstructured data. Big Data represent a large spectrum of problems and techniques used for application domains that collect and maintain large volumes of raw data for domain-specific data analysis. Within the CBR paradigm, Deep Learning models can benefit from the available amounts of data, but the integration between CBR, Big Data and Deep Learning faces challenges that propagated from each research field (CBR, Big Data, DL) [3]. The age of Big Data poses novel ways of thinking to address technical challenges. With Deep Learning neural networks extracting meaningful abstract representations from raw data. While Deep Learning can be applied to learn from large volumes of labeled data, it can also be attractive for learning from large amounts of unlabeled/unsupervised data [4–6], making it attractive for extracting meaningful representations and patterns from Big Data.

The research approach in this paper aims to assess the effect of combining CBR with Deep Learning on overcoming the challenges that come with highly-complex, highly-noisy domains. Our proposed work has been mainly designed and implemented to support Help-Desk engineers in prioritizing and solving new, raw-content tickets as they come from customers. We present a hybrid Textual Case-based reasoning (hTCBR) approach using Deep Neural Networks and Big Data Technologies. hTCBR poses two main advantages: (a) it does not rely on manually constructed similarity measures as with traditional CBR and (b) it does not require domain expertise to decode the domain knowledge.

This paper is structured as follows: First we describe the application domain and the main limitations of the processes in place. Section 3 explains our approach, our faced challenges and the followed solution architecture. Section 4 presents the carried-out evaluation with domain experts to ensure the efficiency of our proposed approach. In Sect. 5 we discuss the related work followed by the summary, conclusion and future work in Sect. 6.

2   Application Domain

Most companies have a dedicated internal Help-Desk team for customer support since service quality is usually measured via customer satisfaction. For this work the implemented application and any used data is a joint application between the German Research Center for Artificial Intelligence (DFKI) and a Multinational Automotive Company (the company) located in Munich, Germany with branches all over the world. Inside the company, most of the help-desk tickets come through emails to a dedicated help-desk team. Once received help-desk agents prioritize the tickets and assign them to specialist engineers inside the team to work on it. The company had several historical datasets describing a plethora of issues they have happened in the past along with proposed solutions to those. A historical case could be represented in the form of Problem Description, Solution and Keywords. When new tickets arrive, a help desk engineer should search within the company's knowledge base to confirm whether any solution(s) exists or not. As reported by domain experts, their processes in place were suffering from the following issues:

1. A help-desk agent prioritizes or routes the ticket in the wrong way. Such an action can lead to longer times to a successful ticket resolution.
2. Lack of enough experience or deep knowledge from a help-desk engineer
3. It is not easy to find proposed solutions from a historical knowledge base and engineers find it detrimentally time consuming and not always leading to a solution

3   Hybrid Textual CBR Approach on Ticket Management System

3.1   The Methodology

Text is used to express knowledge. Text is a collection of words in any well-known language that can convey a meaning (i.e., ideas) when interpreted in aggregation [8]. To build a textual CBR system we discussed the system process and how normally the help-desk agents prioritize and route tickets. From this process four attributes were identified as key ones to make a decision. These were: 1. Email Subject 2. Email Content 3. Email Sender Group (The company was organized internally in different groups and each group had its own applications and systems) 4. The initial priority of the ticket assigned by the team who reported it. Based on the above attributes, a help-desk agent would decide how to proceed with this ticket. Based on those discussions with experts we decided our CBR approach as follows:

1. Case Generation: Since there were not too many attributes, cases were generated with flat attribute-value representation features.
2. Case Retrieval: Due to the complexity of Natural Language Processing (NLP) case similarities required a rich context-aware similarity measure. As such a trained neural network for identifying and recommending solutions from the historical case base was selected.
3. Case Adaptation: Adaptation rules are not included during this implementation but should be added in the next phases.

3.2   The Challenges

After analyzing the application domain and the data we received, we identified the following challenges:

1. Building cases was a tedious and extremely time consuming task for domain experts. Experts were not able to add much effort, and hence we resorted to as much automation during the build-up of the CBR system as possible.
2. Any existing knowledge base and new tickets were received in a bilingual format (English, German, or both), which added more complexity in the text analysis and pre-processing to build cases or retrieve similar cases.
3. Tickets were primarily written by non-native English or German speakers and they could have contained several grammar mistakes or vague domain abbreviations.

Due to the last two challenges it was not possible to use any traditional NLP frameworks for text understanding like TwitterNLP and Stanford NLP, since their application did not lead to promising results. Therefore, we decided to use Deep Neural Networks and Word Embeddings to improve the text pre-processing and similarity measures.

Sections 3.3 and 3.4 describe the proposed solution architecture along with the tools and methodologies we have applied to overcome the aforementioned challenges.

3.3   DeepTMS: The Solution Architecture

DeepTMS solution architecture consists of three main modules (See Fig. 1):

1. Input Process (Data Generation) Module: This module is responsible for generating and simulating the emails (tickets) stream.
2. Map/Reduce -Hadoop- Cluster (Data Processing & Retrieval): This module is responsible for receiving the tickets and doing the ticket content pre-processing/processing, then retrieve the similar tickets from the Case Base (Case Generation, Retrieval & Retain).
3. Graphical User Interface (Data Visualization): This module is responsible for visualizing the results to the system end-users.

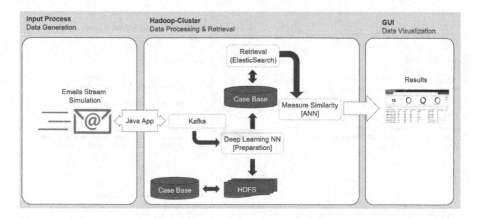

Fig. 1. DeepTMS solution architecture

3.4   The Hybrid CBR Approach

The first decision we had to make in the development of DeepTMS was how we are going to handle the challenges mentioned before, and which approach we should apply. The selected approach combines a Deep Neural Network with CBR to capture and decode domain knowledge. Our approach uses Deep Learning algorithms in the context of Natural Language Processing (NLP). More specifically it applies them throughout the task of prioritizing emails based on their content and it measures text similarity based on their semantics. We, therefore, present several Neural Network types to represent a sequence of sentences as a convenient input for our different models. First, we divided the emails into sub-groups based on the business sectors they were coming from. The first stage was the ticket pre-processing, which divided into five main processes (see Fig. 2).

1. P1: Input Process (Data Generation): was responsible for generating and simulating the emails (tickets) stream
2. P2: Prioritization process: was prioritizing incoming tickets based on historical cases and their recorded priorities
3. P3: Greedings filter: which identified and eliminated any unnecessary text (ex. greetings, signatures etc.) from any email
4. P4: Stemming and stop words elimination: in either German or English language
5. P5: Text vectorization

In the beginning, our approach was to use Support Vector Machines (SVM) and Vectorization to prioritize emails. Early results from this approach were promising but not in sub-group cases. When we performed a more intensive test with large volume of emails, it failed to prioritize with high accuracy. Therefore, we decided to build several state of the art neural network models: Convolutional Neural Networks (CNNs), Recurrent Neural Network (RNNs), and Long Short-Term Memory (LSTMs) [16] to test and compare their results. Deep neural

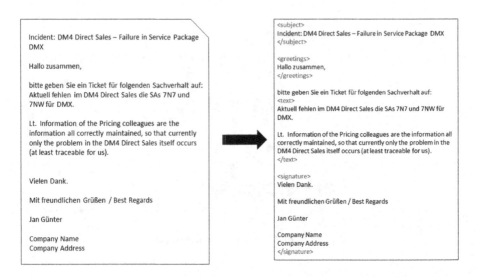

Fig. 2. Ticket pre-processing

network applications seemed to perform substantially better on all sub-groups (Detailed results will be shown in the next section).

3.4.1 Vocabulary Containers

Vocabulary is one of the knowledge containers and represents the information collected from the domain to express knowledge [17]. By filling in this container we identify terms that are useful for the main system tasks. The acquisition of the domain vocabulary has direct effect on the system performance, and that's why it is usually done with intensive help from domain experts. As mentioned in Sect. 3.2 utilizing several experts to manually assist with decoding domain knowledge was rather expensive, therefore an alternative was sought. In order to improve the acquired vocabulary, we followed the typical three methods described in [7]. We have used neural networks to remove irrelevant words and extracted the main features that represent certain text using the Word2Vec models [12]. In the next section we describe how exactly Word2Vec worked to build neural word embeddings.

3.4.2 Neural Word Embedding

Most of the Deep Learning models aren't able to process strings or plain text. They require numbers as inputs to perform any sort of job, classification, regression, etc. Many current NLP systems and techniques treat words as atomic units, therefore, in order to apply a Deep Learning model on NLP, we need to convert words to vectors first. Word embedding is the process of converting text into a numerical representation for further processing. The different types of word embeddings can fall into two main categories:

1. **Frequency-based embedding (FBE):**
   FBE algorithms focus mainly on the number of occurrences for each word, which requires a lot of time to process and exhaustive memory allocation to store the co-occurrence matrix. A severe disadvantage of this approach is that quite important words may be skipped since they may not appear frequently in the text corpus.

2. **Prediction-based embedding (PBE):**
   PBE algorithms are based on Neural Networks. These methods are prediction based in the sense that they assign probabilities to seen words. PBE algorithms seem the present state of the art for tasks like word analogies and word similarities.

PBE methodologies were known to be limited in their word representations until Mitolov et al. introduced Word2Vec to the NLP community [12]. Word2vec consists of two neural network language models: A Continuous Bag of Words (CBOW) and Skip-gram. In both models, a window of predefined length is moved along the corpus, and in each step the network is trained with the words inside the window. Whereas the CBOW model is trained to predict the word in the center of the window based on the surrounding words, the Skip-gram model is trained to predict the context based on the central word. Once the neural network has been trained, the learned linear transformation in the hidden layer is regarded as the word representation. In this work we have used Skip-gram model since it demonstrates better performance in semantic task identification [13].

3.4.3   Text Pre-Processing

In the Text Pre-Processing stage, raw text corpus preparation tasks are taking place in anticipation of text mining or NLP. We trained our Word2Vec model over the ticket corpus overall to build cases used in similarity measures. As any text pre-processing tasks, we have two main components: 1. Tokenization, 2. Normalization. Tokenization is a step which splits longer strings of text into smaller pieces, or tokens. Normalization generally refers to a series of related tasks meant to put all text on a level playing field: converting all text to the same case (upper or lower), removing punctuation, converting numbers to their word equivalents, and so on. Normalization puts all words on equal footing, and allows processing to proceed uniformly. Normalizing text can mean performing a number of tasks, but for our approach, we will apply normalization in four steps: 1. Stemming, 2. Lemmatization 3. Eliminating any stopping words (German or English) 4. Noise Removal (e.g. greetings & signatures). In essence we can consider the Word2Vec model or any other model that could be built as a substitution to the traditional taxonomies.

3.4.4   Similarity Measures

Similarity measures are highly domain dependant and used to describe how cases are related to each other. In CBR, comparison of cases can be performed along multiple important dimensions [9,11]. Cases that only match partially, can be

adapted to a problem situation, using domain knowledge contained in the system
[10]. Thus, methods, like in particular Information Retrieval, which are based
only on statistical inferences over word vectors, are not appropriate or sufficient.
Instead, mechanisms for mapping textual cases onto a structured representation are required. A basic assumption for applying the principle for similarity
measures is that both arguments of the measure follow the same construction
process. This allows us comparing the corresponding sub-objects in a systematic way. For our system we defined the two types of similarity measures: Local
Similarity Measures and Global Similarity Measures. Local Similarity Measures
describe the similarity between two attributes and the Global Similarity Measures describe the similarity between two complete cases. In the next section we
elaborate how we applied the Local Similarity Measures followed by the Global
Similarity Measures.

Local Similarity Measures: Based on the collected data and the discussions
with experts, we defined the local similarity measures. We have mainly four
attributes which are distinctive except for the email subject and content. For
the Priority (integer) and Sending Groups (distinctive strings) we used distance
functions. For the email subject and content, we counted upon the Word2Vec
model to give us the similarity degrees between different texts, after applying all
the aforementioned prepossessing tasks.

Global Similarity Measures: The Global Similarity Measure defines the relations between attributes and gives an overall weight to the retrieved case. The
weight of each attribute demonstrates its importance within the case. We decided
to use the weighted euclidean distance for the calculation of the global similarity
as applied in [15]. The weight of each attribute has been defined in collaboration
with the domain experts. We decided to use a weight range between 1 and 5.
The most important values are weighted with 5.0 and 4.0 determined by the
experts on which attribute value they would use to evaluate the case. They have
decided to give the following weights to the attributes (Priority = 2.0, Email
Content = 4.0 or 5.0, Email Subject = 2.0 or 3.0, Sending Group = 3.0 or 4.0).
After giving the weights to the attributes we then sum up the given weights to
come up with the overall global case similarity.

4   Experimental Evaluation

Our system evaluation is divided into two parts:

1. The case priority given by the neural network
2. The retrieved cases and suggested solutions to the new case

During our system testing and evaluation phase, we decided to use different
Neural Network models to explore, validate and compare accuracy results for

each and every model. We applied three Neural Network models: CNNs, RNNs, and LSTMs [16]. Word2Vec was applied to vectorize text input and build word representations in the vector space (See Fig. 3). Sequences of such vectors were processed using various neural net architectures.

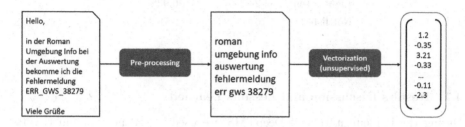

Fig. 3. Text vectorization

Word2Vec was built using 300,000 historical tickets in an unsupervised training mode. All networks were built with one hidden layer, and utilised the Word2Vec model we have already built. To train the three different neural net models, we have also used 300,000 old tickets with known priorities in a supervised learning process. An additional 10,000 tickets were used to evaluate the models in prioritizing the test tickets automatically. Table 1 summarizes the prioritizing stage results.

The second evaluation part is retrieving similar cases based on the similarity measures we defined before, and using Word2Vec model to give the degree of similarity between two texts. Since the LSTM model showed the best results in prioritizing the tickets, we continued to build our solution with LSTM models. In the **Results Discussion** section, we are presenting details about the difference between the three applied models. The evaluation was done with company experts and technicians. DeepTMS suggested ten solutions to a new ticket, and then experts were called to decide where the most relevant solution was positioned among the retrieved ten. We defined also four levels that the most relevant solution could belong to. These were: 1. **one:three** 2. **four:seven** 3. **eight:ten** 4. **Not Listed**. For the evaluation we used the same 10000 Test Tickets that were used in the Prioritization stage. Table 2 shows the results for this stage.

Table 1. Prioritization results

Neural network model	Accuracy	Precision	Recall	F1
Convolutional Neural Network **(CNN)**	82.67%	82.52%	82.64%	82.58%
Recurrent Neural Network **(RNN)**	89.28%	89.19%	89.27%	89.23%
Long Short-Term Memory Network **(LSTM)**	92.35%	92.13%	92.23%	92.16%

Table 2. Retrieval results

Level	Number of cases	Percentage
One : Three	7764	77.64%
Four : Seven	1468	14.68%
Eight : Ten	692	6.92%
Not listed	76	0.76%

4.1   Results Discussion and Lessons Learned

During the implementation of DeepTMS, we used neural networks in tickets pre-processing to eliminate the redundant text and pass the most relevant text to deep neural networks for prioritization purposes. For both tasks, LSTMs outperformed all the other neural network models we used. It is recommended to use LTSM for text related tasks, but it is also important to mention that it takes longer time both for its training phase, and for text processing afterwards. CNNs are more appropriate for image-related tasks. However, we investigated them since the literature suggests them as appropriate to areas where changes take place in the network architecture and can give promising results in text processing as well [18]. CNNs are faster in training and processing phases than RNNs and LSTMs. Since an LSTM is a special RNN case they seemed to perform well on text tasks, better t standard CNNs and worse than LSTMs. In terms of training and processing performance they take longer than CNNs and less time compared to LSTMs.

For building the Word Embedding using Word2Vec and use them within the neural networks models, the performance is pretty good and it always gets improved with more text we use in building the model, since it expands the word corpus and improves the ability to find relationships between words. We started building the Word2Vec model with 50000 tickets, and the results were worse compared to training with 6 times more tickets.

5   Related Work

The related work to this research, is defined on the following three axes: 1. Text processing issues with incorrect sentences and mixed languages 2. Help-desk CBR systems 3. Automation of text relation extraction.

Text processing and analysis is considered a "must-have" capability due to the immense amount of text data available on the internet. Textual CBR is the type of CBR systems where the cases are represented as text. The text representation brings several challenges when the text is unstructured or has grammatically incorrect sentences. The task of the approach described in our research can be compared to the work presented in [19–21], the authors used a hybrid CBR approach where they combined CBR with NLP frameworks to be able to process the knowledge written in free text. They mentioned to the issues they faced with the free text or to extract features and build accurate similarity measures. In our work, NLP frameworks were not able to process text spanned across different languages and there were several issues related to accurate sentence parsing. Therefore, we applied a different approach using Deep Neural Networks to ease the task of finding similarities between cases and automate the knowledge from textual cases.

HOMER [22, 23] is a help desk support system designer for the same purpose of DeepTMS. HOMER used an Object Oriented approach to represent cases and used a question-answering approach to retrieve cases. HOMER showed very good results when it first presented in 1998 and after its further improvement in 2004. However any existing fast-pace work environments demand solutions that are able to deal with big amounts of data in real time with minimum human interference. Comparing to DeepTMS, we focused more on how to automate the extraction of similarities and deal with unstructured or mixed-languages text, but this approach also can't be automated to be integrated in the real business environments.

Finding the relation between text and extract features are key criteria in the success of any textual CBR system. These tasks require a lot of effort and normally can take a long time to be done accurately. Different approaches have been presented to build text similarities and find higher order relationships [24]. The work of automating knowledge extraction using Neural Networks can be compared to the work presented in [25] where authors represented the text using dubbed Text Reasoning Relevant work has been seen in Graph (TRG), a graph-based representation with expressive power to represent the chain of reasoning underlying the analysis as well as facilitate the adaptation of a past analysis to a new problem. The atuhors have used manually constructed lexico-syntactic patterns developed by Khoo [26] to extract the relations between texts.

6 Summary

This paper presents DeepTMS, a hybrid CBR system that uses Deep Neural Networks to assist in automatic feature extractions from text and define similarity across text. DeepTMS is able to automate the building of text similarity without exhaustive expert involvement and work in real-time on new tickets to suggest the most relevant solutions. However, such an approach hides part of the explainability capability of CBR approaches. Our main goal through this research was to show how a hybrid approach using deep learning and CBR can ease in dealing with complex tasks. Such an approach seems appropriate to deal with high volume data that need to be processed fast and in real-time.

7 Future Work

DeepTMS is a starting point towards similarity measures extraction. In the near future we plan to use the fastText text classifier presented by Facebook

[27]. Recurrent Siamese Network models are also considered to improve the efficiency of text similarity measures [28]. DeepTMS is not dealing with too many attributes and the text in the emails is not too long. The results from our presenting implementation are promising, however, it should be tested in more complex environments to show how a hybrid CBR approach can scale. Additional layers to the deep neural networks might be required to be added or more complex models should be applied for better results. The built models can be used to find similarity for any new additional attributes.

References

1. Brynjolfsson, E., McElheran, K.: Data in Action: Data-Driven Decision Making in U.S. Manufacturing, Center for Economic Studies (CES), January 2016
2. Aamodt, A., Plaza, E.: Case-based reasoning: foundational issues, methodological variations, and system approaches. AI Commun. **1**(7), 39–59 (1994)
3. Chen, X.-W., Lin, X.: Big data deep learning: challenges and perspectives. IEEE Access **2**, 514–525 (2014)
4. Bengio, Y.: Deep learning of representations: looking forward. In: Dediu, A.-H., Martín-Vide, C., Mitkov, R., Truthe, B. (eds.) SLSP 2013. LNCS (LNAI), vol. 7978, pp. 1–37. Springer, Heidelberg (2013). https://doi.org/10.1007/978-3-642-39593-2_1
5. Bengio, Y., LeCun, Y.: Scaling learning algorithms towards, AI. In: Bottou, L., Chapelle, O., DeCoste, D., Weston, J., (eds.) Large Scale Kernel Machines, vol. 34. pp 321–360. MIT Press, Cambridge (2007)
6. Bengio, Y., Courville, A., Vincent, P.: Representation learning: a review and new perspectives. IEEE Trans. Patt. Anal. Mach. Intell. **35**(8), 1798–1828 (2013). https://doi.org/10.1109/TPAMI.2013.50
7. Richter, M.M.: Introduction. In: Lenz, M., Bartsch-Sporl, B., Burkhard, H.D., Wess, S. (eds.) Case-Based Reasoning Technology. LNCS (LNAI), vol. 1400, pp. 1–16. Springer, Heidelberg (1998)
8. Richter, M.M., Weber, R.: Case-Based Reasoning: A Textbook. Springer-Verlag GmbH, Heidelberg (2016)
9. Ashley, K.: Modeling Legal Argument, Reasoning with Cases and Hypotheticals. MIT-Press, Cambridge (1990)
10. Aleven, V.: Teaching Case-Based Argumentation through a Model and Examples. Ph.D. Dissertation, University of Pittsburgh, Intelligent Systems Program (1997)
11. Brninghaus, S., Ashley, K.D.: How machine learning can be beneficial for textual case-based reasoning. In: Proceedings of the AAAI-98/ICML-98 Workshop on Learning for Text Categorization (AAAI Technical report WS-98-05), Madison, WI, pp. 71–74 (1998)
12. Mikolov, T., Chen, K., Corrado, G., Dean, J.: Efficient estimation of word representations in vector space. In: NIPS 2013 Proceedings of the 26th International Conference on Neural Information Processing Systems, vol. 2 (2013)
13. Altszyler, E., Sigman, M., Slezak, D.F.: Comparative study of LSA vs Word2vec embeddings in small corpora: a case study in dreams database (2016)
14. Maddern, M., Maull, R., Smart, A.: Customer satisfaction and service quality in UK financial services. Int. J. Prod. Oper. Manag. **27**, 998–1019 (2007)

15. Bach, K., Althoff, K.-D., Newo, R., Stahl, A.: A case-based reasoning approach for providing machine diagnosis from service reports. In: Ram, A., Wiratunga, N. (eds.) ICCBR 2011. LNCS (LNAI), vol. 6880, pp. 363–377. Springer, Heidelberg (2011). https://doi.org/10.1007/978-3-642-23291-6_27

16. Hochreiter, S., Schmidhuber, J.: Long Short-term Memory. Neural Comput. **9**(8), 1735–1780 (1997)

17. Richter, M.M., et al.: Introduction. In: Lenz, M., Burkhard, H.-D., Bartsch-Spörl, B., Wess, S. (eds.) Case-Based Reasoning Technology. LNCS (LNAI), vol. 1400, pp. 1–15. Springer, Heidelberg (1998). https://doi.org/10.1007/3-540-69351-3_1

18. Kim, Y.: Convolutional neural networks for sentence classification. In: Conference on Empirical Methods in Natural Language Processing (2014)

19. Stram, R., Reuss, P., Althoff, K.-D.: Weighted one mode projection of a bipartite graph as a local similarity measure. In: Aha, D.W., Lieber, J. (eds.) ICCBR 2017. LNCS (LNAI), vol. 10339, pp. 375–389. Springer, Cham (2017). https://doi.org/10.1007/978-3-319-61030-6_26

20. Reuss, P., Witzke, C., Althoff, K.-D.: Dependency modeling for knowledge maintenance in distributed CBR systems. In: Aha, D.W., Lieber, J. (eds.) ICCBR 2017. LNCS (LNAI), vol. 10339, pp. 302–314. Springer, Cham (2017). https://doi.org/10.1007/978-3-319-61030-6_21

21. Reuss, P., et al.: FEATURE-TAK - framework for extraction, analysis, and transformation of unstructured textual aircraft knowledge. In: Goel, A., Díaz-Agudo, M.B., Roth-Berghofer, T. (eds.) ICCBR 2016. LNCS (LNAI), vol. 9969, pp. 327–341. Springer, Cham (2016). https://doi.org/10.1007/978-3-319-47096-2_22

22. Roth-Berghofer, T.R.: Learning from HOMER, a case-based help desk support system. In: Melnik, G., Holz, H. (eds.) LSO 2004. LNCS, vol. 3096, pp. 88–97. Springer, Heidelberg (2004). https://doi.org/10.1007/978-3-540-25983-1_9

23. Göker, M., et al.: The development of HOMER a case-based CAD/CAM help-desk support tool. In: Smyth, B., Cunningham, P. (eds.) EWCBR 1998. LNCS, vol. 1488, pp. 346–357. Springer, Heidelberg (1998). https://doi.org/10.1007/BFb0056346

24. Öztürk, P., Prasath, R.R., Moen, H.: Distributed representations to detect higher order term correlations in textual content. In: Szczuka, M., Kryszkiewicz, M., Ramanna, S., Jensen, R., Hu, Q. (eds.) RSCTC 2010. LNCS (LNAI), vol. 6086, pp. 740–750. Springer, Heidelberg (2010). https://doi.org/10.1007/978-3-642-13529-3_78

25. Sizov, G., Öztürk, P., Štyrák, J.: Acquisition and reuse of reasoning knowledge from textual cases for automated analysis. In: Lamontagne, L., Plaza, E. (eds.) ICCBR 2014. LNCS (LNAI), vol. 8765, pp. 465–479. Springer, Cham (2014). https://doi.org/10.1007/978-3-319-11209-1_33

26. Khoo, C.S.G.: Automatic identification of causal relations in text and their use for improving precision in information retrieval. Ph.D. thesis, The University of Arizona (1995)

27. Joulin, A., Grave, E., Bojanowski, P., Mikolov, T.: Bag of Tricks for Efficient Text Classification, dblp Computer Science Bibliography (2017)

28. Mueller, J., Thyagarajan, A.: Siamese recurrent architectures for learning sentence similarity. In: Proceedings of the Thirtieth AAAI Conference on Artificial Intelligence (AAAI 2016) (2016)

CEC-Model: A New Competence Model for CBR Systems Based on the Belief Function Theory

Safa Ben Ayed[1,2(✉)], Zied Elouedi[1(✉)], and Eric Lefèvre[2(✉)]

[1] LARODEC, Institut Supérieur de Gestion de Tunis,
Université de Tunis, Tunis, Tunisie
`zied.elouedi@gmx.fr`
[2] Univ. Artois, EA 3926, LGI2A, 62400 Béthune, France
`safa.ben.ayed@hotmail.fr`, `eric.lefevre@univ-artois.fr`

Abstract. The high influence of case bases quality on Case-Based Reasoning success gives birth to an important study on cases competence for problems resolution. The competence of a case base (CB), which presents the range of problems that it can successfully solve, depends on various factors such as the CB size and density. Besides, it is not obvious to specify the exactly relationship between the individual and the overall cases competence. Hence, numerous Competence Models have been proposed to evaluate CBs and predict their actual coverage and competence on problem-solving. However, to the best of our knowledge, all of them are totally neglecting the uncertain aspect of information which is widely presented in cases since they involve real world situations. Therefore, this paper presents a new competence model called *CEC-Model (Coverage & Evidential Clustering based Model)* which manages uncertainty during both of cases clustering and similarity measurement using a powerful tool called the belief function theory.

Keywords: Case-based reasoning · Competence model
Cases coverage · Belief function theory · Uncertainty · Clustering

1 Introduction

Among the main concerns within the knowledge engineering field is to offer techniques aiming to assess informational resources. In particular, the community of Case-Based Reasoning (CBR) provides a specific interest to evaluate case bases since their quality presents the key factor's success of CBR systems. In fact, the higher the quality of this knowledge container, the more "competent" it is. Actually, the competence (or coverage) of a CBR system refers to its cabability to solve target problems. That's why, the notion of *case competence* is widely used, also, within the field of Case Base Maintenance (CBM), where most of the CBM policies ([8,16–19], etc.) do their best to maintain the most competent cases. However, this key evaluation criterion is difficult to predict since

© Springer Nature Switzerland AG 2018
M. T. Cox et al. (Eds.): ICCBR 2018, LNAI 11156, pp. 28–44, 2018.
https://doi.org/10.1007/978-3-030-01081-2_3

the true character of competence within CBR as well as its sources are not well comprehensible [1]. Moreover, even if we could estimate the competence of an individual case, the estimation of the global case base competence remains complex because of the lack of clarity towards the relationship between local and global competence contribution. By this way, we find several research, over the years, that are interested on case base competence notion, where some of them offer case competence models for CBs evaluation. Typically, case competence models divide cases into competence groups, then estimate cases coverage using similarity measures. Their theoretical contributions are obviously well defended. However, the embedded imperfection in cases was totally neglected within this area, especially that each case refers to one real world experience. Evidently, events and situations occured within our world are full of uncertainty and imprecision. Therefore, we propose, in this paper, a new case competence model, called *CEC-Model* encoding "Coverage & Evidential Clustering based Model", that aims to accurately evaluate the overall case base coverage using the belief function theory [2,3]. This theory offers all the necessary tools to manage all the levels of uncertainty in cases. Through Fig. 1, it is straightforward to show the different fields intersection leading to build and construct our new competence model. In a nutshell, CEC-Model divides the case base into groups using the evidential clustering technique called ECM [6]. Then, it uses a distance within the belief functions framework that leads, ultimately, to estimate the global coverage of the case base. Like the competence model on which we are based [1] to estimate the relation between local case competence and global CB competence, our CEC-Model makes some assumption; First, we assume that the set of cases in the CB presents a representative sample of the set of target problems. Second, we assume that the problem space is regular, where we are based on the CBR hypothesis "Similar problems have similar solutions".

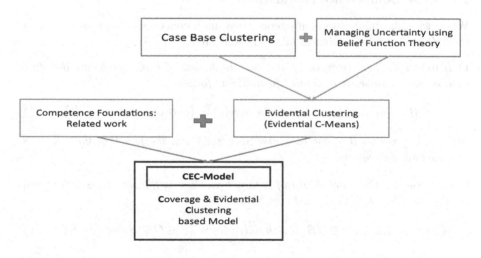

Fig. 1. Towards CEC-model

The reminder of this paper is organized as follows. In Sect. 2, we overview the related work of the Competence concept by offering its foundation, defining the basic factors affecting the case base competence, and presenting some competence models. Section 3 offers the basic concepts of the belief function theory as well as the used evidential tools for building our model. Throughout Sect. sec4, our new CEC-Model is described in details through its different steps. Finally, our model is supported in Sect. 5 using an experimental analysis.

2 General Outlook on Case-Base Competence

A case base is said to be "effective" when it is able to offer solutions efficiently and successfully to solve as many target problems as possible. To evaluate the case base effectiveness for CBR systems, two criteria are generally used: Performance (Definition 1) and Competence (Definition 2).

Definition 1. *The Performance is the answer time that is necessary to generate a solution to a target problem.*

Definition 2. *The Competence is the range of target problems that can be successfully solved.*

Contrary to the competence, the performance criterion for a case base can be straightforward measured. Hence, we will focus, in the following of this Section, on the competence criterion by presenting its foundations (Subsect. 2.1), its influencing factors (Subsect. 2.2) and some existing models to predict the overall case base competence (Subsect. 2.3).

2.1 Case Competence Foundations

When we talk about case competence, two main concepts arise: case Coverage (Definition 3) and case Reachability (Definition 4).

Definition 3. *The coverage of one case is the set of target problems that this case is able to solve. It is defined formally as follows [8]:*

$$CB = \{c_1, .., c_n\}, c \in CB, Coverage(c) = \{c' \in CB/Solves(c, c')\} \quad (1)$$

where CB presents the case base and $Solves(c, c')$ is the fact that the case c is able to solve the case c'.

Definition 4. *The reachability of a target problem is the set of cases that can be used to solve it. It is defined such that [8]:*

$$CB = \{c_1, .., c_n\}, c \in CB, Reachability(c) = \{c' \in CB/Solves(c', c)\} \quad (2)$$

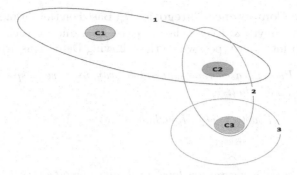

Fig. 2. Concepts of cases Coverage & Reachability

These two latter definitions are based on the assumption that the case base presents the representative sample of all target problems. In fact, it is impossible in the reality to define and fix the entire set of all the target problems. Besides, in that step, we are not intended to explicitly define the predicate "Solves".

For the sake of clarity regarding Definitions 3 and 4, we illustrate in Fig. 2 an example. Let c_1, c_2 and c_3 three cases, and their coverage are labeled with $1, 2$ and 3 respectively. Therefore, $Coverage(c_2) = \{c_2, c_3\}$ and $Reachability(c_2) = \{c_2, c_1\}$. Logically, we assign more interest to cases having a large coverage an a small rechability set. In this paper, we restrict the competence of the case base to its overall coverage. However, the interaction between local competences is necessary to well estimate the entire case base's coverage. Moreover, several factors can influence the prediction of this criterion.

2.2 Basic Factors Influencing Case Base Competence

Building an appropriate competence model requires an awareness on the different factors influencing CB's competence as well as understanding how they affect it. Actually, several factors have been studied in the literature. On the one hand, we find statistical properties such that the CB's size, distribution and density of cases [7,9,10]. On the other hand, the competence is naturally relied to the problem solving properties such as vocabulary, similarity and adaptation knowledge [11,12], as well as individual cases coverage [1,7,13].

Similarly to some other research [1,9], we focus in this paper to understand and measure this competence through case base size and density factors as well as the coverage concept.

2.3 Case Competence Modeling

In the literature, various ways are proposed to model cases competence in order to evaluate the ability of case bases on problem solving. Besides, these models can be the basis of numerous case base maintenance approaches. Hence, we present in what follows three among the most known case competence models.

Model 1: Case Competence Categories [7]: Based on the notions of coverage and reachability, Smyth & Keane classify cases according to their competence characterization into four types, where the following Definitions arise.

Definition 5. *Pivotal cases represent single way to solve a specific problem. They are defined such that:*

$$Pivot(c) \quad iff \quad Reachability(c) - \{c\} = \emptyset \tag{3}$$

Definition 6. *Auxiliary cases are totally subsumed by other cases. They do not influence the global competence at all. Hence, they are defined such that:*

$$Auxiliary(c) \quad iff \quad \exists c' \in Reachability(c) - \{c\}/$$
$$Coverage(c) \subset Coverage(c') \tag{4}$$

Definition 7. *Spanning cases do not directly influence the CB competence. They link together regions covered by the two previous types of cases (Pivotal and Auxiliary).*

Definition 8. *Support cases exist in groups to support an idea. Each support case in a support group provides the same coverage as the other cases belonging to the same group. They are formally defined such that:*

$$Support(c) \quad iff \quad \exists c' \in Reachability(c) - \{c\}/Coverage(c') \subseteq Coverage(c) \tag{5}$$

For further clarification, and by returning to Fig. 2, we mention according to the four previous Definitions that c_1 represents a Pivotal case, c_2 presents a Spanning case, and c_3 is an Auxiliary case. Concerning Support cases, Fig. 3 illustrates three examples of them that cover the same space.

Model 2: Coverage Model Based on Mahalanobis Distance and Clustering (CMDC) [14]: Based on the idea that the CB's competence is proportional to individual case's contribution, CMDC defines the overall case base competence as follows:

$$Comp\%(CB) = |1 - \frac{\sum_{j=1}^{K} \sum_{i=1}^{N} Cov(c_{ij})}{SizeCB}| \tag{6}$$

where K is the number of groups building the CB, N is the size of the jth group, and $Cov(c_{ij})$ represents the coverage of case i towards cluster (group) j.

After applying the DBSCAN-GM algorithm [15] for clustering cases belonging to the CB, this model proposes a classification of cases into three types in order to calculate $Cov(c_{ij})$ used in Eq. 6. The first type concerns *Noisy* cases where their coverage is null since they are considered as a distortion of values.

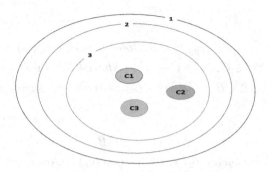

Fig. 3. Example of Support cases towards one Support group

The second type concerns a closely group of cases existing on the core of one cluster and named *Similar* cases. The coverage of Similar cases is equal to their cardinality within each group. Finally, *Internal* cases represent cases that are situated in the border of each cluster. They only cover themselves and their coverage is equal to one (See Fig. 4).

Actually, this model was the basis of several policies aiming to maintain case bases for CBR systems, such that [16, 18, 19], etc.

Model 3: Smyth & McKenna (S&M) Model [1]: Basically, S&M model tries to estimate the competence by finding and encoding the crucial relationship between individual case (local) and the entire CB (global) competence. To do, S&M identifies the fundamental unit of competence as the *competence group* of cases. In fact, within a very traditional point of view, this unit was "the case" only. To recognize these groups, authors in [1] define a competence group as the set of cases that have a shared coverage. Formally, this is defined such that:

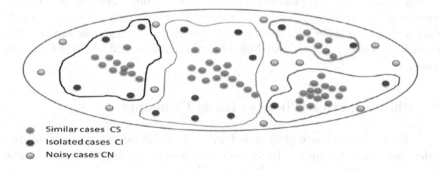

Similar cases CS
Isolated cases CI
Noisy cases CN

Fig. 4. Cases types defined by CMDC model [14]

$$For\ G = \{c_1, .., c_p\} \subseteq CB, CompetenceGroup(G)\ iff$$
$$\forall c_i \in G, \exists c_j \in G - \{c_i\} : SharedCoverage(c_i, c_j) \tag{7}$$
$$\wedge \forall c_k \in CB - G, \neg \exists c_l \in G : SharedCoverage(c_k, c_l)$$

where

$$For\ c_1, c_2 \in CB$$
$$SharedCoverage(c_1, c_2)\ iff\ Coverage(c_1) \cap Coverage(c_2) \neq \emptyset \tag{8}$$

To ease the concept of competence group, we indicate using Fig. 2 that the different cases c_1, c_2 and c_3 present only one coverage group since they share their coverage (similarly for Fig. 3).

Furthermore, S&M model allocate a considerable interest to identify Coverage groups since the larger group coverage means a larger ability to solve target problems. By this way, authors in [1] affirm that it is mainly depending on the *size* and *density* of cases. Obviously, the first factor is straightforward calculated. However, the density of cases is defined such that:

$$GroupDensity(G) = \frac{\sum_{c \in G} CaseDensity(c, G)}{|G|} \tag{9}$$

where $CaseDensity(c, G)$ presents the local density of the case c within the group $G \subset CB$, and $|G|$ is the number of cases belonging to G.

Since the coverage of a group must be directly proportional to its size and inversely proportional to its density, the current model defines it as follows:

$$GroupCoverage(G) = 1 + [\,|G|\,(1 - GroupDensity(G))\,] \tag{10}$$

Undoubtedly, the proposed contributions to model cases competence are interesting. However, they remain limited by their disability to manage uncertainty within knowledge, especially for real experiences (cases). The next Section presents, therefore, a powerful tool used for this matter called the Belief function theory.

3   Belief Function Theory: Basic Concepts

The belief function theory [2,3], also known by Evidence theory or Dempster-Shafer theory, is a theoretical framework for reasoning under partial and unreliable (uncertain and imprecise) information. It was introduced by Dempster and Shafer [2,3], and then studied by Smets [4,5]. As a generalization of other uncertainty management theories [20–22], belief function theory proved to be effective in various applications. The rest of this Section will recall the main definitions and concepts and the used tools offered within this theory.

Let ω be a variable taking values in a finite set $\Omega = \{w_1, .., w_K\}$ named the frame of discernment. The mass function $m(.)$, which represents the uncertainty and imprecision knowledge about the actual value of ω, is defined as an application from the power set of Ω (2^Ω) in $[0, 1]$ and satisfying

$$\sum_{A \subseteq \Omega} m(A) = 1 \tag{11}$$

Actually, $m(A)$ can be viewed as the degree of belief committed exactly to the subset of events A. A is called focal element if $m(A) > 0$, and the mass function m is equivalent to a probability distribution when all the focal elements are singletons. It is then called Bayesian mass function.

Since two events within the belief function theory are mainly described by their mass functions, it is also interesting to measure the similarity and distance between them. One of the most known and used distances between two pieces of evidence is called the Jousselme Distance of evidence [23].

Given two pieces of evidence m_1 and m_2 on the same frame of discernment, the Jousselme distance between them is defined as follows:

$$d(m_1, m_2) = \sqrt{\frac{1}{2}(\overrightarrow{m_1} - \overrightarrow{m_2})^T \underline{\underline{D}} \, (\overrightarrow{m_1} - \overrightarrow{m_2})} \tag{12}$$

where $\underline{\underline{D}}$ is a $2^K \times 2^K$ matrix whose its elements are calculated as follows:

$$D(A, B) = \begin{cases} 1 & if \;\; A = B = \emptyset \\ \dfrac{|A \cap B|}{|A \cup B|} & \forall \;\; A, B \in 2^\Omega \end{cases} \tag{13}$$

To make decision towards the value of ω, the mass function m can be transformed into a pignistic probability distribution $BetP$ [4] such as:

$$BetP(A) = \sum_{B \subseteq \Omega} \frac{|A \cap B|}{|B|} \frac{m(B)}{1 - m(\emptyset)} \quad \forall A \in \Omega \tag{14}$$

Finally, the decision is made by choosing the variable with the highest $BetP$ value.

Concerning the evidential clustering of n objects, the partial knowledge in that time will concern the membership of objects to clusters. Hence, the frame of discernment Ω, in that case, contains the set of all clusters. Basically, an $n \times 2^{|\Omega|}$ credal partition matrix is generated after applying an evidential clustering technique. It offers n mass functions that reflect the membership degrees of belief to each clusters' subset (partition).

The Evidential C-Means (ECM) [6] presents one of the most known evidential clustering techniques. It takes as input the set of n objects and the number K of clusters, and generates as output the credal partition (matrix M) as well as the prototype (center) of each partition (matrix V). Like almost of clustering methods, ECM aims to create dense groups by minimizing distances belonging to the same cluster and maximize those belonging to different ones. To do, ECM method intend to minimize the following objective function:

$$J_{ECM}(M,V) = \sum_{i=1}^{n} \sum_{j/A_j \neq \emptyset, A_j \subseteq \Omega} |A_j|^{\alpha} m_{ij}^{\beta} d_{ij}^2 + \sum_{i=1}^{n} \delta^2 m_{i\emptyset}^{\beta} \qquad (15)$$

subject to

$$\sum_{j/A_j \subseteq \Omega, A_j \neq \emptyset} m_{ij} + m_{i\emptyset} = 1 \qquad \forall i = 1...n \qquad (16)$$

where d_{ij} represents the euclidean distance between the object i and the center of the partition j, the parameter α controls the degree of penalization allocated to partitions with high cardinality, and δ and β are two parameters aiming to treat noisy objects.

To minimize the above objective function, an alternation between two steps is performed. The first one consists of supposing that the matrix of centers V is fixed and solving Eq. 15 constrained by Eq. 16 using the Lagrangian technique. Then, the second phase consists to fix the credal partition M and minimize the unconstrained problem defined only by Eq. 15.

During this Section, we only focused on the necessary background within the belief function framework that allow to understand our contribution presented hereafter. More details can be found in [2–6,23].

4   Coverage and Evidential Clustering Based Model (CEC-Model)

The purpose of this Section is to present our new case competence model dedicated for this paper. This model is named CEC-Model and able to manage uncertainty within the base knowledge. It also uses the coverage concept as well as the mathematical relation between the competence of a group and the local competence contribution of its individual cases [1] to provide as output a prediction of the global case base competence. Our model can serve, on the one hand, at evaluating the quality of any given case base. On the other hand, it can be the basis for maintaining case bases by finding, for instance, the combination of cases that offer a maximum rate of global competence offered by CEC-Model. For the sake of simplicity, the global process followed by our model to reach its objective in estimating the CB competence rate while managing uncertainty is shown in Fig. 5. First of all, we perform the evidential clustering technique to offer a credal partition of cases that allows to manage uncertainty not only towards the membership of cases to clusters, but also towards their membership to all possible subsets of clusters (partitions). At the second level, the credal partition generated during Step 1, which is a way to model cases membership uncertainty, will be used then, during Step 2, to measure the similarity between cases. Besides, it will be transformed using the pignistic probability (Eq. 14), during Step 3, to make the decision about the membership of cases to groups.

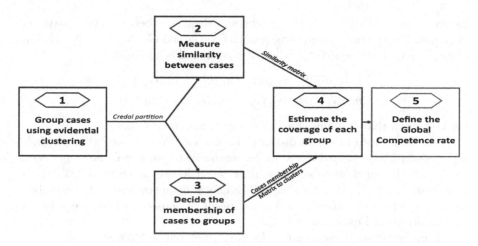

Fig. 5. CEC-Model steps for CB's competence estimation

The outcome of both Steps 2 and 3 will serve then to calculate the individual cases densities regarding their groups, the density rate of each group, and the coverage of the different groups. Finally, the global competence rate of the overall case base defines the purpose of Step 5, where it is estimated by the average of normalized coverages of all groups composing the case base. In what follows, within the reminder of this Section, we will present in more details every step composing our CEC-Model.

4.1 Step 1: Group Cases Using Evidential Clustering

In our first Step, we aim to group cases according to their similarities. The more two cases are similar, the more they are able to cover each others. In fact, similarly to several research in competence modeling [1,14], the idea is that the coverage of one case is defined by the range of cases that are similar to it. Hence, applying a clustering technique based on distances computing offers a simple and reasonable solution to devise the case base into a number of coverage groups. However, the amount of imperfection that is commonly presented in cases knowledge do not allow us to be certain about the membership of cases to the different clusters. For that reason, we make use of the belief function theory and the evidential clustering, more accurately the Evidential C-Means (ECM) technique (see Subsect. 3). The idea consists on creating coverage groups with degrees of belief. Finally, the output of this Step is a credal partition containing n pieces of evidence m_i describing the belief's degrees of membership.

4.2 Step 2: Measure Similarity Between Cases Within the Evidential Framework

At this Step, we aim to take advantage of the offered credal partition to measure the similarities between every couple of cases. A case is therefore characterized by its mass function that defines the membership degrees of belief to every partition of groups. For instance, given three groups G_1, G_2 and G_3, the mass function of case c_i is presented as a vector where it has the following form:

$$m_i = [m_i(\emptyset) \quad m_i(G_1) \quad m_i(G_2) \quad m_i(G_1, G_2)$$
$$m_i(G_3) \quad m_i(G_1, G_3) \quad m_i(G_2, G_3) \quad m_i(\Omega)] \tag{17}$$

Let us remind that the sum of all its elements are equal to one.

Now, we have to calculate distances between every two cases through their corresponding pieces of evidence. To do, we choose to use a well known powerful tool within the belief functions community called Jousselme Distance [23], which offers results in $[0, 1]$. Therefore, we build an $n \times n$ distances matrix that we called $CredDist$, where $CredDist(c_i, c_j)$ is the result of Jousselme Distance between m_i and m_j using Eqs. 12 and 13.

Then, the similarity matrix $CredSim$ is generated as follows:

$$CredSim = Ones - CredDist \tag{18}$$

where $Ones$ is an $n \times n$ matrix filled by 1.

4.3   Step 3: Decide the Membership of Cases to Groups

After computing cases distances with taking into account the uncertainty presented in cases, we move on now from the credal level to the pignistic level where we have to make decision about the membership of cases to the different groups. To do, we transform the mass function of each case to a pignistic probability using Eq. 14. Then, we put each case in the group offering the highest pignistic probability value.

4.4   Step 4: Estimate the Coverage of Each Group

The challenge of this step consists on finding the best configuration to model the relationship between a local (individual case) and the global (entire CB) competence contributions. As mentioned in Subsect. 2.2, several factors are affecting the interaction between them. For our model, and based on [1], the combination to build the global competence properties of case bases is influenced by two main factors: *Size* and *Density*.

As specified in the Introduction, we assume that the problem space is regular. Hence, cases with high density imply a high degree of mutual similarity. Per contra, sparse cases present low degree of mutual similarity. Consequently, our model calculate the local density of a case c towards the group $G \subseteq CB$ in which it belongs as follows:

$$CaseDensity(c, G) = \frac{\sum_{c' \in G - \{c\}} CredSim(c, c')}{|G| - 1} \tag{19}$$

Afterwards, we calculate the density of each group as the average of all its corresponding cases density using Eq. 9.

Ultimately, and based on [1], we define the relationship between the density and the coverage of each group. In fact, dense groups cover smaller target problems space (Density factor). In contrast, groups with higher size cover larger problem space (Size factor). Consequently, we calculate the coverage of each group using Eq. 10.

4.5   Step 5: Define the Global Case Base Competence Rate

Last but not least, we aim at estimating the global competence of case bases based on groups coverage computed during the previous step. In S&M model [1], the global competence is calculated as the sum of all the coverage measurements of groups building the CB. However, we aim in our model to estimate the global competence as a percentage. Then, the proposed global competence rate is calculated as follows:

$$Comp(CB)\% = \frac{\sum_{k=1}^{|\Omega|} GroupCov_n(G_k)}{|\Omega|} \tag{20}$$

where $GroupCov_n(G_k)$ is the normalized coverage of the kth group, defined such that:

$$GroupCov_n(G_k) = \frac{GroupCoverage(G_k) - 1}{|G_k|} \tag{21}$$

The demonstration that gives birth to groups coverage normalization formula (and then the global CB competence rate) is presented as follows:
Let Ω be the frame of discernment containing K groups G_k. $CB = \{c_1, .., c_n\}$ is then divided into $|\Omega|$ groups:

We have:
$$0 \leq CredSim(c, c_i) \leq 1$$
$$0 \leq \sum_{c_i \in G - \{c\}} CredSim(c, c_i) \leq |G| - 1$$
$$0 \leq \frac{\sum_{c_i \in G - \{c\}} CredSim(c, c_i)}{|G| - 1} \leq 1$$
$$0 \leq CaseDensity(c, G) \leq 1$$
$$0 \leq \frac{\sum_{c \in G} CaseDensity(c, G)}{|G|} \leq 1$$
$$0 \leq GroupDensity(G) \leq 1$$
$$1 \leq 1 + [|G|(1 - GroupDensity(G))] \leq 1 + |G|$$
$$1 \leq GroupCoverage(G) \leq 1 + |G|$$
$$0 \leq \frac{GroupCoverage(G) - 1}{|G|} \leq 1$$
$$0 \leq GroupCov_n(G) \leq 1$$
$$0 \leq \sum_{G \in \Omega} GroupCov_n(G) \leq |\Omega|$$
$$0 \leq \frac{\sum_{G \in \Omega} GroupCov_n(G)}{|\Omega|} \leq 1$$
$$0 \leq Comp(CB) \leq 1$$

5   Experimental Analysis

During the previous Sections, we reviewed the main definitions for competence and coverage modeling, and we proposed a novel model for case bases competence estimation within the frame of belief function theory and evidential clustering. In this Section, we need to support our model using an empirical evidences. The idea is to demonstrate experimentally that our model competence rate predictions are sufficiently match to the actual competence measurements such as the Percentage of Correct Classification (accuracy). Furthermore, it is more reasonable to define the correlation between their values than focusing on which criterion has the highest values. To start, we present the setup of experimentation. Then, we show how to proceed to support our CEC-Model.

5.1   Experimental Setup

Our CEC-Model algorithm was developed using Matlab R2015a, and tests were performed on real data sets taken from UCI repository [24]. In this paper, we share results offered by three data sets[1] that are described in Table 1. In fact, within the context of CBR, attributes are considered as problems description and the class characterizes their solutions. Besides, default values of the ECM algorithm are taken, and the number of clusters is equal to the number of solutions in the CB. Since we will support our model basing on the accuracy criterion, we measure it by applying 10-folds cross validation using the following formula:

$$PCC(\%) = \frac{Number\ of\ correct\ classifications}{Total\ number\ of\ classifications} \times 100 \qquad (22)$$

where we used the 1-Nearest Neighbor as a classification method.

Table 1. UCI data sets characteristics

Case base	Attributes	Instances	Classes	Class distribution
Mammographic mass	6	961	2	516/445
Ionosphere	34	351	2	226/125
Iris	4	150	3	50/50/50

5.2   Evaluation Criteria

Our experimental study is divided into two parts, where each one carries on one evaluation criterion. Firstly, we are interested to know the correlation between the actual CB's competence (Accuracy) and the estimated global competence rates predicted by our CEC-Model. The different values are the results of a randomly incremental evolution of case bases. Actually, the higher a positive correlation, the more our model is supported. Hence, we measure this correlation using the *Pearson's correlation coefficient* [25] which is bounded between −1 and 1, and defined as follows:

---

[1] Other CBs are offering similar results but are not presented here due to lack of space.

$$r = \frac{\sum_{i=1}^{n}(a_i - \overline{a})(b_i - \overline{b})}{\sqrt{\sum_{i=1}^{n}(a_i - \overline{a})^2} \sqrt{\sum_{i=1}^{n}(b_i - \overline{b})^2}} \tag{23}$$

where a_i (respectively b_i) are the values of the actual CB's competence (respectively the predicted global competence by CEC-Model), and $\overline{a}$ (respectively $\overline{b}$) presents the mean value of a_i (respectively b_i) measurements.

During the second part of our experimentation, we opt to measure the error rate between CEC-Model estimated competence and the PCC values, such that:

$$Error(\%) = \frac{|EstimatedComp - PCC|}{PCC} \times 100 \tag{24}$$

5.3   Results and Discussion

For the first part of our experimentation, results are shown in Fig. 6, where the actual and estimated competence are plotted against the size of three different case bases. These results provide a high support in favor of our CEC-Model. In fact, it seems to be an almost perfect closely relationship between every two curves (problem-solving accuracy and CB's competence), and hence a strong correlation between them. For the sake of precision, we further measured this correlation for every CB using Eq. 23 and we found high results reflecting a good match between the predicted and the true competence (0.91 for Mammographic Mass, 0.8 for Ionosphere, and 0.83 for Iris). Let us remind that the closer the value to one, the higher the correlation is.

In the second results part, we note from Table 2 that our CEC-Model offers close competence estimation to the actual accuracy regarding the totality of the different three tested case bases. Actually, this closeness was measured formally using the error rate criterion (Eq. 24), where competitive results were provided comparing to those offered by S&M [1] and CMDC [14] models. For instance, we offered the minimum error rate for Iris data set which is estimated to 0.8%. Besides, the error rate for Mammographic Mass is estimated to environ 5.9%, where it is measured as 21.1% with S&M and environ 13.8% with CMDC (S&M and CMDC models are reviewed in Subsect. 2.3).

Table 2. Results in term of error rate (%)

Case base	S& M	CMDC	CEC-Model
Mammographic mass	21.10	13.820	5.928
Ionosphere	3.544	0.287	1.779
Iris	4.010	0.927	0.807

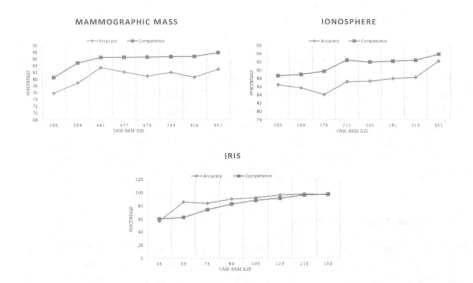

Fig. 6. Comparing estimated competence using our CEC-Model to the CB's accuracy for Mammographic Mass, Ionosphere, and Iris data sets

6 Conclusion

The evaluation of knowledge resources are regularly a concern of widespread interest in knowledge management systems. In CBR systems, modeling case base competence with managing uncertainty within knowledge is essential to find the real coverage of cases. In this paper, we proposed a new competence model based on a previous work [1] with joining the ability to manage all levels of cases membership uncertainty towards groups building the case base, as well as to satisfy the need of imperfection handling when measure similarities and cases density. To support our model, we tested on data sets from UCI repository [24] with varying their size. Actually, competence estimations offered by our model are quite closely to the actual competence measurement (Accuracy) with a relatively high positive correlation between them.

Since the competence of CBR systems case bases presents the basis of the Case Base Maintenance (CBM) policies, we can, as future work, use our new competence model CEC-Model at the aim of maintaining CBs in order to well detect useless cases for target problems resolution.

References

1. Smyth, B., McKenna, E.: Modelling the competence of case-bases. In: Smyth, B., Cunningham, P. (eds.) EWCBR 1998. LNCS, vol. 1488, pp. 208–220. Springer, Heidelberg (1998). https://doi.org/10.1007/BFb0056334

2. Dempster, A.P.: Upper and lower probabilities induced by a multivalued mapping. Ann. Math. Stat. **38**, 325–339 (1967)
3. Shafer, G.: A Mathematical Theory of Evidence, vol. 1. Princeton University Press, Princeton (1976)
4. Smets, P.: The transferable belief model for quantified belief representation. In: Smets, P. (eds.) Quantified Representation of Uncertainty and Imprecision. Handbook of Defeasible Reasoning and Uncertainty Management Systems, vol. 1, pp. 267–301. Springer, Dordrecht (1998). https://doi.org/10.1007/978-94-017-1735-9_9
5. Smets, P.: The combination of evidence in the transferable belief model. IEEE Trans. Patt. Anal. Mach. Intell. **12**(5), 447–458 (1990)
6. Masson, M.H., Denœux, T.: ECM: an evidential version of the fuzzy c-means algorithm. Patt. Recogn. **41**, 1384–1397 (2008)
7. Smyth, B., Keane, M.T.: Remembering to forget: a competence-perserving deletion policy for CBR systems. In Proceedings of the Thirteenth International Joint Conference on Artificial Intelligence (IJCAI), pp. 377–382 (1995)
8. Smyth, B., McKenna, E.: Competence models and the maintenance problem. Comput. Intell. **17**(2), 235–249 (2001)
9. Lieber, J.: A criterion of comparison between two case bases. In: Haton, J.-P., Keane, M., Manago, M. (eds.) EWCBR 1994. LNCS, vol. 984, pp. 87–100. Springer, Heidelberg (1995). https://doi.org/10.1007/3-540-60364-6_29
10. Riesbeck, C.K., Schank, R.C.: Inside Case-Based Reasoning. Psychology Press, London (2013)
11. Arshadi, N., Jurisica, I.: Feature selection for improving case-based classifiers on high-dimensional data sets. In: FLAIRS Conference, pp. 99–104 (2005)
12. Ayeldeen, H., Hegazy, O., Hassanien, A.E.: Case selection strategy based on k-means clustering. In: Mandal, J.K., Satapathy, S.C., Sanyal, M.K., Sarkar, P.P., Mukhopadhyay, A. (eds.) Information Systems Design and Intelligent Applications. AISC, vol. 339, pp. 385–394. Springer, New Delhi (2015). https://doi.org/10.1007/978-81-322-2250-7_39
13. Smyth, B.: Case-base maintenance. In: Pasqual del Pobil, A., Mira, J., Ali, M. (eds.) IEA/AIE 1998. LNCS, vol. 1416, pp. 507–516. Springer, Heidelberg (1998). https://doi.org/10.1007/3-540-64574-8_436
14. Smiti, A., Elouedi, Z.: Modeling competence for case based reasoning systems using clustering. The 26th International FLAIRS Conference, the Florida Artificial Intelligence Research Society, USA, pp. 399–404 (2013)
15. Smiti, A., Elouedi, Z.: DBSCAN-GM: an improved clustering method based on Gaussian means and DBSCAN techniques. In: 16th International Conference on Intelligent Engineering Systems (INES), pp. 573–578. IEEE (2012)
16. Smiti, A., Elouedi, Z.: SCBM: soft case base maintenance method based on competence model. J. Comput. Sci. **25**, 221–227 (2018)
17. Smyth, B., McKenna, E.: Building compact competent case-bases. In: Althoff, K.-D., Bergmann, R., Branting, L.K. (eds.) ICCBR 1999. LNCS, vol. 1650, pp. 329–342. Springer, Heidelberg (1999). https://doi.org/10.1007/3-540-48508-2_24
18. Ben Ayed, S., Elouedi, Z., Lefevre, E.: ECTD: evidential clustering and case Types Detection for case base maintenance. In: The 14th ACS/IEEE International Conference on Computer Systems and Applications (AICCSA), pp. 1462–1469 (2017)
19. Ben Ayed, S., Elouedi, Z., Lefevre, E.: DETD: dynamic policy for case base maintenance based on EK-NNclus algorithm and case types detection. In: The 17th International Conference on Information Processing and Management of Uncertainty in Knowledge-Based Systems (IPMU). Springer (2018, to appear)

20. Feller, W.: An Introduction to Probability Theory and Its Applications, vol. 2. Wiley (2008)
21. Zadeh, L.A.: Fuzzy sets. In: Fuzzy Sets, Fuzzy Logic, And Fuzzy Systems: Selected Papers by Lotfi A Zadeh, pp. 394–432 (1996)
22. Dubois, D., Henri, P.: Possibility Theory. Computational Complexity, pp. 2240–2252. Springer, New York (2012)
23. Jousselme, A.L., Grenier, D., Bossé, É.: A new distance between two bodies of evidence. Inf. Fusion **2**(2), 91–101 (2001)
24. Blake, C.: UCI repository of machine learning databases (1998). http://www.ics.uci.edu/mlearn/MLRepository.html
25. Pearson, K.: Mathematical contributions to the theory of evolution. III. Regression, heredity, and panmixia. In: Philosophical Transactions of the Royal Society of London, pp. 253–318 (1896)

The Case for Case Based Learning

Isabelle Bichindaritz[(✉)]

Computer Science Department, SUNY Oswego,
Shineman 396A, 7060 New York 104, Oswego, NY 13126, USA
ibichind@oswego.edu

Abstract. Case-based reasoning (CBR) systems often refer to diverse machine learning functionalities and algorithms to augment their capabilities. In this article we review the concept of case based learning and define it as the use of case based reasoning for machine learning. We present some of its characteristics and situate it in the context of the major machine learning tasks and machine learning approaches. In doing so, we review the particular manner in which case based learning practices declarative learning, for its main knowledge containers, as well as dynamic induction, through similarity assessment. The central role of analogy as a dynamic induction is highlighted as the cornerstone of case based learning that makes it a method of choice in classification and prediction tasks in particular. We propose a larger understanding, beyond instance-based learning, of case based learning as analogical learning that would promote it as a major contributor of the analogizer approach of machine learning.

Keywords: Case based learning · Machine learning · Analogy
Induction

1 Introduction

Case-based reasoning (CBR) systems have tight connections with machine learning and knowledge discovery as exemplified by their description in data mining (Han et al. 2012) and machine learning (Mitchell 1997) textbooks. They have been tagged by machine learning researchers as *lazy* learners because they defer the decision of how to generalize beyond the training set until a target new case is encountered (Mitchell 1997), by opposition to most other learners, tagged as *eager*. Even though most inductive inferences is definitely performed at *Retrieve* time in CBR (Aha 1997), mostly through sophisticated similarity assessment, most CBR systems also perform inductive inferences at *Retain* time. This article proposes to define case based learning (CBL) as the use of case based reasoning for machine learning and highlights the role of analogical inference as a dynamic induction. It reviews the main machine learning tasks, both supervised and unsupervised, and how case based learning can be applied to performing these tasks either standalone or in cooperation/complement with other machine learning approaches. This article also reviews the five tribes of machine learning and situates CBL within the *analogizers'* tribe. Based on these foundations, this article presents, beyond the instance-based learning label, a broader scope for CBL based on the concept of analogical learning, which could be a unifying theme for analogizers.

© Springer Nature Switzerland AG 2018
M. T. Cox et al. (Eds.): ICCBR 2018, LNAI 11156, pp. 45–61, 2018.
https://doi.org/10.1007/978-3-030-01081-2_4

2 Machine Learning

From the formal definition of Tom M. Mitchell (1997), "A computer program is said to learn from experience E with respect to some class of tasks T and performance measure P if its performance at tasks in T, as measured by P, improves with experience E", machine learning algorithms fitting this definition are numerous since the field was launched after the term was coined in 1959 by Arthur Samuel. Machine learning systems learn from experience, represented by data, to improve their performance in tasks, the most classical one being prediction. Therefore, the main focus in machine learning is to improve the performance of a particular artificial intelligence (AI) system.

Machine learning shares much interest with the field of data mining, being the field of data science analyzing observational data sets to find unsuspected and interesting relationships and to summarize the data in novel ways that are both understandable and useful to the data owner (Hand et al. 2001). Traditionally described as a misnomer, knowledge discovery is a preferred term. Since knowledge discovery is involved in learning or improving knowledge and AI systems generally contain knowledge, in knowledge containers, the goals of knowledge discovery can all serve AI, and in particular machine learning. Therefore, the major tasks afforded by knowledge discovery are also attributed to machine learning, among which (Han et al. 2012):

- **Classification/prediction:** classification is a supervised knowledge discovery method applied to datasets containing an expert labeling in the form of a categorical attribute, called a class; when the attribute is numeric, the method is called prediction. Examples of classifiers include neural networks, support vector machines, naïve Bayes, and decision trees.
- **Association Mining:** association mining mines for frequent itemsets in a dataset, which can be represented as rules. It is an unsupervised method. The most famous algorithm in this category is a priori algorithm.
- **Clustering:** clustering finds groups of similar objects in a dataset, which are also dissimilar from the objects in other clusters, although not all methods are based on similarity. In addition to the similarity-based methods like K-Means, some methods use density-based algorithms or hierarchical algorithms.
- **Dimensionality reduction:** when an abundance of features is available (high dimensionality), systems may select pertinent features to improve efficiency and overall performance.
- **Optimization:** optimization focuses on finding the optimal value of a parameter.

Considerations for evaluating the mining results vary across methods, however a set of quality measurements are traditionally associated with each, for example accuracy or error rate for classification, and lift or confidence for association mining.

These core functionalities can be combined and applied to several data types, with extensions to the underlying algorithms or completely new methods to complement the classical nominal and numeric data types. Well researched data types are graphs, texts, images, time series, networks, etc. We refer to these extensions as multimedia mining.

Other types of functionalities, generally combined with the core ones, are for example sampling, where the goal is to select a subset of input samples, and characterization, where the goal is to provide a summary representation of a set of samples, for example those contained in a cluster.

3 Case Based Learning

We propose to define case based learning (CBL) as the use of case based reasoning for machine learning.

Machine learning researchers have often reported on how case-based reasoning relates to machine learning. CBR systems satisfy the definition of machine learning systems because they afford classification or prediction tasks (Nilsson and Funk 2004). From a set of data – called cases in CBR – the classification or prediction achieved gives the case base the competency of an expert system. If CBR systems are in par with other data mining systems in such tasks as classification and prediction, there is, though, an important difference. CBR systems start their reasoning from knowledge units, called cases, while data mining systems most often start from raw data. This is why case mining, which consists in mining raw data for these knowledge units called cases, is a data mining task often used in CBR.

Machine learning researchers consider case-based reasoning systems as either analogical reasoning systems (Michalski 1993) or instance based learners (Mitchell 1997).

For Mitchell, CBR systems belong to instance based learning systems in the field of machine learning. CBR systems, learning from the cases or experiences in their memory, often incrementally, are examples of machine learning systems according to Mitchell's definition. They are problem-solving systems following an analogical reasoning cycle illustrated in Fig. 1. Most machine learning systems abstract a model through their learning process – a process called *induction* – and can forget the experiences from which the model was abstracted. Instance-based learning systems are different because they keep their memory of experiences to reuse them later on for solving new problems. Mitchell labels these systems as *lazy* learners because they defer the decision about how to generalize beyond the training data until each new query instance is encountered (Aha 1997). This allows CBR systems to not commit to a global approximation once and for all during the training phase of machine learning, but to generalize specifically for each target case, therefore to fit its induction bias, to the case at hand. He points here to the drawback of overgeneralization, or overfitting, that is well known for *eager* learners, from which instance based learners are exempt (Mitchell 1997).

Other machine learning authors have classified case-based learning as a special kind of inductive learning where the inductive inferences are performed *dynamically* instead of *declaratively* as when a model is induced. Michalski (1993) presents the analogical inference, at the basis of case-based retrieval, as a dynamic induction performed during the matching process.

These authors focus their analysis on the inferential aspects of learning in case-based reasoning. Historically CBR systems have evolved from the early work of Schank in the theory of the dynamic memory (Schank 1982), where this author proposes to design intelligent systems primarily by modeling their memory. Ever since Schank's precursory work on natural language understanding, one of the main goals of case-based reasoning has been to integrate as much as possible memory and inferences for the performance of intelligent tasks. Therefore, focusing on studying how case-based reasoning systems learn, or mine, their memory structures and organization can prove at least as fruitful as studying and classifying them from an inference standpoint.

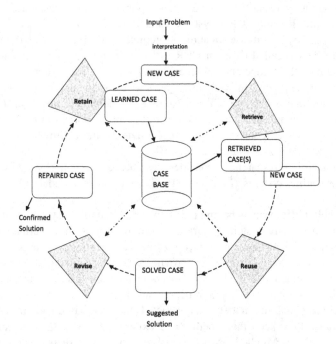

Fig. 1. The classical CBR reasoning cycle (Aamodt and Plaza 1994)

From a memory standpoint, learning in CBR consists in the creation and maintenance of the knowledge containers, namely vocabulary and knowledge representation language, retrieval knowledge, adaptation knowledge, and the case base (Richter 1998). In the general cycle of CBR, learning takes place within the reasoning cycle (Fig. 1), in an *incremental* manner. It is possible to fix it after a certain point, but it is not a tradition in CBR: *learning is an emergent behavior from normal functioning* (Kolodner 1993). When an external problem-solving source is available, CBR systems start reasoning from an empty memory, and their reasoning capabilities stem from progressively learning from the cases processed. Aamodt and Plaza (1994) further state that *case-based reasoning favors learning from experience*. Thus often the decisions about each case or structure in memory, to memorize it or not, enable the system to evolve progressively toward states as different as ongoing learning, in novice mode, and its termination, in expert mode. Case based learning anticipates the conditions of cases recall (or retrieval). As the theory of the dynamic memory showed, recall and learning are closely linked (Schank 1982): *the memory is directed toward the future* both to avoid situations having caused a problem and to reinforce the performance in success situations.

Learning in case-based reasoning is multi-faceted and can be organized around the knowledge containers (Richter 1998):

1. Case representation: the process of *case mining* can learn features and parts to include in a case from raw data or relational databases.
2. Retrieval knowledge: choosing the indices or *index mining* consists in anticipating *Retrieval*, the first reasoning step. Some systems modify their similarity measure through in particular *weight learning* or situation assessment refinement.
3. Adaptation knowledge: some systems *learn adaptation rules*, for example d'Aquin et al. (2007), through knowledge discovery.
4. Case base: often referred to as case base maintenance (Wilson and Leake 2001), it can take the form of:

   - *adding a case* to the memory, which is at the heart of CBR systems and traditionally one of the main phases in the reasoning cycle - *Retain* (Aamodt and Plaza 1994). It is the most primitive learning kind, also called learning by consolidation, or rote learning.
   - *learning memory structures*: these may be learned by generalization from cases or be provided from the start to hold the indices for example. These learned memory structures can play additional roles, such as facilitating reuse or retrieval.
   - *organizing the memory* in a network of cases, or given memory structures, and learned memory structures, organized in efficient ways. Flat and hierarchical memories have been traditionally described.
   - *refining cases* by updating them based upon the CBR result.
   - *discovering knowledge* or metareasoning: the knowledge at the basis of the case-based reasoning can be refined.

4 Case Based Learning Tasks

As explained in Sect. 2, machine learning involves or encompasses different tasks, which provide an informative view of its capabilities:

4.1 Classification/Prediction and CBL

CBL systems can perform classification or prediction tasks on their own, or in combination with other classifiers. Ensemble learning often combines the CBL expertise with other classification/prediction algorithms. Another type of combination of classifiers is to use several CBL systems as input to another classifier, for example a support vector machine, applied to the task of predicting business failure (Li and Sun 2009).

Another notable synergy with classification consists in resorting to other classifiers to learn or improve a knowledge container. For example, *decision tree induction* may organize a case memory, like in INRECA (Auriol et al. 1994). This project integrated CBR and decision trees by preprocessing the case base by an induction tree algorithm.

4.2 Association Mining and CBL

Association mining, although not looking closely related to CBR, can be resorted to in several scenarios. Main uses are for case mining and case base maintenance. For example, Wong et al. (2001) use fuzzy association rule mining to learn cases from a web log, for future reuse through CBR. Liu et al. (2008) use frequent item sets mining to detect associations between cases, and thus detect cases candidate for removal from the case base and its reduction (Retain step).

4.3 Clustering and CBL

Memory structures in CBR are foremost cases. A case is defined as a contextualized piece of knowledge representing an experience that teaches a lesson fundamental to achieving the goals of a reasoner (Kolodner 1993). For many systems, cases are represented as truthfully as possible to the application domain. Additionally, clustering or pattern recognition methods have been applied to learn cases themselves (case mining), features (feature mining), and generalized cases (prototype mining). These techniques can be applied concurrently to the same problem, or selectively. If the trend is now to use them selectively, it is expected that in the future CBL systems will use these methods more and more concurrently.

Case Mining

Case mining refers to the process of mining potentially large data sets for cases (Yang and Cheng 2003). Researchers have often noticed that cases simply do not exist in electronic format, that databases do not contain well-defined cases, and that the cases need to be created before CBR can be applied. Instead of starting CBR with an empty case base, when large databases are available, preprocessing these to learn cases for future CBR permits to capitalize on the experience dormant in these databases. Yang and Cheng (2003) propose to learn cases by linking several database tables through *clustering* and *Support Vector Machines*. The approach can be applied to learning cases from electronic medical records (EMRs).

Generalized Case Mining

Generalized case mining refers to the process of mining databases for generalized and/or abstract cases. Generalized cases are named in varied ways, such as prototypical cases, abstract cases, prototypes, stereotypes, templates, classes, ossified cases, categories, concepts, and scripts – to name the main ones (Maximini et al. 2003). Although all these terms refer to slightly different concepts, they represent structures that have been abstracted or generalized from real cases either by the CBR system, or by an expert. When these prototypical cases are provided by a domain expert, this is a knowledge acquisition task. More frequently they are learned from actual cases. Prototypical cases are often learned to structure the memory.

In medical domains, many authors mine for *prototypes*, and simply refer to *induction* for learning these (Armengol and Plaza 1994) (Bellazzi et al. 1998). Schmidt and Gierl (1998) point that prototypes are an essential knowledge structure to fill the gap between general knowledge and cases in medical domains. The main purpose of this prototype learning step is to guide the retrieval process and to decrease the amount of storage by erasing redundant cases. A generalization step becomes necessary to learn the knowledge contained in stored cases.

Others specifically refer to *generalization*, so that their prototypes correspond to generalized cases (Malek 1995) (Portinale and Torasso 1995) (Kolodner 1993).

Finally, many authors learn *concepts* through *conceptual clustering* (Bichindaritz 1995) (Perner 1998). Díaz-Agudo et al. (2003) use *formal concept analysis* (FCA) – a mathematical method from data analysis - as another induction method for extracting knowledge from case bases, in the form of *concepts*. Napoli (2010) stresses the important role FCA can play for classification purposes in CBR, through learning a case hierarchy, indexing, and information retrieval.

Mining for Memory Organization

Efficiency at case retrieval time is conditioned by a judicious memory organization. Two main classes of memory are presented here: unstructured – or flat – memories, and structured memories.

Flat memories are memories in which all cases are organized at the same level. Retrieval in such memories processes all the cases in memory. Classical nearest neighbor (kNN) retrieval is a method of choice for retrieval in flat memories. Flat memories can also contain prototypes, but in this case the prototypical cases do not serve as indexing structures for the cases. They can simply replace a cluster of similar cases that has been deleted from the case base during case base maintenance activity. They can also have been acquired from experts. Flat memories are the memories of predilection of kNN retrieval methods (Aha 1997) and of so-called memory-based systems.

Among the different structured memory organizations, the accumulation of generalizations or abstractions facilitates the evaluation of the situation and the control of indexation. Structured memories, when they are dynamic, present the advantage of being declarative. The important learning efforts in declarative learning are materialized in the structures and the dynamic organization of the memory, in particular through incremental concept learning (Perner 1998) (Bichindaritz 1995). By learning memory structures in the form of concepts, the classical CBR classification task improves, and at the same time the system extracts what it has learnt, thus adding a knowledge discovery dimension to the classification tasks performed.

Another important method, presented in CHROMA (Armengol and Plaza 1994), is to organize the memory like a hierarchy of objects, by *subsumption*. Retrieval is then a classification in a hierarchy of objects, and functions by substitution of values in slots. CHROMA uses its prototypes, induced from cases, to organize its memory.

Other types of memory organization include the *formal concept lattice* (Díaz-Agudo et al. 2003) organizing the case base around *Galois lattices*. Retrieval step is a classification in a concept hierarchy, as specified in the FCA methodology, which provides such algorithms (Napoli 2010). The concepts can be seen as an alternate form of indexing structure.

Yet other authors take advantage of the *B-tree structure* implementing databases and retrieve cases using database SQL query language over a large case base stored in a database (West and McDonald 2003).

4.4 Feature Selection and CBL

Feature mining refers to the process of mining data sets for features. Many CBR systems select the features for their cases, and/or generalize them. Wiratunga et al. (2004) notice that transforming textual documents into cases requires dimension reduction and/or feature selection, and show that this preprocessing improves the classification in terms of CBL accuracy – and efficiency. These authors induce a kind of decision tree called boosted *decision stumps,* comprised of only one level, in order to select features, and *induce rules* to generalize the features. Montani et al. (2004) reduce their cases time series dimensions through *Discrete Fourier Transform*, approach adopted by other authors for time series (Nilsson and Funk 2004). Niloofar and Jurisica propose an original method for generalizing features. Here the generalization is an abstraction that reduces the number of features stored in a case (Niloofar and Jurisica 2004).

5   Case Based Learning as an Analogizer

Another way of studying the relationship between CBL and machine learning is to characterize its approach. Domingos (2015) have clustered the different ML approaches into five major tribes. He presents the overall goal of machine as answering empiricist philosopher Hume's question: "How can we ever be justified in generalizing from what we've seen to what we haven't?", thus defining induction as a major research paradigm. Following Domingos's theory, a machine learning approach can be characterized by three main tenants: the representation formalism it uses, its evaluation paradigm, and its optimization component, focused on the search for the highest scoring model. The five major machine learning approaches can be represented more precisely along these three dimensions (see Fig. 2):

1. Symbolists: the symbolist school is based on the assumption that intelligence can be simulated by manipulating symbols like mathematicians and logicians do and knowledge can be represented in a declarative manner through rule-based knowledge representation. Main examples in this family are decision trees and rule learning algorithms such as ID3 or C4.5.
2. Connectionists: the connectionist school is based on the assumption that intelligence can be simulated by representing the brain in artificial neural networks and knowledge can be represented in simulated neurons and the connections between neurons. Main examples in this family are deep learning approaches such as artificial neural networks (ANNs) and their evolution into convolutional neural networks (CNNs).

3. Bayesians: the Bayesian school is based on the assumption that intelligence can be simulated by probabilistic inference and knowledge can be represented in graphical models. Main examples in this family are belief networks, also called Bayesian networks, and hidden Markov models (HMMs).
4. Analogizers: the analogy school is based on the assumption that intelligence can be represented by analogical reasoning. Main examples in this family are the nearest-neighbor algorithm and support vector machines (SVMs).
5. Evolutionaries: the evolutionary school is based on the assumption that intelligence can be simulated by modeling the process of evolution and natural selection. The family of evolutionary algorithms encompasses genetic algorithms, genetic programming, and learning classifier systems.

Fig. 2. The five proposed main approaches to machine learning (Domingos 2015), the representation in the inner circle, the evaluation in the middle circle, and the optimization in the outer circle

Although a master algorithm unifying all these machine learning tribes has not been completely designed yet, and maybe never will, there is more synergy and hybridization between these different methods than ever.

Case-based learning is also based on the concept of analogical inference and thus belongs to the analogizer family. Domingos comments that this group is the least cohesive of all ML groups and that it would benefit from making common cause around the central idea of similarity. He also foresees the possibility that deep analogy will in the future rule ML.

Among the concepts grounding analogy research are analogical argument and analogical rule. An *analogical argument* has the following form (Copi and Cohen 2005). Given *S* being a source domain and *T* being a target domain, where we define a domain as a set of objects and an interpreted set of statements about them:

(1) *S* is similar to *T* in certain (known) respects.
(2) *S* has some further feature *Q*.
(3) Therefore, *T* also has the feature *Q*, or some feature *Q** similar to *Q*.

(1) and (2) are premises. (3) is the conclusion of the argument. The * notation refers to features in the target domain and the unstarred symbols refer to symbols in the source domain. The argument form is inductive; the conclusion is not guaranteed to follow from the premises. Formally, an analogy between *S* and *T* is a one-to-one mapping between objects, properties, relations and functions in *S* and those in *T*. Not all of the items in *S* and *T* need to be placed in correspondence. Commonly, the analogy only identifies correspondences between a select set of items. In practice, we specify an analogy simply by indicating the most significant similarities (and sometimes differences).

Keynes (1921) introduced some terminology related to *positive analogy* (accepted or known similarities), *negative analogy* (accepted or known differences), and *neutral analogy* (propositions of unknown status). These concepts allow us to provide a characterization for an individual analogical argument as follows:

SOURCE (S)	TARGET (T)	
P	P*	[positive analogy]
A	~A*	[negative analogy]
~B	B*	
Q		
	Q*	(plausibly)

An analogical argument may thus be summarized by: It is plausible that Q* holds in the target because of certain known (or accepted) similarities with the source domain, despite certain known (or accepted) differences.

Analogical inference uses a source analog to form a new conjecture, and is the fundamental purpose of analogical reasoning (Holyak 2017). Although there is no current complete formalization of analogical inference, the most complete form proposed can be represented by the equation (Bartha 2016):

> Suppose S and T are the source and target domains. Suppose P_1, ..., P_n (with $n \geq 1$) represents the positive analogy, A_1, ..., A_r and $\sim B_1$, ..., $\sim B_s$ represent the (possibly vacuous) negative analogy, and Q represents the hypothetical analogy. In the absence of reasons for thinking otherwise, infer that Q* holds in the target domain with degree of support $p > 0$, where p is an increasing function of n and a decreasing function of r and s.

In order to make this formula computationally actionable, formal models have been designed to represent retrieval, mapping, transfer, and learning (see Fig. 3). Analogical inference can then permit to derive knowledge about a target situation from data and knowledge about a known similar situation (the source). Such an inference is neither true- nor false-preserving. Analogical machine learning is essentially an axiomatic machine learning approach close to explanation-based learning.

Analogical learning starts with analogical reasoning as defined by:

- Retrieval: the retrieval of potential analogous sources are recognized through their similarities with the target, which are properties P.
- Mapping: the mapping consists in determining the properties Q that can be transferred from the source to the target. Mapping serves to highlight correspondences between the source and target, including "alignable differences"– the distinct but corresponding elements of the two analogs. These correspondences provide the input to an inference engine that generates new target propositions.
- Transfer: the properties $Q[S]$ are transferred to the target T, yielding properties Q $[T]$. The basic form of analogical inference has been called "copy with substitution and generation" (CWSG; Holyoak 1997). CWSG involves constructing target analogs of unmapped source propositions by substituting the corresponding target element, if known, for each source element, and if no corresponding target element exists, postulating one as needed. All major computational models of analogical inference use some variant of CWSG. CWSG is critically dependent on variable binding and mapping; hence, models that lack these key computational properties (e.g., traditional connectionist models) fail to capture even the most basic aspects of analogical inference (Doumas and Hummel 2005).

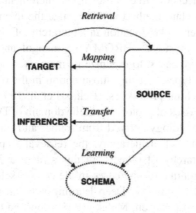

Fig. 3. Major components of analogical reasoning from (Holyak 2017)

CBR researchers have stressed the essential role of analogy in CBR. De Mantaras et al. (2005) emphasize that the main difference between CBR and analogical reasoning resides in the engineering and practical focus of CBR, to build specific working systems, while analogical reasoning is mostly interested in cognitive modeling in general, although recently computational analogy has contributed to bridging the gap between CBL and analogy (Besod and Plaza 2015). If CBL has much in common with computational analogical learning, it also brings a rich research in adaptation (Ontanón and Plaza 2012) that complements well the extensive mapping and transfer theories of analogy (Falkenhainer et al. 1989). In the grander scheme of machine learning, the analogy framework provides a broader field of action to case-based learning that is advantageous to broaden CBL beyond the instance-based learning paradigm. Indeed, through analogical learning CBL can propose a general learning model for the analogizer family. For example, Domingos proposed a unified algorithm between instance based learning and rule based learning where a rule would not match only entities that satisfies all its preconditions but also any entity that is more similar to it than any other rule (Domingos 1996). Through analogical learning, CBL can occupy a more central stage within the analogizer family of machine learning. SVM can be situated within this framework as an instance-based learner (Domingos 2015) where the instances are support vectors and the kernel function serves as a similarity function between a new case to solve and a support vector. The nearest support vectors serve as the source cases for further reasoning.

Synergies between CBL and the other ML tribes are frequent. We can provide several examples:

1. Symbolists and CBL synergy: some early models of this synergy encompass for example the INRECA project (Auriol et al. 1994), which studied how to integrate CBR and decision tree induction by preprocessing the case base by an induction tree, namely a decision tree. The system is based on a similar approach in KATE and PATDEX from the authors. Later refined into an INRECA tree, which is a hybrid between a decision tree and a k-d tree, this method allows both similarity based retrieval and decision tree retrieval, is incremental, and speeds up the retrieval. Another important method is to organize the memory like a hierarchy of objects. Retrieval is then a classification in a hierarchy of objects, and functions by substitution of values in slots. CHROMA (Armengol and Plaza 1994) uses its prototypes, induced from cases, to organize its memory. The retrieval step of CBR retrieves relevant prototypes by using subsumption in the object oriented language NOOS to find the matching prototypes. (Bellazzi et al. 1998) also show a memory organization around classes of prototypes in the domain of Diabetes Mellitus. Every knowledge-based methodology derived from frames and semantic nets rely on that type of knowledge. In such a hierarchy, the retrieval step is two folded: first a classification in a hierarchy of objects, in this system a Bayesian classification, followed by a NN technique on the cases in the classes selected by the first step.

2. Connectionists and CBL synergy: Deep learning synergies with CBL have been studied for a long time. Earlier on, Malek (1995) proposed to use a *neural network* to learn the prototypes in memory for a classification task, such as diagnosis, therefore as a method for learning the memory structure, and also for generalized case mining. CNNs can also be used for feature selection and dimensionality reduction, which can be combined with CBR as well. Retrieval is another area where CNNs have been successfully applied. (Cheng and Ma 2015) propose to use CNN as a non-linear method for attribute similarity local distance to retrieve green building certified design cases.

3. Bayesians and CBL synergy: Bennacer et al. (2015) apply a combination of Bayesian Network (BN) and CBR to the diagnostic task of fault diagnosis. The proposed mechanism allows the identification of the root cause with a finer precision and a higher reliability. At the same time, it helps to reduce computation time while taking into account the network dynamicity. The BN serves as a retrieval method by calculating the distance between a new case and those in the case base.

4. Analogizers and CBL synergy: CBL represents in and of itself a machine learning method of choice, through in particular the instance-based learning methods of kNN (Aha 1997), the synergies between analogy and machine learning, and between case-based reasoning and support vector machines (Li and Sun 2009).

5. Evolutionaries and CBL: synergies between evolutionary algorithms and CBL have long been studied as well. Genetic algorithms methods have been proposed for retrieval purposes, to optimize the search for the most pertinent cases to retrieve (Shin and Han 1999), and for adaptation purposes, to optimize the adaptation of reused case(s) and propose innovative forms of reuse (Floyd et al. 2008).

6 Building the Case and Future Directions

In summary, traditionally case-based learning has been associated with instance-based learning (Mitchell and Aha 1987). However, situating it within the broader scope of the analogical inference, at the core of case-based reasoning, we can more fully take advantage of the promises attached to analogy for human cognition, which includes the ability to learn (Hofstadter 2001).

An important consideration is also the concept of master/slave situation between CBL and other ML methods. This article has presented many synergies between CBL and ML, showing that ML methods can be used in a slave situation for CBL in terms of learning its knowledge containers. It has also presented many synergies between ML approaches and CBL that show that generally CBL has a master role, and less often an equally important role, except in Ensemble methods, or as a slave.

Table 1. CBL and ML tasks map

	Classification/ prediction	Association mining	Clustering	Feature selection
Metareasoning	Ensemble learning			
Retrieval knowledge				Indexing/Weight learning
Adaptation knowledge	Adaptation rule mining			
Case base	Memory organization	Case mining/ Case base reduction	Case mining/ Generalized case mining/ Memory organization	Feature mining/Case refinement

Table 1 represents the mapping between CBL and ML tasks, where we notice that the knowledge containers benefitting the most from ML are retrieval knowledge and case base knowledge. Interesting areas to explore could be feature selection functionality for case mining, or metareasoning. Retrieval knowledge and Adaptation knowledge could also explore more fully the use of knowledge discovery and some work has started in these areas (Badra et al. 2009). For retrieval, in addition to weight learning, learning a similarity measure (Stahl 2005), or improving on an existing one, would be valuable. These synergies could take place during the Retain step, but also in an opportunistic fashion during the Retrieve and/or Reuse steps.

Overall, CBL works synergistically very well with any ML approach. Table 2 summarizes the main ideas coming from studying the major synergies with the five approaches to machine learning. The table highlights that the greatest synergies contribute to the retrieval of cases, and some methods also contribute to the reuse step to bring creativity (evolutionary methods) or knowledge-based approaches (symbolist methods) while other methods contribute to the retain step through memory organization and memory structures. As for the other aspects of CBL, the contribution of different ML methods has been less studied, which could open new fields of research for the future.

Table 2. CBL and other ML approaches map

	Symbolist	Connectionist	Bayesian	Analogizer	Evolutionary
Retrieve	X	X	X	X	X
Reuse	X				X
Revise	X				
Retain	X	X			

By combining the two considerations – the approach and the task, we get a clearer picture that ML is often used in CBL in a non-traditional way – to extend the CBL capability beyond the traditional retrieval, reuse or retain methods.

7 Conclusion

In this paper, we presented the considerable synergies existing between ML tasks and approaches and CBL, and how there is much promise in extending them in the future, in particular with connectionist approaches, to exploit their high performance in imaging in particular, and Bayesian approaches, in domains such as medicine where probabilities are highly regarded. A promising research area is to broaden the framework of case-based learning to analogical learning, while enriching it with reuse theories, which would free CBL from some of the limitations of strict instance-based learning paradigm and extend the notion of case to concept, support vector, or prototype. Indeed, through analogical learning CBL can propose a general learning model for the analogizer family and occupy a more central stage within this family of machine learning. Future steps could tackle how to represent in this broader framework major elements of the analogizer approach of ML such as SVMs, how to develop more fully metareasoning for CBL, and how to develop the promising concept of deep analogy.

References

Aamodt, A., Plaza, E.: Case-based reasoning: foundational issues, methodologies variations, and systems approaches. AI Commun. **7**(1), 39–59 (1994)

Aha, D.W.: Lazy Learning. Artif. Intell. Rev. **11**, 7–10 (1997)

d'Aquin, M., Badra, F., Lafrogne, S., Lieber, J., Napoli, A., Szathmary, L.: Case base mining for adaptation knowledge acquisition. IJCAI **7**, 750–755 (2007)

Armengol, E., Plaza, E.: Integrating induction in a case-based reasoner. In: Keane, M., Haton, J. P., Manago, M. (eds.) Proceedings of EWCBR 94, pp. 243–251. Acknosoft Press, Paris (1994)

Auriol, E., Manago, M., Althoff, K.D., Wess, S., Dittrich, S.: Integrating induction and case-based reasoning: methodological approach and first evaluations. In: Keane, M., Haton, J.P., Manago, M. (eds.) Proceedings of EWCBR 94, pp. 145–155. Acknosoft Press, Paris (1994)

Badra, F., Cordier, A., Lieber, J.: Opportunistic adaptation knowledge discovery. In: McGinty, L., Wilson, D.C. (eds.) ICCBR 2009. LNCS (LNAI), vol. 5650, pp. 60–74. Springer, Heidelberg (2009). https://doi.org/10.1007/978-3-642-02998-1_6

Bartha, P.: Analogy and Analogical Reasoning, the Stanford Encyclopedia of Philosophy (Winter 2016 Edition), Zalta, E.N. (ed.). https://plato.stanford.edu/archives/win2016/entries/reasoning-analogy/

Bellazzi, R., Montani, S., Portinale, L.: Retrieval in a prototype-based case library: a case study in diabetes therapy revision. In: Smyth, B., Cunningham, P. (eds.) EWCBR 1998. LNCS, vol. 1488, pp. 64–75. Springer, Heidelberg (1998). https://doi.org/10.1007/BFb0056322

Bennacer, L., Amirat, Y., Chibani, A., Mellouk, A., Ciavaglia, L.: Self-diagnosis technique for virtual private networks combining Bayesian networks and case-based reasoning. IEEE Trans. Autom. Sci. Eng. **12**(1), 354–366 (2015)

Besold, T.R., Plaza, E.: Generalize and blend: concept blending based on generalization, analogy, and amalgams. In: ICCC, pp. 150–157 (2015)

Bichindaritz, I.: A case-based reasoner adaptive to different cognitive tasks. In: Veloso, M., Aamodt, A. (eds.) ICCBR 1995. LNCS, vol. 1010, pp. 391–400. Springer, Heidelberg (1995). https://doi.org/10.1007/3-540-60598-3_35

Cheng, J.C., Ma, L.J.: A non-linear case-based reasoning approach for retrieval of similar cases and selection of target credits in LEED projects. Build. Environ. **93**, 349–361 (2015)

Copi, I., Cohen, C.: Introduction to Logic, 12th edn. Prentice-Hall, Englewood Cliffs (2005)

De Mantaras, R.L., et al.: Retrieval, reuse, revision and retention in case-based reasoning. Knowl. Eng. Rev. **20**(3), 215–240 (2005)

Díaz-Agudo, B., Gervás, P., González-Calero, P.A.: Adaptation guided retrieval based on formal concept analysis. In: Ashley, K.D., Bridge, D.G. (eds.) ICCBR 2003. LNCS (LNAI), vol. 2689, pp. 131–145. Springer, Heidelberg (2003). https://doi.org/10.1007/3-540-45006-8_13

Domingos, P.: Unifying instance-based and rule-based induction. Mach. Learn. **24**(2), 141–168 (1996)

Domingos, P.: The Master Algorithm. Basic Books, New York (2015)

Doumas, L.A., Hummel, J.E.: Approaches to modeling human mental representations: what works, what doesn't and Why. In: Holyoak, K.J., Morrison, R.G. (eds.) The Cambridge Handbook of Thinking and Reasoning, pp. 73–94 (2005)

Falkenhainer, B., Forbus, K.D., Gentner, D.: The structure-mapping engine: algorithm and examples. Artif. Intell. **41**(1), 1–63 (1989)

Floyd, M.W., Esfandiari, B., Lam, K.: A case-based reasoning approach to imitating RoboCup players. In: FLAIRS Conference, pp. 251–256 (2008)

Han, J., Kamber, M., Pei, J.: Data Mining Concepts and Techniques. Morgan Kaufmann, Waltham (2012)

Hand, D., Mannila, H., Smyth, P.: Principles of Data Mining. The MIT Press, Cambridge (2001)

Hofstadter, D.R.: Analogy as the Core of Cognition. The Analogical Mind: Perspectives from Cognitive Science, pp. 499–538 (2001)

Holyak, K.J.: Analogy, the Cambridge Handbook of Thinking and Reasoning, pp. 117–142. Cambridge University Press, New York (2017)

Keynes, J.M.: A Treatise on Probability. Macmillan, London (1921)

Kolodner, J.: Case-Based Reasoning. Morgan Kaufmann Publishers, San Mateo (1993)

Li, H., Sun, J.: Predicting business failure using multiple case-based reasoning combined with support vector machine. Expert Syst. Appl. **36**(6), 10085–10096 (2009)

Liu, C.H., Chen, L.S., Hsu, C.C.: An association-based case reduction technique for case-based reasoning. Inf. Sci. **178**(17), 3347–3355 (2008)

Malek, M.: A connectionist indexing approach for CBR systems. In: Veloso, M., Aamodt, A. (eds.) ICCBR 1995. LNCS, vol. 1010, pp. 520–527. Springer, Heidelberg (1995). https://doi.org/10.1007/3-540-60598-3_48

Maximini, K., Maximini, R., Bergmann, R.: An investigation of generalized cases. In: Ashley, K. D., Bridge, D.G. (eds.) ICCBR 2003. LNCS (LNAI), vol. 2689, pp. 261–275. Springer, Heidelberg (2003). https://doi.org/10.1007/3-540-45006-8_22

Michalski, R.S.: Toward a Unified Theory of Learning. In: Buchanan, B.G., Wilkins, D.C. (eds.) Readings in Knowledge Acquisition and Learning, Automating the Construction and Improvement of Expert Systems, pp. 7–38. Morgan Kaufmann Publishers, San Mateo (1993)

Mitchell, T.M.: Machine Learning. Mc Graw Hill, Boston (1997)

Montani, S., Portinale, L., Bellazzi, R., Leonardi, G.: RHENE: a case retrieval system for hemodialysis cases with dynamically monitored parameters. In: Funk, P., González Calero, P. A. (eds.) ECCBR 2004. LNCS (LNAI), vol. 3155, pp. 659–672. Springer, Heidelberg (2004). https://doi.org/10.1007/978-3-540-28631-8_48

Napoli, A.: Why and how knowledge discovery can be useful for solving problems with CBR. In: Bichindaritz, I., Montani, S. (eds.) ICCBR 2010. LNCS (LNAI), vol. 6176, pp. 12–19. Springer, Heidelberg (2010). https://doi.org/10.1007/978-3-642-14274-1_2

Arshadi, N., Jurisica, I.: Maintaining case-based reasoning systems: a machine learning approach. In: Funk, P., González Calero, P.A. (eds.) ECCBR 2004. LNCS (LNAI), vol. 3155, pp. 17–31. Springer, Heidelberg (2004). https://doi.org/10.1007/978-3-540-28631-8_3

Nilsson, M., Funk, P.: A case-based classification of respiratory sinus arrhythmia. In: Funk, P., González Calero, P.A. (eds.) ECCBR 2004. LNCS (LNAI), vol. 3155, pp. 673–685. Springer, Heidelberg (2004). https://doi.org/10.1007/978-3-540-28631-8_49

Ontañón, S., Plaza, E.: On knowledge transfer in case-based inference. In: Agudo, B.D., Watson, I. (eds.) ICCBR 2012. LNCS (LNAI), vol. 7466, pp. 312–326. Springer, Heidelberg (2012). https://doi.org/10.1007/978-3-642-32986-9_24

Perner, P.: Different learning strategies in a case-based reasoning system for image interpretation. In: Smyth, B., Cunningham, P. (eds.) EWCBR 1998. LNCS, vol. 1488, pp. 251–261. Springer, Heidelberg (1998). https://doi.org/10.1007/BFb0056338

Portinale, L., Torasso, P.: ADAPtER: an integrated diagnostic system combining case-based and abductive reasoning. In: Veloso, M., Aamodt, A. (eds.) ICCBR 1995. LNCS, vol. 1010, pp. 277–288. Springer, Heidelberg (1995). https://doi.org/10.1007/3-540-60598-3_25

Richter, M.M.: Introduction. In: Lenz, M., Burkhard, H.D., Bartsch-Spörl, B., Wess, S. (eds.) Case-Based Reasoning Technology. Lecture Notes in Computer Science, vol. 1400, pp. 1–15. Springer, Heidelberg (1998). https://doi.org/10.1007/3-540-69351-3_1

Schank, R.C.: Dynamic Memory. A Theory of Reminding and Learning in Computers and People. Cambridge University Press, Cambridge (1982)

Shin, K.S., Han, I.: Case-based reasoning supported by genetic algorithms for corporate bond rating. Expert Syst. Appl. **16**(2), 85–95 (1999)

Schmidt, R., Gierl, L.: Experiences with prototype designs and retrieval methods in medical case-based reasoning systems. In: Smyth, B., Cunningham, P. (eds.) EWCBR 1998. LNCS, vol. 1488, pp. 370–381. Springer, Heidelberg (1998). https://doi.org/10.1007/BFb0056348

Stahl, A.: Learning similarity measures: a formal view based on a generalized CBR model. In: Muñoz-Ávila, H., Ricci, F. (eds.) ICCBR 2005. LNCS (LNAI), vol. 3620, pp. 507–521. Springer, Heidelberg (2005). https://doi.org/10.1007/11536406_39

West, G.M., McDonald, J.R.: An SQL-based approach to similarity assessment within a relational database. In: Ashley, K.D., Bridge, D.G. (eds.) ICCBR 2003. LNCS (LNAI), vol. 2689, pp. 610–621. Springer, Heidelberg (2003). https://doi.org/10.1007/3-540-45006-8_46

Wilson, D.C., Leake, D.B.: Maintaining case-based reasoners: dimensions and directions. Comput. Intell. J. **17**(2), 196–213 (2001)

Wiratunga, N., Koychev, I., Massie, S.: Feature selection and generalisation for retrieval of textual cases. In: Funk, P., González Calero, Pedro A. (eds.) ECCBR 2004. LNCS (LNAI), vol. 3155, pp. 806–820. Springer, Heidelberg (2004). https://doi.org/10.1007/978-3-540-28631-8_58

Wong, C., Shiu, S., Pal, S.: Mining fuzzy association rules for web access case adaptation. In: Workshop Proceedings of Soft Computing in Case-Based Reasoning Workshop, Vancouver, Canada, pp. 213–220 (2001)

Yang, Q., Cheng, H.: Case mining from large databases. In: Ashley, Kevin D., Bridge, Derek G. (eds.) ICCBR 2003. LNCS (LNAI), vol. 2689, pp. 691–702. Springer, Heidelberg (2003). https://doi.org/10.1007/3-540-45006-8_52

Case Based Reasoning as a Model
for Cognitive Artificial Intelligence

Susan Craw[1]($\boxtimes$)(iD) and Agnar Aamodt[2](iD)

[1] School of Computing Science and Digital Media,
Robert Gordon University, Aberdeen, UK
`s.craw@rgu.ac.uk`
[2] Department of Computer Science,
Norwegian University of Science and Technology, Trondheim, Norway
`agnar@ntnu.no`
`http://www.rgu.ac.uk/dmstaff/craw-susan`
`http://www.ntnu.edu/employees/agnar`

Abstract. Cognitive Systems understand the world through learning and experience. Case Based Reasoning (CBR) systems naturally capture knowledge as experiences in memory and they are able to learn new experiences to retain in their memory. CBR's retrieve and reuse reasoning is also knowledge-rich because of its nearest neighbour retrieval and analogy-based adaptation of retrieved solutions. CBR is particularly suited to domains where there is no well-defined theory, because they have a memory of experiences of *what* happened, rather than *why/how* it happened. CBR's assumption that '*similar problems have similar solutions*' enables it to understand the contexts for its experiences and the 'bigger picture' from clusters of cases, but also where its similarity assumption is challenged. Here we explore cognition and meta-cognition for CBR through self-reflection and introspection of both memory and retrieve and reuse reasoning. Our idea is to embed and exploit cognitive functionality such as insight, intuition and curiosity within CBR to drive robust, and even explainable, intelligence that will achieve problem-solving in challenging, complex, dynamic domains.

1 Introduction

Cognition is human-like understanding[1] of the world, context, etc., and cognitive systems aim to understand the world in a way similar to what humans do, through senses, learning, and experience [1]. Langley's 2012 article in the inaugural issue of Advances in Cognitive Systems [2] highlighted the need for AI to refocus on the human intelligence aspect from its early days. Recently there has been an upsurge of interest in cognition in AI with special issues of the AAAI AI

---

[1] We use the term '*understanding*' in the sense of '*interpret in order to give meaning*' for the system involved.

© Springer Nature Switzerland AG 2018
M. T. Cox et al. (Eds.): ICCBR 2018, LNAI 11156, pp. 62–77, 2018.
https://doi.org/10.1007/978-3-030-01081-2_5

Magazine and IEEE Intelligent Systems [3–5]. These papers highlight the importance of understanding, context and analogy for Future Intelligent Technologies (FIT)[2].

In early 2017 Launchbury published DARPA's perspective on AI [6] where he reflected on 3 waves of AI: the early approaches relying on handcrafted knowledge, and later statistical learning, and the need now for new advances in contextual adaptation. In contrast to Launchbury's historical timeline, Domingos proposes 5 'tribes' (i.e. classes) of learning algorithms: symbolic, connectionist, evolutionary, bayesian and analogical [7]. He suggests that Machine Learning in around 10 years will be dominated by deep analogy, and envisions a *Master Algorithm* that combines nearest neighbour, Support Vector Machines (SVMs) and analogical reasoning [8]. Forbus and Hinrichs' *Companion Cognitive Architecture* [9] also highlights the key role of analogical reasoning and the utility of qualitative representations. Case Based Reasoning (CBR) already takes advantage of many of these ideas: cases capture the context in which the experience occurs, retrieval uses nearest neighbour, adaptation is a key part of reuse, and analogy is the basis of reasoning in CBR.

Kahneman [10] proposes a classification of reasoning as *'Fast Thinking'* with intuitive, quick, stereotypical decisions, or *'Slow Thinking'* with deliberative, calculating, logical reasoning. 'Fast Thinking' may easily lead to errors, and Kahnemann gives many examples of that, while 'Slow Thinking', being more deep and elaborate, can act as a censor and make necessary corrections. We may think of CBR with a simple retrieve & reuse reasoning as replicating 'Fast Thinking' because of its assumption of intuition that similar problems will have similar solutions. In contrast, 'Slow Thinking' CBR is when similarity knowledge is complex, retrieved cases are conflicting, when adaptation is complicated or computationally demanding, etc. A CBR system is able to do both 'Fast Thinking' or 'Slow Thinking' depending on the complexity of retrieval and reuse. Its 'Fast Thinking' errors are when similar problems do NOT have similar solutions!

Gartner's dimensions of machine smartness [11] highlight the need for cognitive intelligence: handling complexity; making confidence-based predictions; learning actively/passively; acting autonomously; appearing to understand; and reflecting a well-scoped purpose. These match the three 'Ls' of cognitive computing, *Language, Learning* and (confidence) *Levels* [12]. Case-based systems go some way towards Gartner's complexity, confidence and passive learning criteria [11]. More ambitious self-reflection, introspection, and curiosity is needed to advance towards Gartner's active learning criteria and the demands of complex/changing contexts.

This paper considers the explicit knowledge in cases, but also the similarity and adaptation knowledge, in order to explore the system's *understanding* of its knowledge. This approach also broadens the CBR system's understanding to implicit knowledge from *collections* of cases, and *interactions* between case,

---

[2] EPSRC   FIT   Priority   www.epsrc.ac.uk/research/ourportfolio/themes/ict/introduction/crossictpriorities/futureintelligenttechnologies/.

retrieval and reuse knowledge. This will enable the system to exploit 'Fast Think-ing' when possible and to streamline 'Slow Thinking' when necessary. For this we take advantage of both cognition and meta-cognition, using Cox's interpreta-tion of Minsky's World and Self models [13]. The rest of this paper is organised as follows. Section 2 considers the knowledge sources of a CBR system and its knowledge of itself. Sections 3 and 4 explore the system's understanding of its knowledge and of itself, through cognition and meta-cognition, and how this understanding can be used for self-adaptation. The impact of cognitive CBR through its knowledge and understanding is discussed in Sect. 5. Section 6 high-lights related work from a variety of angles, before we draw some conclusions about cognitive CBR as a model for cognitive AI in Sect. 7.

2   What a CBR System Knows

A CBR system has knowledge of the world it models, but it also has knowl-edge of itself. Its world knowledge comprises its cases, and in addition rea-soning knowledge through similarities and adaptations. CBR contains explicit knowledge represented as symbolic structures in some knowledge representa-tion format. The reasoning knowledge may be explicit, allowing for meta-level reasoning, or implicit in the underlying procedures. CBR's world knowledge is well-understood. Richter's notion of knowledge containers [14] identifies four different types of knowledge (vocabulary, cases, similarities and adaptations). Richter also highlights the interactions between containers, and the possibility of moving knowledge between these, as shown in Fig. 1. We shall take advantage of interactions between knowledge containers in the following sections.

CBR's self knowledge is that its memory of cases contains things it believes to be true, its similarity assumption that similar problems will have similar

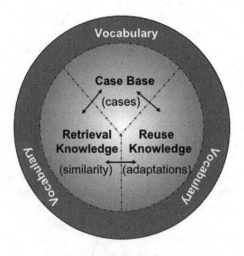

Fig. 1. Knowledge containers (adapted from [14])

solutions, and that differences between query and retrieved cases may/should be reflected in the new solution.

The notions of world and self knowledge fit well with Donald Rumsfeld's (in)famous statement on 'Knowns/Unknowns' [15]:

" ... there are no 'knowns'. There are things we know that we know [Known Knowns]. There are Known Unknowns. That is to say there are things that we now know we don't know. But there are also Unknown Unknowns. There are things we don't know we don't know."

We add the missing combination *Unknown Knowns* for 'things we don't know we know' to Rumsfeld's list.

Figure 2 shows a problem-solving space where the horizontal axis is the system's knowledge about the *world*: what it knows towards the right, and what it does not know on the left. Similarly what the system knows about *itself* is on the vertical axis, with what it knows in the lower half, and what it does not know above. The shaded areas place the four Known/UnKnown combinations in the appropriate quadrant. For CBR the lower right Known Knowns quadrant contains things the system knows it knows; e.g. the cases in memory. The upper Unknown Knowns quadrant is information that the system does not know it knows; e.g. these may be problems that are not in the case base and CBR does not know if nearest neighbour retrieval will generate the right solution. The lower left Known Unknowns quadrant contains things the system knows it does not know; e.g. these may be problems where similar cases contain very different solutions so CBR is not confident of the solution. The upper Unknown Unknowns quadrant is information that the system does not know it does not know; e.g. these may be problems that are outliers or not similar enough to cases in the case base.

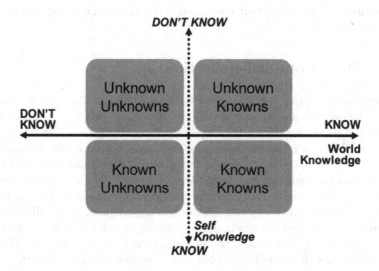

Fig. 2. Self vs World Knowledge from 'Known Knowns' to 'Unknown Unknowns'

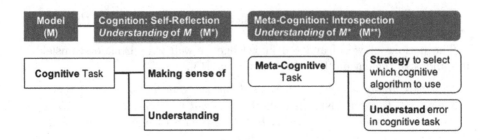

Fig. 3. Cognition and Meta-cognition

This paper will explore a CBR system's understanding of the world knowledge 'it knows it knows' to enable better cognition in the other quadrants. For this we shall view a CBR system as a case based memory of experiences and its retrieve and reuse reasoning. Both memory and reasoning are essentially knowledge based representations [14], and so cognition in one area may enable refinements in this area or others.

We shall take advantage of Cox's work on cognition and meta-cognition [13]. Cox associates cognition with self-reflection as a system understands or makes sense of what it knows. Metacognition is cognition about cognition, or making sense of understanding, and is knowledge about when and how to use particular strategies for problem-solving. Cox associates meta-cognition with introspection. Figure 3 illustrates these ideas. Cognition is shown as 'making sense of' or 'understanding', and Meta-Cognition as 'selection strategies' or 'understanding errors'. Cognition for a model M is self-reflections or understanding of M (denoted M*), and meta-cognition is introspection or understanding of M* (M**). This diagram will be used to underpin the following 2 sections to explore cognition and meta-cognition for a CBR system composed of a case based memory and retrieve & reuse reasoning.

3   Cognition from Self-Reflection

In this section we explore cognition for a CBR system by looking at the system's understanding of its memory of cases and its reasoning, and how it makes sense of its case and reasoning knowledge. Figure 4 applies cognition in Fig. 3 to a CBR system, describing cognition as context for each case, insight of the domain from collections of cases, intuitive reasoning from nearest neighbour, and analogy to take account of problem differences. Reflections on memory provide understanding of each experience as a whole and the relationships among its various facets, and the landscape captured by the collection of experiences. This will enable an understanding of implicit knowledge corresponding to 'what you don't know you know'. Understanding the reasoning will exploit the fundamental assumption of case based systems that 'similar problems have similar solutions', but that some differences are significant and alter the solution.

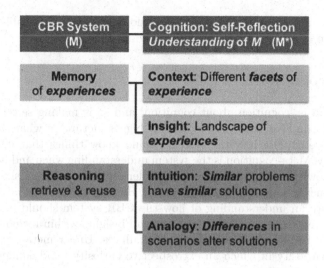

Fig. 4. Cognition with CBR

A case captures a collection of related facets for an experience, and different combinations of facets can be used as a specification or scenario in order to retrieve solutions or suggestions contained in the other facets. Learning relationships between sets of facets within clusters or neighbourhoods of the case base allows the identification of important concepts and relationships between them, and so an understanding of the different contexts in which each case is relevant.

The collection of cases offers an opportunity to understand the landscape for the domain. Areas where there are many similar cases could validate the contents of individual experiences but it also shows where reuse of similar experiences is less risky. In contrast, areas where the problem and solution spaces are not well aligned mean the landscape is complex and more reasoning is needed to reuse these cases. Competence and complexity models for CBR maintenance [16,17] use a similar approach, but these identify redundant or noisy cases whereas here we are interested in areas where 'slow reasoning' may be needed.

Case based systems assume that 'similar problems have similar solutions' and so understanding the reasoning becomes understanding the alignment of cases in similarity space. In areas of regularity, where similar problems do indeed have similar solutions, an intuitive reasoning that reuses similar cases is appropriate, but in complex areas a more sophisticated reasoning is needed. A more complex, finer-grained local similarity can be learned [18], or an uncertainty-based reuse of multiple similar cases is needed by mining neighbourhoods.

The use of analogy to exploit cases beyond their areas of intuitive reasoning may require reuse that includes significant adaptation to take account of differences across the neighbourhood. Understanding when differences between cases in similarity space become significant allows adaptations that reflect the differences in scenarios as alterations to solutions. This is based on learning adaptation knowledge by understanding relationships among cases; e.g. ensemble learning for adaptation [19], or gradient learning for adaptation [20].

4   Meta-cognition

Meta-cognition is 'cognition about cognition' and so is making sense of cognition. Cognition in Sect. 3 has developed the 'bigger picture' of what the system knows; here we explore how the system should know things that it currently solves wrongly. Meta-cognition is the system understanding when and how to use particular knowledge and strategies for problem-solving. Figure 5 shows meta-cognition from Fig. 3 applied to a CBR system. Here we explore how introspective models capture an understanding of how the CBR system should know something, by making sense of different contexts and insights within memory, and by understanding retrieve and reuse reasoning failures. Under meta-cognition we also include curiosity in which an extrospective curiosity builds understanding from external sources.

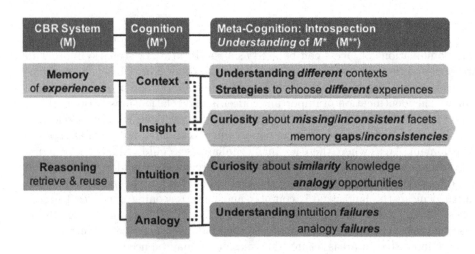

Fig. 5. Meta-cognition with CBR

4.1   Meta-cognition from Introspection

Introspection for CBR memory focuses attention on understanding different contexts in cases. Clusters of similar cases in the problem space allows different selections of facets or features to be identified as key features for similarity matching. Areas of redundancy in the case base enables rich alternative views of the context of an experience. Clusters of similar cases in the solution space can identify dimensions in the problem space where similarity is found. By taking advantage of similarity in the problem or solution spaces, we can define feature selection strategies to create different contexts from these cases. Figure 6 shows two different views of 5 cases comprising problem-solution pairs (P_i, S_i). The left diagram shows a circle of neighbouring problems P_1, P_2, P_3 in the problem space, and a less regular cluster of the corresponding solutions S_1, S_2, S_3. P_4 is a neighbouring problem whose solution S_4 is closer to the others than S_3. P_4 can give important pointers about features and similarity in the problem space in relation to P_1 and $P2_2$ and in comparison with P_3. The diagram on the right shows the same cases but now focuses on the neighbourhood S_1, S_2, S_5 in the solution space. This highlights P_5 as a potentially useful neighbour of P_1 and P_2. In a similar way as previously, P_5 can help to highlight important features and similarity in the P_1, P_2, P_3 region of the case base.

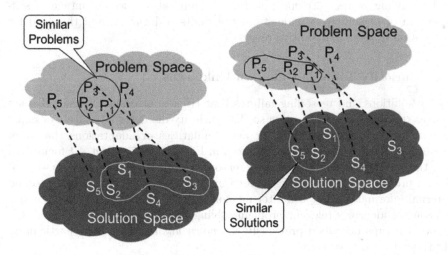

Fig. 6. Problem-solution alignment

By understanding how different facets or experiences are relevant, new selection strategies can be learned. Richter's knowledge containers allow knowledge to be shifted between containers. So it is natural that a given selection strategy can be implemented within different knowledge containers; e.g. a different memory selection can be achieved by altering the representation (different facets) or the retrieval knowledge. For areas of complexity in the case base, cases with similar problems do not have similar solutions. We might take advantage of the contexts learned from other areas of the case base to reduce this complexity by feature/context selection. Alternatively we could identify this region as needing more focused search or more deliberative reasoning. Memory introspection takes advantage of self-reflection for reasoning to associate faulty solutions with the need to learn selection strategies that use alternative contexts or more narrowly focused regions within complex regions of the landscape of cases.

Introspection for retrieve and reuse reasoning in Fig. 5 highlights understanding the failures to identify similar cases or to use analogy to adapt retrieved cases. So here we explore the system's understanding of faulty solutions where the reasoning, rather than memory, is to blame. These methods should go beyond explaining the failure, to understanding what may have caused the failure. The similarity based retrieval may be the cause of the failure, and understanding will involve repairing faulty retrieval knowledge or refining it by adding new similarity knowledge. If the reuse of the retrieved cases is to blame then the adaptation knowledge should be repaired or refined. As before, the interaction between different knowledge containers means that equivalent refinements or repairs can be achieved in similarity or reuse knowledge. An important aspect of understanding reasoning failures is exploring which options are available and where do changes have least potential impact and are most natural for future understanding issues. Introspection for reasoning also takes advantage of self-reflection of reasoning to understand the limits of intuition and the need for adaptation in more deliberative reuse.

4.2   Curiosity Towards Unknown Unknowns

Faulty solutions and reasoning failures that trigger introspection may also act as cues to instigate extrospection so that curiosity discovers new facets or experiences to expand the memory, or new similarities or adaptations that alter retrieval or reuse from memory, as shown in Fig. 5. Whereas Sect. 4.1 focuses on how the current memory and existing reasoning can resolve failures, here we consider a proactive outward facing understanding, where curiosity searches to find external information that will alter memory and/or reasoning. Exploring external sources identifies relevant problem-solving knowledge that fills some of the knowledge gaps described previously as *known unknowns* and the particularly elusive *unknown unknowns*.

Curiosity-inspired learning may be triggered in response to faulty reasoning highlighted during problem-solving. However curiosity about gaps or inconsistencies in memory and reasoning knowledge can also come naturally from self-reflection in Sect. 3. Proactive learning strategies may be applied based on the system's awareness of its own competencies; e.g. in identifying relevant trending stories in social media. Introspective processes may help identify the type of information needed, but curiosity-driven learning will provide autonomous reasoning that interrogates web based memories to refine existing knowledge and assemble latent cases. Trust and provenance will play an important role in selecting knowledge sources that range from trusted, well established, domain relevant ontologies, through to unstructured, uncorroborated content on social media. Mixed strategies based on provenance, previous performance and extent of verification is needed to select and verify suitable sources.

5   Understanding in Cognitive CBR

The previous sections have explored cognitive extensions to CBR to enable understanding of CBR's memory and reasoning at different levels: self-reflection for cognition, introspection for meta-cognition and curiosity for exploration beyond the CBR system itself to discover relevant new knowledge and understanding. These cognitive enhancements have built on the multiple, and interacting, sources of knowledge in a CBR system, the knowledge containers.

Cognitive CBR can have *insights* from the collection of cases in its memory. Relationships between cases can uncover different facets that offer alternative scenarios for retrieval. Collections of cases offer a problem-solving landscape where localised generalisation makes sense. This enables it to develop *intuition* by knowing which contexts are relevant and where similar problems have similar solutions. However it also has an understanding of when and why a more *deliberative* reasoning is needed and how to apply relevant similarity based retrieval and analogy based reuse knowledge. *Curiosity* stems from an understanding that the memory should explore relevant external knowledge or that the reasoning needs to discover similarity or analogy knowledge that is not already available in the CBR system.

Figure 7 demonstrates our ideas of CBR and its cognitive enhancements superimposed on the (Un)Known (Un)Knowns diagram in Fig. 2. The CBR system's memory contains the things *it knows it knows* about the world, the Known Knowns. Adding Self-Reflection offers an understanding of *what* the CBR system knows to discover what the system did not know it knew; i.e. its insights and intuition to uncover Unknown Knowns. Introspection provides an understanding of its

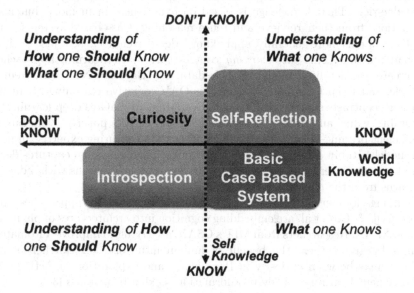

Fig. 7. Cognitive CBR

understanding and so an understanding of *how* it *should* know things, the Known Unknowns. Curiosity takes steps towards Unknown Unknowns by understanding *how* it *should* know *what* it *should* know!

6 Related Work

IBM Watson demonstrates cognitive behaviour in the way it reasons about the facts that it has learned from the Web to 'flesh out' its concept model for a domain. It was able to reason about some '*Unknown Knowns*' when winning the Jeopardy! game show in the US [21]. Watson's Jeopardy! success depended on its DeepQA question-answering cognitive knowledge engine [22]. DeepQA combines Natural Language Processing, Machine Learning and Evidence-based Experimentation to reason about the meaning of queries, to discover relevant information from its memory of extracted facts, and to gather evidence to rank the candidate answers [23, 9:1–12,10:1–14,14:1–12]. IBM's vision for Watson is to exploit DeepQA to underpin decision support in specialised domains. However, priming Watson to understand a new domain is a significant challenge, as found with Healthcare Watson [24]. It must be able to extract meaning from new text content, to understand new questions/scenarios, and to reason about new concepts [25]. Although IBM Watson Knowledge Studio[3] is designed to allow experts to teach Watson about a new domain, this instruction is quite knowledge poor – annotating texts to highlight domain entities and relationships. Nevertheless, Goel's application *Jill Watson*, the virtual teaching assistant, has been highly successful for supporting students during learning because its knowledge source of previous years student queries and answers is well matched to its task [26].

Case-based systems are a different sort of cognitive system; they are already knowledge-rich. Their knowledge is based on experiences in memory, but also explanations from their retrieve and reuse reasoning. Case-based systems, and cognitive systems more generally, apply knowledge-driven, localised, just-in-time search at run-time. This '*lazy learning*' contrasts with other learning approaches that create a generalised model of their data; e.g. Bayesian Networks, Neural Networks and Deep Learning. Watson DeepQA's cognitive reasoning about its knowledge contrasts sharply with Google DeepMind AlphaGo's deep learning of inscrutable 'value' and 'policy' networks [27], and CMU's poker-playing Libratus' efficient pruning of game trees [28]. Rather than capturing expertise in network models, Rubin & Watson's case-based poker-playing system captures decisions of expert players and its knowledge-driven approach reasons with, adapts, and learns from the play of experts [29,30].

Planning domains are particularly amenable to cognitive approaches and Muñoz-Avila & Cox et al. are embedding cognition into architectures of planning systems [31,32]. Researchers from MIT's CSAIL are trying to improve automated planners by giving them the benefit of human intuition [33]. Gottlieb et al. highlight links between curiosity in Psychology, and exploration in Active and Reinforcement Learning, as key to information-seeking behaviours [34].

---

[3] https://www.ibm.com/watson/services/knowledge-studio/.

The ideas in this paper have built on existing areas of research in CBR. Cognition and meta-cognition for memory relates to case base maintenance and TCBR indexing. Memory based reflection has been useful to identify redundant or noisy cases for case base maintenance [17,35,36]. Memory based introspection has been used in facet learning and case indexing. Meta-level reasoning has been used in a clinical decision support system for combining reasoning methods at run-time [37]. This was later extended to an architecture for learning how to select reasoning methods dynamically during execution time, using a lazy learning approach [38]. For recommendation, Smyth et al. have used opinion mining from reviews to learn relevant features for the products to be recommended [39,40]. Curiosity builds on previous work on case discovery and case indexing [41,42]. Cognition and Meta-Cognition for reasoning relates to CBR research in introspective learning of retrieval knowledge in changing environments [43], self-reflection for improving retrieval and reuse [44,45], and introspective learning of adaptation knowledge to reuse retrieved solutions [46–48]. Introspection for reasoning also builds on previous research in textual contexts through understanding failures [49].

7 Conclusions

In this paper we have explored the possibility of extending CBR to embed cognition and meta-cognition. CBR offers a suitable framework for this enhancement because CBR comprises local independent cases in its memory and a just-in-time localised generalisation at run-time. Both its memory and reasoning are driven by explicit qualitative knowledge that allows experimentation and refinement. Compared to the generalised models of other AI systems, CBR is able to understand its knowledge and reasoning, and update it as needed. In this way CBR can use its existing framework to capture self-reflection and introspection.

Cognitive CBR may also address the features of Domingos' proposed Master Algorithm: nearest neighbour, SVMs and analogical reasoning [7]. CBR already uses nearest neighbour retrieval and analogical reasoning in its R^4 Retrieve-Reuse-Revise-Retain approach [50,51]. Self-reflection and introspection enables cognitive CBR to achieve feature/facet learning, case refinement and local similarity learning. These could be thought of as learning the efficient problem solving representation corresponding to SVM's planes.

Self-understanding through reflection and introspection offers both cognition and meta-cognition, and thus provides opportunities for adaptive self-improvement towards a cognitive system with high competence and robust intelligence. Understanding of both self- and world-knowledge will also contribute to explainability. Cognitive CBR will underpin Explainable CBR (XCBR) since the system has its (self) understanding of its knowledge and problem-solving. Thus explainability for a human is transformed into interpreting the system's understanding and explanation into understanding in the human's view. There are links between cognition and the important AI goals of explainability, competence, and robustness. As a result Cognitive CBR could make a valuable contribution to an XAI that is robust in complex and changing environments.

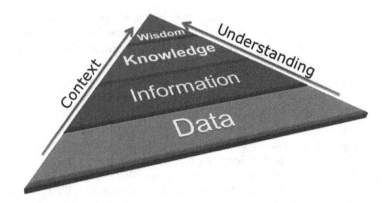

Fig. 8. Data – Information – Knowledge – Wisdom Pyramid

The well-known Data – Information – Knowledge – Wisdom Pyramid [52] shown in Fig. 8 demonstrates the need for increased understanding and context as systems fit in the higher layers of Knowledge and Wisdom compared to Data and Information nearer the base. A CBR system certainly fits in the Knowledge layer through its knowledge in cases, the patterns and relationships captured by similarity based retrieval, and analogy-based adaptations in reuse. So does cognitive CBR achieve wisdom? Its understanding of the CBR system at the knowledge layer builds additional context, insight and intuition and so extends cognitive CBR beyond knowledge. We argue that cognitive CBR captures some aspects of Wisdom in its understanding and higher level reasoning, but human wisdom may include other more perceptive or emotional aspects not yet found in cognitive CBR.

Acknowledgments. Susan Craw wishes to thank Stewart Massie for very helpful discussions of cognition and curiosity during the early stages of developing a research proposal on cognitive CBR that underpins this paper. Agnar Aamodt wishes to thank Enric Plaza for discussions of CBR, analogy, and cognition relevant to this paper, in preparing an invited talk at ICCBR 2017.

References

1. Kelly III, J.E., Hamm, S.: Smart Machines: IBM's Watson and the Era of Cognitive Computing. Columbia University Press, New York (2013)
2. Langley, P.: The cognitive systems paradigm. In: Advances in Cognitive Systems, vol. 1, pp. 3–13 (2012)
3. Nirenburg, S.: Cognitive systems: towards human-level functionality. AI Mag. **38**(4), 5–12 (2017)
4. Langley, P.: Interactive cognitive systems and social intelligence. IEEE Intell. Syst. **32**(4), 22–30 (2017)
5. Langley, P.: Meta-algorithms in cognitive computing. IEEE Intell. Syst. **32**(4), 35–39 (2017)

6. Launchbury, J.: A DARPA perspective on artificial intelligence (2017). http://www.darpa.mil/attachments/AIFull.pdf, http://machinelearning.technicacuriosa.com/2017/03/19/a-darpa-perspective-on-artificial-intelligence
7. Domingos, P.: The Master Algorithm: How the Quest for the Ultimate Learning Machine Will Remake Our World. Basic Books, New York (2015)
8. Vasant, D., Pedro, D.: Pedro domingos on the master algorithm: a conversation with vasant dhar. Big Data 4(1), 10–13 (2016). https://doi.org/10.1089/big.2016.29003.pdo
9. Forbus, K., Hinrichs, T.: Analogy and qualitative representation in the companion cognitive architecture. AI Mag. 38(4), 5–12 (2017)
10. Kahneman, D.: Thinking, Fast and Slow. Farrar Straus Giroux, New York (2011)
11. Austin, T., LeHong, H.: Digital business innovation with smart machines. Report G00265758, Gartner, Stamford, CT, August 2014. http://www.gartner.com/doc/2818821/digital-business-innovation-smart-machines
12. Spohrer, J., Banavar, G.: Cognition as a service: an industry perspective. AAAI Artif. Intell. Mag. Winter 36, 71–86 (2015)
13. Cox, M.T.: Metacognition in computation: a selected research review. Artif. Intell. 169(2), 104–141 (2005). https://doi.org/10.1016/j.artint.2005.10.009
14. Richter, M.M.: Knowledge containers. http://pages.cpsc.ucalgary.ca/~mrichter/Papers/Knowledge%20Containers.pdf
15. Rumsfeld, D.: Press Conference, NATO HQ, Brussels, June 2002. http://www.nato.int/docu/speech/2002/s020606g.htm
16. Smyth, B., McKenna, E.: Competence models and the maintenance problem. Comput. Intell. 17(2), 235–249 (2001). https://doi.org/10.1111/0824-7935.00142
17. Craw, S., Massie, S., Wiratunga, N.: Informed case base maintenance: a complexity profiling approach. In: Proceedings of the 22nd AAAI Conference on Artificial Intelligence, Vancouver, Canada, pp. 1618–1621. AAAI Press (2007). http://www.aaai.org/Papers/AAAI/2007/AAAI07-258.pdf
18. Jarmulak, J., Craw, S., Rowe, R.: Self-optimising CBR retrieval. In: Proceedings of the 12th IEEE International Conference on Tools with AI, Vancouver, Canada, pp. 376–383. IEEE Press (2000). https://doi.org/10.1109/TAI.2000.889897
19. Jalali, V., Leake, D., Forouzandehmehr, N.: Learning and applying case adaptation rules for classification: an ensemble approach. In: Proceedings of the 26th International Joint Conference on Artificial Intelligence (IJCAI), Melbourne, Australia, pp. 4874–4878. AAAI Press (2017). http://static.ijcai.org/proceedings-2017/0685.pdf
20. McDonnell, N., Cunningham, P.: A knowledge-light approach to regression using case-based reasoning. In: Roth-Berghofer, T.R., Göker, M.H., Güvenir, H.A. (eds.) ECCBR 2006. LNCS (LNAI), vol. 4106, pp. 91–105. Springer, Heidelberg (2006). https://doi.org/10.1007/11805816_9
21. Murdock, J.W.: Structure mapping for jeopardy! clues. In: Ram, A., Wiratunga, N. (eds.) ICCBR 2011. LNCS (LNAI), vol. 6880, pp. 6–10. Springer, Heidelberg (2011). https://doi.org/10.1007/978-3-642-23291-6_2
22. Ferrucci, D., et al.: Building watson: an overview of the DeepQA project. AAAI Artif. Intell. Mag. Fall 31, 59–79 (2010)
23. Murdock, (ed.) J.W.: This is Watson (Special Issue). IBM J. Res. Dev. 56(3–4) (2012)
24. Ferrucci, D., Levas, A., Bagchi, S., Gondek, D., Mueller, E.: Watson: beyond jeopardy!. Artif. Intell. 199–200, 93–105 (2013). https://doi.org/10.1016/j.artint.2012.06.009

25. Kalyanpur, A., Murdock, J.W.: Unsupervised entity-relation analysis in IBM Watson. In: Proceedings of the Third Annual Conference on Advances in Cognitive Systems, pp. 12:2–12:12 (2015). http://www.cogsys.org/papers/ACS2015/article12.pdf

26. Goel, A.K., Polepeddi, L.: Jill watson: a virtual teaching assistant for online education. Presented to the Learning Engineering for Online Learning Workshop, Harvard University (2017). http://smartech.gatech.edu/handle/1853/59104

27. Silver, D., Huang, A., et al.: Mastering the game of Go with deep neural networks and tree search. Nature **529**(7587), 484–489 (2016). https://doi.org/10.1038/nature16961

28. Brown, N., Kroer, C., Sandholm, T.: Dynamic thresholding and pruning for regret minimization. In: Proceeding of the 31st AAAI Conference on Artificial Intelligence, San Francisco, CA, pp. 421–429. AAAI Press (2017). http://aaai.org/ocs/index.php/AAAI/AAAI17/paper/view/14855/13793

29. Rubin, J., Watson, I.: On combining decisions from multiple expert imitators of performance. In: Proceedings of the 22nd International Joint Conference on Artificial Intelligence (IJCAI), Barcelona, Spain, pp. 344–349. AAAI Press (2011). http://ijcai.org/Proceedings/11/Papers/067.pdf

30. Rubin, J., Watson, I.: Decision generalisation from game logs in No Limit Texas Hold'Em. In: Proceedings of the 23rd International Joint Conference on Artificial Intelligence (IJCAI), Beijing, China, pp. 3062–3066. AAAI Press (2013). http://dl.acm.org/citation.cfm?id=2540128.2540578

31. Cox, M.T., Alavi, Z., Dannenhauer, D., Eyorokon, V., Muñoz-Avila, H., Perlis, D.: MIDCA: a meta cognitive, integrated dual-cycle architecture for self-regulated autonomy. In: Proceedings of the 30th AAAI Conference on Artificial Intelligence, Phoenix, AZ, pp. 3712–3718. AAAI Press (2016). http://www.aaai.org/ocs/index.php/AAAI/AAAI16/paper/view/12292/12151

32. Muñoz-Avila, H., Dannenhauer, D., Cox, M.T.: Towards cognition-level goal reasoning for playing real-time strategy games. In: Annual Conference on Advances in Cognitive Systems: Workshop on Goal Reasoning, pp. 120–132 (2015). http://smartech.gatech.edu/handle/1853/53646

33. Kim, J., Banks, C., Shah, J.: Collaborative planning with encoding of users high-level strategies. In: Proceeding of the 31st AAAI Conference on Artificial Intelligence, San Francisco, CA, pp. 955–961. AAAI Press (2017). http://aaai.org/ocs/index.php/AAAI/AAAI17/paper/view/14840/13867

34. Gottlieb, J., Oudeyer, P.Y., Lopes, M., Baranes, A.: Information-seeking, curiosity, and attention: computational and neural mechanisms. Trends Cogn. Sci. **17**(11), 585–593 (2013). https://doi.org/10.1016/j.tics.2013.09.001

35. Lupiani, E., Massie, S., Craw, S., Juarez, J.M., Palma, J.: Case-base maintenance with multi-objective evolutionary algorithms. J. Intell. Inf. Syst. **46**(2), 259–284 (2016). https://doi.org/10.1007/s10844-015-0378-z

36. Jalali, V., Leake, D.: Adaptation-guided case base maintenance. In: Proceedings of the 28th AAAI Conference on Artificial Intelligence, Quebec, Canada, pp. 1875–1881. AAAI Press (2014). http://www.aaai.org/ocs/index.php/AAAI/AAAI14/paper/download/8360/8824

37. Houeland, T.G., Aamodt, A.: An introspective component-based approach for meta-level reasoning in clinical decision-support systems. In: Proceedings of the 1st Norwegian Artificial Intelligence Symposium (NAIS 2009), Trondheim, Tapir Forlag, pp. 121–132 (2009)

38. Houeland, T.G., Aamodt, A.: A learning system based on lazy meta reasoning. In: Progress in Artificial Intelligence (In Press, Online November 2017). https://doi. org/10.1007/s13748-017-0138-0
39. Dong, R., OMahony, M.P., Schaal, M., McCarthy, K., Smyth, B.: Combining similarity and sentiment in opinion mining for productrecommendation. Intell. Inf. Syst. **46**(2), 285–312 (2016). https://doi.org/10.1007/s10844-015-0379-y
40. Dong, R., Schaal, M., O'Mahony, M.P., Smyth, B.: Topic extraction from online reviews for classification and recommendation. In: Proceedings of the 23rd International Joint Conference on Artificial Intelligence (IJCAI), Beijing, China, pp. 1310–1316. AAAI Press (2013). http://dl.acm.org/citation.cfm?id=2540128.2540317
41. Massie, S., Craw, S., Wiratunga, N.: Complexity-guided case discovery for case based reasoning. In: Proceedings of the 20th National Conference on Artificial Intelligence (AAAI 2005), Pittsburgh, PA, pp. 216–221. AAAI Press (2005). http:// www.aaai.org/Papers/AAAI/2005/AAAI05-035.pdf
42. Recio-Garcia, J.A., Wiratunga, N.: Taxonomic semantic indexing for textual casebased reasoning. In: Bichindaritz, I., Montani, S. (eds.) ICCBR 2010. LNCS (LNAI), vol. 6176, pp. 302–316. Springer, Heidelberg (2010). https://doi.org/10. 1007/978-3-642-14274-1_23
43. Craw, S., Jarmulak, J., Rowe, R.: Maintaining retrieval knowledge in a case-based reasoning system. Comput. Intell. **17**(2), 346–363 (2001). https://doi.org/10.1111/ 0824-7935.00149
44. Sizov, G., Öztürk, P., Aamodt, A.: Evidence-driven retrieval in textual CBR: bridging the gap between retrieval and reuse. In: Hüllermeier, E., Minor, M. (eds.) ICCBR 2015. LNCS (LNAI), vol. 9343, pp. 351–365. Springer, Cham (2015). https://doi.org/10.1007/978-3-319-24586-7_24
45. Murdock, J.W., Goel, A.: Meta-case-based reasoning: self-improvement through self-understanding. J. Exp. Theor. Artif. Intell. **20**(1), 1–36 (2008). https://doi. org/10.1080/09528130701472416
46. Craw, S., Wiratunga, N., Rowe, R.C.: Learning adaptation knowledge to improve case-based reasoning. Artif. Intell. **170**(16–17), 1175–1192 (2006). https://doi.org/ 10.1016/j.artint.2006.09.001
47. Arcos, J.L., Mulayim, O., Leake, D.B.: Using introspective reasoning to improve CBR system performance. In: Meta reasoning: Thinking about Thinking, pp. 167–182. MIT Press (2011). https://doi.org/10.7551/mitpress/9780262014809.003.0011
48. Leake, D., Powell, J.: A general introspective reasoning approach to web search for case adaptation. In: Bichindaritz, I., Montani, S. (eds.) ICCBR 2010. LNCS (LNAI), vol. 6176, pp. 186–200. Springer, Heidelberg (2010). https://doi.org/10. 1007/978-3-642-14274-1_15
49. Jayanthi, K., Chakraborti, S., Massie, S.: Introspective knowledge revision in textual case-based reasoning. In: Bichindaritz, I., Montani, S. (eds.) ICCBR 2010. LNCS (LNAI), vol. 6176, pp. 171–185. Springer, Heidelberg (2010). https://doi. org/10.1007/978-3-642-14274-1_14
50. Aamodt, A., Plaza, E.: Case-based reasoning: foundational issues, methodological variations, and system approaches. AI Commun. **7**(1), 39–59 (1994). citeseerx.ist.psu.edu/viewdoc/summary?doi=10.1.1.39.1670
51. de Mántaras, R.L., et al.: Retrieval, reuse, revision, and retention in case-based reasoning. Knowl. Eng. Rev. **20**(3), 215–240 (2005). https://doi.org/10.1017/ S0269888906000646
52. Rowley, J.: The wisdom hierarchy: representations of the DIKW hierarchy. J. Inf. Sci. **33**(2), 163–180 (2009). https://doi.org/10.1177/0165551506070706

Explainable Distributed Case-Based Support Systems: Patterns for Enhancement and Validation of Design Recommendations

Viktor Eisenstadt[1]($\boxtimes$), Christian Espinoza-Stapelfeld[1], Ada Mikyas[1],
and Klaus-Dieter Althoff[1,2]

[1] Institute of Computer Science Intelligent Information Systems Lab (IIS),
University of Hildesheim, Samelsonplatz 1, 31141 Hildesheim, Germany
{viktor.eisenstadt,christian.espinoza-stapelfeld,ada.mikyas}
@uni-hildesheim.de
[2] German Research Center for Artificial Intelligence,
Trippstadter Strasse 122, 67663 Kaiserslautern, Germany
klaus-dieter.althoff@dfki.de

Abstract. This paper addresses the issues of explainability of case-based support systems, particularly structural CBR systems dominated by knowledge-rich comprehensive cases and domain models. We show how explanation patterns and contextually enriched explanations of retrieval results can provide human-understandable insights on the system behavior, justify the shown results, and recommend the best cases to be considered for further use. We applied and implemented our approach as an agent-based system module within a case-based assistance framework for support of the early conceptual phases in architectural design, taking a single floor plan as a case with a high number of attributes. For the retrieval phase, a semantic search pattern structure, Semantic Fingerprint, was applied, whereas the explanation generation phase is controlled by a number of explanation patterns adapted from already existing explanation goals. Rulesets, case bases, and natural language generation are used for construction and automatic revision of explanation expressions. A contextualization feature categorizes the results into different context classes and includes this information into the explanation. A user study we conducted after the implementation of the explanation algorithm resulted in good acceptance by the representatives of the architectural domain, a quantitative experiment revealed a high rate of valid generated explanations and a reasonable distribution of patterns and contexts.

Keywords: Case-based design · Knowledge-supported design
Explainable artificial intelligence · Pattern recognition
Contextualization · Human-computer interaction

© Springer Nature Switzerland AG 2018
M. T. Cox et al. (Eds.): ICCBR 2018, LNAI 11156, pp. 78–94, 2018.
https://doi.org/10.1007/978-3-030-01081-2_6

1   Introduction

Users of modern AI-based decision support systems are usually not provided with a sufficient amount of information about the system's inner processes that lead to the presented result, solution, or recommendation. However, often, a particular requirement of users of such intelligent information systems is to have a possibility to understand and even reconstruct the system's behavior in order to follow its reasoning process. This is helpful for both, users and the system, if it is planned by developers that interaction with the system should be based on users' trust in the system. Some systems try to satisfy this requirement by including a feature to track the system's behavior, e.g., by providing the users and/or developers with comprehensive documentation or a special API endpoint that can return some explanation data with a certain grade of transparency. In many cases, however, an additional action from the user is required, which is not always desirable from the usability and user experience point of view.

In this paper, we present an automatic approach for explaining of design support system's actions, based on special explanation patterns that can be detected in the user query and the corresponding retrieval results. Our approach consists of three main steps – *pattern recognition, validation,* and *contextualization* (PRVC) – and is implemented in *MetisCBR* [6], a case-based framework for support of early design phases in architectutre, as the underlying technique for its results explanation module, the *Explainer*. This work is a continuation, further development, and enhancement of our pilot research into explanation of case-based design recommendations [3] (see also Sect. 4.1). In this paper, we describe a much more detailed approach that deals with deep properties of cases and builds a contextual relation between result sets from the same user session.

This paper is structured as follows: in Sect. 2, we describe our previous work in the domain of case-based support of the early conceptual phases in architecture and other related research in the domain of explainable AI. In Sect. 3, we shortly describe the MetisCBR framework, followed by the Sect. 4, where we provide a detailed description of our new explanation approach and its application within the framework. Finally, in the last two sections, we present the results of the user study and the quantitative experiment that evaluated the approach, and conclude the paper with a short review of this work and our future research.

2   Related Work

Foundations of explainability of CBR-based software were defined in a seminal work [24] that described current and future issues of this domain in relation to other CBR tasks, such as retrieval and retention. Some of these issues are highly related to our work presented in this paper and are described later in this section. However, before being summarized by Roth-Berghofer [24], earlier work on explanations in CBR has been published, e.g., Aamodt described explanation-driven case-based reasoning [1]. Explanations were also mentioned as an important feature of CBR systems in a survey [9] of functions of all four steps (Retrieve, Reuse, Revise, Retain) of the CBR cycle. In a series of work about explanation-aware systems [8, 25, 27, 28], explanation patterns were presented that formalize the explainable system knowledge by means of applying a control structure with a collection of patterns that represent *explanation problem frame*. Problem frames themselves are a core concept presented by Jackson [13]. For recommender systems, explainability-themed research was conducted as well [19, 29, 30].

In the last decades, multiple research initiatives were started to support design process in creative engineering domains; issues of *case-based design* (CBD) were examined [18]. Especially in architecture, methods of CBD made a big progress with seminal projects such as PRECEDENTS [20], ARCHIE [32] SEED [11], or FABEL [31]. Later, a number of approaches continued research into this topic: DIM [14], VAT [17], or CaseBook [12]. Some of them had an explicit explanation facility implemented and established this fucntionality in CBR-CAAD approaches: ARCHIE contains explanations in the cases as 'outcomes' (goal satisfaction summary) and 'lessons to be learned' (contextual performance of the cases), CaseBook contains a *similarity explanation report* (no information is available about its concrete functionality or algorithms). One of the most recent research projects that worked on further research into the topic of (distributed) CBR-based design support, is *Metis* (funded by German Research Foundation). The focus of Metis were the graph-based and case-based retrieval methods. MetisCBR, the framework for which the explanation component presented in this paper was developed, was initially one of these methods. Others were the adapted VF2 graph matching method and the index-based retrieval in a graph database [26].

Explainability of AI systems has become an emerging topic during the last years, based on the wide distribution of such systems in a multitude of research/application domains. Initiatives, such as workshops [2, 16, 21–23] collect the current trends and newest approaches. In contrast to many other AI fields, case-based reasoning, as mentioned earlier in this section, explored and emphasized the importance of explanations even before the most well-known 4R-structure (Retrieve, Reuse, Revise, Retain) was presented. Roth-Berghofer's work on foundational issues of explainability in CBR [24] argued that the (commercial) CBR systems provide, if implemented, only simplistic types of explanations (why-, how-, and purpose-explanations). What these systems often do not provide are the so-called *cognitive explanations* that, inter alia, aim at answering the question of how the results are related to each other in different dimensions (*contexts*, in our case).

Our approach in this paper is an effort to combine all of these types of explanations to provide a versatile and universal algorithm for construction of reasonable explanations in structural CBR systems and to establish further the tradition of explanation facility in CBR-CAAD systems.

3 MetisCBR

MetisCBR[1] is a distributed system for case-based support of the early conceptual phases in archtecture. A case in MetisCBR is a floor plan that has attributes according to the Rooms+Edges+Metadata domain model [5] (see Fig. 2). The system's core functionality is the *case-based retrieval with semantic fingerprints*, where the fingerprints (FPs), based on a hierarchical description structure [15], represent a collection of attributes according to structural/relational floor plan abstractions, thus acting as semantic search patterns. For each query, the FPs selected by the user are distributed among the *retrieval containers* to decrease the complexity of search. The currently implemented FPs are shown in Fig. 1.

Fingerprint	Label / Specifics	Fingerprint	Label / Specifics
FP1	**Room Count** No connections between rooms and no labels specified	FP5	**Adjacency** Rooms information is complete, no edge labels
FP2	**Relation Count** No room information specified	FP6	**Accessibility** Edge information is complete, no room labels
FP3	**Room Graph** Anonymous representation (no labels) of rooms & edges	FP7	**Full Graph** All information about rooms and edges available
FP4	**Room Types** No room connections, only room labels are specified	FP8	**Natural Light** Light condition attributes

Fig. 1. Current semantic fingerprints of MetisCBR. FP1, FP2, FP4, FP8 are metadata-based (non-graph-based), FP3, FP5-7 are graph-based. Figure from [3].

4 PRVC Methodology for Explanation Generation

In this section, we present our methodology for creation of explanations for design recommendations. We think that this methodology might be of use not only for floor plan cases, but also for cases from other domains and other structural CBR systems. The only requirement to adapt this methodology for other domains and systems is a domain model that can hierarchically differentiate between cases, concepts, and attributes, or similar structures. Firstly, however, we give a definition of explanation as we use it in our support system.

Definition 1. *Explanation is a quadruple $E = (P, V, C, R)$, where P is the set of explanation patterns, V is the vocabulary for explanation expressions, C is the set of case contexts, and R is the set of mapping rules between P, V, and C.*

---

[1] http://veisen.de/metiscbr/.

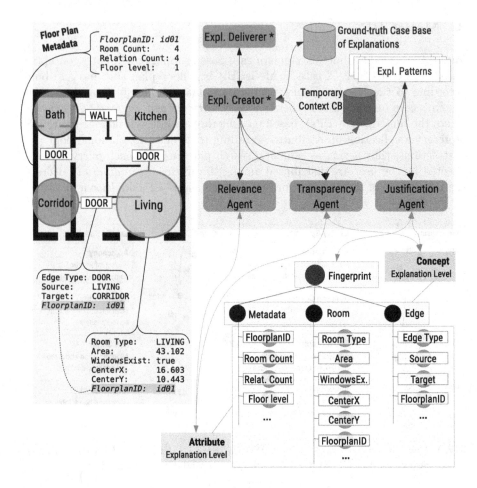

Fig. 2. Left: the domain model *Rooms+Edges+Metadata* and an exemplary case (floor plan) that consists of 4 rooms and 4 edges connected with a common floor plan ID. Bottom right: the general structure of an explanation tree with the explanation levels for a single retrieval result. Top right: the current Explainer module (asterisk marks the agents from the previous version of the module).

4.1 Previous Explainability Function in MetisCBR

The previous explainability function in MetisCBR is described in detail in our previous work [3]. In this section, only a brief overview of this previous/first version of the explanation module, the *Explainer*, is given to present its features relevant for the purposes of this paper. As shown in Fig. 2, two agents govern the process of generation of explanations. The first one is the *Explanation Deliverer* agent whose task is to receive the explanation request for a result and to forward it for further processing, and to receive the results enriched with explanations for forwarding them for displaying in the user interface. The second agent is the *Explanation Creator* agent who is responsible for actual creation/generation of explanations for the results forwarded by the Deliverer. The Creator tries to detect explanation patterns within the query-result object, that consists of the user query and the corresponding results, and generates an *explanation expression* based on the patterns detected (more on explanation patterns is provided in the next sections). After that, the explanation expression is validated against a set of ground-truth expressions, and, if valid, is added to the result.

4.2   Pattern Recognition Phase

The first phase of the PRVC methodology deals with detection of explanation patterns in the previously mentioned *query-result object*. This part of the explanation generation process works with a so-called *explanation tree*, which is created for each single result, and where each *explanation level* of the tree corresponds to an abstraction level of the domain model (see also Fig. 2):

1. *Fingerprint Level* – represents the highest possible abstraction level of the hierarchy and corresponds to the semantic fingerprint selected by the user.
2. *Concept Level* – this level stands for the core structural concepts of the domain model: Floor plan metadata, Room, and Edge.
3. *Attribute Level* – contains attributes of the core concepts according to the fingerprint (i.e., only the attributes of the FP are considered for explanation).

As shown in Fig. 2, the explanation levels are distributed among the *explanation agents* which in turn represent an explanation pattern. In the next sections, these patterns and the procedures for their detection and analysis are presented more in detail. First, however, we give a short description of the theory behind the explanation problem frames and patterns.

Explanation Problem Frames and Patterns. The *explanation patterns* [8] provide a means for abstracted description of explanation-aware computing problems when it comes to dealing with the question of how the reasoning process of an intelligent information system should be made understandable to the user. The concept of explanation patterns is a derivation from the original concept of generic software engineering problem frames [13], and thus an adaptation of these frames for the explanation-aware computing domain. Therefore, the explanation patterns can also be considered *explanation problem frames*. The general structure of an explanation pattern consists of a machine (representation of the software component that creates the explanation), domain (representation of the application area), and requirements (criteria of the proper solution space for a problem, in this case a space of possible explanations). Our rationale for use of explanation patterns for the explanation component was the similarity of their concept to the concept of semantic fingerprints, so that our knowledge and expertise in work with patterns could be transferred. As a result of our work on this transfer, a new *Fingerprint* machine was created [3] that connects the semantic fingerprints of architecture to the explanation patterns of *Relevance*, *Justification*, and *Transparency* [10].

Relevance Pattern. The *Relevance* pattern was conceptualized to justify the questions that system asks the user if certain requirements have not been met. For example, if not enough relevant information was provided to properly answer the query, the system may ask the user for more relevant information and display a message why it needs this information, e.g., why the answer/result may be inexact or incorrect in the current context (the *purpose*-question [24]).

To provide the new version of the Explainer with abilities to detect queries and cases that could not be considered for a proper similarity assessment because of their incompleteness or inexactness, we implemented a rule-based proving mechanism that checks each structural entity of the query and of the result, i.e., each room (node) and room connection (edge), for the *structural completeness* requirement. Currently, the structural completeness requirement for rooms is considered met if the room is *not isolated* – that is, each node has to be connected to *at least one* other node, and if the room label is in the list of enabled labels, such as Working, Living, Sleeping, or Corridor. For edges, this requirement employs a ruleset that checks their *source* and *target* rooms for the same label availability requirement – i.e., each edge has to have both source and target to be considered structurally correct. Depending on the outcome of this check, each entity in the result gets an additional *relevance label* that corresponds to its structural correctness (i.e., RelevanceQuery, RelevanceResult, or RelevanceNone). The relevance score *relScore* for rooms ($relScore_r$) or edges ($relScore_e$) is then:

$$relScore = \frac{|R_Q| + |R_R|}{|R_N| + |R_Q| + |R_R| + e} \tag{1}$$

where R_Q is the set of entities labeled with RelevanceQuery, the same for R_R (RelevanceResult), and R_N (RelevanceNone). e is the error rate for entities whose relevance could not be determined. The entire result floor plan then gets its own relevance label depending on condition resolving shown in Algorithm 1.

Data: $relScore_r$, $relScore_e$, Relevance threshold t_{rel}, Floor plan f, Floor plan relevance rel_f, Expression vocabulary E, Relevance expression set $E_{rel} \subseteq E$

if $relScore_r > t_{rel}$ *or* $relScore_e > t_{rel}$ **then**

   $rel_f = $ **true**

   if $relScore_r >= relScore_e$ **then**

      $e_{rel} = e_{rel}^{rooms} \in E_{rel}$

   else

      $e_{rel} = e_{rel}^{edges} \in E_{rel}$

   end

else

   $rel_f = $ **false**

end

Algorithm 1: Rule-based relevance determination for a result floor plan.

The outcome of this algorithm, if the relevance pattern has been detected for the entire result (i.e., $rel_f = \texttt{true}$), is an expression e_{rel} from the corresponding subset of expressions that should help the user understand why more data is needed by the system to ensure proper similarity assessment for this query or result. Some examples of such expressions are:

- *'This database floor plan may not have enough structural information about room connections for proper similarity assessment.'*
- *'Not enough information has been provided about room configuration to properly assess similarity for this query. Please provide more structural information for the room configuration.'*

Justification Pattern. Reasoning of why a result might be good/helfpul is the task of the *Justification* pattern (*why*-question [24]). For the proper implementation of this pattern in the new Explainer, we relied on our previously applied reasoning premise: a possibly helfpul result is a result whose overall similarity should be at least over the threshold of a sufficient similarity grade. Like in the first version of the Explainer [3] (and for results of the retrieval phase [5]), we applied the following similarity grades: *very similar* if result's overall similarity $Sim \geq 0.75$, *similar* if $0.75 > Sim \geq 0.5$, *sufficiently similar* if $0.5 > Sim \geq 0.25$, and *unsimilar* if $Sim < 0.25$. For the extension and more detailed recognition of possibly helpful designs we introduced an additional justification score $jstScore$:

$$jstScore = \frac{1}{2}\left(\frac{1}{n}\sum_{i=1}^{n} s_{e_i} + \frac{1}{m}\sum_{i=1}^{m} s_{r_i}\right) \tag{2}$$

where $s_e \in S_E$ are the similarity values of edge entities of a result, the same for rooms with $s_r \in S_R$. It is important to notice, however, that the $jstScore$ computation and all other justification operations are only executed if the *Relevance* pattern has not been detected (i.e., if $rel_f = \texttt{false}$, see Algorithm 1). After the computation of $jstScore$, the justification expression is added to the explanation text of the result, depending on conditions shown in Algorithm 2:

Data: $jstScore$, Threshold set T_{jst}, Floor plan f, Floor plan justification jst_f, Expression vocabulary E, Justification expression set $E_{jst} \subseteq E$, Similarity grades G, Justification classes $C_{jst} = \{0 : high, 1 : middle, 2 : low\}$
if $jstScore > t_{jst}^{high} \in T_{jst}$ **then**
  | $jst_f = \texttt{true}$; $c_{jst} = 0$
else if $jstScore > t_{jst}^{middle} \in T_{jst}$ **then**
  | $jst_f = \texttt{true}$; $c_{jst} = 1$
else
  | $jst_f = \texttt{false}$; $c_{jst} = 2$
end
$e_{jst} = mapping(c_{jst}, g_f \in G, E_{jst})$
Algorithm 2: Justification expression determination for a result floor plan.

Where T_{jst} is a set of threshold values for classification of justification depending on its $jstScore$. Currently, following values are used: $t_{jst}^{high} = 0.6$, $t_{jst}^{middle} = 0.3$. The mapping function assigns the proper justification expression for the given justification class c_{jst} and the similarity grade $g_f \in G$ of the result floor plan.

Transparency Pattern. The last implemented explanation pattern is the *Transparency* pattern (the *how*-question [24]), whose task is to provide a means for decoding of the system's pathways to find a result. We think that the users of our system should be informed in as much detail as possible, but at the same time we are aware of the fact that they know how the system works in general. Therefore, we came to a conclusion that a summary of similarity assessment on the attribute level is the best way to provide the users with sufficient information about this procedure. To ensure this, a completely new approach has been implemented for the *Transparency* pattern that takes all the local similarity values from the entity pre-selection step of the retrieval strategy [5] into account. Generally, the transparency reasoning process consists of the following tasks:

1. *Collect* all information of the entity comparison history, i.e., how often and for which entity of the query the entity of the result has been object of comparison, and include the corresponding similarity values.
2. *Reason* about this data, that is, produce an understandable, human-readable summary of this data according to the user requirements and techical terms.

From the collected data, the transparency agent tries to derive the relevant similarity data for each of the attributes for the currently selected fingerprint and summarizes this data by grouping the attributes with the same overall similarity grade. The outcome of the reasoning process is a summarized statistical expression about the attributes' local similarity assessment (*local transparency*) followed by a detailed list of the mean similarity grades for each attribute for each entity. The same procedure is also conducted for the complete result set and is handled as the *global transparency*, and placed on top of the result set. Some examples of such outcomes are provided below (attribute overview omitted):

- '*This floor plan provides a sufficient grade of similarity in terms of passages, room functionalities, and light.*' (local transparency, FP 6 `Accessibility`)
- '*This result set has an overall high value of similarity for room area, and light condition. Low similarity has been determined for door connections.*' (global)

4.3   Validation

The basic principles of the validation process already introduced in [3] remained unchanged, especially because of its good performance: the complete explanation undergoes a feature extraction process, these features build together a case, i.e., become the attributes of this case which in turn becomes a query and is compared with the cases from the ground-truth (i.e., 'golden standard') explanation case base. The value of similarity with the most similar 'golden standard' case then becomes the *validation similarity* v_{max}. The explanation is considered *valid* if

v_{max} exceeds the specified threshold. For the new version of the Explainer, we modified the attributes of the explanation case and replaced the explanation text with the *fingerprint label* (see Fig. 1) and the overall FP similarity value. The detected explanation patterns remained the main similarity assessment feature for the validation. However, to provide a more exact comparison for the patterns as well, we now take into account the *undetected patterns* too, and do not use the detected ones exclusively. The following weighted sum is now in use for validation:

$$v = \omega_l l + \omega_o o + \sum_{i=1}^{n} \omega_{p_i} p_i \qquad (3)$$

Where $v \in V$ ($v_{max} = max(V)$), and $\omega \in \Omega$ are the weights, where ω_l is the weight of the FP label similarity l, ω_o is the weight of the overall FP similarity value o, and ω_p are the weights for the similarity values of the patterns.

4.4 Contextualization

The last step of the PRVC methodology, and the completely new feature of the Explainer, is *Contextualization*, which is responsible for classification of the results into different contexts of the user session (see Fig. 3), and is intended to provide a means for cognitive explanations mentioned in Sect. 2. The inspiration for this feature came from the experience with different internet services such as Flickr or Netflix, where the automatic tagging of pictures and categorization of movies/series are the well-known features. To adapt this feature for our cases, we consider each user request to the system an action of a conceptualization process according to the definition of *Process* defined in our previous work on transfer of cognitive processes of architectural domain representatives into the system [4].

Definition 2. *Process is a triple $P = (S, t, A)$, where S is a set of retrieval strategies, t is the type of the process (e.g., sequential, semi-sequential, enclosing iteration), and A is the set of actions. $A = A_s \cup A_i \cup A_e$ (actions can be of starting, ending, and intermediate type), where $A_s \wedge A_e \neq \varnothing$. Strategies are linked to actions with a surjective mapping $S \twoheadrightarrow A$, i.e., $\forall a \in A \exists s \in S$.*

The basic mode of operation of the contextualization process is based on *feature extraction* from a single result: the main semantic and structural properties, such as room and edge count, room types, or a number of identical room types between query and result, are extracted from the result data and mapped with different contextual classes. These classes represent an abstract expression about the floor plan, some examples are:

- `SparseConnection` - represents floor plans where the number of connections is in the interval from lower to marginally higher as the number of rooms.
- `RoomCount`, `EdgeCount` - number of rooms and/or room connections is equal to the corresponding average value of the complete result set.

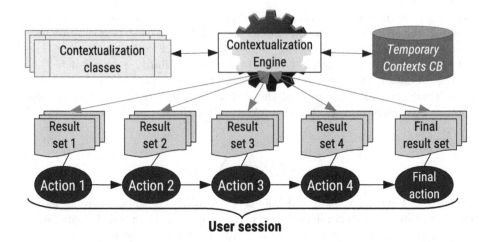

Fig. 3. Contextualization of the results of a sequential process.

- RoomTypeDominance - floor plans where a certain room type dominates the room configuration (e.g., {Living, Living, Living, Kitchen,
Sleeping}).

Additionally to the classification step, for each user session a special temporary case base is created that contains cases where the attributes represent
the extracted features named above, with corresponding values. For each unique
floor plan result from a session, such a case with a count as label is created (if
this case is already available then its count gets increased). For each new single
result, a context similarity value $sim_{context}$ is then calculated as follows and
categorized into a similarity grade (f is a feature, F is the set of all available
features):

$$sim_{context} = \frac{1}{n} \sum_{i=1}^{n} sim_{f_i} \quad f \in F \tag{4}$$

The result of the contextualization process is a contextual expression that
contains information about contexts available in the single result, providing the
user with additional information about differences and commonalities regarding
the configuration of all results. Exemplary contextual expressions are:

- '*This result has a high grade of contextual connection to the previous retrieval
results of this session. Available contexts for this result are:* Room Type
Dominance, Sparse Connections.'
- '*This result has a very low grade of contextual connection within this session.
No contexts could be determined.*'

The $sim_{context}$ value is then combined with the overall similarity of the result,
thus influencing its position in the overall result ranking within the result set.

Other influence is the previously mentioned *case label*, that works as a *boost value* for results whose final similarity values are identical.

4.5 Explanation Algorithm

Summarizing all of the steps described above we present the algorithm for generation of explanations within MetisCBR, that can be transferred or adapted for other systems. The concrete implementation depends on the domain and the corresponding domain model, however, the adaptation should not be difficult, as many structural CBR systems use the attribute-value-based structure for cases (Fig. 4).

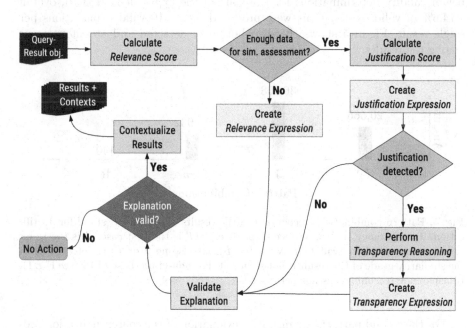

Fig. 4. Algorithm for generation, validation, and contextualization of explanations.

5 User Study and Quantitative Evaluation

To evaluate the new, PRVC-based, Explainer module, we conducted two studies: the first one was a quantitative experiment that aimed at examination of the new Explainer for validity of explanations and distribution of detected patterns. Additionally, we examined the context similarity and contexts distribution of the result floor plans. In the subsequent user study, we presented the representatives of the architectural domain with the explanation module and asked them to rate the produced explanation expressions and context classes.

5.1   Quantitative Experiment

The quantitative test was performed on a case base of 119 floor plans. We used 18 different queries and produced 47 requests (≈3 randomly selected FPs per query) that returned an overall number of 5189 results. 14 ground-truth explanations were used for validation, i.e., the explanation of each single result was validated 14 times. A threshold of 0.5 was applied to determine the validity. Overall, the constructed explanations were validated 72646 times for these results. 58408 (80,4%) of them resulted in a valid outcome – an expectable slightly lower value than in the previous version [3] (84.825% for 225 cases), considering the more restricted handling of patterns (inclusion of undetected patterns) and addition of a new validation attribute. For the theoretical maximum number of validity determinations for this part of the experiment (78302), overall ≈74,6% of valid explanations were produced, i.e., ≈10 valid explanations per single result. Figure 5 shows the distribution of detected and absent patterns among the results.

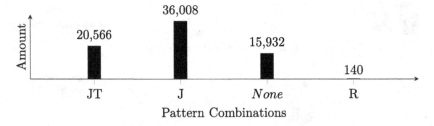

Fig. 5. Pattern combinations recognized in the results. J, T, and R stand for Justification, Transparency, and Relevance respectively. JT is the best case, R is the worst case (not enough data available), *None* (no R, but also no J or T) is detected when the similarity grade of the result is not sufficient. For non-graph-based FPs (see Fig. 1), transparency reasoning was not performed.

For the second part, the quantitative evaluation of the contextualization process, we first examined the overall context similarity $sim_{context}$ of the results, which revealed an average similarity value of ≈0.31, where from the total number of 5189, 2280 results had $sim_{context}$ of 0.35, 1934 results had $sim_{context}$ of 0.15, and 944 results had $sim_{context}$ of 0.55. Further, we examined the overall count of the detected classes during contextualization. Similar to the patterns examination, we show how the contexts were distributed among the results (Fig. 6).

5.2   User Study

For the subsequent user study, we used the same floor plan data set as for the quantitative experiment. The participants, $n = 5$, were asked to answer a specific questionnaire that contained questions regarding the understandability of explanations and their opinion on the contextualization feature. Before the

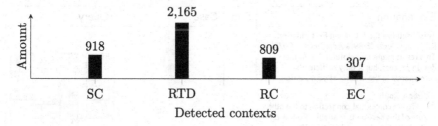

Fig. 6. Context classes recognized in the results. *SC, RTD, RC*, and *EC* stand for Sparse Connections, Room Type Dominance, Room Count, and Edge Count respectively.

rating process, each of the participants was asked to run a self-sketched or one of the already existing queries against the data set and get the corresponding results and explanations (see Fig. 7). 2 FPs should be used for either type of the query. On average, we spent ≈1.5 h per experiment session for each participant. Following questions (Q[n]) were included in the rating questionnaire:

1. Are the explanation expressions and their purpose understandable?
2. *(After the concept of explanation patterns was explained)*:
   Is it easy to recognize which partial expression belongs to which pattern?
3. Specific pattern questions:
   (a) `Justification:` are more reasons for recommendation required/advisable?
   (b) `Transparency:` Is more statistical data required, why and what exactly?
   (c) `Relevance:` is it understandable why the system needs more data?
4. Is the context-awareness and classification of results easy to recognize?
5. *(After the contextualization process was explained)*:
   Is it understandable how the classification/contextualization feature works and how would you estimate the helpfulness of the current contexts?

Generally, for Q1, experienced users who already knew how the system works and participated in one or more of our previous studies, found that the textual explanations are only partly helfpul and wished an additional visualization between query and result (which is already available for one of the MetisCBR-compatible user interfaces [7]). They also wished more detailed transparency explanation, e.g., for each attribute of each room and room connection. The inexperienced participants, i.e., architects who did not work with MetisCBR before (but at least knew the general concepts of CBR), found the textual explanations adequate and could recognize their purpose directly. The expressions themselves were also considered adequate and understandable.

For pattern questions (Q2-Q3), all of the participants were able to recognize which textual part is responsible for which explanation pattern. The positioning of the justification explanation before all others was considered a good decision, the length of the corresponding justification text was also considered good. Besides the already mentioned more detailed transparency data for experienced

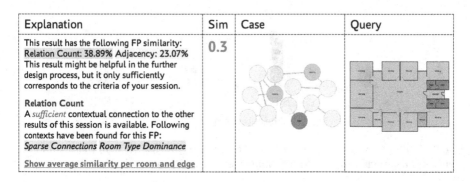

Explanation	Sim	Case	Query
This result has the following FP similarity: Relation Count: 38.89% Adjacency: 23.07% This result might be helpful in the further design process, but it only sufficiently corresponds to the criteria of your session. **Relation Count** A *sufficient* contextual connection to the other results of this session is available. Following contexts have been found for this FP: ***Sparse Connections Room Type Dominance*** Show average similarity per room and edge	0.3		

Fig. 7. Query, case, and explanation of a result with a 'sufficiently similar' similarity grade as they appeared to the participants. Blank lines separate texts for Justification and Contextualization, the last line contains a link for opening the statistical expression (Transparency).

users, a filter function for an 'entity-for-entity' comparison was requested. The purpose of systems' questions in case of lack of sufficient data was also found adequate.

The last examined feature, the contextualization of results (Q4-Q5), was considered interesting and most enriching. All of the participants could recognize the context classes and their purpose for the explainability. The fact that the participants were already familiar with similar concepts from internet services and portals played a big role. However, some of the contexts, i.e., which features exactly they represent, were not always clear (e.g., *What does 'sparse connections' mean?*). Suggestions for new contexts also were made, e.g., RoomDominance, for floor plans where a certain room has a dominant area value.

6   Conclusion and Future Work

In this work we presented a new, extended, version of our results explanation approach for architectural design recommendations, which now works by means of applying the PRVC (pattern recognition, validation, contextualization) methodology. The complete methodology was presented in detail, including algorithms for partial steps and the overall explanation algorithm. Detection of explanation patterns, automatic validation of generated explanations, and the contextualization of results are the main aspects of the approach. We evaluated the new Explainer module with a quantitative expriment and a user study with participation of the architectural domain representatives.

Our future work will be concentrated on a better analysis of explanations (e.g., how the validation and the context classes change over time). Additionally, we will improve each of the steps, especially by applying an improved, more domain-oriented wording (e.g., Space Syntax) for explanations and context classes.

References

1. Aamodt, A.: Explanation-driven case-based reasoning. In: Wess, S., Althoff, K.-D., Richter, M.M. (eds.) EWCBR 1993. LNCS, vol. 837, pp. 274–288. Springer, Heidelberg (1994). https://doi.org/10.1007/3-540-58330-0_93
2. Aha, D., Darrell, T., Pazzani, M., Reid, D., Sammut, C., Stone, P.: IJCAI-17 Workshop on Explainable AI (XAI) (2017)
3. Ayzenshtadt, V., Espinoza-Stapelfeld, C.A., Langenhahn, C., Althoff, K.D.: Multi-agent-based generation of explanations for retrieval results within a case-based support framework for architectural design. In: Proceedings of the 10th International Conference on Agents and Artificial Intelligence (ICAART 2018). Scitepress (2018)
4. Ayzenshtadt, V., Langenhan, C., Bukhari, S., Althoff, K.-D., Petzold, F., Dengel, A.: Extending the flexibility of case-based design support tools: a use case in the architectural domain. In: Aha, D.W., Lieber, J. (eds.) ICCBR 2017. LNCS (LNAI), vol. 10339, pp. 46–60. Springer, Cham (2017). https://doi.org/10.1007/978-3-319-61030-6_4
5. Ayzenshtadt, V., Langenhan, C., Bukhari, S.S., Althoff, K.D., Petzold, F., Dengel, A.: Distributed domain model for the case-based retrieval of architectural building designs. In: Petridis, M., Roth-Berghofer, T., Wiratunga, N. (eds.) Proceedings of the 20th UK Workshop on Case-Based Reasoning (UKCBR-2015), 15–17 December, Cambridge, United Kingdom (2015)
6. Ayzenshtadt, V., Langenhan, C., Bukhari, S.S., Althoff, K.D., Petzold, F., Dengel, A.: Thinking with containers: a multi-agent retrieval approach for the case-based semantic search of architectural designs. In: Filipe, J., van den Herik, J. (eds.) 8th International Conference on Agents and Artificial Intelligence (ICAART-2016), 24–26 February, Rome, Italy. SCITEPRESS (2016)
7. Bayer, J., et al.: Migrating the classical pen-and-paper based conceptual sketching of architecture plans towards computer tools - prototype design and evaluation. In: Lamiroy, B., Dueire Lins, R. (eds.) GREC 2015. LNCS, vol. 9657, pp. 47–59. Springer, Cham (2017). https://doi.org/10.1007/978-3-319-52159-6_4
8. Cassens, J., Kofod-Petersen, A.: Designing explanation aware systems: the quest for explanation patterns. In: ExaCt, pp. 20–27 (2007)
9. De Mantaras, R.L., et al.: Retrieval, reuse, revision and retention in case-based reasoning. Knowl. Eng. Rev. **20**(3), 215–240 (2005)
10. Espinoza, C.: Analysis of Identification of Explanation Patterns for an Explanation Module for Support of Design Phase in Architectural Domain. Project report. University of Hildesheim (2017)
11. Flemming, U.: Case-based design in the SEED system. Autom. Constr. **3**(2), 123–133 (1994)
12. Inanc, B.S.: Casebook. an information retrieval system for housing floor plans. In: The Proceedings of 5th Conference on Computer Aided Architectural Design Research (CAADRIA), pp. 389–398 (2000)
13. Jackson, M.: Problem analysis using small problem frames. S. Afr. Comput. J. **22**, 47–60 (1999)
14. Lai, I.C.: Dynamic idea maps: a framework for linking ideas with cases during brainstorming. Int. J. Arch. Comput. **3**(4), 429–447 (2005)
15. Langenhan, C., Petzold, F.: The fingerprint of architecture-sketch-based design methods for researching building layouts through the semantic fingerprinting of floor plans. Int. Electron. Sci. Educ. J. Arch. Mod. Inf. Technol. **4**, 13 (2010)

16. Lim, B., Smith, A., Stumpf, S.: ExSS 2018: workshop on explainable smart systems (2018)
17. Lin, C.J.: Visual architectural topology. In: Open Systems: Proceedings of the 18th International Conference on Computer-Aided Architectural Design Research in Asia, pp. 3–12 (2013)
18. Maher, M., Balachandran, M., Zhang, D.: Case-Based Reasoning in Design. Lawrence Erlbaum Associates, Mahwah (1995)
19. Muhammad, K., Lawlor, A., Rafter, R., Smyth, B.: Great explanations: opinionated explanations for recommendations. In: Hüllermeier, E., Minor, M. (eds.) ICCBR 2015. LNCS (LNAI), vol. 9343, pp. 244–258. Springer, Cham (2015). https://doi.org/10.1007/978-3-319-24586-7_17
20. Oxman, R., Oxman, R.: Precedents: memory structure in design case libraries. CAAD Futures **93**, 273–287 (1993)
21. Pereira-Fariña, M., Reed, C.: Proceedings of the 1st Workshop on Explainable Computational Intelligence (XCI 2017) (2017)
22. Roth-Berghofer, T.: Explanation-aware computing exact 2012. In: Proceedings of the Seventh International ExaCt workshop (2012)
23. Roth-Berghofer, T., Tintarev, N., Leake, D.B.: Explanation-aware computing exact 2011. In: Proceedings of the 6th International ExaCt workshop (2011)
24. Roth-Berghofer, T.R.: Explanations and case-based reasoning: foundational issues. In: Funk, P., González Calero, P.A. (eds.) ECCBR 2004. LNCS (LNAI), vol. 3155, pp. 389–403. Springer, Heidelberg (2004). https://doi.org/10.1007/978-3-540-28631-8_29
25. Roth-Berghofer, T.R., Cassens, J.: Mapping goals and kinds of explanations to the knowledge containers of case-based reasoning systems. In: Muñoz-Ávila, H., Ricci, F. (eds.) ICCBR 2005. LNCS (LNAI), vol. 3620, pp. 451–464. Springer, Heidelberg (2005). https://doi.org/10.1007/11536406_35
26. Sabri, Q.U., Bayer, J., Ayzenshtadt, V., Bukhari, S.S., Althoff, K.D., Dengel, A.: Semantic pattern-based retrieval of architectural floor plans with case-based and graph-based searching techniques and their evaluation and visualization. In: 6th International Conference on Pattern Recognition Applications and Methods (ICPRAM 2017), 24–26 February, Porto, Portugal (2017)
27. Sørmo, F., Cassens, J.: Explanation goals in case-based reasoning. In: Proceedings of the ECCBR 2004 Workshops, pp. 165–174. No. 142–04 (2004)
28. Sørmo, F., Cassens, J., Aamodt, A.: Explanation in case-based reasoning-perspectives and goals. Artif. Intell. Rev. **24**(2), 109–143 (2005)
29. Tintarev, N., Masthoff, J.: A survey of explanations in recommender systems. In: 2007 IEEE 23rd International Conference on Data Engineering Workshop, pp. 801–810. IEEE (2007)
30. Tintarev, N., Masthoff, J.: Designing and evaluating explanations for recommender systems. In: Ricci, F., Rokach, L., Shapira, B., Kantor, P.B. (eds.) Recommender Systems Handbook, pp. 479–510. Springer, Boston (2011). https://doi.org/10.1007/978-0-387-85820-3_15
31. Voss, A.: Case design specialists in FABEL. In: Issues and Applications of Case-Based Reasoning in Design, pp. 301–335 (1997)
32. Zimring, C.M., Pearce, M., Goel, A.K., Kolodner, J.L., Sentosa, L.S., Billington, R.: Case-based decision support: a case study in architectural design (1992)

Tangent Recognition and Anomaly Pruning to TRAP Off-Topic Questions in Conversational Case-Based Dialogues

Vahid B. Eyorokon(✉), Pratyusha Yalamanchili, and Michael T. Cox(ID)

Department of Computer Science, Wright State University, Dayton, OH, USA
{eyorokon.3,yalamanchili.23,michael.cox}@wright.edu
http://mcox.org/colab2/

Abstract. In any knowledge investigation by which a user must acquire new or missing information, situations often arise which lead to a fork in their investigation. Multiple possible lines of inquiry appear that the users must choose between. A choice of any one would delay the user's ability to choose another, if the chosen path proves to be irrelevant and happens to yield only useless information. With limited knowledge or experience, a user must make assumptions which serve as justifications for their choice of a particular path of inquiry. Yet incorrect assumptions can lead the user to choose a path that ultimately leads to dead-end. These fruitless lines of inquiry can waste both time and resources by adding confusion and noise to the user's investigation. Here we evaluate an algorithm called Tangent Recognition Anomaly Pruning to eliminate false starts that arise in interactive dialogues created within our case-based reasoning system called Ronin. Results show that Tangent Recognition Anomaly Pruning is an effective algorithm for processing mistakes when reusin case reuse.

Keywords: Tangential case-based reasoning
Knowledge investigation · Conversational case-based reasoning
Textual case-based reasoning · Case reuse

1 Introduction

Search for information on complex issues and topics is challenging as well as ubiquitous in a modern society and the knowledge economy. Much like a criminal investigation, a *knowledge investigation* revolves around a series of key questions or knowledge goals that seek to provide answers related to a central purpose of the investigation. As a person asks questions, their investigation often increases in complexity until the user eventually reaches a new state of knowledge and understanding, that is, they achieve their set of knowledge goals. Yet if a person's problem is sufficiently difficult and they are sufficiently inexperienced, mistakes are likely to occur. These mistakes can be costly and often delay the person's ability to achieve their goals and can potentially introduce confusion and frustration. Finally, knowledge investigations in many domains are often repetitive

© Springer Nature Switzerland AG 2018
M. T. Cox et al. (Eds.): ICCBR 2018, LNAI 11156, pp. 95–109, 2018.
https://doi.org/10.1007/978-3-030-01081-2_7

with a few patterns of questions covering the majority of the information tasks performed by an investigator. As such, experience from past investigations (particularly expert experience) can potentially inform and guide new problems or information needs, making a search effective and avoiding false directions in one's information plan.

Case-based reasoning (*CBR*) systems leverage their experience of interactions with past users to provide guidance for future users [1,5,13,19]. Each time a user concludes a novel interaction, the system uses the information collected from that interaction to form a data structure to preserve the problem the user had and the solution they found. This problem-solution pair comprises a case stored by the system in a case-base which functions similarly to a database. When a new user begins an interaction, the system compares the new user's problem with those of previous cases from the case-base. The system then retrieves the most relevant case so that it can be revised or adapted to the user's current problem and reused to help the new user find a solution. During reuse, this case acts like a template the guide the current user to a solution for their problem. *Conversational CBR* (*CCBR*) systems [2,4] are often designed to incrementally build a dialogue through iterative user interactions.

Mistakes manifest in CCBR systems as off-topic questions which we call *tangents*. Tangents manifest as anomalies in a hyper-dimensional similarity space generated from a dialogue's comprising questions using a technique we will discuss. We call this process *tangent recognition*. Once detected, anomalies can then be pruned or removed via a separate process we call *anomaly pruning*. By developing an algorithm to recognize these tangents as they occur, a system can better assist its user in a knowledge investigation and help users avoid tangents in real-time. This creates an opportunity to save the user time on an otherwise protracted search for new information. Additionally, it affords a system with the ability to identify precisely where a user made a mistake and a chance to give the user immediate feedback. We evaluate an algorithm for tangent recognition combined with anomaly pruning that enables a system to TRAP unrelated questions as a user asks them.

We begin by outlining a definition for knowledge goals followed by a case representation of dialogues as goal trajectories within our case-based reasoning system called Ronin. Next, we propose a simple definition of tangents and the two types we consider. Next, we then cover four separate approaches for measuring the similarity between text. Then, we evaluate the performance of *Tangent Recognition Anomaly Pruning* (*TRAP*) when using each of the described similarity methods. We review the performance of TRAP with each similarity method in two complex domains: military and concierge, discuss the results and then conclude.

2   Knowledge Goals and Trajectories in Ronin

A *knowledge goal* is the needed information or knowledge that would satisfy the user's desired state of knowledge [3,17]. By acquiring the missing information, the user's state of knowledge transitions to a new state where they have learned the previously missing information and the user's knowledge goal is said to have been satisfied. Knowledge goals often can be expressed in the form of the utterance or a question, where the utterance is the most superficial part of the knowledge goal. However, the question is not the synonymous with the knowledge goal. By chaining together these knowledge goals as shown in Fig. 1, we create a *goal trajectory*. This text-based goal trajectory then becomes a case in our case-base [6]. The key difference between a dialogue and a goal trajectory is that a goal trajectory is the case representation of knowledge goals in series within a similarity space but the two terms may sometimes be used interchangeably.

Fig. 1. Shows a case as a knowledge goal trajectory.

Ronin is our conversational CBR system that shares fundamental problems found in natural language and text processing as it incorporates unstructured textual data. *Textual CBR* involves systems whereby cases are largely comprised on unstructured text [18,24,25]. Users interact with Ronin by asking a series of questions each of which represents the utterance of a knowledge goal [7]. When posing these questions, or knowledge goals in a series of text, users create dialogues [9] that preserve the order in which individual knowledge goals were asked. These dialogues can sometimes contain tangents as shown in Fig. 2. In our system, knowledge goals can also capture relationships to their answers, but here we instead explore the overall knowledge investigation and the effect that tangents have in goal trajectories.

2.1   Tangents in Goal Trajectories

When an individual begins their knowledge investigation to acquire new information in response to a problem, it is often the case that their current understanding of the problem itself is ill-defined either through a lack of experience or because the problem domain is challenging. This makes it difficult for the user to phrase questions correctly and accurately enough for their question to sufficiently capture their need for specific information. Without an accurate question, a system's ability to assist the user is bounded. Additionally, it is not always the case that individuals are afforded the option of having a more experienced and knowledgeable person to guide them through their investigation thereby introducing more exposure to mistakes. The medium through which knowledge investigations are performed can be laborious, boring, time consuming or otherwise tiresome as they are often performed through search engines, research journals or basic question and answer systems thereby adding to the stress of

Fig. 2. Shows a case where a question (q2) is off-topic in the dialogue.

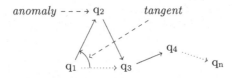

Fig. 3. The second question, q2, is recognized as an anomaly and is shown as a tangent (i.e., the angle between the dotted arrow and the solid arrow).

the user's investigation. Each scenario can cause mistakes or tangents. Figure 3 shows a simple representation of recognizing tangents within a dialogue.

While not all knowledge investigations suffer from all of these properties, we believe it is reasonable to assume that each one increases the chances for mistakes. Figure 4 shows a tangent being removed from a dialogue. In order to recognize tangents, it is important to consider the types of tangents that exist. Simply put, some tangents are more obvious than others. We use a simple distinction for tangents with two classifications: hard and soft. Our evaluation for this paper will cover hard tangents.

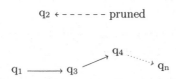

Fig. 4. The second question is dropped from the dialogue.

2.2   Soft Tangents

Soft tangents are unrelated questions that are from the same domain. Simply put, these questions are not relevant to the current knowledge investigation, but they are related to the overall domain in which the knowledge investigation exists. Consider an example in the Concierge Domain where a person asks about restaurants nearby. She might ask the concierge for a general list of nearby restaurants. She would then refine this list asking about cost, distance, speed of service and possibly even inquire about specific dietary options. But suppose at some point, the thought of entertainment and museums occurred to her and so she asked about art museums. This question about museums is certainly within the concierge domain, however, it is irrelevant to her current goal of finding a suitable restaurant. For this reason, it is a soft tangent.

2.3 Hard Tangents

Hard tangents are unrelated questions from an unrelated domain. Because hard tangents are from an entirely unrelated domain, intuitively we can surmise that they are easier to detect over soft tangents since soft tangents at least share a similar domain. For hard tangents, we used questions from a political domain. Questions in this domain ask about various global leaders, general practices of democratic systems and laws. When considering our previous example of a person investigating nearby restaurants, a hard tangent would have manifested had she asked about the voting age, the number of senators in the senate or results of the latest general election.

3   Similarity Measures

Ronin can use four different ways of measuring similarity between text. Such similarity measures are also used in case trajectory retrieval as described in [8]. The first of these is Term Frequency Inverse Document Frequency which is a statistical, bag-of-words approach. The second is Word2Vec which is a neural network that generates vectors for a word by considering its surrounding words. The third is called SkipThoughts and uses a neural network similar to Wod2Vec. These vector representations can be compared to measure the similarity between words and yield a similarity score when using cosine similarity. We will discuss later how word vectors can be used to measure similarity between sentences. The fourth measure uses a semantic net, along with corpus statistics and is an algorithm based on the work done by which we refer to as NetSim. We will discuss each similarity measure, their advantages and their drawbacks in the remainder of this section.

3.1   Term Frequency Inverse Document Frequency

Term Frequency Inverse Document Frequency (TFIDF) [26] requires a rich corpus of text for the bag-of-words approach to be effective. For this, our system relies on parsing the noun and verb phrases from each utterance and querying the phrases to Wikipedia. This query usually returns a related page from which our system extracts the first three sentences. These sentences are added to the original text of the question's utterance to build a question document. This process is done for each utterance in the database and TFIDF is performed using the resulting question documents instead of the utterances alone and allows us to gain a better under-standing of conceptual terms in the question [11]. However, this process of querying Wikipedia introduces the issue of disambiguation.

Sometimes, Wikipedia will return a list of possible results that are related to the queried phrase instead of a single page. To disambiguate these results would require a sophisticated algorithm or constant human supervision. Given the challenges of disambiguation and since our research focuses on retrieval, we default to the result Wikipedia suggests is the best matching. Yet this is sometimes incorrect.

3.2   Word2Vec

Word2Vec [16] is a neural network trained on a large corpus of textual data collected by Google. This approach creates a vector representation for words that considers surrounding words. When an utterance is provided, each word in the string is converted into a vector [20]. After gathering the vector representations for each word in the utterance, we averaged these vectors into a single vector for the entire utterance. That is, given a vector for each individual word in a sentence we compute the sum of all vectors divided by the number of words in the sentence to form a sentence vector [22]. The main insight in this method is to obtain the individual word embedding vectors in a question/sentence and form a sentence embedding by averaging vectors. By using the cosine similarity [14] between two questions vectors we calculate the similarity. We obtain each word embedding from the Word2Vec skip-gram model which was pre-trained on Google News vectors containing a corpus of 3 billion words. Word2Vec's skip-gram algorithm predicts whether a word belongs to the surrounding window of words, from a three-layer neural network with one hidden layer while both input and output layers being the unique bag of words thereby forming a word embedding.

3.3   Skip-Thoughts

The Skip-thought model draws inspiration from the skip-gram structure in the word2vec model. It consists of a neural network that is trained to reconstruct the surrounding sentences that share syntactic and semantic properties [12]. This model is based on an encoder-decoder architecture where encoder maps natural language sentences into fixed length vector representations. Then given the vector representation of a sentence, the encoder is built using recurrent neural network layers, bi-directional recurrent neural network layers, or a combination of both. This captures the temporal patterns of continuous word vectors. Hidden states of the encoder are fed as a representation into two separate decoders. Again each decoder uses another set of recurrent layers. These decoders share the same look-up table with the encoder and then predict the preceding and subsequent sentences.

3.4   NetSim

NetSim uses a semantic net along with corpus statistics to measure the similarity between two sentences [15]. The semantic net factors into account two measures:

semantic and syntactic similarity. Semantic similarity looks at the synonyms words have in common, the distance from one word to an-other in the semantic net and the depth of a word in the semantic net. Since depth of a word relates to the specialization of a word, distance alone cannot be used. To understand why depth is important, consider the following example. The word 'human' may appear closer to the word 'boy' than the word 'babysitter' but a knowledge goal about humans may be less relevant than one about 'babysitters'. Since words become more specialized as we go down the semantic net, depth is factored into the similarity measure. Syntactic similarity for NetSim considers the position of words in one utterance and the distance from related words in another utterance. Additionally, inverse document frequency (IDF) is used to establish an information content of each word. This is a statistical measure where words that are common in the corpus have a low information content and thus a lower IDF score, while less occurring words have a higher IDF score. Finally, the semantic and syntactic scores are multiplied by weights and added together yielding a scalar value for similarity. The semantic and syntactic weights for our evaluation were set to 70% and 30% respectively. It should be noted that the use of a semantic net has drawbacks since they only capture is-a relationships and while similarity using NetSim is powerful, it is also bounded as we will see from the evaluation.

4   Tangent Recognition Anomaly Pruning (TRAP)

We refer to Ronin's ability to recognize irrelevant questions in the user's dialogue as *tangent recognition*. The goal of tangent recognition is not merely to represent goal trajectories as a series of Bag-of-Word vectors, but to move beyond this and represent the user's knowledge investigation itself and reason about their goals [21]. Tangents manifest as anomalies in a hyper-dimensional similarity space and can then be pruned or removed.

$$D = \left[\begin{array}{ccccc} q_1 & q_2 & q_3 & \cdots & q_n \end{array} \right]$$

Fig. 5. Shows dialogue D represented as a vector of questions.

The process begins by first creating a vector representation for a dialogue D as shown in Fig. 5. Converting each of the dialogue's questions into a vector yields a dialogue matrix that can then be used to recognize tangents and prune anomalies. Each of the following four subsections correspond to the four major functions called by TRAP shown in Algorithm 1.

Algorithm 1. Tangent Recognition Anomaly Pruning

1: **function** QUESTIONVECTOR(*origQuestion, goalTrajectory*)
2:     *questionVec* ← []
3:     **for each** *question* ∈ *goalTrajectory* **do**
4:         *sim* ← *Similarity*(*question, origQuestion*)
5:         *Append*(*questionVec, sim*)
6:     **return** *questionVec*
7: **function** DIALOGUEMATRIX(*goalTrajectory*)
8:     *dialogueMatrix* ← []
9:     **for each** *question* ∈ *goalTrajectory* **do**
10:         *questionVec* ← QUESTIONVECTOR(question, goalTrajectory)
11:         *Append*(*dialogueMatrix, questionVec*)
12:     **return** *dialogueMatrix*
13: **function** TANGENTRECOGNITION(*goalTrajectory, threshold*)
14:     *dialogueMatrix* ← DIALOGUEMATRIX(goalTrajectory)
15:     i, j ← 0, 1
16:     **while** j ≤ length(goalTrajectory) **do**
17:         *pairwiseCosineSim* ← COSINESIM(goalTrajectory[i], goalTrajectory[j])
18:         **if** *pairwiseCosineSim* < *threshold* **then**
19:             **return** [i, j]
20:         INCREMENT(i,j)
21:     **return** −1
22: **function** ANOMALYPRUNING(*goalTrajectory, threshold*)
23:     *tangentFree* ← *goalTrajectory*
24:     **do**
25:         *anomalies* ← TANGENTRECOGNITION(tangentFree,threshold)
26:         REMOVE(*tangentFree, tangentFree*[*anomalies*[*length*(*anomalies*) − 1]])
27:     **while** *anomalies* ≠ −1
28:     **return** *tangentFree*
29: **function** TRAP(*goalTrajectory, threshold*)
30:     *tangentFree* ← ANOMALYPRUNING(goalTrajectory,threshold)
31:     **return** *tangentFree*

4.1   Question Vector

Each question comprises an atomic part of the overall dialogue. Therefore, the dialogue itself can be represented as a list of its comprising questions. Since the dialogue, or goal trajectory itself can be represented as a list of questions, by comparing a particular original question to each question in the goal trajectory, we can get a sense of the original question's relevance to the overall dialogue. By measuring the similarity of the original question to each question in the goal trajectory denoted as s, we create a *question vector* that represents that particular question's relevance to the entire goal trajectory. See the *QuestionVector* function in Algorithm 1 which returns such a representation as that shown in Fig. 6.

$$q_1 = \begin{bmatrix} s_{q_1,q_1} & s_{q_1,q_2} & s_{q_1,q_3} & \cdots & s_{q_1,q_n} \end{bmatrix}$$

Fig. 6. Shows question q_1 represented as a vector of similarity scores between itself and each question in the dialogue (i.e., D from Fig. 5.)

4.2 Dialogue Matrix and Similarity Hyper-Space

This question vectorization process is repeated for every question in the goal trajectory and returns in a symmetrical square n x n matrix where n is equal to the number of questions in the goal trajectory. After we completing this question vectorization process for all questions in the dialogue, we get a square *dialogue matrix* where the number of columns and rows are equal to the number of questions in the dialogue. See the *DialogueMatrix* function in Algorithm 1 which returns the dialogue matrix representation shown in Fig. 7. In such a matrix, each question becomes both a sample and a feature. This matrix represents a multidimensional space of similarity for its comprising questions. By modeling the user's goal trajectory in a multi-dimensional similarity space, tangents manifest as divergent points along the overall direction of the goal trajectory through the similarity space.

$$\begin{bmatrix} q_1 & q_2 & q_3 & \cdots & q_n \end{bmatrix} \rightarrow \begin{bmatrix} [s_{q_1,q_1} & s_{q_1,q_2} & s_{q_1,q_3} & \cdots & s_{q_1,q_n}] \\ [s_{q_2,q_1} & s_{q_2,q_2} & s_{q_2,q_3} & \cdots & s_{q_2,q_n}] \\ [s_{q_3,q_1} & s_{q_3,q_2} & s_{q_3,q_3} & \cdots & s_{q_3,q_n}] \\ \vdots & \vdots & \vdots & \vdots & \vdots \\ [s_{q_n,q_1} & s_{q_n,q_2} & s_{q_n,q_3} & \cdots & s_{q_n,q_n}] \end{bmatrix}$$

Fig. 7. Shows the conversion of each question into a question vector to create a similarity matrix.

4.3 Tangent Recognition

To detect these diverging points, we calculate the pairwise cosine similarity values between row vectors in the similarity matrix. Cosine similarity yields a scalar value between 0 and 1 corresponding to the similarity of the two vectors in this multi-dimensional space where 0 is no similarity and 1 is perfect similarity. We then compare this value against a tunable threshold. Any values less than this threshold indicate that one of the two vectors is anomalous and represents an off-topic question. See the *TangentRecognition* function in Algorithm 1.

4.4 Anomaly Pruning

Once a tangent has been recognized, we next need to identify the anomaly. The challenge here is that cosine similarity represents a score between two vectors, but it does not tell us which vector is the anomalous or irrelevant question. Additionally, the length of the pairwise cosine similarity vector is one less than the length of our dialogue. For this we have chosen to make a simple assumption which is one that allowed us to proceed with our evaluation and that we plan to revisit at a later point.

Our assumption is that the first question of the dialogue is never a tangent. Therefore, when given a cosine score that is less than our threshold for determining tangents, the second question of the pair is always selected as the anomaly. See the *AnomalyPruning* function in Algorithm 1. It should be clear that this assumption lacks consistency in all scenarios as the first question could also be a tangent. For this reason we plan to explore more robust methods of identifying anomalies like *idealization* which will be discussed in future work.

After the anomaly has been removed or pruned, the similarity space is reduced accordingly by removing the row and column that corresponded to the anomalous question. After reducing the similarity space, pairwise cosine similarity is recalculated and TRAP repeats until all tangents have been removed.

5   Empirical Evaluation of TRAP

To evaluate the TRAP algorithm within Ronin, we used existing dialogues/cases from two separate domains: a concierge and a military domain. While TRAP works in real-time, for our evaluation we used existing dialogues to approximate the effect of a tangent in a dialogue to evaluate the TRAP algorithm. As previously mentioned, in the concierge domain, Ronin took the role of a hotel concierge who answered questions from various hotel guests as they inquire about nearby entertainment, food, activities, safety and other assorted tourism related themes. In the military domain, Ronin assisted analysts with answering intelligence questions. We took each dialogue and iteratively inserted hard tangents from a political domain in the middle of the dialogue from one to three consecutive hard tangents. We evaluated TRAP's performance with removing all inserted tangents. The closer the accuracy was to 100%, the better TRAP performed. Conversely, the closer the false positive rate was to 0%, the better.

Here we evaluated the effectiveness of four separate measures: Word2Vec, NetSim, TFIDF and SkipThoughts when used in our TRAP algorithm. Each dialogue in our evaluation was at least 5 questions long. In the middle of each dialogue, we iteratively inserted one tangent until a total of three were inserted. We refer to the number of tangential questions as the tangent length at the time TRAP was performed and the tangent length appears on the X axis. We performed TRAP using each similarity method and averaged the number of the tangents caught across all dialogues of that iteration's tangent length. This averaged value for the tangent length is shown on the Y axis. We then recorded the number of false positives for that iteration. The best any similarity measure could do, was an average accuracy of 100% and a false positive rate of 0%.

In the military domain, 21 dialogues were used at 3 separate tangent lengths for a total of 63 TRAP trials each for Word2Vec, NetSim, TFIDF and

SkipThoughts. A grand total of 252 TRAP trials were performed in the military domain. In the military domain, TRAP with Word2Vec performed the best with an accuracy of 100% with a tangent length of 1 as shown in Fig. 8. Similarly when TRAP used SkipThoughts, the performance resembled Word2Vec on tangent length of one, but fell below Word2Vec as the tangent grew. TFIDF performed the second best and NetSim consistently scored the lowest. Most generally worsened as the tangent length increased with TRAP's performance when using NetSim following an arc as it improved on tangent size 2.

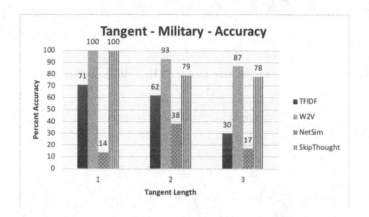

Fig. 8. Shows the accuracy of TRAP in the military domain.

All similarity measures generally had similar false positive rates with the exception of TRAP when using SkipThoughts. TRAP with SkipThoughts had a consistently higher false positive rate than all other similarity measures. These results are reflected in Fig. 9.

In the concierge domain, 19 dialogues were used at 3 separate tangent lengths for a total of 57 TRAP trials each using Word2Vec, NetSim, TFIDF and SkipThoughts. A grand total of 228 TRAP trials were performed in the concierge domain. Figure 10 shows that TRAP with Word2Vec again performed better than TRAP with TFIDF, NetSim or SkipThoughts with all generally worsening as the tangent length grew. The exception to this again was TRAP with NetSim which followed a similar arch in performance as it did in the military domain.

The false positive rates for TFIDF generally fell as the tangent length grew see Fig. 11. This could be because as the tangent length grew, TFIDF had fewer cosine scores above the threshold thereby making catching fewer tangents but also flagging fewer non-tangential questions. When TRAP used Word2Vec, the false positive rate grew with it's highest score being 6% at a tangent length of 3. TRAP with NetSim performed significantly worse in the concierge domain with the false positive rate being four times higher than in the military domain on a tangent length of 2. TRAP with NetSim also had the highest false positive rates on tangent sizes 1 and 2, but fell below TRAP with SkipThoughts on a tangent of size 3.

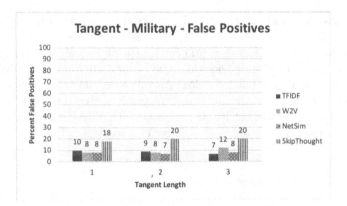

Fig. 9. Shows the false positive rate for TRAP in the military domain.

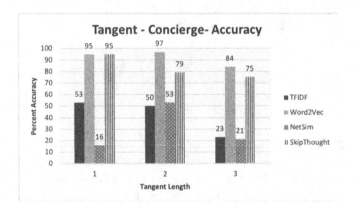

Fig. 10. Shows the accuracy of TRAP in the concierge domain.

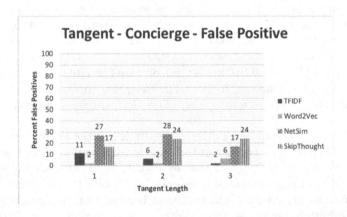

Fig. 11. Shows the false positive rate of TRAP in the concierge domain.

6   Related Research

The work done in [10] is relevant as the goal of identifying off topic answers to questions with TRAP. Their work focuses on content vector analysis (CVA) and unlike TRAP which uses cosine similarity and a hyperspace for tangent recognition, CVA uses a variant of the inverse document frequency score and cosine similarity to measure the relationship between the answer and the question. While both approaches use cosine similarity, TRAP uses a different vector representation that is determined by the surrounding questions in a dialogue.

In doing so, the number of dimensions grows as the number of questions in the dialogue increases. CVA uses a vector representation that is based on the content of the question and the answer supplied by the student. Furthermore, the vector representation generated by TRAP is dependent on the similarity measure used by TRAP. CVA as described by the paper, only uses a variant of TFIDF. While TFIDF can be used with TRAP, so too can Word2Vec, NetSim and Skip-Thoughts. The decoupling of the similarity measure and the algorithm make TRAP more versatile and less susceptible to shortcomings of any one similarity measure.

The work done in [23] is also relevant as the dialogue nature of telephone speech is similar to the dialogue interface in Ronin. Their work focuses on a machine learning algorithmic approach aimed at automating the identification of irrelevance within dialogues. In doing so, theyve built a classifier that identifies important features of dialogues. Since their approach incorporates a series of text over a period of time, this shares similarities to Ronins goal trajectory data structure. Yet Ronins approach differs in that Ronin neither uses a classifier or any other machine learning technique for detecting off-topic text.

7   Future Work and Conclusion

The issue of capturing a tangent where the anomaly is the first question in the dialogue has been a challenge for our evaluation. For this reason, we adopted the simple assumption that the first question was not a tangent. However, while this assumption allowed us to proceed with an initial evaluation to gauge the relevance and utility of TRAP, it is not robust or realistic. For this reason, we are continuing to explore options for adding context to determine the substance of the first question. One such aforementioned approach is what we refer to as idealization. This approach extracts the highest non-perfect score from each column in the dialogue to create an ideal vector. In a sense this would be a question that is highly related to all other questions in the dialogue if such a thing existed and is therefore an ideal. By inserting this vector before the first question vector in the dialogue, we provide initial context in which to evaluate the first question. While this approach remains to be evaluated the underlying challenge does underscore the non-triviality of capturing a tangent whose anomaly is the first question.

The degree to which a case-based reasoning system can assist a user in finding solutions to novel problems largely rests on the systems capacity to retain, retrieve, revise and reuse its experiences. Yet those experiences which the system has acquired through interactions with past users often contain the mistakes their users also made. To maximize the positive impact a system has while minimizing it's negative affects requires a system to both recognize past mistakes and prevent those mistakes from being repeated. Indeed, a system which accumulates cases that routinely commit the same mistakes is a system that can be improved to say the least. By modeling cases in the form of trajectories through a multi-dimensional space, these mistakes can manifest in diverging tangents. Therefore, combining both tangent recognition and pruning of the anomalies which created them leads to an overall better experience for users. TRAP combined with the Word2Vec neural network has been shown to be effective at removing tangents from natural language dialogues while having a low false positive rate. These features make TRAP suitable for processing error from cases to be efficiently reused to find future solutions.

Acknowledgments. This material is based on research sponsored by the Air Force Research Laboratory, under agreement number FA8650-16-C-6763. This research was also supported by ONR grant N00014-18-1-2009. The U.S. Government is authorized to reproduce and distribute reprints for Governmental purposes notwithstanding any copyright notation thereon. The views and conclusions contained herein are those of the authors and should not be interpreted as necessarily representing the official policies or endorsements, either expressed or implied, of the Air Force Research Laboratory or the U.S. Government. We would like to also thank David Aha, Venkatsampath Gogineni, Srikanth Nadella, James Schmitz and the anonymous reviewers for their feedback. Special thanks is given to NSF grant 1834774 for support in funding the first author's travel to and attendance at ICCBR 2018.

References

1. Aamodt, A., Plaza, E.: Case-based reasoning: foundational issues, methodological variations, and system approaches. AI Commun. **7**(1), 39–59 (1994)
2. Aha, D., Breslow, L., Muoz-Avila, H.: Conversational case-based reasoning. Appl. Intell. **14**(1), 125 (1999)
3. Bengfort, B., Cox, M.: Interactive reasoning to solve knowledge goals. In: Aha, D.W. (ed.) Goal Reasoning: Papers from the ACS Workshop, GT-IRIM-CR-2015-001: 1025. Georgia Institute of Technology, Atlanta, GA, Institute for Robotics and Intelligent Machines, May 2015
4. Branting, K., Lester, J., Mott, B.: Dialogue management for conversational case-based reasoning. In: Funk, P., González Calero, P.A. (eds.) ECCBR 2004. LNCS (LNAI), vol. 3155, pp. 77–90. Springer, Heidelberg (2004). https://doi.org/10.1007/978-3-540-28631-8_7
5. De Mantaras, R.L., et al.: Retrieval, reuse, revision and retention in case-based reasoning. Knowl. Eng. Rev. **20**(3), 215–240 (2005)
6. Dufour-Lussier, V., Le Ber, F., Lieber, J., Nauer, E.: Automatic case acquisition from texts for process-oriented case-based reasoning. Inf. Syst. **40**, 153–167 (2014)
7. Eyorokon, V., Bengfort, B., Panjala, U., Cox, M.: Goal trajectories for knowledge investigations. In: Coman, A., Kapetanakis, S. (eds.) Twenty-Forth International Conference on Case-Based Reasoning Workshop Proceedings: Synergies between CBR and Knowledge Discovery, vol. 1815, pp. 202–211. Atlanta, Georgia (2016)

8. Eyorokon, V., Gogineni, B., Pratyusha, Y., Cox, M.: Case Retrieval Using Goal Similarity for Knowledge Investigations. Unpubl. Data (2018)
9. Gu, M., Aamodt, A.: Dialogue learning in conversational CBR. In: Proceedings of the Nineteenth International Florida Artificial Intelligence Research Society Conference, pp. 358–363, Melbourne Beach, Florida, January 2006
10. Higgins, D., Burstein, J., Attali, Y.: Identifying off-topic student essays without topic-specific training data. Nat. Lang. Eng. **12**, 145 (2006). https://doi.org/10. 1017/s1351324906004189
11. Huang, A., Milne, D., Frank, E., Witten, I.H.: Clustering documents using a wikipedia-based concept representation. In: Theeramunkong, T., Kijsirikul, B., Cercone, N., Ho, T.-B. (eds.) PAKDD 2009. LNCS (LNAI), vol. 5476, pp. 628–636. Springer, Heidelberg (2009). https://doi.org/10.1007/978-3-642-01307-2_62
12. Kiros, R., Zhu, Y., Salakhutdinov, R., Zemel, R., Torralba, A., Urtasun, R., Fidler, S.: Skip-thought vectors. arXiv preprint arXiv, 3, 4 (2015)
13. Kolodner, J.L.: Case-Based Reasoning, p. 1993. Morgan Kaufmann Publishers, San Mateo (1993)
14. Kryszkiewicz, M.: The cosine similarity in terms of the euclidean distance. In: Encyclopedia of Business Analytics and Optimization, pp. 2498–2508. https://doi. org/10.4018/978-1-4666-5202-6.ch223.
15. Li, Y., McLean, D., Bandar, Z., O'shea, J., Crockett, K.: Sentence similarity based on semantic nets and corpus statistics. IEEE Trans. Knowl. Data Eng. **18**(8), 1138–1150 (2006)
16. Mikolov, T., Sutskever, I., Chen, K., Corrado, G., Dean, J.: Distributed representations of words and phrases and their compositionality (2013)
17. Ram, A., Hunter, L.: The use of explicit goals for knowledge to guide inference and learning. Appl. Intell. **2**(1), 47–73 (1992)
18. Recio-Garcia, J.A. Diaz-Agudo, B., Gonzlez-Calero, P.A. Textual CBR in jCOLIBRI: from retrieval to reuse. In: Proceedings of the ICCBR 2007 Workshop on Textual Case-Based Reasoning: Beyond Retrieval, pp. 217–226 (2007)
19. Riesbeck, C.K., Schank, R.C. (eds.): Inside Case-Based Reasoning. Lawrence Erlbaum Associates, Hillsdale (1989)
20. Salton, G., Wong, A., Yang, C.: A vector space model for automatic indexing. Commun. ACM **18**(11), 613–620 (1975)
21. Schumacher, P., Minor, M., Walter, K., Bergmann, R.: Extraction of procedural knowledge from the web. In: Workshop Proceedings, WWW 2012, Lyon, France (2012)
22. Singhal, A.: Modern information retrieval: a brief overview. IEEE Data Eng. Bull. **24**(4), 35–43 (2001)
23. Stewart, R, Danyluk, A, Liu, Y.: Off-topic detection in conversational telephone speech. In: Proceedings of the HLT-NAACL 2006 Workshop on Analyzing Conversations in Text and Speech, ACTS 09 (2006). https://doi.org/10.3115/1564535. 1564537
24. Weber, R., Martins, A., Barcia, R.: On legal texts and cases. In: Textual Case-Based Reasoning: Papers from the AAAI 1998 Workshop, pp. 40–50 (1998)
25. Weber, R.O., Ashley, K.D., Brninghaus, S.: Textual case-based reasoning. Knowl. Eng. Rev. **20**(3), 255–260 (2005)
26. Zellig, H.: Distributional structure. Word **10**(2–3), 146–162 (1954)

Combining Case-Based Reasoning with Complex Event Processing for Network Traffic Classification

Manuel Grob[1(✉)], Martin Kappes[1], and Inmaculada Medina-Bulo[2]

[1] Frankfurt University of Applied Sciences, Nibelungenplatz 1,
60318 Frankfurt, Germany
{manuel.grob,kappes}@fb2.fra-uas.de
[2] Universidad de Cádiz, Avda. de la Universidad de Cádiz 10,
11519 Puerto Real, Spain
inmaculada.medina@uca.es

Abstract. In this paper we present an approach for combining Case-based Reasoning (CBR) and Complex Event Processing (CEP) in order to classify network traffic. We show that this combination has a high potential to improve existing classification methods by enriching the stream processing techniques in CEP with the capability of historic case reuse in CBR by continuously analysing the application layer data of network communication.

Keywords: Traffic classification · CEP · CBR

1 Introduction

Monitoring network traffic is a crucial part for planning and maintaining large scale computer networks. Especially, classifying network traffic according to its service is an important task with respect to traffic management and security control. Traditionally, port-based methods were used to classify traffic where the combination of source and destination ports are used to determine the traffic class. However, many protocols, such as Voice-over-IP (VoIP) communications, are able to use ephemeral ports negotiated during the session establishment and thus prevent those techniques to reliably determine the kind of service class. Also, many applications, like Instant Messaging services, offering the possibility to encapsulate their protocol into well-known protocols like HTTP in order to prevent from being blocked by firewalls when using a custom port.

Moreover, due to novel Cloud services, like Content Delivery Networks (CDNs), IP addresses cannot be reliably used for traffic classification as well. An application served through a CDN has a distributed architecture where the

This work was supported by the German Federal Ministry of Education and Research within the funding program Forschung an Fachhochschulen (contract number 13FH019IA6).

© Springer Nature Switzerland AG 2018
M. T. Cox et al. (Eds.): ICCBR 2018, LNAI 11156, pp. 110–123, 2018.
https://doi.org/10.1007/978-3-030-01081-2_8

service is provided through geographically spread machines such that a user communicates with the nearest instance of it. This way, contents can be served with a high performance and a high availability as short communication paths are used between the two endpoints. As a consequence, a particular application may use different IP addresses depending on where the service is used.

To improve the situation for classifying traffic in such highly dynamic environments, content-based techniques have been developed, e.g. Deep Packet Inspection (DPI) or heuristic techniques using statistical properties. These techniques inspect the content of applications (i.e. OSI Layer 4 payloads) to reason about the kind of service being used. However, this process is heavy weighted and time consuming in contrast to port-based approaches as sophisticated algorithms have to be used.

Event-driven stream processing techniques, like Complex Event Processing (CEP), have proven to cope with such situations, where dealing with large amounts of data transferred through computer networks are necessary to analyse traffic [6]. The CEP paradigm enables handling such traffic by means of generating network events, where each packet produces an event which can be gradually aggregated, combined and processed into higher-level events, until the desired level of abstraction is reached to reason about the traffic.

While CEP is therefore suitable for the application in the field of network traffic analysis, it lacks the possibility of using historic data for reasoning about a particular traffic flow. The Case-based Reasoning (CBR) methodology has sophisticated techniques to close this gap. As a knowledge-based system, it is able to use historic cases for improving the reasoning task over the captured network flows to classify traffic. Also, CBR enables the possibility to continuously extend parts of the system by including new measurements and functionality [14].

In this work, we discuss a prototypical implementation which combines CEP and CBR for network traffic classification. In a first step, we use the CEP system to aggregate captured network traffic and provide it to the CBR component. The CBR component holds historic instances of aggregated traffic and gradually learns changes within the payload to maintain a high degree of service matching even though the actual contents of an application are subject to change over time. Eventually, the CBR system is used to define pattern matching rules in the CEP system in order to classify the network traffic according to its service.

The remainder of this work is organised as follows: after an explanation of the related work used by this paper we give a brief overview of the fundamentals of this work. Then we introduce the CEP part of the architecture, covering the traffic capturing and processing within the CEP engine. Afterwards, we discuss the CBR component by explaining our approach for solution finding, learning new cases and providing feedback to the CEP system. Then, we show in an experiment how our prototype behaves within a simulated network which provides access to distributed services.

2 Related Work

The Complex Event Processing paradigm has proven to work efficiently with network traffic in large network environments. For example, in [7] the authors presented an event hierarchy for determining network-based attacks, e.g. TCP SYN-flooding, and showed how CEP can be used to detect such kind of intrusions. Furthermore, based on the aforementioned work, in [5] the authors showed, how event hierarchies and CEP can be used to well-perform in larger scale networks by discussing a distributed approach of their proposed data processing techniques.

However, CEP currently lacks support of using background knowledge learnt or provided by historical data for using it during the event processing [1]. To circumvent this shortcoming, combining CEP with Case-based Reasoning is a suitable approach. For example, Gay et al. [8] described a system which combines both technologies to make use of historical data preserved in the CBR part of the system and the real-time capabilities of CEP. They used the CBR part to predict forthcoming events on the basis of recently occurred event patterns. The predicted event in turn will then be raised in the CEP system.

With respect to network classification techniques, port-based detection approaches by means of using the IANA port number registry [9] is one of the most common techniques for determining kinds of network traffic. It is still common to use for specifying firewall rules and therefore restrict the communication between two networks. However, this kind of classification has limitations, as more and more applications are served over well-known protocols such as HTTP and thus using port numbers which are not dedicated to the particular service.

To leverage this situation, novel techniques for network traffic classification have been developed. Deep Packet Inspection (DPI), for example, parses the actual application payload often with the use of regular expressions for analysing the protocol. However, those kinds of systems require an extensive base of definitions for recognising the syntax and semantics of a protocol and often suffer from performance issues [11].

Furthermore, there are statistical approaches [2,3] which aim to circumvent the expensive parsing of application payloads by using statistical properties of the payload, such as packet lengths, number of packets, etc. In particular, Chung et al. [3] describes a similarity function based on the cosine similarity of payloads. In our experimental implementation we used this approach as similarity metric for comparing payloads in order to classify network traffic. We will discuss the function in the next section.

3 Fundamentals

Before we discuss our approach, we give a brief introduction of the CEP paradigm as well as an overview of our chosen similarity function.

3.1   Complex Event Processing

Complex Event Processing is a paradigm for processing information in form of events which are produced by data sources [12]. Those data sources produce so-called "raw events" which are occurrences in the system that are of interest with respect to the desired application domain. The raw events are consumed by the CEP system—which is also referred to as CEP engine—as a continuous stream of events. In essence, CEP enables analysing and processing those raw events by extracting necessary parts and combining it with other events that occur in the system. This enables the creation of higher-order, i.e. more meaningful, events, which are derived from the aggregation of the event stream.

Within the CEP engine the processing includes extraction and filtering of information from events and combining the therefore aggregated data with other events. The engine is instructed by using the "Event Processing Language" (EPL), a language which is based on the Structured Query Language (SQL) extended with correlation capabilities [4]. Furthermore, an "event pattern" defines a complete statement expressed in the EPL. Besides the usual SQL elements, e.g. "select", "from" or "where", the EPL has abilities to describe sequences of events in terms of their temporal occurrence. For example, such a sequence can define the matching of two events E_1 and E_2, where E_1 occurs before E_2. Such an expression could be stated by the "followed by" operator $\rightarrow$. The corresponding pattern for the aforementioned events E_1 and E_2 can then be expressed as $E_1 \rightarrow E_1$.

An EPL pattern can also be used to create a new, complexer event which is produced of the aggregation of the events on the level below. These aggregations can be expressed in an event hierarchy which shows the levels of abstractions of each pattern application. An example for such an event hierarchy is depicted in Fig. 1.

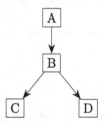

Fig. 1. Example event hierarchy

The example hierarchy has four layers which denote the abstraction levels of the respective events. In this case, A is the raw event which is produced by a system belonging to the application domain. With the occurrence of A event B can be derived by processing the information contained in A. After event B appears in the event stream, events C and D are again produced by transformation steps defined in the CEP engine.

3.2   Similarity Function for Traffic Classification

In our prototypical implementation we used the classification metric discussed in [3] as our similarity function for the CBR system. The authors thereby proposed a classification method based on the similarity between flows of packets, i.e. the similarity of certain properties within a complete protocol session.

In their paper, the authors use a Payload Flow Matrix (PFM) to represent a complete traffic flow for an application. Each row in the matrix represents a network packet within the flow and contains a term-frequency vector of counted words within the payload, whereas a word is a sequence of overlapping bytes within the payload.

Chung et al. determine the overall similarity between two PFMs by calculating the cosine similarity between each payload vector of the corresponding rows. In their experiment, they use a exponentially decreasing weighting scheme for the calculating global similarity.

4   Our Approach

Our approach entails a CBR system with the stream processing capabilities of CEP by reusing historical cases of network traffic payloads and continuously learning divergences of such payloads to constantly classify network traffic.

We use the CEP engine to aggregate network traffic—which is acquired through traffic capturing on the low-layer network stack of a system—into events representing entire and successful TCP sessions. Afterwards, this complex event is used to form a query problem for the CBR part. The CBR system then reasons about the kind of service contained in the TCP session and creates a corresponding EPL pattern for that particular service class. Also, as part of the reasoning cycle, the CBR component learns the ongoing changes within the payloads by creating new cases. Figure 2 shows an overview of the prototypical implementation we propose.

In the remainder of the section the functions of the two CEP-related parts are discussed in detail.

4.1   Event Producers

In our prototype, event producers are systems which capture network packets on the low-level networking stack of a operating system. This way, we ensure all necessary information which is required for the further processing is available and can be used during the forthcoming procedure. Each captured packet is comprised of the stacked headers and payloads of the layers two to seven of the ISO OSI network stack [10].

After a packet is captured, the producer forwards it to the CEP engine. It therefore produces a continuous stream of network packets which are the raw events consumed by the CEP engine. The producer forwards the captured traffic in the order of their arrival, i.e. the order of the packets is preserved.

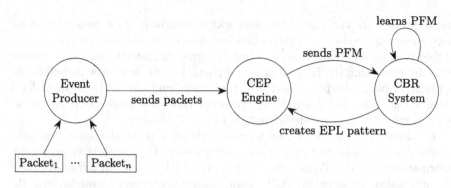

Fig. 2. Overview of the prototype

4.2 Event Processing

The event processing takes place in the CEP engine. Raw events received from
the producers are consumed in a compound event stream, i.e. events are not
separately processed for each event producer. The entire processing within the
engine is comprised of several disjunct steps; each step is triggered by the occurrence of an event of a certain type, which is produced as a result of a previous
processing step. During the processing, the previously produced events are used
in order to combine and aggregate their information.

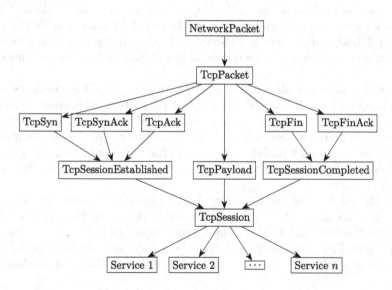

Fig. 3. Event hierarchy for a TCP session

In our approach, we use the event hierarchy shown in Fig. 3 which describes
the different abstraction layers by means of a TCP session. The root of the

hierarchy denotes the raw event NetworkPacket which is an incoming packet from the event producers. This occurrence also acts as the first processing step of the event aggregation. Each raw event is aggregated into the next higher-order event by extracting the IP addresses and ports, i.e. the flow data, as well as the application payload which consists of the header and the actual payload for a given application. For determining the occurrence of a single TCP packet we apply a filter for the corresponding field in the IP header.

Downwards the hierarchy, each event type on a particular layer consumes events of one or more event types of the layer above. Thus, each layer aggregates information until the TcpSession event is produced, which—in our case—holds the information of an entire TCP session. Thereby, on every hierarchy layer the flow data and application payload is preserved.

Besides the hierarchy of event types, the order of the occurring events has to be taken into account when deriving higher-order events. E.g. for establishing a TCP connection, the three-way-handshake has to be fulfilled in the proper temporal order. Therefore, the following EPL pattern has to match for a successful established TCP connection:

$$\text{TcpSessionEstablished} = \text{TcpSyn} \rightarrow \text{TcpSynAck} \rightarrow \text{TcpAck}$$

In case of a TCP session, the pattern looks for the three consecutive events, i.e. TcpSyn, TcpSynAck and TcpAck. Each event is raised if the corresponding flag or combination of flags within the TCP header of an incoming TCP packet are present which was processed on the layer below within the event hierarchy. As soon as the pattern matches, the engine creates a new and dedicated data window for recording packets belonging to the new TCP session. A TCP session is closed if both parties send a FIN flag and acknowledge the session closing. A second pattern recognises this termination and raises a TcpSessionCompleted event.

After a session completion has been recognised, the CEP engine raises a TcpSession event which is also defined as an EPL pattern. This event represents the occurrence of a complete and successful TCP session of a service which has been recorded. This event type aggregates all events of the aforementioned data window containing packets belonging to the particular session and thus is comprised of all parts of the application layer payload as well as the flow data of the connection.

The highest level of our hierarchy defines the service events. These events denote the recognition of a service on the application level. Each service which has to be classified has thus a unique event type. As part of our approach, corresponding EPL patterns for matching the services are created from the CBR system as the result of the reasoning cycle. We will discuss this in the forthcoming section.

5   CBR System

In our prototype, we use a CBR-based approach to classify network traffic according to the application layer payload. Chung et al. [3] developed a traffic classification method based on the similarity of payload vectors. We enhance this method by adopting it to a CBR approach for distinguishing different kinds of services within a protocol.

A reasoning cycle is started when a TCP connection has been successfully completed. A query problem is therefore generated each time the aforementioned TcpSession event is raised in the CEP engine of the system. When the event appears, the system extracts the payload parts of the TCP session event and creates the PFM according to its definition above. This PFM is used as the query problem for the reasoning cycle.

Along with the actual query problem, the CBR system receives meta data of the TCP session in question. This meta data is comprised of the destination IP address and port from the initial TCP handshake of the session which is extracted out of the TcpSession event. This information is used later on to define the EPL pattern in the CEP engine.

5.1   Case Base and Case Design

The problem description of a case in our CBR system consists of a collected PFM of a particular service. As part of the PFM, the payload vector of each TCP packet contained in the session is included. The vectors are aligned in the order they appear in the TCP stream, i.e. payload vector$_n$ belongs to the nth packet in the corresponding TCP stream containing application layer payload.

In the solution part, the kind of service is described as well as the corresponding IP address and port are stated (Fig. 4).

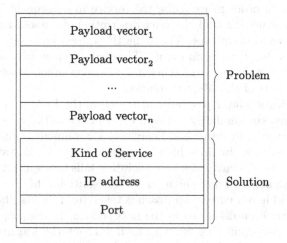

Fig. 4. Case representation

When the system is started (i.e. the system is used for the first time) a predefined case base consisting of cases with recognised PFMs in the problem description on one hand and the corresponding kind of service in the solution part on the other is initialised. As the system runs, new cases are deduced during the learning step, which is described below.

5.2 Similarity and Case Retrieval

The similarity function is taken from the aforementioned work from Chung et al. It calculates the cosine similarity between the PFM contained in the query problem and each case from the case base and returns a value between 0 and 1, whereas 0 means no similarity at all and 1 denotes a perfect match.

The retrieval function for finding the best solution for the query problem is simple: the solution of the case containing a PFM which is most similar to the PFM in the query problem is selected as the overall solution of the retrieval function. The solution describes the kind of service of the TCP session.

5.3 Case Reuse and Learning

After the retrieval function returns a solution, the chosen case is reused in order to adapt it to the query problem. As the adaptation rule we replace the IP address and port within the solution part of the case with the meta data provided by the CEP engine while maintaining the description of the kind of service. This way, after the adaptation the solution represents the actual classification of the network traffic along with the IP address and port of the device which provides the service.

By now, the adapted solution can be used to create a new EPL pattern within the CEP engine in order to recognise the service in subsequent TCP sessions. Therefore, we first use the kind of service description of the solution as the name of the newly derived event type. Then, the IP address and port is used as the filtering criterion for TcpSession events. This way, we now have a pattern that produces a new event when it matches a TcpSession event which contains the IP address and port of the adapted solution.

As the application layer payload and therefore the PFM of a service might change over time, the similarity between cases of the initial case base and the query problem eventually decreases. Therefore, a continuous learning of changed PFMs is required to maintain a high similarity. In our CBR system, we learn new cases when the similarity of a found solution falls below a certain threshold. This way, we are able to keep a high service recognition rate.

The threshold in our current approach is taken from the results of our proto-typical implementation described in the next section. In essence, the threshold was determined by simulating our approach without the learning step in the CBR reasoning cycle. We defined the threshold by 95%, meaning new cases will be learnt if the similarity of the chosen solution case and the query problem is less than this threshold. Thus, if a solution case has less than 95% similarity the adopted solution along with the PFM of the query problem forming the new problem description is included as a case in the case base. As a result, reasoning cycle for a subsequent query problem containing an again changed PFM of the same service will now select the newly created case.

We want to remark, that the reasoning cycle is done every time a TcpSession event is raised in the CEP engine, whereas the EPL pattern creation only appears when there is no pattern registered which matches the service with the corresponding IP address and port. On the other hand, the ongoing execution of the reasoning cycle ensures a continuous learning of the changing payloads of the services in the case base.

6   Experiment

In order to evaluate our proposed architecture, we simulated a Content Delivery Network (CDN) which provides HTTP-based services. This way, we mimic a HTTP-based service which is accessible through different nodes within the same network. We ensure the service uses a synchronised content container such that all nodes providing a service share the same content database. In our test, we use nine CDN nodes each of them providing one HTTP service, i.e. three nodes for each service.

Furthermore, the contents served by a node continuously change on each request from a client and therefore differ between two connections. Between each request, the content randomly changes by 5% from the one served before. Thus, we force a variation of the application payload for each request and ensure the learning capabilities of our system is used.

The nodes of the CDN are provided by virtual containers connected to a dedicated virtual network which ensures we are able to capture the entire traffic. The capturing process itself takes place on the host system where the prototype of the CEP engine and CBR system runs on.

The HTTP-based services provided by the CDN are dynamically created HTML pages with session tracking, i.e. a previous access of an HTTP client is recognised in order to identify it across the simulation. Each session tracks the current state of the dynamic HTML page by means of the delivered content of the page. This way we ensure the aforementioned variation of the content is consistent over all connections of a client. The sessions are synchronised across all nodes of the CDN of a particular HTTP service and thus ensures a client is identified throughout the entire CDN.

If a client connects to a service for the first time, i.e. no previous session exists, the CDN delivers an initial version of the HTML page which is the same for all new clients. During the simulation, the delivered contents diverge for each client as the changes of the HTML page are random.

Before the simulation of client accesses takes place, we initialise the CEP engine and CBR system. In the Complex Event Processing component we set up the aforementioned event hierarchy with their respective recognition patterns for aggregating TCP sessions. The CBR component is set up with a initial case base of three cases—one case for each service. Each case has a Payload Flow Matrix containing payload vectors for one service in the problem description, which was captured prior to the simulation. In the solution part, the name identifying the service is present as well as the IP address and the port of a known service endpoint.

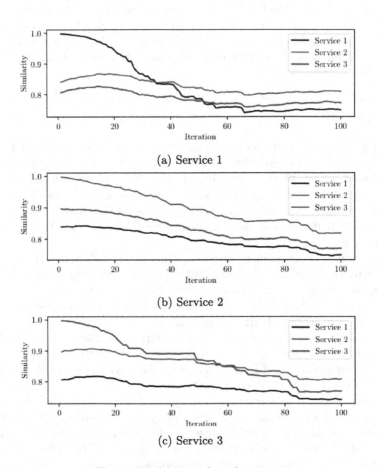

Fig. 5. Similarity without learning

For determining the threshold which leads to creating new cases, we run the simulation without using the learning step of the CBR system. This way, no new cases in case base appear and the similarity between the PFMs in the query problem and the correct solution diverges as shown in Fig. 5. The chart shows the similarities between the query problems and all cases in the case base. In case of service 1 and 3 (Fig. 5a and c), at a certain point the similarity of the correct case (i.e. solution case "Service 1" and "Service 3" respectively) falls below the similarity of the case containing the PFM for service 2. In this case, the solution of our retrieval function continuously returns the wrong kind of service. We therefore chose to take a high threshold percentage of 95% to circumvent this situation. Of course, using a constant and high threshold leads to a more frequent case creation. Likewise, while in our simulation the learning function worked out well, we will considering in using more elaborated methods for more precise thresholds.

For the simulation, each service was accessed 300 times and the CDNs of a service were randomly chosen. We recorded the accesses by monitoring the occurrence of events in the CEP engine. This way, we were able to track all events of our event hierarchy, especially those produced by the EPL patterns of the CBR engine. The results for the simulation with and without learning enabled are shown in Table 1. The results show the false positive and false negative rates between the selected solution of the CBR system and the correct service as well as the overall accuracy as defined in [3]. The false positive rate for service 1 and 3 without learning are both 0% whereas it is 61.3% for service 2. This reflects the aforementioned decrease of the similarity of the correct service classification.

The sum of the false negatives of service 1 and 3 is the false positive rate of service 2 which shows service 2 is falsely chosen as the solution of the reasoning cycle after the similarity rate decreases over time. Service 1 has a higher false negative rate as service 3 due to the fact the wrong service classification was earlier chosen than for service 3.

Table 1. Results

Service name	Without learning			With learning		
	False positives	False negatives	Accuracy	False positives	False negatives	Accuracy
Service 1	0%	36.6%	63.4%	0%	0%	100%
Service 2	61.3%	0%	38.7%	0%	0%	100%
Service 3	0%	24.7%	75.3%	0%	0%	100%

The results indicate a drastic increase of the accuracy of the traffic classification when the CBR system learns new cases. We explain the accuracy of 100% with the choice of a high learning threshold of 95% which was determined by running the simulation without the learning step as mentioned before. However, since our simulation uses fixed number of HTTP-based services, we expect variations of the accuracy when new cases of unknown services are included in the system. Using real-world traffic data would therefore better allow to evaluate the performance of our approach. However, labelled real-world traffic data of Content Delivery Networks is currently—to the best of our knowledge—not publicly available.

7   Conclusion

In this work, we introduced an approach for an architecture which combines Complex Event Processing with Case-based Reasoning in order to classify network traffic.

We discussed the three parts of the architecture: traffic capturing, flow recognition and traffic classification. Network traffic is captured through event producers which operate on the low-level networking stack of the operating system. The producer forwards network packets as raw events to the CEP engine, which processes and aggregates the traffic. We showed the processing and aggregation of TCP sessions as an example for our event hierarchy.

Afterwards, we introduced our CBR system where a reasoning cycle starts every time a successful TCP session occurred in the CEP system. We measure the similarity between two services by determining the cosine similarity between the PFM of the query problem and the PFMs in the case base. The solution of the cycle is comprised of the kind of service being used and the IP address and port of the network node which provides the service. The CBR system then instructs the CEP engine to create a new EPL pattern in order to recognise forthcoming TCP sessions which access the service.

For maintaining a high recognition rate, we learn new cases by creating them each time the similarity of a selected solution falls below a certain, currently predefined, threshold. We showed that this approach helps to minimise wrong classification of network services.

In our experiment, we discussed how the system behaves in a simulated CDN with three HTTP services. We showed the problem of changing application payloads which appear every time the service is accessed. As a result, the output of the retrieval process chose the wrong case as the similarity between the correct initial case the query problem differed too much. We showed, that learning new cases based on the current PFM instance of a service PFM increased the correct retrieval.

We see this work as an initial step towards a more elaborated traffic classification system. We claim that there is a high potential in our approach as the combination of CEP and CBR with respect to network traffic analysis enables new fields of research in that area. In particular, in our forthcoming work we will investigate in more dynamic techniques for determine the threshold when new cases are learnt as well as in maintaining the case base by means of forgetting learnt cases and including unknown service definitions.

References

1. Anicic, D., et al.: Stream reasoning and complex event processing in ETALIS. In: Semantic Web 3.4, pp. 397–407, 1st January 2012. ISSN 15700844. https://doi. org/10.3233/SW-2011-0053. https://content.iospress.com/articles/semantic-web/ sw053. Accessed 05 Apr 2018
2. Bernaille, L., Teixeira, R., Salamatian, K.: Early application identification. In: Proceedings of the 2006 ACM CoNEXT Conference, CoNEXT 2006, New York, NY, USA, pp. 6:1–6:12. ACM (2006). ISBN 978-1-59593-456-7. https://doi.org/10. 1145/1368436.1368445. Accessed 05 Apr 2018
3. Chung, J.Y., Park, B., Won, Y.J., Strassner, J., Hong, J.W.: Traffic classification based on flow similarity. In: Nunzi, G., Scoglio, C., Li, X. (eds.) IPOM 2009. LNCS, vol. 5843, pp. 65–77. Springer, Heidelberg (2009). https://doi.org/10.1007/978-3-642-04968-2_6

4. EsperTech, Inc., Esper Reference Documentation. http://esper.espertech.com/release-7.1.0/esper-reference/html/index.html. Accessed 24 Apr 2018
5. Gad, R., et al.: Hierarchical events for efficient distributed network analysis and surveillance. In: Proceedings of the 2nd International Workshop on Adaptive Services for the Future Internet and 6th International Workshop on Web APIs and Service Mashups, pp. 5–11. ACM (2012). ISBN 1-4503-1566-6
6. Gad, R., et al.: Leveraging EDA and CEP for integrating low-level network analysis methods into modern, distributed IT architectures. In: VII Jornadas de Ciencia e Ingeniería de Servicios (JCIS-SISTEDES 2012), Almería (2012)
7. Gad, R., et al.: Employing the CEP paradigm for network analysis and surveillance. In: Proceedings of the Ninth Advanced International Conference on Telecommunications, pp. 204–210. Citeseer (2013)
8. Gay, P., López, B., Meléndez, J.: Sequential learning for case-based pattern recognition in complex event domains. In: Proceedings of the 16th UK Workshop on Case-Based Reasoning, pp. 46–55 (2011)
9. IANA: Service Name and Transport Protocol Port Number Registry, 27th March 2018. https://www.iana.org/assignments/portnumbers. Accessed 04 May 2018
10. ITU Telecommunication Standardization Sector. Information Technology - Open Systems Interconnection - Basic Reference Model: The Basic Model (1994). http://handle.itu.int/11.1002/1000/2820. Accessed 27 Apr 2018
11. Lin, P.C., et al.: Using string matching for deep packet inspection. Computer **41**(4), 23–28 (2008). https://doi.org/10.1109/MC.2008.138. ISSN 0018-9162
12. Luckham, D.: The power of events: an introduction to complex event processing in distributed enterprise systems. In: Bassiliades, N., Governatori, G., Paschke, A. (eds.) RuleML 2008. LNCS, vol. 5321, pp. 3–3. Springer, Heidelberg (2008). https://doi.org/10.1007/978-3-540-88808-6_2
13. Nguyen, T.T.T., Armitage, G.: A survey of techniques for internet traffic classification using machine learning. IEEE Commun. Surv. Tutor. **10**(4), 56–76 (2008). https://doi.org/10.1109/SURV.2008.080406. ISSN 1553-877X
14. Richter, M.M.: Case-Based Reasoning: A Textbook, 1st edn. Springer, New York (2013). https://doi.org/10.1007/978-3-642-40167-1. ISBN 978-3-642-40166-4

AI-VT: An Example of CBR that Generates a Variety of Solutions to the Same Problem

Julien Henriet[1(✉)] and Françoise Greffier[2]

[1] FEMTO-ST Institute, Univ. Bourgogne-Franche-Comté, CNRS, DISC,
16 route de Gray, 25030 Besançon, France
`julien.henriet@univ-fcomte.fr`
[2] ELLIADD, Univ. Bourgogne-Franche-Comté, 16 route de Gray, 25030 Besançon,
France
`francoise.greffier@univ-fcomte.fr`

Abstract. AI-Virtual Trainer (AI-VT) is an intelligent tutoring system based on case-based reasoning. AI-VT has been designed to generate personalised, varied, and consistent training sessions for learners. The AI-VT training sessions propose different exercises in regard to a capacity associated with sub-capacities. For example, in the field of training for algorithms, a capacity could be "Use a control structure alternative" and an associated sub-capacity could be "Write a boolean condition". AI-VT can elaborate a personalised list of exercises for each learner. One of the main requirements and challenges studied in this work is its ability to propose varied training sessions to the same learner for many weeks, which constitutes the challenge studied in our work. Indeed, if the same set of exercises is proposed time after time to learners, they will stop paying attention and lose motivation. Thus, even if the generation of training sessions is based on analogy and must integrate the repetition of some exercises, it also must introduce some diversity and AI-VT must deal with this diversity. In this paper, we have highlighted the fact that the retaining (or capitalisation) phase of CBR is of the utmost importance for diversity, and we have also highlighted that the equilibrium between repetition and variety depends on the abilities learned. This balance has an important impact on the retaining phase of AI-VT.

Keywords: Case-based reasoning · Intelligent tutoring system
Diversity · Capitalisation · Personalised learning

1 Introduction

We are interested in the issue of the personalisation of learning through training sessions. For us, a training session is a list of exercises suited to each learner. Motivation and repetition are key aspects in teaching. Nevertheless, repetition causes learners to be bored and to turn themselves off. Consequently, teachers must introduce originality and diversity and adapt the exercise level and nature

© Springer Nature Switzerland AG 2018
M. T. Cox et al. (Eds.): ICCBR 2018, LNAI 11156, pp. 124–139, 2018.
https://doi.org/10.1007/978-3-030-01081-2_9

to the learners' acquired skills. Furthermore, teachers must propose varied exercises and consistent sessions while providing training for the same skill over a given number of weeks. Thus, the elaboration of a cycle training session, suited to one particular learner, is a reasoning based on analogy in which it is necessary to introduce some kind of originality. Indeed, on the one hand, this elaboration is based on the past experiences of the trainer as well as the exercises previously proposed to the learner, and on the other hand, the exercises proposed to the learner must not be always the same. As a consequence, a case-based reasoning (CBR) system [11], based on analogy reasoning, is a good answer to these kind of systems, but must be adapted in order to introduce diversity in the solutions to be proposed (the training sessions). In addition, this diversity varies from one domain to another. Indeed, the frequency with which an exercise must be proposed to learners in the field of sports is not the same as for learners in the field of algorithmics, for example. As a matter of fact, basic exercises will be proposed often by sports trainers since the body must practise a lot before integrating basic movements and attitudes. On the contrary, proposing an algorithmic exercise that the learner has already successfully completed twice will bore the learner.

2   Related Works

This paper presents Artificial Intelligent - Virtual Trainer (AI-VT), a multi-agent system (MAS) that uses CBR to provide consistent training sessions with widely differing progressions. CBR is widely employed in e-learning systems and intelligent tutoring systems (ITS) [8]. Kolodner [12] distinguished two types of CBR-inspired approaches to education: goal-based scenarios [19] where learners achieve missions in simulated worlds, and learning by design [13], in which learners design and build working devices to obtain feedback. CBR is actually well-suited to the latter type of system [10], as well as to other tools using artificial intelligence (AI) and distributed AI (DAI) systems, such as genetic algorithm (GA) [2], Artificial Neural Network (ANN) [5] and MAS [21]. Baylari and Montazer focused on the adaptation of tests to obtain a personalised estimation of a learner's level [5]. They used an ANN in order to correlate learners' answers to the tests and the exercises proposed by teachers. The CBR- and GA-based e-learning system proposed by Huang et al. also provides lessons taking into account the curriculum and the incorrect-response patterns of a pre-test given to the learner [9]. Rishi et al. designed an ITS based on agents and a CBR system [18] in which a Personal Agent is responsible for determining learner level. A Teaching Agent then determines the educative strategy with the help of CBR according to the description of the transmitted learner level. Finally, a Course Agent provides and revises the lessons and exercises corresponding to the strategy proposed by the system with the help of a tutor. All these tools provided by AI would therefore produce exactly the same exercises and lessons for training a single given skill, or would propose a large set of exercises as an answer to the diversity requirement and leave the teachers or the learners to choose the most adapted exercises themselves. In this particular domain, repetitive activities are a drawback, yet lesson planning is a process based on adaptation of past experiences.

AI-VT tries to address the problem of balance between repetitiveness and the variety of the solutions proposed. Indeed, even if the exercises must be selected by analogy with previously proposed ones, the same exercise proposed too often to one learner may bore her/him. Moreover, the number of propositions varies according to the domain (algorithmic vs. sports, for example) and the level reached by the learner. The problem of variety in CBR-systems is close to the creativity one addressed in the literature [4,6,7,14,17]. Muller and Bergmann proposed the introduction of novelty combining different solutions during the adaptation phase [17]. In their approach, source case solutions are decomposed into elementary activities and elements and combined in original ways. This approach allows introduction of diversity and novelty in the solutions proposed by their system. Diversity is also addressed in applications dedicated to recommender systems [3,15,16,20]. These systems select products or services for customers in electronic commerce. In these approaches, the systems select and deliver a set of similar cases and their solutions. In this set, these systems also integrate cases which present some dissimilarities with the described problem part of the target case. The dissimilarities are computed according to different metrics, and the sets of cases are refined successively. In our problem, dissimilarity is not sufficient since the level acquired by the learner must be taken into account, as well as the ease with which each previously proposed exercise has been solved by the considered learner. More recent works go further into the introduction of unexpected results in order to surprise and retain attention. Gero and Maher present the basis of a new approach based on Deep Learning in order to introduce creativity [4]. Grace et al. went further with Deep Learning and proposed creative and unexpected concepts which were then adapted to a CBR-cycle process in order to generate original recipes [6,7]. This neural network is trained to introduce novelty (new ingredients) into a set of preferences by the end-user in order to give recipes with new ingredients [14]. Actually, in these approaches, creativity and originality are treated during the description and adaptation phases of the target case, whereas AI-VT addresses this particular aspect during the retaining and adaptation phases, giving much importance to these CBR-system phases.

3   Presentation of AI-VT

AI-VT is based on pedagogy which proposes repetition of exercises in order to attain levels of capacities. Once a lack of knowledge is detected by the teacher or the learner, she/he can decide to train for many weeks in order to reach this level. Then, when the user asks the AI-VT for a training session on a particular capacity with a specific duration, the system generates a session organised into sub-capacities and proposes exercises with regard to each sub-capacity. We also considered two different domains of application: practical (sports - Aïkido) and

Table 1. Examples of capacities and their associated sub-capacities

Domain	Sports - Aïkido	Algorithmic
Capacity	Using a grip	Design an algorithm
Associated sub-capacities	Break the partner's posture	Find inputs and outputs
	Relax despite a grip	Give a formula for the calculus
	Make the partner loose balance	Associate a type with a variable
	Pivote around a grip	Display a clear message

theoretical (computer science - algorithmics). As examples shown in Table 1, in the field of Aïkido, a capacity could be *"Using a grip"*, and *"Relaxing despite a grip"* and *"Pivoting around a grip"* could be two associated sub-capacities. In the field of algorithmics, *"Design an algorithm"* is an example of capacity, and *"Find inputs and outputs"* and *"Associate a type with a variable"* are two sub-capacities which can be associated with it. In the first part of this section, we detail the session structure and the requirements of AI-VT. The distributed architecture and the data flows are presented in the second part. Finally, in the third part, we examine how a session is designed.

3.1 Lesson Structure

In this sub-section, we describe the way a teacher elaborates a training session, the parameters and the way this generation is done, and the behaviour AI-VT should imitate.

We considered activities that guide each training session by reaching one capacity [22] divided into sub-capacities. These capacities and their order of appearance are decided at the beginning of each session. One specific skill can consequently be assigned to some consecutive sessions. The chosen capacity is then divided into elementary abilities (sub-capacities) that have to be mastered by the learner. We considered that in sports in particular, each skill may be shared by more than one capacity. In all the domains of application we considered (in sports training like Aïkido and theoretical disciplines like algorithmics), the mastery of each skill is a time-consuming process that is reached through the repetition of exercises [1]. Some will learn faster than others, and thus the teacher must adapt each session to the level of the learner.

AI-VT must (1) propose pertinent sub-capacities and exercises according to the capacity decided and the level already reached by the learner, (2) ensure that no exercise is proposed more than once during a given training session and that the sessions in the same training cycle are varied, and (3) build a consistent training session that begins with the simplest exercise and then continues with a list of exercises that relate sufficiently to the preceding and following ones.

3.2 System Architecture and Communication Model

Figure 1 presents the architecture of AI-VT modelled as a multi-agent system (MAS). A MAS constitutes a paradigm designed to handle distributed systems.

In a MAS, an agent is a physical or abstract entity having certain specific characteristics: perception of its environment (including itself and the other agents),
the capacity to act (upon itself or the environment) and autonomy in its decisions
and actions. In AI-VT, the choice of sub-capacities regarding a given capacity
takes place via an autonomous process, as does the determination of exercises
regarding a sub-capacity, or of any other exercises chosen and their priority levels.
The initial choice of exercises regarding a sub-capacity must be an autonomous
process: each agent's autonomy ensures a wise and free selection of the most suitable exercises. These processes can be undertaken simultaneously, coming after
the determination of sub-capacities. In addition, each one must interact with the
other processes and take their choices into account: the solution proposed by one
agent influences the choices made by the others.

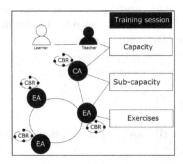

Fig. 1. Overview of AI-VT Architecture

As shown in Fig. 1, the system is composed of four types of agents: the
teacher, the learner, the capacity agent (CA) - which is responsible for choosing
the sub-capacities regarding a capacity requested by the teacher - and the exercise agents. Each of these agents is responsible for proposing the exercises best
suited to a given sub-capacity. CAs are directly connected to exercise agents,
and they can exchange messages. The CA sends the set of sub-capacities it has
chosen to one of the exercise agents. This first-contacted exercise agent (EA)
endorses the role of coordinator between the CA and the other EAs. This EA
assumes responsibility for the first-proposed sub-capacity, and then creates and
sends the list to another EA which assumes the second sub-capacity, and so
on. The EAs then communicate and share information in order to prepare the
requested training session. Each EA proposes exercises concerning its assigned
sub-capacity. Each EA takes into account the choices proposed by the other EAs:
for example, one of the system's requirements is that each exercise is to be done
only once during the entire training session. Thus, the choices of the EAs are
shared. The referent version of the training session is transmitted from EA to
EA until it fulfills all the requirements. Finally, the EA initially contacted by
the CA sends the referent version of the training session back to the CA.

3.3   Determination of Sub-capacities

The CA is responsible for choosing the set of sub-capacities and their duration. Once the training session has been chosen by the teacher, and after having analysed any additional learner needs, the CA follows the CBR approach to make these choices according to the sub-capacities already achieved and to the learners' degree of assimilation.

For the CA, a case is a set comprised of two parts: a problem and a solution.

Each problem part is composed of a capacity C, and the solution part of a set of $(SC, D_{SC,C})$ where SC is a sub-capacity and $D_{SC,C}$ the duration required to reach this SC regarding C. Thus, formally, a source case s is expressed as $s = (C, \bigcup\{SC, D^{S}_{SC,C}\})$. The durations $D_{SC,C}$ are initialised by the teacher at the beginning of the season and updated by AI-VT after the training session, taking into account the evaluation of the learner's acquired level. Since learner levels of expertise rise, we can consider that durations decrease and thus call them 'remaining durations'. Indeed, if the teacher has considered that 60 min of training is usually necessary in order to master one sub-capacity, and after the learner has successfully trained herself/himself 20 min in this specific sub-capacity, we consider the average learner will then (after this training) need $60 - 20 = 40$ min during the next sessions for the considered sub-capacity.

First, all the sub-capacities associated with C are retrieved. The similarity between each source case s and the target case t is computed as follows: $SIM_{SC}(t, s) = \begin{cases} 1 \text{ if } C_t = C_s \\ 0 \text{ if } C_t \neq C_s \end{cases}$ where C_s (respectively C_t) is the capacity of s (respectively t).

In order to illustrate this phase, we can consider the cases stored in the case base reported in Table 2. In this example taken from an Aïkido training session, sub-capacities 'Breaking the partner's posture', 'Relaxing despite a grip', 'Making the partner lose balance' and 'Pivoting around a grip' have been associated with the capacity 'Using a grip' by the trainer in the initial process or in previous training sessions. Thus, if the capacity of t is C_t = 'Using a grip', the sub-capacities of Source Case 1 are reminded by analogy, since $SIM_{SC}(t, 1) = 1$ and $SIM_{SC}(t, 2) = 0$.

The adaptation phase consists of computing the duration of each sub-capacity. We assumed that these durations are somehow linked to the importance of practising each sub-capacity. We also assumed that these durations may depend at times on the given capacity. Indeed, one sub-capacity may be associated with two different capacities. And maybe, the considered sub-capacity may have to be mastered in order to master one capacity and only be known in order to master another capacity. As an example, "Give the types of simple variables" must be practised often in order to master the capacity "Design a simple algorithm", and only revised once or twice during the practice of the capacity "design object oriented algorithms". Actually, this is more frequently observed in sports training for which capacity progression is less linear than theoretical disciplines: in sports, capacities can be practised without a clear order ("using a grip" can be practised before of after "breaking a grip" in the season) whereas in theoretical fields there is usually a clearer order for mastering the capacities ("*design simple algorithms*" comes after "*design object oriented algorithms*"). Consequently, the adaptation module sorts the set of sub-capacities according to $D_{SC,C}$ (descending order). Then, the proposed durations are calculated according to the number of sub-capacities the teacher wants to work on and the duration of the entire session.

Following the training session, the teacher and the learner evaluate the learner's acquired level of mastery (mark and duration spent on each exercise). Before the training session begins, each selected sub-capacity is transmitted to one EA that will have to associate the corresponding exercises. After the training session, each sub-capacity duration is modified in proportion to the evaluation from 0 to 10 of the learner-s level for the proposed sub-capacity.

Finally, during the retaining (or capitalisation) phase, the system subtracts the durations from all the durations of the source cases for which the practised sub-capacity appear. During capitalisation, the effective time spent by the learner to resolve the sub-capacity exercises may differ from the resolution time (estimated time to be spent by the learner on the considered sub-capacity) initially allocated by the teacher. Since this difference between time really spent and time initially allocated gives information on the difficulties of the learner and the integration of the sub-capacity, it has been taken into account into the remaining time to spend on the sub-capacity.

The remaining duration of each worked sub-capacities is computed as follows:

$$D_{SC} = D_{SC} - \frac{M_{SC}}{10} \times \frac{d_{SC}^{alloc}}{d_{SC}^{real}},$$

where M_{SC} is the mark (out of 10) obtained by the learner, d_{SC}^{alloc} is the predicted duration allowed to finish the exercises of the sub-capacity and d_{SC}^{real} is the real duration spent by the learner on the sub-capacity exercises.

Table 2. Example of modifications of durations after a training session.

Source case	Capacity	Sub-capacities	Initial duration (min)	Teacher's mark (points)	Stored duration (min)
1	Using a grip	Breaking the partner's posture	90	7/10	$90 - \frac{7}{10} \times \frac{20}{20} = 76$
		Relaxing despite a grip	90	3/10	$90 - \frac{3}{10} \times \frac{20}{20} = 84$
		Making the partner lose balance	80	4/10	$80 - \frac{4}{10} \times \frac{20}{20} = 72$
		Pivoting around a grip	80	–	80
2	Breaking a grip	Breaking a single grip	90	–	90
		Relaxing despite a grip	70	3/10	$70 - \frac{3}{10} \times \frac{20}{20} = 64$

Table 2 presents two source cases of the tests performed by one of the trainers (an Aïkido teacher) who evaluated AI-VT. The trainer chose three different sub-capacities per training session and decided that the total duration of the training session must be 60 min. Since the trainer chose the capacity '*The learner becomes capable of using a grip*' for this training session, the CA recalled Case 1. The adaptation process then sorted the sub-capacities according to their durations and proposed the three first sub-capacities, allocating $D_{SC} = \frac{60}{3} = 20$ min to 3 each sub-capacity. In this example, the times really spent were all equal to the times allocated. It was usual for sports training tests, but very unusual for algorithm trainings. Consequently, after capitalisation, the new durations were those reported in the last column of Table 2. Thus, the less assimilated sub-capacities ('*Relaxing despite a grip*' and '*Pivoting around a grip*') became the most immediate ones. We also note that, as required for the system specification, when the same capacity ('*Using a grip*') was selected again, another set of sub-capacities (composed of the less assimilated ones, and others) were selected. Thus, as required, the proposed solutions changed even if the same capacity was requested again later.

3.4 Selection of Varied Exercises

This subsection presents how the exercises are chosen regarding the selected sub-capacities. At the allocation of its sub-capacity, each EA selects a set of exercises according to the CBR-cycle. For each EA, a source case is noted:

$$\sigma = (SC, \bigcup\{(EX, AD^{\sigma}_{EX}, RD^{\sigma}_{EX,SC})\}),$$

where AD^{σ}_{EX} is the estimated duration that must be allocated to the learner to resolve the exercise EX, and $RD^{\sigma}_{EX,SC}$, the estimated remaining duration to spend on this exercise EX before reaching the sub-capacity SC. Each source case σ contains the exercises possible regarding SC. Assuming $Card(Sol_{\sigma})$ is the number of exercises of the solution part of σ, the target case τ_i (i.e. the part of the training session that will be proposed) taken into account by the EA EA_i is noted:

$$\tau_i = (SC_i, \bigcup_{n \in \{1..Card(Sol_{\sigma})\}}\{(EX_n, AD^{\tau_i}_{EX_n}, RD^{\tau_i}_{EX_n,SC_i})\}).$$

Each EA_i then retrieves the source case corresponding to SC_i.

The similarity between source case σ and target case τ_i is computed as follows:

$$SIM_{EX}(\tau_i, \sigma) = \begin{cases} 1 \; if \; SC_i = SC \\ 0 \; if \; SC_i \neq SC \end{cases} \tag{1}$$

The adaptation phase orders the exercises of the training session. Selected exercises for which the RD is the highest are proposed first. If two agents select the same exercise, the one with the highest RD_{EX,SC_i} prevails, and the one with the lowest must be changed. Then, exercises are ordered according to their complexity (ascending order). Finally, distances between consecutive exercises are computed, and permutations between consecutive exercises may occur in order to minimise these distances between one proposed exercise and the next one. This final adaptation step creates consistency for the training session.

During the revision phase, the teacher and learner evaluate the answers (give a mark between 0 and 10) proposed by the learner and give the real duration spent on each exercise.

Table 3. Example of exercises initially retrieved by AI-VT.

Sub-capacities/Exercises	Dist. with next ex.	Complex.	RD
— Sub-capacity SC_3: *Give a formula*			20
EX_6: Retrieve the total price before taxe of product using knowing its price including taxe and taxe rate. Give the formula.	18	18	10
EX_7: Compute the fuel consumption of car knowing the distance and its mean speed. Give the formula	18	18	10
— Sub-capacity SC_1: *Find inputs & outputs*			15
EX_2: Retrieve the total price before taxe of product using knowing its price including taxe and taxe rate. Give the inputs & outputs	18	18	10
EX_1: Compute a rectangle perimeter. Give inputs & outputs		5	5

Table 4. Example of exercises finally proposed by AI-VT.

Sub-capacities/Exercises	Dist. next	Complex.	RD
— Sub-capacity SC_1: *Find inputs & outputs*			15
EX_1: Compute rectangle perimeter. Give ...	18	5	5
EX_2: Retrieve the total price before taxe of product using ...	5	18	10
— Sub-capacity SC_3: *Give a formula*			20
EX_6: Retrieve the total price before taxe of product using ...	18	18	10
EX_7: Compute the fuel consumption of car knowing the ...		18	10

As an example, Tables 3 and 4 illustrate the adaptation of a training session dedicated to algorithms. Table 3 shows the sub-capacities retrieved by AI-VT. These sub-capacities are ordered by AI-VT according to their *RD* (descending order). In this Table 3, the first exercise (EX_6) deals with economy and has the highest complexity (18), the second exercise (EX_7) deals with another context and has the same complexity. The third exercise (EX_2) deals with economy (like EX_6) and has a complexity of 18, and the last proposed exercise (EX_1) deals with geometry and is the simplest exercise (complexity is equal to 5). Thus, this first proposal begins with the most complex exercises and ends with the simplest one, and the context always changes. As it can be observed in Table 4, the adaptation process places the same exercises in a different order: the adapted training session will begin with the easiest exercise (EX_1) and the exercises that deal with economy $(EX_2$ and $EX_6)$ are grouped.

At the end of the CBR cycle, capitalisation will allow the system to prepare the next training session. Indeed, even if the same sub-capacities are required next, the system will have to propose a different set of exercises. Thus, the retaining phase of AI-VT is very important since it will give the history of the performed exercises. Furthermore, if one exercise has not been understood or successfully solved, or even solved but with great difficulty by the learner, the system must have the possibility to choose this exercise again. Otherwise, if one exercise has been successfully solved with no difficulty, AI-VT must not propose it again in the case of a theoretical knowledge acquisition.

In addition, if an exercise has been done with much difficulty by an athlete, the duration of practice must not change. On the contrary, for a theoretical training, if the learner has spent a lot of time on an exercise and did not solve it, this exercise should be proposed once again to the learner with a higher resolution time.

Consequently, AI-VT must capitalise cases of theoretical-domain training and cases of physical training differently.

In the case of physical training, only the RD is modified as follows:

$$\forall SC, \forall EX, RD^{\sigma}_{EX,SC} = max(0, (RD^{\sigma}_{EX,SC} - \frac{M_{EX}}{10} \times AD^{\tau}_{EX,SC})).$$

In that case, the remaining duration of practise of the exercises are only decreased from the time spent over it during the training session.

And in the case of training on theoretical skills, AD and RD are modified as follows:

$$\forall SC, \forall EX, AD^{\sigma}_{EX,SC} = max(0, (AD^{\sigma}_{EX,SC} - \frac{M_{EX}}{10} \times \frac{AD^{Real}_{EX,SC}}{AD^{\tau}_{EX,SC}})),$$

$$\forall SC, \forall EX, RD^{\sigma}_{EX,SC} = max(0, (RD^{\sigma}_{EX,SC} \times (1 - \frac{M_{EX}}{10} \times \frac{AD^{Real}_{EX,SC}}{AD^{\tau}_{EX,SC}}))),$$

where M_{EX} is the mark (out of 10) obtained by the learner for excise EX and $AD^{Real}_{EX,SC}$ the real time spent over this exercise. For these types of learning, we considered that the time spent by the learner over an exercise $(AD^{Real}_{EX,SC})$ can differ from the initial time allocated $(AD^{\tau}_{EX,SC})$.

In order to illustrate the performance of AI-VT, Table 5 presents the different durations $(RD, AD$ and real time spent) of the exercises proposed in the last training session and the durations of other exercises stored in the case base. We can see that the retaining phase modifies the priorities of the exercises stored in the case base. Indeed, the RDs of the successfully resolved exercises fall to 0: EX_1 and EX_2 will not be proposed next time. In addition, since EX_6 has been partially resolved (mark 5/10) with high difficulty (time spent 12 min instead of 8 min planned), its RD becomes inferior to other exercises in the case base: it could be proposed another time, but other exercises of the same sub-capacity

Table 5. Example of capitalisation proposed by AI-VT.

Exercises	Initial AD	Initial RD	Mark	Real time spent	Capitalised AD	Capitalised RD
Ex. of SC_1:						
EX_1 (proposed)	5	5	10	5	$5 - \frac{10}{10} \times \frac{5}{5} = 4$	$5 \times (1 - \frac{10}{10} \times \frac{5}{5}) = 0$
EX_2 (proposed)	5	10	10	5	$5 - \frac{10}{10} \times \frac{5}{5} = 4$	$10 \times (1 - \frac{10}{10} \times \frac{5}{5}) = 0$
EX_3 (case base)	5	5	–	–	5	5
EX_4 (case base)	5	5	–	–	5	5
Ex. of SC_3:						
EX_6 (proposed)	8	10	5	12	$8 - \frac{5}{10} \times \frac{12}{8} = 7$	$10 \times (1 - \frac{5}{10} \times \frac{15}{8}) = 3$
EX_7 (proposed)	8	10	0	15	$8 - \frac{0}{10} \times \frac{15}{8} = 8$	$10 \times (1 - \frac{0}{10} \times \frac{15}{8}) = 10$
EX_8 (case base)	8	10	–	–	8	10

will be selected first for the next training session. Finally, EX_7 has not been resolved at all (mark 0/10), and the learner has spent much time on it (15 min instead of 8 min planned). Consequently, its AD and RD stay the same, and it will most probably be proposed next time with EX_8.

4   Results

AI-VT has been tested in two very different contexts: sports training (Aïkido, a traditional Japanese martial art) and algorithmics (computer science).

For the context of sports training, we asked seven Aïkido teachers to evaluate 10 consecutive training sessions for the same capacity. This corresponds to five weeks of training, with two 90-min sessions per week. They evaluated the system through two aspects: the consistency of the proposed training sessions, and the diversity of the proposed exercises. It is important to note that all the trainers had different sessions and had initialised the system with different sub-capacities and exercise associations. Indeed, each trainer had his/her own way of teaching Aïkido and a set of favourite techniques.

For the second evaluation, we proposed to seven learners of computer science to use AI-VT for their training. These learners at our university (first year of studies) were having difficulties with algorithmics, and they were taking tutoring sessions. We proposed to them to resolve the exercises generated by AI-VT over four consecutive weeks for one 60-min session per week. After each training session, we asked the learners to evaluate the session generated by the system through the same aspects: consistency and diversity of the proposed exercises.

Since there were two methods of capitalisation, we first compare and analyse the diversities obtained, and then we present the evaluations of AI-VT made by Aïkido trainers and university learners in algorithmics.

Table 6 presents the measures obtained for the diversity in both of the contexts of use. Since each Aïkido trainer asked for 10 training sessions and each university learner asked for four training sessions, AI-VT proposed more exercises in the context of Aïkido than in the context of algorithmics. Nevertheless,

Table 6. Measures of the diversities obtained

User	NB of EX	Frequency	User	NB of EX	Frequency
Aïkido Trainer #1	19	**3.16**	Algorithmic Student #1	18	1.39
#2	37	1.62	#2	25	1.72
#3	39	**1.54**	#3	21	**1.14**
#4	34	1.76	#4	17	**2.00**
#5	22	2.73	#5	21	1.86
#6	24	2.72	#6	25	1.48
#7	26	2.31	#7	31	1.32

the difference is not so important: 28.71 exercises on average for Aïkido and 22.57 for algorithmic, whereas there are more than twice the sessions in Aïkido. This is due to the difference between both of the retaining processes: in the context of algorithmics, AI-VT ensures a greater turn-over of the exercises.

We observe that, in compliance with the requirements, an exercise is proposed more frequently in the context of Aïkido than in the context of algorithmics. Indeed, Table 6 shows that each Aïkido exercise was generally proposed 1.54 times (Trainer #3) to 3.16 times (Trainer #1), and each exercise was globally proposed 2.26 times. In the context of algorithmics, each exercise was generally proposed 1.14 times (Student #3) to 2.0 times (Student #4), and each exercise was globally proposed 1.56 times.

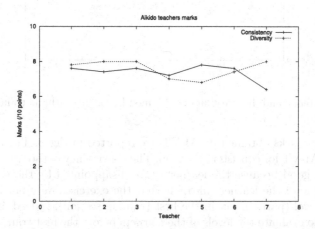

Fig. 2. Consistency and diversity marks obtained by the Aïkido training sessions

Figure 2 presents the evaluations of the Aikido trainers obtained by the training sessions generated by AI-VT. The mean marks obtained for each trainer are reported in this figure. The trainers were asked to give a mark from 0 to 10 for the consistency of the successive generated training sessions: 0 if the trainer felt that the exercises proposed in a session were not consistent at all with regard to the capacity and the sub-capacities trained, and 10 if the trainer was satisfied with the exercises proposed. The mean marks are reported in this figure. Six trainers considered the session consistencies between 7.2 and 7.8. Only the last trainer considered the mean consistency of the sessions was about 6.4. This was because AI-VT replaced many exercises with others deemed less important in the eyes of this trainer in the two last sessions.

The mean marks for the diversities of the training sessions are also reported in Fig. 2. Six of the trainers gave mean marks between 7.4 and 8 for this aspect. There was only one mark of 6.8 for one trainer. This was due to the second session generated for this trainer, in which most of the exercises were the same as the ones proposed in the first session. This was due to the initialisation of the RD of the exercises and sub-capacities. Indeed, if these RD are too high for some sub-capacities and exercises, AI-VT will propose them until other exercises have a higher RD.

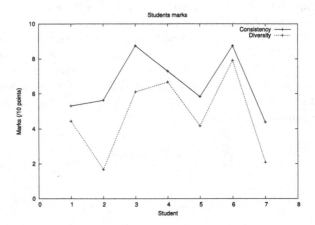

Fig. 3. Consistency and diversity marks obtained by the algorithmic training sessions

The mean marks obtained by AI-VT are reported in Fig. 3. The mean mark obtained by AI-VT for consistency is 6.56. The consistency of the training session was not very good because the learners were disappointed by the repetition of exercises. Some of the learners also felt that the exercises were not adapted to their initial level (particularly in the first training session). Indeed, it would be appropriate to evaluate the levels of the learners before the first training sessions in order to propose exercises with appropriate levels of difficulty before the first time a capacity is worked on. This is the main reason why there are so many differences for AI-VT evaluations from one learner to another.

5 Discussion

The diversity of the AI-VT-generated solutions has been measured and evaluated by different kinds of users. In the case of Aïkido training, AI-VT generally mixed 28 to 29 exercises over 10 training sessions, and each exercise was proposed two to three times in all the sets of generated training sessions. Six out of the seven trainers who evaluated AI-VT were satisfied with the diversity and the consistency of the generated solutions (the mean mark obtained by AI-VT was 7.4/10). This proves the pertinence of the system for Aïkido training: in the particular field of sports training, the system can propose varied and consistent training sessions for many weeks even if the same capacity is requested several times consecutively. The consistency of the set of exercises proposed for each training session is guaranteed by the introduction of complexities and distances between the different exercises. Hence, these distances allow the system to propose exercises that were not initially chosen by the trainers and to sort the exercises in each session. The diversity introduced by the system may sometimes poorly influence the consistency of one session. Indeed, AI-VT may substitute an exercise with a less appropriate one in regard to the performed sub-capacity in order to satisfy the diversity requirement.

The performance of the system is less satisfactory for algorithmic training. The measures obtained show that 22 to 23 exercises were proposed to the learners during the four sessions it was tested for, and each exercise was proposed, on average, 1.56 times to each learner. This measure proves that the retaining phase of AI-VT allows the system to propose the same exercise less often than Aïkido. Nevertheless, as shown by the qualitative evaluation, we must develop further the diversity of the training sessions proposed. In that particular field, even if the learners who tested AI-VT were globally satisfied, they were very disappointed when the system proposed the same exercise twice or more. The diversity felt by the learners did not match the measured one. As a consequence, we will study some possible modifications for the formulas for the retaining phase so that exercises that were partially resolved or even resolved with high difficulty should not be proposed more than twice to the learners, and not proposed in consecutive training sessions. Nevertheless, in algorithmics, all the training sessions were consistent, and all the proposed exercises were appropriate. Other approaches like the one of Smyth and McClave [20] propose the introduction of dissimilarity measures in the retrieved phase. That kind of approach is focused on the extension of the scope covered by the set of retrieved cases, whereas ours deals with the variety of the successive sets of retrieved cases. In AI-VT, the dissimilarity is not sufficient; other parameters linked to the acquired level of the learner, the fact that an exercise has already been proposed, and the ease with which it has been solved are of the utmost importance and must be added to the metrics used to select the cases.

AI-VT establishes a link between the adaptation and capitalisation of CBR-systems. Capitalisation is of the utmost importance in this system, which is required to give varied and creative solutions each time. Indeed, we have designed a way to use estimations of the levels acquired by users during the revision phase (based on the marks and the times really spent by learners on each exercise and sub-capacity) in order to enhance the accuracy of the adaptation process of CBR-systems. In addition, the introduction of remaining durations is of the utmost importance since it allows AI-VT to build varied solutions by analogy and thus to never propose the same session twice.

In addition, the initialisation process of AI-VT is time-consuming for the teacher. Indeed, the teacher has to organise sessions and exercises into capacities and sub-capacities and give the distances and the complexity of the exercises stored. In addition, the diversity of the exercises proposed in the training sessions depends on the number of stored exercises. For that reason, we will study the possibility of generating exercises and durations automatically and a way to help the trainer to initialise the system.

6   Conclusion

We have designed a system based on case-based reasoning dedicated to the generation of varied training sessions for learners. AI-VT meets one of the most important requirements: its ability to generate varied training sessions. With this implementation of AI-VT, we highlighted the importance of the retaining phase of CBR for system diversity. Indeed, this retaining phase stores what the learners have used, i.e. the training sessions and training exercises stored. The process that stores these training sessions has an impact on whether an exercise should be proposed once again or not. In addition, we proved AI-VT's ability to adapt the diversity of the training-session exercises generated to the context of use. Indeed, the retaining phase of AI-VT is adapted to the context and type of learning it is used for. The results obtained for sports training are very different from the ones obtained for theoretical learning, like algorithmics. In the case of sports, learning can be based on repetition of the same exercises time after time. Indeed, even if an exercise is proposed at the beginning of each training session, it helps make certain actions automatic. On the contrary, being confronted with the same algorithmic exercise twice or more is disappointing for learners since they already have the resolution of the exercise stored somewhere on their computers. As a consequence, even if the process of generating a training session is based on analogy with past situations, an accurate balance between repetition and diversity is proposed by AI-VT, depending on the learned field.

Acknowledgement. The authors wish to thank the FR-EDUC (*Research Federation for EDUCation*) of University of Franche-Comté for their financial help, and Mary Moritz (WordStyle Traductions) for her help with the English language.

References

1. Bernstein, N.: The Co-ordination and Regulation of Movements. Pergamon Press, Oxford (1966)
2. Biswas, G., Leelawong, K., Schwartz, D., Vye, N., The Teachable Agents Group at Vanderbilt: Learning by teaching: a new agent paradigm for educational software. Appl. Artif. Intell. **19**(3–4), 363–392 (2005)
3. Bridge, D., Kelly, J.P.: Ways of computing diverse collaborative recommendations. In: Wade, V.P., Ashman, H., Smyth, B. (eds.) AH 2006. LNCS, vol. 4018, pp. 41–50. Springer, Heidelberg (2006). https://doi.org/10.1007/11768012_6

4. Gero, J.S., Maher, M.L.: Modeling Creativity and Knowledge-Based Creative Design. Psychology Press, Cambridge (2013)
5. Gisolfi, A., Loia, V.: Designing complex systems within distributed architectures: an intelligent tutoring systems perspective. Appl. Artif. Intell. **8**(3), 393–411 (1994)
6. Grace, K., Maher, M.L.: Surprise-triggered reformulation of design goals. In: AAAI, pp. 3726–3732 (2016)
7. Grace, K., Maher, M.L., Wilson, D.C., Najjar, N.A.: Combining CBR and deep learning to generate surprising recipe designs. In: Goel, A., Díaz-Agudo, M.B., Roth-Berghofer, T. (eds.) ICCBR 2016. LNCS (LNAI), vol. 9969, pp. 154–169. Springer, Cham (2016). https://doi.org/10.1007/978-3-319-47096-2_11
8. Graesser, A.C., Conley, M.W., Olney, A.: Intelligent tutoring systems. In: The APA Educational Psychology Handbook, vol. 3, pp. 451–473 (2012)
9. Huang, M.J., Huang, H.S., Chen, M.Y.: Constructing a personalized e-learning system based on genetic algorithm and case-based reasoning approach. Expert Syst. Appl. **33**(3), 551–564 (2007)
10. Jamsandekar, P., Patil, M.: Online learning - CBR approach. Int. J. Res. Comput. Sci. Inf. Technol. **1**, 111–113 (2013)
11. Kolodner, J.: Case-Based Reasoning. Morgan Kaufmann, San Mateo (1993)
12. Kolodner, J.L., Cox, M.T., González-Calero, P.A.: Case-based reasoning-inspired approaches to education. Knowl. Eng. Rev. **20**(03), 299–303 (2005)
13. Kolodner, J.L., Owensby, J.N., Guzdial, M.: Case-based learning aids. In: Handbook of Research on Educational Communications and Technology, vol. 2, pp. 829–861 (2004)
14. Maher, M.L., Grace, K.: Encouraging curiosity in case-based reasoning and recommender systems. In: Aha, D.W., Lieber, J. (eds.) ICCBR 2017. LNCS (LNAI), vol. 10339, pp. 3–15. Springer, Cham (2017). https://doi.org/10.1007/978-3-319-61030-6_1
15. McGinty, L., Smyth, B.: On the role of diversity in conversational recommender systems. In: Ashley, K.D., Bridge, D.G. (eds.) ICCBR 2003. LNCS (LNAI), vol. 2689, pp. 276–290. Springer, Heidelberg (2003). https://doi.org/10.1007/3-540-45006-8_23
16. McSherry, D.: Diversity-conscious retrieval. In: Craw, S., Preece, A. (eds.) ECCBR 2002. LNCS (LNAI), vol. 2416, pp. 219–233. Springer, Heidelberg (2002). https://doi.org/10.1007/3-540-46119-1_17
17. Müller, G., Bergmann, R.: Workflow streams: a means for compositional adaptation in process-oriented CBR. In: Lamontagne, L., Plaza, E. (eds.) ICCBR 2014. LNCS (LNAI), vol. 8765, pp. 315–329. Springer, Cham (2014). https://doi.org/10.1007/978-3-319-11209-1_23
18. Rishi, O., Govil, R., Sinha, M.: Distributed case based reasoning for intelligent tutoring system: an agent based student modeling paradigm. World Acad. Sci. Eng. Technol. **5**, 273–276 (2007)
19. Schank, R.C., Fano, A., Bell, B., Jona, M.: The design of goal-based scenarios. J. Learn. Sci. **3**(4), 305–345 (1994)
20. Smyth, B., McClave, P.: Similarity vs. diversity. In: Aha, D.W., Watson, I. (eds.) ICCBR 2001. LNCS (LNAI), vol. 2080, pp. 347–361. Springer, Heidelberg (2001). https://doi.org/10.1007/3-540-44593-5_25
21. Tan, X.h., Shen, R.m., Wang, Y.: Personalized course generation and evolution based on genetic algorithms. J. Zhejiang Univ. Sci. C **13**(12), 909–917 (2012)
22. Tyler, R.W.: Statistical methods for utilizing personal judgments to evaluate activities for teacher-training curricula. Ph.D. thesis, University of Chicago (1927)

A Textual Recommender System
for Clinical Data

Philipp Andreas Hummel[1,2(✉)], Frank Jäkel[1], Sascha Lange[1],
and Roland Mertelsmann[3]

[1] PSIORI, Freiburg, Germany
philipp@psiori.com
[2] Institute of Cognitive Science, University of Osnabrück, Osnabrück, Germany
[3] Department for Haematology and Oncology, University Hospital Freiburg,
Freiburg, Germany

Abstract. When faced with an exceptional clinical case, doctors like to
review information about similar patients to guide their decision-making.
Retrieving relevant cases, however, is a hard and time-consuming task:
Hospital databases of free-text physician letters provide a rich resource of
information but are usually only searchable with string-matching methods. Here, we present a recommender system that automatically finds
physician letters similar to a specified reference letter using an information retrieval procedure. We use a small-scale, prototypical dataset to
compare the system's recommendations with physicians' similarity judgments of letter pairs in a psychological experiment. The results show
that the recommender system captures expert intuitions about letter
similarity well and is usable for practical applications.

Keywords: Case-based reasoning · Information retrieval
Recommender system · Clinical decision making
Psychological evaluation · Medical decision support system

1 Introduction

1.1 Motivation

Publishing and reading case reports of interesting patients is a popular pastime
among medical doctors. But as the scientific value of single case reports has
been questioned [20], the number of case reports has declined steadily for the
most prestigious medical journals. However, in response, several new journals
dedicated exclusively to case reports have emerged [12][1] and many people have
argued for the continued importance of case reports [8, 24, 27]. Case reports offer

---

[1] e.g., Journal of Medical Cases: http://www.journalmc.org/index.php/JMC/index,
British Medical Journal Case Reports: http://casereports.bmj.com/site/about/
index.xhtml, American Journal of Medical Case Reports: http://www.sciepub.com/
journal/AJMCR.

© Springer Nature Switzerland AG 2018
M. T. Cox et al. (Eds.): ICCBR 2018, LNAI 11156, pp. 140–152, 2018.
https://doi.org/10.1007/978-3-030-01081-2_10

practitioners an in-depth understanding of specific disease courses and provide educational material for students [23]. Although case reports lack the validity of large-scale experimental studies, medical doctors often strongly believe in their usefulness and they report using past clinical records of similar patients to guide problem-solving for their current patients. In particular, when faced with hard or unusual cases, doctors seek information about similar patients from hospital records. While this only shows that physicians think that reviewing similar cases helps them in their work, research in cognitive science suggests that case-based reasoning is indeed important for medical problem-solving.

Cognitive scientists have found that in specific experimental settings reasoning processes are clearly based on single examples [4, 22] and these reasoning processes have also been studied in more real-world scenarios. For example, Klein [13] reviews models for decision-making under real-world conditions and finds that experts interpret a situation based on its resemblance to remembered situations. Once a sufficiently similar situation has been retrieved from memory, experts apply the solution from the recalled situation to the current problem in a thought experiment. They evaluate whether or not this solution strategy will lead to success and adjust it, if necessary. In case no way to adequately adjust the solution can be found, another situation is retrieved from memory. This process is repeated until a sufficiently good solution is found. Information about similar cases should, therefore, aid doctors' decision-making in an actual clinical setting.

Research in cognitive science has also directly addressed the medical domain. Elstein et al. [10] have concluded that for medical problem-solving reasoning processes can be divided into two distinct categories. For cases perceived as easy doctors apply a kind of pattern recognition based on the examples they have encountered before and use solutions stored in memory. For harder cases, however, doctors need to rely on a more elaborate reasoning process. They have to consciously generate and eliminate hypotheses to be able to solve the problem. It is plausible that hypothesis generation, as well as hypothesis falsification, is also guided by the doctor's experience with earlier patients. From a more theoretical perspective, Kolodner and Kolodner [14] have specifically argued that "[i]ndividual experiences act as exemplars upon which to base later decisions" in medical problem-solving. Their research was partially driven by the desire to understand the way in which clinicians perform problem-solving but also by the goal of building artificial systems that can aid in this process. They argue that both humans and machines can learn from specific examples and use them to reason about new problems.

Case-Based Reasoning (CBR) is, of course, the branch of Artificial Intelligence that developed from these ideas. Researchers have successfully built systems—used in real-world applications—that reason from example cases [1] and, not surprisingly, medical problem solving is one of the major applications areas [2].

Given the practical, psychological, and theoretical reflections above, we believe that it is, indeed, helpful for practitioners to be able to review cases of similar patients. One particularly well-suited source for the retrieval of relevant cases is a hospital's records of physician letters. Physician letters provide concise summaries of the specifics of a patient that matter in practice. Search in these free-text databases is, however, often limited to string-matching and therefore provides limited practical value for doctors. We, therefore, designed a prototypical recommender system to automatically retrieve only relevant physician letters. We also evaluated this system in a psychological experiment.

Our approach differs substantially from most CBR applications in that we do not aim to fully automate medical problem-solving. The CBR workflow can usually be described as a four-step process [1]. Retrieving the most similar cases, reusing this information to find a solution for the current problem, revising this solution and retaining (part of) the solution for future problem-solving. In our application, we aim to only automatize the first step. All subsequent reasoning is still done by the doctors themselves. We focus on supplying the physician with relevant information instead of solving the medical problem automatically, thereby making the system more acceptable for doctors. Tange et al. [26] experimented with a manual version of medical document search. They tested human information retrieval performance when presenting free-text sections in different ways. Another approach to automatic retrieval of similar medical cases was pursued by Greenes et al. [11]. However, they did not work on free-text documents but on structured medical information. Díaz-Galiano et al. [7] used an ontology to do query expansion to improve an information retrieval system for annotated medical images. Our approach differs from the others in that our recommender system works on free-text documents, created without restrictions from our side.

1.2 Dataset

Physician letters are free-text documents written by doctors to keep record of patients' visits. They usually include information about a patient's age, sex, diagnosed diseases, therapeutical history, current complaints, and many more medical details like blood counts, but also personal information like names and birth dates. In the dataset used here, great care was taken to remove any personal information from the letters. It was therefore not feasible to acquire a large set of letters. The dataset comprises 286 letters of 269 individual patients of the hematology and oncology department of the University Hospital Freiburg. For 17 patients two letters of two distinct points during therapy are included, which we refer to as follow-up letter pairs.

1.3 Use Case Scenario

The recommender system we ultimately envision is built into the clinical workflow of doctors. During the visit of a patient, physicians write a new or modify an existing letter. Already in this writing phase, the system should retrieve letters of similar patients and present them on demand. Thereby, doctors' decision-making processes can be guided by these similar cases if the doctor deems this necessary. The perceived suitability of the retrieved letters has to be exceptionally high as physicians' time resources are usually very limited. Therefore, the recommender system will only be used in practice if almost all recommendations are considered useful.

In the following we will describe our recommender system and the information retrieval methods that were used in more detail. Then we present an experiment and corresponding evaluation we conducted to understand the performance of the system. Finally, we discuss problems, but also future steps for an implementation of the system.

2 Recommender System

For the purpose of retrieving similar letters from a database we make use of information retrieval methods that represents every document as a vector in a vector space. Document similarity is measured in this vector space and similar letters can thus be retrieved.

2.1 Term Frequency-Inverse Document Frequency

The conceptually simplest vector space model of documents is the Bag of Words Model (BOW) [19]. A set of documents is mapped to a set of vectors in the following manner: First, the vocabulary V of the corpus (i.e. set of documents) is identified. The vector space for embedding the documents has dimensionality $|V|$. Every dimension of this space represents one word of the vocabulary. Every document vector's dimension represents the absolute frequency of a word (called term frequency (TF)) in the document. Consider the two exemplary documents $d_1 = $ "A minor disease" and $d_2 = $ "A major disease". Their bag of words vector representations $\mathbf{v}_{d_1}$ and $\mathbf{v}_{d_2}$ are:

$$\mathbf{v}_{d_1} = \begin{pmatrix} 1 \\ 1 \\ 0 \\ 1 \end{pmatrix} \quad \mathbf{v}_{d_2} = \begin{pmatrix} 1 \\ 0 \\ 1 \\ 1 \end{pmatrix} \quad \begin{matrix} \text{a} \\ \text{minor} \\ \text{major} \\ \text{disease} \end{matrix}$$

A common problem with the bag of words model is that some words or terms appear frequently across texts in a corpus, i.e. have a high term frequency, yet do not constitute a good feature for discrimination between texts. Therefore, a scaling factor for the term frequencies is required that captures the intuition that words that appear frequently in a few texts but rarely in others are good discriminative features for those texts. Term Frequency–Inverse Document Frequency (TF-IDF) downscales the importance of frequent words, while upscaling the importance of rare words.

Term frequency $\text{tf}(t, d)$ of term t in document d is defined as in the BOW model. Inverse document frequency $\text{idf}(t, C)$ of term t and corpus C can be computed as

$$\text{idf}(t, C) = \log_2 \left(\frac{|C|}{|\{d \in C : t \in d\}|} \right) \tag{1}$$

where $|C|$ is the total number of documents in the corpus and $|\{d \in C : t \in d\}|$ is the number of documents in which term t appears at least once. Term frequency–inverse document frequency $\text{tfidf}(t, d, C)$ is then calculated as

$$\text{tfidf}(t, d, C) = \text{tf}(t, d) \cdot \text{idf}(t, C) \tag{2}$$

TF-IDF can be used as a feature for the representation of the document that is more robust to uninformative changes in the distribution of common words and more expressive for rare words [19]. We therefore use TF-IDF, instead of the vanilla BOW model, in our system.

The similarity of two documents can now be defined as the cosine similarity of the corresponding TF-IDF vectors

$$s_{\cos}(\mathbf{v}_1, \mathbf{v}_2) = \frac{\langle \mathbf{v}_1, \mathbf{v}_2 \rangle}{||\mathbf{v}_1|| \cdot ||\mathbf{v}_2||} \tag{3}$$

where $\langle \mathbf{v}_1, \mathbf{v}_2 \rangle$ is the scalar product of $\mathbf{v}_1$ and $\mathbf{v}_2$ and $||\mathbf{v}||$ is the norm of vector $\mathbf{v}$. Using this similarity measure, the recommender system can retrieve the documents from the database that are most similar to the reference letter of the current patient.

3   Experimental Evaluation

To measure the performance of the recommender system we conduct a psychological experiment with medically trained subjects. More precisely, we compare the subjects' similarity ratings of letter pairs to the cosine similarity of the TF-IDF embeddings.

3.1   Experimental Setup

The experiment has 32 trials. In each trial subjects have to compare one so-called "reference letter" to five so-called "comparison letters". More precisely, we select 32 letters from our dataset as reference letters and ask subjects to rate the similarity between the reference letters and five other letters each. Thus, we collect ratings for 160 letter pairs. Half of the reference letters are selected such that they have a follow-up letter in our database. The remaining 16 reference letters are selected randomly among the letters without follow-ups present in our dataset. Four of the five comparison letters of a trial are selected based on the cosine similarity between the reference letter and all other letters in our dataset. Having the highest cosine similarity, these four are the best matches to the reference letter according to the TF-IDF recommender system. The fifth comparison letter is randomly selected from all other letters. The order of the reference and comparison letters is random, but the same for all subjects. During a trial, subjects are presented with one reference and one comparison letter at a time. After rating the similarity of the pair, they are presented with the next comparison letter. Having rated the five pairs the trial is completed and the next trial starts. Subjects have to give a rating in the range of 1 (very dissimilar) to 7 (very similar) for each letter pair. Trials with a follow-up letter as reference letter are called "follow-up trials" and letter pairs of follow-ups are called "follow-up pairs". The first two trials are practice trials. Trial one is a follow-up trial and trial two is a non-follow-up trial. These trials cover very similar and very dissimilar pairs so that participants can adapt their numerical responses to the full range of similarities in the experiment. Practice trials are excluded from the analysis. Four experts (oncologists with at least five years of practical experience) and two novices (medical students more than halfway through their study course) participated in the experiment.

3.2   Inter-rater Agreement

We first analyze the inter-rater agreement among participants. It is not trivial for subjects to rate letter pairs for similarity because it is not obvious along which dimension similarity is to be judged, a problem well known from the cognitive science literature [21]. One might, for example, judge similarity based on diagnosis or based on therapy. Experts and novices (or students) usually base their judgments on different features. Experts generally have higher agreement when categorizing stimuli than novices and usually use more abstract, less accessible features [5,16,17]. In line with these results, we find that the inter-rater agreement is higher among the experts than among the students (Spearman rank correlation coefficient [25] for expert agreement: 0.76; student agreement: 0.59). As we are interested in expert judgments we discarded the student data and only used the expert ratings for further analysis.

For the following analyses we furthermore exclude data of follow-up pairs, except where explicitly stated otherwise. Subjects rate the similarity of these pairs as very high and almost any information retrieval system will find them to be similar. Including them would positively improve correlation statistics in our analysis, although retrieving them is useless in practice. We will show later that our recommender can, however, easily distinguish them from non-follow-up pairs.

3.3   Are Recommendations Better Than Chance?

The first step of assessing the quality of the recommender system is to evaluate whether the recommendations are better than chance. For this we compare the average subject rating of the letter with the highest cosine similarity and the random comparison letter for each trial. Figure 1 shows a histogram of the differences in subject rating of the most cosine-similar and the randomly selected letter pairs. The figure also shows the mean difference and the 95% confidence interval (based on the standard error of the mean). As the mean and the whole confidence interval are well above zero, the recommendations of the system are significantly better than random recommendations.

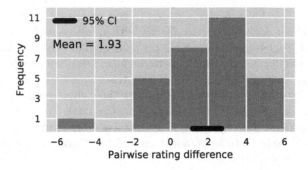

Fig. 1. Histogram of differences in rating of the "best" and the random comparison letter for each trial. The mean and the 95% confidence interval is shown.

3.4   Cosine Similarity and Subject Ratings

Next we analyze the relationship of the cosine similarity and the average subject ratings of letter pairs more directly. We group the letter pairs by the subjects' ratings and plot the mean cosine similarity of each group in Fig. 2. The data show a positive, close to linear correlation (Pearson correlation: 0.96) of those two variables, suggesting that the cosine similarity of TF-IDF vectors captures at least some aspects of the participants' perceived similarity.

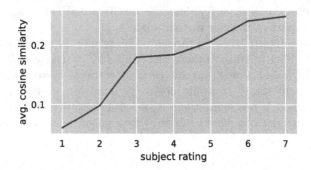

Fig. 2. Averaged cosine similarity of all letter pairs that were rated into one of the seven possible rating categories.

In Fig. 3 each letter pair is visualized as a point. The y-value is the average rating (over subjects) and the x-value the cosine similarity of a pair. Follow-up pairs are marked as green circles, random comparison letter pairs as red triangles, and all the remaining pairs as blue squares. The figure shows that follow-up letters can easily be distinguished from other letter pairs as they have a much higher cosine similarity. The randomly selected pairs mostly have a low cosine similarity as expected. However, surprisingly, several random pairs are still rated as being rather similar by the subjects.

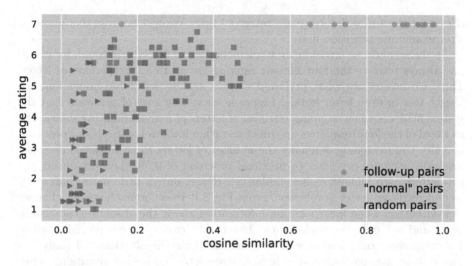

Fig. 3. Average subject rating versus cosine similarity of all letter pairs.

3.5 Considerations of Precision and Recall

The quality of an information retrieval system is usually evaluated by precision and recall. All documents are classified as either relevant or irrelevant given a current information need or query [18]. In our case, a query is a reference letter and we analyze whether a comparison letter is relevant or irrelevant given this reference letter. Precision is then a measure of the correctness of the retrieved results. In probabilistic terms, it is the probability that a document is relevant given that it is retrieved $P(relevant|retrieved)$. Recall is a measure of completeness of the retrieved results and can be expressed as the probability of being retrieved given that the document is relevant $P(retrieved|relevant)$. Both quantities usually exhibit an inverse relationship. One can trade higher precision for lower recall and vice versa. We classify letter pairs with an average rating of five or higher as relevant and the remaining ones as irrelevant. This threshold is somewhat arbitrary but was set after consulting with the contributing physicians.

We can assess the precision of our system in different scenarios. Recall, however, is impossible for us to measure. This is because we do not know the set of relevant letters for a given information need (i.e. reference letter) and therefore cannot compute $P(retrieved|relevant)$. Precision is arguably the more interesting measure for our use-case anyway. For applicability and acceptance by doctors in a clinical setting, it is crucial that a large fraction of recommended letters is deemed useful. Recall on the other hand, is perhaps not as crucial. Doctors will only have time to look at very few of the recommended letters and hence finding a large fraction of all relevant documents is less important. However, an interesting question, somewhat related to recall, is whether or not the *most* relevant letters in a database are retrieved first. We will address this question after examining precision first.

In the scenario we envision, an implementation of the system could, for example, always retrieve the four highest ranking letters to a given reference letter. Thus, we investigate what precision we can achieve when recommending the "best" four or even fewer letters. Figure 4a shows the level of precision that the system achieves when stopping retrieval of letters at a given rank. As shown, the retrieval of the four best letters results in a rather low level of precision (precision = 0.55). Unfortunately, reducing the number of letters to be retrieved does not markedly increase precision (a maximal precision of 0.59 when presenting the two letters with highest cosine similarity). Hence, only a little more than every second retrieved letter is relevant. From Fig. 3 it is apparent, however, that we can do better, when incorporating information about the absolute cosine similarity and not only the ranks of the letters. We can achieve a precision up to 1 if we present only letters with a cosine similarity higher than 0.4 (only letters with an average rating of at least five are retrieved in that situation). This, in turn, means that only for a portion of the reference letters any comparison letters are retrieved. In Fig. 4b we examine this relationship more closely. We restrict the system to retrieve up to four letters (remember that we only have human judgments for the top four) but only if their cosine similarity is bigger than a threshold. We now plot the precision of retrieved letters as a function of varying this cosine similarity threshold. Instead of labeling the x-axis with the threshold we show the average number of retrieved letters per query or reference letter. In this way we can visualize the trade-off between higher precision and fewer retrieved letters. Increasing precision is thus easy to achieve. It comes at the cost though of not retrieving any comparison letters for some reference letters. Unfortunately, it is likely that the recommender system will be of highest value to doctors for patients with very rare diseases. In those cases, however, it is least likely to find other letters with a high cosine similarity in the database. Therefore, a large corpus will be required to reliably retrieve relevant comparison letters.

Next, we turn to the question whether the most relevant letters are retrieved first. This is hard to answer, since through our experiment we only know the similarity of five comparison letters for each of the reference letters. We do not know which similarity ratings participants would have assigned to the other letters from our database. However, comparing the ranking computed by the algorithm with the ranking by the experts can provide some insight into this problem. The correlation between the algorithm's and experts' ranking on the five comparison letters can be used as an approximate measure of the correlation between their ranking for all comparison letters. This correlation in turn can provide insight into whether the most relevant letters are retrieved first. Given a high correlation it would be plausible to assume that the most relevant letters are often retrieved before less relevant letters. We compute this correlation with the Spearman rank correlation coefficient. Additionally we estimate the 95% confidence interval for the correlation by a non-parametric bootstrap [9],

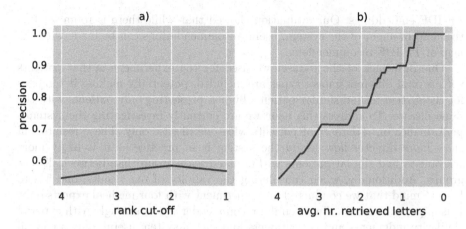

Fig. 4. (a): Precision as a function of rank cut-off. **(b):** Precision as function of a varying cosine similarity threshold. The x-axis shows the average number of retrieved letters per reference letter at the threshold instead of the threshold itself. Note that both plots **(a)** and **(b)** start at the same point, where all letters with rank four or lower are retrieved, and share a common y-axis.

i.e. by randomly resampling with replacement the dataset at hand. The correlation between the ranking given by the average expert rating and the ranking of the algorithm is 0.39 (95% CI: [0.22, 0.56]). While this is not particularly high, it is still far better than chance (Spearman coefficient of 0). The inter-rater agreement among the experts when calculated accordingly (i.e. without follow-up pairs) is 0.71 (95% CI: [0.63, 0.79]). We also directly estimate the difference between inter-expert agreement and algorithm-to-expert agreement. On average the algorithm-to-expert agreement lies 0.33 below the inter-expert agreement (95% CI: [0.15, 0.52]). While our system performs substantially worse than the human gold standard, its ranking is well above chance. Therefore it seems plausible that the most relevant letters will be retrieved much earlier than expected by chance.

4 Discussion

Facing challenging cases medical doctors are likely to benefit from reviewing information about similar patients. In this paper we have built a tool for automatic retrieval of physician letters similar to a reference letter. These similar cases ought to help guide a physician's decision-making. Our prototype uses the Term Frequency–Inverse Document Frequency (TF-IDF) vector space embedding of texts, a standard tool from Information Retrieval, to compute the similarity between documents and to find the most similar letters from a database. The performance of this prototype was assessed in a psychological experiment by comparing expert judgments of letter similarity to the cosine similarity of

TF-IDF embeddings. Our evaluation showed that while there is room for further improvement of the system, useful recommendations can be made with the help of TF-IDF recommenders.

One drawback of the dataset we used for the experiment is that patients with several different cancer types are included, potentially making it too easy for the system to find similar patients by just presenting only patients with the same disease. To address this issue we are currently investigating the system's performance on a dataset of patients with one disease only. These results will show more directly how useful the system is in practice as it is likely more relevant to find similar patients within one disease group than between disease groups. Additionally, when considering the validity of our results, one has to keep in mind that we conducted our experiment with four medical experts only. It is important to note that even if a recommender agrees strongly with experts' similarity judgments and practitioners find such a system useful, only a clinical trial can establish whether using such a system also improves clinical treatment for patients.

In any case, while we find a reasonable correlation between cosine similarity and experts' judgments, there is reason to believe that the recommender will work even better on a larger database. In a much larger database there will be more documents with a higher cosine similarity for each reference letter. And a high absolute cosine similarity seems to be a much better predictor for a high perceived similarity than the relative rank as shown in Fig. 4, which suggests that using a larger database will directly improve recommendations.

To increase the performance of the system further one can imagine using other embedding methods or a combined similarity measure created out of the similarity measures of single embeddings. We already performed some experiments with three additional embedding methods: Latent Semantic Analysis [6], Latent Dirichlet Allocation [3] and Paragraph Vector [15]. None of these methods outperformed the TF-IDF embedding but we got encouraging results when using a combination of Paragraph Vector and TF-IDF embeddings. These two methods seem to be sufficiently dissimilar in their embedding procedure that useful additional information can be gained by combining them.

As already described in the introduction, Klein [13] describes real-world decision-making in the following way: Experts generate hypotheses for the current problem at hand based on examples of previous problems stored in memory. The example-solutions are applied to the current problem and refined or discarded if necessary. It is quite compelling to believe that the quality of decisions will increase if more relevant examples are retrieved. In our application scenario, the examples are provided by our algorithm rather than retrieved from memory and we showed that our system indeed retrieves useful instances. We can thus extend the physician's retrieval memory to the whole database of the hospital.

References

1. Aamodt, A., Plaza, E.: Case-based reasoning: foundational issues, methodological variations, and system approaches. AI Commun. **7**(1), 39–59 (1994). https://doi.org/10.3233/AIC-1994-7104

2. Begum, S., Ahmed, M.U., Funk, P., Xiong, N., Folke, M.: Case-based reasoning systems in the health sciences: a survey of recent trends and developments. IEEE Trans. Syst. Man Cybern. Part C (Appl. Rev.) **41**(4), 421–434 (2011). https://doi.org/10.1109/TSMCC.2010.2071862

3. Blei, D.M., Ng, A.Y., Jordan, M.I.: Latent dirichlet allocation. Mach. Learn. Res. **3**, 993–1022 (2003)

4. Brooks, L.R., Norman, G.R., Allen, S.W.: Role of specific similarity in a medical diagnostic task. J. Exp. Psychol. **120**(3), 278–287 (1991)

5. Chi, M.T.H., Feltovich, P.J., Glaser, R.: Categorization and representation of physics problems by experts and novices. Cognit. Sci. **5**(2), 121–152 (1981)

6. Deerwester, S., Dumais, S.T., Furnas, G.W., Landauer, T.K., Harshman, R.: Indexing by latent semantic analysis. Am. Soc. Inf. Sci. **41**(6), 391–407 (1990)

7. Díaz-Galiano, M.C., Martín-Valdivia, M.T., Ureña-López, L.A.: Query expansion with a medical ontology to improve a multimodal information retrieval system. Comput. Biol. Med. **39**(4), 396–403 (2009). https://doi.org/10.1016/j.compbiomed.2009.01.012

8. Dib, E.G., Kidd, M.R., Saltman, D.C.: Case reports and the fight against cancer. J. Med. Case Rep. **2**(1), 39 (2008). https://doi.org/10.1186/1752-1947-2-39

9. Efron, B.: Bootstrap methods: another look at the jackknife. Ann. Stat. **7**(1), 1–26 (1979)

10. Elstein, A.S.: Clinical problem solving and diagnostic decision making: selective review of the cognitive literature. BMJ **324**(7339), 729–732 (2002). https://doi.org/10.1136/bmj.324.7339.729

11. Greenes, A.R., Octo Barnett, G., Klein, S.W., Robbins, A., Prior, R.E.: Recording, retrieval and review of medical data by physician-computer interaction. N. Engl. J. Med. **282**(6), 307–315 (1970). https://doi.org/10.1056/NEJM197002052820605

12. Kidd, M., Hubbard, C.: Introducing journal of medical case reports. J. Med. Case Rep. **1**(1), 1 (2007). https://doi.org/10.1186/1752-1947-1-1

13. Klein, G.: Naturalistic decision making. Hum. Factors J. Hum. Factors Ergonomics Soc. **50**(3), 456–460 (2008). https://doi.org/10.1518/001872008X288385

14. Kolodner, J.L., Kolodner, R.M.: Using experience in clinical problem solving: introduction and framework. IEEE Trans. Syst. Man Cybern. **17**(3), 420–431 (1987)

15. Le, Q., Mikolov, T.: Distributed representations of sentences and documents. In: International Conference on Machine Learning, vol. 32, pp. 1188–1196 (2014). https://doi.org/10.1145/2740908.2742760

16. León-Villagrá, P., Jäkel, F.: Categorization and abstract similarity in chess. In: Proceedings of the 35th Annual Meeting of the Cognitive Science Society, pp. 2860–2865. Cognitive Science Society, Berlin (2013). https://escholarship.org/uc/item/4jr8r7x1

17. Linhares, A., Brum, P.: Understanding our understanding of strategic scenarios: what role do chunks play? Cognit. Sci. **31**(6), 989–1007 (2007). https://doi.org/10.1080/03640210701703725

18. Manning, C.D., Raghavan, P., Schütze, H.: Evaluation of unranked retrieval sets. In: Introduction to Information Retrieval, vol. 8, pp. 154–157. Cambridge University Press, Cambridge (2008)

19. Manning, C.D., Raghavan, P., Schütze, H.: Scoring, term weighting and the vector space model. In: Introduction to Information Retrieval, vol. 6, pp. 117–120. Cambridge University Press, Cambridge (2008)
20. Mason, R.A.: The case report - an endangered species? Anaesthesia **56**(2), 99–102 (2001)
21. Medin, D.L., Goldstone, R.L., Gentner, D.: Respects for similarity. Psychol. Rev. **100**(2), 254–278 (1993). https://doi.org/10.1037/0033-295X.100.2.254
22. Medin, D.L., Schaffer, M.M.: Context theory of classification learning. Psychol. Rev. **85**(3), 207–238 (1978). https://doi.org/10.1037/0033-295X.85.3.207
23. Nissen, T., Wynn, R.: The clinical case report: a review of its merits and limitations. BMC Res. Notes **7**(1), 264 (2014). https://doi.org/10.1186/1756-0500-7-264
24. Sandu, N., Chowdhury, T., Schaller, B.J.: How to apply case reports in clinical practice using surrogate models via example of the trigeminocardiac reflex. J. Med. Case Rep. **10**(1), 84 (2016). https://doi.org/10.1186/s13256-016-0849-z
25. Spearman, C.: The proof and measurement of association between two things. Am. J. Psychol. **15**(1), 72 (1904). https://doi.org/10.2307/1412159
26. Tange, H.J., Schouten, H.C., Kester, A.D.M., Hasman, A.: The granularity of medical narratives and its effect on the speed and completeness of information retrieval. J. Am. Med. Inform. Assoc. **5**(6), 571–582 (1998). https://doi.org/10.1136/jamia.1998.0050571
27. Williams, D.D.R.: In defence of the case report. R. Coll. Psychiatr. **184**(1), 84–88 (2004)

Harnessing Hundreds of Millions of Cases:
Case-Based Prediction at Industrial Scale

Vahid Jalali[1]([☒]) and David Leake[2]

[1] Walmartlabs, Sunnyvale, CA 94086, USA
vjalali@walmartlabs.com
[2] School of Informatics, Computing, and Engineering, Indiana University,
Bloomington, IN 47408, USA
leake@indiana.edu

Abstract. Building predictive models is central to many big data applications. However, model building is computationally costly at scale. An appealing alternative is bypassing model building by applying case-based prediction to reason directly from data. However, to our knowledge case-based prediction still has not been applied at true industrial scale. In previous work we introduced a knowledge-light/data intensive approach to case-based prediction, using ensembles of automatically-generated adaptations. We developed foundational scaleup methods, using Locality Sensitive Hashing (LSH) for fast approximate nearest neighbor retrieval of both cases and adaptation rules, and tested them for millions of cases. This paper presents research on extending these methods to address the practical challenges raised by case bases of hundreds of millions of cases for a real world industrial e-commerce application. Handling this application required addressing how to keep LSH practical for skewed data; the resulting efficiency gains in turn enabled applying an adaptation generation strategy that previously was computationally infeasible. Experimental results show that our CBR approach achieves accuracy comparable to or better than state of the art machine learning methods commonly applied, while avoiding their model-building cost. This supports the opportunity to harness CBR for industrial scale prediction.

Keywords: Big data · Case based reasoning
Ensemble of adaptations · Locality sensitive hashing · Skewed data

1 Introduction

Predicting future customer actions is integral to e-commerce competitiveness. For example, the success of retailers is closely tied to predicting customer behaviors to maximize effectiveness of the supply chain, inventory management, and marketing. The standard method for such prediction is to abstract data into mathematical models to apply to the prediction task (e.g., a firm might train a logistic regression model to predict whether a customer will make an electronics purchase within the next month). The staggering growth of digital data has

© Springer Nature Switzerland AG 2018
M. T. Cox et al. (Eds.): ICCBR 2018, LNAI 11156, pp. 153–169, 2018.
https://doi.org/10.1007/978-3-030-01081-2_11

made a plethora of training instances available, increasing prediction opportunities but making model building computationally challenging. This challenge is commonly addressed at two stages: First, by applying sampling methods to select a manageable-size subset of the data to use as a training set (e.g., [26]), and second, by applying optimization techniques such as stochastic learning (e.g., [4]) or parallelization (e.g., [31]) to expedite the model-building process.

In contrast to model-based approaches, case-based reasoning's lazy learning approach skips the model building step entirely, to retrieve cases on demand and predict directly from them. This avoids the cost of model building but shifts cost to retrieval. Often retrieval costs are not a practical impediment [9]. However, successful industrial-scale CBR will depend on controlling them. A rich current of CBR research develops methods for controlling retrieval costs by compressing the case base (see Leake, Smyth, Wilson and Yang [18] for some examples). However, applying even carefully-crafted competence-driven methods (e.g., [30]) has two major drawbacks. First, deletion of cases may unavoidably lose information. Second, compression can impose a considerable pre-processing cost penalty [9]. Standard compression methods generally have $O(n^2)$ complexity [30], making them prohibitively expensive to apply to case bases at scale.

In previous work [11] we argued that using retrieval methods from big data frameworks can enable scaling up CBR without compression. That work introduced large scale case/rule retrieval and adaptation generation methods for regression and classification tasks, using Locality Sensitive Hashing (LSH) [10] for efficient approximate nearest neighbor retrieval, based on examining a subset of candidate cases (those in the same hash bucket as the query) rather than the entire case base. Evaluations supported that the methods were practical for large case bases (tests included a case base of two million cases), but also revealed that handling larger case bases would require going beyond those methods alone. It is now common to deal with data sets with several hundreds of millions of instances [1], and is not unheard of to handle billions of instances [19,23]. Consequently, new methods are needed.

This paper discusses the primary challenges of extending the LSH-based case-based prediction approach to the next level, of hundreds of millions of cases, and how we addressed them. The testbed domain for this work is an important e-commerce application: predicting the propensity of the users of an e-commerce platform to engage with a marketing vehicle (e.g., to open a marketing email) or to make a transaction within a certain set of departments over a certain period of time in future. These tasks require predicting probabilities ranging from 0 to 1. The data in this domain is skewed and the labels are imbalanced. Skewed data is a common problem in real-world domains and has been the subject of considerable study in machine learning (e.g., [3,5]), but has received only limited consideration in CBR (e.g., [20,21]).

This paper proposes and evaluates a set of case-based predictors able to retrieve sufficiently efficiently to handle case bases two orders of magnitude larger than previously tested and to deal with skewed data. It proposes three new methods for efficient large-scale retrieval by LSH when handling skewed data, hierarchical LSH, prototype-based case retrieval, and capping the number of cases within a hash bucket. It presents an CBR approach applying these methods, *Ensembles of Adaptations at ScalE* (EASE), building from our previous work using automatically generated ensembles of adaptations [11–13,15], and tests an implementation for a sampling of variant methods.

The rest of the paper is organized as follows. First, it reviews existing work on large scale case-based reasoning. Next, it introduces EASE. It then presents an evaluation of four different configurations of EASE, to identify the contributions of different design choices, as well as evaluation of a new configuration of our ensemble-based adaptation learning/application method, enabled by the new retrieval methods, exploiting much larger sets of automatically-generated adaptation rule ensembles than in our previous work. The paper closes with a summary of contributions and future directions.

2   Background: Retrieval Cost and Case-Base Growth

2.1   Speedup Through Maintenance

The CBR community has long been aware that case base growth can impair system efficiency, due to the utility problem as retrieval cost grows due to increased case base size (e.g., [28]). This has led to much research on case-base maintenance methods for controlling case base size, such as selective retention of cases (e.g., [24,27]) and competence-based case deletion/selection (e.g., [29,30,32]). Retention strategies have also been developed to control growth of automatically-generated case adaptation rule sets [16].

However, even state of the art competence-based techniques cannot ensure protection against knowledge loss from deleted cases or rules. As compression increases competence loss can become severe (e.g., [30]). In addition, sophisticated competence-preserving deletion methods are computationally expensive— overwhelmingly so for data at scale—and must be incurred each time the case base is compressed [9]—which may occur routinely in the life cycle of a CBR system. These issues with compression methods motivate replacing compression by retrieval efficient enough to handle complete case bases at scale.

2.2   Speedup by Big Data Methods

Recent work on applying big data methods to CBR provides a first step towards large-scale retrieval without knowledge loss, but has limitations. Some existing methods enable rapid retrieval of exact matches, enabling efficiency and accuracy to be achieved simultaneously when similarity-based matching can be sacrificed. For example, Dumoulin [2] applied a MapReduce based retrieval method to perform efficient exact match retrieval on a case base of several million cases.

However, CBR normally requires searching for nearest neighbors of a case, for partially-matching neighbors. In these scenarios, locality-sensitive hashing (LSH) is a natural candidate for practical approximate nearest neighbor search.

Locality Sensitive Hashing: Locality Sensitive Hashing (LSH) [10] is an efficient method for mapping data points into "buckets." With appropriate parameter settings LSH is likely to place similar points in the same bucket. LSH is often used to speed up nearest neighbor search by narrowing down the search space for a given query to a subset of cases—those in the bucket associated with that query—rather than the whole case base. LSH is an approximation method; it does not guarantee that all nearest neighbors of a case will be grouped into the same bucket nor does it guarantee that all cases in the same bucket will be similar to each other. However, LSH has been shown sufficiently accurate to be an effective practical approach for finding nearest neighbors of a case [6], and the trade-off between accuracy and efficiency can be tuned as needed (e.g. [17]). Various schemes have been developed to improve its core method [6,7,17].

Integrating LSH with CBR: We began to explore LSH for similarity-based retrieval in our work on BEAR [11], which applied LSH using p-stable hashing [6] for retrieval for case-based numerical prediction (regression) tasks. BEAR was tested on case bases with up to two million cases. We recently introduced EACH [12], a locality sensitive hashing scheme for domains with both categorical and numeric input features/target values, and used it as the basis of fast large-scale retrieval in EACX, a scalable case-based classifier. This work showed that applying ensembles of adaptations to adjust the approximate nearest neighbor solutions can help compensate for the lower retrieval quality of LSH retrieval compared to full nearest neighbor retrieval [11,12].

3   Ensembles of Adaptations at Scale (EASE)

3.1   Foundations of EASE

The EASE method builds on succession of knowledge-light approaches for improving CBR performance by automatically generating adaptation rules from the case base and applying ensembles of those solutions for problem-solving and classification [11–13,15]. Experimental results support that these methods significantly increase accuracy over baselines. Here we summarize the two most relevant variants for the prediction tasks of this paper: EAR (Ensembles of Adaptations for Regression) [15], which developed the basic approach, and BEAR (Big Data Ensembles of Adaptations for Regression) [11], which scaled up the approach. However, the scaleup methods from this paper could be applied to the classification variants as well.

EAR uses the *Case Difference Heuristic* (CDH) [8] approach to generate adaptations from pairs of cases in the case base. Each resulting rule has two parts, a description of differences in the input features of the two cases and a description of the differences between their solutions (here, values or labels). EAR generates adaptations by comparing pairs of cases, selected by one of three strategies:

1. Local cases - Local neighbors: Generate adaptations by comparing every pair of cases in the local neighborhood of the input query. Because this approach considers few cases, it is practical for lazy generation of adaptation rules on demand.
2. Global cases - Local neighbors: Generate adaptations by comparing every case in the case base with its few top nearest neighbors.
3. Global cases - Global cases: Generate adaptations by comparing every possible pair of cases in the case base.

EAR solves input problems by retrieving a relevant prior case or cases, according to a selection strategy, and applying ensembles of automatically-generated adaptations to generate sets of solutions to combine.

BEAR scales up EAR by using LSH for fast approximate nearest neighbor retrieval. For any retrieval task, the appropriate LSH method is dictated by the input features' data types in the underlying domain; BEAR used p-stable hashing. BEAR developed foundations for case-based predictors at scale, handling millions of cases. However, it did not address the scale and skewed data issues of our e-commerce domain.

3.2   EASE

EASE extends BEAR to handle arbitrarily large case bases, where the limitation is only the storage capacity of the underlying big data platform—*the expected look up time remains constant as the size scales up, even for skewed data*. To reduce computation costs, EASE dedupes cases with identical input features and uses collision handling methods to handle cases with non-identical but similar features.

Case/Adaptation Deduping: In our e-commerce domain, cases often have identical input features. For example, when predicting customer propensity to engage with marketing emails, based on cases for past customer actions, it is likely that many customers never opened or clicked a marketing email, yielding identical features (here, zero opened or clicked marketing emails over any of a range of time periods). EASE handles such cases through a deduping process, separate from the skewed data process that applies to distinct cases/adaptations whose similar input features result in their being hashed to the same hash bucket. Deduping cases with identical input features serves two purposes. First, deduping improves efficiency. Cases with identical input features in the training data have the same performance effect on LSH as skewed data, because excessive numbers of cases in the same hash bucket make nearest neighbor retrieval inefficient within the hash bucket. Second, duplicate cases can degrade the accuracy of prediction if there is high variation in their labels. For example, if there are millions of such cases with numeric target values with very high variance, randomly selecting a few of these cases as the nearest neighbors of the input query will result in high variance for predictions. In addition, if all nearest neighbors of an input query have identical input features, then EASE's automatic adaptation generation would generate the same difference vector for comparing the input query with its nearest neighbors, which in turn would reduce diversity in the adaptation rules to be applied and decrease the benefit of ensemble adaptation.

Deduping in EASE is done at both training and solution building stages and is applied to both cases and adaptation rules. At training, cases/adaptations with identical features are grouped and form a prototype case whose solution is a function of all participating cases' solutions (e.g. the mean or median). Techniques such as outlier removal could be used to generate a better estimate of the prototype case's solution in presence of noise.

Deduping during solution-building is done differently depending on whether EASE is run in batch mode or to process streaming problems. In batch mode all input queries are known to the system in advance. In the streaming mode, input queries are introduced to the system successively and not known to the system in advance. At the solution building stage, in the batch mode, only one version of cases with identical features is retained. The calculated solution is then replicated for all cases with identical input features. In the streaming mode, the solutions for previously solved problems are stored and each new incoming problem is looked up in the pool of previously solved problems.

Collision Handling: The main novelty of EASE's approach is its collision handling module. The collision handling module controls the number of cases per hashing bucket with the aim of keeping the number of cases per bucket within a desired range to ensure efficient case/rule retrieval. We have identified two families of methods for collision handling for EASE, one lossy and one lossless. To the best of our knowledge, neither has been proposed previously.

Lossy Collision Handler: The lossy handler deletes cases in a bucket to keep the number of cases below a threshold. This approach may seem incompatible with EASE's claim of avoiding the information loss associated with case-based compression. However, case deletion in EASE is mainly targeting skewedness in the data, with the premise that given many cases with similar input features, keeping all those cases does not improve prediction accuracy. We propose two types of lossy collision handlers, competence-based and sampling-based:

- Competence-based Collision Handler: Uses competence-based deletion methods to control the number of cases per bucket. For example, a footprint deletion policy [29], or—more relevant to the ensemble and adaptation-based nature of EASE—adaptation-guided maintenance [16] could be applied.
- Sampling-based Collision Handler: Uses sampling methods to control the number of cases per bucket. The most naive such method is random sampling. However, more advanced sampling techniques such as clustering or density-sensitive sampling [25] could also be used. Random sampling has the advantage of low time complexity compared to advanced sampling techniques or competence-based alternatives. We note that an overly expensive collision handling step could easily become a new bottleneck, nullifying speed gains from EASE.

Lossless Collision Handler: Another approach to deal with a high collision rate is to keep all cases, but to further split the cases into new buckets to guarantee the limit on the maximum bucket size. LSH controls the number of cases in each bucket thorough the *sensitivity* of the chosen hashing functions. Increasing the sensitivity increases the total number of buckets while decreasing the average number of cases per bucket; decreasing the sensitivity reduces the number of buckets and increases the average number of cases per bucket. For large case bases with skewed data distributions, two conflicting factors pose a problem for LSH. Increasing sensitivity results in a large number of buckets with few cases per bucket, potentially making it unlikely there will be enough candidate cases/rules for ensemble-based solution building by EASE. On the other hand, decreasing sensitivity results in a manageable number of buckets, but a few of these buckets will still contain a large number of cases. For cases hashed to those buckets the retrieval process may have excessive computational cost. We address this with a method we call *Hierarchical LSH*.

Hierarchical LSH: The main idea of *Hierarchical LSH* is to use a moderate sensitivity to hash cases initially, and then to apply additional rounds of hashing with higher sensitivity to buckets with high collision level (i.e. buckets with large number of cases). This results in a density sensitive LSH that tunes the sensitivity for different subspaces according to their case distribution densities. We note that adding more levels of hashing can potentially increase the look up time, but practically speaking the time complexity should be comparable with one level LSH. If there are i cases in a skewed hash bucket and if r, is the number of cases per bucket considered manageable, then the number of required hash levels will be $O(\log_r i)$.

These collision handling methods apply to both batch and streaming scenarios. In streaming scenarios, reservoir sampling can be used for random sampling. Both footprint and adaptation-guided collision handling apply directly to streaming settings. Because hierarchical LSH keeps all cases in the case base, it requires no special treatment for streaming scenarios. However, because of cost of competence-based maintenance, random sampling and hierarchical LSH are the most promising collision-handling methods for very large case bases. The following experiments test EASE with random sampling.

3.3 Adaptation Generation and Building the Solution

EASE uses two adaptation generation alternatives: Local cases - Local neighbors (henceforth local-local), and Global cases - Local neighbors (henceforth global-local). Because the extreme large size of the case base, Global cases - Global cases would impose overwhelming computational costs. In terms of space complexity, Local cases - Local neighbors requires constant storage, and Global cases - Local neighbors requires storage of the order of the case base size.

Algorithm 1 summarizes EASE's solution building process. First, the input query is hashed, using the chosen hashing method, and assigned to a case bucket. EASE then does nearest neighbor search among the cases in the same bucket as

---

Algorithm 1. EASE's basic algorithm

Input:
Q: query
n: number of source cases to adapt to solve query
r: number of adaptation rules to apply per source case
CB: case base
sample: whether or not to sample the training data
mode: rule generation mode (local-local or global-local)

Output: Estimated solution value for Q

    //Begin Preprocessing ....
    if *sample* then
       $CB \leftarrow$ StratifiedSampler(CB)
    end if
    $HashedCaseBase \leftarrow$ LSH(CB)
    if *mode* == global-local then
       $rules \leftarrow$ RuleGenerator($HashedCaseBase$)
       $HashedRules \leftarrow$ LSH($rules$)
    end if
    //End Preprocessing ....
    if *mode* == local-local then
       $rules \leftarrow$ RuleGenerator($HashedCaseBase$, Q)
       $HashedRules \leftarrow$ LSH($rules$)
    end if
    $CasesToAdapt \leftarrow$ ApproximateNeighborhoodSelector(Q,n,$HashedCaseBase$)
    for c in $CasesToAdapt$ do
       $RulesToApply \leftarrow$ ApproximateNeighborhoodSelector($HashedRules$,c,Q)
       $SolutionEstimate(c) \leftarrow$ MajorityRuleVote($RulesToApply$, c, r)
    end for
    return MajorityVote($\cup_{c \in CasesToAdapt} SolutionEstimate(c)$)

---

the input query. By comparing the features of the input query and its nearest neighbors (here the source cases), EASE generates a set of difference descriptors. These difference descriptors are hashed and assigned to the corresponding adaptation buckets. Nearest neighbor search is done within each adaptation bucket and the top K nearest adaptation rules (for a pre-set K) are retrieved for each difference descriptor. For each source case, the new values proposed by the adaptations are aggregated and used to adjust the source case values. The adjusted values for each source case are combined to form the final solution.

3.4   EASE Architecture

Figure 1 presents the EASE architecture, for the configuration in which adaptations are generated by comparing each case with its top nearest neighbors (global-local). The architecture for other variations of EASE is very similar, with slightly simpler flow.

As a preprocessing step, cases in the case base are hashed into different buckets. The input query is hashed using the same mechanism to identify the relevant bucket for the query. The "approximate nearest neighbor retriever" selects its approximate nearest neighbors, whose solutions are adjusted and used to build the final solution. The collision handler module ensures that the number of cases within each hash bucket does not exceed a pre-set threshold, to guarantee acceptable run time. Adaptations are generated by comparing cases in the same hash bucket and form the rule base.

As described in detail in Jalali and Leake [13,15], the EAR/EAC approach automatically generates adaptation rules from cases, indexed analogously to cases; this enables applying the same retrieval process to cases and rules. The rule base is partitioned into different buckets using LSH, and as for the hashed case base, the collision handler ensures that the number of adaptations per bucket does not exceed a certain limit. To generate adaptation rules, the input query and source cases retrieved by the "approximate nearest neighbor retriever" query are compared and their feature differences are generated and hashed. To generate a solution for an input query, the solution of each source case is adjusted by applying an ensemble of adaptations addressing problems with differences similar to those between the input query and that source case. The final solution is built by combining the adjusted values of the retrieved source cases.

4   Evaluation

Our evaluations test the accuracy and efficiency of different variants of EASE and compare them to two classic machine learning approaches for industrial big data, Logistic Regression and Random Forest. Specifically, the evaluations address the following questions:

1. Comparative accuracy: How does the accuracy of different variants of EASE compare to each other and baselines?
2. Effect of preprocessing sampling on performance: How sensitive is the accuracy of EASE to using the whole training data without any preprocessing compared to preprocessing the data with stratified sampling?
3. Comparative execution time: How does the execution time of EASE compare to baseline methods?

4.1   Experimental Design

We tested EASE for two data sets from real-world problems. The first is the Kaggle Real Time Bidding data set[1], which is publicly available and contains one million cases. Kaggle data sets are posted as practical challenges for predictive modeling and analytics competitions. The second is data for building propensity models for Walmart.com, an e-commerce platform with hundreds of millions of users. Because this data contains several hundred million cases, it far exceeds

---

[1] https://www.kaggle.com/zurfer/rtb/data.

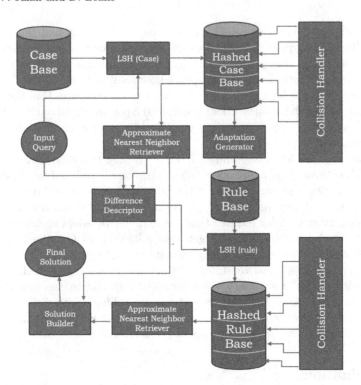

Fig. 1. EASE architecture

the scope of previous CBR applications. We respect corporate practice by not providing precise proprietary details such as the exact size or features. However, because we report the relative performance of the tested methods compared to baselines applied to the same data, comparative performance can be assessed, and these relative results can be compared to the fully replicable results on the Real Time Bidding data set.

Evaluation Tasks: The first task is to predict whether a user will open a marketing email within seven days from receiving it. We will refer to this task as engagement propensity. The input features to predict engagement propensity are mainly related to users' previous interactions with marketing email, such as how many emails they have historically received, opened or clicked. Each user case includes tens of such features. The second task is to predict whether a user will make a purchase within the health and beauty departments in the next 30 days. We refer to this task as purchase propensity. The input features to predict purchase propensity are mainly related to user past purchases and browsing behavior. Each user case includes hundreds of such features. The two tasks are specifically selected to study EASE's performance under different ratios of label values where the class imbalance issue is more severe for propensity prediction. The third task is to predict whether a user will click on an ad (e.g. banner on a webpage). We refer to this task as click prediction. There are 88 input features in the click prediction domain. The data is anonymized by Kaggle; PCA was applied to the original features and 0.99 of the linear explanatory power was retained. The original features included browser, operating system or time of the day the user is online, etc. There are 1908 cases with label 1 and the rest of the cases in this domain have 0 as their labels.

Evaluation Methodology: For engagement and purchase propensity models we pick training labels from one week and one month of user activities respectively and evaluate the models on the activities of the users over the following week and month. For click prediction we randomly split the data to 70% training and 30% test. Because the tests deal with class imbalance, we use the area under the Precision-Recall (PR) curve to evaluate different methods rather than accuracy, AUC or other metrics. The PR curve is especially informative if propensity predictions are used to pick customers to receive a marketing campaign where the objective is to maximize the number of customers that convert (open an email or make a purchase in a specific set of departments). In this case the PR curve can give us the expected number of customers that convert at different recall levels which can be translated to segment sizes (i.e. number of recipients of the marketing campaign).

Implementation: We implemented all EASE variations in Apache Spark and used BucketedRandomProjectionLSH class from Apache Spark MLlib [22] for LSH. We used 0.25 as the sensitivity of the LSH across all variations of EASE. This was selected experimentally based on the bucket size distributions it yields for the e-commerce data. We set the number of hash tables in BucketedRandomProjectionLSH to six; i.e., every case/rule is hashed using six hash functions. These two parameters (i.e. sensitivity and number of hash tables) could be treated as hyper parameters, but in order to narrow down the search space (for hyper parameter tuning) we picked their values experimentally. Spark MLlib provides built-in functionality for grid search, which we used for hyper parameter tuning. It also contains classic predictors such as Logistic Regression (LR) and Random Forest (RF) which we have used in our evaluations. The hyper parameters we tuned for LR are the maximum number of iterations and the regularization parameter; for RF they are the number of the tress and their maximum depth. In our evaluations we used entropy as the underlying impurity measure in RF. The area under the PR curve is calculated using the BinaryClassificationMetrics class from Spark MLlib. We used random sampling within buckets as the underlying collision handling method in our implementation of EASE. We implemented and tested four variants of EASE:

1. EASE-Strat-Local: Uses LSH for approximate nearest neighbor search for case and rule retrieval. It uses the stratified version of the case base as the training set and generates adaptations from the local neighborhood of the input query only. The hyper parameters of EASE-Strat-Local are: number of approximate nearest neighbors to use, number of adaptations to apply, and maximum number of cases per bucket.

2. EASE-Full-Local: Differs from EASE-Strat-Local in using the whole training set rather than the stratified version of the training data.
3. EASE-Strat-Global: Differs from EASE-Strat-Local in generating adaptations by comparing each case with its approximate nearest neighbors, rather than from the local neighborhood of the input query. In addition to the hyper parameters listed for EASE-Strat-Local, EASE-Strat-Global requires tuning the number of approximate nearest neighbors of cases to be used in adaptation learning.
4. EASE-Full-Global: Differs from EASE-Strat-Global in using the whole training set rather than the stratified version of the training data.

In addition to these variants, we used an extreme approximate predictor as the baseline. This baseline uses LSH to hash cases in the training set and creates prototype cases by averaging the input features of all cases in the same hash bucket and averaging of their labels. The only hyper parameter for this baseline is the number of nearest prototypes to use building the solution.

4.2   Experimental Results

Questions 1 and 2: Comparative Accuracy and Effect of Preprocessing: We conducted experiments to evaluate the accuracy (in terms of area under PR curve) of different variations of EASE, LR, and RF compared to the baseline method. Table 1 shows the gain in area of these methods over the baseline.

Table 1. Gain in area under PR curve of EASE-Strat-Local, EASE-Full-Local, EASE-Strat-Global, EASE-Full-Global, LR and RF over the baseline for engagement and purchase propensity prediction tasks

Task name	EASE Strat-Local	EASE Full-Local	EASE Strat-Global	EASE Full-Global	LR	RF
Engagement propensity	8.02%	7.42%	5.92%	5.17%	10.30%	**12.02%**
Purchase propensity	19.13%	29.01%	49.94%	**65.41%**	20.58%	11.54%
Click prediction	20.68%	39.72%	118.39%	**145.86%**	83.32%	72.30%

The experiments show the superior performance of EASE compared to other methods under class imbalance settings. For purchase propensity, EASE-Full-Global shows 65% improvement over the baseline method while LR and RF only show 21% and 11% improvement over baseline respectively. For click prediction EASE-Full-Global shows 146% improvement over the baseline while LR and RF show 83.32% and 72.30% improvement respectively. The absolute values of area under PR curve for EASE-Strat-Local, EASE-Full-Local, EASE-Strat-Global, EASE-Full-Global, LR and RF is 0.0027, 0.0031, 0.0049, 0.0055, 0.0041, and 0.0039 respectively. We hypothesize that the superior performance of EASE using global-local adaptation generation (i.e. EASE-Strat-Global and EASE-Full-Global) over EASE with local-local adaptation generation (i.e. EASE-Strat-Local and EASE-Full-Local) arises because, when there are very few instances with a certain label values in the case base (i.e. class imbalance), it becomes less likely to have enough of these instances in the local neighborhood of the input query and therefore, the generated adaptations will be more homogenous. However, with global-local adaptation generation there will be more diversity in the generated adaptations, providing more benefit from ensemble adaptation. We hypothesize that the superior performance of EASE over model-based machine learning methods such as LR and RF for class imbalance follows from its lazy nature, which enables considering the whole case base rather than abstracting a portion into the mathematical models.

When class labels are more evenly distributed (i.e. engagement propensity setting), the gap between EASE performance compared to classic machine learning models such as LR and RF is smaller and in fact LR and RF slightly outperform EASE but the difference is not drastic (compared to EASE-Strat-Local, 2% for LR and 4% for RF). Among EASE variants, using the local-local method for generating adaptations yields relatively better performance, as shown in Table 1. We hypothesize that sufficient learning opportunities in vicinity of the input query and lack of consideration of context in the global-local method (cf. [14]) are the main reasons for local-local method's superior performance in this case.

The experiments also show that for engagement propensity prediction, there is only a modest difference between using the stratified version versus using the full the training data, with the stratified version showing relatively better performance. In the purchase propensity task, the strong class imbalance setting, the non-stratified versions of EASE show better performance and this gap is especially marked when the global-local method is used for generating the adaptations. Overall, we conclude that pre-processing the case base with stratified sampling is not necessary for EASE. This can save time and computational resources, and is made feasible in practice by the scalability of EASE.

Question 3: Execution Time: The execution time of different methods depends on the underlying technology used to implement them. We implemented EASE in spark to be able to code everything ranging from LSH, to grid search, to evaluation metrics in the same environment. Benchmarking the performance of EASE implemented in Spark versus in other technologies such as NoSQL databases is out of the scope of this work; we only report results based on Spark execution times. We ran Spark on an Apache Mesos cluster with hundreds of workers, several thousands of CPU units and Terabytes of memory. Preprocessing the case base of several hundreds of millions of cases and conducting stratified sampling takes tens of minutes processing time and building a single model (characterizing a single set of departments, e.g., health and beauty) usually takes a few minutes. Scaling these up to a scenario in which more models are required for different super department sets or engagement with different marketing vehicles, the execution time for the model-based approach can go beyond several hours. Using EASE makes it possible to avoid the preprocessing and model building steps and to save this time and computational resources.

Building the solution for an input query usually takes several to several hundreds of milliseconds for model based approaches such as LR or RF depending on the number of features and the complexity of the model. This value increases to a few seconds for EASE's implementation in Spark. However, we believe by using NoSQL databases the run time of EASE can be reduced to a few lookups and a few mathematical operations such as calculating the distance between cases, picking the top nearest neighbors and taking the average of a few values. Considering that a lookup only costs a few milliseconds in NoSQL databases, we believe that the whole solution building process can be kept below a second using the appropriate storage solution. We expect the result to be that EASE will provide much shorter preprocessing time and comparable solution building time to model-building methods.

5   Conclusion and Future Work

This paper introduced Ensemble of Adaptations at ScaleE (EASE), a case-base predictor for industrial big data settings that can handle skewed data. A central goal of this project is to scale up CBR to handle case base sizes far beyond those of previous studies and make CBR methods competetive for large-scale big data prediction tasks.

EASE uses locality sensitive hashing to perform approximate nearest neighbor search. LSH nearest neighbor sacrifices some accuracy for the sake of efficiency. However, the ensemble-based nature of EASE is able to compensate for its accuracy loss. EASE uses deduping and collision handling to maintain efficiency for retrieval from arbitrarily large case bases. We evaluated EASE both for a public real-time bidding domain with one million cases used for a Kaggle challenge, and for building propensity models for an e-commerce platform with hundreds of millions of customers. Experimental results showed superior performance for EASE compared to sample classic machine learning models under class imbalance settings and showed comparable performances under more even label value distribution scenarios. However, compared to other model-based predictors EASE saves time and computational resources by skipping the model building and training data preprocessing step.

The future directions for this work include more extensive performance benchmarking under different levels of class imbalance and for implementations using different platforms such as Apache Spark, NoSQL or an index-based solution such as Elasticsearch. Another direction is adding contextual considerations to adaptation retrieval when adaptations are generated from the entire case base [14]. Yet another is to study the efficiency and performance effects of our alternative proposed collision handling mechanisms such as hierarchical LSH.

References

1. Auer, S., Bizer, C., Kobilarov, G., Lehmann, J., Cyganiak, R., Ives, Z.: DBpedia: a nucleus for a web of open data. In: Aberer, K. (ed.) ASWC/ISWC -2007. LNCS, vol. 4825, pp. 722–735. Springer, Heidelberg (2007). https://doi.org/10.1007/978-3-540-76298-0_52

2. Beaver, I., Dumoulin, J.: Applying mapreduce to learning user preferences in near real-time. In: Delany, S.J., Ontañón, S. (eds.) ICCBR 2013. LNCS, vol. 7969, pp. 15–28. Springer, Heidelberg (2013). https://doi.org/10.1007/978-3-642-39056-2_2

3. Bi, Z., Faloutsos, C., Korn, F.: The "DGX" distribution for mining massive, skewed data. In: Proceedings of the Seventh ACM SIGKDD International Conference on Knowledge Discovery and Data Mining, KDD 2001, pp. 17–26. ACM, New York (2001)

4. Bottou, L.: Large-scale machine learning with stochastic gradient descent. In: Lechevallier, Y., Saporta, G. (eds.) Proceedings of COMPSTAT 2010, pp. 177–186. Physica-Verlag HD, Heidelberg (2010). https://doi.org/10.1007/978-3-7908-2604-3_16

5. Chawla, N.V.: Data mining for imbalanced datasets: an overview. In: Maimon, O., Rokach, L. (eds.) Data Mining and Knowledge Discovery Handbook, pp. 875–886. Springer, Boston (2010). https://doi.org/10.1007/0-387-25465-X_40

6. Datar, M., Immorlica, N., Indyk, P., Mirrokni, V.S.: Locality-sensitive hashing scheme based on p-stable distributions. In: Proceedings of the Twentieth Annual Symposium on Computational Geometry, SCG 2004, pp. 253–262. ACM, New York (2004)

7. Gionis, A., Indyk, P., Motwani, R.: Similarity search in high dimensions via hashing. VLDB **99**, 518–529 (1999)

8. Hanney, K., Keane, M.T.: Learning adaptation rules from a case-base. In: Smith, I., Faltings, B. (eds.) EWCBR 1996. LNCS, vol. 1168, pp. 179–192. Springer, Heidelberg (1996). https://doi.org/10.1007/BFb0020610

9. Houeland, T.G., Aamodt, A.: The utility problem for lazy learners - towards a non-eager approach. In: Bichindaritz, I., Montani, S. (eds.) ICCBR 2010. LNCS (LNAI), vol. 6176, pp. 141–155. Springer, Heidelberg (2010). https://doi.org/10.1007/978-3-642-14274-1_12

10. Indyk, P., Motwani, R.: Approximate nearest neighbors: towards removing the curse of dimensionality. In: Proceedings of the Thirtieth Annual ACM Symposium on Theory of Computing, STOC 1998, pp. 604–613. ACM, New York (1998)

11. Jalali, V., Leake, D.: CBR meets big data: a case study of large-scale adaptation rule generation. In: Hüllermeier, E., Minor, M. (eds.) ICCBR 2015. LNCS, vol. 9343, pp. 181–196. Springer, Cham (2015). https://doi.org/10.1007/978-3-319-24586-7_13

12. Jalali, V., Leake, D.: Scaling up ensemble of adaptations for classification by approximate nearest neighbor retrieval. In: Aha, D.W., Lieber, J. (eds.) ICCBR 2017. LNCS (LNAI), vol. 10339, pp. 154–169. Springer, Cham (2017). https://doi.org/10.1007/978-3-319-61030-6_11

13. Jalali, V., Leake, D., Forouzandehmehr, N.: Ensemble of adaptations for classification: learning adaptation rules for categorical features. In: Goel, A., Díaz-Agudo, M.B., Roth-Berghofer, T. (eds.) ICCBR 2016. LNCS, vol. 9969, pp. 186–202. Springer, Cham (2016). https://doi.org/10.1007/978-3-319-47096-2_13

14. Jalali, V., Leake, D.: A context-aware approach to selecting adaptations for case-based reasoning. In: Brézillon, P., Blackburn, P., Dapoigny, R. (eds.) CONTEXT 2013. LNCS, vol. 8175, pp. 101–114. Springer, Heidelberg (2013). https://doi.org/10.1007/978-3-642-40972-1_8

15. Jalali, V., Leake, D.: Extending case adaptation with automatically-generated ensembles of adaptation rules. In: Delany, S.J., Ontañón, S. (eds.) ICCBR 2013. LNCS, vol. 7969, pp. 188–202. Springer, Heidelberg (2013). https://doi.org/10.1007/978-3-642-39056-2_14

16. Jalali, V., Leake, D.: Adaptation-guided case base maintenance. In: Proceedings of the Twenty-Eighth Conference on Artificial Intelligence, pp. 1875–1881. AAAI Press (2014)

17. Kulis, B., Grauman, K.: Kernelized locality-sensitive hashing for scalable image search. In: IEEE International Conference on Computer Vision ICCV (2009)

18. Leake, D., Smyth, B., Wilson, D., Yang, Q. (eds.): Maintaining Case-Based Reasoning Systems. Blackwell, Malden (2001). Special issue of Computational Intelligence 17(2) (2001)

19. Leetaru, K., Schrodt, P.A.: GDELT: global data on events, location, and tone. ISA Annual Convention (2013)

20. Lin, Y.B., Ping, X.O., Ho, T.W., Lai, F.: Processing and analysis of imbalanced liver cancer patient data by case-based reasoning. In: The 7th 2014 Biomedical Engineering International Conference, pp. 1–5, November 2014

21. Malof, J., Mazurowski, M., Tourassi, G.: The effect of class imbalance on case selection for case-based classifiers: an empirical study in the context of medical decision support. Neural Netw. 25, 141–145 (2012)

22. Meng, X., et al.: MLlib: machine learning in apache spark. CoRR abs/1505.06807 (2015)

23. Mühleisen, H., Bizer, C.: Web data commons - extracting structured data from two large web corpora. In: Bizer, C., Heath, T., Berners-Lee, T., Hausenblas, M. (eds.) WWW 2012 Workshop on Linked Data on the Web, Lyon, France, 16 April 2012. CEUR Workshop Proceedings, vol. 937. CEUR-WS.org (2012)

24. Ontañón, S., Plaza, E.: Collaborative case retention strategies for CBR agents. In: Ashley, K.D., Bridge, D.G. (eds.) ICCBR 2003. LNCS, vol. 2689, pp. 392–406. Springer, Heidelberg (2003). https://doi.org/10.1007/3-540-45006-8_31

25. Palmer, C.R., Faloutsos, C.: Density biased sampling: an improved method for data mining and clustering. SIGMOD Rec. 29(2), 82–92 (2000)

26. Rojas, J.A.R., Kery, M.B., Rosenthal, S., Dey, A.: Sampling techniques to improve big data exploration. In: 2017 IEEE 7th Symposium on Large Data Analysis and Visualization (LDAV), pp. 26–35, October 2017

27. Salamó, M., López-Sánchez, M.: Adaptive case-based reasoning using retention and forgetting strategies. Knowl. Based Syst. 24(2), 230–247 (2011)

28. Smyth, B., Cunningham, P.: The utility problem analysed. In: Smith, I., Faltings, B. (eds.) EWCBR 1996. LNCS, vol. 1168, pp. 392–399. Springer, Heidelberg (1996). https://doi.org/10.1007/BFb0020625

29. Smyth, B., Keane, M.: Remembering to forget: a competence-preserving case deletion policy for case-based reasoning systems. In: Proceedings of the Thirteenth International Joint Conference on Artificial Intelligence, pp. 377–382. Morgan Kaufmann, San Mateo (1995)

30. Smyt, B., McKenna, E.: Footprint-based retrieval. In: Althoff, K.-D., Bergmann, R., Branting, L.K. (eds.) ICCBR 1999. LNCS, vol. 1650, pp. 343–357. Springer, Heidelberg (1999). https://doi.org/10.1007/3-540-48508-2_25

31. Upadhyaya, S.R.: Parallel approaches to machine learning a comprehensive survey. J. Parallel Distrib. Comput. **73**(3), 284–292 (2013). Models and Algorithms for High-Performance Distributed Data Mining

32. Zhu, J., Yang, Q.: Remembering to add: competence-preserving case-addition policies for case base maintenance. In: Proceedings of the Fifteenth International Joint Conference on Artificial Intelligence, pp. 234–241. Morgan Kaufmann (1999)

Case Base Elicitation for a
Context-Aware Recommender System

Jose Luis Jorro-Aragoneses$^{(\boxtimes)}$, Guillermo Jimenez-Díaz$^{(\boxtimes)}$,
Juan Antonio Recio-García$^{(\boxtimes)}$, and Belén Díaz-Agudo$^{(\boxtimes)}$

Department of Software Engineering and Artificial Intelligence,
Universidad Complutense de Madrid, Madrid, Spain
{jljorro,gjimenez,jareciog,belend}@ucm.es

Abstract. Case-based reasoning can resolve new problems based on remembering and adapting the solution of similar problems. Before a CBR system can solve new problems it must be provided with an initial case base covering the problem space with a sufficient number of representative seed cases with solutions that are known to be correct. We use a CBR module to recommend leisure plans in Madrid based on user preferences and contextual information. This paper deals with the problem of how to build and evaluate an initial case base of leisure experiences in Madrid for the recommender system.

Keywords: Case-based reasoning · Cold start
Context-aware recommender system · Knowledge acquisition

1 Introduction

Case-based reasoning (CBR) addresses new problems by remembering and adapting solutions previously used to solve similar problems [18]. CBR is also a theory of skill and knowledge acquisition that overcomes some of the traditional bottlenecks of expert systems [30]. The main argument for using CBR in general is that it does not need an extensive and deep domain model and relies instead on experience-based, compiled knowledge, which humans are known to gather during and after problem solving [26]. Before a CBR system can solve new problems it must be provided with an initial case base covering the problem space with a *sufficient* number of representative *seed* cases with solutions that are known to be correct. Populating the initial case base is a hard, domain-dependent and time-demanding task. Although seed cases are typically provided by a domain expert, there are approaches of (semi)-automated acquisition [2,9,19,24,25,32]. In fact, case acquisition from raw data is one of the challenges of the CBR research [11].

Supported by the Spanish Committee of Economy and Competitiveness (TIN2014-55006-R, TIN2017-87330-R); the UCM (Group 921330) and the funding provided by Banco Santander, in cooperation with UCM, in the form of a predoctoral scholarship (CT17/17-CT17/18).

M. T. Cox et al. (Eds.): ICCBR 2018, LNAI 11156, pp. 170–185, 2018.
https://doi.org/10.1007/978-3-030-01081-2_12

The CBR system begins with this initial case base and then each experience of solving a new problem becomes the basis for a new case and enriches the experiential memory. These experiences are learnt for potential reuse in future similar problems, despite the utility problem [28]. Thus, CBR favors incremental learning from experience and acquisition of expertise rather than exhaustive extraction of domain knowledge [11].

This paper deals with the problem of how to build an initial case base of leisure experiences in Madrid for a contextual recommender system implemented as a CBR system. Contextual recommender systems have the capability to appreciate its environment and assess the situation in which the cases are to be recommended [1].

When a tourism recommender system is in cold start [15] the system could compose a plan as a sequence of activities – Point of Interests (POIs) or events– based on given composition rules. However, this kind of recommendation would require specific domain rules to capture dependencies and intrinsic congruence between the activities. Besides, it would be difficult to adjust the plan to the context restrictions. Another option to avoid the cold start situation is using a set of prototypical routes provided, for example, from a tourism expert, with the limitations described above. In this paper, we propose an approach taking advantage of the wisdom of the crowd [33] where the case base is created from a crowd of people. We use a pseudo-random method to generate the seed case base and then let the crowd vote to select and filter the best cases using an Elo test [10]. With this method we obtain a case base with diversity, congruence between the activities, and collective knowledge that is independent from a domain expert.

The rest of the paper is organized as follows. Section 2 describes the structure of the cases and an brief overview of the recommendation process. Next, Sect. 3, explains the process to generate a large set of candidate cases, and the use of the *Elo test* to obtain a ranking of the best cases. After generating and selecting the initial seed cases, in Sect. 4 we describe how this case base is evaluated using coverage measures. Section 5 details some related works about techniques to acquire knowledge in recommender systems. Finally, Sect. 6 concludes the paper.

2   The CBR Recommendation Process

The CBR module of the recommender system generates a personalized plan by retrieving and adapting the most similar plans according to the user context and preferences. In order to recommend suitable plans, the system case base stores the plan details and the contextual information associated to its activities and points of interests (POIs). This contextual knowledge is useful to avoid unavoidable plans (i.e. outdoor activities when raining). In this paper, we will describe the case structure, and the retrieval stage of the CBR system. A complete description of the system is available in [14].

The cases in the case base are plans with the typical structure description-solution, $\mathcal{C} = <\mathcal{D}, \mathcal{S}>$. In the retrieval step the case description is compared with the query and the solution, that includes the details of the route and the sequence of activities, events and POIs in the plan, is reused. The case description is defined using two groups of attributes. The first group represents the activities, events and POIs contained in the plan (d_a). The second group of attributes represents the contextual restrictions (d_{ctx}) to perform the plan such as time, transportation availability, budget, etc. Table 1 shows an example of a case in our system. The list of attributes that defines the contextual restrictions listed in Table 2.

Table 1. The information contained in a case

	Attribute	Value
Description d_{ctx} context setup	Time	11:05–16:35
	Transport	Public transport
	First location	(−3.709, 40.411)
	Estimated cost	25 €
	Weather	Sunny
	Out/indoor	Outdoor
Description d_a Act. categories	Categories	Park, Restaurant, Italian Food, Museum, Art
Solution	Activities	Park "El campo de la cebada" (11:05–12:05) Restaurant "Saporte di Pizza" (12:15–13:30) Queen Sofia Museum (13:45–16:35)

These details of each plan are stored in the case solution ($\mathcal{S}$). Basically, the case solution is the list of activities contained in the plan. In addition, it contains the time when the user started the activity and when she finished it.

The retrieval process is a k-NN algorithm using a weighted average to combine the local similarities between attributes. It calculates the average of the similarity of all attributes defined in cases and the query. These similarity functions are divided in contextual similarity (sim_{ctx}) and activities similarity (sim_a).

$$similarity(\mathcal{C}, \mathcal{Q}) = \alpha \cdot sim_{ctx}(d_{ctx}^c, d_{ctx}^q) + (1 - \alpha) \cdot sim_a(d_a^c, d_a^q) \qquad (1)$$

The contextual similarity function sim_{ctx} is the average of the contextual attributes described in Table 2. Analogously, the similarity of activities, sim_a, compares the type of activities in the plan (museums, restaurants, cinemas, parks, ...).

3 Case Base Acquisition

This section describes our approach to generate synthetically a case base that captures certain wisdom of crowds knowledge [33] about the congruence and

Table 2. Attributes representing contextual information in the cases.

Start-time	It contains the time when the user started the leisure plan
Duration	It is the time spent by a user to complete all activities of the plan
Location	This attribute defines the location where the user started to visit the activities
Out/indoor	It defines the type of location of every activity in the plan. The location type values can be *indoor* or *outdoor*
Weather	It represents the weather requirements to perform the plan
Cost	It is an estimation of the cost to realize all the activities
Transport	It stores the transport used by the user when he/she visited the activities. This transport type can be: *walking*, *public transport* or *car*
Social	This attribute defines the social information associated with the plan, i.e., what are the social conditions when the user did the leisure plan. Its possible values are: *alone*, *couple*, *family*, *friends* and *business*

common sense in the sequence of activities in a plan. This refers to social non algorithmic knowledge associated to a touristic route, for example, leg fatigue, crowed streets in certain seasons like Christmas, delays in big groups of people, alternate between physical and quiet activities, the best lighting conditions for visiting a POI, and others. Firstly, a large number of cases are pseudo-randomly generated complying basic restrictions about distances, timetables, activities, etc. Next, real users rank those cases according to their congruency with the context and their global quality a as a plan. It is important to note that users do not take into account their personal preferences when voting.

To perform this ranking we have used the Elo rating system [10], a well known method for calculating the relative skill levels of players in zero-sum games such as chess.

Following subsections detail the process. Firstly, we generate a large set of cases synthetically. These cases are candidates for the initial case base. Then, the next step uses the *Elo test* to obtain a ranking of the best cases.

3.1   Case Base Generation

The first step consists on generating a large set of candidate plans from a dataset of activities. These activities were obtained from the Madrid's council Open Data portal[1] that contains a large dataset of leisure activities in Madrid. Concretely, we used around 1000 restaurants, more than 300 POIs (monuments, buildings, etc.) and nearly 1300 events.

From this dataset, cases are generated randomly but according to certain restrictions, timetables, types of activities and distances. Cases are generated

---

[1] https://datos.madrid.es.

according to a simulated user context. A plan cannot contain two consecutive restaurants, restaurants are scheduled at certain times, plans of the same context start at the same POI, the maximum distance of the complete plan is limited depending on the public transport in the area, or in the use of private car or walking distance as indicated in the context. We generated randomly 30 different contextual setups. For each contextual setup we define concrete values for the attributes presented in Sect. 2 and described in Table 2. For example, if the simulated context defines bad weather, the generated plan does not contain outdoor activities. Although case generation was driven by the context, only some of its attributes were used to select the activities of the plan as it is not possible to model every possible restriction. This way, the generation stage returns a large set of cases, syntactically correct but, may be, semantically incorrect. We will use the Elo ranking, to filter these cases and select those ones that are good plans and congruent with the context. At the end of this step we generated 10 plans by contextual setup. In total, we generated 300 plans to evaluate as described next.

3.2   Case Base Selection

The main goal of this second step is to capture good plans according to the wisdom of crowd knowledge. To capture this knowledge we used a test based on the *Elo ranking*, that is simple and does not require technical skills, like other approaches such as Likert scales. This method allows determination of the best plans faster than other methods because scoring is very simple. Given a context, it just presents two options (plans) to the user and let her choose the best option for this situation.

In the Elo ranking, each player's performance in a game is modeled as a normally distributed random variable. The mean of that random variable reflects the player's skill and is called the player's Elo rating. If a player wins, her Elo rating goes up, otherwise it goes down. The use of the Elo rating system offers many advantages: it is a simple and fast, it has only a small number of parameters that need to be set, and it also provides comparable performance to more complex models. This way, it has been used for different purposes such as eliciting user preferences [13] or ranking posts in online forums [7]. For our concrete domain, the Elo ranking allows us to obtain cases that have a higher diversity than those generated by an expert. And these cases are not biased by the scorings of other users as they perform the Elo ranking independently contributing with their own opinion. The Elo system aggregates their scorings to obtain a global ranking that summarizes them.

A condition to apply the Elo ranking is that the scored items comply the zero-sum property, meaning that each item's gain or loss of utility is exactly balanced by the losses or gains of the utility of the other items. Therefore, we can apply the Elo ranking to score the quality of touristic plans if we assume that this ranking is also a zero-sum game, in our case, that two plans cannot have the same utility given a concrete context and user preferences. Therefore, for our CBR system a plan is always better than the others when being compared to the query.

We applied this method to select the best cases according to their congruence with the context and its quality as a leisure plan. To do that, we created a test where every user selects the best plan between two options for the same contextual setup. For every couple of plans being shown to the user, the corresponding context used to guide the generation of both plans is also described.

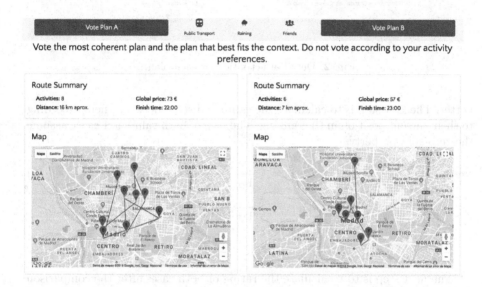

Fig. 1. Map and summary of contextual information for both plans

Figure 1 shows an example of voting using our implementation of the Elo test. First of all, the test shows 2 buttons to vote the corresponding plan; and in the middle of both it shows the contextual information to take into account when choosing the best plan (transport availability, weather conditions, traveling alone, with family, friends, ...). Next, the test shows a summary of each plan: number of activities, total cost, total distance and finishing time. Below, the system shows the route for each plan in a map. Finally, the system shows the list of activities for each plan. Figure 2 shows an example of these lists. Both are ordered according to the starting time of every activity. For each one, relevant attributes are shown to the user: title, short summary and a set of tags that describes the price, location (outdoor/indoor) and the category of the activity.

When a user reads and compares both plans, she selects one of them. Then, the application shows another couple of plans and this process is repeated in loop. Every time the user votes, our test calculates the Elo rating for both plans using the method explained next.

The Elo method calculates a rating for each case (R_x). This rating is updated when 2 cases (A and B) are compared, i.e., the user has selected which case is

Fig. 2. Detail of activities for each plan.

better. The first step is to calculate the estimated score between them according to their current position in the ranking. The sum of both values is 1 as we assume the zero-sum property.

$$E_A = \frac{1}{1 + 10^{(R_A - R_B)/400}} \qquad (2)$$

$$E_B = \frac{1}{1 + 10^{(R_B - R_A)/400}}$$

$$where$$

$$E_A + E_B = 1$$

The next step is to recalculate the rating of both cases after the comparison (R'_x). Elo ranking uses a constant K to adjust the lineal proportion between the estimated points and the final score. For chess players, this value changes depending on the number of matches of the player. In our experiment, we choose a value of 40 as an estimation of the average votes (both positive and negative) that every case could get. The final rating depends on the result of the vote (S_x): 1 to the winner plan or 0 to the looser plan.

$$R'_A = R_A + K * (S_A - E_A) \qquad (3)$$

$$R'_B = R_B + K * (S_B - E_B)$$

$$where$$

$$S_x = \begin{cases} 1 \; if \; x = \text{``}win\text{''} \\ 0 \; if \; x = \text{``}lost\text{''} \end{cases}$$

In the following section, we explain the results obtained by our experiment where we collected 1705 votes from 71 users.

4   Case Base Evaluation

After running the experiment with users we obtained an ordered list of cases according to their Elo rating. The next step consists on filtering this list using the Elo scores that represent their congruency with the context and their quality as a plan. The main goal of this step is to evaluate the case according to several metrics to conclude if its global quality is similar to a case base that was not synthetically generated. And therefore, if the approach presented in this paper is valid to obtain the seed cases for a CBR system.

The Elo test had 1705 votes from 71 users. Firstly, we filtered invalid votes, for example, those votes that the answer time of the user is less than 5 s. After applying this filter, we obtained 814 valid votes. In addition, some candidate cases had not enough votes to be ranked properly. Therefore, we only considered cases with more than 4 votes (positive or negative). At the end of this pre-filtering, there were 222 remaining cases in our case base. This is the initial case base of our analysis, denoted as CB^0.

We will analyze the case base using different metrics. First, we will filter cases according to Elo ranking. Next, we will analyze the similarity, and coverage of the case base taking into account the contextual setups. And finally, we present a global analysis of the case base as a whole.

All analysis explained in this and next sections, with the dataset and their results, have been published in a public GitHub repository[2].

4.1 Elo-Based Similarity

The first analysis in our evaluation was to calculate the Elo ranking based on the user votes. The result of this ranking is shown in Fig. 3. As we can observe, around the 50% of the evaluated cases has a positive Elo score. We can consider these cases as good candidates to be in our initial case base. The leisure plans contained in these cases are supposed to be good plans and congruent with their context according to the opinion of the users.

The resulting case base once we have removed the cases with negative Elo score has 116 cases. We will refer to this case base as CB^2.

4.2 Similarity Analysis

The following analysis tries to evaluate the quality of the retrieval of cases. To do so, we study the performance of the similarity function described in Eq. 1 and detailed in [14].

Figure 4 shows the distribution of the pairwise similarity of every case in CB^1. This figure presents the results obtained for different values of the α parameter in Eq. 1. In this figure we can observe that similarity follows a normal distribution and most of the cases have a low similarity ($\mu \approx 0.2, \sigma \approx 0.1$). It is an indicator of the sparseness and diversity of the case base. As our goal is to obtain the seed cases for our CBR system, these values can be considered as positive because seed cases should not be very similar in order to provide a higher coverage. This

---

[2] https://github.com/UCM-GAIA/Case-Base-elicitation-for-a-context-aware-recommender-system.

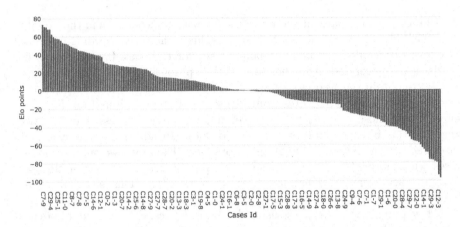

Fig. 3. Analysis of the Elo ranking of CB^0

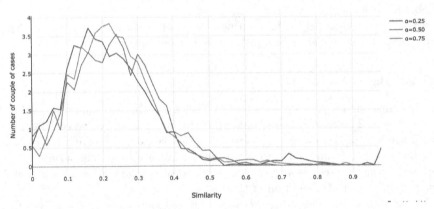

Fig. 4. Distribution of the pairwise similarity distances in CB^1

conclusion will be also corroborated by the following analysis that evaluates the coverage of the case base.

Regarding the impact of the α parameter, results do not show significant differences. This can be interpreted as a positive indicator about the quality of the similarity function in Eq. 1. Meaning that both components of the equation, the contextual similarity (sim_{ctx}) and the activities similarity (sim_a), compensate to each other. This way, there is not a predominant component when comparing cases: the context is as important as the plan itself.

We have also analyzed the pairwise similarities between cases according to the 30 different contextual setups that were used to generate them. Figure 5 shows a heatmap with the results. Every point represents the similarity of every possible couple of cases in the case base from white (no similarity) to dark blue (full similarity). Cases are organized according to the contextual setup, so we can observe similar groups of points in the form of small rectangles. The blue line in the diagonal of the figure corresponds to the comparison of every case with itself. And the (mostly) blue rectangles around the diagonal line represent the similarities of cases from the same contextual setup. As expected, cases sharing the same contextual setup have a high similarity.

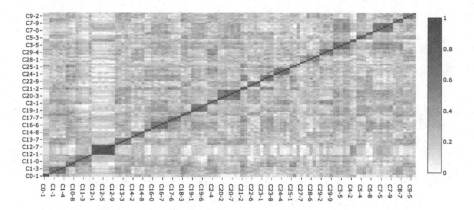

Fig. 5. Distribution of the pairwise similarity distances in CB^1 segmented by contextual setups, from white (no similarity) to dark blue (full similarity). (Color figure online)

Once we have analyzed the case base from the point of view of the similarity metric, we can extend this analysis by using the coverage metrics as explained next.

4.3 Coverage Analysis

The coverage metrics analyze the case base to find out their capability to solve new problems. These metrics have been extensively studied in the literature [17,27]. We have chosen the method described in Smyth et al. [29]. This metric is based on finding groups of cases and estimating their *density*, that averages the intra-group similarity. Having a high density it is more likely to find a proper case to be reused. In our case, it is straightforward to adapt this group-based metric to our case base, where cases are organized according to their contextual restrictions.

The *density* of a group is the average of the case densities of each group, where a group G represents a set of cases with the same contextual restrictions.

$$coverage(G) \quad = \quad \frac{1}{|G|} \sum_{c \in G} density(c, G) \tag{4}$$

$$where$$

$$density(c, G) \quad = \quad \frac{1}{|G| - 1} \sum_{c' \in G - \{c\}} similarity(c, c')$$

The blue line in Fig. 6 shows the coverage of each group defined in our case base CB^1 when using density to estimate coverage. As we can observe the coverage of some groups is really low. This result has two possible explanations: (1) there are not enough cases per group, or (2) we are not taking into account the adaptation stage of the CBR cycle.

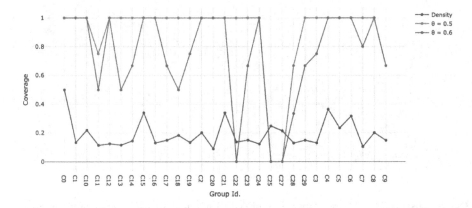

Fig. 6. Group coverage of the case base CB^1.

The probability that the same leisure plan could be repeated by another user is really low. For example, some plans contain temporal activities like a music concert or a football match. To reuse this plan, the system will change this activity because, most probably, this event is not available at the moment of the recommendation. Therefore, the adaptation stage is very important for our CBR system and needs to be incorporated into the coverage metric as explained next.

4.4   Enhanced Coverage Analysis

In our recommender system, the solution obtained by the CBR module needs to be adapted. Díaz et al. [8] describe the two main methods to transform a case solution: *transformational adaptation* and *constructive adaptation*. The first method consists of modifying the solution of the most similar case. On the other hand, the constructive adaptation creates a new solution by combining solutions from the most similar cases. Here, the key issue is the similarity of the cases with respect to the query. If cases are similar enough, the adaptation method would find a proper solution to the query. It is the basic assumption of CBR systems: similar problems have similar solutions.

Actually, coverage metrics in the literature also include the adaptation when evaluating the coverage. Therefore we redefine the coverage of a case base as the probability of being able to solve a new problem. And this probability can be estimated using the similarity of the most similar cases. Thus, we can assume that a new problem would be solved if there are cases with a minimum similarity threshold. It can be formulated as follows:

$$coverage'(G) \quad = \quad \frac{1}{|G|} \sum_{c \in G} resolvability(c, G) \qquad (5)$$

$$where$$

$$resolvability(c, G) \quad = \quad \begin{cases} 1 \; if \; highestSim(c, G) >= \theta \\ 0 \; if \; highestSim(c, G) < \theta \end{cases}$$

The $highestSim(c, G)$ function returns the similarity of the most similar case to c in G. As Fig. 6 shows, when including the adaptation in the coverage metric the performance of the case base increases significantly. Assuming that a solution can be found when the most similar case has a similarity over 0.6 the coverage improves up to 65% on average. Moreover, if we decrease this limit to 0.5 the coverage is complete for almost every context.

Although we have analyzed the case base segmented by contextual setups, we can also analyze it a as whole. Next, we will provide some insights about its features when leaving aside the contextual restrictions.

4.5   Global Analysis

We can also analyze the case base as whole leaving aside the contextual setups. This way, we can apply the *coverage'* metric (Eq. 5) to CB^1 and study the impact of the θ parameter. We have applied this coverage metric for different θ thresholds, from 0.5 to 1.0. The Fig. 7 shows the obtained results. As expected, and according to the results shown in Fig. 6, the best coverage is achieved with a minimum similarity threshold of $\theta = 0.5$ (70% of coverage). It corroborates our hypothesis about the relevance of the adaptation step. Consequently, the coverage decreases when the similarity threshold grows.

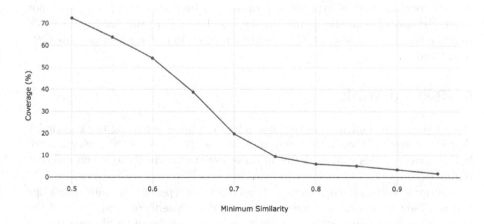

Fig. 7. Case base coverage respect different minimum similarities.

The last analysis tries to figure out the impact of the filtering according to the Elo scores of the original case base CB^0. Hypothetically, we could improve coverage by adding those cases that were deleted because of their low Elo score. We recalculated the coverage again but now we considered different sizes for the case base. We start to measure the coverage with the original CB^0 and repeated it but removing one-by-one the cases with worst Elo rating. The results of this experiment are shown summarized Fig. 8.

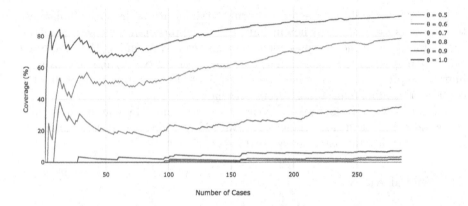

Fig. 8. Case base coverage respect different minimum similarities and the size of the case base.

These results show us that by using more cases we could improve the coverage up to approximately 20% as the coverage with $\theta = 0.6$ similarity threshold is closed to 80%, and the previous results were 65%. However, it is important to note that when including cases with low Elo scores, we are adding cases that do not make sense to the users and do not represent congruent plans. Therefore, we can conclude that a hypothetical maximum improvement of 20% does not worth the loss of semantic quality in the case base. This way, we can conclude that the filtering of cases in CB^0 according to the Elo ranking that obtains CB^1 is justified.

5   Related Work

One of the main challenges in recommender systems is acquiring the knowledge that is required to accurately recommend items [22]. Most of the research work in this area proposes capturing this information automatically based on different resources.

The growth of online resources and social networks permits acquire knowledge because they have a large amount of information. Aizenberg et al. [3] used the information from online radio stations to create a collaborative filtering recommender of music. In addition, Gottschlich et al. [12] proposed a decision support system for investment decision using the votes from online communities. Social networks are used to acquire the knowledge used in recommender systems for groups [6,21,23]. Other works use online resources to create the knowledge for a recommender system like [4]. They created an ontology based on multiple taxonomies for profiling scholar's background knowledge of recommender systems.

In the last years, there have been many approaches to acquire the knowledge in context-aware recommender systems for tourism. Wang et al. [31] proposed a demographic recommender system of tourist attractions. They trained different machine learning methods to obtain the predicted rating and classify the demographic features to provide recommendations. To do that, they used the Tripadvisor reviews. Another similar work is proposed by Palumbo et al. [20] who created a neural network based on the FourSquare data to create a recommender system for point of interests. Other works have created some questionaries to acquire the knowledge of recommender system for tourism. For example, in [16] authors studied the influence of each context element in the recommendation of tourist items. A similar work is presented in [5]. They determined which contextual attribute is the most influential at the time of scoring a tourist activity.

All the works enumerated here need to train their systems to create the recommendations. By contrast, the use of a CBR system based on experience and learning avoids the training stage. Besides, our method deals with knowledge acquisition for contextual systems.

6   Conclusions

Contextual recommender systems have the capability to appreciate its environment and assess the situation in which the cases are to be recommended. They provide accurate recommendations that are better adjusted to a given situation or context. We have designed a contextual recommender system for leisure activities in Madrid using a CBR approach, where plans are stored and reused for similar situations. In this paper, we have discussed the knowledge acquisition difficulties of the system and how to solve the cold start situation when we have not plans to retrieve and reuse in a certain context. We have proposed a method where we first generate the candidate cases and then let the crowd vote to select and filter the best cases using an Elo test. With this method we obtain a case base with diversity, congruence between the activities, and collective knowledge that is independent from a domain expert. We have evaluated the case base using different metrics. We have analyzed the similarity, and coverage of the case base taking into account the contextual setups with and without adaptation, and we have presented a global analysis of the case base as a whole. The proposed method is generic, reusable and captures the wisdom of crowd method.

References

1. Adomavicius, G., Tuzhilin, A.: Context-aware recommender systems. In: Ricci, F., Rokach, L., Shapira, B. (eds.) Recommender Systems Handbook, pp. 191–226. Springer, Boston (2015). https://doi.org/10.1007/978-1-4899-7637-6_6
2. Aha, D.W.: The omnipresence of case-based reasoning in science and application. Knowl. Based Syst. **11**(5–6), 261–273 (1998)
3. Aizenberg, N., Koren, Y., Somekh, O.: Build your own music recommender by modeling internet radio streams. In: Proceedings of the 21st International Conference on World Wide Web 2012, p. 1. ACM Press, New York
4. Amini, B., Ibrahim, R., Shahizan, M., Ali, M.: Expert systems with applications a reference ontology for profiling scholar's background knowledge in recommender systems. Expert. Syst. Appl. **42**(2), 913–928 (2015)
5. Braunhofer, M., Ricci, F.: Selective contextual information acquisition in travel recommender systems. Inf. Technol. Tour. **17**(1), 5–29 (2017)
6. Carrer-Neto, W., Hernández-Alcaraz, M.L., Valencia-García, R., García-S'anchez, F.: Social knowledge-based recommender system. Application to the movies domain. Expert. Syst. Appl. **39**(12), 10990–11000 (2012)
7. Das Sarma, A., Das Sarma, A., Gollapudi, S., Panigrahy, R.: Ranking mechanisms in twitter-like forums. In: Proceedings of the third ACM International Conference on Web Search and Data Mining, pp. 21–30. ACM (2010)
8. Díaz-Agudo, B., Plaza, E., Recio-García, J.A., Arcos, J.-L.: Noticeably new: case reuse in originality-driven tasks. In: Althoff, K.-D., Bergmann, R., Minor, M., Hanft, A. (eds.) ECCBR 2008. LNCS, vol. 5239, pp. 165–179. Springer, Heidelberg (2008). https://doi.org/10.1007/978-3-540-85502-6_11
9. Dufour-Lussier, V., Le Ber, F., Lieber, J., Nauer, E.: Automatic case acquisition from texts for process-oriented case-based reasoning. Inf. Syst. **40**, 153–167 (2014)
10. Elo, A.E.: The Rating of Chess Players, Past and Present. Arco, New York (1978)
11. Goel, A.K., Díaz-Agudo, B.: What's hot in case-based reasoning. In: Proceedings of the Thirty-First AAAI Conference on Artificial Intelligence, San Francisco, California, USA, 4–9 February 2017, pp. 5067–5069 (2017)
12. Gottschlich, J., Hinz, O.: A decision support system for stock investment recommendations using collective wisdom. Decis. Support. Syst. **59**(1), 52–62 (2014)
13. Hacker, S., Von Ahn, L.: Matchin: eliciting user preferences with an online game. In: Proceedings of the SIGCHI Conference on Human Factors in Computing Systems, pp. 1207–1216. ACM (2009)
14. Jorro-Aragoneses, J.L., Díaz-Agudo, B., Recio-García, J.A.: Madrid live: a context-aware recommender system of leisure plans. In: 2017 International Conference on Tools with Artificial Intelligence, pp. 796–801 (2017)
15. Lam, X.N., Vu, T., Le, T.D., Duong, A.D.: Addressing cold-start problem in recommendation systems. In: Proceedings of the 2nd International Conference on Ubiquitous Information Management and Communication, ICUIMC 2008, pp. 208–211. ACM, New York (2008)
16. Laß, C., Herzog, D., Wörndl, W.: Context-aware tourist trip recommendations. In: CEUR Workshop Proceedings, vol. 1906, pp. 18–25 (2017)
17. Leake, D., Wilson, M.: How many cases do you need? Assessing and predicting case-base coverage. In: Ram, A., Wiratunga, N. (eds.) ICCBR 2011. LNCS (LNAI), vol. 6880, pp. 92–106. Springer, Heidelberg (2011). https://doi.org/10.1007/978-3-642-23291-6_9

18. Leake, D.B.: CBR in context: the present and future. In: Case-Based Reasoning, Experiences, Lessons & Future Directions, pp. 1–30 (1996)
19. Manzoor, J., Asif, S., Masud, M., Khan, M.J.: Automatic case generation for case-based reasoning systems using genetic algorithms. In: 2012 Third Global Congress on Intelligent Systems (GCIS), pp. 311–314. IEEE (2012)
20. Palumbo, E., Rizzo, G., Baralis, E.: Predicting your next stop-over from location-based social network data with recurrent neural networks. In: 2nd ACM International Workshop on Recommenders in Tourism (RecTour 2017) RECSYS 2017, CEUR Proceedings, Como, Italy, 27–31 August 2017, vol. 1906, pp. 1–8 (2017)
21. Quijano-Sanchez, L., Recio-Garcia, J.A., Diaz-Agudo, B.: An architecture and functional description to integrate social behaviour knowledge into group recommender systems. Appl. Intell. **40**(4), 732–748 (2014)
22. Ricci, F., Rokach, L., Shapira, B.: Recommender systems: introduction and challenges. In: Ricci, F., Rokach, L., Shapira, B. (eds.) Recommender Systems Handbook, pp. 1–34. Springer, Boston, MA (2015). https://doi.org/10.1007/978-1-4899-7637-6_1
23. Shang, S., Hui, P., Kulkarni, S.R., Cuff, P.W.: Wisdom of the crowd: incorporating social influence in recommendation models. In: Proceedings of the International Conference on Parallel and Distributed Systems - ICPADS, pp. 835–840. IEEE, December 2011
24. Shokouhi, S.V., Skalle, P., Aamodt, A.: An overview of case-based reasoning applications in drilling engineering. Artif. Intell. Rev. **41**(3), 317–329 (2014)
25. Shokouhi, S., Aamodt, A., Skalle, P.: A semi-automatic method for case acquisition in CBR a study in oil well drilling, pp. 263–270, January 2010
26. Sizov, G., Öztürk, P., Štyrák, J.: Acquisition and reuse of reasoning knowledge from textual cases for automated analysis. In: Lamontagne, L., Plaza, E. (eds.) ICCBR 2014. LNCS, vol. 8765, pp. 465–479. Springer, Cham (2014). https://doi.org/10.1007/978-3-319-11209-1_33
27. Smiti, A., Elouedi, Z.: Modeling competence for case based reasoning systems using clustering (2013)
28. Smyth, B., Keane, M.: Remembering to forget: a competence-perserving deletion policy for CBR systems. In: Proceedings of the Thirteenth International Joint Conference on Artificial Intelligence, Montreal, Canada (1994)
29. Smyth, B., McKenna, E.: Building compact competent case-bases. In: Althoff, K.-D., Bergmann, R., Branting, L.K. (eds.) ICCBR 1999. LNCS, vol. 1650, pp. 329–342. Springer, Heidelberg (1999). https://doi.org/10.1007/3-540-48508-2_24
30. Sussman, G.J.: A Computer Model of Skill Acquisition. Elsevier Science Inc., New York (1975)
31. Wang, F.H.: On extracting recommendation knowledge for personalized web-based learning based on ant colony optimization with segmented-goal and meta-control strategies. Expert. Syst. Appl. **39**(7), 6446–6453 (2012)
32. Yang, C., Farley, B., Orchard, B.: Automated case creation and management for diagnostic CBR systems. Appl. Intell. **28**(1), 17–28 (2008)
33. Zhang, S., Lee, M.: Cognitive models and the wisdom of crowds: a case study using the bandit problem. In: Proceedings of the Annual Meeting of the Cognitive Science Society, vol. 32 (2010)

The SECCO Ontology for the Retrieval and Generation of Security Concepts

Andreas Korger[1]($\boxtimes$) and Joachim Baumeister[2,3]

[1] Angesagt GmbH, Dettelbachergasse 2, 97070 Würzburg, Germany
a.korger@angesagt-gmbh.de
[2] denkbares GmbH, Friedrich-Bergius-Ring 15, 97076 Würzburg, Germany
[3] University of Würzburg, Am Hubland, 97074 Würzburg, Germany

Abstract. Due to the development of the global security situation, the existence and implementation of security concepts became an important aspect of public events. The definition and writing of a security concept demands domain knowledge and experience. This paper describes an approach for the automated retrieval and generation of security concept templates based on reliable examples. We use ontologies for the conceptualization of textual security concepts, and we employ case-based reasoning for the retrieval and generation of new security concepts.

Keywords: Case-based reasoning · Experience management
Knowledge management · SKOS ontology

1 Introduction

Recently, a number of terror attacks changed the international security situation of public events, such as festivals and Christmas markets. Consequently, the implementation of security concepts for these events became an essential prerequisite. The development of security concepts requires domain knowledge and experience. Yet before, especially major events required sophisticated planning to minimize security risks. Therefore, a security concept is mandatory for the official approval of larger events. This paper describes the SECCO ontology (SECurity Concept Ontology) for the modeling and the description of official security concepts for public events. Further, we show how this ontology can be used for the retrieval and generation of security concepts by using case-based reasoning. A security concept describes the parameters of an event in textual form, i.e., how incidents can be avoided because of precaution and how to react to an actual occurrence of incidents. At least in Germany, a general specification of a security concept with respect to structure and content does not formally exist. However, several recommendations on how to write a security concept were published. In this paper we present a general approach to structure security concepts for public events according to diverse recommendations. We present an ontology-based framework to make relevant content of such concepts accessible, comparable, and finally interchangeable. Furthermore, we use case-based

© Springer Nature Switzerland AG 2018
M. T. Cox et al. (Eds.): ICCBR 2018, LNAI 11156, pp. 186–201, 2018.
https://doi.org/10.1007/978-3-030-01081-2_13

retrieval and adaptation for the generation of new security concepts appropriate for a given event.

First, we introduce the domain of security concepts and give a general idea of their characteristics. A security concept is a textual document most commonly published as an open text file or PDF-Document. The document length ranges from one page to more than 100 pages. On the one hand, contextual information like location-based data, individual-related data or data concerning traditions and customs play a major role. On the other hand, there exist entangled abstract patterns which are very similar for every public event and thus are transferable. Fire safety or means of escape, for example, are general concepts adaptable to different applications. We developed a framework having the actual textual document and its constituent parts as a core. The approach does not provide a generic model for a public event. Also, (at this point of research) it does not give deep semantic analysis of the documents to, e.g., automatically find the topic structure. As there are several recommendations how a security concept should be structured [12, 13, 18] we selected one as a baseline for further considerations. We chose a popular recommendation [18], which is published by the German institute for standardization (DIN) [10], the major national authority in matters of standardization. Based on the DIN specification we created a *master structure MST*$_1$ for topics contained in security concepts represented as a feature model [15] as shown in Fig. 1.

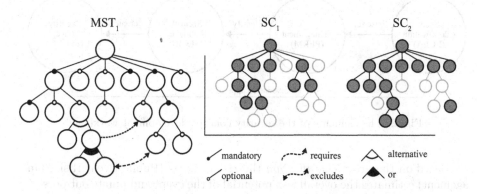

Fig. 1. Subtree structures of a given master structure tree.

We transfer the general topics of the documents into a hierarchical conceptual graph structure, which is always a substructure of the master structure. The hierarchical structure is defined as a set $C = \{c_1, .., c_n\}$ of disjunctive real world concepts linked by a generalization property. Nodes denote disjunctive concepts, edges the hierarchical relation between these concepts. The graphs SC_1 and SC_2 show the structure of two real security concepts. The subgraphs are constructed as follows. Given C_{SC1} a subset of C, for each $(c_i, c_j) \in C_{SC1}$, an edge is inserted when (c_i, c_j) has an edge in MST_1. As seen in SC_2, nodes may not necessarily be linked and the inherent logic needs not to be fulfilled necessarily. The subgraph is then incomplete and incorrect. This can be solved by deleting conflicting nodes and virtually inserting missing nodes and relating them until the next existing concept is reached and the nodes of the tree are fully connected. Similarly, C_{SC1} can be arranged according to another master structure MST_2. That way, we are able to dynamically adapt to different recommendations found in an analogous space of concepts. Additionally, the previous efforts lead to a higher formalization [6] of the knowledge encoded in a security concept. As a result, the formalization gives the option to define characteristics of a security concept like connectivity, completeness, grade of detail, and simplicity. It helps us to answer the question of how "well" a security concept is built up concerning quality and quantity.

2   Ontological Representation of Security Concepts

A security concept describes highly interdependent and linked content. It has to be shareable and diverse stakeholders need to formally agree. To achieve more flexibility, we chose an ontology-based approach for the representation. The creation of a security concept follows a general workflow [18]. The four steps of the workflow are depicted in Fig. 2.

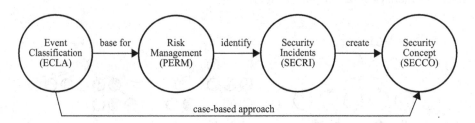

Fig. 2. The elements of the security concept development workflow.

Based on the *event classification* the *risk analysis* (Public Event Risk Management) estimates the overall risk potential of the event and points out possible threats in detail. Threats are organized in the third partition *security incidents* (SECurity Relevant Incidents). The security concept itself is defined in step four. The *security concept* should cover precaution tasks to avoid identified threats of step two and three, and it should give action advice in case of the occurrence of a threat [18]. Furthermore, the concept should mention basic information about the event as well as other subject areas. All this information is formalized hierarchically. This paper presents a way to abbreviate the workflow by the use of case-based techniques to generate security concepts directly from the event classification via adaptation of existing concepts.

2.1   The Security Concept Ontology (SECCO)

Since a security concept aggregates and hierarchically organizes event-related knowledge, we used the SKOS ontology (Simple Knowledge Organization System) [23] as an upper-ontology. The security concept ontology models the actual security concept in OWL2 [22]. The class *secco:SecurityConcept* is defined as a *subclass* of a *secco:Document*, and merges the textual and conceptual character of a security concept. Therefore, *secco:Document* is a subclass of *skos:Concept* and *prov:Entity* [24] in order to interlink the semantics of this concepts as depicted in Fig. 3. This clarifies that we consider a real document (*prov:Entity*) but also a hierarchical concept within a formal knowledge system (*skos:Concept*). The PROV ontology [17] provides access to model documental information and document provenance in a standardized manner. A security concept has one or more authors (*prov:Agent*) and a final version developed step by step releasing intermediate versions through modification (*prov:Activity*). The document substructure is refined by *secco:Chapter* as a subclass of *skos:Concept*. This enriches the document by the conceptual hierarchy according to a given master structure as explained in the introduction. We now are able to model a document made up of several concepts but also other corresponding documents.

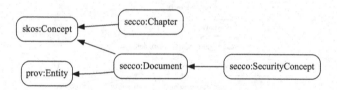

Fig. 3. The hierarchical structure of security concepts.

The domain-specific hierarchy shown partially in Fig. 4 is modeled by the property *secco:partOf*, a sub property of *skos:broader*. In a first step, we model the hierarchy consistently by the relation *partOf* (what equates using exclusively optional edges in the feature model) [15], even if there were more specific relations fitting better in special cases.

Nevertheless, we use specific relations (not included in SKOS) for additional purposes, for instance to model a mandatory, causal or sequential relation. Having in mind, that there are different recommendations, the presented ontology may be refined by using sub-properties of *secco:partOf*. For instance, the property *secco:partOfBavarianGovRecommendations* refines the *partOf* relation with respect to a recommendation of the Bavarian Government (state in Germany) as can be seen in Fig. 5.

To explicitly define a security concept for a given public event, an instance of every class of the master structure is created if covered by the security concept. The property *secco:hasAnnotation* allows to link each concept with specific parts of the textual document.

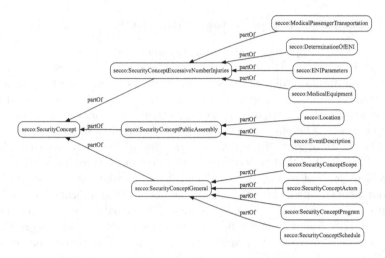

Fig. 4. Excerpt of the SECCO ontology master structure (14 of 278 concepts).

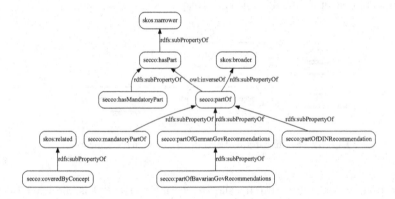

Fig. 5. Properties linking concepts.

2.2   Event Classification (ECLA)

The classification of public events is encapsulated in a separate package with the prefix *ecla*. The architecture follows a similar pattern as used for modeling the security concept. That way, the event classification may either be used stand-alone, but can also be integrated into the security concept by using the property *secco:partOf*. The class *ecla:Component* is defined as a subclass of *skos:Concept*. The top-level class of the event classification is *ecla:EventClassification*; itself a subclass of *ecla:Component*.

The hierarchical structure linking event classification components is implemented by using the property *ecla:partOf*. Its inverse property *ecla:hasPart* is

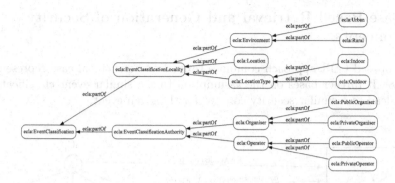

Fig. 6. Excerpt of the event classification hierarchy (16 of 136 concepts).

used to directly assign abstract classification components to an instantiated *ecla:EventClassification*. This simplifies the instantiation of concrete events.

2.3 Security Relevant Incident (SECRI)

Security relevant incidents are defined in a distinct namespace (*secri*) and thus can be also used separately. A special use case during the modeling is the definition of preventive measures and actions taken for considered incidents which is a subpart of the actual security concept (Fig. 7).

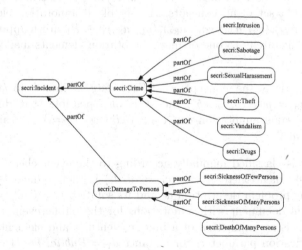

Fig. 7. Excerpt of the event classification hierarchy (16 of 136 concepts).

The formalization of incidents allows for the inclusion of external ontologies, that structure incidents (e.g. DO4MG [14]) or to extend these structures when appropriate.

3 Case-Based Retrieval and Generation of Security Concepts

The proposed CBR approach combines textual and structural case representations [8]. It further bases on the assumption that a similar event classification should lead to a similar security concept for the given event.

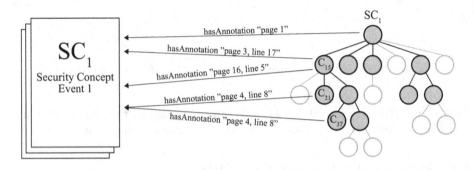

Fig. 8. Semantic annotation of a textual security concept.

The textual document (the concrete security concept) is annotated by instances of the hierarchical master structure of concepts. The annotation process $A(SC_i)$ for a security concept SC_i of an event i is described by a relation $R_i \subseteq C \times A$, $C =$ set of all concepts, $A =$ set of all annotation elements. For instance $\{(c_{21}, a_{43}), (c_{37}, a_{43}), (c_{15}, a_{34}), (c_{15}, a_{35})\} \in R_1$ are mapping concepts of the SECCO hierarchy to one or more annotation elements made for SC_1 as depicted in Fig. 8.

Example 1. In Fig. 8 the concept $c_{15} = FireSafety$ is linked to $a_{34} = $ "page3, line17" and $a_{35} = $ "page16, line5", but it is also possible that different concepts have the same annotation e.g. $c_{21} = Audience$, $c_{37} = Artists$ are linked to $a_{43} = $ "page4, line8".

Each event is classified manually according to the event classification hierarchy previously mentioned. A case $c_i = (d_i, l_i)$ is then defined by the event classification as problem description d_i and its solution $l_i = (SC_i, A(SC_i))$ the concrete textual document with annotations for the public event i. The problem description is a conjunction of a unique identifier and elements of the set of event classification parameters for instance $d_1 = PublicEvent1 \wedge Outdoor \wedge PublicOperator \wedge FreeAdmission \wedge StreetFestival$. The case base is the collection of all cases c_i for security concepts SC_i. A query q to the case base is a conjunct subset of the event classification parameters. For instance, a company wants to organize an indoor sport event SportEvent2 and searches for security concepts describing an indoor sport event hosted by a private organizer, then the query is $q_{SE2} = PrivateOrganizer \wedge Indoor \wedge SportEvent$. To retrieve

cases, we either search the case base for problem descriptions d_i exactly matching the query or if this is not possible, then find most similar cases. At this
point the model is built exclusively using symbolic attributes. Thanks to the
ontological structuring process, numeric attributes are yet mapped to symbolic
classes. For instance, the number of visitors is represented by five classes like
AttendanceBelow5000 meaning less than 5000 visitors. To define a similarity
function, we divided the event classification into n parts. One part would be,
e.g., the *EventLocalityClassification* shown in Fig. 6. Each part is then processed
by a local similarity measure. The local similarity measures are aggregated by an
aggregation function to form a global similarity measure. Therefore, each local
similarity function of two security concepts k, l is weighted (ω_j) and summed
up as depicted in the following equation:

$$Sim_{glob}(SC_k, SC_l) = \sum_{j=1}^{n} \omega_j * Sim_j(SC_k, SC_l) \qquad (1)$$

For the local similarity calculation, the symbolic types are sorted according to
the hierarchy represented by the event classification structure. Each concept is
assigned with a likelihood symbolizing the similarity of its sub-concepts. The
similarity of the leaf-node-concepts is set to *1*. The similarity of the root is *0*
and the similarity increases with depth d of the concept in the hierarchy and is
calculated by $sim_d = 1 - 1/2^d$ [4]. An example of the event type classification
with similarity values is shown in Fig. 9.

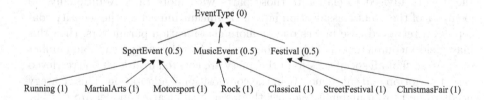

Fig. 9. Excerpt of the event type taxonomy.

Please note that this only holds for sticking to one master structure. If concepts are rearranged to fit an alternative master structure the likelihood values
of the concepts have to be adjusted. We emphasize the two classification parameters *real-world location* and the *number of visitors*. The real-world location is
not subject to an abstract event classification hierarchy but to location-based
data. We also take into account that public events taking place on the same
event location have much in common themselves. All factors influencing the
security concept caused by the event location are the same. The number of visitors (*attendance*) is separately treated as well because the number has direct
legal consequences and the classes are derived from an integer value and should
thus have an order and a different similarity than implemented by a taxonomy.

3.1   Using Case-Based Adaptation to Generate Security Concepts

The generation of new security concepts can become necessary for the following reasons: First, someone wants to host an event and needs to define a security concept from scratch. Second, someone already wrote a security concept and wants to improve the concept with respect to new requirements. As textual cases are difficult to adapt [8], we use the annotations with descriptive information of the structural concepts.

Generation of New Security Concepts. To generate a completely new security concept the user specifies the event according to the event classification structure (see Sect. 2.2). Then, the case base is queried with those parameters to find the most similar security concept. The retrieved security concept is a draft for the new one. The user does the actual transformational adaptation via revision of the textual document and manual adaptation to his needs. The user is supported in his decisions by the explanatory content of the knowledge description in the ontology and has to replace context-based information in the retrieved security concept by the information of his own context. The cost of leaving out parts of a retrieved security concept is lower than self-reliant adding topics. With this regard a more satisfying adaptation strategy would be a compositional adaptation of several retrieved security concepts, e.g., the three most similar ones. The structure of those concepts is merged to a new structure as depicted for two merged concepts in Fig. 10. Concepts covered by both merged security concepts (black nodes in SC_{NEW}) seem to be more "important" and the user is advised to elaborate those parts with more care. Additionally, all elements of the event classification have a significant impact on the security concept. If a retrieved case misses one or more classification parameters, then this may yield incompleteness. This can be resolved by retrieving a suitable number of cases, so that all specifications of the query are covered in at least one retrieved case description and subsequently in the compositional adaptation. This strategy needs to be proven manually against the logic of the feature model MST_1. The usage of, e.g., graph operators makes it possible to automate the process [21] what we leave to future work.

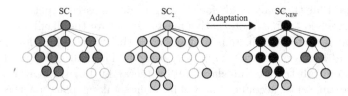

Fig. 10. Generation of a new security concept from two existing concepts. In SC_{NEW} black means SC_1 and SC_2 cover the node, dark grey SC_1 and light grey SC_2.

The user may decide for each topic between the different annotations, skip those he/she does not find adequate and adapt those fitting his event. After the event has taken place, the security concept is annotated and retained in the case base together with the event classification specified in the beginning making up a new case.

Adapt Existing Security Concepts to New Requirements. The second scenario of improving an existing security concept is more complex. For each concept covered in the old security concept the author has to make the decision if it is still required in the new security concept.

Example 2. In Fig. 11 a security concept SC_{OLD} shall be adapted because the event location changed from outdoor to indoor. To generate the new security concept SC_{NEW} the following strategy for adaptation is suggested:

1. Adjust the event classification and thus query to new user requirements
2. Retrieve x most similar cases according to Sim_{glob} mentioned before
3. Add concepts found in more than y of x most similar cases
4. Delete concepts only found in less than z of x most similar cases
5. Insert missing edges and nodes according to MST_1
6. For each concept: filter out cases that do not cover the concept
7. Among remaining cases present the annotation ranked by the similarity of the case as decision support.

This strategy may be adjusted by the parameters x of retrieved security concepts taken into account and the threshold $0 \le y < x$ of adding and $0 < z \le x$ of deleting nodes. With increasing number y for given x this strategy integrates less concepts into the new security concept and deletes more from the old one with increasing z (in the example: $x = 2$, $y = 0$, $z = 1$). This strategy implements a kind of common sense. What many people do is ok, what nobody does isnt' necessary.

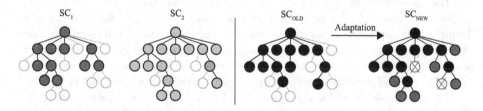

Fig. 11. Adaptation of SC_{OLD}, In SC_{NEW} black symbolizes remaining nodes, dark grey new nodes and dashed lines symbolize deleted nodes.

4   Case Study

We started the case study by analyzing the DIN recommendation [18] of security concepts for public events. The informal knowledge encoded in this recommendation was extracted and formalized in order to make up a hierarchical master structure for the case-based processing of security concepts. Subsequently, we collected and analyzed real world security concepts. The most evident facts were the document length, the city, the author, and the type of event described. With this insight to the domain knowledge an ontology was implemented. The development of the ontology builds on the W3C standards SKOS and PROV, that were extended to fit the domain-specific requirements. For the construction and maintenance of the ontology the semantic wiki KnowWE [7] was used. The application provides an environment for the distributed development of ontologies, with efficient editing functionalities, SPARQL querying, visualization plugins and debugging.

In total, 30 real world security concepts were collected (all in German language). A data pool was created by manually annotating (the most meaningful) 15 of the 30 security concepts of different events, for instance Christmas markets, carnival parades, and city festivals. The coverage of 278 domain specific characteristics where annotated. The major part of the topics as well as their hierarchical structure were derived from the DIN recommendation previously mentioned. For each characteristic, the annotation declared whether a topic was covered by the concept and roughly where this characteristic was mentioned in the document, referencing to a page number and the area on that page. At a first glance, the similarity of the documents is clearly depending rather on the origin (e.g. author or city), than on the type of event. From a knowledge management-oriented point of view, the type of event should be the base to develop a security concept. The DIN recommendation provides an event classification model which is also represented in the ontology. This event classification model was instantiated for each of the 15 annotated security concepts. The classification of one event together with the ontological representation and the text document defines one distinct case. The case base of the corpus finally contains 15 cases representing the 15 selected events. As a technical platform for the case-based part the application myCBR [5] was used. The tool is an environment for efficient and intuitive development of case-based reasoning applications. To develop a sound similarity measure for the usage in case-based reasoning the event classification was split into parts. For the case-based retrieval and adaptation, we transferred the ontology and security concept corpus from KnowWE into myCBR (Fig. 12).

The case-based model was evaluated and refined by a post-mortem analysis. The classification of each of the 15 security concepts was used as a query to the case base. For each of these 15 queries the results were analyzed by 3 domain experts to refine the case model and similarity functions. The results using the developed basic model are shown in Fig. 13. Besides the similarity values the document length in pages is shown as well as the percentage of 278 concepts covered by the particular security concept. The underlying case model divides the event classification into six parts (*attendance, authority, locality, spatial,*

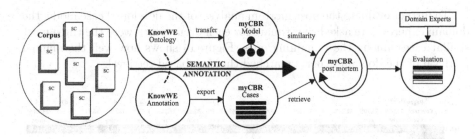

Fig. 12. Case study workflow

type, visitors). For the attribute *attendance* the similarity values were set individually. All other attributes were built as taxonomies as subtrees of the event classification ontology. The taxonomy was set to allow multiple values and inner nodes as values. The similarities of the nodes were set as mentioned in Chap. 3. The model does not involve location-based information. The weights were set to $w = 2$ for the attributes attendance and type and to $w = 1$ for all other attributes. This setting respects the importance of the number of visitors and the obvious influence of the type of event. The model yielded satisfactory classification results. For example, the instance *ecla5* is a carnival parade in a city; the most similar cases are another carnival parade, a music parade and a city festival which are indeed the most similar events. Additionally, *case 8* covers twice as many concepts as *case 5*, which gives a good chance of improving the security concept of *case 5* through adaptation of *case 8*. Having costs in mind then again *case 5* may also help to lighten the security concept of *case 8*. The *cases 13* and *14* are not rated very similar to the remaining cases: Here, the arena and the university campus are indeed very different to all other events and event locations, respectively.

Event	Case	ecla0	ecla1	ecla2	ecla3	ecla4	ecla5	ecla6	ecla7	ecla8	ecla9	ecla10	ecla11	ecla12	ecla13	ecla14
Pages		17	30	31	41	58	72	26	10	64	4	4	9	2	47	16
Coverage		11,90%	23,70%	23,70%	18,00%	22,30%	14,40%	15,50%	16,20%	30,22%	13,31%	12,23%	13,67%	16,91%	25,18%	23,38%
Event		christm	wine	wine	folk	city	carne	folk	music	carne	fair	fair	running	camp	arena	campus
christm	ecla0	x	0.63	0.5	0.6	0.6	0.6	0.75	0.6	0.6	0.65	0.65	0.35	0.34	0.59	0.34
wine	ecla1	0.63	x	0.65	0.6	0.48	0.48	0.75	0.35	0.48	0.65	0.53	0.35	0.4	0.34	0.34
wine	ecla2	0.53	0.65	x	0.57	0.4	0.4	0.65	0.28	0.4	0.75	0.63	0.33	0.5	0.44	0.44
folk	ecla3	0.6	0.6	0.57	x	0.68	0.68	0.6	0.68	0.68	0.54	0.45	0.5	0.33	0.57	0.33
city	ecla4	0.6	0.48	0.4	0.68	x	0.75	0.6	0.75	0.75	0.53	0.4	0.43	0.28	0.43	0.18
carne	ecla5	0.6	0.48	0.4	0.68	0.75	x	0.6	0.75	0.75	0.53	0.53	0.43	0.28	0.46	0.21
folk	ecla6	0.75	0.75	0.65	0.6	0.6	0.6	x	0.6	0.6	0.62	0.53	0.35	0.4	0.65	0.4
music	ecla7	0.6	0.35	0.28	0.68	0.75	0.75	0.6	x	0.75	0.24	0.28	0.43	0.28	0.46	0.21
carne	ecla8	0.6	0.48	0.4	0.68	0.75	0.75	0.6	0.75	x	0.53	0.53	0.43	0.28	0.46	0.21
fair	ecla9	0.65	0.65	0.75	0.54	0.53	0.53	0.62	0.24	0.53	x	0.75	0.33	0.44	0.38	0.38
fair	ecla10	0.65	0.53	0.63	0.45	0.4	0.53	0.53	0.28	0.53	0.75	x	0.33	0.44	0.44	0.44
running	ecla11	0.35	0.35	0.33	0.5	0.43	0.43	0.35	0.43	0.43	0.33	0.33	x	0.33	0.48	0.23
camp	ecla12	0.34	0.4	0.5	0.33	0.28	0.28	0.4	0.28	0.28	0.44	0.44	0.33	x	0.38	0.63
arena	ecla13	0.59	0.34	0.44	0.57	0.43	0.46	0.65	0.46	0.46	0.38	0.44	0.48	0.38	x	0.5
campus	ecla14	0.34	0.34	0.44	0.33	0.18	0.21	0.4	0.21	0.21	0.38	0.44	0.23	0.63	0.5	x

Fig. 13. Results of the post mortem analysis for event classifications.

To further evaluate the post mortem analysis of the developed case model the domain experts were asked to estimate for each event which were the three most similar cases among the remaining ones. Figure 14 shows how well the manual retrieval of the domain experts matched the case-based retrieval.

Event	Case	ecla0	ecla1	ecla2	ecla3	ecla4	ecla5	ecla6	ecla7	ecla8	ecla9	ecla10	ecla11	ecla12	ecla13	ecla14
Pages		17	30	31	41	58	72	26	10	64	4	4	9	2	47	16
Coverage		11,90%	23,70%	23,70%	18,00%	22,30%	14,40%	15,50%	16,20%	30,22%	13,31%	12,23%	13,67%	16,91%	25,18%	23,38%
Event		christm	wine	wine	folk	city	carne	folk	music	carne	fair	fair	running	camp	arena	campus
christm	ecla0	x	1-2-3	1-2-3				0					0-1-2-3	0		
wine	ecla1	1-2-3	x	0-1-2-3		2		0					1-3	0		
wine	ecla2	1-2-3	0-1-2-	x	3			0					1-2-3	0		
folk	ecla3				x	0-1-2	0	1-2-3	0-7	0-2	1-3					
city	ecla4				1-2	x	0-2-3	1	0	0-2-3	1		3			
carne	ecla5		1			0-2-3	x		0-1-2	0-1-2-3			3			
folk	ecla6	0	0-2	0	1-2-3	1-2		x	3		1-3				0	
music	ecla7				3	0-2	0-1-2	3	x	0-1-2			3		1	
carne	ecla8		1			0-2	0-1-2-3		0-1-2-	x	3		3			
fair	ecla9	0-1	0-2	0-2	1-3			1			x	0-2-3	3			
fair	ecla10	0-1	0-1-2-3	1-2-3							0-2-3	x				
running	ecla11				0	0-2-3	0-2-3		0-2	0-3	1		x	1	0	1
camp	ecla12		0		0						0-1-2-3	0-2-3	1-2	x		0-1-3
arena	ecla13	0			0-2		1		0-2	1	3	2	3		x	3
campus	ecla14				0	1-2					1-3	0-2-3		0-1-3	0-2	x

Fig. 14. Evaluation results comparing automatic vs. manual domain expert ranking. 0 = cbr, 1 = domain expert 1, 2 = de2, 3 = de3.

The domain experts were completely informed about the event parameters and that they should estimate the similarity regarding to the writing of a security concept for those events. For the case-based part it was not always possible to cut the three most similar cases because of equal similarity values. We decided to extend the threshold in those cases and consider all cases with equal similarity. This leads to a slightly better performance of the case based evaluation. The proposed similarity of two event classifications is symmetrical. What we can see is that the domain experts sometimes do not rate symmetrically (e.g. *ecla7/ecla8*, *ecla9/ecla11*, *ecla13/ecla14*). Additionally we can observe that the domain experts are more conformable, when there is another event of the same type. For instance *ecla1* is related by all to the other wine event *ecla2*. Precision and recall [19] show how well the intuitive manual measure matches the objective measure. For the calculation we merged the evaluation of the three experts into one by neglecting multiple classifications and just considering whether an event was rated by one of the three experts as depicted in Fig. 15. As recall and precision just switch when we want to estimate how well the case based classification matches the manual classification we did not depict this information.

The domain experts were interviewed how they came to their decision. They had informed themselves about the events via the events websites. They described a rating based on several factors similar to the event classification but furthermore admitted that they had handled the task intuitively. We see this as a main reason for the divergence of the analyzed security concepts and as a validation of the need for more formalization in the domain. At this point of work we estimate the presented case-based approach as capable of giving satisfactory decision support even to people with deep domain knowledge and experience.

Pages		17	30	31	41	58	72	26	10	64	4	4	9	2	47	16			
Coverage		11,90%	23,70%	23,70%	18,00%	22,30%	14,40%	15,50%	16,20%	30,22%	13,31%	12,23%	13,67%	16,91%	25,18%	23,38%			
Event		christm	wine	wine	folk	city	carne	folk	music	carne	fair	fair	running	camp	arena	campus			
Event	Case	ecla0	ecla1	ecla2	ecla3	ecla4	ecla5	ecla6	ecla7	ecla8	ecla9	ecla10	ecla11	ecla12	ecla13	ecla14	Precision	Recall	F1
christm	ecla0		1	1	x	0						0-1	0						%
wine	ecla1	1	x	0-1	1		0				1	0							%
wine	ecla2	1	0-	x	1		0				1	0							%
folk	ecla3				x	0-1	0	1	0-1	0-	1	1							%
city	ecla4				1	x	0-1	1	0	0-	1	1	1						%
carne	ecla5		1			0-1	x		0-1	0-1	1								%
folk	ecla6	0	0-			1	1	0	1	1	x	1			0				%
music	ecla7				1	0-1	0-1	1	x	0-1	1			1	1				%
carne	ecla8		1			0-1	0-1		0-	x	1		1						%
fair	ecla9	0-1	0-1	0-1		1		1			0-		1	1					%
fair	ecla10	0-1	0-	1	1					0-	x	1							%
running	ecla11				0	0-1	0-1		0-1	0-1	1		x	1	0	1	57%	66%	61%
camp	ecla12		0							0-1	0-1	1	x		0-1	75%	75%	75%	
arena	ecla13	0			0-1		1	0-1	1	1		1	1	x	1	22%	66%	33%	
campus	ecla14		0		1						0-1	1	0-1	0-1	x	60%	75%	67%	

Fig. 15. Precision and recall of the evaluation, 0 = cbr, 1 = aggregated domain experts.

What we do not see at the moment is the capability of replacing a team of experts elaborating a sophisticated security concept going through the complete workflow of Fig. 2.

5   Conclusions

In this paper, we introduced an ontology approach for the representation of security concepts. We implemented case-based reasoning for the generation of new security concepts based on existing ones and the adaptation of existing security concepts motivated by changed requirements. In a case study we demonstrated the plausible use of the approach and compared the automated results with the results of a manual domain expert rating. We see two fields of related work to the presented work. The first field is subjected to the formalization and hierarchical structure of knowledge according to a master structure. The second field describes the domains public events, mass gatherings, and security incidents either by ontology or case-based representations. The work of Roth-Berghofer et al. [20] towards case acquisition from text inspired the presented overall workflow and shows how this work can be further extended to automatic case acquisition. Very similar to the presented approach, Delir Haghighi [14] introduces the ontology DO4MG (Domain Ontology for Mass Gatherings), that describes mass gatherings and case-based reasoning to give decision support for medical emergencies. The author mentions the problem of not having official standards in the domain of mass gatherings. This problem is mitigated by a unified vocabulary covering synonyms to improve case retrieval. The approach misses the capability of adaptation either in the ontological as well as in the case-based part. Khaled and Lu [2] developed an ontology-based CBR system for mobile-based emergency response. They address the issue of needing a unified vocabulary but are also giving no information about adaptation. For the definition and interchange of vocabularies there exist thesauri for different domains. For instance, EuroVoc [11], the multilingual thesaurus of the European Union and in the agricultural domain AgroVoc [1] a thesaurus maintained by the United Nations. Both build up on the SKOS standard. Maintaining a thesaurus is promising in our approach to improve decision support via building a unified and thus adaptable vocabulary. Assem et al. [3] provide substantial advice on how to transform a thesaurus into SKOS. How the basic SKOS standard may be extended to special needs can be seen for instance in the work of Cotton et al. [9], who developed an extension of SKOS to be capable of describing statistical classification. They uncovered limitations of the standard. Similar to their approach we also refined the properties for domain-specific linkage of concepts. There exists various work towards the similarity of hierarchical structures in general. For instance, Lakkaraju et al. [16] propose a way to calculate document similarity based on a concept tree distance. In the future, we are planning a number of extensions of the presented approach. Not only event classification can be a base for case definition but also the classification of security incidents. We are expecting that its implementation is feasible in an analogous way and yields improvement to the case retrieval but also adaption step. In general, this would result in the merge of different case definitions into one case-based system. The development of a conversational case-based approach would be also promising. It could be generated automatically from the ontology structure by bringing the concepts into a question and answer form. We also want to interlink the thesaurus structure in the future, e.g., to model time, causal relations, and process information. In the next step we want to use this information for further improvements of the case retrieval and adaptation.

References

1. AgroVoc. https://www.aims.fao.org/standards/agrovoc
2. Amailef, K., Lu, J.: Mobile-based emergency response system using ontology-supported information extraction. In: Lu, J., Jain, L.C., Zhang, G. (eds.) Handbook on Decision Making. Intelligent Systems Reference Library, vol. 33, pp. 429–449. Springer, Heidelberg (2012). https://doi.org/10.1007/978-3-642-25755-1_21
3. van Assem, M., Malaisé, V., Miles, A., Schreiber, G.: A method to convert thesauri to SKOS. In: Sure, Y., Domingue, J. (eds.) ESWC 2006. LNCS, vol. 4011, pp. 95–109. Springer, Heidelberg (2006). https://doi.org/10.1007/11762256_10
4. Bach, K., Althoff, K.-D.: Developing case-based reasoning applications using myCBR 3. In: Agudo, B.D., Watson, I. (eds.) ICCBR 2012. LNCS, vol. 7466, pp. 17–31. Springer, Heidelberg (2012). https://doi.org/10.1007/978-3-642-32986-9_4
5. Bach, K., Sauer, C., Althoff, K.D., Roth-Berghofer, T.: Knowledge modeling with the open source tool myCBR. In: Proceedings of the 10th International Conference on Knowledge Engineering and Software Engineering, KESE 2014, vol. 1289, pp. 84–94. CEUR-WS.org, Aachen (2014)
6. Baumeister, J., Reutelshoefer, J., Puppe, F.: Engineering intelligent systems on the knowledge formalization continuum. Int. J. Appl. Math. Comput. Sci. (AMCS) **21**(1), 27–39 (2011)
7. Baumeister, J., Reutelshoefer, J., Puppe, F.: KnowWE: a semantic wiki for knowledge engineering. Appl. Intell. **35**(3), 323–344 (2011)
8. Bergmann, R.: Experience Management. Springer, Heidelberg (2002). https://doi.org/10.1007/3-540-45759-3

9. Cotton, F., Gillman, D.W., Jaques, Y.: XKOS: extending SKOS for describing statistical classifications. In: Proceedings of the 1st International Workshop on Semantic Statistics Co-located with 12th International Semantic Web Conference, Sydney, Australia (2013)

10. DIN: German Institute of Standardization. https://www.din.de

11. EuroVoc. https://www.eurovoc.europa.eu

12. Gundel, S.: Security for Places of Public Assembly and Events. Richard Boorberg Verlag, Stuttgart (2017)

13. Gutsche, H., Riemann, J., Sommer, S.: Security Concepts. VHZ Verlagshaus Zitzmann Nrnberg (2016)

14. Haghighi, P.D., Burstein, F., Zaslavsky, A., Arbon, P.: Development and evaluation of ontology for intelligent decision support in medical emergency management for mass gatherings. Decis. Support. Syst. **54**(2), 1192–1204 (2013)

15. Kang, K.C., Cohen, S.G., Hess, J.A., Novak, W.E., Peterson, A.S.: Feature-oriented domain analysis (FODA) feasibility study. Carnegie Mellon University, Technical report (1990)

16. Lakkaraju, P., Gauch, S., Speretta, M.: Document similarity based on concept tree distance. In: Proceedings of the Nineteenth ACM Conference on Hypertext and Hypermedia, HT 2008, pp. 127–132. ACM, New York (2008)

17. Moreau, L., Groth, P.: Provenance: An Introduction to PROV. Synthesis Lectures on the Semantic Web: Theory and Technology. Morgan and Claypool, San Rafeal (2013)

18. Paul, S., Ebner, M., Klode, K., Sakschewski, T.: Security Concepts for Events. DIN Beuth, Berlin (2014)

19. Perry, J.W., Kent, A., Berry, M.M.: Machine literature searching X. machine language; factors underlying its design and development. Am. Doc. **6**(4), 242–254 (1955)

20. Roth-Berghofer, T., Adrian, B., Dengel, A.: Case acquisition from text: ontology-based information extraction with SCOOBIE for myCBR. In: Bichindaritz, I., Montani, S. (eds.) ICCBR 2010. LNCS, vol. 6176, pp. 451–464. Springer, Heidelberg (2010). https://doi.org/10.1007/978-3-642-14274-1_33

21. Segura, S., Benavides, D., Ruiz-Cortés, A., Trinidad, P.: Automated merging of feature models using graph transformations. In: Lämmel, R., Visser, J., Saraiva, J. (eds.) GTTSE 2007. LNCS, vol. 5235, pp. 489–505. Springer, Heidelberg (2008). https://doi.org/10.1007/978-3-540-88643-3_15

22. W3C: OWL2 Profiles, April 2009. http://www.w3.org/tr/owl2-profiles/

23. W3C: SKOS Simple Knowledge Organization System Reference, August 2009. http://www.w3.org/TR/skos-reference

24. W3C: PROV-O: The PROV Ontology, April 2013. http://www.w3.org/TR/prov-o

Exploration vs. Exploitation in Case-Base Maintenance: Leveraging Competence-Based Deletion with Ghost Cases

David Leake[(✉)] and Brian Schack

School of Informatics, Computing, and Engineering, Indiana University,
Bloomington, IN 47408, USA
{leake,schackb}@indiana.edu

Abstract. Case-base maintenance research has extensively studied strategies for competence-retaining case base compression. Such approaches generally rely on the *representativeness assumption* that current case base contents can be used as a proxy for future problems when determining cases to retain. For mature case bases in stable domains, this assumption works well. However, representativeness may not hold for sparse case bases during initial case base growth, for dynamically changing domains, or when a case base built for one task is applied to cross-domain problem-solving in another. This paper presents a new method for competence-preserving deletion, Expansion-Contraction Compression (ECC), aimed at improving competence preservation when the representativeness assumption is only partially satisfied. ECC precedes compression with adaptation-based exploration of previously unseen parts of the problem space to create "ghost cases" and exploits them to broaden the range of cases available for competence-based deletion. Experimental results support that this method increases competence and quality retention for less representative case bases. They also reveal the unexpected result that ECC can improve retention of competence and quality even for representative case bases.

Keywords: Case base maintenance · Competence
Knowledge containers · Representativeness assumption

1 Introduction

Much case-based reasoning research focuses on how to develop compact, competent case bases (*e.g.*, [1,2,7,19,27,34,38]. The desire for compact, competent case bases arose from retrieval efficiency concerns (*e.g.*, [9,32,35]). Such efficiency concerns remain an issue for CBR applied to big data, and case base compression remains important for other reasons as well. Compact case bases are easier for humans to maintain, and compact case bases may facilitate knowledge sharing

© Springer Nature Switzerland AG 2018
M. T. Cox et al. (Eds.): ICCBR 2018, LNAI 11156, pp. 202–218, 2018.
https://doi.org/10.1007/978-3-030-01081-2_14

and reasoning about the competence of other agents in distributed case-based reasoning [30].

Many methods have been developed for controlling case base growth. Because case deletion may result in unrecoverable knowledge loss, a central focus has been selective deletion aimed at maximum competence preservation, starting with seminal work by Smyth and Keane [33] and continuing with many other methods (*e.g.*, [19,20,27,34]). Retention methods generally estimate the competence contribution of each case, to prioritize retention decisions according to maximum competence contributions. Estimating the future competence contributions of a case is difficult because it depends on predicting the problems a CBR system will encounter. Smyth and McKenna proposed addressing this with the *representativeness assumption* [34] that the prior problems are representative of the problems to be encountered in the future. Under this assumption, the future competence contribution of a case can be estimated as its competence contribution in the existing case base. Although the assumption may not always hold, Smyth and McKenna advanced a compelling argument for its appropriateness for CBR systems: Because CBR is based on the assumption that future problems will resemble previous problems (problem-distribution regularity [23]), domains for which the representativeness hypothesis fails would be ill-suited for CBR.

Case-base compression relying on the representativeness assumption has been shown effective in many domains. However, in domains for which only a small part of the problem space has yet been encountered, or in which concept drift shifts the problem distribution [5], representativeness may not hold, and in turn, competence may suffer [26]. Likewise, if a case base generated for one task is applied to a new task for cross-domain problem-solving [21], there is no guarantee that the problems of the first space will be representative of problems in the second.

A well-known strength of CBR is that it can draw on multiple knowledge containers whose contributions overlap, in the sense that strengths in one can compensate for weaknesses in another [31]. This paper investigates how a CBR system can draw on adaptation knowledge to handle experience gaps when building a case base. By adapting cases already in the case base, a CBR system can pre-populate sparsely populated regions of the case base—transferring some of the knowledge of its adaptation component into the case component to expand the set of cases. This in turn enables the system to generate the compressed case base from a set of candidates larger than its retained experience. This can be seen as shifting from maintenance that only exploits existing experiences, to maintenance that explores the space of future problems. Combining case base exploitation with problem space exploration is a novel step for case-base maintenance.

To combine exploitation and exploration for case-base compression, this paper proposes the new method *expansion-contraction compression* (ECC). ECC adapts existing cases to generate additional candidate cases, which we call "ghost cases," providing a more diverse set of cases for compression to consider. In ECC, the union of the case base and ghost cases is then provided to the condensed nearest neighbor algorithm (CNN) [11] in order of competence contribution. This provides competence-based deletion with a wider set of cases from which to select that can include cases from unseen but solvable parts of the problem space. If case adaptation is considered sufficiently reliable, the result of ECC can be used as-is. Otherwise, the selected ghost cases can become targets for verification, *e.g.*, by asking a human expert in an active learning process, or provenance information [22] about the origin of ghost cases could be used to predict confidence when they are used.

This paper presents an evaluation of ECC for four standard data sets manipulated to enable controlled comparisons with CNN for case bases with varying representativeness. We hypothesized that ECC would provide better competence retention than CNN as representativeness decreased and observed this in the results. We also hypothesized that ECC would not provide benefit for standard case bases and would even impose a competence penalty, due to ghost cases increasing the coverage density for non-representative problems at the expense of coverage density for representative problems. Surprisingly, however, ECC often improved competence retention even for standard case bases. We attribute this to the addition of ghost cases providing CNN with more extensive choices, enabling it to select a more effective mix of cases.

2   Background

2.1   Compressing the Case Base

A primary early motivation for case-base compression was the swamping utility problem for CBR (*e.g.,* [9,32,35]). As the case base grows, case retrieval costs generally increase, while case adaptation costs tend to decrease due to the increased similarity of retrieved cases. The swamping utility problem occurs when the increased retrieval cost swamps the adaptation cost savings. Recent arguments propose that current computing resources and limited case base sizes for many tasks can make this less important in practice [14]. However, CBR for domains such as big data health care (*e.g.,* [13]) and large-scale e-commerce, for which customer data can measure in the hundreds of millions of cases will continue to face challenges (cf. [15] for an alternative approach to addressing the utility problem, based on big data retrieval methods). Likewise, provenance capture for e-science can result in extremely large provenance cases [4] making case-base compression potentially important for sheer case size. In addition, controlling size can be important even without extreme size, if maintenance requires manual intervention or if the case-bases will be transmitted or replicated, as possible in distributed CBR.

2.2   Knowledge Container Transfer

The relationship of the four CBR knowledge containers—vocabulary, similarity measure, case base, and adaptation knowledge—has given rise to much research on knowledge container transfer, such as improving adaptation knowledge by transfer from cases [10, 16, 17, 28, 29, 36], and from adaptation knowledge to similarity [18]. Whenever a case-based problem-solver adapts a previous case and stores the result, it can be seen as transferring some of its adaptation knowledge into the case base, in a lazy manner, on demand. ECC, which generates ghost cases by adapting existing cases and adding them to the case base, can be seen as performing eager knowledge transfer from the adaptation component to the case base.

2.3   Exploration of the Problem Space Versus Exploitation of Cases in the Case Base

The notion of exploration versus exploitation concerns how an agent should allocate effort between exploiting existing resources versus exploring in search of others. The explore/exploit trade-off has proven a useful framework in many fields [12]. In traditional case-base maintenance, all maintenance effort is focused on exploitation of existing cases; the ECC process of generating ghost cases using adaptation knowledge explores the space of potential cases. ECC provides both existing cases and the fruits of exploration to CNN to select those cases expected to be most valuable in the compressed case base.

Contrasts Between Ghost Case Generation and Adaptation on Demand: Both ECC and normal CBR do adaptation, but the effect of ECC is different from simply compressing the original case base and adapting the retained cases to solve new problems. For ECC, the system selects new problems to solve. This could potentially be guided by trend detection, to hypothesize areas in which additional case coverage is especially important. For example, the system could note shifts in the types of problems the system is solving [37] to focus ghost case generation there.

When a CBR system adds ghost cases to the case base, it must do so without benefit of the feedback that often enables CBR systems to detect and repair solution flaws. Consequently, the solutions of ghost cases are not guaranteed to be correct. However, because the ghost case is generated in advance, there is an opportunity to seek confirmation of its solution to avoid future failure. (Note that even if the solution proposed by the ghost case remains unverified, and if later application of the ghost case results in an erroneous solution, the same failure would have occurred if the case had been adapted on the fly.)

Benefits of Exploration: Augmenting the case base with ghost cases prior to compression has four primary potential benefits:

1. Potential to improve competence preservation: We hypothesize that for less representative case bases, ECC will enable increased compression for a given competence retention level. We test this hypothesis in Sect. 6. (We expect results to depend on the representativeness of the original case base and on the density of the original case base: If the original case base covers only

a small region but all problems fall within that region, adding ghost cases for problems outside that region might exact a penalty as relevant cases are "crowded out" by the ghost cases.)

2. Potential to improve adaptation efficiency: If ECC applies a performance-based criterion for case retention that reflects not only competence but also adaptation cost [24], an ECC-compressed case base could enable more efficient problem-solving, by adding ghost cases useful for decreasing expected adaptation cost. Where adaptation is not fully reliable but reliability can be estimated by similarity distance, such ghost cases can be chosen to reduce expected average similarity distances, and, consequently, to increase expected solution reliability.

3. Potential to focus active learning/external pre-verification of adaptations: If case adaptation is unreliable, the quality of ghost cases is not guaranteed. However, by selecting useful ghost cases, ECC identifies good candidates for external case acquisition/verification. For example, an expert could be asked to provide the solutions to these problems, or to review system-generated solutions (this may be easier than solution generation, *e.g.*, verifying the routing of pipes in the design of a house is easier than finding a routing).

4. Potential to extend the reach of adaptation: Many CBR systems restrict the adaptation of any problem to a single adaptation step, limiting the problems they can solve (cf. [6]). When ghost cases are generated by applying an adaptation, future adaptations can start from that adapted state, effectively enabling two-step paths for adaptations going through that case. Generating ghost cases from longer adaptation paths further extends the range of problems and decreases adaptation costs.

3   The Expansion-Contraction Compression Algorithm

The ECC algorithm is described in Algorithm 1. Inputs to the algorithm include the maximum length of adaptation paths for generating ghost cases (*ghostSteps*) and the criterion for whether a case can be adapted to solve a given problem (*coverageCriterion*), which we implement as a similarity threshold. ECC first expands the case base by adapting selected cases, according to an adaptation procedure which selects adaptations to perform.

Because ECC performs adaptations in the absence of a specific problem to solve, many strategies are possible for choosing the adaptation, *e.g.*, selecting a random adaptation, selecting a high confidence adaptation, selecting an adaptation expected to produce the greatest difference between old and new solutions, etc. Also, when generating a ghost case, ECC must adjust not only the solution, but also the problem description of the case, to keep the new problem and solution consistent. The adjustment is derived from the problem description part of the chosen adaptation rule—if the rule normally addresses a given difference D between an input problem and a retrieved case, the problem part of the ghost case should be the problem of the current case, adjusted by D.

After generating ghost cases, ECC then compresses the expanded case base by CNN, presenting cases in order of decreasing coverage (other ordering criteria, such as relative coverage [34], could be used as well). If the resulting case base size is below the size limit, ECC "fills out" the additional capacity by adding cases up to the size limit, prioritized by estimated competence contribution.

Algorithm 1. The ECC Algorithm

Input:

caseBase: The case base to compress

ghostSteps: the maximum number of adaptation steps for generating ghost cases from the case base.

targetSize: the target number of cases in the compressed case base

coverageCriterion: test for whether a case can be adapted to solve another case

Output: Compressed case base

$expandedCaseBase \leftarrow caseBase$
$ghostCases \leftarrow \emptyset$
for $ghostLevel = 0$ to $ghostSteps$ **do**
   for all $case$ in $expandedCaseBase$ **do**
      $ghostCases \leftarrow ghostCases \cup adapt(case)$
   end for
   $expandedCaseBase \leftarrow expandedCaseBase \cup ghostCases$
end for
$expandedCaseBase \leftarrow sort(expandedCaseBase, coverage, descending)$
$contractedCaseBase \leftarrow cnn(expandedCaseBase, targetSize, coverageCriterion)$
$additionalCases \leftarrow limit(expandedCaseBase - contractedCaseBase,$
    $targetSize - size(contractedCaseBase))$
$contractedCaseBase \leftarrow contractedCaseBase \cup additionalCases$
return $contractedCaseBase$

---

4 Evaluation

4.1 Experimental Questions

To evaluate expansion-contraction compression, we considered five questions. For the first four, because our tests used standard domains without associated adaptation knowledge, we modeled adaptation based on similarity. Our experiments considered effects of compression on both competence (measured by number of test problems solved) and solution quality (average similarity between problems and the cases retrieved for them):

1. How does ECC affect preservation of quality compared to conventional competence-based compression, for varying levels of representativeness?
2. How does the ECC affect preservation of competence compared to conventional competence-based compression, for varying levels of representativeness?

3. How does the number of steps in the adaptation path to generate ghost cases affect competence retention of ECC, and how does competence compare to CNN?
4. How does sparsity of the initial case base affect the relative preservation of competence of ECC and CNN?

We then tested ECC in a standard domain augmented with automatically generated adaptation rules, to examine:

5. How does ECC affect preservation of competence, quality, and accuracy when applying generated adaptation rules?

5 Experimental Design

Data: The evaluation used five data sets: Houses, with 781 cases and 8 features, from the Datasets Wiki of the California Polytechnic University Computer Science Department [3], and four from the UCI Machine Learning Repository [8]: Iris, with 150 cases and 5 features, Wine, with 178 cases and 14 features, Car Evaluation, with 1,728 cases and 7 features, and Wine Quality, with 1,599 cases and 12 features.

Generating the Case Base and Problem Stream: Each trial partitioned each case base into three random subsets of equal size: (1) training cases (33%), (2) testing cases (33%), and (3) potential ghost cases (33%). Because of the random selection of the subsets, initially the training cases have normal representativeness for the data (the effectiveness of standard competence-based compression suggests that these are reasonably representative). To test the effect of decreased representativeness, one of the experimental conditions modifies the case bases to place a gap in a region of the case base (as might exist, for example, if cases reflected seasonally varying outcomes and no problems had yet been encountered for a particular season). The gap generation process picks a random case as the starting point for the gap, and then removes all of the problems from the training case base within a given similarity threshold (the gap radius). The testing cases and potential ghost cases remain in their original distribution, without an added gap.

Modeling Adaptation and Generating Ghost Cases: None of the data sets include adaptation knowledge. The first four experiments simulate adaptation-driven generation of ghost cases as follows. The experiment repeatedly picks a random case in the training data and filters the set of potential ghost cases for cases within a similarity threshold (the coverage criterion) required for adaptability from the selected training case. Those cases are then treated as the result of an adaptation and stored as ghost cases. This simulates deriving new cases by applying adaptation rules of limited power to the training case base. To test the effects of more powerful adaptation, additional experiments apply this process recursively, with selection of sequences of successive cases to simulate applying chains of one, two, or three adaptation steps.

Generating Adaptation Rules: For the fifth experiment, we applied the case difference heuristic approach [10] to automatically generate a set of adaptation rules from the data. These rules were then used to generate ghost cases by adaptation, rather than drawing on potential ghost cases as in experiments one through four.

Our rule generation approach repeatedly selects two random cases, ascribes the difference in their solutions to the difference in their problems, and forms a rule to apply the same difference to a solution. The rule is applied when the input problem and the problem of the retrieved case have a difference similar to the one from which the rule was generated. Given a problem and retrieved case, the single rule for the most similar difference was applied. For similarity, categorical features in problem descriptions were only considered to match if identical. The rules adjusted the solution values by the proportional difference of the solution values of the cases from which they were generated.

Experimental Procedure: Compression by condensed nearest neighbor [11] was compared to compression by ECC. For comparisons with CNN, we use a version of CNN that, like ECC, "fills out" the case base up to the size limit, so that both methods have access to the same number of cases.

For both ECC and CNN, cases were sorted in descending order of coverage. Compression was done in steps of 10% from 100% to 10% of the size of the uncompressed case base. Each level of compression starts from the uncompressed case base (not the result of the previous level of compression). Each experiment runs for ten trials with different randomly chosen partitions, with results averaged over those runs.

6   Experimental Results

Q1: Relative preservation of quality for different representativeness levels: Figure 1 compares the absolute quality between CNN and ECC strategies for the Houses case base. The coverage criterion for deriving ghost cases and solving testing problems is 5%. Each of the four graphs in Fig. 1 uses a different value for the gap radius. When there is no gap, this value is 0%, a small gap is 5%, a medium gap is 10%, and a large gap is 20%. The size of the gap is measured not in the number of cases that the experiment can remove but in the similarity distance to the most different case that the experiment can remove. The horizontal axis shows the proportionate case base size of the compressed case base, ranging from 100% to 10% in steps of 10%.

In all four graphs of Fig. 1, ECC uses adaptation paths with a maximum length of two steps. The vertical axis shows the quality of the compressed case base. Note that similarity of a retrieved case counts towards the average quality even when the coverage criterion is not met. Quality can fall anywhere in the range from 0 to 1, inclusive. The top and bottom graphs use different scales for the vertical axis (0.91 to 0.97 on the top, and 0.87 to 0.95 on the bottom) in order to "zoom in" on the difference between the strategies.

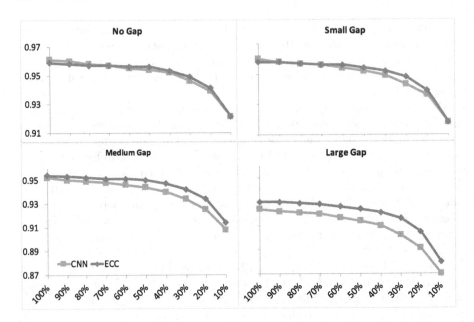

Fig. 1. Absolute quality for condensed nearest neighbor and expansion-contraction compression on House data set, for four different gap sizes in the training data.)

When the training case base has no gap (top left), CNN outperforms ECC from 100% to 80% of the size of the original case base. However, from 70% to 10% size, ECC leads. Because neither the set of training cases nor the set of testing problems has a gap, the training case base is expected to be approximately representative of the testing problems. Therefore, in this graph, we believe that the addition of ghost cases cannot be improving quality by improving representativeness, and must be doing so simply by providing a wider pool of cases from which CNN can select alternatives. This was a small effect, but the benefit of the increased choice is an interesting result that contradicted our initial hypothesis. The Question 2 results show a similar but more dramatic effect on competence.

When the training case base has a small gap (top right), CNN outperforms ECC only at 100% of the size of the original case base. Thereafter, from 90% to 10%, the expansion-contraction strategy leads. For the medium (bottom left) and large gap (bottom right), ECC dominates CNN throughout. Overall, as the size of the gap increases, and the training case base less represents the testing problems, the quality difference increases between CNN and ECC. This suggests that part of the benefit comes from the choice of additional cases for retention (as with the no-gap graph in the top left), and that part of the benefit comes from correction for nonrepresentativeness.

Q2: Relative preservation of competence for different representativeness levels: Figure 2 compares the relative competence between CNN and ECC. The results are based on using the Houses case base and a coverage cri-

terion of 5% both for deriving ghost cases and for solving testing problems. As
for Figs. 1 and 2 includes four graphs showing different sizes for the gap in the
training case base, and the horizontal axis shows the size of the case base. However, in Fig. 2, the vertical axis shows the relative competence, the ratio of the
observed competence to the maximum competence observed with any strategy
and any case base size (intuitively, the maximum competence might be expected
to be at maximum size, but this need not always hold). The top and bottom
graphs use different scales for the vertical axis (60% to 100% on the top, and
20% to 100% on the bottom) in order to "zoom in" on the difference between
the strategies.

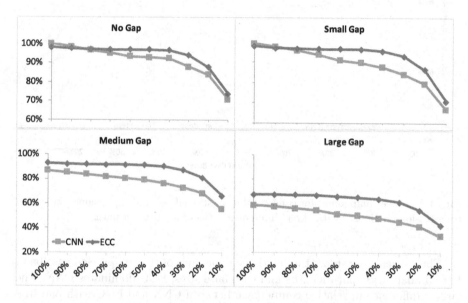

Fig. 2. Relative competence for condensed nearest neighbor and expansion-contraction
compression on Houses data set with four different representativeness levels

As shown in the no gap (top left) and small gap (top right) graphs, CNN
outperforms ECC at 100% and 90% of the size of the original case base. Thereafter, from 80% to 10%, ECC leads over condensed nearest neighbor. For the
medium gap (bottom left) and large gap (bottom right) graphs, ECC dominates
CNN throughout all case base sizes. The amount of the difference between the
strategies increases as the size of the gap increases.

**Question 3: Effect of length of adaptation path for generating ghost
cases:** Figure 3 presents the relative competence using CNN and ECC for the
Houses case base. The gap radius for this figure is 20% (a large gap). The coverage criterion for deriving ghost cases and solving testing problems is 5%, i.e.,
simulated adaptations can adapt solutions to address problem differences of up to
5%. Therefore, an adaptation path could require up to four steps to cross the

gap. The horizontal axis shows the relative size of the case base decreasing from 100% to 10% in steps of 10%. Each of the lines shows a different upper limit to the number of adaptations in the adaptation path to derive ghost cases. No adaptation, which is equivalent to CNN, is the baseline strategy.

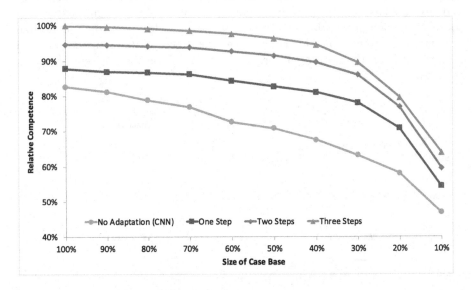

Fig. 3. Relative competence for condensed nearest neighbor and expansion-contraction compression on Houses with three different lengths of adaptation paths

The vertical axis shows the relative competence of the compressed case base. For all adaptation path lengths and case base sizes, ECC dominates CNN. The largest difference in relative competence between CNN and ECC with one step of adaptation is 15% at 30% of the size of the original case base. The smallest difference between these two strategies is 5.1% at 100% size. The relative competence for each adaptation path length varies consistently, with longer paths associated with greater competence retention. The largest difference in relative competence between CNN and ECC with three steps of adaptation is 27% at 40% of the size of the original case base. The smallest difference is 17% at 10% size.

Question 4: Effect of case base sparsity: Figure 4 compares the relative competence between CNN and ECC with a sparse case base; the sparse case base models a case base in the early phases of case base growth. The basic presentation of results follows Fig. 2, but the underlying experiment uses different proportions for the partitions for training, testing, and ghost cases. As described in the experimental design (Sect. 5), the partitions for Figs. 1, 2, and 3 are equal thirds, but for Fig. 4, the proportions are 10% training, 70% testing, and 20% potential ghost cases. The competence trend resembles Fig. 2 but decreases more steeply because the case base begins with fewer cases.

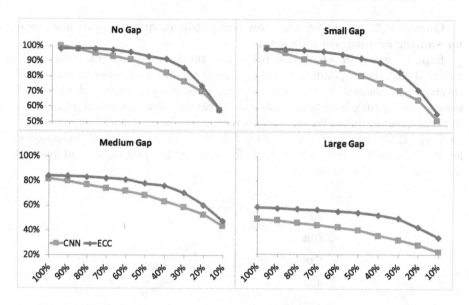

Fig. 4. Relative competence for condensed nearest neighbor and expansion-contraction compression on Houses with a sparse initial case base and four different representativeness levels

Table 1 shows the relative competence difference between CNN and ECC on five different case bases, each modified by adding a medium gap in the training data, making it non-representative. For all five, the gap radius is set to twice the coverage criterion (for House, this corresponds to the lower left graph in Fig. 2). ECC outperformed CNN on four of the five case bases (Houses, Iris, Wine, and Wine Quality), but not on Car Evaluation. This suggests that the expansion-contraction strategy might benefit compression across many domains and raises the question of which factors determine whether it will be beneficial.

Table 1. Difference in relative competence between ECC and CNN on five different case bases

Case base	No compression	33% compression	67% compression
Houses	6.6%	11.2%	15.8%
Iris	1.2%	7.6%	7.0%
Wine	2.8%	9.6%	13.4%
Car evaluation	−3.5%	0.0%	−8.0%
Wine quality (Red)	9.4%	13.4%	14.9%

Question 5: Effect of ECC on competence, quality, and accuracy for sample adaptation rule sets:

Experiments with adaptation rules used the Houses data set, with a gap radius of 20% (corresponding to a large gap in the previous experiments), a 5% coverage criterion, and 40 automatically-generated rules for each trial. ECC used the adaptation rules both to generate ghost cases and to adapt solutions. Figure 5 shows the average preservation of competence and quality during compression by ECC and CNN. ECC outperformed CNN in both dimensions at all compression levels. Thus ECC was beneficial both for modeled adaptation and adaptation with generated adaptation rules.

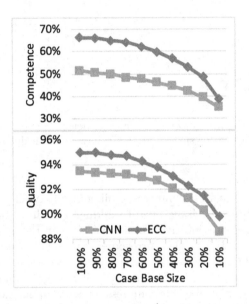

Fig. 5. Competence and quality for ECC and CNN on Houses data with adaptation rules.

7 Future Work

In our experiments, ghost case generation is an unguided process, generating ghost cases from randomly-selected cases using randomly-generated adaptations. In addition, ghost cases are generated within neighborhoods of existing cases, making ghost cases most likely to be added near regions that are already densely populated. Ghost cases can be useful there, for example, as spanning cases [33], bridging two competence regions. However, such placement may not help to populate a distant sparse region. Identifying and targeting sparse regions on which to focus ghost case generation might increase the benefit of ECC. On the other hand, populating such regions might be detrimental if representativeness generally holds. Thus determining guidance strategies for ghost case generation and assessing their effects is an interesting area for future study.

For example, areas to target for ghost generation could be selected by dividing the case base into regions and applying Monte Carlo methods to assess case base density [25]. Another interesting direction would be to develop maintenance strategies that tracked, reasoned about, and responded to expected future case distributions, to explicitly determine the expected utility of exploring areas of the unseen case space.

8 Conclusion

This paper proposed a new approach to case-base compression, Expansion-Contraction Compression (ECC), aimed at achieving better competence retention when the representativeness assumption may not hold. The ECC approach contrasts with previous approaches, which focus on how best to exploit the cases in the case base, in going outside problems addressed by the case base to explore the larger problem space as licensed by case adaptation knowledge. ECC can be seen as applying a knowledge container transfer strategy: It uses adaptation knowledge to generate new case knowledge, ghost cases, which are then added to the pool of cases available to the compression algorithm. Chosen ghost cases can be retained as-is or can be used to guide verification or active learning of new cases. Experiments support the expected result of ECC improving competence retention for less-representative case bases. Surprisingly, ECC also often improved competence retention even for standard case bases. Thus the ECC approach appears promising. Interesting questions remain for studying factors affecting ECC performance and guiding ghost case generation to maximize the effectiveness of ECC.

References

1. Angiulli, F.: Fast condensed nearest neighbor rule. In: Proceedings of the Twenty-second International Conference on Machine Learning, pp. 25–32. ACM, New York (2005)
2. Brighton, H., Mellish, C.: Identifying competence-critical instances for instance-based learners. In: Liu, H., Motoda, H. (eds.) Instance Selection and Construction for Data Mining, vol. 608, pp. 77–94. Springer, Berlin (2001). https://doi.org/10.1007/978-1-4757-3359-4_5
3. Houses Data Set, May 2009. https://wiki.csc.calpoly.edu/datasets/wiki/Houses
4. Cheah, Y.-W., Plale, B., Kendall-Morwick, J., Leake, D., Ramakrishnan, L.: A noisy 10GB provenance database. In: Daniel, F., Barkaoui, K., Dustdar, S. (eds.) BPM 2011. LNBIP, vol. 100, pp. 370–381. Springer, Heidelberg (2012). https://doi.org/10.1007/978-3-642-28115-0_35
5. Cunningham, P., Nowlan, N., Delany, S., Haahr, M.: A case-based approach to spam filtering that can track concept drift. Technical report. TCD-CS-2003-16, Computer Science Department, Trinity College Dublin (2003)

6. D'Aquin, M., Lieber, J., Napoli, A.: Adaptation knowledge acquisition: a case study for case-based decision support in oncology. Comput. Intell. **22**(3/4), 161–176 (2006)

7. Delany, S.J., Cunningham, P.: An analysis of case-base editing in a spam filtering system. In: Funk, P., González Calero, P.A. (eds.) ECCBR 2004. LNCS, vol. 3155, pp. 128–141. Springer, Heidelberg (2004). https://doi.org/10.1007/978-3-540-28631-8_11

8. Dheeru, D., Karra Taniskidou, E.: UCI Machine Learning Repository (2017). http://archive.ics.uci.edu/ml

9. Francis, A.G., Ram, A.: A comparative utility analysis of case-based reasoning and control-rule learning systems. In: Lavrac, N., Wrobel, S. (eds.) ECML 1995. LNCS, vol. 912, pp. 138–150. Springer, Heidelberg (1995). https://doi.org/10.1007/3-540-59286-5_54

10. Hanney, K., Keane, M.T.: Learning adaptation rules from a case-base. In: Smith, I., Faltings, B. (eds.) EWCBR 1996. LNCS, vol. 1168, pp. 179–192. Springer, Heidelberg (1996). https://doi.org/10.1007/BFb0020610

11. Hart, P.E.: The condensed nearest neighbor rule. IEEE Trans. Inf. Theory **14**, 515–516 (1968)

12. Hills, T., Todd, P., Lazer, D., Redish, A., Couzin, I.: Exploration versus exploitation in space, mind, and society. Trends Cogn. Sci. **19**(1), 46–54 (2015)

13. Hoover, W.: Transforming health care through big data. Technical report, Institute for Health Technology Transformation (2013)

14. Houeland, T.G., Aamodt, A.: The Utility problem for lazy learners - towards a non-eager approach. In: Bichindaritz, I., Montani, S. (eds.) ICCBR 2010. LNCS, vol. 6176, pp. 141–155. Springer, Heidelberg (2010). https://doi.org/10.1007/978-3-642-14274-1_12

15. Jalali, V., Leake, D.: Harnessing hundreds of millions of cases: case-based prediction at industrial scale. In: Ram, A., Wiratunga, N. (eds.) Case-Based Reasoning Research and Development, ICCBR 2018, vol. 6880. Springer, Berlin (2018). https://doi.org/10.1007/978-3-642-23291-6

16. Jalali, V., Leake, D., Forouzandehmehr, N.: Ensemble of adaptations for classification: learning adaptation rules for categorical features. In: Goel, A., Díaz-Agudo, M.B., Roth-Berghofer, T. (eds.) ICCBR 2016. LNCS, vol. 9969, pp. 186–202. Springer, Cham (2016). https://doi.org/10.1007/978-3-319-47096-2_13

17. Jalali, V., Leake, D.: Extending case adaptation with automatically-generated ensembles of adaptation rules. In: Delany, S.J., Ontañón, S. (eds.) ICCBR 2013. LNCS, vol. 7969, pp. 188–202. Springer, Heidelberg (2013). https://doi.org/10.1007/978-3-642-39056-2_14

18. Leake, D., Kinley, A., Wilson, D.: Linking adaptation and similarity learning. In: Proceedings of the Eighteenth Annual Conference of the Cognitive Science Society, pp. 591–596. Lawrence Erlbaum, Mahwah (1996)

19. Leake, D., Schack, B.: Flexible feature deletion: compacting case bases by selectively compressing case contents. In: Hüllermeier, E., Minor, M. (eds.) ICCBR 2015. LNCS, vol. 9343, pp. 212–227. Springer, Cham (2015). https://doi.org/10.1007/978-3-319-24586-7_15

20. Leake, D., Schack, B.: Adaptation-guided feature deletion: testing recoverability to guide case compression. In: Goel, A., Díaz-Agudo, M.B., Roth-Berghofer, T. (eds.) ICCBR 2016. LNCS, vol. 9969, pp. 234–248. Springer, Cham (2016). https://doi.org/10.1007/978-3-319-47096-2_16

21. Leake, D., Sooriamurthi, R.: Managing multiple case-bases: dimensions and issues. In: Proceedings of the Fifteenth International Florida Artificial Intelligence Research Society Conference, pp. 106–110. AAAI Press, Menlo Park (2002)

22. Leake, D., Whitehead, M.: Case provenance: the value of remembering case sources. In: Weber, R.O., Richter, M.M. (eds.) ICCBR 2007. LNCS, vol. 4626, pp. 194–208. Springer, Heidelberg (2007). https://doi.org/10.1007/978-3-540-74141-1_14

23. Leake, D.B., Wilson, D.C.: When experience is wrong: examining CBR for changing tasks and environments. In: Althoff, K.-D., Bergmann, R., Branting, L.K. (eds.) ICCBR 1999. LNCS, vol. 1650, pp. 218–232. Springer, Heidelberg (1999). https://doi.org/10.1007/3-540-48508-2_16

24. Leake, D.B., Wilson, D.C.: Remembering why to remember: performance-guided case-base maintenance. In: Blanzieri, E., Portinale, L. (eds.) EWCBR 2000. LNCS, vol. 1898, pp. 161–172. Springer, Heidelberg (2000). https://doi.org/10.1007/3-540-44527-7_15

25. Leake, D., Wilson, M.: How many cases do you need? Assessing and predicting case-base coverage. In: Ram, A., Wiratunga, N. (eds.) ICCBR 2011. LNCS, vol. 6880, pp. 92–106. Springer, Heidelberg (2011). https://doi.org/10.1007/978-3-642-23291-6_9

26. Lu, N., Zhang, G., Lu, J.: Concept drift detection via competence models. Artif. Intell. **209**, 11–28 (2014)

27. Mathew, D., Chakraborti, S.: Competence guided model for casebase maintenance. In: Proceedings of the Twenty-Sixth International Joint Conference on Artificial Intelligence, pp. 4904–4908. International Joint Conferences on Artificial Intelligence (2017)

28. McDonnell, N., Cunningham, P.: A Knowledge-light approach to regression using case-based reasoning. In: Roth-Berghofer, T.R., Göker, M.H., Güvenir, H.A. (eds.) ECCBR 2006. LNCS, vol. 4106, pp. 91–105. Springer, Heidelberg (2006). https://doi.org/10.1007/11805816_9

29. McSherry, D.: An adaptation heuristic for case-based estimation. In: Smyth, B., Cunningham, P. (eds.) EWCBR 1998. LNCS, vol. 1488, pp. 184–195. Springer, Heidelberg (1998). https://doi.org/10.1007/BFb0056332

30. Plaza, E., McGinty, L.: Distributed case-based reasoning. Knowl. Eng. Rev. **20**(3), 315–320 (2005)

31. Richter, M.: Knowledge Containers (2005). http://pages.cpsc.ucalgary.ca/mrichter/Papers/Knowledge%20Containers.pdf

32. Smyth, B., Cunningham, P.: The utility problem analysed. In: Smith, I., Faltings, B. (eds.) EWCBR 1996. LNCS, vol. 1168, pp. 392–399. Springer, Heidelberg (1996). https://doi.org/10.1007/BFb0020625

33. Smyth, B., Keane, M.: Remembering to forget: a competence-preserving case deletion policy for case-based reasoning systems. In: Proceedings of the Thirteenth International Joint Conference on Artificial Intelligence, pp. 377–382. Morgan Kaufmann, San Mateo (1995)

34. Smyt, B., McKenna, E.: Footprint-based retrieval. In: Althoff, K.-D., Bergmann, R., Branting, L.K. (eds.) ICCBR 1999. LNCS, vol. 1650, pp. 343–357. Springer, Heidelberg (1999). https://doi.org/10.1007/3-540-48508-2_25
35. van Someren, M., Surma, J., Torasso, P.: A utility-based approach to learning in a mixed case-based and model-based reasoning architecture. In: Proceedings of the Second International Conference on Case-Based Reasoning, pp. 477–488. Springer, Berlin (1997)
36. Wilke, W., Vollrath, I., Bergmann, R.: Using knowledge containers to model a framework for learning adaptation knowledge. In: ECML Workshop Notes. LIS, Faculty of Informatics and Statistics (1998)
37. Wilson, D., Leake, D.: Maintaining case-based reasoners: dimensions and directions. Comput. Intell. **17**(2), 196–213 (2001)
38. Wilson, D., Martinez, T.: Reduction techniques for instance-based learning algorithms. Mach. Learn. **38**(3), 257–286 (2000)

Dynamic Detection of Radical Profiles in Social Networks Using Image Feature Descriptors and a Case-Based Reasoning Methodology

Daniel López-Sánchez[1]([⊠]), Juan M. Corchado[1,2], and Angélica González Arrieta[1]

[1] BISITE Digital Innovation Hub,
University of Salamanca. Edificio Multiusos I+D+i, 37007 Salamanca, Spain
{lope,corchado,angelica}@usal.es
[2] Osaka Institute of Technology, Osaka, Japan

Abstract. Nowadays, security forces are challenged by a new type of terrorist propaganda which occurs in public social networks and targets vulnerable individuals. The current volume of online radicalization messages has rendered manual monitoring approaches unfeasible, and effective countermeasures can only be adopted through early detection by automatized tools. Some approaches focus on mining the information provided by social users in the form of interactions and textual content. However, radical users also tend to exhibit distinctive iconography in their profile images. In this work, we propose the use of local image descriptors over profile images to aid the detection and monitoring of online radicalization processes. In addition, we complement this approach with an interaction-based formula for risk assessment, so candidate profiles can be selected for image-analysis based on their interaction with confirmed radical profiles. These techniques are combined in the context of a Case-Based Reasoning framework which, together with the feedback provided by the end-user, enables a continuous monitoring of the activity of radical users and eases the discovery of new profiles with a radicalization agenda.

Keywords: Image analysis · Social network analysis · Security

1 Introduction

In the recent years, several terrorist groups have started to make an intensive use of the Internet and various online social networks to spread their message and radicalize vulnerable individuals [8]. Their goal involves encouraging others, especially young people, to support their terrorist organizations, to take part in the conflicts of Middle East and even to commit acts of violence in western countries when traveling is not possible. For this reason, terrorist propaganda

© Springer Nature Switzerland AG 2018
M. T. Cox et al. (Eds.): ICCBR 2018, LNAI 11156, pp. 219–232, 2018.
https://doi.org/10.1007/978-3-030-01081-2_15

targets young western individuals and adopts their channels of communication and language. In this context, security forces are in charge of detecting and monitor ongoing radicalization processes, which often take place publicly, in social networks such as Twitter. Unfortunately, effective countermeasures can only be taken through early detection, which is not always possible due to the growing amount of information to be analyzed [6]. Motivated by this challenge, several researchers have turned their attention towards the problem of automatic detection of online radicalization processes and extremist profiles. In addition, several studies have been conducted trying to provide insight into the habits and language patterns used by radical profiles to spread their radical ideology.

In this paper, we focus on the task of radical user sub-network detection and monitoring in Twitter. In this scenario, a number of related radical social network profiles are manually identified, and the system must monitor their activity in the social network in order to (1) identify other radical profiles who share their radicalization agenda and (2) identify vulnerable users surrounding the sub-network of radical profiles who might be in risk of radicalization. Therefore, the input of the system is a set of confirmed radical users along with a reference image of the corresponding radical iconography, and its output is a prioritized list with suggestions of new radical users, which evolves as the monitored radical users interact with adjacent profiles in the social network and new profiles are added to the monitoring system after their extremist nature is confirmed by an human expert. As discussed later, this cyclic process of radical profile suggestion, confirmation by the human expert and automatic monitoring can be naturally modeled as a Case-Based Reasoning (CBR) methodology. This early detection of radicalization processes and new extremist profiles seeks to enable security forces to adopt countermeasures in a timely manner, while also reducing the amount of time human experts have to spend manually monitoring the activity of radicals in social networks. In particular, our proposed framework is based on two types of techniques; namely an interaction-based candidate profile selection process and an image-analysis mechanism to prioritize candidate profiles. Our experimental results focus on comparing different image-description algorithms in the context of radical iconography detection. In addition, we provide an example case study with a group of ISIS-supporting accounts.

2   Related Work

With the emergence of the online-radicalization phenomenon, several researchers have turned their attention towards the problem of automatic detection of online radicalization processes and profiles. Particularly, several studies have been conducted trying to provide insight into the habits and language patterns used by radical profiles to spread their radical ideology. For instance, in [7] the authors manually identified a set of radical Youtube profiles and used different social network and natural language processing techniques to analyze the messages they published in the social network. This study revealed significant gender differences in the language and habits of radical users. Other authors have focused on the automatic detection of radical profiles. Most of these proposals focus solely on the textual content of individual publications, rather than analyzing the social interactions between confirmed radical users and users in risk of radicalization. For example, in [2] the authors adopted a machine-learning classification approach to detect ideologically extremist tweets based on linguistic and stylistic text features. However, in the recent years it has become apparent that, in order to fully characterize the behavior of radical social network users, it is necessary to consider not only the textual content of messages but also the patterns in the interactions between social users. It has been shown that users in social networks interact in a homophilic manner [10]; that is, they tend to maintain relationships with people who are similar to themselves, as characterized by age, race, gender, religion and ideology. For instance, in [12] the authors analyzed different community detection techniques to cluster users according to their political preferences, showing that users in the social network Twitter tend to form very cohesive networks when talking about political issues.

More recently, researches have started to focus on the potential of mining visual content from social networks and profile images specifically [14]. For instance, some researchers suggest that profile images can even be used to estimate the intelligence of users [16]. Other authors have proposed using image analysis to detect bullying in image-centered social networks such as Instagram [17]. While image analysis might not entirely replace text and interaction-based methods, it has become increasingly clear that profile images contain a lot of information which can be key for many automated social network analysis tasks.

Regarding the use of a CBR methodology, several authors have proposed applying this methodology to deal with terrorism-related issues due to its adaptation capabilities and the importance of learning from past experiences in this domain. Some examples include the use of a case-based approach for modeling and simulating terrorist decision-making processes [15], or to support emergency decision makers in the event of a terrorist attack [4].

3   Proposed Framework

As mentioned before, the goal of our Case-Based Reasoning (CBR) framework is to produce a dynamic list of possible radical users, which must be revised by human experts in order to confirm their radical nature. This list of suggested users is generated and updated over-time based on a set of confirmed radical users who are monitored by the platform. Figure 1 shows the overall architecture of the proposed framework. As shown in the schematic view, the core of the framework is the Interaction Case-Base. Essentially, the Interaction Case-Base stores the most recent publications made by the set of monitored radical users, along with their profile meta-data which includes their lists of followings and followers.

As opposed to the standard CBR workflow, where the retrieve stage is triggered by the arrival of a new case which must be solved, the CBR phases in our framework are executed periodically, as new information is added to the Interaction Case-Base. In particular, the system works is the following manner:

First, the human expert provides the framework with an initial set of radical users to be monitored, and a reference image displaying the typical iconography associated to the target radical ideology. With this information, the system initializes the interaction Case-Base by extracting all the available publications of the monitored users from Twitter's API. Then, the CBR stages are triggered for the first time. More details about the role of each stage are provided in the following sections, but essentially the retrieve and reuse stages use the Interaction Case-Base and image analysis methods to provide the human expert with a set of possible radical users somehow related to the ones currently being monitored. In the revise and retain stages, the human expert decides whether the suggested profiles should be incorporated into the group of monitored users. In addition, a periodical update mechanism keeps the Interaction Case-Base updated by downloading the latest publications of the monitored users. The Retrive and Reuse stages are also executed periodically, so the list of suggested candidate profiles for the human expert is updated dynamically as the monitored users engage with other profiles and exhibit new interactions.

Apart from generating the list of candidate radical profiles, the information stored in the Interaction Case-Base can be used to produce different visualizations which provide insight into how radical users behave in the social network, their publication rates, relationships, etc. In addition, it is possible to create alerts to notify the human experts managing the system when the monitored users publish a message containing a certain keyword.

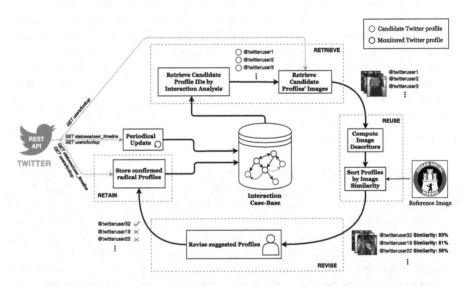

Fig. 1. Architecture of the proposed CBR framework. The primary goal of the system is to provide the human expert with a dynamically updated list of possible radical profiles, based on the set of confirmed radical profiles being monitored and a reference image.

3.1   Retrieve Stage

As mentioned before, our framework deals with the task of monitoring a set of confirmed radical users with the goal of identifying new radical users or users under an immediate risk of radicalization. In this context, our system works under the assumption that new radical profiles can often be discovered by looking at the profile images of adjacent[1] users. However, trying to analyze the profile images of all the users who have interacted in some manner with one of the monitored radical profiles is too inefficient. Consider that, very often, Twitter profiles have thousands of followers. Furthermore, we are not only limited by the computational power required to analyze the profile images but also by the rate-limits of Twitter's API, which imposes a maximum number of requests per hour. For this reason, our framework applies a prior stage to image analysis where a number of candidate profiles are selected based on their interaction with the monitored radical users. Conveniently, once the information about the monitored users (i.e., their followers, tweets, followings, etc.) has been downloaded and stored into the Interaction Case-Base, the candidate adjacent profiles can be identified without any further query to the social network's API.

Interaction Case-Base

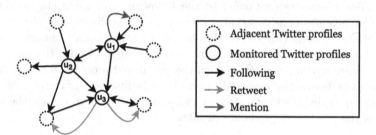

Fig. 2. Contents of the Interaction Case-Base represented as a directed graph with different types of arcs and nodes.

Formally, at a particular point in time the Interaction Case-Base consists of a set of monitored user profiles $\{u_1, u_2, \cdots, u_n\}$ for which their followers, followings and tweets have been extracted from Twitter's API. The tweets published by the monitored users are analyzed, identifying re-tweets $\{RT_1, RT_2, \cdots, RT_r\}$ and mentions $\{M_1, M_2, \cdots, M_m\}$ (see Fig. 2). Then, the prioritized list of adjacent users is generated by scoring each user profile which has interacted with the monitored users according to the following formula:

---

[1] In this context, adjacent profiles are social users who have recently interacted with the set of confirmed radical users under monitoring (e.g., their followers, mentioned users, users who retweet their posts, etc.).

$$Score(u) = \sum_{i=1}^{n} follows(u, u_i) + \sum_{i=1}^{n} follows(u_i, u) \tag{1}$$

$$+ \sum_{i=1}^{r} RT_i.to(u) + \sum_{i=1}^{m} M_i.to(u) \cdot |sentiment(M_i)|$$

Note that the contribution of mentions to the overall score is weighted by the absolute value of the automatically estimated sentiment of the mention's text. This reflects the informal observation that mentions with a strong sentimental load (either positive or negative) may indicate a more personal interaction. To estimate the sentiment of mentions $sentiment(M_i) \in [-1, 1]$ our framework uses the automatic sentiment analysis tool SentiStrength[2], which is compatible with a variety of languages [13]. As mentioned before, the major advantage of this scoring approach is that, once the information of the monitored users has been extracted form Twitter, the score of adjacent users can be computed without any further query to Twitter's API.

Once the list of users which have interacted with the group of monitored radical profiles has been sorted according to the above described score, the k top candidate users are selected for further analysis. In general, increasing k will improve the chances of detecting new relevant profiles. However, the number k of profiles which are forwarded to the following processing stages must be selected taking into consideration Twitter's API rate limits and the available computational power. Our interaction-based scoring approach guarantees that the k candidate profiles analyzed by the subsequent stages are the ones which exhibit a more intense interaction with the monitored profiles, thus maximizing the chances of discovering new radical profiles. The final step of the retrieve stage consists of querying Twitter's API *users/lookup* endpoint to obtain the profile images of the k selected candidate profiles.

3.2   Reuse Stage

The reuse stage of the proposed CBR framework is in charge of sorting the k candidate profiles selected in the retrieve stage based on the presence of radical iconography in their profile images. To achieve this, our framework uses a local feature description algorithm to compare candidates' profile images with a reference image provided by the human expert using the system. Over the years, numerous local feature descriptors have been proposed. Some of the most popular alternatives include:

- Scale-Invariant Feature Transform (SIFT), introduced in [9], is arguably one of the most effective and widely used local image descriptors. The major drawback of this algorithm is its computational cost, being significantly slower than alternative methods.

---

[2] http://sentistrength.wlv.ac.uk/.

- Root-SIFT, popularized by a 2012 paper [5], is a simple extension of the SIFT descriptor which can potentially boost the results by simply L1-normalizing the SIFT descriptors and taking the square root of each element.
- Speeded Up Robust Features (SURF), proposed in [11], was conceived as a faster alternative to SIFT which sacrificed little or none of the accuracy of its predecessor. Nowadays SURF is almost as popular as SIFT, and the results for both methods are comparable with the exception that SURF is thought to be slightly faster.
- Oriented FAST and Rotated BRIEF (ORB), introduced more recently [11], is a computationally efficient alternative to SIFT and SURF. In addition, as opposed to SIFT and SURF, ORB is not patented so it is free to use. The major difference with SIFT and SURF is that ORB uses binary descriptors to achieve its remarkable efficiency.
- Accelerated-KAZE (AKAZE) was proposed as a faster version of KAZE [3] seeking to emulate the efficiency of methods like ORB while reducing the effectiveness gap with SIFT and SURF.

In Sect. 4, we present experimental results suggesting that among these local feature descriptors SIFT is the best performing alternative, with the possible drawback of being computationally demanding. Nevertheless, they can be used interchangeably since they all work in an analogous way. Essentially, the reuse stage of our framework performs the following operations:

- First, each profile image of the candidate users is analyzed to detect the key-points. These are points in the image with a characteristic visual appearance than can be useful to detect similar images. In this regard, each compared descriptor has its own key-point detection strategy and more information can be found in the corresponding references.
- Secondly, a feature descriptor is generated for each key-point. The descriptors are vectors of fixed-length whose contents describe the appearance of the previously detected key-points.
- Then, to determine the presence of the selected radical iconography in a profile image, the descriptors of both the reference and the profile images are compared finding the best matches in terms of Euclidean distances (or normalized Hamming distances for ORB) between the descriptors. Valid matches are determined using the ratio test proposed by Lowe in [9] with a 0.8 threshold.
- The candidate profiles are sorted according to the number of valid matches. A threshold can be set to determine which profile images contain the reference radical iconography.

Figure 3 shows the result of the above described matching process on a reference and target image. The red polygon of the image on the right side shows the estimated position and perspective of the detected iconography. This is achieved by computing an estimated homography matrix for the point matches between the reference and the target image. Note that this is only computed to improve the explainability of the recommendations of the system, since the candidate profiles are prioritized simply based on the number of matches. For more details

Fig. 3. Example matching of a reference image (left) with a real-world image containing radical iconography (right). The matches found with the SIFT algorithm are depicted in green. The red polygon corresponds to the automatically estimated position of the reference image (found using homography estimation from key-point matches). (Color figure online)

about the homography calculation process see [1]. After executing these steps, the reuse stage provides the human expert with a prioritized list of twitter users whose profile images contain radical iconography.

3.3   Revise and Retain Stages and the Periodical Update Mechanism

Once the human expert receives the prioritized list of candidate profiles, he can manually revise the suggested profiles to determine whether some of them should be incorporated into the set of monitored radical users. The profiles selected to be incorporated into the monitoring process by the human expert are forwarded to the retain stage, which emits a series of queries to Twitter's API *statuses/user_timeline* endpoint, extracting their published tweets and incorporating them into the Interaction Case-Base.

As mentioned before, a very important feature of the proposed framework is its ability to keep an updated record of the Interactions generated by the monitored users in the social network. This is achieved by periodically polling Twitter's API for updates and new published tweets by the monitored users. The new tweets and meta-data are then incorporated to the Interaction Case-Base, so they are taken into consideration during the next execution of the CBR stages, possibly altering the list of suggested radical users.

4   Experimental Results

To evaluate the accuracy of the different image descriptors considered in the previous section, we collected a dataset of real-word occurrences of radical iconography. In particular, we selected three radical groups with characteristic iconography. Namely the Islamic State (ISIS), Golden Dawn (GD) and "Hogar Social Madrid" (HSM). First, we selected a representative image for the iconography of each group. These are the images that the human experts might provide to our tool as the reference. The selected reference images are shown in Fig. 4, alongside with their detected key-points (SIFT).

GD   ISIS   HSM

Fig. 4. Reference images for Golden Dawn, Islamic State and "Hogar Social Madrid" (left to right), and key-points as detected by the SIFT algorithm (second row).

After selecting the reference images, we collected a database with real-world occurrences of the corresponding radical symbols. In total, we collected 300 images distributed over 50 GD images, 90 ISIS images and 90 HSM images. Additionally, 70 images were collected containing no occurrence of the reference symbols. These 70 images were selected from a variety of topics to account for the inherent variability of online images. Figure 5 shows some sample images from each category. To evaluate the different feature descriptors discussed in the previous section, we computed the descriptors of each of the reference images, and then used them to try to retrieve all the images with the same iconography from the collected dataset by executing the steps described in Sect. 3.2. In each experiment, the images containing iconography of the same group as the reference image were considered as positive, while images containing iconography of other groups were considered as negative together with the images containing no iconography at all. For each experiment, we computed the ROC curves (Fig. 6) and the corresponding AUCs (Table 1). Another important aspect to consider when selecting the feature description algorithm is the computational efficiency. In this regard, Table 2 provides the time required by each algorithm to process the 300 images in our dataset, along with the average number of key-points detected per image. Surprisingly, SURF was slower than SIFT, while it was originally proposed as a faster variant of SIFT. The reason for this might be that, in this case, SURF detected 26% more key-points on average than SIFT, so more descriptors had to be computed. In addition, it has been suggested that the implementation of SURF in the OpenCV library we used could be further optimized[3].

---

[3] http://boofcv.org/index.php?title=Performance:SURF.

GD   ISIS   HSM   None

Fig. 5. Some sample images for each category in our evaluation dataset.

Table 1. ROC AUCs and FPRs at 0.8 TPR for different radical groups and image description algorithms.

Group	ROC AUC					FPR at 0.8 TPR				
	SIFT	r-SIFT	SURF	ORB	AKAZE	SIFT	r-SIFT	SURF	ORB	AKAZE
GD	0.866	0.817	0.878	0.770	0.800	0.330	0.280	0.244	0.441	0.399
ISIS	0.951	0.947	0.751	0.781	0.908	0.035	0.010	0.348	0.457	0.141
HSM	0.958	0.984	0.823	0.814	0.871	0.015	0.015	0.303	0.510	0.205

Table 2. Execution time of local feature descriptors on 300 images and average number of key-points detected (OpenCV implementation running on an Intel Core i5-4460).

	SIFT	r-SIFT	SURF	ORB	AKAZE
Time (s)	68.86	69.32	77.23	4.57	40.28
Avg. key-points	3503	3503	4427	493	2370

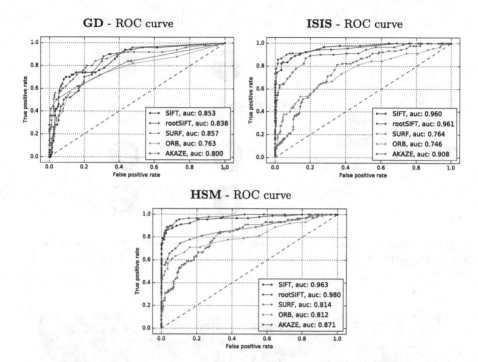

Fig. 6. ROC curves for the detection of radical iconography of GD, ISIS and HSM groups.

5   A Case Study with ISIS Supporters

To provide further insight into the effectiveness of the proposed framework, we present an illustrative case study with ISIS supporting Twitter profiles. In this case study, the system was provided with four manually found ISIS-supportive Twitter profiles (see Fig. 7). The reference image in this case was the same ISIS flag used in our previous experiments. After the first execution of the CBR stages, our system produced a list with eight candidate radical profiles. In this case, no false positives were registered, and all the suggested users did exhibit ISIS's flag in their profiles. Note that the three suggested profiles which do not exhibit a variation of the ISIS flag in their profile image (i.e., @Sracp_1, @ssds03 and @KMjahd) do exhibit it in their banner or profile-background image which is also analyzed by the latest version of our system.

To assess whether our system had neglected any adjacent users exhibiting ISIS's flag, we manually checked every following/follower of the monitored users. In total, the monitored users had 1.403 followings and followers. After manually inspecting all these profiles, we identified 7 new users displaying ISIS's flag either in their profile images or banners, which had not been detected by our system. However, in all these cases the flag appeared in a very small region of the image,

Monitored Users   **Suggested profiles**

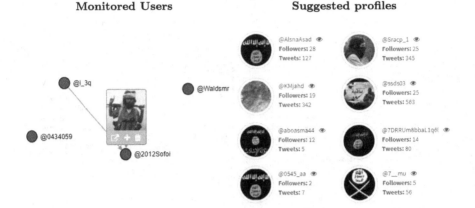

Fig. 7. Example Case Study with ISIS-supportive Twitter users. The monitored users are shown on the left side, and the list of suggested radical profiles is shown on the right side.

Fig. 8. Some sample profile images with radical iconography which were not detected by the proposed framework due to the low quality, size or distortion of the images.

with a notably poor quality, or partially blended with other images. Figure 8 shows some examples of these profile images where the system failed to recognize the radical iconography.

6   Discussion and Future Work

The experimental results presented in the previous section evidence the potential of local feature descriptors in the task of detecting radical iconography in unconstrained real-world images. Looking at Fig. 6 we can see that the retrieval accuracy was significantly greater for HSM and ISIS than for GD. We believe this is a consequence of the low visual complexity of the iconography associated to GD. The absence of distinctive visual features makes it harder for all the descriptors evaluated to retrieve the correct images. In addition, our results show that except for the case of GD, SIFT greatly outperformed SURF and ORB descriptors. This suggest that SIFT might be the best option to detect iconography of extremist groups in online images, as long as its computational cost is admissible in the specific application case. Regarding the comparison between SIFT and Root-SIFT, no conclusive results were found, and further experimentation is required to determine whether Root-SIFT out-performs SIFT in this context.

During our experiments, we have also identified some possible drawbacks of the described approach. For instance, some of the images containing the flag of ISIS were actually of Iraqi soldiers holding the flag upside-down as a sign of victory after recapturing Mosul. In this case, users sharing this image are unlikely to be ISIS-supporters. However, as the image descriptors applied are rotation invariant, this image is detected as a positive match by our approach (see Fig. 9). This type of particularities require a certain degree of expert knowledge to be decided and shall probably be left to the judgement of the human expert whose work is being assisted by the automatic system. This highlights the potential of the proposed CBR framework, where the machine automatizes most of the tedious, repetitive work and the human expert provides their expertise to make decisions in hard cases like the one described above.

Fig. 9. ISIS's flag detected in a picture of Iraqi soldiers holding it upside-down as a sign of victory after recapturing Mosul. Human expert knowledge is necessary to clarify this case.

As for future research lines, we intend to evaluate the proposed framework in a real application scenario. While our experimental results evidence the potential of image analysis to detect radical iconography in unconstrained images and provide insight into the performance of the different algorithmic alternatives, further evaluation is required before the system can be put into production. We also intend to explore the role of reciprocity in social interactions for radicalization risk assessment. For instance, mentions from confirmed radical users to profiles who never answer them and have a significantly higher number of followers might not be indicative of possible ongoing radicalization processes.

Acknowledgment. The research of Daniel López-Sánchez has been financed by the Ministry of Education, Culture and Sports of the Spanish Government (University Faculty Training programme (FPU), reference number FPU15/02339). In addition, this work was supported by the Spanish Ministry of Economy and FEDER funds. Project SURF: Intelligent System for integrated and sustainable management of urban fleets TIN2015-65515-C4-3-R.

References

1. Basic Concepts of the Homography Explained with Code. https://docs.opencv.org/3.4.1/d9/dab/tutorial_homography.html. Accessed 27 Apr 2018
2. Agarwal, S., Sureka, A.: Using KNN and SVM based one-class classifier for detecting online radicalization on Twitter. In: Natarajan, R., Barua, G., Patra, M.R. (eds.) ICDCIT 2015. LNCS, vol. 8956, pp. 431–442. Springer, Cham (2015). https://doi.org/10.1007/978-3-319-14977-6_47
3. Alcantarilla, P.F., Solutions, T.: Fast explicit diffusion for accelerated features in nonlinear scale spaces. IEEE Trans. Pattern Anal. Mach. Intell. **34**(7), 1281–1298 (2011)
4. Amailef, K., Jie, L.: Ontology-supported case-based reasoning approach for intelligent m-government emergency response services. Decis. Support Syst. **55**(1), 79–97 (2013)
5. Arandjelović, R., Zisserman, A.: Three things everyone should know to improve object retrieval. In: 2012 IEEE Conference on Computer Vision and Pattern Recognition (CVPR), pp. 2911–2918. IEEE (2012)
6. Berger, J.M.: The ISIS Twitter census: making sense of ISIS's use of Twitter. The Brookings Institution (2015)
7. Bermingham, A., Conway, M., McInerney, L., O'Hare, N., Smeaton, A.F.: Combining social network analysis and sentiment analysis to explore the potential for online radicalisation. In: International Conference on Advances in Social Network Analysis and Mining, ASONAM 2009, pp. 231–236. IEEE (2009)
8. Blaker, L.: The Islamic state's use of online social media. Mil. Cyber Affairs **1**(1), 4 (2015)
9. Lowe, D.G.: Distinctive image features from scale-invariant keypoints. Int. J. Comput. Vis. **60**(2), 91–110 (2004)
10. McPherson, M., Smith-Lovin, L., Cook, J.M.: Birds of a feather: homophily in social networks. Ann. Rev. Soc. **27**(1), 415–444 (2001)
11. Rublee, E., Rabaud, V., Konolige, K., Bradski, G.: ORB: an efficient alternative to sift or surf. In: 2011 IEEE International Conference on Computer Vision (ICCV), pp. 2564–2571. IEEE (2011)
12. Sánchez, D.L., Revuelta, J., De la Prieta, F., Gil-González, A.B., Dang, C.: Twitter user clustering based on their preferences and the louvain algorithm. In: Trends in Practical Applications of Scalable Multi-Agent Systems, the PAAMS Collection. AISC, vol. 473, pp. 349–356. Springer, Cham (2016). https://doi.org/10.1007/978-3-319-40159-1_29
13. Thelwall, M.: The heart and soul of the web? Sentiment strength detection in the social web with sentistrength. In: Hołyst, J.A. (ed.) Cyberemotions. UCS, pp. 119–134. Springer, Cham (2017). https://doi.org/10.1007/978-3-319-43639-5_7
14. Tominaga, T., Hijikata, Y.: Exploring the relationship between user activities and profile images on twitter through machine learning techniques. J. Web Sci. **3**(1) (2017)
15. Weaver, R., Silverman, B.G., Shin, H., Dubois, R.: Modeling and simulating terrorist decision-making: a 'performance moderator function' approach to generating virtual opponents. Center for Human Modeling and Simulation, p. 22 (2001)
16. Wei, X., Stillwell, D.: How smart does your profile image look? Estimating intelligence from social network profile images. In: Proceedings of the Tenth ACM International Conference on Web Search and Data Mining, pp. 33–40. ACM (2017)
17. Zhong, H., et al.: Content-driven detection of cyberbullying on the instagram social network. In: IJCAI, pp. 3952–3958 (2016)

Segmentation of Kidneys Deformed by Nephroblastoma Using Case-Based Reasoning

Florent Marie[1(✉)], Lisa Corbat[1], Thibault Delavelle[1], Yann Chaussy[2], Julien Henriet[1], and Jean-Christophe Lapayre[1]

[1] FEMTO-ST Institute, University Bourgogne-Franche-Comté, CNRS, DISC, 16 route de Gray, 25030 Besançon, France
{florent.marie,lisa.corbat,julien.henriet,
jean-christophe.lapayre}@univ-fcomte.fr
thibault.delavelle@edu.univ-fcomte.fr
[2] CHRU Besançon, 2 boulevard Fleming, 25000 Besançon, France
ychaussy@chu-besancon.fr

Abstract. Image segmentation is a hot topic in image processing research. Most of the time, segmentation is not fully automated, and a user is required to guide the process in order to obtain correct results. Yet, even with programs, it is a time-consuming process. In a medical context, segmentation can provide a lot of information to surgeons, but since this task is manual, it is rarely executed because of time. Artificial Intelligence (AI) is a powerful approach to create viable solutions for fully automated treatments. In this paper, we define a case-based reasoning (CBR) that can enhance region-growing segmentation of kidneys deformed by nephroblastoma. The main problem with region-growing methods is that a user needs to place the seeds in the image manually. Automated methods exist but they are not efficient every time and they often give an over-segmentation. That is why we have designed an adaptation phase which can modify the coordinates of seeds recovered during the retrieval phase. We compared our CBR approach with manual region growing and Convolutional Neural Networking (CNN) to segment kidneys and tumours of CT-scans. Our CBR system succeeded in performing the best segmentation for the kidney.

Keywords: Case-based reasoning · Convolution Neural Network
Segmentation · Cancer tumour · Healthcare imaging
Artificial Intelligence

1 Introduction

Nephroblastoma, also called Wilms tumour, is the abdominal tumour most frequently observed in children (generally 1- to 5-year-old boys and girls). This cancer disease represents 5 to 14% of malignant paediatric tumours. As indicated by its name, this type of tumour is situated in the kidney. Most of the

© Springer Nature Switzerland AG 2018
M. T. Cox et al. (Eds.): ICCBR 2018, LNAI 11156, pp. 233–248, 2018.
https://doi.org/10.1007/978-3-030-01081-2_16

time, its initial diagnosis is based on imaging. Generally, ultrasound observations are planned first in order to confirm its existence and approximate its position. Then, a medical scanner provides its position, and the healthy tissues and organs are reached with a higher accuracy. Radiologists and surgeons need 3-Dimensional (3D) representation of the tumour and the border organs in order to establish the diagnosis, plan the surgery (estimated quantity of blood, specialized equipment needed, estimation of the duration of the surgery, etc.), and also in order to guide the actions of the surgeon during the surgery.

Segmentation is one of the key steps of the construction of this type of 3D representation. During this process, each pixel of every scan has to be affected to one, and only one, region. radiologists and surgeons must guide and verify the segmentation of more than 200 scans manually, which is out of the question in practice. Our ambition is to introduce a process based on the knowledge and experience of experts in order to guide the segmentation process. This paper presents a case-based reasoning (CBR) system which can enhance segmentations of kidneys deformed by nephroblastoma.

The originality of the present approach resides in the way our CBR system adapts the solutions of past situations. The principle of region-growing segmentation consists of placing seeds on different points of the image that must be segmented, and then verifying if the pixels around these seeds have grey levels close enough to be integrated into the same region following a local threshold (difference between the candidate pixel and its neighbourhood) and a global threshold (difference between the candidate pixel and the regional mean). This algorithm makes each region grow until each pixel of the considered picture belongs to one and only one region. The main problem with the region-growing method is that a user needs to place the seeds in the image manually. Automated methods exist but are not efficient every time and often give over-segmentation. Our idea consists in using a CBR system, which places the seeds at the correct places, and then performing region-growing segmentation. In addition, our system can modify the position of a seed during the adaptation phase in order to choose a pixel which matches the expected/average grey level of a kidney better.

After this introduction, this paper presents the CBR system we have designed in order to compensate the unpredictability of tumoural kidney shapes: its case representation and all the phases of the system, emphasising the adaptation phase. The third part of this paper presents the performance of our method, and these results are then discussed regarding the general purpose of the project.

2   Related Work

There is a lot of research relative to segmentation enhanced by AI in literature. In [8] CBR is used with a watershed algorithm to segment pictures. Litjens et al. [18] wrote an survey for Deep learning in medical applications which is a mark of the popularity of Deep learning for segmentation. Other techniques are also availables: genetic algorithm [10], knowledge stored in ontologies [26] or Random Markov Fields [15]. Deep learning (like Convolutional Neural Network

(CNN)) is one of the most efficient and promising tools, and it is widely used. CNN were used in order to perform segmentation of healthy kidneys [3,25]. Nevertheless, they did not try to perform segmentations of kidneys with tumours, which introduces a difficulty. Actually, convolutional networks must be firstly trained to recognize the shapes of these organs. Since these two works focused on healthy organs, their shapes and areas are more or less the same from one subject to another. On the contrary, our work aims at performing segmentation of tumoural kidneys with unpredictable shapes and positions from a patient to another. Even if deep learning seems to give the most accurate results in recent studies, this technique requires a lot of data in order to be trained. By contrast, CBR takes advantage of knowledge and enriches itself following its experiments [16]. A large number of CBR systems designed for Health Science (CBR-HS) can also be found [2,6,13,14,20,22,24]. In particular, Perner designed a system for segmentation of brain images with a cut histogram method [23] and Frucci *et al.* adapted and improved this system with a watershed method [8]. We chose to implement a CBR system with a region growing method but, to place seeds at the optimum position, we need an adaptation phase.

Many adaptation strategies can be found in the literature. Adaptation using Adaptation Rules [21] consists of computing a solution for a target case by applying a function that takes the target case as parameters, a source case that presents some similarities, and its solution. Differential Adaptation [9] is based on evaluation of the variations between the source and target cases: an approximate solution of the target case is computed by applying the variations between the two cases to the solution for the source case under consideration. Conservative Adaptation [17] is based on the Revision Theory, which considers knowledge updates. This kind of adaptation consists of minimising the modifications to be applied to knowledge, and has been applied to the resolution of spatial and temporal problems [7] as well as in oncology [5]. A. Cordier *et al.* [4] used influence functions that link variations in problem descriptors to those in solution descriptors. In the CBR-HS EquiVox, an adaptation based on rules defined by experiences by experts and Artificial Neural Networks (ANN) has been implemented and enhanced by a precision combination vector [11,12]. In this work, the neighbourhood of the seeds are explored in order to match the desired grey levels as much as possible. Consequently, our adaptation is a kind of Conservative Adaptation lead by rules.

3   Materials and Methods

This part of the paper presents the CBR system defined for image segmentation with the region-growing method, summarized in Fig. 1. All the CBR phases are explained below. Our system comes from a CT-scan and looks for the closest stored image already segmented in the case base. It calculates a similarity value for each stored case and extracts the source case with the highest similarity during a retrieval phase. Then, extracted parameters of segmentation are adapted to the current case through an adaptation phase. These adapted parameters are used to perform a new segmentation. Finally, the result is evaluated by an expert and stored in the case base as new source case if segmentation is relevant.

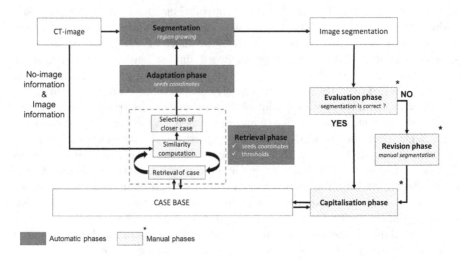

Fig. 1. Overview of our CBR system

3.1 Case Model Approach

A case is composed of two parts: the *Problem* and the *Solution*. The *Problem* part describes the characteristics of the problem to be resolved, and the *Solution* part gives the way to solve it. The case model of the CBR is discribed in Fig. 2.

In our study, the *Problem* part has to describe the CT-images, i.e. some descriptors that provide information about the structure or the statistics of the image. The *Solution* part should give the locations of seeds and the thresholds for the region-growing algorithm.

Like [1,2], the *Problem* part of our cases is composed of:

- meta-data representing the information for the patient: sex, age, height and weight;
- statistical image information: mean, kurtosis, skewness and variance;

The *Solution* part of our cases contains the values of the thresholds (local and global) for each structure to segment, a list of positions for the seeds, and a list of pre-treatments (giving the order of the filters to apply and their parameters). We use three different pretreatments in order to enhance the contrast of the images: histogram equalization, median filter and unsharp mask. Each image has its own characteristics, thus it is necessary to add pre-processing to the *Solution part*, in order to fit each case.

$$Case = \begin{bmatrix} patient\ sex \\ patient\ age \\ patient\ height \\ patient\ weight \\ image\ mean \\ image\ kurtosis \\ image\ skewness \\ image\ variance \end{bmatrix} + \begin{bmatrix} thresholds\ for\ each\ structure \\ list\ of\ pretreatments \\ 2D\ coordinates\ of\ kidney\ seeds \end{bmatrix}$$

Description of problem part   Description of solution part

Fig. 2. The case model of the CBR: problem part and solution part

3.2 Retrieval Phase

This section describes how the retrieval phase is performed using a similarity calculation between the stored cases and the new problem.

As we explained in the last section, our case base is composed of two types of data: meta-data and image characteristics (see Sect. 3.1). We tested two variants of a similarity formula between two images x and y. First, we used Perner's formula as in [23], called $s_1(x,y)$ with a component $SM_d(x,y)$ for meta-data (a derivation of Tversky index) and another $SI(x,y)$ for image information. The second is a hybrid formula called $s_2(x,y)$. It takes back the meta-data formula of Perner $SM_d(x,y)$ but uses MSSIM (Mean Structural SIMilarity) [27] criteria ($MSSIM(x,y)$) for the image characteristics. The MSSIM criteria are an improvement of the SSIM (Structural Similarity) criteria that are commonly used in image compression. MSSIM uses an iterative windowing to increase the capacity of structural comparison on images (i.e. each window describes a ROI (Region Of Interest) which is compared independently). The following formulas show the construction of both similarity calculations between two images x and y ($s_1(x,y)$ and $s_2(x,y)$):

$$s_1(x,y) = \frac{1}{2}(SM_d(x,y) + SI(x,y)) \tag{1}$$

$$s_2(x,y) = \frac{1}{2}(SM_d(x,y) + MSSIM(x,y)) \tag{2}$$

The meta-data component is computed as follows:

$$SM_d(x,y) = \frac{|A_i|}{\alpha|A_i| + \beta|D_i| + \gamma|E_i|} \tag{3}$$

where A_i is the number of common features between x and y, D_i the features only in x and E_i the features only in y. α, β and γ are weight factors such as $\alpha = \beta = 1$ and $\gamma = 0.5$. Weight values come from Perner's work [23].

The image component in $s_1(x,y)$ is:

$$SI(x,y) = \frac{1}{K}\sum_{i=1}^{K} w_i \left| \frac{C_{ix} - C_{imin}}{C_{imax} - C_{imin}} - \frac{C_{iy} - C_{imin}}{C_{imax} - C_{imin}} \right| \tag{4}$$

C_{ix} and C_{iy} are the ith feature of both images x and y. C_{imin} and C_{imax} are the minimum and the maximum of the ith feature in the case base respectively. w_i is a weight factor which allows to weight each image features. In our study, all weight factors are set to 1.

The image component in $s_2(x, y)$ is:

$$MSSIM(x, y) = \frac{1}{M} \sum_{i=1}^{M} SSIM(x_i, y_i) \tag{5}$$

where M is the number of windows and SSIM is

$$SSIM(x, y) = \frac{(2\mu_x \mu_y + C_1) + (2\sigma_{xy} + C_2)}{(\mu_x^2 + \mu_y^2 + C_1)(\sigma_x^2 + \sigma_y^2 + C_2)} \tag{6}$$

where μ is the mean, σ is the standard deviation and $C_1 = 0.01 * L$ and $C_2 = 0.03 * L$ with $L = 255$.

3.3   Adaptation Phase

The adaptation consists of positioning the seeds correctly. Since the tumour form and position are unpredictable, the position of the kidney is vulnerable to errors. Moreover, the kidney is a relatively small region, especially if the tumour crushes it. Consequently, the retrieved case is not always exactly the same as the new case we want to solve. So, the position of the seeds has to be adapted, especially for small regions.

We assumed that after the retrieval phase, the position of a seed is inside or close to its dedicated region. After applying our pre-treatments, we figured out that the grey-level intensity of an object to segment is almost always the same. Therefore, we can automatically infer the correct position of seeds, considering the grey-level intensity I of the pixel. We defined a coherence interval CI for each object to segment, corresponding to an interval of grey-level intensity a seed must be in. We can define a procedure to verify if a seed belongs to its dedicated region by performing this test:

$$\forall seed, \; isCorrectlyPlaced(seed) = true$$
$$if \; I(seed) \in CI_{kidney}/CI_{kidney} = [220, 255] \tag{7}$$

From this test, we defined an algorithm that can place the seed in a correct position on the image (i.e. in a pixel belonging to the kidney). Figure 3 illustrates the iterative extending of the neighbours from the initial position of seed. The main idea is to evaluate the neighbours of the seed (8-connected) and check the coherence of these neighbours using the test presented above. If no candidate satisfies the test, we iteratively expand the scope of the neighbours until we find a coherent pixel. On Fig. 3, each square represents a pixel of the image: in the first iteration, we evaluate the direct neighbours of the white seed; in the second one, we increase the scope to the pixels at a distance of two from the seed, and so on.

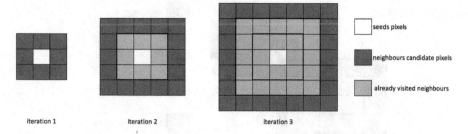

iteration 1   iteration 2   iteration 3

seeds pixels

neighbours candidate pixels

already visited neighbours

Fig. 3. Overview of the evaluated neighbours during the execution of the adaptation algorithm (for the position of the seeds) on 3 iterations

Algorithm 1 presented below gives the details of this process. Giving a seed S and CI, it returns the 2D coordinate representing the adapted position of the seed. For each evaluated neighbour, the test presented above is performed to check if the pixel is coherent, and at each iteration, the scope (α) is increased.

Algorithm 1. Adaptation algorithm of the position of the seeds

---

inputs : a seed S (with its 2D coordinates in the image $S.x$ et $S.y$) and the
intensity coherence interval for dedicated region of $S : CI$
output: a 2D Point describing the new position of the seed S
$\alpha \leftarrow 1$;
while $intensity(S.x, S.y) \notin CI$ **do**
    for i *from* $-\alpha$ *to* α *step of* 2α **do**
        for j *from* $-\alpha$ *to* α *step of* 2α **do**
            if $intensity(S.x + i, S.y + j) \in CI$ **then**
                return the point of coordinates $(S.x + i, S.y + j)$;
            end
        end
    end
    $\alpha + +$;
end
return error "no candidate satisfies the coherence interval";

Figure 4 shows an example of execution of the algorithm. From the initial seed (in white), we expand two times until a coherent candidate is found (the black pixel) that is part of the kidney region according to its grey-level intensity (> 220).

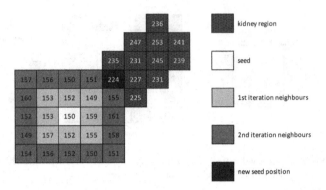

Fig. 4. Execution example of the adaptation algorithm to find a new correct seed

3.4 Revision and Capitalization Phases

As presented in Fig. 1, all these phases are carried out by an expert. The expert evaluates the results of segmentation, visually, and decides to perform it again if necessary with a region growing process manually guided. The capitalisation phase is systematic; we enrich the case base after every relevant segmentation obtained. Ideally, a satisfaction measure would determine if a resolved case could be added to the base in order to have an automatic system.

4   Results

We have tested the performance of our system on a set of 10 scans from one patient. We used a cross-validation method with a series of 10 tests. For each test, one image was used as a target case, and the nine others were stored as source cases.

Then, we carried out tests in order to compare our approach with others for segmentation: region growing, watershed, threshold-based segmentation, and also FCN [19] which is a Convolutional Neural Network (deep-learning method).

4.1   Coefficients for Evaluation of Results

We used two scientific indicators in order to compare the results. The Dice and the IU. The Dice is commonly used by experts of medical imaging, and the IU is an index commonly used by the imaging community.

The DICE coefficient, also known as the Sorensen coefficient, gives a similarity value (on $[0,1]$) between two sets X and Y. In our case, X represents the pixels of the ground truth (i.e. the desired segmentation) and Y represents the pixels of the calculated segmentation given by our system. The above formula gives the details to calculate the value of the coefficient:

$$DICE = \frac{2 * |X \cap Y|}{|X| + |Y|} \tag{8}$$

The IU (Intersection over Union, also called Jaccard index) is the mean of the IU_i of all the regions, and the IU_i of region i is given by the equation below:

$$IU_i = \frac{|X \cap Y|}{|X \cup Y|} = \frac{n_{ii}}{n_{ii} + n_{ji} + n_{ij}} \tag{9}$$

where:

- n_{ii} is the number of pixels correctly placed in region i,
- n_{ji} is the number of pixels that should have been in region i but are not,
- n_{ij} is the number of pixels that are in region i but should not have been.

4.2 Evaluation of Similarity Metrics

Table 1 shows the different similarity values according to the formulas mainly used in image processing with each source case. The last column shows the retrieved case for each target case and each similarity measure. The retrieved case is the case with the higher similarity value, excluding the target case (a case cannot retrieve itself). The results are equivalent for the both similarity measures and, for each case, the retrieved case is the same. There are only two differences. On the one hand, Perner's formula seems more discriminative, with a higher difference between the similarities from one image to another. But on the other hand, MSSIM seems more accurate because the similarity of two identical cases is equal to 1. Consequently, the MSSIM similarity was chosen.

Table 1. Comparison of two similarity measures (MSSIM and Attig and Perner's formulas) for each case during the cross validation

	Best s_1	Best s_2	Retrivied case
Case 1	0.908	0.995	6
Case 2	0.945	0.995	7
Case 3	0.920	0.997	8
Case 4	0.929	0.997	9
Case 5	0.944	0.996	10
Case 6	0.908	0.995	1
Case 7	0.945	0.995	2
Case 8	0.920	0.997	3
Case 9	0.929	0.997	4
Case 10	0.944	0.996	5

4.3   System Adaptation

In order to illustrate the effects of this adaptation algorithm, Fig. 5 shows a comparison between an execution of our program with and without the adaptation phase. The kidney has a light grey label and the tumour has a dark grey label. From left to right we have a CT-image, segmentation without the adaptation phase, and finally segmentation with adaptation phase. For the segmentation without an adaptation process, the seed was placed outside the top part of the kidney. Consequently, the top part was not correctly segmented and the result has become irrelevant. Our adaptation phase helps to avoid this situation and improves the precision of segmentation.

Fig. 5. Comparison between an execution of our system with and without the adaptation phase (from left to right, CT-Scan, segmentation without adaptation and segmentation with adaptation)

Without adaptation, the seed was only placed at the correct position in 60% of our tested cases. Through the adaptation process, we improved the placement of seeds to 100% at the correct position.

Table 2 shows the results for kidney segmentation with DICE and IU. Using cross validation, the number corresponds to the tested scan as the target case, with the nine others as source cases. We highlighted in grey cases presenting an improvement after the adaptation process. To check the efficiency of the adaptation process only, we compared CBR results with a ground truth, which is the result of a manual region growing. We highlighted in grey cases presenting an improvement after the adaptation process. Most of the time, the CBR process succeeded in recovering the correct coordinates to place a seed in the kidney. For these cases, adaptation did not improve the results because the CBR did not need it. However, some segmentations (2, 3, 6 and 9) did not work well with just a CBR process and seeds were placed at the wrong coordinates (outside the kidney). Thanks to an adaptation step, we observed a clear improvement of results (up to 99.8% for Case 6).

Table 2. DICE and IU for kidney segmentation with CBR-region growing

	Case	1	2	3	4	5	6
CBR RG	DICE	0.998	0.559	0.843	0.894	0.997	0.000
	IU	0.995	0.388	0.728	0.809	0.995	0.000
CBR RG +	DICE	0.998	0.999	0.993	0.894	0.997	0.998
adaptation	IU	0.995	0.999	0.987	0.809	0.995	0.997
	Case	7	8	9	10	Mean	Median
CBR RG	DICE	0.927	1.000	0.936	0.998	0.815	0.931
	IU	0.865	1.000	0.879	0.996	0.765	0.872
CBR RG +	DICE	0.927	1.000	0.973	0.998	0.978	0.997
adaptation	IU	0.865	1.000	0.948	0.996	0.959	0.995

Table 3. Mean errors for retrieved thresholds: local and global

	Retrivied case	Global threshold error (%)	Local threshold error (%)
Case 1	6	0.0	0.0
Case 2	7	0.0	0.0
Case 3	8	0.0	0.0
Case 4	9	20.9	17.5
Case 5	10	3.6	0.0
Case 6	1	0.0	0.0
Case 7	2	0.0	0.0
Case 8	3	0.0	0.0
Case 9	4	29.7	14.5
Case 10	5	0.0	0.0

Table 3 shows the error rates for each segmented case during the retrieval phase. Errors were computed with respect to thresholds determined during manual region-growing segmentation and are a mean between all seeds of the kidney (each seed has its own threshold and error rate). For most of them, we have a null error rate because the similarity between the problem case and the retrieved case is very high. So, thresholds are the same. But for some cases, we can observe a higher error rate (Cases 4 and 9) from 14.5 to 29.7%. It could explain why cases 4 and 9 do not have high scores in Table 2. It shows the main limitation of our CBR system without the adaptation phase for thresholds. This adaptation process represents an important perspective to improve its robustness. Case 7 has the lowest result in spite of an error rate of 0%. This is because the thresholds used are closely related to the seed position. As the retrieved position is not the same as the seed position during manual region growing, it is logical that the scores are different. Furthermore, the best parameters are not always determined manually. Thus, by coincidence, the CBR solution can be better and has a score lower than 1 because of differences.

4.4 Comparison with Other Approaches

In order to compare our CBR system with other classical approaches, we carried out a segmentation with a manual level set with ImageJ software and a CNN. For the CNN, we implemented FCN-8s architecture from Long *et al.* [19], trained with a training set of 10 slices (CT-Scans) corresponding to our case base and according to a cross-validation strategy to have the same conditions as CBR. Table 4 shows our results from these different methods. The CBR system version evaluated is the one with a Region-Growing (RG) and adaptation phase. As before, evaluation was done with a DICE and IU computation but, this time, we computed them from true ground truths carried out manually by paediatric surgeons.

As presented in Table 4, the best results were obtained with our CBR system. Indeed, we succeeded in having results very close to manual RG with a mean DICE of 0.83. A Level-Set technique shows good results for most of the cases, but it failed to segment Case 8 correctly. Globally, RG (manual or with CBR) performs more pertinent segmentations. CNN has the worst scores, with a mean DICE of only 0.59. This is a logical result since CNNs are based on experiences and require a large database to yield interesting segmentations. CBR is another approach based on knowledge, which requires much less data in order to work well.

Table 4. Comparison of our CBR system and some other approaches. DICE and IU were calculated for segmentation of deformed kidney

	CBR		RG		Level set		FCN-8s	
	DICE	IU	DICE	IU	DICE	IU	DICE	IU
Case 1	0.92	0.85	0.92	0.85	0.93	0.87	0.73	0.58
Case 2	0.89	0.80	0.88	0.79	0.88	0.79	0.78	0.64
Case 3	0.74	0.59	0.75	0.60	0.73	0.58	0.65	0.48
Case 4	0.74	0.59	0.79	0.65	0.75	0.60	0.52	0.35
Case 5	0.84	0.72	0.84	0.72	0.83	0.71	0.53	0.36
Case 6	0.95	0.90	0.95	0.90	0.90	0.83	0.47	0.31
Case 7	0.82	0.70	0.82	0.69	0.76	0.62	0.59	0.42
Case 8	0.76	0.62	0.76	0.62	0.18	0.10	0.60	0.42
Case 9	0.86	0.76	0.86	0.76	0.84	0.73	0.73	0.57
Case 10	0.76	0.61	0.77	0.63	0.73	0.58	0.35	0.21
Mean	**0.83**	**0.71**	**0.83**	**0.72**	**0.75**	**0.64**	**0.59**	**0.43**
Median	**0.83**	**0.71**	**0.83**	**0.70**	**0.79**	**0.66**	**0.59**	**0.42**

5   Discussion

Our results prove that our CBR system can enhance and guide segmentations of organs and structures deformed by a singularity (the tumour). Indeed, using this technique, the deformed tumoural kidneys of our scans were widely retrieved and better segmented than with all the other tested methods. This mainly comes from our adaptation phase ensuring that seeds are placed at the right place. Nevertheless, this adaptation is based on a coherence of pixel intensity and, unfortunately, different structures can have similar grey levels. Thus, it is possible that the adaptation selects the wrong pixel and places seeds in the spine or ribs, for example. Most of the time, kidneys are close enough to avoid this situation, but it could theoretically occur. In that respect, it would be interesting to enhance our adaptation phase to prevent this possibility. One way of doing that would be to drive the pixel research in the direction of kidney, rather than visiting all the neighbours around the initial seed. Another improvement would be the design of another adaptation phase for adjustment of the thresholds recovered from the source case.

Globally, RG produced better segmentations than the Level-Set (LS) technique although results are close for the most of cases. Yet, for some cases, LS parametrisation is easier and faster. This could permit designing a CBR system with both approaches: a case would be composed by the segmentation technique as well (RG or LS), following the best way determined during the manual step. In this way, a CBR system could retrieve the segmentation approach used to solve a case and not only the parameters of a particular technique. In our approach, CNNs have poor results because of the lack of data (only 10 images). The main advantage of CBR with respect to CNN is that CBR is simultaneously an experience approach and a knowledge approach, where CNN is just based on experience. This is the reason why CBR can perform interesting results even with a small data set. Actually, CNNs may give better results with larger data set. However, the limited number of elements is one of the constraints we have to deal with. Moreover, CNNs encounter many difficulties segmenting little structures, such as deformed kidneys, but could lead to results accurate enough with larger structures such as tumours. This helps to envisage a hybrid system, with a CBR system to segment kidneys and a CNN to segment tumours.

In addition, for surgeons, the segmentation of kidneys and tumours is not sufficient. Surgeons also need to visualise other small structures, such as blood vessels (artery, vein, etc.) in order to evaluate the difficulty of the surgery. Yet, it can be very difficult to segment them because of the lack of visibility. Due to their small size, placing a seed inside is not allowed. Deep learning could be a good option.

In regards with these results, inspired by the Trzupek et al. approach [26], we want to go further and integrate a real ontology which could guide the position of the seeds for all the other structures.

6   Conclusion

We have designed a system based on CBR, which can guide segmentation of tumoural kidneys. We have also compared this approach to classical ones (commonly used in hospitals) and very recent ones (deep learning). These very promising results proved that we must delve further into this approach, and that we are on the correct path to automatic segmentation of all the organs in this part of the abdomen. Our ambition is now to evaluate our method over a larger data set.

The difficulty of our problem resides in the fact that tumoural kidneys are deformed and moved by a totally unpredictable structure (the tumour). Nevertheless, our system can retrieve the positions of these organs.

Further work will consist of defining an ontology of this part of the body, including fuzzy information of the positions of the different structures. Moreover, an interesting future work would be the design of a hybrid segmentation system, with CBR and CNNs, to segment all of them.

Acknowledgements. The authors wish to thank Pr Frédéric Auber, Dr Marion Lenoir-Auber of the *Centre Hospitalier Régional Universitaire de Besançon* for their expertise with nephroblastoma and Loredane Vieille for achieving the manual segmentations. The authors thank *European Community* (*European FEDER*) for financing this work by the *INTERREG V*, the *Communauté d'Agglomération du Grand Besançon* and the *Cancéropóle Grand-Est*. The authors also wish to thank Mary Moritz (WordStyle Traduction) for her help with the English language.

References

1. Attig, A., Perner, P.: A study on the case image description for learning the model of the watershed segmentation. Trans. Case-Based Reason. **2**(1), 41–53 (2009)
2. Attig, A., Perner, P.: Incremental learning of the model for watershed-based image segmentation. In: Barneva, R.P., Brimkov, V.E., Aggarwal, J.K. (eds.) IWCIA 2012. LNCS, vol. 7655, pp. 209–222. Springer, Heidelberg (2012). https://doi.org/10.1007/978-3-642-34732-0_16
3. Çiçek, Ö., Abdulkadir, A., Lienkamp, S.S., Brox, T., Ronneberger, O.: 3D U-Net: learning dense volumetric segmentation from sparse annotation. In: Ourselin, S., Joskowicz, L., Sabuncu, M.R., Unal, G., Wells, W. (eds.) MICCAI 2016. LNCS, vol. 9901, pp. 424–432. Springer, Cham (2016). https://doi.org/10.1007/978-3-319-46723-8_49
4. Cordier, A., Fuchs, B., Mille, A.: Engineering and learning of adaptation knowledge in case-based reasoning. In: Staab, S., Svátek, V. (eds.) EKAW 2006. LNCS (LNAI), vol. 4248, pp. 303–317. Springer, Heidelberg (2006). https://doi.org/10.1007/11891451_27
5. d'Aquin, M., Lieber, J., Napoli, A.: Adaptation knowledge acquisition: a case study for case-based decision support in oncology. Comput. Intell. **22**(3–4), 161–176 (2006)
6. Diaz, F., Fdez-Riverola, F., Corchado, J.M.: Gene-CBR: a case-based reasonig tool for cancer diagnosis using microarray data sets. Comput. Intell. **22**(3–4), 254–268 (2006)

7. Dufour-Lussier, V., Le Ber, F., Lieber, J., Martin, L.: Adapting spatial and temporal cases. In: Agudo, B.D., Watson, I. (eds.) ICCBR 2012. LNCS (LNAI), vol. 7466, pp. 77–91. Springer, Heidelberg (2012). https://doi.org/10.1007/978-3-642-32986-9_8
8. Frucci, M., Perner, P., di Baja, G.S.: Case-based reasoning for image segmentation by watershed transformation. In: Perner, P. (eds.) Case-Based Reasoning on Images and Signals, vol. 73. Springer, Berlin (2008). https://doi.org/10.1007/978-3-540-73180-1_11
9. Fuchs, B., Lieber, J., Mille, A., Napoli, A.: An algorithm for adaptation in case-based reasoning. In: Proceedings of the 14th European Conference on Artificial Intelligence, pp. 45–49. IOS Press (2000)
10. Golobardes, E., Llora, X., Salamó, M., Martı, J.: Computer aided diagnosis with case-based reasoning and genetic algorithms. Knowl.-Based Syst. **15**(1), 45–52 (2002)
11. Henriet, J., Chatonnay, P.: Introduction of a combination vector to optimise the interpolation of numerical phantoms. Expert Syst. Appl. **40**(2), 492–499 (2013)
12. Henriet, J., Chatonnay, P., Leni, P.E.: An iterative precision vector to optimise the cbr adaptation of equivox. Eng. Appl. Artif. Intell. **35**, 158–163 (2014)
13. Henriet, J., Lang, C.: Introduction of a multiagent paradigm to optimize a case-based reasoning system designed to personalize three-dimensional numerical representations of human organs. Biomed. Eng. Appl. Basis Commun. **26**(05), 1450060 (2014)
14. Henriet, J., Leni, P.E., Laurent, R., Salomon, M.: Case-based reasoning adaptation of numerical representations of human organs by interpolation. Expert Syst. Appl. **41**(2), 260–266 (2014)
15. Kato, Z., Zerubia, J., et al.: Markov random fields in image segmentation. Found. Trends ® Signal Process. **5**(1–2), 1–155 (2012)
16. Kolodner, J.: Case-Based Reasoning. CA Morgan Kaufmann, Massachusetts (1993)
17. Lieber, J.: Application of the revision theory to adaptation in case-based reasoning: the conservative adaptation. In: Weber, R.O., Richter, M.M. (eds.) ICCBR 2007. LNCS (LNAI), vol. 4626, pp. 239–253. Springer, Heidelberg (2007). https://doi.org/10.1007/978-3-540-74141-1_17
18. Litjens, G., et al.: A survey on deep learning in medical image analysis. Med. Image Anal. **42**, 66–88 (2017)
19. Long, J., Shelhamer, E., Darrell, T.: Fully Convolutional Networks for Semantic Segmentation. arXiv:1411.4038v2 (2015)
20. Marling, C., Montani, S., Bichindaritz, I., Funk, P.: Synergistic case-based reasoning in medical domains. Expert Syst. Appl. **41**(2), 249–259 (2014)
21. Melis, E., Lieber, J., Napoli, A.: Reformulation in case-based reasoning. In: Smyth, B., Cunningham, P. (eds.) EWCBR 1998. LNCS, vol. 1488, pp. 172–183. Springer, Heidelberg (1998). https://doi.org/10.1007/BFb0056331
22. Montani, S.: Case-based reasoning for managing noncompliance with clinical guidelines. Comput. Intell. **25**(3), 196–213 (2009)
23. Perner, P.: An architecture for a CBR image segmentation system. Eng. Appl. Artif. Intell. **12**(6), 749–759 (1999)
24. Perner, P., Attig, A.: Using prototype-based classification for automatic knowledge acquisition. In: Pattern Recognition, Machine Intelligence and Biometrics, pp. 197–212. Springer, Heidelberg (2011). https://doi.org/10.1007/978-3-642-22407-2_8
25. Thong, W., Kadoury, S., Piché, N., Pal, C.J.: Convolutional networks for kidney segmentation in contrast-enhanced CT scans. In: Computer Methods in Biomechanics and Biomedical Engineering: Imaging & Visualization, pp. 1–6 (2016)

26. Trzupek, M., Ogiela, M.R., Tadeusiewicz, R.: Intelligent image content semantic description for cardiac 3D visualisations. Eng. Appl. Artif. Intell. **24**(8), 1410–1418 (2011)
27. Wang, Z., Bovik, A.C., Sheikh, H.R., Simoncelli, E.P.: Image quality assessment: from error visibility to structural similarity. IEEE Trans. Image Process. **13**(4), 600–612 (2004)

FITsense: Employing Multi-modal Sensors in Smart Homes to Predict Falls

Stewart Massie[1]([⊠]) , Glenn Forbes[1], Susan Craw[1] , Lucy Fraser[2], and Graeme Hamilton[2]

[1] School of Computing Science and Digital Media, Robert Gordon University, Aberdeen, UK
{s.massie,g.forbes6,s.craw}@rgu.ac.uk
[2] Albyn Housing Society Ltd, Invergordon, UK
https://www.rgu.ac.uk/dmstaff/massie-stewart,
https://www.rgu.ac.uk/dmstaff/forbes-glenn,
https://www.rgu.ac.uk/dmstaff/craw-susan

Abstract. As people live longer, the increasing average age of the population places additional strains on our health and social services. There are widely recognised benefits to both the individual and society from supporting people to live independently for longer in their own homes. However, falls in particular have been found to be a leading cause of the elderly moving into care, and yet surprisingly preventative approaches are not in place; fall detection and rehabilitation are too late. In this paper we present FITsense, which is building a Smart Home environment to identify increased risk of falls for residents, and so allow timely interventions before falls occurs. An ambient sensor network, installed in the Smart Home, identifies low level events taking place which is analysed to generate a resident's profile of activities of daily living (ADLs). These ADL profiles are compared to both the resident's typical profile and to known "risky" profiles to allow evidence-driven intervention recommendations. Human activity recognition to identify ADLs from sensor data is a key challenge. Here we compare a windowing-based and a sequence-based event representation on four existing datasets. We find that windowing works well, giving consistent performance but may lack sufficient granularity for more complex multi-part activities.

Keywords: Human activity recognition · Smart Homes · Sensors

1 Introduction

In this work we examine the opportunities to support assisted living environments with ambient sensors in a Smart House solution to monitor health trends in the home. A Case-Based Reasoning (CBR) approach is proposed which exploits the pattern of activities identified by the sensors to infer information about the health of the resident. In particular, the initial solution aims to predict

© Springer Nature Switzerland AG 2018
M. T. Cox et al. (Eds.): ICCBR 2018, LNAI 11156, pp. 249–263, 2018.
https://doi.org/10.1007/978-3-030-01081-2_17

increased risk of falls for residents of 16 Smart Homes being built near Inverness in Scotland.

The country is facing an ageing population with many people living longer. 10 million people in the UK are currently over 65 with a further increase of 5.5 million projected over the next 20 years. 3 million people are aged over 80 which is expected to double by 2030 [1]. An ageing population puts additional strains on health and social services with both a smaller proportion of working population available to support services, and with the elderly having more complex medical needs. Furthermore, with modern lifestyles, carers from within the family are less available. More people are tending to live alone as families live further apart with increased levels of relocation for work. In this changing scenario it is important that we help people with mobility or social needs to live independently for longer, and so reduce their reliance on more expensive health care solutions.

In particular, falls are an ongoing problem accounting for over 4 million bed days a year in the UK [2]. They are the most common cause of death for over 65s [3] with on average 35,848 fall-related deaths occurring annually in the EU between 2010 and 2012 [4]. One study performed in Torbay found 28% of falls proved to either be fatal or became so within 12 months, highlighting that research into preventative measures may be a more promising approach than rehabilitation after falls have occurred. Identifying preventative measures to be taken against falls could reduce morbidity, while also reducing costs and workload on health services. In addition to direct physical health concerns, falls have a lasting psychological effect which can reduce a person's confidence in their independent abilities, leading to an increase in sedentary behaviour and depression [5]. Effective methodologies for anticipating falls would be invaluable and the benefits associated with prevention appear to outweigh those of rehabilitation.

Recent developments in a number of technologies (sensors, Internet of Things, Cloud Computing, and increased computational power), along with reduced costs have resulted in substantial interest in the development of Smart Homes for automation, security and to a lesser extent health. Smart Homes offer a ubiquitous computing solution, in which a house utilises many sensors to deliver a safer environment. The core design of the common devices (e.g. IR, magnets, temperature) have remained unchanged over the last decade although size, cost and efficiency have all improved. Newer technologies are also beginning to be relevant, such as Wi-Fi and radar. Ambient sensors are practical for continuous monitoring in health application; lacking the overhead associated with wearables, or privacy concerns with video.

In this paper, we explore the use of everyday, low-cost ambient sensors installed in new-build Smart Homes with the aim of supporting tenants to live independently for longer. Specifically, we identify and discuss the main challenges in designing and deploying a real-world health monitoring system that senses and predicts the level of risk of falling attributed to Smart Home residents. Data is captured by a range of sensors installed in specially-designed, technology-enabled "FitHomes". Targeting specific activities identified as precursors to falls, the system analyses data derived from these sensors to identify patterns of activity, and changes in these patterns which could be linked to an increased risk of falling. It is hoped that evidence-based alerts will enable families and agencies to intervene with preventative measures before incidents occur. An outline solution is developed and initial experiments are undertaken to evaluate alternative approaches to classifying activity with low level, raw data inputs from multiple multi-modal sensors. The key contributions of the work are:

- to outline a novel CBR solution for identifying the risk of falls for residents in Smart Homes; and
- to evaluate alternative representations for activity recognition from the low-level, data inputs delivered from sensors.

The remainder of this paper describes our approach to employing ambient, non-intrusive sensors for monitoring and predicting risk of falls in purpose-built assisted homes, and presents experiments that evaluate alternative representations for activity recognition. In Sect. 2 we review existing research on the use of Smart Homes for health monitoring and risk of fall prediction. Section 3 discusses, in more detail, the specific scenario being faced in this real world development along with the associated challenges that we plan to address. Our proposed 2-part solution, which first employs Machine Learning (ML) to generate a more abstract case-structure on which we can then build an effective CBR system is outlined in Sect. 4. In Sect. 5 we introduce four datasets that we use to evaluate alternative feature representations for our initial activity recognition task. Finally, we draw our conclusions in Sect. 6.

2   Related Work

Activities of Daily Living (ADLs) are events in daily life which would be considered intrinsic to a person's ability to live independently. Typical ADLs include being able to dress oneself, get out of bed, and feed oneself. Katz [6] originally proposed the term along with a scale for rating a person's independent ability using their performance in simple ADLs. He suggests that there may be a procedural decline in ADL capability. While this was not proven, the concept of losing ADLs as we age has influenced future research in the field by identifying that specific ADLs are more indicative of reduced capability than others. Observing variances in ADL performance, such as missing a key step in an activity or performing steps out of order, can aid the identification of degenerative mental and physical capability which in turn may contribute to an increased risk of falling.

Physiological expressions, such as movement, can also be used to identify an increased risk of falling. Vestergaard [7] performed a study in which a relationship between performance in a 400-meter walk test and subsequent mortality in older adults was observed. This test (and other shorter variants) is usually performed in laboratory or hospital conditions, in which a physician would also be able to consider the patients condition and other metrics from the test. These include but are not limited to, whether or not a break was taken, variation in lap times and existing health conditions. However, lab-based testing is time consuming, costly and impractical for many patients, especially those with mobility issues. In addition, some studies have been able to identify risk of falling, and other potential health issues, in the elderly using gait velocity alone [8–10]. So while gait and other expressions of movement are indicative of many underlying conditions, measuring all aspects of gait such as swing and stride length requires specialist equipment, e.g. vision-based sensors. Gait velocity, however, can be measured using simpler equipment and still provides excellent insight into subject movement. For instance, Rana [11] performed a study in which gait velocity was estimated using simple infra-red motion sensors. We plan to adopt this approach and, while lab-based testing can provide higher accuracy, we hope accessible in-home testing can contribute to early detection of health problems.

Housing installations with ubiquitous simple sensors offer an opportunity to provide continuous behavioural and physiological monitoring of residents. These simple sensors can range from binary magnetic switches [12], to IoT-monitored motion sensors [13], all of which can provide insight into behavioural and physiological expressions. ADLs can then be reconstructed and modelled by identifying temporal patterns in these sensor outputs.

Modelling and classifying activities from sensor data typically involves applying ML techniques best adapted for pattern recognition. Several manually annotated datasets taken from Smart Home installations have been produced for the purpose of activity recognition [12,14,15]. Tapia made use of an extended Naive Bayes classifier to identify activities in their labelled dataset, whereas Kasteren made use of Hidden Markov Models (HMM) and Conditional Random Fields (CRF). All these techniques have demonstrable strengths in activity recognition, however the use of generative methods, such as HMMs and CRFs allow for the use of sequential data to train a model based on successive activities [16]. We use these existing datasets in our experiments to explore the effectiveness of alternative modelling and ML approaches.

3   FitHomes and Predicting Falls

FitHomes is an initiative, lead by Albyn Housing Society Ltd (AHS) in partnership with Carbon Dynamic, that aims to support independent living with the supply of custom-built Smart Homes fitted with integrated non-invasive sensors. 16 houses are being built and near completion at Alness near Invergordon. These houses are part of a development cycle with a further 32 FitHomes, funded by the Inverness City Deal, planned to be built within the Inverness area within 3 years. FITsense is a one year Data Lab[1] funded project that aims to exploit the sensor data to develop a prototype fall prediction system for these FitHomes.

3.1   Sensors

One of the first considerations in designing a Smart Home focused on health monitoring is the choice of what type and mix of sensors to use in order to

---

[1] The Data Lab, Scotland. https://www.thedatalab.com/.

provide a cost-effective solution that is also acceptable to residents. AHS have conducted initial research and it was clear that their tenants wanted an unobtrusive system that supported them in their homes, but did not take over. Both video and wearables were considered too intrusive for continuous in-home use; video due to privacy issues and wearables due to the ongoing overhead associated with 24 h operation. As a result, the focus in this project has been on simple everyday sensors, many of which are already widely used in security and automation applications. FITsense is an applied project and with this approach we can establish the limits of existing technology now, rather than developing new solutions for the future. A plug and play design will be adopted such that new sensors can be easily integrated as new technologies become main stream. A further benefit is provision of a low cost solution from the hardware perspective but with additional challenges for the data analysis.

FITsense aims to identify increased risk of falls and so a key focus for monitoring is to identify activity levels, patterns and speeds. However, the monitoring can go beyond just movement to consider other factors that have been shown to be related to falls, including dehydration, tiredness and mental health. Gaining information on these additional factors requires monitoring to also capture data on more general activities such as eating & drinking behaviours, sleep patterns, and toileting & grooming habits. With these criteria in mind a range of sensors have been selected for the FitHomes, that include:

- IR motion sensors that capture movement in each room;
- contact sensors to capture room, cupboard, and fridge door opening/closing;
- pressure sensors that identify use of the bed and chairs;
- IR beam break sensor to identify gait speed;
- electricity smart meters to identify power usage pattern;
- float sensors identifying toilet flushing;
- humidity sensors to identify shower use; and
- temperature sensors integrated with the humidity sensors.

Figure 1 shows typical sensors being used, including from left to right: a motion sensor; a presence sensor, being considered to identify presence of carers; a contact sensor; and electricity usage sensor, being considered for specific electrical items.

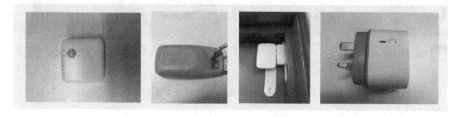

Fig. 1. Example of the sensors used in FITsense

Most of the sensors chosen have a binary output that simply activate when the event they are monitoring takes place e.g. a door opening; however others output continuous readings provided at fixed polling rates. The data fusion task across multiple sensors with different output modes becomes one of the main challenges in employing large numbers of sensors.

3.2 Smart Homes

The FitHomes are factory manufactured and supplied on-site ready to connect to site services, providing a cost effective build method for multiple properties. Sensor installation currently takes place on-site. Positioning and orientation of the sensors is important to give as much information as possible but also to consider building constraints, for example to give access to an electricity connection and remove reliance on battery usage. Figure 2 gives a plan layout view of the FitHomes with positioning identified for many of the sensors, including 6 motion sensors (one in each room), contact & pressure sensors, humidity & temperature sensors, electricity meter, and a float sensor in the toilet.

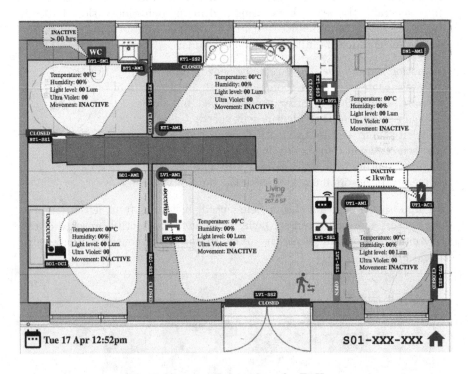

Fig. 2. Annotated floorplan of a FitHome

A Samsung SmartThings hub is used as the data centre to collect output from the sensors via ZigBee and pass the data on over the internet to cloud storage that allows API access for data analysis at a later date as required. The key challenge in employing multiple ambient sensors of varying types is to transform the low-level largely event-driven individual sensor activations (e.g. movement in kitchen) into meaningful activities on which to reason (e.g. food preparation).

4   Case-Based Approach

The elements of the CBR solution are first to identify patterns in the data that allow us to create representations from the low-level, raw sensor data that capture the residents' activities and behaviours of daily living, e.g. sleeping, dressing, showering, cooking etc., and then to assemble these activities into personalised daily and weekly profiles. The second stage is the analysis of these activity profiles to enable both the identification of changing trends in the resident's activities over time and to make comparisons with data collected from other similar residents. Changes in the Smart Home resident's own activity patterns over time can then be used to detect deterioration in health linked to falls, while comparisons with the patterns of other Smart Home residents can provide benchmark measures of health. The data thus supports evidence-driven intervention tailored to the resident and their specific circumstances.

4.1   Classifying ADLs

Human Activity Recognition (HAR) to identify ADLs is challenging in Smart Home scenarios because large volumes of data is generated from multi-modal sensors in real time making patterns associated with specific activities difficult to identify. Simple sensors (e.g. door open/closed sensors) are binary and record events, while more complex sensors (e.g. electricity consumption meters) poll data at fixed intervals to produce single or multi-dimensional time series outputs.

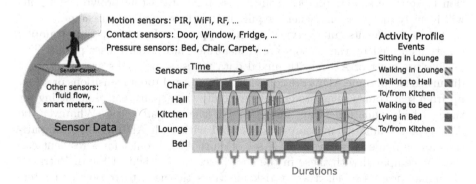

Fig. 3. Identifying activities from sensor activations

Figure 3 shows a diagram with examples of sensor activations for motion sensors in a hall, kitchen and lounge together with pressure sensors on the chair and bed. Simple events can be inferred from this data to generate activities. A mix of approaches will be adopted to identify activities and to then generate the residents daily activity profile. For the simple activities shown (e.g. time sitting, time in bed, number of toilet visits, number of room transitions) only one or two sensor activations are required to identify the activity; a rule-based approach with simple human generated rules is sufficient to identify the activity. Where effective this approach will be adopted.

However, more complex activities can only be recognised by the interaction of several sensors e.g. food preparation, showering, grooming, disturbed sleep. For these more complex activities a ML approach will be adopted. HAR typically employs a windowing approach to create a single aggregated vector representation on which ML (e.g. kNN, Support Vector Machines or Naive Bayes) can be applied for classification. These approaches can work well but are perhaps less able to handle the data fusion scenarios from Smart Homes because of difficulties in selecting appropriate time windows for different activities; and due to the loss of information when the sequence of events is not maintained, by aggregating within a window. In this paper we investigate using a sequence-based representation, in which the events are placed in order based on their time stamp.

4.2   Reasoning with ADLs

Identifying ADLs in themselves does not give an indication of health. However, it has been shown that one of the best ways to evaluate the health status of older adults is through functional assessment [17]; ADLs are lost as we age and in FITsense the plan is to monitor changes in ADL activity as an indicator of deteriorating health and increased risk of falls. To do this a CBR approach is adopted. With CBR, new problems are solved by retrieving similar, previously solved problems and reusing their solutions. In our scenario, a set of ADL templates (together with contextual information) will be used as the problem representation to retrieve similar profiles from a case base of existing profiles. Solutions will identify interventions, where required, and their previous outcomes.

Figure 4 presents an overview of our approach. Low-level, time-stamped events identified by the sensors are transformed into a daily user profile. The profiles are a set of ADLs with mixed data types: some ADLs are binary, e.g. disturbed sleep; some ADLs are counts, e.g. number of room transitions or stand up from seat count; some are cumulative daily time spans, e.g. time sitting, or time in bed; while others are numeric, e.g. average gait speed. Whatever the data type a similarity measure is associated with each ADL so that comparison can be made between them. A set of daily ADL profiles for a resident can then be compared with those in the case base, on the right of Fig. 4. Retrieval of similar profiles labelled as at risk identifies the need to recommend intervention, and falling similarity with the user's own previous profiles identifies changing behaviours. Importance in determining similarity for FITsense is given to ADLs known to correlate with falls. For other health conditions the similarity knowledge could be refined to reflect specific conditions e.g. gait for falls, erratic behaviour for Dementia, general physical activity level for obesity, etc.

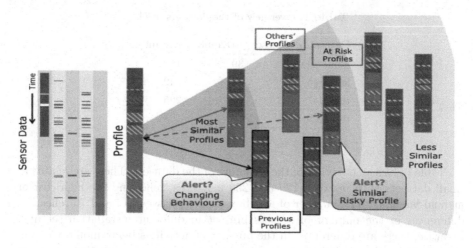

Fig. 4. CBR Approach to Identifying 'Risky' Behaviours

A key challenge is to identify risky or deteriorating behaviour. Labelled positive cases (identifying a fall is likely) are rare because people don't fall that often. The initial approach is to generate template solutions with guidance from health care professionals. Then, as real data becomes available, we can learn/refine/supplement these hand-crafted templates with the addition of real experiences as they occur in the data generated both by the user and by others.

5   Evaluation

The initial task is to assess our effectiveness at classifying ADLs from raw sensor data. We do not yet have live data being generated by tenants from the FitHomes, so for this evaluation we use existing datasets. The aim of the evaluation is to compare the performance of different ML algorithms when applied to the window-based and sequence-based representations.

5.1   Datasets

Four publicly available datasets are used in our experiments: CASAS[2] (adl-normal), Van Kasteren[3] (kasteren) and two from the Massachusetts Institute of Technology[4] (tapia1/2). These datasets share similar properties to that expected from the FitHomes with a focus on activity recognition using simple sensors in Smart Home installations. They all capture binary sensor activation data from the homes and have been labelled with class information, i.e. the ADL identified during the specified time period. The activities are of varying length.

---

[2] http://casas.wsu.edu/datasets/adlnormal.zip.

[3] https://sites.google.com/site/tim0306/kasterenDataset.zip.

[4] http://courses.media.mit.edu/2004fall/mas622j/04.projects/home/thesis_data_txt. zip.

Table 1. Overview of the datasets used.

Dataset	Classes	Attributes	Instances
adlnormal	5	39	120
kasteren	7	14	242
tapia1	22	76	295
tapia2	24	70	208

Table 1 gives an overview of the structure of the datasets. These are relatively small datasets with between 120 and 295 instances, reflecting the high cost of manual labelling. The number of attributes varies between 14 and 76 reflecting differences in the number of sensors present in different installation set ups. Likewise, there are differences in the number of activities being monitored (i.e. classes) depending on the focus of the particular study; tapia in particular has a large number of different activity labels, some of which would not be relevant for predicting falls. Some activities are more popular than others and as a result most datasets do not have balanced class distributions. In Table 2, the activity classes present in each dataset are shown, along with a count of the number of times the activity is recorded in the dataset.

Table 2. Details on the distribution of activities across datasets.

Dataset	Activities (in order of expression)
adlnormal	24 × Phone_Call, 24 × Wash_hands, 24 × Cook, 24 × Eat, 24 × Clean
kasteren	34 × Leave_House, 113 × Use_Toilet, 23 × Take_Shower, 23 × Go_to_Bed, 20 × Prepare_Breakfast, 10 × Prepare_Dinner, 19 × Get_Drink
tapia1	1 × Going_out_for_entertainment, 15 × Preparing_a_snack, 19 × Doing_laundry, 4 × Dressing, 1 × Washing_hands, 8 × Washing_dishes, 3 × Watching_TV, 14 × Preparing_breakfast, 12 × Going_out_to_work, 2 × Putting_away_dishes, 37 × Grooming, 9 × Cleaning, 2 × Putting_away_groceries, 18 × Bathing, 8 × Preparing_dinner, 17 × Preparing_lunch, 1 × Other, 2 × Putting_away_laundry, 2 × Going_out_for_shopping, 1 × Lawnwork, 15 × Preparing_a_beverage, 84 × Toileting
tapia2	4 × Talking_on_telephone, 1 × Lawnwork, 3 × Cleaning, 5 × Dressing, 16 × Preparing a snack, 2 × Home_education, 17 × Listening_to_music, 2 × Grooming, 37 × Toileting, 15 × Watching_TV, 2 × Other, 14 × Taking_medication, 13 × Preparing_breakfast, 5 × Working_at_computer, 3 × Going_out_for_shopping, 20 × Preparing_lunch, 20 × Washing_dishes, 1 × Preparing_a_beverage, 1 × Putting_away_groceries, 1 × Going_out_for_entertainment, 3 × Bathing, 3 × Putting_away_dishes, 1 × Putting_away_laundry, 14 × Preparing_dinner

The average sequence length of activities identified in the datasets varies between 4.7 in kasteren and 34.4 in adlnormal, as can be seen in Table 3. The datasets feature complete representations of sensor activations, including timestamps and durations, which allows us to build both a window-based and sequence-based representation.

The window-based representation is a fixed-length vector which does not change with varying activity lengths. If we count the number of sensors in the installation there will be one problem-side attribute for each sensor. The attribute value being a count of the number of times the sensor is activated during an activity timespan. The solution is a single class label, namely the labelled activity.

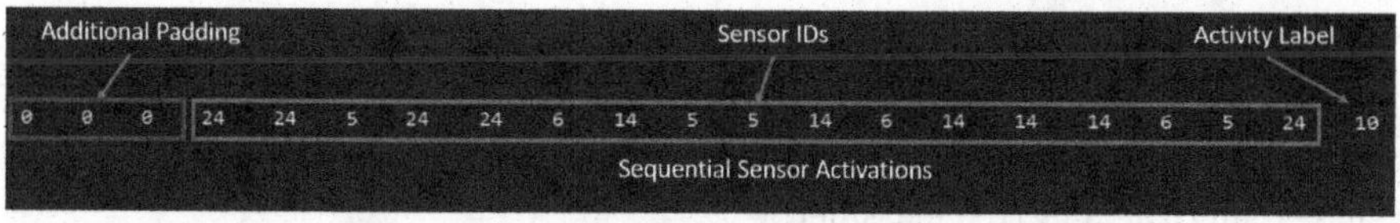

Fig. 5. Example Sequence-based representation for a shortened kasteren dataset.

The sequence-based representation captures temporal relationships between attributes. The intuition is that this additional information will aid activity classification performance, with the ordered sequences of sensor activations allowing more detailed understanding of activities and the underlying sensor network in the installation. A fixed length representation set to the length of the longest activity sequence in the dataset is used. Hence, as shown in Fig. 5, each problem-side attribute in a case is a sensor activation identified by its unique id, or a null padding value. As with the window-based representation, the solution is a single class label, identifying the activity. The longest activity length in the shortened "kasteren" example, is 20, and a sequence of 17 sensor activations is recorded in this activity. Hence, the first 3 attributes are null. As the maximum activity length increases, the number of null attribute values in shorter activities (which form the majority of datasets) will increase.

Table 3. Average and maximum length of activities.

Dataset	Sequence length		Temporal length	
	Avg (cnt)	Max (cnt)	Avg time (sec)	Max time (sec)
adlnormal	34.4	127	203.3	658
kasteren	4.7	92	8588.4	38193
tapia1	9.4	156	732.5	8132
tapia2	9.4	184	1824.5	14936

5.2 Experiment Set-Up

Popular ML algorithms that delivered good performance on these datasets were selected from the default Weka library to run on the window-based representation of each dataset [18]. These were compared to CRFs run on both the window-based and sequential-based representation. CRFs were selected for use with sequence-based representation as they can train based on the probability of previous sequences reoccurring. By modelling state-to-state dependencies the context of a sequence within a meta-sequence can be considered during training. Weka does not natively support learning with CRFs, and so for CRF learning, the CRF++ toolkit was used. Both tools make use of different data formats, so each dataset was converted to ARFF (for use in Weka), and CSV (for use with CRF++).

- Bayes Network: Using the BayesNet bayes classifier.
- k-NN: Using the IBk lazy classifier (with k = 3).
- SVM: Using the SMO function classifier.
- J48: Using the J48 tree classifier.
- CRF-Win: Using CRFs on the window-based representation.
- CRF-Seq: Using CRFs on sequenced-based representation.

Given the limited data available, Leave-One-Out cross validation was applied on all experiments. In addition to recording average accuracy results, confusion matrices were plotted for each dataset and ML algorithm combination using Matplotlib[5] (for CRFs), and Weka (for other algorithms).

Table 4. Experiment results (in accuracy %).

Dataset	BayesNet	k-NN	SVM	J48	CRF-Win	CRF-Seq
adlnormal	**98.3**	91.6	92.5	92.5	95.0	96.7
kasteren	92.6	**94.2**	81.0	93.4	80.6	93.0
tapia1	50.8	54.2	56.3	54.2	**61.0**	55.6
tapia2	28.3	34.6	35.1	**47.1**	**47.1**	42.0

5.3 Results and Discussion

The performance of BayesNet, k-NN, SVM, J48 and CRFs when used with Windowed data, and CRFs when used with Sequenced data are compared. The results can be seen in Table 4 with the highest accuracy achieved on each dataset in bold.

On the window-based representation, high accuracies, generally in excess of 90%, are achieved on adlnormal and kasteren compared to highs of 61% and 47%

---

[5] https://matplotlib.org/.

on tapia1 and 2 respectively. The differences reflect that both tapia datasets present a much harder classification task with over 20 fine grained activities, many of which are hard to distinguish even with over 70 sensors. adlnormal and kasteren have fewer activities being identified (5 and 7 respectively) and fewer sensors (39 and 14 respectively). kasteren in particular is more in line with the type of activities and sensor network we plan for FITsense.

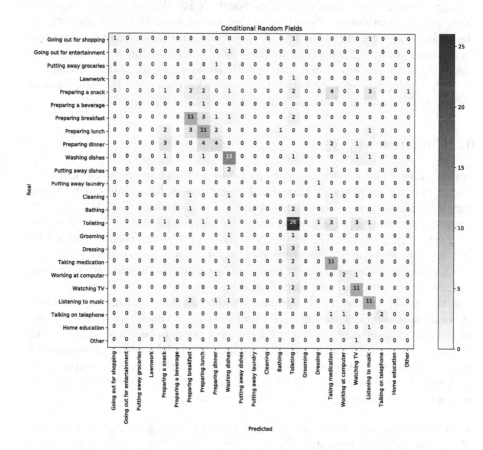

Fig. 6. Confusion matrix for CRFs on tapia1 windowed data.

With the algorithms applied to the window-based representation, there is not a clear winner. BayesNet, k-NN and J48 all provide good performance on the simpler datasets (adlnormal and kasteren); k-NN gives highest accuracy on kasteren which having the fewest sensors and shortest activity sequences is likely to have few noisy attributes. BayesNet gives highest accuracy on adlnormal which is distinguished by having long sensor sequences associated with activities. CRF-Win gives highest accuracies on the more complex tapia datasets, which seems to indicate that the relationship between sensor activations becomes more important for distinguishing similar activities from each other.

On the sequence-based dataset representation, CRF-Seq outperformed CRF-Win on the simpler datasets, although it was beaten by BayesNet on adlnormal and k-NN on kasteren. On the tapia datasets CRF-Seq did not perform as well as CRF-Win, although its performance was competitive with the other algorithms. These results are slightly surprising as we anticipated that knowledge of sensor activation sequence would improve classification.

Figure 6 shows an example confusion matrix (CRF-Win on tapia1). This view of the results identifies specific activities that get miss-classified and interestingly the activity they get miss-classified as. There are errors that might be expected, for example confusing preparing breakfast with preparing lunch and vice-versa. Generally, activities associated with specific sensors such as Taking Medication or Toileting tend to classify better than activities performed in shared spaces with several sensors used across many activities e.g. preparing dinner.

6   Conclusions

In this paper we have presented a Smart Home approach to predicting increased risk of falls for residents in 16 assisted living houses being built in Scotland. Simple ambient sensors are employed to monitor activities of daily living. We propose a two stage approach in which activities are first classified based on low level sensor data inputs. Daily/weekly activity profiles are then assembled for each resident and compared to their own past data and known risky profiles.

Overall, the initial experiment results on activity classification are promising and we can expect accurate identification of activities in FITsense, providing that the classes are not too fine-grained. It appears that the window-based representation is sufficient for effective classification, although the results are not clear and additional comparisons will be made when data becomes available from FitHomes. It may be that a hybrid approach is required with the assumption that attributes are independent being an effective simplification for simple activities; but for more complex activities, methods that take advantage of attribute interaction and event sequences may be more effective.

Acknowledgements. This work was part funded by The Scottish Funding Council via The Data Lab innovation centre. Thanks also to Matt Stevenson at Carbon Dynamic and Angus Watson at NHS Highland, Inverness for their support of the FITsense project.

References

1. Population Division, United Nations Department of Economic and Social Affairs: World population ageing (2015)
2. NHS Improvement: The incidence and costs of inpatient falls in hospitals (2017)
3. Tian, Y., Thompson, J., Buck, D., Sonola, L.: Exploring the System-Wide Costs of Falls in Older People in Torbay, pp. 1–12. The King's Fund, London (2013)

4. Turner, S., Kisser, R., Rogmans, W.: Falls among older adults in the EU-28 : key facts from the available statistics. Technical report, Swansea University, EuroSafe (2015)
5. Arfken, C.L., Lach, H.W., Birge, S.J., Miller, J.P.: The prevalence and correlates of fear of falling in elderly persons living in the community. Am. J. Public Health 84(4), 565–570 (1994)
6. Katz, S., Ford, A.B., Moskowitz, R.W., Jackson, B.A., Jaffe, M.W.: Studies of illness in the aged. the index of ADL: a standardized measure of biological and psychosocial function. J. Am. Med. Assoc. 185, 914–919 (1963)
7. Vestergaard, S., Patel, K.V., Bandinelli, S., Ferrucci, L., Guralnik, J.M.: Characteristics of 400-meter walk test performance and subsequent mortality in older adults. Rejuvenation Res. 12(3), 177–184 (2009)
8. Stone, E.E., Skubic, M.: Unobtrusive, continuous, in-home gait measurement using the Microsoft Kinect. IEEE Trans. Biomed. Eng. 60(10), 2925–2932 (2013)
9. Jiang, S., Zhang, B., Wei, D.: The elderly fall risk assessment and prediction based on gait analysis. In: 2011 IEEE 11th International Conference on Computer and Information Technology, pp. 176–180 (2011)
10. Montero-Odasso, M., et al.: Gait velocity as a single predictor of adverse events in healthy seniors aged 75 years and older. J. Gerontol. 60A, 1304–1309 (2005)
11. Rana, R., Austin, D., Jacobs, P.G., Karunanithi, M., Kaye, J.: Gait velocity estimation using time-interleaved between consecutive passive IR sensor activations. IEEE Sens. J. 16(16), 6351–6358 (2016)
12. Tapia, E.M., Intille, S.S., Larson, K.: Activity recognition in the home using simple and ubiquitous sensors. In: Ferscha, A., Mattern, F. (eds.) Pervasive 2004. LNCS, vol. 3001, pp. 158–175. Springer, Heidelberg (2004). https://doi.org/10.1007/978-3-540-24646-6_10
13. Suryadevara, N.K., Mukhopadhyay, S.C.: Wireless sensor network based home monitoring system for wellness determination of elderly. IEEE Sens. J. 12(6), 1965–1972 (2012)
14. Van Kasteren, T., Noulas, A., Englebienne, G., Kröse, B.: Accurate activity recognition in a home setting. In: Proceedings of the 10th International Conference on Ubiquitous Computing, pp. 1–9. ACM (2008)
15. Cook, D.J., Schmitter-Edgecombe, M.: Assessing the quality of activities in a smart environment. Methods Inf. Med. 48(5), 480 (2009)
16. Kim, E., Helal, S., Cook, D.: Human activity recognition and pattern discovery. IEEE Pervasive Comput. 9(1), 1–14 (2010)
17. Cook, D.J., Schmitter-edgecombe, M., Cook, D.J., Schmitter-edgecombe, M., Dawadi, P.: Analyzing activity behavior and movement in a naturalistic environment using smart home techniques. 19, 1882–1892 (2015)
18. Hall, M., Frank, E., Holmes, G., Pfahringer, B., Reutemann, P., Witten, I.H.: The WEKA data mining software: an update. SIGKDD Explor. 11(1), 10–18 (2009)

Embedded Word Representations for Rich Indexing: A Case Study for Medical Records

Katherine Metcalf and David Leake[✉]

School of Informatics, Computing, and Engineering, Indiana University,
Bloomington, IN 47408, USA
{metcalka,leake}@indiana.edu

Abstract. Case indexing decisions must often confront the tradeoff between rich semantic indexing schemes, which provide effective retrieval at large indexing cost, and shallower indexing schemes, which enable low-cost indexing but may be less reliable. Indexing for textual case-based reasoning is often based on information retrieval approaches that minimize index acquisition cost but sacrifice semantic information. This paper presents JointEmbed, a method for automatically generating rich indices. JointEmbed automatically generates continuous vector space embeddings that implicitly capture semantic information, leveraging multiple knowledge sources such as free text cases and pre-existing knowledge graphs. JointEmbed generates effective indices by applying *pTransR*, a novel approach for modelling knowledge graphs, to encode and summarize contents of domain knowledge resources. JointEmbed is applied to the medical CBR task of retrieving relevant patient electronic health records, for which potential health consequences make retrieval quality paramount. An evaluation supports that JointEmbed outperforms previous methods.

Keywords: Case-based reasoning for medicine
Electronic health records · Indexing · Textual case-based reasoning
Vector space embedding

1 Introduction

Textual case-based reasoning (TCBR) (e.g., [32]) enables case-based reasoning to exploit textual case information captured for human use. Electronic health records (EHRs) provide a high-impact information source for TCBR. National initiatives have encouraged the adoption of such records, and in the United States a majority of doctors and hospitals keep their records in electronic form. If harnessed effectively, EHRs could provide a vast resource for assisting with tasks such as diagnosis, early disease detection, and treatment decision support. However, indexing such records for effective retrieval is challenging. When reasoning about patient conditions, relational information is important (e.g. how and

M. T. Cox et al. (Eds.): ICCBR 2018, LNAI 11156, pp. 264–280, 2018.
https://doi.org/10.1007/978-3-030-01081-2_18

which symptoms are related to which illnesses); case retrieval should reflect such relations. Common textual retrieval approaches, such as bag-of-words (BoW) [5] and word frequency counts [33], while successful in many domains, do not represent relational or semantic information, resulting in crucial loss of information about connections between symptoms and between illnesses. Incorporating relational and semantic knowledge into TCBR indices can substantially improve performance [32], but traditionally requires drawing on knowledge and computationally expensive natural language processing (NLP) tools at query time.

This paper presents research on mining and capturing semantic and relational information for indexing textual cases, tested on the EHR domain. The approach we propose automatically represents knowledge as word embeddings. Our system, JointEmbed, extends research on distributed continuous vector space embeddings, which represent words using a real-valued vector. Such embeddings, especially those learned using the *word2vec* approach, have been shown to encode useful semantic characteristics of words, and indexing has been done via word embeddings that encode semantic and relational information. We extend the existing *word2vec* framework to enable JointEmbed simultaneously to encode both semantic and relational information.

JointEmbed can leverage multiple knowledge sources, ranging from free text to knowledge graphs, to learn word embeddings. It applies *pTransR*, a new method which we developed to model and incorporate information from knowledge graphs within the embeddings learned using the existing *word2vec* framework. The resulting word embeddings are a single resource that encodes and summarizes the information across knowledge resources. We hypothesize that our method will result in a more robust and generalizable indexing scheme for EHRs compared to other word embeddings techniques [7,9,25,27,34]. This hypothesis is tested with the word embeddings used to represent physician notes for indexing, and with PubMed article abstracts, Unified Medical Language System (UMLS), MeSH, clinical trial reports, and the Merck Manuals used as the sources of background knowledge. The performance of JointEmbed's indexing scheme is scored according to the quality of cases retrieved, following methods of Moen and colleagues [20], with the goal of taking a new patient record as input and retrieving cases able to support patient diagnosis. The performance of JointEmbed highlights the benefit of leveraging domain knowledge that is external to the knowledge contained in the cases to learn continuous space vector embeddings.

2 Motivation

The goal of this work is to develop domain-independent methods for learning word representations that encode the important semantic and relational information for retrieving useful cases. The proposed method relies on an objective function for jointly learning word embeddings across free text and structured knowledge sources. The word embeddings are then used as the indexing scheme to encode rich and robust information about words in text.

Indexing text is challenging because word-based representations do not encode the semantic meaning or function of words they represent. Continuous space vector embeddings encode a word's meaning or function. Recently it has been shown that algorithms such as *skip-gram* [16], a highly efficient version of *word2vec*, can encode some degree of semantic information, and that algorithms such as TransE [4] can encode relational information. Learning word representations that are solely based on word co-occurrences, as in *word2vec*, ignores existing information available in the form of knowledge graphs. Our method aims to address this issue by learning word embeddings that represent both the raw, unstructured information and the formal, structured information that knowledge graphs may provide for a given word.

3   Task Domain

When making decisions, medical practitioners rely on prior experience with similar patients, the information given in a patient's medical history file, and a vast wealth of medical knowledge formalized, refined, and maintained by the community. The importance of experiential knowledge immediately points to the usefulness of CBR and has lead to extensive research in CBR and medicine (e.g., [2]). However, especially as case complexity increases and case bases grow, achieving reliable and efficient retrieval may be challenging. Electronic health records (EHRs) are complex sources of data that are temporally extended and consist of multiple data modalities, such as phycisian's notes, blood tests, and heart rate readings. As case data, our work uses the EHRs from the MIMIC-III (Medical Information Mart for Intensive Care) database [11]. MIMIC-III contains information about patients admitted to critical care units. Each patient's visit is described according to the data collected, procedures done, and the final diagnosis and/or treatment. Our cases contain the database's physician notes and the "ICD-9" label assigned to each visit indicating its outcome. This information could be used in many ways, but for purposes of our studies, we consider the reasoning task to be predicting the visit outcome from the physician notes.

Domain knowledge includes several medical knowledge sources as additional background knowledge: PubMed Central journal articles[1], the Merck Manuals [26], clinical trials information[2], the Unified Medical Language System (UMLS) knowledge graph [3], and the Medical Subject Headings (MeSH) metathesaurus[3]. The PubMed Central articles, the Merck Manuals, and the clinical trials fall under the category of formal, unstructured knowledge sources. While semi-structured knowledge is associated with these sources, it was not used for the purposes of this paper. UMLS and MeSh explicitly define relations between different medical concepts and fall under the category of formal, structured knowledge sources. WordNet [19] was used to provide background knowledge for words that are not specific to medicine.

---

[1] http://www.ncbi.nlm.nih.gov/pmc/tolls/openftlist.

[2] https://clinicaltrials.gov.

[3] https://www.ncbi.nlm.nih.gov/mesh.

4   Background

Textual CBR (TCBR): Many methods have been proposed for indexing textual information. Frequently these approaches draw from information retrieval and incorporate IR techniques such as using the information retrieval (IR) term vector space model [32]. Similarly to our method, a number of approaches use both statistical and background information, combining IR and NLP. Typically a statistical method is used when doing the initial retrieval pass, and then a more knowledge intensive approach is used during the second pass, e.g. in FAQ-Finder [6]. Other approaches reason about word counts/statistics or tree representations derived from the text, e.g. FALLQ [14]. In FAQ-Finder and FallQ cases are entirely textual. However, there are domains in which cases contain both text and non-text features resulting in additional challenges; the textual information needs to be related to the non-textual information. Statistical IR methods are a common way to relate the textual and non-textual information, e.g. in the DRAMA design support system [34].

Rich representations often depend on knowledge engineering to craft a case representation and define the similarity metric [23,28]. This imposes a heavy burden, motivating development of methods for automatically identifying and mining meaningful features from the text. Such features can take forms such as graphs [7,27,29], semantic themes (e.g. SOPHIA [25]), propositional clauses [34], and predicate logic (e.g. FACIT [9]). Domain independent methods have been proposed for extracting such features, but constructing graphs and extracting relevant information can be computationally expensive at query time.

Learning Continuous Space Vector Representations from Texts: Distributed and reduced representations capture global properties of words by mapping them to a continuous, high-dimensional space that encodes the contexts in which they occur, which in turn reflect their semantics. Several techniques have been used to learn word context representations, such as latent semantic indexing (LSI) [8,24], random indexing (RI) [12], and *word2vec* [16–18].

Word2vec is currently considered to be the state-of-the-art for learning continuous space vector embeddings of words. The most efficient version of *word2vec* is *skip-gram* [13]. During training, the goal of *skip-gram* is to learn word representations that can be used to predict which other words are likely to occur nearby. The objective is based on the idea that a word's context should be predictive of that word. In the case of *skip-gram*, a word's context is those words that occur within some fixed window to its left and right [17].

A variant of *word2vec* [13] that learns vector representations for words, sentences, paragraphs, and entire documents has been used to evaluate query and document similarity within a clinical decision support (CDS) system [36]. The CDS system retrieves relevant biomedical articles given a user query. Continuous space vector embeddings are learned to represent the user queries and the biomedical articles, and are then used to evaluate the semantic similarity between the queries and the articles. The word and paragraph vectors are learned according to the method of Le and Mikolov [13]. Queries are compared against existing documents by computing the cosine similarity between the query vector representation and the vector representation of each document. Documents are then ranked according to the similarity score. A similar approach was later taken by Moen and colleagues [20, 21] where queries were entire patient health records and relevant patient cases were retrieved.

Learning Continuous Space Vectors from Knowledge Graphs: Multiple methods exist for learning continuous space vectors from knowledge graphs. The methods treat knowledge graphs as being composed of relational triplets and take inspiration from the *word2vec* algorithm. One category of approach learns a single vector per relation and considers the relationship between two entities to be a translation [4, 10, 15, 31, 35]; *pTransE* [30] and *TransR* [15] are specific instances of this approach and provide the basis for the new algorithm presented in this paper, *pTransR*. In general, the different approaches operate under the premise that when a relation, r, between two objects, h and t, holds, translating an entity vector, $\mathbf{h}$, representing h by the relation vector $\mathbf{r}$ should result in a vector, $\mathbf{t}$, near t. For example, given the relation (cough symptom_of cold), translating the vector for "cough" by the relation vector "symptom_of" should result in a vector very similar to the one for "cold." Typically, the first object in the relation, "cough," is referred to as the head of the relation and the second object, "cold," is referred to as the tail of the relation.

Each of the approaches defines a scoring function that evaluates how true the relation $(\mathbf{h}, \mathbf{r}, \mathbf{t})$ is, but they differ according to exact mechanism by which $\mathbf{h}$ and $\mathbf{t}$ are compared and according to the loss and objective functions used to learn the embeddings. *pTransE* uses a log-likelihood objective function and translates objects by relations by adding the relation vector, $\mathbf{r}$, to the object vector, $\mathbf{h}$. *TransR* uses a SVM-like objective function and projects the object vector, $\mathbf{h}$, into the relation's semantic space before adding the relation and object vectors together.

While learning the embeddings, the objective is to predict the object that participates in relation with the head object. At the core of each approach is a scoring function that applies a linear combination to the head $\mathbf{h} \in \mathbb{R}^d$ and the relation $\mathbf{r} \in \mathbb{R}^d$, and computes the resulting vector's distance from the tail $\mathbf{t} \in \mathbb{R}^d$. The distance is computed using either the L_1 or L_2 norm. How the head, relation, and tail embeddings are computed varies across approaches.

5   Methods

JointEmbed treats each knowledge source as independently contributing to and constraining the meaning of the word representations (embeddings). Specifically, the free text provides information about word co-occurrences and the knowledge graphs define more complex relations (e.g. "is an instance of" or "is a synonym of"). The contribution of the free text knowledge sources is modelled using *skip-gram* [16], which learns word representations that are predictive of word co-occurrences. To jointly model the information provided by the knowledge graphs with that provided by the free text we developed *pTransR*, described in detail in a following subsection.

A single set of word embeddings was learned across knowledge sources. However, a unique set of relation embeddings was learned per knowledge graph as the relations in each graph were considered to occupy distinct semantic spaces. For example, a knowledge graph about heart attacks will define a space of information about blood pressure that is different from that defined by a knowledge graph about diabetes. The concept "blood pressure" is shared between the knowledge graphs, but its implications and relations vary. Constraining the word embeddings according to a set of semantically distinct relations results in embeddings that are both robust to, and generalizable across, different medical domains. The need for unique relation embeddings per knowledge graph becomes clear when the procedure for learning the embeddings is discussed in Sect. 5.

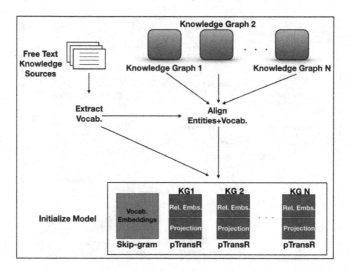

Fig. 1. Overview of data processing and model initialization.

Preparing JointEmbed: Figure 1 presents an outline of training data pre-processing, alignment of free text words and knowledge graph entities, and extracting the vocabulary and relation statistics needed to initialize the joint embedding model. The data is pre-processed by applying MetaMap [1] to associate National Library of Medicine concepts with each sentence; cleaning the text by removing stopwords, punctuation, digits, and XML/HTML mark-up language; correcting spelling mistakes; splitting the texts up into sentences; and removing all words that occur less than 50 times, which is standard practice. The embedding vocabulary and vocabulary statistics are then extracted and aligned with the entities in the knowledge graphs. The model is then initialized according to the vocabulary, vocabulary statistics, and the set of relations. A single vocabulary embedding matrix is created; relation embedding matrices and projection matrices are created for each relation in the set of knowledge graphs.

The resulting vocabulary set, vocabulary statistics, relation sets, and relation statistics are used to initialize the embeddings model. All embedding matrices are initialized according to a uniform distribution over $(-\frac{1}{\sqrt{6}}, \frac{1}{\sqrt{6}})$ [13]. The number of rows in the word embedding matrix is equal to the number of words in the vocabulary. The number of rows in the relation embedding matrix for a knowledge graph is equal to the number of unique relations in the knowledge graph. The number of columns in each embedding matrix is equal to the desired dimensionality of the embeddings (e.g. 20, 50, 100). The projection tensor is used to project the word embeddings into the semantic space occupied by the relation embeddings. The tensor contains a matrix per unique relation in the knowledge graph.

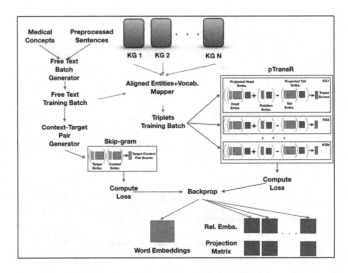

Fig. 2. Overview of training the embedding model.

Training the Model: The process by which the word embeddings are learned is outlined in Fig. 2. The training process consists of 5 main steps:

1. Extract a mini-batch from the set of training sentences and medical concepts;
2. Find all triplets in which the words in the mini-batch participate (these triplets become part of the context for that word);
3. Create the target-context word pairs from the list of medical concepts and the words in the sentence;
4. Create the target-context pairs from the words in the sentence;
5. Update the model following Eq. (9) (below).

A word is considered to participate in a triplet if it plays the role of head, tail, or relation. The extracted triplets act as the structured context for the words in the sentence and the list of medical concepts. The target-context word pairs for the sentence are generated using the *skip-gram* method. Each word within some predefined window of the target word is part of that word's context. The context for the words in the list of medical concepts is the set of words in the sentence.

The model is updated according to Eq. (9). The scores and the loss for each target-context word pair and for each triplet are computed and used to update the embeddings. The model is updated via stochastic gradient descent. The above process is repeated until model convergence is reached.

Modeling Free Text: The free text knowledge sources were modelled according to *skip-gram* [16,17]. The objective function is defined as the average log-probability over all T words:

$$\frac{1}{T}\prod_{t=1}^{T}\sum_{-c\leq j\leq c,\, j\notin\{0,t\}}\log p(w_{t+j}|w_t),\tag{1}$$

where c is the maximum number of words to consider to the left and the right of the target, i.e. the context window. For each word in the text w_t, the objective maximizes the likelihood of the c words to the left and the c words to the right. The constraint on j, $j\notin\{0,t\}$, ensures that a given word is not its own context. The probability of a target word's context is evaluated according to:

$$p(w_c|w_t)=\frac{\exp\left(v_c\cdot v_t\right)}{\sum_{c'\in C}\exp\left(v_{c'}\cdot v_t\right)}.\tag{2}$$

where C is the set of all possible context words, v_c is the n-dimensional vector for context word w_c and v_t is the n-dimensional vector for target word w_t. As a result, the matrix of word embeddings is defined according to $|V|\cdot n$ real-valued numbers, where V is the set of all unique vocabulary words and, typically, $V=C$. Given a large vocabulary the denominator of Eq. 2 becomes computationally intractable. Therefore, $\log p(w_c|w_t)$ is estimated according to Negative Sampling (NEG) [16], which converts the objective into a binary classification problem where the goal is to distinguish between the positive and negative target-context word pairs. Every time an embedding is moved closer to its neighbors, it is tugged away from j embeddings sampled from a distribution over all embeddings.

The log-probability is re-defined accordingly:

$$\log p(w_c|w_t)=\log\sigma(v_c^\top v_t)+\sum_{i=1}^{j}\mathbb{E}_{w_i\sim P_n(w)}[\log\sigma(-v_i^\top v_t)],\tag{3}$$

where $v_t, v_c, v_i \in \mathbb{R}^n$ are the vector embeddings for the target word, the positive context word, and the negative context word sampled; j is the number of negative samples to draw for each positive target and context word pair; and $P_n(w)$ is the noise distribution over context words. The exact noise distribution over context words is a free variable. In practice, the unigram distribution (i.e. frequency of word occurrences) raised to the $\frac{3}{4}$ power works well [17]. For small data set 15 to 20 negative sample works well and two to five works well for large data sets [17].

Modeling Relations – pTransR: We developed *pTransR* as a new method for modeling the knowledge graphs. *pTransR* combines elements of *TransR* [15] and *pTransE* [30] in order to benefit from the strengths of both. *TransR* considers entities (i.e. graph nodes) to exist in different semantic spaces than relation embeddings, preventing combining them into rich indices. To address this problem, the entity embeddings are projected into the semantic space occupied by the relations. However, *TransR* uses a margin-based objective function. *pTransE* does not project entity embeddings into the same semantic space as relations, but it uses a likelihood-based objective function. By combining the two approaches, *pTransR* uses the same type of objective function as *skip-gram* while computing word similarity in a shared semantic space.

$$\frac{1}{T}\prod_{t=1}^{T}\left[\sum_{g\in G}\sum_{(h,r,l)\in \mathbf{g}(w_t)}\log\left(p(h|r,l)p(l|r,h)p(r|h,l)\right)\right]. \tag{4}$$

For each vocabulary word in the free text, the set of triplets $\mathbf{g}(w_t)$ in which the word participates is extracted and the likelihood of each triplet (h,r,l) is maximized. The objective function for *pTransR* is given in Eq. (4), where T is the number of words in the training text and G is the set of knowledge graphs defining the relations between the vocabulary words. The likelihood of a triplet is further expanded as the joint probability of each component of the triplet given the other two. For example, the probability of the head given the relation and the tail is:

$$p(h|r,l)=\frac{\exp \mathbf{z}(v_h, u_r, v_l)}{\sum_{h'\in \mathbb{V}}\exp \mathbf{z}(v_{h'}, u_r, v_l)}, \tag{5}$$

where $v_h, v_l \in \mathbb{R}^n$ are the vector embeddings of the head and tail words, $u_r \in \mathbb{R}^m$ is the vector embedding for the relation, $\mathbf{z}(v_h, u_r, v_l)$ computes the distance between the head-relation pair and the tail in the embedding space, and V is the set of other possible words filling the role of the tail. This definition follows that used in *pTransE* [30].

The scoring function comes from *TransR* [15] and relies on projection matrices ($M_r \in \mathbb{R}^{n\times m}$) to shift the word embeddings to the semantic space occupied by the relations. Each relation occupies a distinct semantic space, therefore each relation r has its own projection matrices. The entities are projected according to:

$$\mathbf{h}_r = v_h M_r, \mathbf{l}_r = v_l M_r, \tag{6}$$

where v_h and v_l are the vectors for the head and tail of the relation and $\mathbf{h}_r$ and $\mathbf{l}_r$ are the head and tail vectors projected into r's semantic space. The same projection matrix, M_r, is applied to both the head and the tail embeddings.

The projected embeddings $\mathbf{h}_r$ and $\mathbf{l}_r$ are used to score the triplet according to:

$$\mathbf{z}(v_h, u_r, v_l) = ||\mathbf{h}_r + \mathbf{r} - \mathbf{l}_r||_2^2. \tag{7}$$

The L_2 norm is applied as a constraint on each of the embedding vectors and projection matrices to prevent the embeddings from artificially inflating the scores.

As for *skip-gram*, the denominator in Eq. (5) becomes computationally intractable for large knowledge graphs. Therefore, the *pTransR* log-probability $\log \mathbb{L}((h, r, l))$ is also estimated using Negative Sampling (NEG), making the task a binary classification problem with the goal of distinguishing positive triplets and negative triplets sampled from a noise distribution. The first term in the following equation computes the probability of the given triplet, the second term handles negative sampling for triplet heads, the third handles negative sampling for triplet tails, and the fourth handles negative sampling for triplet relations.

$$\log \left(p(h|r, l) p(l|r, h) p(r|h, l) \right) = 3 \log \sigma(\mathbf{z}(v_h, u_r, v_l))$$
$$+ \sum_{i=1}^{j} \mathbb{E}_{h' \sim P_n(V)} \left[\log \sigma(\mathbf{z}(v_{h'}, u_r, v_l)) \right]$$
$$+ \sum_{i=1}^{j} \mathbb{E}_{l' \sim P_n(V)} \left[\log \sigma(\mathbf{z}(v_h, u_r, v_{l'})) \right]$$
$$+ \sum_{i=1}^{j} \mathbb{E}_{r' \sim P_n(R)} \left[\log \sigma(\mathbf{z}(v_h, u_{r'}, v_l)) \right]. \tag{8}$$

NEG must be applied to each of the probabilities from Eq. 4 to redefine them as Eq. 8, where V is the set of vocabulary words, R is the set of relations, $P_n(V)$ is the noise distribution over negative words, and $P_n(R)$ is the noise distribution over negative relations.

The use of NEG to estimate the log-probability of the triplets highlights the need to model the knowledge graphs and the relations they contain independently. As the relations in the knowledge graph exist in separate semantic spaces, it is inappropriate to sample relations that are part of other knowledge graphs during the negative sampling phase.

JointEmbed: Finally, we developed JointEmbed, an approach for jointly learning word embeddings from free text and knowledge graph information sources. Given the above formalism for *skip-gram* and *pTransR*, combining the two becomes straightforward. By formalizing *TransR* to exist in the same space as *pTransE*, both the *skip-gram* and *pTransR* objective functions attempt to maximize the likelihood of true instances, context-target word pair or relational triplet, the *pTransR* objective function can be incorporated into the *skip-gram* objective function. The *pTransR* objective function is incorporated by adding the *skip-gram* likelihood function and the *pTransR* likelihood functions as follows:

$$\frac{1}{T}\prod_{t=1}^{T}\left[\sum_{-c\leq j\leq c,\, j\notin\{0,t\}}\log p(w_{t+j}|w_t)\right]+\left[\sum_{g\in G}\sum_{(h,r,l)\in \mathbf{g}(w_t)}\log \mathbb{L}(h,r,l)\right], \quad (9)$$

where the summation on the left of Eq. (9) is the *skip-gram* objective function. The nested summation on the right is the *pTransR* objective, introduced below. In the *skip-gram* portion of the equation, $\log p(w_{t+j}|w_t)$ is still expanded using Eq. (3) as defined above in **Modeling Free Text**. In the *pTransR* portion of the equation, $\log \mathbb{L}(h,r,l)$ is expanded according to Eq. (8) defined above. Each knowledge graph incorporated through the *pTransR* objective only contributes to the word embeddings when the knowledge graph contains triplets in which the word participates.

Case Indexing and Retrieval: Cases are indexed in memory according to a summary of their content (Fig. 3). First the word representations of each clinical note are summarized using vector addition over all word embeddings to create a representation for that note; second all clinical note representations are summarized by summing over all note embeddings to create a representation for that patient. Cases are indexed according to these summaries. A new patient is compared first to the patient-level summary for each case in the case base. Once the first set of cases is retrieved, they are further evaluated by comparing them at the level of the clinical note representation. During the first pass, the cosine similarity measure is used because it has been shown to perform well on analogy, word clustering, and word similarity tasks [16–18]. Following Moen and colleagues [20], during the second pass notes are aligned using the Needleman-Wunsch [22] sequence alignment algorithm, which aligns patient cases by their most similar clinical notes. Needleman-Wunsch is used because it maintains the temporal order of the notes when doing alignment. The notes are then compared through a pairwise measure of similarity between note representations for aligned notes. The final similarity score between the current patient and a case in the case base is computed following:

$$\frac{2\cdot\sum_n \cos\left(\mathbf{p_n},\mathbf{c_{i,n}}\right)}{|\mathbf{p}|+|\mathbf{c_i}|}, \quad (10)$$

where the summation is over all pairs of aligned notes n, $\mathbf{p_n}$ represents clinical note n from the current patient's EHR, $\mathbf{c_{i,n}}$ represents clinical note n from case i in the case base, the denominator represents the total number of clinical notes associated with the patient and with the case from the case base. The most similar case returned as the most relevant case in memory.

6   Experimental Design

The effectiveness of the learned word embeddings for indexing was evaluated on MIMIC-III [11], a database containing information from 53,423 distinct adult

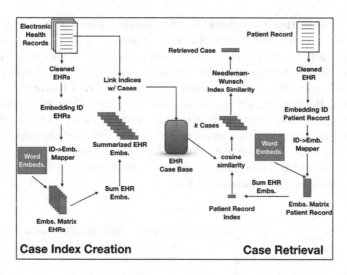

Fig. 3. Overview of extracting case indices and retrieve cases from memory.

patients (16 or older) admitted into hospital critical care units from 2001 to 2012. Additionally, it contains information about 7,870 neonates admitted from 2001 to 2008. The task is to retrieve EHRs that are relevant to the given patient's condition, as recorded in the record, based on the textual clinical notes describing the patient gathered at the time of admission.

We compare the performance of our model against *word2vec* [16] and *word2vec-ICD* [20], a modified implementation of word2vec that incorporates the primary ICD-9 code associated with a clinical note into the context set for each word in the note. The models were trained using the same methods described by Moen and colleagues [20]. The index used to describe a current problem patient record is generated according to the method outlined in Fig. 3.

EHRs represent final physician determinations using ICD-9 codes, a system used to classify patients and their treatment procedures. ICD-9 codes have an internal structure that reflects the classification system, ranging from broad categories down to fine-grained subjects, making them a useful approximation for case relevance. ICD-9 codes served as the gold standard for our evaluation: case retrieval was evaluated based on whether the primary ICD-9 code of the retrieved case matched the ICD-9 code of the patient in the query case. All ICD-9 information from query cases was withheld from index generation.

Forty EHRs were randomly selected to serve as the query episodes during testing, with the requirement that all had different ICD-9 codes and each consisted of a minimum of six clinical notes. Performance is reported using the following metrics: precision at 10 (p@10), R-precision (RPrec), and mean average precision (MAP). P@10 is the proportion of cases with the same ICD-9 code as the current patient that fall within the 10 most similar cases averaged across all 40 test patients. P@10 scores reported are averages over 40 queries. RPrec is the precision at the R-th position in the results, where R is the number of correct entries in the gold standard averaged across all 40 test patients. This metric conveys the proportion of the top-R retrieved episodes with the same ICD-9 code. MAP is the mean of the average precision over the 40 test patients.

The word embeddings were learned using the external resources described in Sect. 3 and the training procedure described in Fig. 2. The word embeddings were updated until convergence was reached. Model parameters for JointEmbed were selected by sweeping different parameter values. Selected parameter settings for the model were: a context window of size four, learning rate of 0.001, a margin value of 5, word embeddings with a dimensionality of 150, and relation embeddings with a dimensionality of 100.

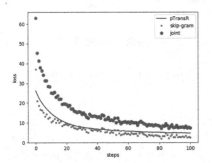

Table 1. Performance evaluation comparison averaged over the 40 test cases.

	MAP	P@10	RPrec
word2vec	0.0647	0.1949	0.0954
word2vec-ICD	0.0938	0.2410	0.1264
JointEmbed	0.5039	0.7175	0.5529

Fig. 4. Training loss in model averaged for each epoch (100 training steps).

7   Experimental Results

The learning curves in Fig. 4 demonstrate that within JointEmbed *skip-gram's* contribution to the loss function was considerably noisier than *pTransR's*. This is likely to be because word co-occurrence is a noisier signal or relation between words to model. For example, many verbs may co-occur with "cough," but there are fewer triplets in which it may participate. However, the loss contributions from both *skip-gram* and *pTransR* decayed nicely allowing the overall joint loss function to decay and converge. The learning curves for the *skip-gram* and *pTransR* loss values have similar shapes and rates of decay indicating that it is possible to constrain word embeddings with relational knowledge graphs without requiring the extra linking structure used in PTransE [10]. This reduces the overall complexity of the learned model.

We compare the performance of our model with that achieved by Moen and colleagues [20] using word2vec [16] and word2vec-ICD. Both models were trained only on the MIMIC-III data, as was done in Moen et al. [20], using the default word2vec settings found at https://code.google.com/p/word2vec/. The MAP, P@10, and RPrec scores for each of the three models is reported in Table 1.

JointEmbed outperformed *word2vec* and *word2vec-ICD* with relative increases of 778.8% and 537.2% in MAP, 368.1% and 297.7% in P@10, and 579.6% and 437.4% in RPrec, respectively. The results indicate that leveraging external knowledge sources, in the form of free text literature and knowledge graphs, and refining on the available EHRs greatly increased the utility of the learned word embeddings.

8   Future Directions

The immediate motivation for our work was to develop an automatic indexing method able to capture and combine implicit semantic information from free text and knowledge graphs. However, the ability to generate embedded representations for CBR based on text and knowledge graphs might potentially have ramifications for supporting CBR tasks beyond indexing, through direct manipulation of those representations. There are intriguing indications that under some circumstances *Word2vec* embeddings can directly support analogical reasoning tasks via vector operations over them, e.g., that the "Paris" embedding minus the "France" embedding plus the embedding for "Spain" yielded an embedding closest to "Madrid" [16], and that the "King" embedding minus the "male" embedding plus the "female" embedding yielded an embedding closest to "Queen" [18]. If this type of direct process were borne out more generally and could be applied in the medical domain, using JointEmbed representations to represent treatments, those representations might help suggest substitution adaptations. As an example, suppose the embedding method were applied to the treatments given to patients, and that the treatment provided to a past patient involved a medication to which the current patient had an allergy. The embedding for the symptoms, minus the embedding for the contraindicated medication and plus the embedding for new symptoms, might suggest a case with a substitution, which could then be used to adapt the treatment plan.

9   Conclusion

The paper has demonstrated the usefulness of indexing textual cases using continuous space vector representations of words in the medical domain. The performance of JointEmbed versus other similar models highlights the usefulness and benefits of leveraging external domain knowledge not contained in the cases. Besides performance alone, our model has several advantages. Learning word representation via available domain knowledge helps to handle the cold start problem that in the absence of a large case base of EHRs it is impossible to learn robust word representations. Additionally, the amount of patient specific information encoded in the learned word embeddings is limited, reducing risks to privacy of sharing them among practitioners. Our next step is to extend JointEmbed and pTransR to other CBR tasks, such as question-answer systems. A long-term goal is to explore the potential of JointEmbed representations to facilitate other aspects of the CBR process, such as applying JointEmbed embeddings to case solutions, to facilitate case adaptation for TCBR.

Acknowledgement. This work is supported by the Indiana University Precision Health Initiative.

References

1. Aronson, A.R.: Effective mapping of biomedical text to the UMLS metathesaurus: the MetaMap program. In: Proceedings of the AMIA Symposium, pp. 17–21. American Medical Informatics Association (2001)
2. Bichindaritz, I., Marling, C.: Case-based reasoning in the health sciences: what's next? Artif. Intell. Med. **36**(2), 127–135 (2006)
3. Bodenreider, O.: The unified medical language system (UMLS): integrating biomedical terminology. Nucl. Acids Res. **32**, 267–270 (2004)
4. Bordes, A., Usunier, N., García-Durán, A., Weston, J., Yakhnenko, O.: Translating embeddings for modeling multi-relational data. In: Advances in Neural Information Processing Systems, vol. 26, pp. 2787–2795 (2013)
5. Brüninghaus, S., Ashley, K.D.: The role of information extraction for textual CBR. In: Aha, D.W., Watson, I. (eds.) ICCBR 2001. LNCS (LNAI), vol. 2080, pp. 74–89. Springer, Heidelberg (2001). https://doi.org/10.1007/3-540-44593-5_6
6. Burke, R.D., Hammond, K.J., Kulyukin, V.A., Lytinen, S.L., Tomuro, N., Schoenberg, S.: Question answering from frequently asked question files: experiences with the FAQ finder system. AI Mag. **18**(2), 57–66 (1997)
7. Cunningham, C., Weber, R., Proctor, J.M., Fowler, C., Murphy, M.: Investigating graphs in textual case-based reasoning. In: Funk, P., González Calero, P.A. (eds.) ECCBR 2004. LNCS (LNAI), vol. 3155, pp. 573–586. Springer, Heidelberg (2004). https://doi.org/10.1007/978-3-540-28631-8_42
8. Deerwester, S.C., Dumais, S.T., Landauer, T.K., Furnas, G.W., Harshman, R.A.: Indexing by latent semantic analysis. JASIS **41**(6), 391–407 (1990)
9. Gupta, K.M., Aha, D.W.: Towards acquiring case indexing taxonomies from text. In: Proceedings of the 17th International Florida AI Research Society Conference, pp. 172–177 (2004)
10. Huang, W., Li, G., Jin, Z.: Improved knowledge base completion by the path-augmented transR model. In: Li, G., Ge, Y., Zhang, Z., Jin, Z., Blumenstein, M. (eds.) KSEM 2017. LNCS (LNAI), vol. 10412, pp. 149–159. Springer, Cham (2017). https://doi.org/10.1007/978-3-319-63558-3_13
11. Johnson, A.E., et al.: MIMIC-III. Scientific data **3**, 160035 (2016)
12. Kanerva, P., Kristoferson, J., Holst, A.: Random indexing of text samples for latent semantic analysis. In: Proceedings of the Annual Meeting of the Cognitive Science Society, pp. 103–106. Erlbaum (2002)
13. Le, Q.V., Mikolov, T.: Distributed representations of sentences and documents. In: Proceedings of the 31st International Conference on Machine Learning ICML, pp. 1188–1196 (2014)
14. Lenz, M., Burkhard, H.-D.: CBR for document retrieval: the FALLQ project. In: Leake, D.B., Plaza, E. (eds.) ICCBR 1997. LNCS, vol. 1266, pp. 84–93. Springer, Heidelberg (1997). https://doi.org/10.1007/3-540-63233-6_481
15. Lin, Y., Liu, Z., Sun, M., Liu, Y., Zhu, X.: Learning entity and relation embeddings for knowledge graph completion. In: Proceedings of the Twenty-Ninth AAAI Conference on Artificial Intelligence, pp. 2181–2187. AAAI Press (2015)
16. Mikolov, T., Chen, K., Corrado, G., Dean, J.: Efficient estimation of word representations in vector space. CoRR abs/1301.3781 (2013). http://arxiv.org/abs/1301.3781

17. Mikolov, T., Sutskever, I., Chen, K., Corrado, G.S., Dean, J.: Distributed representations of words and phrases and their compositionality. Adv. Neural Inf. Process. Syst. **26**, 3111–3119 (2013)
18. Mikolov, T., Yih, W.T., Zweig, G.: Linguistic regularities in continuous space word representations. In: Proceedings of the 2013 Conference of the North American Chapter of the Association for Computational Linguistics, pp. 746–751 (2013)
19. Miller, G.A.: Wordnet: a lexical database for english. Commun. ACM **38**(11), 39–41 (1995)
20. Moen, H., Ginter, F., Marsi, E., Peltonen, L., Salakoski, T., Salanterä, S.: Care episode retrieval: distributional semantic models for information retrieval in the clinical domain. BMC Med. Inf. Decis. Mak. **15**(S-2)–S2 (2015)
21. Moen, H., et al.: Comparison of automatic summarisation methods for clinical free text notes. Artif. Intell. Med. **67**, 25–37 (2016)
22. Needleman, S.B., Wunsch, C.D.: A general method applicable to the search for similarities in the amino acid sequence of two proteins. J. Mol. Biol. **48**(3), 443–453 (1970)
23. Osgood, R., Bareiss, R.: Automated index generation for constructing large-scale conversational hypermedia systems. In: Proceedings of the Eleventh National Conference on Artificial Intelligence, pp. 309–314. AAAI Press, July 1993
24. Papadimitriou, C.H., Raghavan, P., Tamaki, H., Vempala, S.: Latent semantic indexing: a probabilistic analysis. J. Comput. Syst. Sci. **61**(2), 217–235 (2000)
25. Patterson, D.W., Rooney, N., Dobrynin, V., Galushka, M.: Sophia: a novel approach for textual case-based reasoning. In: Proceedings of the Nineteenth International Joint Conference on Artificial Intelligence IJCAI, pp. 15–20 (2005)
26. Porter, R., Kaplan, J.: Merck manual (2012). https://www.merckmanuals.com/professional
27. Proctor, J.M., Waldstein, I., Weber, R.: Identifying facts for TCBR. In: ICCBR 2005 Workshop Proceedings, pp. 150–159 (2005)
28. Schank, R., et al.: A content theory of memory indexing. Tech. Rep. 1, Institute for the Learning Sciences, Northwestern University (1990)
29. Sizov, G., Öztürk, P., Štyrák, J.: Acquisition and reuse of reasoning knowledge from textual cases for automated analysis. In: Lamontagne, L., Plaza, E. (eds.) ICCBR 2014. LNCS (LNAI), vol. 8765, pp. 465–479. Springer, Cham (2014). https://doi.org/10.1007/978-3-319-11209-1_33
30. Wang, Z., Zhang, J., Feng, J., Chen, Z.: Knowledge graph and text jointly embedding. In: Proceedings of the 2014 Conference on Empirical Methods in Natural Language Processing EMNLP, pp. 1591–1601 (2014)
31. Wang, Z., Zhang, J., Feng, J., Chen, Z.: Knowledge graph embedding by translating on hyperplanes. In: Proceedings of the Twenty-Eighth AAAI Conference on Artificial Intelligence, pp. 1112–1119. AAAI Press (2014)
32. Weber, R.O., Ashley, K.D., Brüninghaus, S.: Textual case-based reasoning. Knowl. Eng. Rev. **20**(3), 255–260 (2005)
33. Wiratunga, N., Lothian, R., Massie, S.: Unsupervised feature selection for text data. In: Roth-Berghofer, T.R., Göker, M.H., Güvenir, H.A. (eds.) ECCBR 2006. LNCS (LNAI), vol. 4106, pp. 340–354. Springer, Heidelberg (2006). https://doi.org/10.1007/11805816_26
34. Wiratunga, N., Lothian, R., Chakraborti, S., Koychev, I.: Textual feature construction from keywords. In: ICCBR 2005 Workshop Proceedings, pp. 110–119 (2005)

35. Xie, R., Liu, Z., Jia, J., Luan, H., Sun, M.: Representation learning of knowledge graphs with entity descriptions. In: Proceedings of the Thirtieth AAAI Conference on Artificial Intelligence, pp. 2659–2665. AAAI Press (2016)
36. Yang, C., He, B.: A novel semantics-based approach to medical literature search. In: IEEE International Conference on Bioinformatics and Biomedicine BIBM, pp. 1616–1623 (2016)

Case-Based Data Masking for Software Test Management

Mirjam Minor[1]([⊠]), Alexander Herborn[2], and Dierk Jordan[2]

[1] Business Information Systems, Goethe University,
Robert-Mayer-Str. 10, 60629 Frankfurt, Germany
`minor@cs.uni-frankfurt.de`
[2] R + V Versicherung AG, Wiesbaden, Germany
{`Alexander.Herborn,Dierk.Jordan`}`@ruv.de`

Abstract. Data masking is a means to protect data from unauthorized access by third parties. In this paper, we propose a case-based assistance system for data masking that reuses experience on substituting (pseudonymising) the values of database fields. The data masking experts use rules that maintain task-oriented properties of the data values, such as the environmental hazards risk class of residential areas when masking address data of insurance customers. The rules transform operational data into hardly traceable, masked data sets, which are to be applied, for instance, during software test management in the insurance sector. We will introduce a case representation for masking a database column, including problem descriptors about structural properties and value properties of the column as well as the data masking rule as the solution part of the case. We will describe the similarity functions and the implementation of the approach by means of myCBR. Finally, we report about an experimental evaluation with a case base of more than 600 cases and 31 queries that compares the results of a case-based retrieval with the solutions recommended by a data masking expert.

Keywords: CBR applications · Data protection · Substitution rules
myCBR

1 Introduction

A novel General Data Protection Regulation (GDPR) [1] is effective in the European Union from May 25, 2018. Organizations in non-compliance may face heavy fines. The regulation document states that processing of personal data is lawful if the data subject has given consent [1, p.36]. It recommends encryption or pseudonymisation in cases where the processing is for a purpose that is different from that for which the personal data have been collected [1, p.37]. Apart from the fact that there remains a grey zone which purposes are still based on the data subject's consent, it is quite challenging for organizations to follow this recommendation.

© Springer Nature Switzerland AG 2018
M. T. Cox et al. (Eds.): ICCBR 2018, LNAI 11156, pp. 281–291, 2018.
https://doi.org/10.1007/978-3-030-01081-2_19

Encryption is not feasible for many purposes of data processing, such as data analytics, business process modeling, or software testing, that require unencrypted data with values as realistic as possible. *Pseudonymisation* means "the processing of personal data in such a manner that the personal data can no longer be attributed to a specific data subject without the use of additional information" [1, p.33]. In contrast to pseudonymisation, anonymisation produces data where the personal data is not traceable at all any more [4]. Nulling-out is a sample anonymisation technique. A straight-forward technique of pseudonymisation is to replace data values by arbitrary pseudonyms, for instance, transforming the name Bob into Alice. However, this substitution may lead to a severe loss of information, including task-oriented properties of the data that are necessary to fulfill the intended purpose of data processing. An example is the approximate age of a policyholder that is important for the purpose of testing software in an insurance company. In such scenarios, the date of birth should not be pseudonymised arbitrarily. More sophisticated techniques of pseudonymisation are called data masking. *Data masking* is "a technique applied to systematically substitute, suppress, or scramble data that call out an individual, such as names, IDs, account numbers, SSNs (i.e. social security numbers, editor's note), etc." [7, p.8]. Data masking rules can be specified by data masking experts to identify and transform personal data into pseudonymised target data. This is a time-consuming task that has to be conducted carefully each time a new data source is pseudonymised.

Case-based reasoning (CBR) provides a means to reuse experience in data masking. In this paper, we present a case-based assistance system for specifying masking rules. We demonstrate the feasibility of the approach in the application area of test management for insurance software.

The remainder of the paper is organized as follows. The basic principles and techniques of data masking are introduced in Sect. 2. The case representation is presented in Sect. 3. Section 4 sketches the retrieval with the according similarity functions. In Sect. 5, the approach is evaluated in a lab experiment. Section 6 contains a discussion and a conclusion.

2   Data Masking

A data masking rule transforms personal data into hardly traceable, masked data. In software test management, the source for data masking are operational data with newly created test data sets as target. Following Raghunathan [4, p.172ff], there are various basic techniques for data masking that reduce the information content of the data to different degrees. Deterministic techniques achieve reproducible results. Randomised techniques produce different results for each run. The personal data used by the latter is traceable only by means of log information on the masking process, which blurs the line between pseudonymisation and anonymisation.

Substitution rules replace a data value by another data value. The following variants of substitution are particularly useful for pseudonymisation purposes:

- *Direct substitution* maps a data value directly to a substitute value.
- *Lookup substitution* uses an external list of potential replacements. In lookup substitution with hashing, the list is organised in a hash table. A mapping function assigns a hash-value to each source data value. In contrast, randomised lookup substitution selects a value from the list arbitrarily.
- *Conditional substitution* is an extension of direct or lookup substitution that considers conditions.

Obviously, direct substitution and lookup substitution with hashing are deterministic while randomised lookup substitution is nondeterministic. An example for a conditional substitution is a lookup substitution that maintains a risk class of the data values, such as the environmental hazards risk class of residential areas when masking address data of customers.

Shuffling rules rearrange the data within the same column across different rows. Several data columns can be grouped in order to preserve the relationship of their values. Table 1 depicts an example where postal code, city and street are grouped together during shuffling.

Table 1. Example for data masking by shuffling.

Raw data				
	Customer id	Postal code	City	Street
1	10012	65189	Wiesbaden	Siegfriedring
2	10049	65195	Wiesbaden	Lahnstr
3	10144	55122	Mainz	Saarstr
4	10220	60486	Frankfurt	Solmsstr
5	13002	60594	Frankfurt	Dreieichstr
Masked data				
	Customer id	Postal code	City	Street
1	10012	60594	Frankfurt	Dreieichstr
2	10049	55122	Mainz	Saarstr
3	10144	60486	Frankfurt	Solmsstr
4	10220	65189	Wiesbaden	Siegfriedring
5	13002	65195	Wiesbaden	Lahnstr

Mutation rules produce variations of data values within given boundaries. In case of numeric values, the number variance technique exchanges a number by a randomly generated value within a range. An advanced variance technique randomises the selection of the arithmetic operator or function to mutate the numeric data value. For instance, the mutation of a date value can process the date for a random number x between 0 and 10 as follows:

- $0 \leq x \leq 3$: increase date by 30 days
- $4 \leq x \leq 7$: decrease date by 70 days
- $8 \leq x \leq 10$: increase date by 120 days

A birth date 06/01/1955 is mutated to 03/23/1955 in case x is 5.

The data masking rules are used by an ETL[1] tool within a data masking architecture (see Fig. 1). The source data comprises of database tables. During export, the data are split into tables with the portions of data that contain personal data and tables without personal data. The tables with personal data are loaded into staging data for the ETL tool. The ETL tool applies the masking rules and exports the masked data to be loaded into the target data.

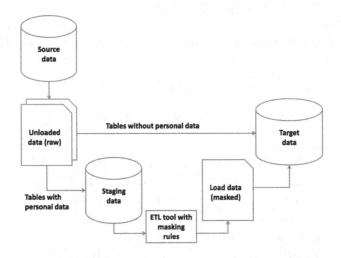

Fig. 1. Architecture for data masking.

3   Representation of a Data Masking Case

A data masking case represents the experience on masking one attribute of a database, i.e. it is used to replace all values of a particular data column in a database table. The problem description comprises a set of descriptors for the data column. The solution is a masking rule that is used to pseudonymise the values of the data row. In addition to the attribute to be masked, the masking rule might require access to several attributes of the database table.

A sample rule for masking the first names while maintaining the gender might use lookup substitution with hashing as follows. The rule expects two attributes namely the salutation and the first name as input. It creates a hash value from the input serving as key for a gender-specific lookup table with first names. It selects the element with the key as pseudonym. Table 2 depicts six sample cases

---

[1] ETL stands for Extract - Transform - Load.

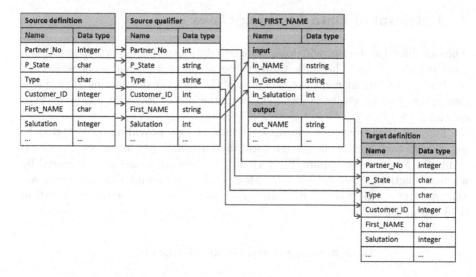

Fig. 2. Sample mapping for the data masking rule RL_FIRST_NAME.

for different attributes. Each row stands for a case with the problem part on the left hand side and the solution part (the masking rule) on the right hand side. Case 2 employs the sample rule described above as the solution for masking the first names.

The problem descriptors of a case represent structure-oriented and value-oriented properties of the data column. In the sample case base (see Table 2), the structure-oriented properties are the column name and the data type of the attribute. The value-oriented properties are the most used value in the column, the frequency of the most used value in percentage of occurrence (value frequency), a regular expression describing the most used pattern, the frequency of this pattern (pattern frequency), and a value that describes the percentage of data values with unique occurrence within the data row (distinct percentage). Michael, for instance, is the most used value in cases 2 and 6. 'XXXXXX' stands for a sequence of six letters. Since Michael has 7 letters, it does not match the most used pattern in cases 2 and 5 (Table 2).

Table 2. Sample cases for different data rows.

	Column name	Data type	Most used value	Value frequency (in %)	Most used pattern	Pattern frequency (in %)	Distinct percentage (in %)	Rule
1	Name	string	Müller	0.54	XXXXXX	17.88	13.86	RL_NAME
2	First_Name	string	Michael	1.2	XXXXXX	20.81	2.05	RL_FIRST_NAME
3	Street	string	Hauptstr	1.8	XXXXXXXX	5.68	2.52	RL_ADDRESS_V6
4	TaxID	string	n.d	0.08	999999999	7.23	48.93	RL_TAXID_V_STR
5	BIC	int	0	10.76	99999999	89.24	21.48	RL_BIC_V5
6	Prename	string	Michael	0.93	XXXXXX	15.76	2.46	RL_FIRST_NAME

4   Retrieval of Data Masking Cases

The case-based system provides assistance to data masking experts in specifying data masking rules. The data table to be pseudonymised is processed automatically resulting in n queries where n is the number of columns. The query descriptors can be easily determined from the data source by means of SQL queries.

The case-based system performs a retrieval process providing the best matching case for each query. The system uses standard similarity measures [2] as local similarity functions (compare Table 4). The percentage values are compared by a linear function. 'Most used value', 'Most used pattern' and 'Column name' are compared by string matching. 'Data type' uses a symbolic similarity function depicted in Table 3.

Table 3. Sample similarity values for data types.

	Date/Time	Decimal	Int	String
Date/Time	1.0	0.0	0.0	0.0
Decimal	0.0	1.0	0.5	0.0
Int	0.0	0.5	1.0	0.0
String	0.0	0.0	0.0	1.0

The values of the local similarity functions are aggregated by a weighted sum [5, p.29]:

$$\sum_{i=1}^{i=n} \left(\frac{\omega_i sim(x_i, y_i)}{k} \middle| 1 \leq i \leq n \right).$$

The weights ω_i for the local similarity values have been specified as depicted in Table 4. The weights are preliminary and intend to estimate the impact of a descriptor for the result. In the recent specification, the value frequency and the pattern frequency are not considered during retrieval.

Table 4. Types and weights of the local similarity functions.

Column name	Data type	Most used value	Value frequency	Most used pattern	Pattern frequency	Distinct percentage
String matching	Symbolic	String matching	Linear	Partial string matching	Linear	Linear
$\omega_1 = 5$	$\omega_2 = 3$	$\omega_3 = 2$	$\omega_4 = 0$	$\omega_5 = 4$	$\omega_6 = 0$	$\omega_7 = 1$

5   Evaluation

The approach is implemented by means of the myCBR tool [6]. The evaluation provides a first proof-of-concept that is guided by the following two hypotheses:

H1 The CBR approach is able to identify columns with personal data in database tables.

H2 The retrieval result provides a solution that is comparable to the data masking rule that is recommended for a column by a human expert.

The evaluation uses an experimental setting with real sample data from the insurance domain. 615 cases have been extracted from an operational database system of the insurance company R + V with the according data masking rules specified by experts from the test management department.

Overall, R + V uses a heterogeneous landscape of database systems, including IBM DB2, Microsoft SQL Server, SAP R/3 and Hana. Today, the experts sift all tables when preparing test data. The tables that include personal data are selected as staging data (cmp. Figure 1) for a detailed review. During review, the experts mark columns of the sensitive tables that need not to be masked and specify rules for the other, sensitive columns. The entire staging data created from R + V's IBM DB2 database serves as the source for our case base in the experimental setup. It includes nearly 200 tables that contain personal data for different insurance products, such as health, life, casualty etc. The experimental case base is created automatically from the 615 columns of the staging data tables. The values of the problem descriptors 'Column name', 'Data type', 'Most used value', 'Value frequency', 'Most used pattern', 'Pattern frequency', and 'Distinct percentage' (cmp. Table 2) are extracted by means of the ETL tool Informatica Analyst and by SQL statements. The solution parts of the cases (the masking rules) are taken directly from the ETL tool as they have been specified for each column by the experts. The experimental case base contains 90 'negative' cases on the 90 columns that have been marked as 'not sensitive' by the experts. For instance, the 'tariff rate' of a particular database table has been excluded from masking. 38 different masking rules have been specified for the columns resulting in 525 'positive' cases. In addition to the case base, the experimental setup comprises a set of queries. 31 queries have been created from two database tables that are actually to be pseudonymised for software testing. Further, the similarity functions are specified in myCBR as described in Sect. 4. In order to investigate the hypotheses H1 and H2, the results of the case-based retrieval are compared to a golden standard provided by the data masking experts for the recent two database tables.

The preparation of the experimental setup from real data allows already some observations with respect to the feasibility of the chosen case representation. As expected, the value-oriented descriptors are useful to understand the experts' rule assignment. Unsurprisingly, some columns with different names refer to matching content and use the same masking rule, such as 'VT_GEB_DAT' and

Test case ID	Column name	Highest similarity value	Most similar column	Rule recommendation by prototype	Rule recommendation by expert
T1	HAUS_NR_ZUSATZ	0.86	Q01T221_MT_HAUS_NR_ZUSATZ	RL_Anschrift_V6	RL_Anschrift_V6
T2	ANREDE	0.79	Q35T806_MT_RUF_NR_ERG	RL_Telefonnummer_V_Text_Robust	none
T3	NATION_KZ	0.87	Q45T503_MT_NATION_KZ	RL_Land_V_Str_Kfz_v2	RL_Land_V_Str_Kfz_v2
T4	HAUS_NR	0.86	Q45T551_MT_UNTERN_HAUS_NR	RL_Anschrift_V6	RL_Anschrift_V6
T5	ORT_ZUS	0.65	Q45T551_MT_UNTERN_ORT	RL_Anschrift_V6	RL_Anschrift_V6
T6	VORNAME	0.85	Q12T120_MT_VORNAME1	RL_Vorname_V2	RL_Vorname_V2
T7	NAME1	0.77	Q55T009_MT_VWB_NAME_1	RL_Nachname_V2	RL_Nachname_V2
T8	STAAT_ZUGEH	0.87	Q01T001_MT_STAAT_ZUGEH	RL_Land_V_Str_Kfz_v2	RL_Land_V_Str_Kfz_v2
T9	STR	0.56	Q80T102_MT_STR	RL_Anschrift_V6	RL_Anschrift_V6
T10	FK_Q01T001UID	0.41	Q45T552_MT_UNTERN_ANPR_TEL01	RL_Telefonnummer_V_Text_Robust	none
T11	GEBURTSDATUM	0.84	Q17T415_MT_GEBURTSDATUM	RL_Geburtstag_V_Dat_V2	RL_Geburtstag_V_Dat_V2
T12	ORT_NAME	0.82	Q17T200_MT_ORT_NAME	RL_Anschrift_V6	RL_Anschrift_V6
T13	PLZ	0.86	Q45T551_MT_UNTERN_PLZ	RL_Anschrift_V6	RL_Anschrift_V6
T14	PR_FAKTOR	0.57	Q12T576_MT_FAX_NR_AKT	RL_Telefon_Num_Vorwahl_Durchwahl	none
T15	BEITR_PRO_A_VTRG	0.54	Q12T576_MT_FAX_NR_AKT	RL_Telefon_Num_Vorwahl_Durchwahl	none
T16	FK_Q35T101RG_TYP	0.63	Q35T811_MT_BTG_FKT_HSNR_ZUS	RL_Anschrift_V6	none
T17	FK_Q35T101RG_TYP_Z	0.65	Q35T811_MT_BTG_FKT_HSNR_ZUS	RL_Anschrift_V6	none
T18	TARIFSATZ	0.55	Q12T576_MT_TEL_VW_TAG	RL_Telefon_Num_Vorwahl_Durchwahl	none
T19	ERF_LFD_NR	0.67	Q35T805_MT_HSNR	RL_Anschrift_V6	none
T20	JAHR_PR	0.56	Q12T516_MT_TEL_VW_VN_PRIV	RL_Telefon_Num_Vorwahl_Durchwahl	none
T21	FK_Q35T101AG	0.62	Q35T811_MT_BTG_FKT_HSNR	RL_Anschrift_V6	none
T22	GRUND_PR	0.59	Q57T305_MT_BERUF_NR	RL_Beruf_in_Unfall_V2	none
T23	H_LFD_NR	0.68	Q35T811_MT_BTG_FKT_HSNR	RL_Anschrift_V6	none
T24	MASCH_UMS_ABR_KZ	0.75	Q17T732_MT_KFZ_AKZ_BUCH	RL_KFZ_V_NUM_Optimiert	none
T25	MIND_PR	0.55	Q12T516_MT_TEL_VW_VN_PRIV	RL_Telefon_Num_Vorwahl_Durchwahl	none
T26	PR_FAKTOR_INTERN	0.53	Q12T576_MT_TEL_NR_AKT	RL_Telefon_Num_Vorwahl_Durchwahl	none
T27	VEREINB_PR_SATZ	0.54	Q35T815_MT_NEG_VER_HSNR	RL_Anschrift_V6	none
T28	FK_Q35T101SACH_VSN	0.54	Q35T122_MT_SICH_BLZ	RL_BIC_IBAN_BLZ_Ktonr_V_BLZ_Ktonr_Num_v5	none
T29	PR_KLASSE	0.7	Q03T110_MT_KORRESPONDENZFELD	ToDo	none
T30	UMS_VOM_DAT_X	0.8	Q17T756_MT_GEB_DAT_VP	RL_Geburtstag_V_Dat_V2	none
T31	UMSATZ_BETR	0.49	Q45T552_MT_UNTERN_KTONR	RL_BIC_IBAN_BLZ_Ktonr_V_BLZ_Ktonr_Num_v5	none

Fig. 3. Evaluation result.

'GEBURTS_DATUM' for birthdays. In some cases, underspecified data types require slightly different masking rules for matching content, for instance 'string' used in the format 'mm/dd/yy' in one column vs. 'dd.mm.yyyy' in another column. In such cases, the value-oriented descriptors differ. Further, some structure-oriented descriptors, such as 'SCHL2' as column name, are not comprehensible at all while the value-oriented descriptors provide further explanation and, thus, are justified.

The evaluation results are depicted in Fig. 3 including the retrieval results for the 31 queries. Queries T1 to T13 are created from the first database table. T14 to T31 origin from the second database table. The right hand side of the table shows the recommendations of the experts for the queries which serve as the golden standard. For 11 queries, the experts recommend a masking rule. For 9 queries, the values of the similarity function are above a threshold of 0.8. This can be interpreted as a hint that the considered data row contains personal data that is to be masked. The comparison of the result of the prototype with the recommendation by the experts shows that it includes three false negatives for T5, T7, and T9. This is not yet satisfactory. Further, the result contains one false positive (T30), which is not so bad. Thus, hypothesis H1 is partially fulfilled.

Including the false negatives, however, the 100% overlap of the recommendations of the CBR system with the golden standard is surprisingly high. The experiments confirm hypothesis H2.

6 Discussion and Conclusion

In this paper, we have introduced data masking as a novel application task for CBR. The case-based assistance system aims at assigning data masking rules to database tables with the goal to mask personal data by pseudonyms. We presented a structural case representation whose problem descriptors are extracted from database columns automatically. We implemented the approach with the tool myCBR for the purpose of software test management in the insurance sector. The results of the preliminary evaluation show that CBR is a promising approach.

The results create manifold opportunities for future work. First, we are planning to conduct further experiments. The weights that specify the relevance of the local similarity functions will be further investigated, for instance from an information theoretical approach. In addition, the dependencies between columns that are already considered in the solution parts (rules) could also serve as contextual information during retrieval. However, masking rules can get quite complex depending on the properties that need to be preserved. For example, the rule RL_ADDRESS_V6 takes customer address data like street name, zip code or city as input and treats it according to the following procedure:

- Check whether the given zip code is valid or not. If not, take the given city name and get the corresponding zip code.

- Use the zip code as a parameter for a lookup to get the information how many streets and ZUERS-entries[2] exist in the lookup-table for that zip code.
- The street name and house number are converted by a deterministic, reproducible hash-algorithm and projected to a number between one and the amount of entries in the lookup-table that have the same zip code and ZUERS-zone as the original value.
- Take the entry of the lookup-table where the index is equivalent to the calculated number and use it to replace the original value.

This procedure ensures that the masked value has the same city and ZUERS-zone as the original value. Thus, a residence insurance at the masked address is guaranteed to cost the same as at the original address. This is required for testing the residence insurance calculation. The rule deals with dependencies between database columns and from external knowledge sources, such as those between zip code, city and ZUERS-code. It requires pre-processing to transform the representation of such dependencies from the rule into contextual information that is accessible during retrieval. Further, the threshold for the global similarity function could be improved or replaced by a machine learning approach that identifies which columns should be masked at all previously to the CBR approach that selects an appropriate masking rule. Larger experiments are required to demonstrate the scalability of the approach for both, an increasing number of database columns and rows. We expect that the number of data entries (rows) can be easily increased since the problem descriptors are determined off-line. A larger number of database columns or entire tables will probably require more sophisticated memory models for the case base.

Reducing the number of persons who have access to personal data means reducing the risk of incidents with data leakage. Today, productive data including personal data are still used also in non-productive systems [3]. The manual efforts for pseudonymisation that maintains task-oriented properties for the non-productive systems are tremendous. CBR has demonstrated a high potential to provide automated assistance for the data masking experts. Decreasing the efforts for pseudonymisation will significantly contribute to the companies' capability to achieve compliance with data protection regulations such as GDPR.

Acknowledgements. The authors would like to thank the data masking experts of R + V who contributed to this work by their rule recommendations. Providing the golden standard for the evaluation, they are vitally important to demonstrate the feasibility of the approach. We highly appreciate their time and efforts.

---

[2] ZUERS is a zoning-system that is determined by the potential risk to become victim of a flooding or a similar environmental hazard. The ZUERS-zone is an important criteria to calculate the insurance rate, e.g. of a residence insurance.

References

1. Regulation (EU) 2016/679 of the European Parliament and of the Council. Official Journal of the European Union, L 119 (2016)
2. Bergmann, R.: Experience Management: Foundations, Development Methodology, and Internet-Based Applications. Springer, Heidelberg (2002). https://doi.org/10.1007/3-540-45759-3
3. Lang, A.: Anonymisierung/Pseudonymisierung von Daten für den Test. In D.A.CH Security Conference 2012, Konstanz (2012). Syssec Forschungsgruppe Systemsicherheit
4. Raghunathan, B.: The Complete Book of Data Anonymization: From Planning to Implementation. CRC Press, Boca Raton (2013)
5. Richter, M.M., Weber, R.O.: Case-Based Reasoning: A Textbook. Springer, Heidelberg (2013). https://doi.org/10.1007/978-3-642-40167-1
6. Stahl, A., Roth-Berghofer, T.R.: Rapid prototyping of CBR applications with the open source tool myCBR. In: Althoff, K.-D., Bergmann, R., Minor, M., Hanft, A. (eds.) ECCBR 2008. LNCS (LNAI), vol. 5239, pp. 615–629. Springer, Heidelberg (2008). https://doi.org/10.1007/978-3-540-85502-6_42
7. Venkataramanan, N., Shriram, A.: Data Privacy: Principles and Practice. CRC Press, Boca Raton (2016)

A CBR Approach for Imitating Human Playing Style in Ms. Pac-Man Video Game

Maximiliano Miranda$^{(\boxtimes)}$, Antonio A. Sánchez-Ruiz, and Federico Peinado

Departamento de Ingeniería del Software e Inteligencia Artificial,
Universidad Complutense de Madrid, c/ Profesor José García Santesmases 9,
28040 Madrid, Spain
{m.miranda,antsanch}@ucm.es,email@federicopeinado.com
http://www.narratech.com

Abstract. Imitating video game players is considered one of the most stimulating challenges for the Game AI research community. The goal for a virtual player is not just to beat the game but to show some human-like playing style. In this work we describe a Case-Based Reasoning approach that learns to play the popular Ms. Pac-Man vs Ghosts video game from the traces of a human player. We evaluate the performance of our bot using both low level standard measures such as accuracy and recall, and high level measures such as *recklessness* (distance to the closest ghost, as it is mapped in our Ms. Pac-Man domain model), *restlessness* (changes of direction), *aggressiveness* (ghosts eaten), *clumsiness* (game steps the player is stuck) and *survival* (lives left). Results suggest that, although there is still a lot of room for improvement, some aspects of the human playing style are indeed captured in the cases and used by our bot.

Keywords: Virtual video game player · Human behavior imitation
Case-based reasoning · Artificial Neural Network
Artificial Intelligence

1 Introduction

Researchers studying Artificial Intelligence (AI) who explore agents that mimic human behavior are always looking for problems that are challenging but feasible at the same time, in order to progress their mission of recreating human intelligence in a computer. Imitating video game players has been considered a stimulating challenge for the Game AI research community, and several competitions on developing believable characters have emerged during the last decade [8].

Usually, in games where there are machine-controlled characters (bots) and they play in a more human-like way, human players perceived the game to be less predictable, more replayable, and more challenging than if the bots were hand-coded [17]. Furthermore, in the Digital Game Industry there is a widespread assumption that wherever there is a machine-controlled character, the game

© Springer Nature Switzerland AG 2018
M. T. Cox et al. (Eds.): ICCBR 2018, LNAI 11156, pp. 292–308, 2018.
https://doi.org/10.1007/978-3-030-01081-2_20

experience will benefit from this character to be controlled by the computer in a less "robotic" and more human-like way. For this reason, player modeling in video games has been an increasingly important field of study, not only for academics but for professional developers as well [24].

There is a wide variety of scenarios where these human-like computer bots come into play. They can be used not only to confront the human player, but also to collaborate with him or to illustrate how to succeed in a particular game level to help players who get stuck. It is reasonable to think that these computer-played sequences will be more meaningful if the bot imitates human-like playing style. Another possible application of these "empathetic" bots is to help during the testing phase in the game production process. Acting as virtual players, these bots could be used to test the game levels, not only checking whether the game crashes or not, but verifying if the game levels have the right difficulty, or finding new ways for solving a puzzle.

Despite the popularity of the Turing test, in the domain of video games there is no formal, rigorous standard for determining how human-like is an artificial agent [7]. Furthermore there is not a clear concept about what a believable AI should achieve, and its expected behavior will vary strongly, depending on what it is supposed to imitate: to emulate the behavior of other players or to create lifelike characters [11]. In the case of this work, we are focused on emulating the playing style of specific human players, assuming that this emulation models the way the player moves (how it reacts) in the game scene given the current situation of his avatar and the other game entities (items and enemies).

For this work we have been focused with case-based reasoning due to its capacity for imitating spatially-aware autonomous agents in a real-time setting [2]. Ms. Pac-Man agent's are able to identify objects that are visible to them in their environment (game items as pills and other agents), and perform actions based on the configuration of those objects (to choose its next direction).

We propose a set of high level metrics such as *recklessness* (distance to the closest ghost), *restlessness* (changes of direction), *aggressiveness* (ghosts eaten), *clumsiness* (game steps the player is stuck) and *survival* (lives left when the level is finished) that are able to capture to some extend different styles of play and skill levels of different players. We considered these high level metrics to be more useful to measure the level of performance of a bot that standard low level metrics such as accuracy or recall since these have been proven to be ineffective to determine whether two behaviors are similar or not when the behaviors are stochastic or require memory of past states [14]. Although these metrics are implemented as specific measures for Ms. Pac-Man domain, similar ideas can be used for other arcade games.

We have implemented two different virtual players, one based on Case-Based Reasoning (CBR) and the other based on an Artificial Neural Network (ANN), and evaluated their performance when they play with knowledge acquired from both naive rational bots and human players. Although the virtual players seem to achieve very high scores in low level metrics such as accuracy with respect to the behavior of human players, our bot based on cases seems to replicate better the style of play of the player it learns from, characterized by the high level metrics already mentioned. These results make us optimistic about the use of CBR to imitate human behaviors in interactive environments such as action video games.

The rest of the paper is structured as follows. Next section summarizes the related work in the field. Section 3 describes the internals of Ms. Pac-Man vs Ghosts framework that we use in our experiments. The following two sections describe the virtual players based on CBR and ANN, respectively. Section 6 describes the setup used in the experiments and the metrics for assessing the performance of our bots. In Sect. 7 we show and discuss the results obtained in all the different scenarios. Finally, we close the paper with some encouraging conclusions about this approach and future lines of research.

2   Related Work

Several works regarding the imitation of behavior in video games can be found in the scientific literature, for imitating human players and also script-driven characters. The behavior of an agent can be characterized by studying all its proactive actions and its reactions to sequences of events and inputs over a period of time, but achieving that involves a significant amount of effort and technical knowledge [23] in the best case. Machine Learning (ML) techniques can be used to automate the problem of learning how to play a video game either progressively using players' game traces as input, in direct imitation approaches, or using some form of optimization technique such as Evolutionary Computation or Reinforcement Learning to develop a fitness function that, for instance, "measures" the human likeness of an agent's playing style [19].

Traditionally, several ML algorithms, like ANNs and Naive Bayes classifiers, have been used for modeling human-like players in first-person shooter games by using sets of examples [5]. Other techniques based on indirect imitation like dynamic scripting and Neuroevolution achieved better results in Super Mario Bros than direct (ad hoc) imitation techniques [15].

Case-based reasoning has used successfully for training RoboCup soccer players, observing the behavior of other players and using traces taken from the game, without requiring much human intervention [3]. Related to CBR and Robotic Soccer, Floyd et al. [2] also noted that when working in a setting with time limits constraints, it is very important to study what characteristics of the cases really impact the precision of the system and when it is better to increase the size of the case base while simplifying the cases. Furthermore, they described how applying preprocessing techniques to a case base can increase the performance of a CBR system by increasing the diversity of the case base.

About how the cases for the case base are obtained, we follow a similar approach as the described by Lam et al. [10], as the cases are generated in an automated manner by recording traces of the player that will be imitated as pairs of *scene* state (scene as a representation of the player's point of view) - player's outputs.

Concerning human-like agents, there have been several AI competitions including special tracks for testing the human likeness of agents using Turing-like tests. One of these competitions is the Mario AI Championship[1], which included a 'Turing test track' where submitted AI controllers compete with each other for being the most human-like player, judged by human spectators [20]. The BotPrize competition [8] focuses on developing human-like agents for Unreal Tournament, encouraging AI programmers to create bots which cannot be distinguished from human players. Finally, Ms Pac-Man vs Ghosts, the framework that we use for this work, has been used in different bot competitions during the last years [12]. After some years discontinued, it returned in 2016[2] to be celebrated yearly [22].

About human behavior imitation in first person shooters, Quake II has also been used in past works for studying what is called Learning from Demostration or Imitation Learning (IL). Within this environment Gorman et al. concluded that IL had the potential to produce more believable game agents than traditional AI techniques using Bayesian Imitation [7].

Bauckhage et al. [18] applied IL while investigating human movements within the game's environment for imitating a reactive behavior, paying attention to strategic decisions of the human player on how to reach certain goals.

Recently the used of Hidden Markov Models to analyze and model individual differences of in-game behaviors using data from an Role-Playing Game called VPAL has been successfully tested for player modeling by Bunian et al. [1].

Finally, in an earlier work [13] we described an experiment with human judges to determine how easy it is, for human spectators, to distinguish automatic bots from human players in Ms. Pac-Man. This work allowed the judges to address characteristics of the playing style that led their conclusions. Some of these characteristics are related to the high level parameters we used in this experiment, as illustrated in Sect. 6.

3   Ms. Pac-Man vs. Ghosts

Pac-Man is an arcade video game produced by Namco and created by Toru Iwatani and Shigeo Fukani in 1980. Since its launch it has been considered as an icon, not only for the video game industry, but for the 20th century popular culture [6]. In this game, the player has direct control over Pac-Man (a small yellow character), pointing the direction it will follow in the next turn. The level is a simple maze full of white pills, called Pac-Dots, that Pac-Man eats gaining points. There are four ghosts (named Blinky, Inky, Pinky and Sue) with different behaviors trying to capture Pac-Man, causing it to lose one live. Pac-Man initially has three lives and the game ends when the player looses all of them. In the maze there are also four special pills, bigger than the normal ones and named Power Pellets or Energizers, which make the ghosts to be "edible"

---

[1] http://www.marioai.org/.
[2] http://www.pacmanvghosts.co.uk/.

during a short period of time. Every time Pac-Man eats one of the ghosts during this period, the player is rewarded with several points.

Two years after the release of the original Pac-Man video game, some students of the MIT, including Doug Macrae and Kevin Curran, developed what would become one of the most popular arcade video games of all time: Ms. Pac-Man. This new arcade was produced by Midway Manufacturing Corporation (distributors of the original version of Pac-Man in the USA) and introduced a female protagonist, Ms. Pac-Man, and some changes in the gameplay: the game is slightly faster than the original one and, in contrast with the prequel, the ghosts do not have a deterministic behavior, being their path through the maze not predefined [9].

Ms. Pac-Man is a real-time, dynamic and non-deterministic environment. Ms. Pac-Man agents must deal with temporal events as well as with an environment consisting of a 2D space (the game level) with pills and other agents (the ghosts) within that space. Every game-step the player is able to analyze the current state of the maze, in order to develop possible strategies and compute reachable paths to succeed. The agent then sends a command to the game in response which indicates the direction it will move towards the next time-step.

Ms. Pac-Man vs Ghosts (see Fig. 1) is a new implementation of Pac-Man's sequel Ms. Pac-Man in Java designed to develop bots to control both the protagonist and the antagonists of the game. This framework has been used in several academic competitions during the recent years [22] to compare different AI techniques. Some of these bots are able to obtain very high scores but their behavior is usually not very human. For example, they are able to compute optimal routes and pass very close to the ghosts while human players tend to keep more distance and avoid potential dangerous situations.

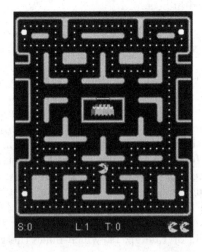

Fig. 1. A screenshot of Ms. Pac-Man vs. Ghosts

The Ms. Pac-Man vs. Ghosts API represents the state of the game as a graph in which each node corresponds to a walkable region of the maze (which visually is a 2×2 pixels square). Each node can be connected to up to other four nodes, one in each direction (north, east, south and west), and can contain a Pac-Dot, a Power Pellet, one or more ghosts, Ms. Pac-Man herself or nothing at all (i.e. the node represents an empty portion of the maze). The full graph representing the state of the first level of the game contains 1293 nodes.

The framework provides a few examples of simple bots that can be used as entry points for developing new ones. A bot for whether the ghosts (as a group) or Ms. Pac-Man herself should implement an interface with a function that offers one direction every game step. The agent can consult the game state (current pills state and situation, other agents position and state, current score and time, etc.) and, with this information, make a decision accordingly, namely chose one direction: up, right, down, left, or neutral.

Among the controllers included for the ghosts there is the *StarterGhosts* controller with which the ghosts have a simple behavior: if the ghost is edible or Ms. Pac-Man is near a Power Pellet, they escape in the opposite direction. Otherwise, they try to follow Ms. Pac-Man with a probability of 0.9, or make random movements with a probability of 0.1. Visually, this makes the controller to appear like having 2 different states: they try to reach Ms. Pac-Man unless they are edible (or Ms. Pac-Man is very close to a Power Pellet) in which case they will try to escape. We use this controller for the ghosts because it does not have a behavior that is neither too complex nor too simple, enriching the game space states with slight variations depending on Ms. Pac-Man situation and some minor random decisions.

4   The CBR Virtual Player

Ms. Pac-Man vs. Ghosts provides the functionality to save the games in text files regardless of whether the games have been played by a human player or by a bot. From these text files we can reproduce the games and extract different features. Typically, a human player needs between 1200 to 1800 cycles or game steps to complete one level of the game depending on his skill level, so each game file contains thousand of pairs (state, action). The full state representation of the game contains 256 different parameters and there are 5 possible actions (left, right, up, down, neutral). It is interesting to note that even a classical arcade game such as Pac-Man hides a very high dimensional feature space that is a challenge for machine learning algorithms.

A case contains an abstract representation of the game state and the direction chosen by the player or bot we aspire to imitate. In particular, each case contains the following features:

- distances to the closest Pac-Dot in each direction (p).
- distances to the closest Power Pellet in each direction (pp).
- distances to the closest ghosts in each direction (g).

- time (game steps) the nearest ghost will remain edible in each direction (**eg**).
- direction chosen by the player in the previous game step (*la*).
- direction chosen by the player in the current game step (*a*).

The first 4 features are four-dimensional vectors containing a scalar value (distance or time) for each direction. The last 2 features are categorical variables with 5 possible values: left, right, up, down, neutral (neutral means to maintain a direction than makes unable to transition to another node of the maze, i.e. the agent is stuck in a corner without selecting a really possible direction). The remaining edible time in each direction is a scalar value ranging from 0 (the closest ghost via that direction is not in an edible) and 200 (Ms. Pac-Man has just eaten a Power Pellet).

The direction chosen in the previous game step deserves some special consideration. The addition of this feature to the cases led to a significant improvement in the performance of our bot. Without this feature, the bots are purely *reactive* meaning that their decisions are based only on the current game state. This feature allows the bot to remember were it comes from so the bot maintains a very simple internal state describing the recent past events. Although limited and short-term, this *memory-based* representation has an important impact in the performance of the bot.

The similarity between cases is computed as a linear combination of the similarities between the vectors which, in turn, is computed as the inverse of the euclidean distance. This way, we can weight the contribution of each feature to the final similarity value. An exception is the direction chosen in the last game step that is compared using an specific similarity measure for that categorical feature:

$$sim(c_1, c_2) = \alpha_1 * sim_e(\boldsymbol{p_1}, \boldsymbol{p_2}) + \alpha_2 * sim_e(\boldsymbol{pp_1}, \boldsymbol{pp_2})$$
$$+ \alpha_3 * sim_e(\boldsymbol{g_1}, \boldsymbol{g_2}) + \alpha_4 * sim_e(\boldsymbol{eg_1}, \boldsymbol{eg_2})$$
$$+ \alpha_5 * sim_a(la_1, la_2)$$
$$sim_e(\boldsymbol{v}, \boldsymbol{w}) = \frac{1}{\|\boldsymbol{v} - \boldsymbol{w}\|}$$

where sim_e is the inverse of the Euclidean distance, and sim_a is 1 if both directions are the same, 0 if they are opposite directions, and 0.25 in other cases.

In our current implementation all the features are weighted the same (0.20). We are confident than with a fine tuning of the weights we could obtain better results, and that adjustment will be part of our future work.

5   The ANN Virtual Player

We use a multi-layer perceptron with a single hidden layer and a sigmoid transfer function because it is a standard configuration that has been proved successfully previously [4].

The input layer has 21 neurons, 16 for the features describing distances and times and 5 for the feature describing the last direction (coded using one-hot). The hidden layer has the same number of neurons. The output layer has 5 neurons, representing each of the directions Ms. Pac-Man can move. The direction of the bot is chosen based on the output neuron with the greatest value.

We use a very simple and standard ANN configuration but our CBR bot is also based on an unweighted similarity measure, and both systems work with the same game state representation.

6   Experimental Setup

We have performed 2 different experiments. In the first one the CBR bot and the ANN bot learn to play from the *Pilling* bot, a very simple bot we created for testing a basic behavior: always going towards the closest Pac-Dot or Power Pellet ignoring the ghosts. In order to make it less predictable, we have modified its behavior slightly so that when there are several Pac-Dots at the same distance, it goes towards one of them randomly. Note that in the original implementation the decisions are deterministic and, since the bot ignores the ghosts, it always traverses the maze using the same route.

In the second experiment we try to learn to play from the traces of two different human players with different style of play and skill level. We expect this second scenario to be much more challenging and we are interested in knowing to what extent the bots are capable of reproducing the different styles of play of each player. In all the experiments we count with samples extracted from 100 games played by each player (bot and humans) in the first level of the game (if the human player or bot was able to complete the first level, the game was force to end).

We evaluate the performance of our learning bots using both low level standard classification measures such as accuracy, recall and f-score, and high level measures characterizing the style of play.

The accuracy, recall and f-score measures are computed using leave-one-out validation on the games (99 games to train and 1 test). This is equivalent to make the bots play the test games and every time they make a wrong decision, relocate Ms. Pac-Man so that the games continue as the original ones. Note that this is a standard approach in learning by imitation [15] because just one different decision can produce a completely different game in a few game cycles.

The evaluation using the high level parameters is different. First, we train the learning bots with the games of the player they are learning from. Then we let the learning bots play 100 new games by themselves and extract the following measures:

– *Score*: the final game score. This values reflect the skill level of the player. For example, good players try to eat several edible ghosts in a row because the game rewards it with extra points.

- *Time*: the duration of the game in game steps. Although good players tend to survive longer, some not-so-good players flee from the ghosts all the time and survive for a long time without getting points.
- *Restlessness*: number of direction changes per second. This parameter captures different ways to navigate the maze.
- *Recklessness*: average distance to the closest ghost. This parameter describes the level of danger that the player is willing to assume.
- *Aggressiveness*: number of ghosts eaten. When the player eats a Power Pellet, he can use the edible time to chase the ghosts or to eat the remaining Pac-Dots or Power Pellets in the maze.
- *Clumsiness*: number of game steps in which the player is stuck against a wall. This situation usually happens because the player made a mistake and chose an impossible direction, but some expert players provoke this situation to have time to evaluate the state of the game.
- *Survival*: the number of lives left when the player completes the first level or 0 if the player died before.

We believe these high level game features are able to capture to some extend different styles of play and skill levels of different players.

7   Results and Discussion

In the first experiment we work with a set of 100 games played by the *PillingRandom* bot. On average, this bot gets a score of 2194 points and survives for 922 game steps. It only complete the first level in 21 of the games, loosing its 3 lives in the remaining 79 games.

Table 1. Low level metrics for the CBR and ANN bots when they try to imitate the Pilling bot and 2 different human players.

	Accuracy	Recall	F-Score
ANN (Pilling bot)	0,9760	0,9824	0,9805
CBR (Pilling bot)	0,9845	0,9872	0,9859
ANN (Human1)	0,9750	0,9468	0,9607
CBR (Human1)	0,9773	0,9066	0,9406
ANN (Human2)	0,9747	0,9562	0,9654
CBR (Human2)	0,9773	0,8892	0,9312

The first 2 rows of Table 1 show the accuracy, recall and f-score values obtained by the CBR and ANN bots. These values were obtained using a leave-one-out evaluation, the ANN bot was trained for 200 epochs using backpropagation and a learning rate of 0.01, and the retrieval in the CBR bot was based on k Nearest

Table 2. High level metrics when the CBR and ANN bots try to imitate the style of play of the Pilling bot. We show the absolute values and the difference with the Pilling bot in percentage (less is better).

	Pilling bot	CBR	CBR Diff	ANN	ANN Diff
Score	922,24	1.188,32	28,85%	333,00	63,89%
Time	2.194,00	2.523,10	15,00%	185,30	91,55%
Restlessness	1,28	1,15	10,40%	1,46	13,45%
Recklessness	42,16	34,33	18,58%	56,35	33,67%
Aggressiveness	1,10	1,75	59,09%	0,10	90,91%
Clumsiness	0,00	0,00	0%	0,02	n/a
Survival	0,45	0,06	86,67%	0,00	100,00%

Neighbor with k = 5 where the final decision was made by majority vote. As we can see, both bots obtain very high values of accuracy and recall.

In view of these results we could expect both bots to replicate the behavior of the Pilling bot very closely. However, when we make them play 100 new games the performance is not as expected. Table 2 shows the high level metrics that characterize the style of play when the CBR and ANN bots try to imitate the Pilling bot. The table also shows the difference in percentage for each metric respect to the imitated bot (less difference is better).

Although the CBR bot makes a much better job than the ANN bot in all the metrics, the results are far from good. The difference in score is 28,85% and in survival time 15% compared to the original bot (the ANN bot performs worse, 63,89% and 91,55% respectively). The worst results are in Aggressiveness (distance to the closest ghost) and Survival (remaining lives). These results are also shown graphically in Fig. 2.

How is it possible to obtain so high accuracy values and however to behave so differently? We think that it is due to the dynamic nature of the game. Every wrong decision leads the imitating bot to new game states that are probably more different than the ones it learn from. This way, the probability of making a new wrong decision increases taking the bot further to even more unknown situations. The underlying problem is that the original bot always plays in the same way, so the train game set only covers a small part of the possible game scenarios. This problem has been addressed recently [16] and emerges when the "training set" and "test set" do not come from the same distribution, since the "test set", when the agent actually plays, depends on the agent's policy, thus violating the i.i.d. assumption of supervised learning. As we will show next, this problem also arises when we try to imitate human players.

In the second experiment we want to imitate two different human players with different skill level and style of play. We asked both player to play 100 times the first level of Ms. Pac-Man and recorded their traces. On average, Human 1 got 3113 points, survived for 1838 game steps and was able to finish the first

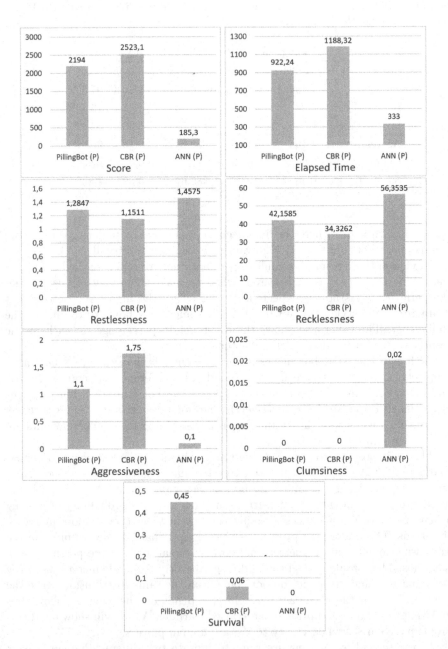

Fig. 2. High level metrics when the CBR and ANN bots try to imitate the style of play of the Pilling bot.

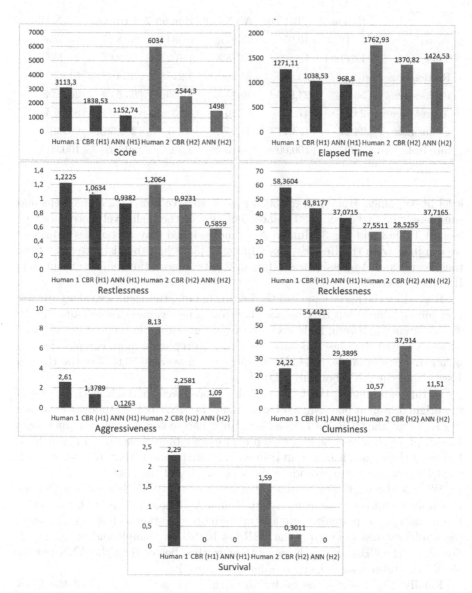

Fig. 3. High level metrics when the CBR and ANN bots try to imitate the style of play of Human 1 (H1) and Human 2 (H2).

Table 3. High level metrics when the CBR and ANN bots try to imitate the style of play of two human players. We show the original values obtained by the human players and the difference in percentage for the bots.

	Human 1	CBR Diff	ANN Diff	Human 2	CBR Diff	ANN Diff
Score	3.113,30	40,95%	62,97%	6.034,00	57,83%	75,17%
Time	1.271,11	18,30%	23,78%	1.762,93	22,24%	19,20%
Restlessness	1,22	13,01%	23,26%	1,21	23,48%	51,43%
Recklessness	58,36	24,92%	36,48%	27,55	03,54%	36,90%
Aggressiveness	2,61	47,13%	95,16%	8,13	72,20%	86,59%
Clumsiness	24,22	124,77%	21,35%	10,57	258,66%	08,89%
Survival	2,29	100,00%	100,00%	1,59	80,50%	100,00%

level in 95 games. Human 2 got 6034 points, survived for 1762 game steps and completed the first level in 80 games. The rest of the high level metrics can be seen in Table 3 and Fig. 3. Human 2 is a more skilled player who likes danger as we can infer from the Recklessness (Human 2 plays half the distance away from the ghosts) and Aggressiveness (Human 2 eats 3 more time edible ghosts than Human 1) metrics.

Regarding the performance of the imitating bots, the accuracy values are also very high (Table 1) but they do not play so well new games (Table 3 and Fig. 3). The difference in several high level metrics is bigger than in the first experiment, as we expected, because the bots are trying to replicate more complex human behaviors. For example, the CBR bot obtains on average 59,05% of the Human 1 score and the ANN bot only 37,03%.

In this experiment, the CBR bot also reproduces the high level metrics of the original human player much better than the ANN bot. Actually, we can see in Fig. 3 that the CBR bot (second column in each color) gets more points, lasts longer, plays closer to the ghosts and eats more edible ghosts when learns from Human 2 than when learns from Human 1. So we conclude that, to some extend, the CBR bot is able to reproduce the style of play of the player.

Why is the CBR bot so much better than the ANN bot in new games? Probably because we are using a very simple ANN and we could obtain better results using a deep architecture and modern optimization techniques. However, the similarity measure used in the CBR bot is also very simple and unoptimized. Somehow, the CBR approach seems to generalize better than the ANN but we should run several more tests in order to confirm it.

Finally, Fig. 4 shows the evolution of the accuracy and recall of the CBR bot as we incorporate new cases to the case base. Is interesting to note that, with very few cases (around 241, 1/4 of a game) the bot reaches an accuracy of 0,9554. However we must be careful when interpreting these results because, as we have seen, precision and recall are probably not the best indicators of the performance in new games.

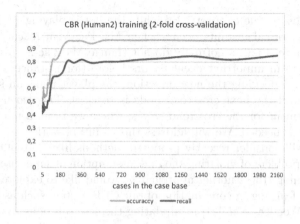

Fig. 4. CBR evaluation of the Human 2 game states.

8   Conclusions

As part of our research on imitation of human playing style in video games, we are interested in the role that the CBR approach can play in solving this complex challenge. In this work we have proposed a set of high level metrics such as *recklessness* and *aggressiveness* that are able to capture to some extend different styles of play and skill levels of different players. We have shown that these metrics are more meaningful to measure the performance of a bot in IL problems that standard low level metrics such as accuracy and recall.

We have implemented two different virtual players, one based on CBR and the other based on ANN, and evaluated their performance when they learn from both simple bots and human players. The CBR approach seems to generalize better to new scenarios and is able to replicate, to some extend, different ways of playing. There is still a lot of room for improvement, however, specially when we try to learn from human players because they exhibit complex behaviors and advanced strategies that are difficult to replicate.

Despite the modest results concerning the high level metrics, the bot is able to reproduce *human errors* unlikely to be made by simpler scripted bots. For example, in many of the games we use as training set, the human player sometimes makes an obvious mistake consisting in when heading straight for a pill, change the direction just before Ms. Pac-Man could pick it, return again after noticing that the pill was not gained, gather the pill and finally change again towards the opposite direction. Our CBR bot is able to replicate this slight portions of human playing-style thanks to not being purely *reactive*.

As part of our future work, we would like to create a CBR agent implementing the full CBR cycle. There are several locations in the system were we can incorporate domain knowledge such as the similarity measure or the adaptation strategy. We also need to pay attention to case base indexing and maintenance because the bot needs to play in real time.

When analyzing the case retrieval while the bot is playing we have noticed that the most critical instants occurs when Ms. Pac-Man reaches a crossroad node in the maze. Players normally do not change Ms. Pac-Man's direction in corridors unless an important event occurs before (for instance a ghost is too close), and when deciding the new direction, the player plans an strategy that will execute until the next crossroad node is reached. This led us to consider a special treatment for the crossroad states, where we think a more exhaustive representation is needed. We will address this as future work.

Also, we will consider recently proposed methods like DAGGER in order to overcome the problem of violating the i.i.d. assumption of supervised learning in imitation learning [16]. Another approach we would like to explore is the use of reinforcement learning in combination of our CBR system such as the proposal presented by Wender et al. [21] for updating the case solutions. As it served for a 2D spacial navigation system with goal-driven agents while avoiding enemies.

Finally, for the purpose of comparing our CBR system with a more sophisticated ML bot, we plan to use a deep architecture and modern optimization techniques.

Acknowledgements. This work has been partially supported by the Spanish Committee of Economy and Competitiveness (TIN2014-55006-R, TIN2017-87330-R) and the UCM (Group 921330), project *ComunicArte: Comunicación Efectiva a través de la Realidad Virtual y las Tecnologías Educativas*, funded by *Ayudas Fundación BBVA a Equipos de Investigación Científica 2017*, and project *NarraKit VR: Interfaces de Comunicación Narrativa para Aplicaciones de Realidad Virtual* (PR41/17-21016), funded by *Ayudas para la Financiación de Proyectos de Investigación Santander-UCM 2017*.

References

1. Bunian, S., Canossa, A., Colvin, R., El-Nasr, M.S.: Modeling individual differences in game behavior using hmm (2017)
2. Floyd, M.W., Davoust, A., Esfandiari, B.: Considerations for real-time spatially-aware case-based reasoning: a case study in robotic soccer imitation. In: Althoff, K.-D., Bergmann, R., Minor, M., Hanft, A. (eds.) ECCBR 2008. LNCS (LNAI), vol. 5239, pp. 195–209. Springer, Heidelberg (2008). https://doi.org/10.1007/978-3-540-85502-6_13
3. Floyd, M.W., Esfandiari, B., Lam, K.: A case-based reasoning approach to imitating robocup players. In: Proceedings of the Twenty-First International Florida Artificial Intelligence Research Society Conference, pp. 251–256, Coconut Grove, Florida, USA, 15–17 May 2008
4. Gallagher, M., Ledwich, M.: Evolving pac-man players: can we learn from raw input? In: Proceedings of the 2007 IEEE Symposium on Computational Intelligence and Games, CIG 2007, pp. 282–287, Honolulu, Hawaii, USA, 1–5 April 2007
5. Geisler, B.: An empirical study of machine learning algorithms applied to modeling player behavior in a "first person shooter" video game. Ph.d. thesis, Citeseer (2002)

6. Goldberg, H.: All Your Base are Belong to Us: How 50 Years of Videogames Conquered Pop Culture
7. Gorman, B., Thurau, C., Bauckhage, C., Humphrys, M.: Believability testing and bayesian imitation in interactive computer games. In: Nolfi, S., et al. (eds.) SAB 2006. LNCS (LNAI), vol. 4095, pp. 655–666. Springer, Heidelberg (2006). https://doi.org/10.1007/11840541_54
8. Hingston, P.: A new design for a turing test for bots. In: Proceedings of the 2010 IEEE Conference on Computational Intelligence and Games CIG 2010, pp. 345–350, Copenhagen, Denmark, 18–21 August 2010
9. Kent, S.: The Ultimate History of Video Games: From Pong to Pokémon and Beyond : the Story Behind the Craze that Touched Our Lives and Changed the World
10. Lam, K., Esfandiari, B., Tudino, D.: A scene-based imitation framework for robocup clients. In: MOO-Modeling Other Agents from Observations (2006)
11. Livingstone, D.: Turing's test and believable ai in games. Comput. Entertain. **4**, 6 (2006)
12. Lucas, S.M.: Ms pac-man versus ghost-team competition. In: Proceedings of the 2009 IEEE Symposium on Computational Intelligence and Games CIG 2009, Milano, Italy, 7–10 September 2009
13. Miranda, M., Sánchez-Ruiz, A.A., Peinado, F.: Pac-man or pac-bot? exploring subjective perception of players' humanity in ms. pac-man. In: Proceedings of the 4th Congreso de la Sociedad Española para las Ciencias del Videojuego, pp. 163–175, Barcelona, Spain, 30 June 2017
14. Ontañón, S., Montaña, J.L., Gonzalez, A.J.: A dynamic-bayesian network framework for modeling and evaluating learning from observation. Expert Syst. Appl. **41**(11), 5212–5226 (2014)
15. Ortega, J., Shaker, N., Togelius, J., Yannakakis, G.N.: Imitating human playing styles in super mario bros. Entertain. Comput. **4**(2), 93–104 (2013)
16. Ross, S., Gordon, G.J., Bagnell, D.: A reduction of imitation learning and structured prediction to no-regret online learning. In: Proceedings of the Fourteenth International Conference on Artificial Intelligence and Statistics AISTATS 2011, pp. 627–635, Fort Lauderdale, USA, 11–13 April 2011
17. Soni, B., Hingston, P.: Bots trained to play like a human are more fun. In: 2008 IEEE International Joint Conference on Neural Networks (IEEE World Congress on Computational Intelligence), pp. 363–369 (2008)
18. Thurau, C., Bauckhage, C., Sagerer, G.: Learning human-like movement behavior for computer games. In: Proceedings of the Eighth International Conference on the Simulation of Adaptive Behavior (SAB04) (2004)
19. Togelius, J., Nardi, R.D., Lucas, S.M.: Towards automatic personalised content creation for racing games. In: 2007 IEEE Symposium on Computational Intelligence and Games, pp. 252–259 (2007)
20. Togelius, J., Yannakakis, G., Shaker, N., Karakovskiy, S.: Believable Bots, chap. Assessing believability, pp. 219–233 (2012). Hingston, p. (Ed.)
21. Wender, S., Watson, I.: Combining case-based reasoning and reinforcement learning for unit navigation in real-time strategy game AI. In: Lamontagne, L., Plaza, E. (eds.) ICCBR 2014. LNCS (LNAI), vol. 8765, pp. 511–525. Springer, Cham (2014). https://doi.org/10.1007/978-3-319-11209-1_36
22. Williams, P.R., Liebana, D.P., Lucas, S.M.: Ms. pac-man versus ghost team CIG 2016 competition. In: IEEE Conference on Computational Intelligence and Games CIG 2016, pp. 1–8, Santorini, Greece, 20–23 September 2016

23. Wooldridge, M.: Introduction to multiagent systems. Cell **757**(239), 8573 (2002)
24. Yannakakis, G.N., Maragoudakis, M.: Player modeling impact on player's entertainment in computer games. In: Ardissono, L., Brna, P., Mitrovic, A. (eds.) UM 2005. LNCS (LNAI), vol. 3538, pp. 74–78. Springer, Heidelberg (2005). https://doi.org/10.1007/11527886_11

Perks of Being Lazy: Boosting Retrieval Performance

Mehmet Oğuz Mülâyim$^{(\boxtimes)}$ and Josep Lluís Arcos

IIIA, Artificial Intelligence Research Institute,
CSIC, Spanish National Research Council, Bellaterra, Spain
{oguz,arcos}@iiia.csic.es

Abstract. Case-Based Reasoning (CBR) is a lazy learning method and, being such, when a new query is made to a CBR system, the swiftness of its retrieval phase proves to be very important for the overall system performance. The availability of ubiquitous data today is an opportunity for CBR systems as it implies more cases to reason with. Nevertheless, this availability also introduces a challenge for the CBR retrieval since distance calculations become computationally expensive. A good example of a domain where the case base is subject to substantial growth over time is the health records of patients where a query is typically an incremental update to prior cases. To deal with the retrieval performance challenge in such domains where cases are sequentially related, we introduce a novel method which significantly reduces the number of cases assessed in the search of exact nearest neighbors (NNs). In particular, when distance measures are metrics, they satisfy the triangle inequality and our method leverages this property to use it as a cutoff in NN search. Specifically, the retrieval is conducted in a lazy manner where only the cases that are true NN candidates for a query are evaluated. We demonstrate how a considerable number of unnecessary distance calculations is avoided in synthetically built domains which exhibit different problem feature characteristics and different cluster diversity.

Keywords: Lazy retrieval · Triangle inequality
Exact nearest neighbor search

1 Introduction

Being a lazy learning methodology, a Case-Based Reasoning (CBR) system will try to generalize its cases at the time a query is made to the system. And a typical CBR retrieval algorithm ends up calculating the similarity of the query to all of the cases in the case base (CB). While a CB grows larger by time as new experiences are incorporated as cases, especially the time spent at the retrieval phase in reasoning episodes is likely to become a performance issue. Computationally expensive distance calculations in the search of nearest neighbors (NNs) eventually leads to the utility problem (a.k.a. swamping problem) which is commonly known within the CBR community. Indeed, the utility problem has proved to be

© Springer Nature Switzerland AG 2018
M. T. Cox et al. (Eds.): ICCBR 2018, LNAI 11156, pp. 309–322, 2018.
https://doi.org/10.1007/978-3-030-01081-2_21

one of the most studied subfields to be able to overcome the issues faced in real world implementations of CBR systems [3,4,7]. Two major approaches to cope with this problem have been smart indexing of the cases and reducing the size of the case base in terms of competence [8,10]. We should note that efficiency in NN search has not been only a problem of the CBR community, and there has been considerable work on finding approximate NNs instead of exact NNs in large-scale high dimensional spaces (for a survey see [12]).

Health sciences are increasingly becoming one of the major focuses for CBR research (for a survey of applications see [1]). A medical CBR system where health records of patients constitute the CB is expected to grow considerably over time and hence, it is prone to face the utility problem if extra care is not taken at the retrieval process.

In such a domain, a new problem is typically an incremental update to its predecessor case in the CB. By saying incremental, we mean that it comprises (partially or completely) the information of its sequentially related predecessors. In the above mentioned medical CBR system, after the initial session for a patient, consecutive sessions would be updates to previous sessions. These sessions would altogether form a sequence of cases, i.e. the case history of the patient (see Fig. 1 for a visual representation of such a CB). A query to find patients with similar health records should take into account these sequences of cases for the patients in the CB. As the cases are appended, the sequence grows longer by time and the incremental difference introduced by the new problem becomes minimal compared to the shared long history between the latest cases of the sequence. Then, it is intuitive to think that a new problem's NNs are very likely to be similar to those of its predecessor case. The basic assumption of CBR that "similar problems have similar solutions" also confirms this thought. Following this intuition, while we are calculating the NNs of a new problem, it makes sense to start from the ranked neighbors of the predecessor. These two suggestions lead us to the thought that if we could have an oracle that showed us to what extent we should be doing the similarity calculations (i.e. making sure that we could not find a nearer neighbor than the last one we have calculated), we could save invaluable time at the retrieval phase, especially if the CB is subject to substantial growth over time as it is in this example and/or the distance calculation is expensive for the domain.

In this work, we introduce a new approach to limit the number of cases assessed in the search of *exact* NNs in domains where a case is sequentially related to another and where the distance measures are metrics. The method leverages the triangle inequality as a cutoff to calculate the NNs of a new problem based on its distance to its predecessor case. In the sense of reducing the number of cases to assess in retrieval, our method bears resemblance to the "Fish and Shrink" strategy [6] which also exploits the triangle inequality to set bounds on similarities between cases. "Fish and Shrink" assumes that "if a case does not fit the actual query, then this may reduce the possible usefulness of its neighbors" and it uses similarity bounds to successively eliminate (shrink) similarity regions. However, our method is unique in its *incremental approach* to use similarities between sequentially related cases to determine the cutoff point in the search of exact NNs.

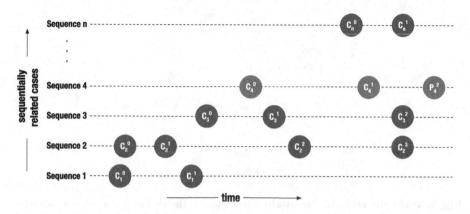

Fig. 1. A visual representation of a case base where a new problem is typically an incremental update of its predecessor case. In a health care CBR system where patient sessions form the cases, each sequence would represent the case history of a different patient. For e.g., P_4^2 would be the new query for the patient with $id{=}4$ for her upcoming third consecutive session. This query would bear implicitly and/or explicitly the information of the prior session's case C_4^1, which in its own right was an update to the initial case C_4^0.

Specifically, we describe how to implement an oracle that indicates the cutoff points in NN search in metric spaces and how to use it in a *Lazy KNN search* algorithm in Sect. 2. Next, in Sect. 3 we describe the experiments conducted in synthetic domains of different problem feature characteristics and different cluster diversity and we report the results in which we can observe the gain in terms of avoided similarity calculations by our algorithm. Finally, in Sect. 4 we conclude with discussion and future work.

2 Lazy Retrieval

In a CB of n cases, for a problem sequence S which has had u updates so far including the initial problem, a standard linear kNN search algorithm would have to make a total number of $u \times n$ similarity calculations to assess the kNNs of the updates of S throughout its evolution, assuming the CB does not change during these u updates. Our aim here is to try to reduce the number of calculations when a new query arrives as an update to S by using the knowledge we have acquired from the calculations made for prior updates.

Our approach to accomplish this objective is to find an oracle in such a domain that can help us carry out as few similarity (or distance) calculations as possible during the assessment of the kNNs. For a new query, if this oracle indicates a point in the CB, onward from which it is useless to search a nearer neighbor (since it guarantees that there is none ahead), we could hope to save some precious time spent for calculations.

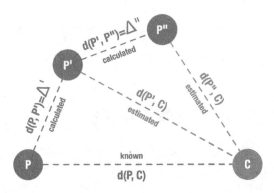

Fig. 2. Using the **triangle inequality** to estimate the distance (as well as the similarity) of two sequential problems to an existing case. Where P' is the incremental update of the problem P, and P'' is the incremental update of the problem P', C is any case in the CB, and d is the distance metric; we have $d(P, C) \leq d(P', C) + \Delta'$ and $d(P, C) \leq d(P'', C) + \Delta' + \Delta''$.

In the following subsection, we propose such an oracle which leverages the triangle inequality in metric spaces and then we introduce our algorithm for the lazy assessment of the kNNs using this oracle.

2.1   Leveraging the Triangle Inequality in kNN Assessment

The most popular metric space used by CBR systems is the Euclidean space and being a metric space, distance metrics used in this space should satisfy the triangle inequality among other axioms [2]. When we already know the similarity of a case to a previous update of a given problem sequence, we show how we exploit this property to calculate the upper-bound of the similarity of this case to the current update of that problem.

Let us use Fig. 2 to illustrate the triangle inequality property. Given three points in the problem space $\langle P, P', C \rangle$, P' being the incremental update of the problem P, and C any case in the CB, and given d as a distance metric, the three points will satisfy the following triangle inequality:

$$d(P, C) \leq d(P, P') + d(P', C)$$

This property also holds for P'' which is the incremental update of the problem P'. Thus, new distances $d(P', C)$ and $d(P'', C)$ are conditioned by the distances among the incremental updates of the problem.[1]

---

[1] Following Fig. 1, you can think of P and P' as the problem parts of the cases C_4^0 and C_4^1 respectively, and P'' as P_4^2, and C as any case C_x^y of any Sequence x where $x \neq 4$.

Finally, since we already know $d(P, C)$, and we may calculate $d(P, P')$ and $d(P', P'')$, using the triangle inequality we may obtain the *upper* limits of similarity of two sequences to a case C, namely $sim(P', C)$ and $sim(P'', C)$ without the need to actually calculate them in the following way:

The triangle inequality allows us to write the following two inequalities:

$$d(P, C) \leq \overbrace{d(P, P')}^{\Delta'} + d(P', C) \tag{1}$$

$$d(P', C) \leq \overbrace{d(P', P'')}^{\Delta''} + d(P'', C)$$

Then, using the latter inequality in the former (1), we get:

$$d(P, C) \leq d(P'', C) + \Delta' + \Delta'' \tag{2}$$

Because we are more interested in similarities rather than distances, we can transform above inequalities into similarity inequalities. When all the distances d are normalized values into the range of $[0, 1]$ in accordance with the common, and most of the times necessary, practice in CBR systems to compare distances and/or similarities in a CB, the inequalities (1) and (2) can be written in terms of similarity as follows where $sim(x, y) = 1 - d(x, y)$:

Following the inequality (1):

$$\underbrace{1 - d(P, C)}_{} \geq \underbrace{1 - d(P', C)}_{} - \Delta'$$

$$sim(P, C) \geq sim(P', C) - \Delta'$$

which leads to:

$$sim(P', C) \leq sim(P, C) + \Delta' \tag{3}$$

Following the inequality (2):

$$\underbrace{1 - d(P, C)}_{} \geq \underbrace{1 - d(P'', C)}_{} - \Delta' - \Delta''$$

$$sim(P, C) \geq sim(P'', C) - \Delta' - \Delta''$$

which leads to:

$$sim(P'', C) \leq sim(P, C) + \Delta' + \Delta'' \tag{4}$$

The inequality (3) gives us the oracle we need. Just by calculating Δ', we know that a new update P' can be more similar to *any* case C than its predecessor P is to C, at best by a degree of Δ'. We see it important to reemphasize the word "*any*" here, because note that Δ' calculation does not involve any case but only the problem P and its update P'.

Consecutively, a following update P'' can be more similar to any case C in the CB than P is to it, at best by a degree of $\Delta' + \Delta''$ as shown in the inequality (4).

Intuitively if we generalize the inequality (4), we have:

$$sim(P^i, C) \leq sim(P^j, C) + \sum_{s=j+1}^{i} \Delta_P^s \qquad (5)$$

where
$$\Delta_P^s = d(P^{s-1}, P^s)$$

Now, we can say that any update P^i of a problem P can get more similar to any case C in the CB, than a prior update P^j is to it, at best by a degree of the sum of Δs calculated between updates $j + 1$ and i (both inclusive).

In the following subsection, we explain how we leverage this knowledge as a cutoff in the search of exact kNNs of the problem updates.

2.2 Lazy Assessment of the kNNs

The working hypotheses are that i) any problem P will be updated many times, ii) the CBR system will have to provide the k-nearest neighbors for each update of P, and iii) we are interested in reducing the retrieval effort as much as possible. As a consequence, the CBR system should keep some information (state) regarding previous calculations in the retrieval step. The simplest state is a ranked list of similarities between a problem and all the cases in the case base.

The first time a new problem P is presented to the system, the retrieval step will be performed as usual: calculating the similarity of the new problem to all cases in the case base[2]. Beside providing the k-nearest cases, the retrieval step will keep this rank ($RANK_P$) for future calculations.

Later, each time the problem P is amended with an update P', the CBR system will exploit the inequality presented in (3) to try to minimize similarity calculations adopting the following strategy:

1. updating the similarities between the current problem P' and, previously calculated k-nearest neighbors in rank $RANK_P$;
2. calculating an upper bound Δ' to determine the best possible improvement in similarity, by computing the similarity between the current problem P' and its previous update (i.e. the initial problem P);
3. adding the Δ' upper bound to all the rest (i.e. starting from the $k + 1^{th}$ neighbor) of similarities previously stored in rank $RANK_P$ to find their "optimistic" similarity values to the current problem;
4. calculating the actual similarity of P' to any such case whose "optimistic" similarity to the current problem surpasses the kth neighbor's calculated similarity (in the first step above) to it.

---

[2] As we will discuss in a following section, this calculus can be improved by introducing some proposals already existing in the CBR literature.

Remembering that $RANK_P$ is a ranked list, the CBR system may iterate the list from the top and stop at a position l when the "optimistic" similarity of case C_l does not beat the similarity calculated for the kth neighbor in $RANK_P$. And this would mean that starting from C_l, the remaining cases ahead in $RANK_P$ certainly cannot beat the kth neighbor in $RANK_P$ either.

The second observation is that, since Δ' depends only on the distance between the current problem P' and its predecessor P, the procedure described above can be improved by delaying the calculation of "optimistic" similarities as much as possible. As presented in (5), when we know the similarities of a group of cases to the problem sequence P^j, we can calculate their "optimistic" similarities to the current problem sequence P^i by adding the sum of all Δs between iteration $j + 1$ and i to their known similarity values in iteration j. Thus, all the similarities calculated in the same iteration i share the same accumulated Δs. As a consequence, instead of updating all "optimistic" similarities in each iteration, it is enough to keep a sub-rank for each iteration.

Finally, above described *Lazy KNN search* algorithm can be found as pseudo-code in Algorithm 1. As it can be seen in the pseudo-code as well, throughout the iterations, we delay the assessment of a case as a nearest neighbor in a *lazy* manner until we consider it as a true candidate for the kNN list.

In the formalization of the upper bound calculation and in the algorithm presented, we have assumed that the CB remains unchanged between the updates of a problem P for the sake of simplicity. To be able to tackle the changes to the CB, the algorithm can be improved easily by adding following behaviors:

1. If new cases are incorporated after the last update P^i, their similarities to the next update P^{i+1} have to be calculated in the $i + 1^{th}$ update;
2. If old cases are modified and if these modifications affect the similarity calculations, these cases should be removed from the $RANK_P$ list and their similarities to the next update P^{i+1} have to be calculated in the $i + 1^{th}$ update;
3. If old cases are deleted, they have to be deleted from the $RANK_P$ list as well.

3   Experimentation

Experiments were performed on a collection of synthetically generated datasets to assess 1) the impact of the distribution of the cases in the CB, and 2) the impact of problem changes in each problem update on the gain in the number of calculations achieved by our algorithm. For NN_P^i the list of cases whose similarity was calculated at iteration i, we define the gain at an iteration i as follows:

$$gain(P^i) = \frac{|CB| - |NN_P^i|}{|CB|}$$

where $|A|$ denotes the cardinality of a set A.

Algorithm 1. Lazy KNN search algorithm.

Where

k is the number of nearest neighbors to be returned;

P^i is the ith update to the problem P, for $i \geq 0$ and P^0 is the initial problem P;

d is the distance metric;

$\Delta_P^i = d(P^{i-1}, P^i)$;

NN_P^i is the list of (c, sim) 2-tuples formed for every case c to which P^i's similarity is actually calculated where $sim = 1 - d(P^i, c)$, this list is ranked in a descending order, the most similar case being at the top;

$NN_P^i[k].similarity$ is the similarity part of the kth 2-tuple in NN_P^i;

$NN_P^i[: k]$ is the list of top k members of NN_P^i, i.e. the kNNs of P^i;

$RANK_P$ is the list of (NN_P^i, Δ_P^i) 2-tuples that are calculated for all occurred updates of the problem P. When P^i arrives, the content of this list is as follows:

$$RANK_P = [(NN_P^{i-1}, \Delta_P^{i-1}), (NN_P^{i-2}, \Delta_P^{i-2}), \ldots, (NN_P^1, \Delta_P^1), (NN_P^0, null)]$$

```
   input : k,
           P^i,
           P^{i-1}, // P^{i-1} = null if P^i ≡ P^0
           RANK_P
   output: (NN_P^i[: k], RANK_P) // 2-tuple
 1 NN_P^i ← [ ]
 2 if P^{i-1} = null then                      // Treatment of the initial problem, P^i ≡ P^0
 3 |   Δ_P^i ← null
 4 |   foreach c in case base do                                      // Linear search
 5 |   |   NN_P^i .append((c, 1-d(P^i,c)))
 6 |   end
 7 |   NN_P^i .sort_descending()
 8 else                                  // Treatment of the following problem updates
 9 |   foreach (c, sim) in NN_P^{i-1}[: k] do        // Calc sims of P^{i-1}'s kNNs to P^i
10 |   |   NN_P^{i-1} .remove((c, sim))
11 |   |   NN_P^i .append((c, 1-d(P^i,c)))
12 |   end
13 |   NN_P^i .sort_descending()
14 |   Δ_P^i ← d(P^i, P^{i-1})
15 |   SumΔ_P ← Δ_P^i
16 |   foreach (NN_P^j, Δ_P^j) in RANK_P do                           // Iterate RANK_P
17 |   |   foreach (c, sim) in NN_P^j do
18 |   |   |   if (sim+SumΔ_P)> NN_P^i[k].similarity then            // c a candidate?
19 |   |   |   |   NN_P^j .remove((c, sim))
20 |   |   |   |   NN_P^i .append((c, 1-d(P^i,c)))                  // Calc the actual sim
21 |   |   |   |   NN_P^i .sort_descending()
22 |   |   |   else
23 |   |   |   |   break                   // Continue with the next 2-tuple in RANK_P
24 |   |   |   end
25 |   |   end
26 |   |   SumΔ_P ← SumΔ_P + Δ_P^j                                   // Accumulate Δs
27 |   end
28 end
29 RANK_P.append((NN_P^i, Δ_P^i))
30 return (NN_P^i[: k], RANK_P)
```

Datasets with a uniform distribution of cases will probably result in higher distances among cases but smoother changes on neighborhoods. Conversely, datasets with dense but distant clusters of cases will present less advantages at the beginning, but significant gains in the long run (see Subsect. 3.2 for a more detailed discussion).

The amount of change among problem updates will determine the margin for deltas. Since we are interested in domains with cases keeping information over long periods of time, we could represent cases with many sequences of tiny updates to guarantee small deltas. However, fragmenting cases in many sequences will result in an increase of calls to the Lazy KNN search algorithm.

3.1 Datasets

To perform comparable experiments, the number of sequences was set to 10,000 and the number of problem features was set to 100 in all datasets. All the experiments were performed using a normalized euclidean similarity as the similarity measure.

To assess the gain effect of the proposed algorithm when the granularity of problem updates varies, we have played with two parameters: the number of the problem updates (U) and the maximum number of feature changes (V). For instance, since each update in a problem sequence is a case, a $U = 40$ would mean that there are $10,000 \times 40 = 400,000$ cases in the CB. And a $V = 10$ means that from one update to another update 10 units will be distributed randomly to increment feature values where one unit represents the minimal change for a feature value. Note that one feature slot may receive more than one unit of change. In a given dataset, V is fixed for all cases and problem updates.

To assess the gain effect of the proposed algorithm over different case base densities, we have introduced a parameter B to control the number of clusters (blobs). A total of number of 48 datasets were generated by combining the values of parameters detailed in Table 1.

To generate the datasets, we have used the blobs generator available in the scikit-learn library [5]. To guarantee the generation of overlapped blobs as B increased, the parameter *cluster_std* was set to 5.0: The generator of blobs was used to obtain prototypes of cases which were later fragmented in sequences of length U with a random distribution of values satisfying V changes from update to update[3].

3.2 Results with Varying CB Densities

The first study conducted was the analysis of the gains with varying case base densities, i.e. varying parameter B, and fixing parameters U and V. The behavior of the gain along U was similar on all configurations of pairs $[U, V]$.

---

[3] Dataset generation code can be found at http://www.iiia.csic.es/~oguz/lazy/.

Table 1. Range of values for each dataset parameter.

Parameter	Values
B	$[1, 5, 10, 20]$
U	$[10, 20, 30, 40]$
V	$[10, 25, 50]$

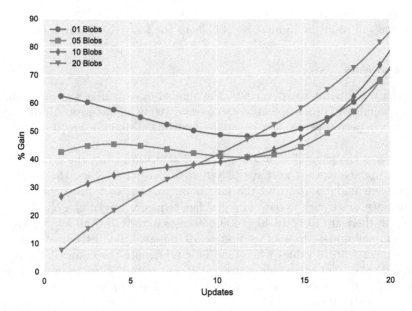

Fig. 3. Impact of the number of blobs $(U = 20,\ V = 10)$.

Take as example[4] Figure 3 where $U = 20$ and $V = 10$. In the first half of iterations, the number of blobs is inversely correlated with the gain. However, as iterations increase, the number of blobs (more blobs imply more sub-regions in the CB) is directly correlated with gains. For datasets generated with a low number of blobs, neighborhoods tend to be less dense and cases more uniformly distributed on the problem space, therefore the change in nearest neighbors is more smooth but more constant. As a consequence, gains start higher than other datasets but remain more constant over time.

Gains on datasets generated with a high number of blobs behave differently. In the beginning many cases are similar enough and this generates the effect of having many nearest neighbor candidates, i.e. at first gains are low, but as time goes by, a subset of nearest neighbors become very close allowing high gains. In Fig. 3 we can observe this extreme behavior for dataset with $B = 20$.

---

[4] A document with supplementary material with figures summarizing all datasets can be found at http://www.iiia.csic.es/~oguz/lazy/.

Table 2. Effect of increasing the number of blobs on accumulated gain ($U = 20$, $V = 10$).

Num. Blobs	Acc. Gain
1	54.95%
5	46.28%
10	43.17%
20	42.91%

In Fig. 3 we can see the gain for each iteration, however the accumulated gains throughout iterations are not evident. We can find summarized accumulated gains in Table 2 where we can observe that the constant gains of datasets generated with less blobs have their reward as a higher accumulated gain in the end.

3.3 Results with Varying Problem Changes

The second study conducted was the analysis of the gains with varying problem changes, i.e. varying parameters U or V, for a fixed parameter B. Because we are using a normalized similarity measure among cases, parameters U and V are correlated. Low values of change (V) together with short problem sequences (smaller U) have a similar effect as high values of change combined with long problem sequences.

Table 3. Effect of increasing the number of iterations on accumulated gain ($B = 10$, $V = 10$).

Num. Iterations	Acc. Gain
10	20.64%
20	43.17%
30	55.93%
40	60.71%

Take as example Fig. 4 where $B=10$ and $V=10$. We can observe that datasets with less iterations depart from lower gains but are able to achieve higher gains in the end. The second observation is that when iterations are long enough (i.e. $U=30$ and $U=40$) the evolution of gains converges to the same behavior. This result is important because the main motivation of the proposed algorithm was to deal efficiently with long sequences of problems, i.e. to take advantage of cases that will be updated many times. Table 3 summarizes the accumulated gains for Fig. 4. As expected, the accumulated gain increases on datasets with longer sequences.

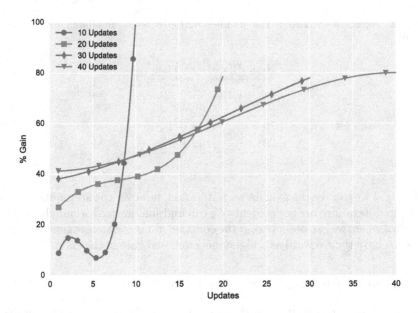

Fig. 4. Impact of the amount of problem updates ($B=10$, $V=10$).

4   Discussion and Future Work

In this article, we have presented a novel approach that can significantly improve the retrieval performance of CBR systems that are designed for domains where a case is typically a sequential update to a prior case in the case base. The improvement is achieved by limiting the number of the cases that are evaluated in the exact k-nearest neighbor (kNN) search for consecutive updates of a problem. And we can reduce the number of calculations thanks to the triangle inequality property which holds for metric spaces.

When a new update of a problem is introduced as a query to the CBR system, we leverage this property to calculate the upper bound of the similarity change for all cases in the case base for which we had calculated their similarities to previous updates of the same problem. Using this optimistic similarity change, we determine which cases are true candidates for the kNN list of the current query.

We have provided a formal description of our methodology and our algorithm for the lazy assessment of the kNNs. Then we have shared the description and results of our experiments that we conducted in synthetically built domains of different problem feature and cluster characteristics. We have demonstrated gains obtained by our algorithm which avoided redundant similarity calculations to a significant degree.

We believe our method can boost the retrieval performance in domains where we deal with large case bases constituted of packages of sequentially related cases as described. We note that although our method is based on metric spaces, non-metric distance measures for which there are ways to transform them into metric measures can also make use of our method. A good example of this could be transforming the popular cosine similarity which is non-metric by nature into a metric distance [11].

At the current implementation, the actual similarity of a problem update to a case is calculated from scratch, i.e. it is treated the same as any initial problem. However, since these updates are incremental in their nature, we can make use of the previously calculated similarity of its predecessor to the same case and only calculate the contribution of change in similarity which is introduced by the current update. As future work, we are planning to implement such an incremental computation of similarity measures for yet a better improvement of retrieval performance in similar domains where this computation is relevant.

A further improvement would come by taking advantage of the *footprint cases* concept in CBR literature [9] in our method. Since a footprint case represents a group of cases sharing a similar competence contribution, our method can choose kNN candidates within these footprint cases instead of a larger group of candidates.

Acknowledgements. This work has been partially funded by project Innobrain, COMRDI-151-0017 (RIS3CAT comunitats), and Feder funds. Mehmet Oğuz Mülâyim is a PhD Student of the doctoral program in Computer Science at the Universitat Autònoma de Barcelona.

References

1. Begum, S., Ahmed, M.U., Funk, P., Xiong, N., Folke, M.: Case-based reasoning systems in the health sciences: a survey of recent trends and developments. IEEE Trans. Syst., Man, Cybern., Part C (Appl. Rev.) **41**(4), 421–434 (2011)
2. Deza, M.M., Deza, E.: Encyclopedia of distances. Springer, Heidelberg (2009). https://doi.org/10.1007/978-3-642-00234-2
3. Francis, A.G., Ram, A.: The utility problem in case-based reasoning. In: Case-Based Reasoning: Papers from the 1993 Workshop, pp. 160–161 (1993)
4. Houeland, T.G., Aamodt, A.: The utility problem for lazy learners - towards a non-eager approach. In: Bichindaritz, I., Montani, S. (eds.) ICCBR 2010. LNCS (LNAI), vol. 6176, pp. 141–155. Springer, Heidelberg (2010). https://doi.org/10.1007/978-3-642-14274-1_12
5. Pedregosa, F., et al.: Scikit-learn: machine learning in Python. J. Mach. Learn. Res. **12**, 2825–2830 (2011)
6. Schaaf, J.W.: Fish and Shrink. A next step towards efficient case retrieval in large scaled case bases. In: Smith, I., Faltings, B. (eds.) EWCBR 1996. LNCS, vol. 1168, pp. 362–376. Springer, Heidelberg (1996). https://doi.org/10.1007/BFb0020623
7. Smyth, B., Cunningham, P.: The utility problem analysed. In: Smith, I., Faltings, B. (eds.) EWCBR 1996. LNCS, vol. 1168, pp. 392–399. Springer, Heidelberg (1996). https://doi.org/10.1007/BFb0020625

8. Smyth, B., Keane, M.T.: Remembering to forget. In: Proceedings of the 14th International Joint Conference on Artificial Intelligence, pp. 377–382. Citeseer (1995)
9. Smyth, B., McKenna, E.: Competence guided incremental footprint-based retrieval. Knowl. Based Syst. **14**(3–4), 155–161 (2001)
10. Smyth, B., McKenna, E.: Competence models and the maintenance problem. Comput. Intell. **17**(2), 235–249 (2001)
11. Van Dongen, S., Enright, A.J.: Metric distances derived from cosine similarity and Pearson and Spearman correlations. arXiv preprint arXiv:1208.3145 (2012)
12. Wang, J., Shen, H.T., Song, J., Ji, J.: Hashing for similarity search: a survey. arXiv preprint arXiv:1408.2927 (2014)

Bayesian-Supported Retrieval in BNCreek: A Knowledge-Intensive Case-Based Reasoning System

Hoda Nikpour$^{(\boxtimes)}$, Agnar Aamodt, and Kerstin Bach

Department of Computer Science, Norwegian University of Science and Technology, Trondheim, Norway
hoda.nikpour@ntnu.no
https://www.ntnu.edu/idi

Abstract. This study presents a case-based reasoning (CBR) system that makes use of general domain knowledge - referred to as a knowledge-intensive CBR system. The system applies a Bayesian analysis aimed at increasing the accuracy of the similarity assessment. The idea is to employ the Bayesian posterior distribution for each case symptom to modify the case descriptions and the dependencies in the model. To evaluate the system, referred to as BNCreek, two experiment sets are set up from a "food" and an "oil well drilling" application domain. In both of the experiments, the BNCreek is evaluated against two corresponding systems named TrollCreek and myCBR with Normalized Discounted Cumulative Gain (NDCG) and interpolated average Precision-Recall as the evaluation measures. The obtained results reveal the capability of Bayesian analysis to increase the accuracy of the similarity assessment.

Keywords: CBR · Bayesian analysis · Similarity assessment

1 Introduction

Knowledge-intensive case-based reasoning (CBR) enables cases to be matched based on semantic rather than purely syntactic criteria. It captures and reuses human experiences for complex problem-solving domains [1], and generates targeted explanations for the user as well as for its internal reasoning process.

Although pure Case-based reasoning is an efficient method for complex domains problem solving, it is not able to generate an explanation for the proposed solution, beyond the cases themselves. Aamodt [2] combined CBR with a semantic network of multi-relational domain knowledge, which allows the matching process to compute the similarity based on semantic criteria, leading to a capability of explanation generation. A challenge with that method was the lack of a formal basis for the semantic network. It makes the inference processes within the network difficult to develop and less powerful than desired. The procedural semantic inherent in that type of network allows for a large degree of

© Springer Nature Switzerland AG 2018
M. T. Cox et al. (Eds.): ICCBR 2018, LNAI 11156, pp. 323–338, 2018.
https://doi.org/10.1007/978-3-030-01081-2_22

freedom in specifying the network semantics underlying the inferences that can be made, such as the value propagation and various forms of inheritance [3]. The disadvantage is that inference methods are implicit and hidden in the code, hence difficult to interpret and compare to other inference methods. In the past network a prototype-based semantic was implemented, as a way to handle uncertainly. The need for a clearly defined semantic and a more formal treatment of uncertainty led to some initial investigations into how a Bayesian Network (BN) model could be incorporated [4,5]. A Bayesian framework includes an inference engine and builds probabilistic models without introducing unrealistic assumptions of independencies. It enables the conditioning over any of the variables and supports any direction of reasoning [6–8].

BNCreek, as a knowledge intensive system, provides a formal basis for the causal inference within the knowledge model, based on Bayesian probability theory.

2   Related Work

Been et al. [9] integrated BN and CBR to model the underlying root causes and explanations to bridge the gap between the machine learning methods and human decision-making strategies. They used case-based classifiers and BN as two interpretable models to identify the most representative cases and important features. Bruland et al. [10] studied reasoning under uncertainty. They employed Bayesian networks to model aleatory uncertainty, which works by assigning a probability to a particular state given a known distribution, and case-based reasoning to handle epistemic uncertainty, which refers to cognitive mechanisms of processing knowledge. Houeland et al. [8] presented an automatic reasoning architecture that employs meta reasoning to detect the robustness and performance of systems, which combined case-based reasoning and Bayesian network. Tran et al. [11] used a distributed CBR system to assist operators in feature solutions for faults by determining the cases sharing common symptoms. Aamodt et al. [4] focused on retrieval and reuse of past cases. They proposed a BN-powered sub-model as a calculation method that works in parallel with general domain knowledge. Kofod-Petersen et al. [5] investigated weaknesses of Bayesian networks in structural and parametric changes by adding case based reasoning functionality to the Bayesian network. Lacave [6] reviewed accomplished studies in Bayesian networks explanation and addressed the remaining challenges in this regard. Koton [12] presented a system called CASEY in which, CBR and a probabilistic causal model are combined to retrieve a qualified case. It takes advantage of the causal model, as a second attempt, after trying a pure CBR to solve the problem.

Aamodt [2] presented a knowledge intensive system called TrollCreek, which is an implementation based on the Creek architecture for knowledge-intensive case-based problem solving and learning targeted at addressing problems in open and weak-theory domains. In TrollCreek, case-based reasoning is supported by a model-based reasoning component that utilizes general domain knowledge. The model of general knowledge constitutes a combined frame system and semantic network where each node and each link in the network are explicitly defined in their own frame object. Each node in the network corresponds to a concept in the knowledge model, and each link corresponds to a relation between concepts. A concept may be a general definitional, prototypical concept or a heuristic rule and describes knowledge of domain objects as well as problem solving methods and strategies. Each concept is defined by its relations to other concepts represented by the set of slots in the concept's frame definition. A case is also viewed as a concept (a situation-specific concept), and hence it is a node in the network linked into the rest of the network by its case features. The case retrieval process in TrollCreek is a two-step process, in line with the two-step MAC- FAC model [14]. The first step is a computationally cheap, syntactic matching process, and the second step is a knowledge-based inference process attempts to create correspondences between structured representations in the semantic network. In the first step, cases are matched based on a weighed number of identical features, while in the second step, paths in the semantic network represent relation sequences between unidentical features, are identified. Based on a specific method for calculating the closeness between two features at the end of such a sequence, the two features are given a local similarity score.

Some of the aforementioned research apply BN in different segments of CBR. The research presented here has been inspired by TrollCreek and is partly based on it. However, it aims to improve the accuracy of the retrieval by taking advantage of both BN and CBR. The main idea behind BNCreek is to inject the Bayesian analysis into a domain ontology (semantic network) to assist the retrieve phase of a knowledge-intensive CBR system. BNCreek and TrollCreek conceptually work on the same ontology and the difference between them stems from the relational strengths, which in Trollcreek are static whereas in BNCreek change dynamically. In the present paper, we investigate the effects of Bayesian inference within the Creek architecture as a specific knowledge intensive CBR system. In Sect. 3, the structure of BNCreek and its retrieve process are presented. Section 4 evaluates our approach by NDCG and interpolated average precision/recall measures. Section 5 discusses the obtained results and Sect. 6 concludes the paper and names the future steps.

3   The BNCreek Methodology

BNCreek is a knowledge-intensive system to address problems in uncertain domains. The knowledge representation in BNCreek is a combination of a semantic network, a Bayesian network, and a case-base, which together constitutes the knowledge model of the system as a three-module structure. The semantic module consists of the ontology nodes, which are connected by structural, causal, etc. relations (e.g., "subclass-of", "part-of", etc.). This module enables the system to conduct semantic inference through various forms of inheritance. The Bayesian module is a sub-model of the semantic module and consists of the nodes that are connected by causal relations. That module enables the system to do the

Bayesian inferences within the knowledge model in order to extract extra knowledge from the causes behind the observed symptoms and to utilize it for the case similarity assessment process. There is an individual module named Mirror Bayesian network, which interacts with the Bayesian module and is responsible for the Bayesian inference computational issues. The Mirror Bayesian network is created to keep the implementation complexity low and provides scalability for the system. The case base layer is connected to the upper layers through the case features (features are nodes of the Bayesian or the semantic networks) each possessing a relevance factor, which is a number that shows the importance of a feature for a stored case [2].

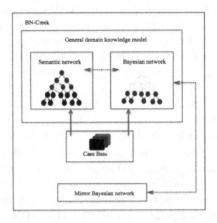

Fig. 1. The graphical representation of BNCreek.

Figure 1 illustrates the graphical representation of the system structure. Each box illustrates one module of the BNCreek, and the inner boxes make up the outer ones, i.e., "semantic network" and "Bayesian network" modules form the "General domain knowledge model"; and the "General domain knowledge model", "Case Base" and "Mirror Bayesian network" form the BNCreek system. The solid arrows show the direction of connecting nodes inside and between modules and the dotted arrow indicates the information flow between the "semantic network", "Bayesian network" and the "Mirror Bayesian network".

3.1   The Retrieve Process

The retrieve process in the current BNCreek system is the mature version of the process earlier outlined for BNCreek1 [13]. In the version presented here, the Bayesian analysis is integrated into the retrieve procedure and is an essential part of it, in contrast with BNCreek1 in which the semantic and Bayesian analysis were working in parallel and their results were combined.

The retrieve process in BNCreek is a master-slave process, which is triggered by observing a new raw case, i.e. knowledge about a concrete problem situation consisting of a set of feature names and features values [2]. In BNCreek the features are of two types:

1. Observed features that are entered into the case by the user (the raw case features).
2. Inferred features that are entered into the case by the system.

Each of the Observed and Inferred features could have three types, i.e., the symptom features (symptoms), the status features (status) and the failure features (failures). Below the retrieve process is presented utilizing a run-through example from the "food domain". The domain description and details can be found in the "System evaluation" section.

Name: Chicken fried steak (Case6)		
Relation	Value	RF
has normal st.	Ok_chicken	0.7
has normal st.	Enough_salt	0.7
has normal st.	Enough_pepper	0.7
has normal st.	Enough_oil	0.7
has normal st.	Enough_milk	0.7
has normal st.	Enough_flour	0.7
has failure	Much_garlic	0.9
has symptom	Juiceless_food	0.9
has symptom	Smelly_food	0.9
has case st.	Unsolved_case	

Name: Fried shrimp & mushroom (Case2)		
Relation	Value	RF
has normal st.	Ok_shrimp	0.7
has failure	Little_butter	0.9
has normal st.	Enough_cream	0.7
has normal st.	Ok_mushroom	0.7
has normal st.	Enough_garlic	0.7
has symptom	Juiceless_food	0.9
has symptom	Smelly_food	0.9
has case st.	Unsolved_case	

Name: Fried shrimp (Case11)		
Relation	Value	RF
has normal st.	Ok_shrimpn	0.7
has failure	Much_salt	0.9
has normal st.	Enough_pepper	0.7
has normal st.	Enough_oil	0.7
has normal st.	Enough_milk	0.7
has normal st.	Enough_flour	0.7
has normal st.	Enough_garlic	0.7
has symptom	Salty_taste	0.9
has case st.	Unsolved_case	

Name: Chicken fried steak (Case6)		
Relation	Value	RF
has failure	LC_chicken	0.9
has normal st.	Enough_salt	0.7
has normal st.	Enough_pepper	0.7
has failure	Little_oil	0.9
has failure	Little_milk	0.9
has failure	Much_flour	0.9
has failure	Little_garlic	0.9
has failure	Not..marinated	0.9
has symptom	Juiceless_food	0.9
has symptom	Smelly_food	0.9
has case st.	Unsolved_case	

Name: Fried shrimp & mushroom (Case2)		
Relation	Value	RF
has failure	LC_shrimp	0.9
has failure	Little_butter	0.9
has normal st.	Enough_cream	0.7
has normal st.	Ok_mushroom	0.7
has failure	Little_garlic	0.9
has failure	Not..marinated	0.9
has symptom	Juiceless_food	0.9
has symptom	Smelly_food	0.9
has case st.	Unsolved_case	

Fig. 2. The upper cases are three sample raw cases from the food domain, and the two lower cases are the corresponding pre-processed cases descriptions. "st." and "LC" stand for status and long cooked, respectively.

As the run-through example, consider a "Chicken fried steak" dish with reported "Juiceless food" and "Smelly food" symptoms as a raw input case. The case is entered by a chef into BNCreek, to find the failures behind the symptoms. The raw case description consists of the dish ingredients like "Enough salt" as a status feature and the reported symptoms, illustrated on the upper left side of Fig. 2.

The master phase is based on inferencing in the Bayesian module. It has three steps.

The first step: The system utilizes the symptoms from the raw case description, i.e., "Juiceless food" and "Smelly food" and applies them to the Bayesian network module. The Bayesian inference results in the network posterior distribution (Algorithm 1, lines 1 and 2) utilizing the Eq. 1, in which "θ", "$p(\theta)$"

and "$p(symptoms|\theta)$" stand for the parameter of distribution, prior distribution and the likelihood of the observations, respectively. The Bayesian module posterior distribution is dynamic in nature, i.e., the probabilities of the dependencies change as a new raw case is entered.

$$p(\theta|symptoms) \propto p(symptoms|\theta) \times p(\theta) \tag{1}$$

The second step: This step extracts informative knowledge from the knowledge model and adds it to the case description.

BNCreek considers the network posterior distribution and extracts the causes behind any of the case description symptoms. Due to the nature of the Bayesian networks, the parent nodes cause the children. So there would be several causes for any symptom that could be extracted. A threshold for the numbers of extracted causes will determine by the expert based on the knowledge model size. In the given example, the symptoms' causes are as follows: "Little oil" causes "Juiceless food"; "LC chicken" causes "Juiceless food"; "Little milk" causes "Juiceless food"; "Much flour" causes "Juiceless food" and "Not enough marinated" causes "Smelly food".

Algorithm 1. Retrieve in BNCreek

Input   : An input raw case.
Output: A sorted list of retrieved failure cases and graphical causal explanations
1 Utilize the symptoms of the input raw case from its case description.
2 In the Bayesian module compute the Bayesian layer posterior beliefs given the symptoms.
3 Extract the cause of the applied symptoms.
4 Modify the raw input case description by adding the extracted causes or adjusting the features.
5 Pass the posterior beliefs from the Bayesian network module into the Semantic network module.
6 Adjust the semantic network module causal strengths utilizing the posterior distribution from the Bayesian network module.
7 **while** *not all the case base is tested* **do**
8   Consider one case from case base.
9   Compute the explanation strength between any pair of input and retrieved case features.
10   Compute the similarity between input and retrieved case.
11 **end**
12 List the matched cases.
13 Generate a graphical causal explanation for the input case.

Then the case description is modified based on the extracted causes and forms what is referred to as a pre-processed case description. The pre-processed case consists of Observed and Inferred features, e.g., "Enough salt" and "Not enough marinated", respectively. Which the "Not enough marinated" is added and the "Little oil" is adjusted from "Enough oil" in the modification process (see the bottom left side of Fig. 2 and Algorithm 1, lines 3 and 4).

The third step: The obtained posterior distribution from the Bayesian network module is passed to the semantic network module (Algorithm 1, line 5).

The slave phase is based on inferencing in the semantic network module. This phase has two steps.

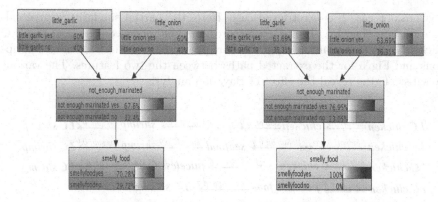

Fig. 3. Part of the Bayesian beliefs before (prior) and after (posterior) applying the symptoms into the network.

The first step: The semantic network causal strengths are adjusted dynamically corresponding to the Bayesian posterior beliefs, in contrast to the other relations in the semantic network module, which are fixed (Algorithm 1, line 6). Figure 3 illustrates part of the Bayesian network prior and posterior distribution, respectively. In which the posterior beliefs will be utilized to adjust the semantic network strengths.

The second step: This step utilizes the adjusted causal strengths and the preprocessed case description and computes the similarity between the input case and the case base.

The similarity assessment in BNCreek follows an "explanation engine" (Fig. 4) with an Activate-Explain-Focus cycle [2]. Activate finds the directly matched features between input and retrieved cases then the Explain tries to account for the not directly matched features of the input and retrieved cases. Focus applies the preferences or external constraints to adjust the ranking of the cases.

Fig. 4. The retrieve explanation cycle.

BNCreek considers each of the case base members at the time and utilizes Dijkstra's Algorithm [15] to extract all possible paths in the knowledge model that represent relation sequences between any features in the input case (f_i) and all the features in the retrieved case (f_j).

Consider case 2 as a retrieved case. Here, the partial similarity degree calculation between "LC shrimp", a feature from the retrieved case, and the "LC chicken", a feature from the input case, are presented. See Fig. 2 for cases descriptions and Fig. 5 for the extracted paths between the two features. The various causal strengths reveal the effect of Bayesian analysis.

LC chicken $\xrightarrow{Sub\ of:\ 0.9}$ *chicken* $\xrightarrow{Sub\ of:\ 0.9}$ *meat* $\xrightarrow{has\ sub:\ 0.9}$ *shrimp* $\xrightarrow{has\ sub:\ 0.9}$ *LC shrimp*

LC chicken $\xrightarrow{Sub\ of:\ 0.9}$ ... $\xrightarrow{Sub\ of:\ 0.9}$ *seafood* $\xrightarrow{has\ sub:\ 0.9}$ *shrimp* $\xrightarrow{has\ sub:\ 0.9}$ *LC shrimp*

LC chicken $\xrightarrow{Sub\ of:\ 0.9}$ *chicken* ... $\xrightarrow{causes:\ 0.6}$ *juiceless food* $\xrightarrow{caused\ by:\ 0.7}$ *LC shrimp*

LC chicken $\xrightarrow{causes:\ 0.7}$ *juiceless food* $\xrightarrow{caused\ by:\ 0.7}$ *LC shrimp*

LC chicken $\xrightarrow{causes:\ 0.7}$ *juiceless food* $\xrightarrow{caused\ by:\ 0.6}$ *early salted beef* ... *LC shrimp*

LC chicken $\xrightarrow{causes:\ 0.7}$ *juiceless food* $\xrightarrow{caused\ by:\ 0.6}$ *early salted beef* ... *LC shrimp*

Fig. 5. All possible paths between "LC chicken" and "LC shrimp" features from the input and retrieved cases, respectively

To explain the similarity strength between any coupled features, Eq. 2 is applied. To compute the *explanation strength*(f_i, f_j), the strength of any path between (f_i) and (f_j) is computed by multiplying its R relation strengths, then all the P path strengths are multiplied. Consider "LC chicken" as f_i, "LC shrimp" as f_j and Fig. 5 for possible paths between them. The $1 - pathstrength$ for the first path in Fig. 5 is $1 - (0.9 * 0.9 * 0.9 * 0.9)$, which is 0.35 and for rest of the paths will be equal to 0.47, 0.71, 0.51, 0.71, 0.71. The multiplication of them is approximately 0.04. Finally the strengths between considered f_i and f_j is $1 - 0.4$, which is 0.96. For the situations where the paired features are the same (exact matched features), the explanation strength is considered as 1.

$$explanation\ strength(f_i, f_j) = 1 - \prod_{p=1}^{P}\left(1 - \prod_{r=1}^{R} relation strength_{rp}\right) \quad (2)$$

$$sim(C_{IN}, C_{RE}) = \frac{\sum_{i=1}^{n}\sum_{j=1}^{m} explanation strength(f_i, f_j) * relevance factor_{f_j}}{\sum_{i=1}^{n}\sum_{j=1}^{m} \beta(explanation strength(f_i, f_j)) * relevance factor_{f_j} + \sum_{j=1}^{m} relevance factor_{f_j}} \quad (3)$$

The similarity between input case (C_{IN}) and the retrieved case (C_{RE}) is computed by summing up all the multiplication of explanation strength of (f_i, f_j) with a relevance factor of f_j divided by the summation of the relevance factor of f_j multiplied by β (explanation strength(f_i, f_j)). β (explanation strength(f_i, f_j)) is a binary function, which is equal to one when explanation strength(f_i, f_j) is not zero. Number of features in input and retrieved cases are shown by 'm' and 'n'. See Eq. 3.

The calculation of the total similarity between case6 and case2 are presented here. For the numerator of Eq. 3, the explanation strength between any coupled features from the input and retrieved cases (e.g. "LC chicken" and "LC shrimp") is multiplied to the relevance factor of the retrieved case feature (i.e., "LC shrimp"), which is 0.96*0.9 and is equal to 0.86. Then the numerator is $1*0.9+1*0.9+1*0.9+0.9*0.89+0.9*0.59+0.9*0.85+0.9*0.47+0.9*0.56+0.9*0.96+0.9*0.67+0.9*0.73+0.7*0.84+0.7*0.65+0.7*0.89+0.7*0.89$, which is rounded to 10. In the denominator, for each feature from the input case, the relevance factors of the retrieved case will be multiplied by the binary function β and add together. β for any explained coupled feature is 1. For the directly matched couples, the relevance factors of the retrieved case will be summed up once. Due to the cases descriptions, cases 6 and 2 have 3 direct matched and 6 explained features. Then the denominator will be $(1*0.9+1*0.7+1*0.7+1*0.9)*6$ for the explained coupled features plus $1*0.9+1*0.9+1*0.7+1*0.9+1*0.7+1*0.9+1*0.9$ for the direct matched coupled features, which is 25. Finally, the total similarity between case6 and case2 is 10/25 that is 0.4.

The system computes the similarity between the input case and all the cases from the case base (Algorithm 1 lines 7 to 11).

3.2 Explanations in BNCreek

There are two uses of explanations in the knowledge-based systems. One is the explanation that a system may produce for the user's benefit, e.g., to explain its reasoning steps or to justify why a particular conclusion was drawn. The other one is the internal explanation a system may construct for itself during problem-solving. BNCreek provides internal explanations for solving the problems, which are related to the "explanation strength" between two concepts in the model. A graphical causal explanation is generated to show the causal chains behind the observed symptoms for the benefit of the user.

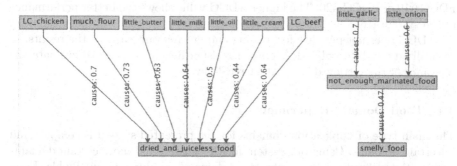

Fig. 6. An explanation structure from which a causal explanation in the food domain can be derived.

Figure 6 demonstrates a graphical causal explanation structure for "Chicken fried steak (case 6)". The explanation is the result of Bayesian analysis given the two observations, i.e., "Juiceless food" and "Smelly food". BNCreek considers the case features and browses into the network to find the related causal chain.

The left part of Fig. 6 explains the seven possible causes for "Juiceless food" in which the "LC chicken", "Little oil", "Little milk" and "Much flour" are related to the case 6 with causal strengths of 0.7, 0.5, 0.64 and 0.73, respectively. The causal strengths demonstrate that "LC chicken" and "Much flour" have the most effect on causing the "Juiceless food". The right part of Fig. 6 shows two causal chains for "Smelly food", i.e., "Little garlic" causes "Not enough marinated" causes "Smelly food" and "Little onion" causes "Not enough marinated" causes "Smelly food" with causal strengths of 0.32 and 0.28, respectively (Algorithm 1 line 13).

The generated explanation in more uncertain domains like oil well drilling, plays a significant role in computing the similarity (by providing explanation paths) and clarifies the proposed solution for the expert.

4   System Evaluation

To evaluate our approach, we set up two sets of experiments. One from the "food domain", a kind of initial toy-domain, and the other one from the "oil well drilling domain" the main investigated domain. Both of the experiments aim to measure the capability of the system to prevent the failures utilizing the observations. The application domains are tested by TrollCreek (version: 0.96devbuild), myCBR (Version: 3.1betaDFKIGmbH) and our implementation of BNCreek. The results from the systems are evaluated against the "ground-truth": domain expert predictions. The evaluation measures in this study are NDCG and Interpolated Average Precision-Recall.

Normalized Discounted Cumulative Gain (NDCG) as a ranked based information retrieval measure, values the highly relevant items appearing earlier in the result list. Usually, NDCG reports at rank cuts of 5, 10 or 20, i.e., nDCG@5, nDCG@10 or nDCG@20. The higher NDCG value shows the better performance of the system [16].

NDCG does not penalize for missing and not relevant cases in the results, so we utilized the Interpolated Average Precision-Recall measure to evaluate the relevance of the retrieved cases at 11 recall levels.

4.1   Food Domain Experiment

The main type of application domains for the presented system is complex and uncertain domains. Using our system for the smaller and more certain domains such as the utilized version of the "food domain" wouldn't be justifiable. However, Due to the simple nature of the "food domain", which leads to a better understanding of the system process, a run-through example from this domain is utilized and a set of evaluating experiments is set up.

Setup. The food domain knowledge model is inspired by "Taaable ontology". Taaable is a CBR system that uses a recipe book as a case base to answer cooking queries [17]. Some modifications are made to fit the ontology to the BNCreek

Export	Case1	Case2	Case3	Case4	Case5	Case6	Case7	Case8	Case9	Case10	case11
Case1		1	1	4	1	1	1	8	7	1	1
Case2	3		7	5	6	8	1	5	3	1	1
Case3	1	7		4	5	6	8	1	3	1	1
Case4	3	5	6		8	6	7	3	1	3	3
Case5	1	5	6	4		8	7	1	3	2	2
Case6	1	5	6	3	8		7	2	4	2	2
Case7	1	7	6	4	5	8		2	4	2	2
Case8	1	7	3	2	1	1	4		2	8	1
Case9	1	8	6	5	6	7	6	1		1	1
Case10	4	3	1	7	1	1	1	2	1		8
Case11	3	2	1	7	4	1	1	8	1	1	

BNCreek	Case1	Case2	Case3	Case4	Case5	Case6	Case7	Case8	Case9	Case10	case11
Case1		15	15	2	8	13	13	11	21	11	12
Case2	15		33	16	25	33	35	10	25	8	13
Case3	15	37		27	42	43	43	20	17	16	19
Case4	2	15	24		29	13	13	26	7	26	18
Case5	9	27	41	31		52	43	23	13	15	17
Case6	14	36	45	13	55		89	16	23	11	16
Case7	14	40	45	14	45	89		16	19	11	16
Case8	10	9	19	26	22	15	15		8	16	18
Case9	21	26	19	8	14	23	20	8		10	15
Case10	11	8	15	19	13	10	10	15	10		19
Case11	13	13	18	16	16	16	16	18	15	17	

myCBR	Case1	Case2	Case3	Case4	Case5	Case6	Case7	Case8	Case9	Case10	case11
Case1		6	10	6	0	0	0	6	0	8	0
Case2	5		5	5	5	8	5	5	5	5	5
Case3	8	6		10	10	10	10	6	6	6	6
Case4	6	6	10		10	10	10	6	0	6	6
Case5	0	6	10	10		10	10	6	8	6	6
Case6	0	6	10	10	10		10	0	8	6	6
Case7	0	8	10	10	10	10		0	8	6	6
Case8	6	6	6	6	6	0	0		6	6	0
Case9	0	6	6	0	8	8	8	6		0	6
Case10	6	6	6	6	6	6	6	6	0		10
Case11	0	6	6	6	6	6	6	0	6	10	

TrollCreek	Case1	Case2	Case3	Case4	Case5	Case6	Case7	Case8	Case9	Case10	case11
Case1		9	6	6	0	0	0	7	0	13	0
Case2	9		0	0	0	6	7	5	6	7	
Case3	6	0		9	16	16	16	5	0	4	5
Case4	6	0	9		24	16	16	5	0	14	5
Case5	0	0	17	23		36	26	5	13	4	12
Case6	0	0	17	16	36		48	0	22	4	29
Case7	0	7	17	16	26	48		0	13	4	40
Case8	8	8	5	5	5	0	0		7	10	0
Case9	0	4	0	0	13	21	13	6		0	15
Case10	14	6	4	14	4	4	4	10	0		11
Case11	0	8	5	5	11	28	39	0	15	11	

Fig. 7. The similarity scores from running BNCreek, myCBR,TrollCreek and the expert prediction in food application domain.

structure, i.e., adding causal relations. The causal relations present the failures of using an inappropriate amount of ingredients. Fifteen recipes are examined and simplified to their basic elements (e.g., Gouda cheese simplified to cheese). The resulted knowledge model consists of 130 food domain concepts and more than 250 relations between them. Eleven failure cases are created and utilized as the queries of the experiment. Each query applies to the case base in leave one out evaluation manner, which results in 11 query sets. The upper side of Fig. 2 demonstrates three samples of raw food failure cases descriptions.

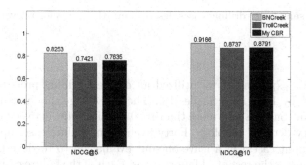

Fig. 8. NDCG values at cuts of 5 and 10 for food domain experiment

Food Experiment Results. Figure 7 demonstrates the similarity scores of BNCreek, myCBR and TrollCreek for the first experiment in a leave one out manner. Utilizing the aforementioned tables, the NDCG values are computed against the expert predictions and reported at NDCG@5 and 10 in Fig. 8.

Figure 8 illustrates that BNCreek with 0.8253 and 0.9186 values at NDCG@5 and 10 ranked the retrieved cases closer to the expert prediction in comparison to the TrollCreek and myCBR with 0.7421, 0.8737 and 0.7635, 0.8791 values.

The overall performance of the three systems is high and not so different, which can be explained by the fact that this experiment is set up on a small case base. Besides that, the BNCreek showed a somewhat better performance than the others in both cuts.

4.2   Oil Well Drilling Domain Experiment

The oil and gas domain is an uncertain domain with a weak theory in which implementing ad hoc solutions frequently leads to a reemergence of the problem and repetition of the cycle. These types of domains are the main application domains addressed by BNCreek.

Name: case17		
Relation	Value	RF
has symptom	Activity Of Tripping In (s)	0.7
has internal...	Cavings On Shaker (j)	0.7
has symptom	Fm Fault Expected (ss)	0.7
has symptom	Fm Hard (s)	0.7
has symptom	Fm Laminated (s)	0.7
has symptom	Fm Soft (s)	0.7
has symptom	Fm Unstable Expected (ss)	0.7
has symptom	HKL High (s)	0.7
has symptom	Losses Seepage (s)	0.7
has symptom	Time Long (s)	0.7
has symptom	Time Of Tripping Long (ss)	0.7
has symptom	Torque High (s)	0.7
has symptom	WBM (ss)	0.7
has symptom	Well Inclination High (s)	0.7
has symptom	Well Openhole Long (ss)	0.7
has symptom	Well P High (s)	0.7
has symptom	Overpull (s)	0.7
has failure	Wellbore Instability ...(f)	0.9
has case status	unsolved case	

Name: case28		
Relation	Value	RF
has symptom	Activity Directional Drilling (s)	0.7
has internal ...	Bit Aggressive (ss)	0.7
has symptom	Wellbore DP Dia Small (ss)	0.7
has symptom	Bit Type Shear Bit (ss)	0.7
has symptom	DLS High (s)	0.7
has symptom	Fm Boundary Expected (ss)	0.7
has symptom	Fm Laminated (s)	0.7
has symptom	Fm Unstable Expected (ss)	0.7
has symptom	HKL High (s)	0.7
has symptom	Mud Weight High (ss)	0.7
has symptom	ROP Decreasing (s)	0.7
has symptom	ROP High (s)	0.7
has symptom	RPM Avg High (s)	0.7
has symptom	RPM String On (s)	0.7
has symptom	SPP Low (s)	0.7
has symptom	Stabilizer Undergauge (ss)	0.7
has symptom	Torque Low (s)	0.7
has symptom	WBM (ss)	0.7
has symptom	Well Depth Shallow (ss)	0.7
has symptom	Well Inclination High (s)	0.7
has symptom	Well Openhole Long (ss)	0.7
has symptom	WOB Spikes (s)	0.7
has symptom	Fm Soft (s)	0.7
has failure	Technical Sidetrack (f)	0.9
has case status	unsolved case	

Fig. 9. Two samples of drilling cases description. RF stands for relevance factor.

Setup. In this experiment, we utilized an oil well drilling process knowledge model created by Prof Paal Skalle [18]. The knowledge model consists of 350 drilling domain concepts and more than 1000 relationships between them, which makes it a very detailed ontology. Forty five drilling failure cases are utilized as the queries (input cases) in a leave-one-out evaluation to retrieve the matched similar ones among the rest of 44 failure cases. Each of the failure cases in average has 20 symptoms and one failure as the case solution that has been removed for the query case. Figure 9 shows two examples of drilling cases.

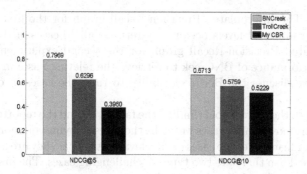

Fig. 10. NDCG values at cuts of 5 and 10

Oil Well Drilling Experiment Results. We report on NDCG at ranks 5 and 10 in Fig. 10. The BNCreek NDCG@5 and 10 are reported as 0.7969 and 0.6713, which significantly outperform TrollCreek with 0.6296, 0.5759 and myCBR with 0.3960, 0.5229, respectively. The ordering produced by BNCreek yields a better NDCG value than the ordering produced by TrollCreek and myCBR at both cuts. This shows the efficiency of the Bayesian inference in case ranking in comparison with the other systems, which do not utilize the Bayesian inference.

Figure 11 demonstrates the three systems interpolated average Precision at 11 Recall levels. In all recall levels, BNCreek has higher precision, which demonstrates the efficiency of the system in retrieving the more similar cases comparing to the other systems.

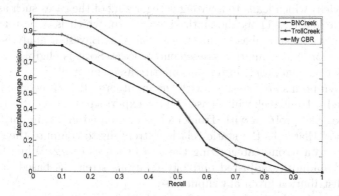

Fig. 11. Interpolated precision/recall graph for the results of BNCreek and TrollCreek

5   Discussion

The higher NDCG values in the two experiments, show the overall ability of BNCreek in ranking the retrieved cases correctly in comparison to TrollCreek and myCBR. The Interpolated Precision-Recall graph for the first experiment would be 1 for all recall levels because we retrieve all 10 cases of the case base. The Interpolated Precision-Recall graph for the second experiment illustrates the higher performance of BNCreek to retrieve the relevant cases in all 11 recall levels. Here we discuss the BNCreek ability to rank the cases in detail by an example.

According to the system goal (finding the failure behind the reported/observed symptoms), the most similar cases would be the cases carrying common symptoms. Then, the other features of the cases are irrelevant as long as they are not failures of the symptoms. Then there are two types of challenging cases. The first type has a similar overall case description but not the same symptoms, and the second one is the cases with the same symptoms but not similar case description, comparing to the input case. The first type should be categorized as not similar and the second type should be categorized as a very similar case.

In Fig. 7, the seventh rows of the four tables demonstrate the similarity degree between case 6 (the input case of the given run-through example) and the case base cases, computed by BNCreek, TrollCreek, myCBR, and the expert.

Case 11, has a similar ingredient with the case 6 and their differences originated in "Ok chicken" being replaced by "Ok shrimp", "Enough salt" being replaced by "Much salt" and their symptoms, which are not the same. Case 11 is categorized as the third most similar case by TrollCreek while, based on the expert's prediction, it is almost the least similar case to case 6. This problem stems from similarity assessment mechanism in TrollCreek which incorporates the raw case descriptions without considering the effect of different symptoms on cases (e.g., a peppery sandwich is more similar to a peppery steak than to a salty sandwich) which leads to a wrong categorizing of the cases such as case 11. BNCreek ranked case 11 as the sixth similar case, which is a better ranking. BNCreek in its master phases, injects the effect of Bayesian analysis into the case description and similarity assessment process. So it is eligible to incorporate the effect of symptoms into the similarity assessment.

Case 2 symptoms are the same with the input case. It is categorised as a not similar case by TrollCreek while, based on the expert's prediction, it is the fourth similar case. The problem with TrollCreek is originated in its similarity assessment method that uses the static relation strengths to compute the similarity which leads to a wrong categorizing the cases such as case 2. While BNCreek, utilizes a dynamically adjusted ontology relations strengths based on the BN posterior distribution given any input case.

myCBR ranked both of the case 2 and 11 as the sixth similar case. It ranks the retrieved cases based on their common features and a fixed similarity table which is determined by the expert. The similarity table could work like a pre computed similarity explanations between the not identical coupled features, if the expert knows all the coupled features similarity degrees, which rarely happens in uncertain domains with several features. This explains the decreased performance of myCBR from the small experiment of the food domain to the drilling domain experiment.

6 Conclusion and Future Work

We studied the effect of Bayesian analysis in the similarity assessment within a knowledge-intensive system. We have developed a knowledge-intensive CBR system, BNCreek, which employs the Bayesian inference method to retrieve similar cases. The Bayesian analysis is incorporated to provide a formal and clear defined inference method for reasoning in the knowledge model.

To evaluate the effectiveness of our approach, we set up two experiments and employed the NDCG and Precision-Recall measures. Over two sets of experiments, we demonstrated that our approach has a better performance in ranking the retrieved cases against the expert prediction compared with the results of TrollCreek and myCBR. This indicates the Bayesian analysis efficiency for similarity assessment, across several application domains.

Although BNCreek showed a better performance in comparison with the other systems, in both of the examples it didn't manage to rank the cases same as the expert. Moreover, comparing the NDCG values in Figs. 8 and 10 shows the decreased performance of the BNCreek by increasing the case base size. A possible further step for this study is designing new metrics that help to rank the cases more accurately in bigger case bases.

Acknowledgement. The authors would like to thank Prof. Paal Skalle for preparing drilling cases and Prof. Helge Langseth and Dr. Frode Sørmo for their useful suggestions.

References

1. Gundersen, O.E., Sørmo, F., Aamodt, A., Skalle, P.: A real-time decision support system for high cost oil-well drilling operations. AI Mag. **34**(1), 21 (2012)
2. Aamodt, A.: Knowledge-intensive case-based reasoning in CREEK. In: Funk, P., González Calero, P.A. (eds.) ECCBR 2004. LNCS (LNAI), vol. 3155, pp. 1–15. Springer, Heidelberg (2004). https://doi.org/10.1007/978-3-540-28631-8_1
3. Sørmo, F.: Plausible inheritance; semantic network inference for case-based reasoning, p. 102. Department of Computer and Information Science, Norwegian University of Science and Technology, Trondheim (2000)
4. Aamodt, A., Langseth, H.: Integrating Bayesian networks into knowledge-intensive CBR. In: AAAI Workshop on Case-Based Reasoning Integrations, pp. 1–6 (1998)
5. Kofod-Petersen, A., Langseth, H., Aamodt, A.: Explanations in Bayesian networks using provenance through case-based reasoning. In: Workshop Proceedings, p. 79 (2010)
6. Lacave, C., Díez, F.J.: A review of explanation methods for Bayesian networks. Knowl. Eng. Rev. **17**(2), 107–127 (2002)
7. Velasco, F.J.M.: A Bayesian network approach to diagnosing the root cause of failure from trouble tickets. Artif. Intell. Res. **1**(2), 75 (2012)
8. Houeland, T.G., Bruland, T., Aamodt, A., Langseth, H.: A hybrid metareasoning architecture combining case-based reasoning and Bayesian networks (extended version). IDI, NTNU (2011)
9. Kim, B., Rudin, C., Shah, J.A.: The Bayesian case model: a generative approach for case-based reasoning and prototype classification. In: Advances in Neural Information Processing Systems, pp. 1952–1960 (2014)

10. Bruland, T., Aamodt, A., Langseth, H.: Architectures integrating case-based reasoning and Bayesian networks for clinical decision support. In: Shi, Z., Vadera, S., Aamodt, A., Leake, D. (eds.) International Conference on Intelligent Information Processing, pp. 82–91. Springer, Heidelberg (2010). https://doi.org/10.1007/978-3-642-16327-2_13

11. Tran, H.M., Schönwälder, J.: Fault resolution in case-based reasoning. In: Ho, T.-B., Zhou, Z.-H. (eds.) PRICAI 2008. LNCS (LNAI), vol. 5351, pp. 417–429. Springer, Heidelberg (2008). https://doi.org/10.1007/978-3-540-89197-0_39

12. Koton, P.A.: Using experience in learning and problem solving. Ph.D. dissertation, Massachusetts Institute of Technology (1988)

13. Nikpour, H., Aamodt, A., Skalle, P.: Diagnosing root causes and generating graphical explanations by integrating temporal causal reasoning and CBR. In: CEUR Workshop Proceedings (2017)

14. Forbus, K.D., Gentner, D., Law, K.: MAC/FAC: a model of similarity-based retrieval. Cogn. Sci. **19**(2), 141–205 (1995)

15. Dijkstra, E.W.: A note on two problems in connexion with graphs. Numer. Math. **1**(1), 269–271 (1959)

16. Järvelin, K., Kekäläinen, J.: Cumulated gain-based evaluation of IR techniques. ACM Trans. Inf. Syst. **20**(4), 422–446 (2002)

17. Badra, F., et al.: Knowledge acquisition and discovery for the textual case-based cooking system WIKITAAABLE. In: 8th International Conference on Case-Based Reasoning-ICCBR 2009, Workshop Proceedings, pp. 249–258 (2009)

18. Skalle, P., Aamodt, A., Swahn, I.: Detection of failures and interpretation of causes during drilling operations. Society of Petroleum Engineers, SPE-183 022-MS, ADIPEC, Abu Dhabi, November 2016

Personalised Human Activity Recognition Using Matching Networks

Sadiq Sani[1]([✉]), Nirmalie Wiratunga[1], Stewart Massie[1], and Kay Cooper[2]

[1] School of Computing Science and Digital Media, Robert Gordon University,
Aberdeen, Scotland AB10 7GJ, UK
[2] School of Health Sciences, Robert Gordon University,
Aberdeen, Scotland AB10 7GJ, UK
{s.sani,n.wiratunga,s.massie,k.cooper}@rgu.ac.uk

Abstract. Human Activity Recognition (HAR) is typically modelled as a classification task where sensor data associated with activity labels are used to train a classifier to recognise future occurrences of these activities. An important consideration when training HAR models is whether to use training data from a general population (subject-independent), or personalised training data from the target user (subject-dependent). Previous evaluations have shown personalised training to be more accurate because of the ability of resulting models to better capture individual users' activity patterns. From a practical perspective however, collecting sufficient training data from end users may not be feasible. This has made using subject-independent training far more common in real-world HAR systems. In this paper, we introduce a novel approach to personalised HAR using a neural network architecture called a matching network. Matching networks perform nearest-neighbour classification by reusing the class label of the most similar instances in a provided support set, which makes them very relevant to case-based reasoning. A key advantage of matching networks is that they use metric learning to produce feature embeddings or representations that maximise classification accuracy, given a chosen similarity metric. Evaluations show our approach to substantially out perform general subject-independent models by at least 6% macro-averaged F1 score.

1 Introduction

Human Activity Recognition (HAR) is the computational discovery of human activity from sensor data and is increasingly being adopted in health, security, entertainment and defense applications [10]. An example of the application of HAR in healthcare is SELFBACK[1], a system designed to improve self-management of low back pain (LBP) by monitoring users' physical activity levels in order to provide advice and guidance on how best to adhere to recommended

---

[1] This work was fully sponsored by the collaborative project SELFBACK under contract with the European Commission (# 689043) in the Horizon2020 framework. Details of this project are available at: http://www.selfback.eu.

M. T. Cox et al. (Eds.): ICCBR 2018, LNAI 11156, pp. 339–353, 2018.
https://doi.org/10.1007/978-3-030-01081-2_23

physical activity guidelines [2]. Guidelines for LBP recommend that patients should not be sedentary for long periods of time and should maintain moderate levels of physical activity. The SELFBACK system uses a wrist-worn sensor to continuously recognise user activities in real time. This allows the system to compare the user's activity profile to the recommended guidelines for physical activity.and produce feedback to inform the user on how well they are adhering to these guidelines. Other information in the user's activity profile include the durations of activities and, for walking, the counts of steps taken, as well as intensity e.g. slow, normal or fast. The categorisation of walking into slow, normal and fast allows us to better match the activity intensity (i.e. low, moderate or high) recommended in the guidelines. HAR is typically modelled as a classification task where sensor data associated with activity labels are used to train a classifier to predict future occurrences of those activities.

An important consideration for HAR is classifier training, where training examples can either be acquired from a general population (subject-independent), or from the target user of the system (subject-dependent). Previous works have shown using subject-dependent data to result in superior performance [5, 7, 19, 21]. The relatively poorer performance of subject-independent models can be attributed to variations in activity patterns, gait or posture between different individuals [12]. However, training a classifier exclusively with user provided data is not practical in a real-world configuration as this places significant burden on the user to provide sufficient amounts of training data required to build a personalised model.

In this paper, we introduce an approach to personalised HAR using matching networks. Matching Networks are a type of neural network architecture introduced for the task of one-shot learning [22] which is a scenario where an algorithm is trained to recognise a new class from just a few examples of that class. Given a (typically small) support set of labelled examples, matching networks are able to classify an unlabelled example by reusing the class labels of the most similar examples in the support set. To apply matching networks for personalised HAR, we require the user to provide a small number of examples for each type of activity. Note that this is no different to the calibration approach which is commonly employed in gesture control devices and is already in use in the Nike + iPod fitness device [12]. The examples provided by the user are treated as the support set used by the matching network to classify future occurrences of the user's activities. In this way, the matching network generates a personalised classifier that is better able to recognise the individual user's activity pattern.

An advantage of matching networks is that they use metric learning in order to produce feature embeddings or representations that maximise nearest neighbour classification accuracy.

At the same time, because classification is only conditioned on the support set, matching networks behave like non-parametric models and can reason with any set of examples that are provided at runtime, without the need for retraining the network. This makes our system able to continuously adapt to changes in the user's context easily which is an important goal of CBR.

The rest of this paper is organised as follows: in Sect. 2, we discuss important related work on personalised HAR and highlight the importance of CBR and k-nearest neighbour in particular for personalisation. Section 3 presents technical details of the steps for training a HAR classifier. In Sect. 4, we formally introduce matching networks and in Sect. 5 we present how we apply this to the task of personalised HAR. A description of our dataset is presented in Sect. 6, evaluations are presented in Sect. 7 and conclusions follow in Sect. 8.

2 Related Work

The standard approach to classifier training for HAR involves using subject-independent examples to create a general classification model. However, comparative evaluation with personalised models, trained using subject-dependent examples, show this to produce more accurate predictions [5,7,21]. In [21], a general model and a personalised model both trained using a C4.5 decision tree classifier are compared. The general model produced an accuracy of 56.3% while the personalised model produced an accuracy of 94.6%, an increase of 39.3%. Similarly, [5,7] reported increases of 19.0% and 9.7% between personalised and general models respectively which are trained using the same classification algorithm. A more recent improvement on standard subject-dependent training which uses online multi-task (OMT) learning is presented in [20]. Here, individual users are treated as separate tasks where each task only contains the respective user's data. Personalised classifiers for each task are then trained jointly which allows the models to influence one-another, thereby improving accuracy. Evaluation shows OMT to perform better than personalised models trained independently. A common disadvantage of all subject-dependent approaches is that they require access to significant amounts of good quality end-user data for training. Such approaches have limited practical use for real-world applications because of the burden they place on users to provide sufficient training data.

An alternative solution is to bootstrap a general model with a small set of examples acquired from the user through semi-supervised learning approaches. Different types of semi-supervised learning approaches have been explored for personalised HAR e.g. self-learning, co-learning and active learning, which bootstrap a general model with examples acquired from the user [12]. Both self-learning and co-learning attempt to infer accurate activity labels for unlabelled examples without querying the user. This way, both approaches manage to avoid placing any labelling burden on the user. In contrast, active learning selectively chooses the most useful examples to present to the user for labelling using techniques such as uncertainty sampling which consistently outperform random sampling [16]. Evaluations show semi-supervised approaches mainly produce improvements in situations where baseline classification accuracy is low but no improvements were observed in situations where baseline accuracy was already very high [12]. In addition, semi-supervised approaches require retraining of the classifier at runtime every time new data needs to be incorporated into the model, which can be very expensive, especially on mobile devices.

Case-based reasoning (CBR) offers a convenient solution to the problem of model retraining at runtime. The k-nearest neighbour (kNN) retrieval approach at the core of CBR does not learn a model, which makes it able to easily assimilate new examples at runtime. However, performance of kNN largely depends on the choice of similarity metric, and manually defining good similarity metrics for specific problems is generally difficult [4].

Metric learning is an approach that is used to automatically learn a similarity metric from data in a way that better captures the important relationships between examples in that data [23]. An important point to note about metric learning is that learning a similarity metric from data is equivalent to transforming the data to a new representation and computing the similarity in this new space using any standard metric e.g. Euclidean [4]. For a comprehensive review of metric learning, we refer the reader to [4,9]. A more recent sub-field of metric learning called deep metric learning uses deep learning algorithms to learn this feature transformation, thereby taking advantage of the ability of deep learning algorithms to extract higher-level, abstract feature representations. Matching networks are an example in this category that are able to incorporate any deep learning architecture e.g. convolutional neural networks [11] or recurrent neural networks [6].

Given the novelty of deep metric learning, very few applications of this are available in case-based reasoning. A very recent work that uses deep metric learning in a Case-based reasoning system for adaptable clickbait detection is [14], where a word2vec model [15] is used in combination with a deep convolutional neural network to learn similarity between clickbait articles. Another CBR system for image-based Web page classification which uses Siamese convolutional neural networks is presented in [13]. Siamese neural networks learn a similarity metric by minimising a contrastive loss which penalises dissimilar example pairs being placed close in the representation space, and rewards similar pairs being placed close together [8]. In this work, we focus on matching networks in particular which have the ability to both learn appropriate feature transformations using metric learning, and at the same time perform nearest neighbour classification using neural attention mechanism [3].

3 Human Activity Recognition

The computational task of HAR consists of three main steps: windowing, feature extraction and classifier training as illustrated in Fig. 1. Windowing is the process of partitioning continuous sensor data into discrete instances of length l, where l is typically specified in seconds. Figure 2 illustrates how windowing is applied to a tri-axial accelerometer data stream with channels: a, b and c. Windows can be overlapped especially at train time in order have better coverage of the data, which also increases the number of examples available for training. We do not overlap windows at test time in order to simulate real-time streaming data.

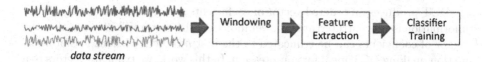

data stream

Fig. 1. Steps of human activity recognition.

The length of windows is an important consideration where very short window lengths typically produce less accurate performance, while longer windows produce latency at runtime due to the fact that several seconds worth of data need to be collected before before making a prediction [18]. In this work, we choose a window length of five seconds which provides a good balance between accuracy and latency. A tri-axial accelerometer partitioned in this way produces a window w_i is comprised of real-valued vectors a_i, b_i and c_i, such that $a_i = (a_{i1}, \ldots, a_{il})$.

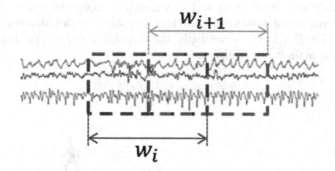

Fig. 2. Illustration of accelerometer data windowing.

Once windows have been partitioned, suitable features need to extracted from each window w_i in order to generate examples x_i used for classifier training. Many different feature extraction approaches have been applied for HAR. These include hand-crafted time and frequency domain features, coefficients of frequency domain transformations, as well as more recent deep learning approaches [17]. One feature extraction approach we have previously found to be both inexpensive to compute and very effective, is Discrete Cosine Transform (DCT) [17]. DCT is applied to each axis (a_i, b_i, c_i) of a given window w_i to produce vectors of coefficients v_a, v_b and v_c respectively that describe the sinusoidal wave forms that constitute the original signal. In addition, we also include the DCT coefficients of the magnitude vector m where each entry m_j in m is computed using the Euclidean norm of corresponding entries in a_j, b_j and c_j as defined in Eq. 1.

$$m_j = \sqrt{a_j^2 + b_j^2 + c_j^2} \tag{1}$$

DCT produces an ordered vector of coefficients such that the most significant information is concentrated at the lower indices of the vectors This means that the vector of coeffcients can be truncated to the first n indices without loss of information, making DCT ideal for compression. In this work, we truncate vectors to a length of $n = 60$. The truncated coefficient vectors v_a, v_b, v_c and v_m are concatenated together to form a single example representation x_i of length 240.

4   Matching Networks

The aim of matching networks is to learn a model that maps an unlabelled example $\hat{x}$ to a class label $\hat{y}$ using a small support set S of labelled examples. To provide a formal definition of matching networks, we define a set of class labels L and a set of examples X. We also define a support set S as shown in Eq. 2,

$$S = \{(x,y)|x \in X, y \in Y \subset L\} \tag{2}$$

i.e. S consists of a subset of classes Y with m examples in each class. Hence, the cardinality of S is $|S| = m \times |Y|$. A matching networks learns a classifier C_s which, given a test instance $\hat{x}$, provides a probability distribution over class labels $y \in Y$ i.e. $P(y|\hat{x}, S)$. Accordingly, the class label $\hat{y}$ of $\hat{x}$ is predicted as the class with the highest probability i.e.

$$\hat{y} = argmax_y P(y|\hat{x}, S) \tag{3}$$

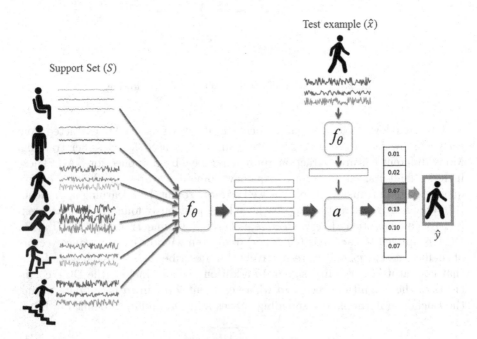

Fig. 3. Illustration of matching network for HAR.

Next we address the question of how to calculate $P(y|\hat{x}, S)$. This can be done using an attention function $a()$ which computes the probabilities in three operations. Firstly, we define an embedding function f_θ, which is a neural network that maps a given input to an embedded representation as shown in Eq. 4 (Fig. 3).

$$f_\theta(x) = x'$$ (4)

The embedding function f_θ is the embedding part of the matching network and it's goal is to produce representations that maximise similarity between examples belonging to the same class. Thus, we define a similarity metric $sim(\hat{x}', x_i')$ which returns the similarity between the embedded representations of our unlabelled example $\hat{x}$ and any example $x_i \in S$. Here, any standard similarity metric e.g. Euclidean, dot product or cosine can be used. An example of sim using cosine similarity is shown in Eq. 5.

$$sim(\hat{x}', x_i') = \frac{\sum \hat{x}_j' x_{i,j}'}{\sqrt{\hat{x}_j'^2}\sqrt{x_{i,j}'^2}}$$ (5)

The last operation of the attention function is to convert the similarity values returned by sim into probabilities. This can be done using the softmax function as shown in Eq. 7.

$$a(\hat{x}', x_i') = e^{sim(\hat{x}', x_i')} / \sum^{|s|} e^{sim(\hat{x}', x_i')}$$ (6)

Using a one-hot encoding vector y to represent any class label y, we can estimate a class probability for $\hat{x}'$ as follows:

$$\hat{y} = \sum^{|S|} a(\hat{x}', x_i') * y$$ (7)

Since y_i has a value of 1 at only the position corresponding to its class (with the rest being zero); the multiplication with a can be viewed as providing a similarity weighted estimate for each candidate class and thereby forming an estimated class distribution.

We can now use this estimated $\hat{y}$ class probability and the actual y class probability (i.e. the one-hot vector) to derive the training loss using a function such as the categorical cross-entropy as shown in Eq. 9.

$$\mathcal{L}(y, \hat{y}) = -\sum_j^{|L|} y_j \, log(\hat{y}_j)$$ (8)

$$\mathcal{L}_{train} = \frac{\sum_i^{|N|} \mathcal{L}(y_i, \hat{y}_i)}{N}$$ (9)

Accordingly the entire matching network can be trained end-to-end using gradient descent.

5   Personalised HAR Using Matching Networks

In this section, we formally describe how we apply matching networks for personalised HAR. Recall that for personalised HAR, our aim is to obtain a network that can classify a particular user's activity using a small set of examples provided by the same user. Therefore, training such a network requires us to define a set of users U where each user $u_j \in U$ is comprised of a set of labelled examples as follows:

$$u_j = \{(x,y)|x \in X, y \in L\} \tag{10}$$

Next we define a set of training instances T_j for each user u_j as follows:

$$T_j = \{(S_j, B_j)\}^l \tag{11}$$

i.e., T_j is made up of user-specific support and target set pairs S_j and B_j respectively, where $S_j = \{(x,y)|x \in u_i, y \in L\}^k$ and $B_j = \{(x,y)|x \in u_j, x \notin S_j\}$. Note that the set of labels in S_j is always equivalent to L because we are interested in learning a classifier over the entire set of activity labels. Accordingly, S_j contains m examples for each class $y \in L$ and the cardinality of S_j is $k = m \times |L|$. Both S_j and B_j are sampled at random from u_j l times to create T_j. Each B_j is used with it's respective S_j by classifying each instance in B_j using S_j and computing loss using categorical cross entropy. This process is illustrated in Fig. 4. The network is trained using stochastic gradient descent and back propagation.

$$T_j = \{(S_j, B_j)\}^l \tag{12}$$

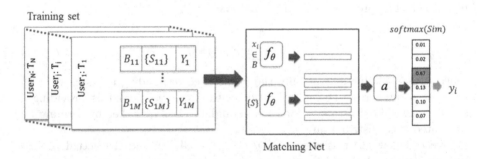

Fig. 4. Training matching network for personalised HAR

The embedding function used in this work is a neural network with one fully-connected layer with 1200 units. Before examples are input into the embedding network, they are passed through Discrete Cosine Transform (DCT) feature extraction. The fully connected layer is followed by a Batch Normalisation layer which reduces covariate shift and has been shown to result in faster training and better accuracy. An illustration of the configuration of the embedding network is presented in Fig. 5.

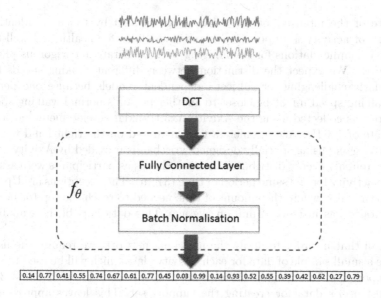

Fig. 5. Details of embedding network

6 Dataset

A group of 50 volunteer participants was used for data collection. The age range of participants is 18–54 years and the gender distribution is 52% Female and 48% Male. Data collection concentrated on the activities provided in Table 1.

Table 1. Description of activity classes.

Activity	Description
Lying	Lying down relatively still on a plinth
Sitting	Sitting still with hands on desk or thighs
Standing	Standing relatively still
Walking Slow	Walking at slow pace
Walking normal	Walking at normal pace
Walking fast	Walking at fast pace
Up stairs	Walking up 4–6 flights of stairs
Down stairs	Walking down 4–6 a flights of stairs
Jogging	Jogging on a treadmill at moderate speed

The set of activities in Table 1 was chosen because it represents the range of normal daily activities typically performed by most people. Three different walking speeds (slow, normal and fast) were included in order to have an accurate estimate of the intensity of the activities performed by the user. Identifying intensity of activity is important because guidelines for health and well-being include recommendations for encouraging both moderate and vigorous physical activity [1]. We expect the distinction between different walking speeds to be particularly challenging for subject-independent models because one person's slow walking speed might be closer to another person's normal walking speed

Data was collected using the Axivity Ax3 tri-axial accelerometer[2] at a sampling rate of 100 Hz. Accelerometers were mounted on the right-hand wrists of the participants using specially designed wristbands provided by Axivity. Activities are roughly evenly distributed between classes as participants were asked to do each activity for the same period of time (3 min). The exceptions are Up stairs and Down stairs, where the amount of time needed to reach the top (or bottom) of the stairs was just over 2 min on average. This data is publicly available on Github[3].

Recall that in order to apply the matching network, we require the user to provide a small sample of data for each activity class which will be used to create the support set. To simulate this with our dataset, we hold out the first 30 s of each test user's data for creating the support set. This leaves approximately 150 s of data per activity which are used for testing, except for "Up Stairs" and "Down Stairs" classes which have about 90 s of test data each.

7   Evaluation

Evaluations are conducted using a hold-out methodology where 8 users were randomly selected for testing and the remaining users' data were used for training. A time window of 5 s is used for signal segmentation and performance is reported using macro-averaged F1 score, a measure of accuracy that considers both precision (the fraction of examples predicted as class c_i that correctly belong to c_i) and recall (the fraction of examples truly belonging to class c_i that are predicted as c_i) for each class. Discrete Cosine Transforms with features are used for data representation.

Our evaluation is composed of two parts. Firstly we explore the performance of our matching network against a number of baseline approaches. Accordingly we compare the following algorithms:

- kNN: Nearest-neighbour classifier trained on the entire training set
- SVM: Support Vector Machines trained on the entire training set
- MLP: A Feed-forward neural network trained on the entire training
- MNet: Our personalised matching network approach

Note that MLP is equivalent to our embedding network with one hidden layer, batch-normalisation and softmax classification layer. The comparison with MLP is meant to provide evidence for the effectiveness of the personalisation approach

---

[2] http://axivity.com/product/ax3.

[3] https://github.com/selfback/activity-recognition/tree/master/activity_data.

of MNet beyond it's use of the embedding network. Note also that increasing the number of hidden layers beyond one for both MNet and MLP did not produce any improvement in performance. For MNet, we use $n = 6$ examples per class. These parameter values are presented in Table 2.

Table 2. Parameter settings.

Parameter	kNN	SVM	MLP	MNet
Similarity metric/Kernel	Cosine	Gaussian	-	Cosine
Neighbours	10	-	-	6
Hidden layers	-	-	1	1
Hidden units	-	-	120	120
Training epochs	-	-	10	20
Batch size	-	-	64	64
Loss function	-	-	Cross entropy	Cross entropy
Optimiser	-	-	Adam	Adam

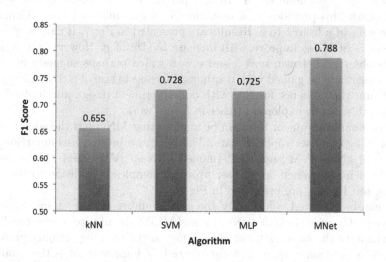

Fig. 6. Evaluation of MNet against popular classifiers.

It can be observed from Fig. 6 that MNet produces the best result; whilst SVM and MLP have comparative performance but kNN comes in last. The poor performance of kNN compared to SVM and MLP is consistent with our previous evaluations [17]. MNet out performs both SVM and MLP by more than 6% which shows the effectiveness of our matching network approach at exploiting personal data for activity recognition.

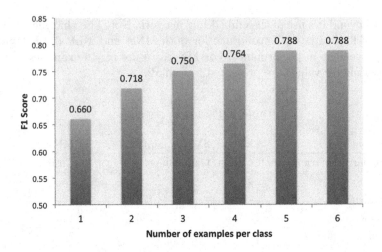

Fig. 7. Results of MNet with different number of samples per class.

The second part of our evaluation explores the influence of the number of examples per class n on classification performance. Recall that the amount "user-provided" data available to us are 30 s per activity. Considering our window length of 5 s, this provides us a maximum of 6 examples per class. Hence, we explore sizes of n from 1 to 6. Results are presented in Fig. 7. It can be observed that results of MNet improve with increase in size of n. However no improvement is observed between $n = 5$ and $n = 6$ which perhaps suggests not much improvement will be gained with continued increase in size of n. Evaluating sizes of n greater than 6 is not feasible with our experiment design and limited data, however, this can be explored further in future work.

A reasonable argument that can be made is that MNet has the added advantage of using end-user supplied data. Therefore, we present a comparison with versions of kNN, SVM and MLP (named kNN+, SVM+ and MLP+ respectively) which are trained on all user provided samples in addition to the entire training set. Results are presented in Fig. 8.

As can be observed, addition of the small number of user samples does not improve performance in kNN+, SVM+ and MLP+. In all three cases, results are approximately the same as those of training on the training set only presented in Fig. 6. An obvious explanation for the lack of improvement is the small size of the user provided data in which case, it can be expected that larger amounts of user data may lead to improved performance. However, the point to note is that the same size of data is sufficient to produce marked improvement in the performance of MNet.

A final point we explored in our evaluation is the significance of creating personalised support sets using the same user's data when training the matching network. In other words, for personalised HAR, do train support sets need to be personalised or can we get similar performance from non-personalised support

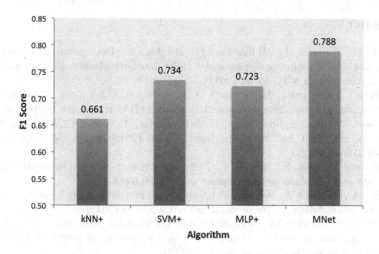

Fig. 8. Evaluation number of examples per class.

sets. The F1 Score using non-personalised support is 0.661 compared to 0.788 with personalised support set. This highlights the importance of matching train conditions to test condition as we have proposed in our methodology.

8   Conclusion

In this paper, we presented a novel approach for personalised HAR using matching networks. Matching networks adopt principles from both metric learning and attention in neural networks to perform effective k-nearest neighbour classification using a small support set of examples. We demonstrated how this support set can be constructed from a small set of labelled examples provided by the user at runtime, which allows the matching network to effectively build a personalised classifier for the user. Evaluation shows our approach to outperform a generals model by at least 6% of F1 score.

There are two main advantages to the approach we presented in this paper. Firstly, our approach is able to achieve high accuracy using only a small set of of user provided examples (30 s in this work) which makes it more practical for real-world applications compared to subject-dependent training which requires the end user to provide large amounts (possible hours) of labelled training data. Secondly, our approach does not require retraining the model at runtime when new data becomes available which makes the approach very adaptable.

The ability of matching networks to learn similarity metrics for particular domains as well as their ability to adapt at runtime make them very relevant for case-based reasoning applications. We hope that this work will inspire further work on adoption of these and similar approaches for application in CBR.

References

1. Abel, M., Hannon, J., Mullineaux, D., Beighle, A.: Determination of step rate thresholds corresponding to physical activity intensity classifications in adults. J. Phys. Act. Health **8**(1), 45–51 (2011)
2. Bach, K., Szczepanski, T., Aamodt, A., Gundersen, O.E., Mork, P.J.: Case representation and similarity assessment in the SELFBACK decision support system. In: Goel, A., Díaz-Agudo, M.B., Roth-Berghofer, T. (eds.) ICCBR 2016. LNCS (LNAI), vol. 9969, pp. 32–46. Springer, Cham (2016). https://doi.org/10.1007/978-3-319-47096-2_3
3. Bahdanau, D., Cho, K., Bengio, Y.: Neural machine translation by jointly learning to align and translate. arXiv preprint arXiv:1409.0473 (2014)
4. Bellet, A., Habrard, A., Sebban, M.: A survey on metric learning for feature vectors and structured data. arXiv preprint arXiv:1306.6709 (2013)
5. Berchtold, M., Budde, M., Gordon, D., Schmidtke, H.R., Beigl, M.: ActiServ: activity recognition service for mobile phones. In: Proceedings of International Symposium on Wearable Computers, pp. 1–8 (2010)
6. Hochreiter, S., Schmidhuber, J.: Long short-term memory. Neural Comput. **9**(8), 1735–1780 (1997)
7. Jatoba, L.C., Grossmann, U., Kunze, C., Ottenbacher, J., Stork, W.: Context-aware mobile health monitoring: Evaluation of different pattern recognition methods for classification of physical activity. In: Proceedings of 30th Annual International eConference of the IEEE Engineering in Medicine and Biology Society, pp. 5250–5253 (2008)
8. Koch, G., Zemel, R., Salakhutdinov, R.: Siamese neural networks for one-shot image recognition. In: Proceedings of International Conference on Machine Learning Deep Learning Workshop, vol. 2 (2015)
9. Kulis, B.: Metric learning: a survey. Found. Trends Mach. Learn. **5**(4), 287–364 (2013)
10. Lara, O.D., Labrador, M.A.: A survey on human activity recognition using wearable sensors. IEEE Commun. Surv. Tutor. **15**(3), 1192–1209 (2013)
11. LeCun, Y., Bottou, L., Bengio, Y., Haffner, P.: Gradient-based learning applied to document recognition. Proc. IEEE **86**(11), 2278–2324 (1998)
12. Longstaff, B., Reddy, S., Estrin, D.: Improving activity classification for health applications on mobile devices using active and semi-supervised learning. In: Proceedings of 4th International Conference on Pervasive Computing Technologies for Healthcare, pp. 1–7 (2010)
13. López-Sánchez, D., Corchado, J.M., Arrieta, A.G.: A CBR system for image-based webpage classification: case representation with convolutional neural networks. In: Proceedings of Florida AI Research Society Conference (2017)
14. López-Sánchez, D., Herrero, J.R., Arrieta, A.G., Corchado, J.M.: Hybridizing metric learning and case-based reasoning for adaptable clickbait detection. Appl. Intell., 1–16 (2017)
15. Mikolov, T., Sutskever, I., Chen, K., Corrado, G.S., Dean, J.: Distributed representations of words and phrases and their compositionality. In: Advances in neural information processing systems, pp. 3111–3119 (2013)
16. Miu, T., Missier, P., Plötz, T.: Bootstrapping personalised human activity recognition models using online active learning. In: Proceedings of IEEE International Conference on Computer and Information Technology; Ubiquitous Computing and Communications; Dependable, Autonomic and Secure Computing; Pervasive Intelligence and Computing, pp. 1138–1147. IEEE (2015)

17. Sani, S., Massie, S., Wiratunga, N., Cooper, K.: Learning deep and shallow features for human activity recognition. In: Li, G., Ge, Y., Zhang, Z., Jin, Z., Blumenstein, M. (eds.) KSEM 2017. LNCS (LNAI), vol. 10412, pp. 469–482. Springer, Cham (2017). https://doi.org/10.1007/978-3-319-63558-3_40

18. Sani, S., Wiratunga, N., Massie, S., Cooper, K.: SELFBACK-activity recognition for self-management of low back pain. In: Bramer, M., Petridis, M. (eds.) Research and Development in Intelligent Systems XXXIII: Incorporating Applications and Innovations in Intelligent Systems XXIV, pp. 281–294. Springer, Cham (2016). https://doi.org/10.1007/978-3-319-47175-4_21

19. Sani, S., Wiratunga, N., Massie, S., Cooper, K.: kNN sampling for personalised human activity recognition. In: Aha, D.W., Lieber, J. (eds.) ICCBR 2017. LNCS (LNAI), vol. 10339, pp. 330–344. Springer, Cham (2017). https://doi.org/10.1007/978-3-319-61030-6_23

20. Sun, X., Kashima, H., Ueda, N.: Large-scale personalized human activity recognition using online multitask learning. IEEE Trans. Knowl. Data Eng. 25(11), 2551–2563 (2013)

21. Tapia, E.M., Intille, S.S., Haskell, W., Larson, K., Wright, J., King, A., Friedman, R.: Real-time recognition of physical activities and their intensities using wireless accelerometers and a heart rate monitor. In: Proceedings of 11th IEEE International Symposium on Wearable Computers, pp. 37–40. IEEE (2007)

22. Vinyals, O., Blundell, C., Lillicrap, T., Wierstra, D.: Matching networks for one shot learning. In: Proceedings of Advances in Neural Information Processing Systems, pp. 3630–3638 (2016)

23. Xing, E.P., Jordan, M.I., Russell, S.J., Ng, A.Y.: Distance metric learning with application to clustering with side-information. In: Proceedings of Advances in neural information processing systems, pp. 521–528 (2003)

Why Did Naethan Pick Android over Apple? Exploiting Trade-offs in Learning User Preferences

Anbarasu Sekar[✉], Devi Ganesan, and Sutanu Chakraborti

Department of Computer Science and Engineering,
Indian Institute of Technology Madras, Chennai 600036, India
{anbu,gdevi,sutanuc}@cse.iitm.ac.in

Abstract. When case-based recommender systems use preference-based feedback, we can learn user preferences by using the trade-off relations between the preferred product and the other products in the given domain. In this work, we propose a representation for trade-offs and motivate several mechanisms by which the identified trade-offs can be used in the process of recommendation. We empirically demonstrate the effectiveness of the proposed approaches in three recommendation domains.

Keywords: Case-based recommendation
Conversational recommender systems · Trade-offs
Preference feedback · Diversity

1 Introduction

A central goal of recommender systems is to make the user aware of the various choices available to her in the product domain. A Conversational Case-Based Reasoning (CCBR) based recommender system attempts to reduce the cognitive load on the user by helping her identify a target while minimizing the number of conversation cycles. This is achieved by discovering the preferences of a user based on her feedback and using it to recommend the right products. CCBR based recommender systems assume no prior knowledge about the user; a setting where most collaborative recommender systems fail [1].

While learning user preferences is very important in the recommendation process and has been elaborately addressed in the literature, we note that it is equally important to consider the relationships among products. In particular, each product in a domain is not always seen as an isolated entity because it is often described in relation to other products in the domain. Therefore, we observe that it is important to consider the relationships among the products while recommending products to the users.

In this work, we present the notion of trade-off as a way of capturing the relationships between products in a domain. Even before a recommender system encounters a user, one can profile a product based on the trade-offs it makes

© Springer Nature Switzerland AG 2018
M. T. Cox et al. (Eds.): ICCBR 2018, LNAI 11156, pp. 354–368, 2018.
https://doi.org/10.1007/978-3-030-01081-2_24

relative to other products, domain knowledge and product specifications. For example, in a car domain, a person who desires a sports car would trade-off mileage for top speed as this statement is independent of any specific user. If we can model trade-off relations between products even before the recommendation process, we can use the trade-off information to recommend right products to the users.

In this work, we propose a representation for capturing relative trade-offs among products and motivate several mechanisms by which user preferences can be combined with the trade-off relations among products to recommend appropriate products to the user. We show empirically that utilizing trade-off information positively affects the length of conversation in the recommendation process thereby reducing the cognitive load on the user. In Sect. 2 we situate our work in relation to past works from the literature. In Sect. 3 we discuss our proposal followed by experiments and results.

2   Background and Related Work

Case-Based Reasoning (CBR) works on the principle that similar problems have similar solutions. Unlike collaborative recommender systems where similar users prefer similar products, CBR based recommender systems are content-based because they use the query and feedback given by a user to recommend products to her. Hence, the recommendation process relies heavily on the similarity of the user's query to the products in the domain[1].

In single shot recommender systems, the recommendation process gets over once a set of products is recommended to the user based on her query. The system does not try to learn if the user is satisfied with the recommendations. In CCBR systems, there is a feedback mechanism that gives users the flexibility to express their view on the set of recommended products. This feedback is in turn used to model user preferences and revise the user's query.

There are several ways in which a user can give her feedback to the system. Critiques [11] and preference feedback [5] are two well-known feedback mechanisms in the literature. In critique-based feedback, the user is allowed to express her view on the individual attributes whereas in preference-based feedback the user chooses her product of preference out of ones recommended. The cognitive load on the user in preference based feedback is less when compared with other feedback mechanisms. In this work, we are interested in CCBR systems with preference-based feedback.

2.1   Similarity and Diversity

In similarity based recommendation, the utility of a product to a user is approximated by the similarity of the product to the user's query. More like This (MLT)

---

[1] We use the terms cases and products; case base and product domain; features and attributes interchangeably.

and weighted More Like This (wMLT) [5] are approaches that use only similarity to recommend products to the users.

Smyth et al. [2] proposed mechanisms by which diverse recommendations can be made without compromising on similarity. The need for diversity in recommendation can be appreciated from the following example. Suppose that a fixed number of products is shown in each cycle of recommendation. While recommending products that are highly similar to the user's query one might end up in a scenario where the recommended products are highly similar to each other. If the user is dissatisfied with one or more features of one recommended product, it is highly likely that the all the similar options suggested to her are not satisfactory as well. If the recommendations are diverse then the likelihood of one of them being satisfactory is more. It is one of the initial works that considered the relation among the products recommended to the users.

McGinty et al. [6] proposed MLT with Adaptive Selection (MLT AS) and demonstrated that introducing diversity methodically in the CCBR system positively affects the conversation length. The authors in [6] identifies that a user could be in two modes of search namely *refine* and *refocus*. In *refine* phase, the user is interested in the products in a small neighbourhood of the query whereas in the *refocus* phase, the user is in exploratory mode and looks out for products that are diverse to the ones suggested to her. The authors show that introducing diversity in refocus phase could improve the efficiency of the system. To enable switching from refine to refocus phase, the product by preferred by a user in one recommendation cycle is introduced in the next cycle too. If the user is not satisfied with any of the products recommended in the current cycle, she would be forced to prefer the same product that she picked in the previous recommendation cycle.

Bounded greedy selection [6] is one of the algorithms proposed by the authors to recommend diverse products. To begin with, a bound B is set on the number of products from which one chooses diverse products, and the top B similar products to query are selected. Next, greedy selection is used to get a diverse set of recommended products. Each time a product is selected greedily, it is done based on a quality measure that ensures diversity. One of the quality measures proposed in [6] is (similarity of the selected product to the query) ∗ (relative dissimilarity of the selected product to the products included so far in the recommended set).

2.2   Coverage

If there is a product in the case base that is interesting to the user then it ought to be recommended to the user. A recommender system should fail only when the right product is not present in the case base and not because of its incapability to fetch the right product. Recommender systems should also ensure that all the options that are available to the user are made known to the user. David McSherry [8] suggests different criteria under which the coverage of the product domain can be defined. Compromise [7] is a criterion that is of interest to our work. Compromise is the sacrifice a user is willing to make in selecting a product.

For example, Camera 2 in Table 1 has compromised with the given query on a manufacturer, while in Camera 1, the compromise is on price. In Compromise-Driven Retrieval (CDR) [7] the products in the domain are categorized into several classes where each class is representative of the kind of sacrifice one has to make in accepting a product of that particular class.

Table 1. A sample recommendation set in camera domain along with user query

	Price ($)	Manufacturer
Camera 1	1000	Sony
Camera 2	500	Canon
Camera 3	300	Olympus
Camera 4	800	Canon
Query	500	Sony

On top of these classes, there is a dominance criterion based on compromise that defines superiority of one class over the other. If a class, say **A**, makes a subset of the compromises made by another class, say **B**, then the products of class **A** are superior to products in class **B** provided they are also similar to the user's query. Within the same class, similarity is used to define the dominance among products. The product that is most similar to the query dominates all the other products in that class. Only the dominant products in each class are recommended to the user thereby covering the product domain.

In some domains, the attributes of the domain can be classified as "More is Better" (MIB) and "Less is Better" (LIB). For example, in the camera domain, resolution is an MIB attribute and price is an LIB attribute. The dominance among the attribute values is based on the classification of the attribute type. In MIB attributes, higher values dominate the lesser values and the converse is true for LIB attributes.

For example, consider the scenario in Table 1. We can have three classes of compromises. Price {Camera 1}, Manufacturer {Camera 2, Camera 3} and Price + Manufacturer {Camera 4}. The class Price refers to the set of products that have compromised only on the attribute price. The class Price and class Manufacturer dominates class Price+Manufacturer. Within the class Manufacturer we have two cameras, Camera 3 dominates Camera 2 as both are of different manufacturers but the price of Camera 3 is better than price of Camera 2. The cameras that would be recommended to the user are Camera 3 and Camera 1. The relations among products are with respect to the user's query. It is evident that if we have a different query we will have different products in each of these classes.

2.3   Compromise Driven Preference Model

The success of a CCBR based recommender system lies in its ability to learn user preferences. In MLT [5], the only information that we have about the user is her query. In each recommendation cycle, the query is revised to reflect the user's preferences. Since MLT uses preference-based feedback, the product that is preferred in the given interaction cycle becomes the query for the next cycle. However, the user may not desire all the attributes in the preferred product. To capture the preferences of the user on individual attributes, in wMLT [5] each attribute is associated with a weight that keeps changing in the process of recommendation. In the sample scenario in Table 1, if the user prefers Camera 1 then the weight that is given to manufacturer is the ratio of the number of alternatives rejected by the user to the total number of alternatives available, which is $(2/2) = 1$, since both the alternatives Canon and Olympus are rejected.

In the wMLT way of modelling user preferences, the attributes are considered independent of each other. In Compromise Driven Preference Model (CDPM) [9], Mouli et al. discuss the disadvantage of such a modelling and motivate the need to relax the independence assumption. They use Multi-Attribute Utility theory (MAUT) [4] to approximate the gain in utility obtained by selecting one product over the other.

Table 2. A pair of products in Camera domain

	Price ($)	Resolution (MP)
Camera X	1000	10
Camera Y	600	8

For example, consider the pair of cameras given in Table 2. When a user is asked to pick one out of them, it is expected that she picks the one that gives her the highest utility. If the user picks Camera X, we infer that the user has traded off price for the gain in resolution. This information is captured by Eq. 1, where $w_{resolution}$ and w_{price} stand for the weights given to resolution and price respectively.

$$(10 - 8) \times w_{resolution} \geq (1000 - 600) \times w_{price} \tag{1}$$

The above linear inequality is treated as a constraint. If there are five products in the recommended set of products and the user gives her choice of product, one can arrive at four such constraints by comparing the preferred product with the each of the rejected products. Apart from these trade-off constraints, there is a general constraint that the feature weights should sum up to one. The region in the feature weight space that satisfies all the constraints is termed as the preference region, from which an appropriate weight vector could be picked as the feature weights for the current interaction cycle.

Though CDPM makes an attempt at using product trade-offs to learn feature weights, the use of linear equations (such as in Eq. 1) to represent trade-offs has some disadvantages. For example, by moving from the trade-off space to feature weight space, we lose out on specific information such as which *set* of attributes may be compromised for which another set. Also, it is not possible to allow partial satisfaction of trade-offs because the preference region is arrived at by modelling all inequalities as hard constraints.

2.4 Dominance Region of Products

In all the above works, computing of feature weights follows a lazy approach i.e. happens only when the query is issued. Instead of learning feature weights at runtime, Anbarasu et al. [12] propose the idea of dominance region, which involves identifying factors useful for recommendation even before a query is issued. The idea is that each product has its own customer base that prefers it over all other products. A set of trade-off constraints is obtained by comparing each product with each of its competitors in a small similarity-based neighbourhood around itself. The region in the feature weight space that satisfies all the trade-off constraints along with the general constraint (see previous section) is termed as the dominance region of the product. Hence, dominance region of a product is that region in the feature weight space where the utility of that product based on MAUT [4] is greater than the utility of its competitors. In the process of recommendation, the preference region computed at a certain interaction cycle is compared with the dominance region of each product to predict the usefulness of a product to the given user.

Though the idea of pre-computing trade-offs has its own advantages the work by Anbarasu et al. [12] uses the same trade-off representation as in [9]. Hence, the drawbacks discussed in CDPM hold for this approach too.

3   Using Trade-offs for Product Recommendation

The contribution of this work is three-fold, first we propose a representation for trade-offs; second, we propose a diversity measure based on trade-offs and third, we show how trade-offs based similarity can be used as a measure of utility. As a part of our second contribution, we introduce two methods that recommend products based on trade-off based diversity. We also introduce a method that recommends products based on trade-off based similarity. The effectiveness of using trade-offs is demonstrated by employing the proposed methods in a conversational recommender setting and comparing it against other methods from literature.

3.1   Trade-offs Representation

Given any pair of products in the case base, we expect that there is a set of attributes in which one product dominates over the other. When we say dominates, we mean dominance based on MIB and LIB classification of attributes. If one product is better than the other product in all attributes, then the latter would eventually disappear from the market.

Definition 1. ***Dominant Set:*** *The set of attributes in which a product is dominant over another product.*

Definition 2. ***Dominated Set:*** *The set of attributes in which a product is dominated by another product.*

For example, for the products given in Table 3, if a user prefers Camera A over Camera B, the Dominant Set would be {resolution} and the Dominated Set would be {price}. By comparing the dominant and dominated attributes between a pair of products, we can predict the traits of a user who would buy a particular product even before the recommendation process begins. For example, when comparing two cars, say a sports car and a commuter car, one can predict that the user who would buy a sports car will be willing to trade-off on the luxury aspects of the car for the gain in performance aspects of the car. The converse is true for the person who would prefer a commuter car.

Table 3. A pair of products in Camera Domain

	Price ($)	Resolution (MP)	Zoom (X)
Camera A	1000	10	10
Camera B	600	8	10
Camera C	2000	15	12
Camera D	1600	12	10

In CDPM [9] the trade-offs are converted to constraints in the feature weights space. As has been discussed earlier in Sect. 2.3, the main drawback of taking trade-offs to feature weight space is that the semantics of which particular set of attributes is traded off for which another set of attributes is lost. In our approach, the dominant and dominated sets enable to preserve these semantics.

It is also important to emphasize that when one product is preferred over another, not all attributes in the dominant set may be preferred equally by the user. Similarly, not all attributes in the dominated Set may be equally repulsive to the user. Hence, it may be detrimental to model the trade-offs using hard constraints as in CDPM.

	Price ($)	Resolution (MP)	Zoom (X)
Camera A	1000	10	10
Camera B	600	8	10
trade-off$_{AB}$	[-1,	1,	0]

Fig. 1. Representation of trade-offs when product A is preferred over product B.

When comparing two products the attributes belonging to the dominant set are represented as 1. The attributes belonging to the dominated set are represented as -1. If both the products have the same value for an attribute it is represented as 0. For the products given in Table 3, Fig. 1 represents trade-offs considering Camera A as the desired product over Camera B. The trade-off$_{AB}$ represented as $[-1, 1, 0]$ conveys that Camera A has been chosen over Camera B in favour of resolution for price. For nominal attributes, if the attribute values are same we represent it as 0 and if the values are different we represent as 1.

Let us consider the representation of the trade-offs as in CDPM [9]. When Camera A is preferred over Camera B the trade-off is represented as given below.

$$2 \times w_{resolution} \geq 400 \times w_{price} \qquad (2)$$

Assuming that the attribute values are normalized the constraint in feature weights space will be $0.2 \times w_{resolution} \geq 0.4 \times w_{price}$. Consider a vector sampled from the feature weights space that satisfies this constraint $(0.7, 0.2, 0.1)$. The weights are suggestive of which attribute is important but the notions of dominant and dominated sets are lost. The set of compromises that a user would be willing to make could be independent of the weights given to individual features [7].

Similarity Measure for Trade-offs. We define the similarity of two trade-offs $T1$ and $T2$, computed between two pairs of products, as a simple matching score between them. In Eq. 3, I is an indicator function that gives a value 1 if the attribute level trade-offs are same and 0 otherwise. Let trade-off$_{AB}$ be $[-1, 1, 0]$ and trade-off$_{CD}$ be $[-1, 1, 1]$. Similarity between these two trade-offs as given by Eq. 3 will be $2/3$.

$$Match(T1, T2) = \frac{\sum\limits_{a \in Attributes} I(T1_a, T2_a)}{|Attributes|} \qquad (3)$$

3.2   Diversity Based on Trade-offs

In this section we propose two diversity measures one based on the local trade-offs and the other based on the global trade-offs. An example of a set of diverse products based on local trade-offs would be {race sports car, street legal sports car}. An example for a set of diverse products based on global trade-offs would be {a sports car, a commuter car}. Each product in the domain is profiled based on the trade-off relationship it has with its neighbours. The intention behind creating these profiles for each product is to help identify products that are diverse based on trade-offs both in the local and global context.

Definition 3. *Local Profile:* *For a product P, its local profile P_{LP} is the list of trade-offs P makes with products in its similarity-based local neighbourhood.*

Definition 4. Global Profile: *For a product P, its global profile P_{GP} is the list of trade-offs that P makes with products sampled from the global product space. Here, we use distance-based probabilisitc sampling - the farther a product from P, the greater is the probability of it being selected for comparison.*

To motivate the semantics of local and global neighbours, imagine two sports cars being compared where one is a race track car and the other being a road legal sports car. The trade-offs that we get out of this comparison would constitute the local profile of a sports car. Whereas, comparing a sports car with a commuter car would result in trade-offs constituting the global profile of a sports car.

Definition 5. User Profile: *For a user, the list of trade-offs obtained by comparing the preferred product with the rejected products are aggregated over interaction cycles and is denoted by UP.*

Approaches Based on Trade-off Based Diversity. The idea of utilizing the overlap between user's profile and product profile is motivated from the work by Anbarasu et al. [12] where the overlap between the preference region computed at a certain interaction cycle and the dominance region of a product is used as a measure to predict the usefulness of a product to the given user. We propose two methods to measure the overlap between the user profile and product profiles. The user profile is in similar lines to the preference region and the product profile is similar to the dominance region of a product. On the basis of the overlap measure used we propose two approaches for product recommendation namely More Like This with Brute Force trade-off Matching (**MLT TM$_{BF}$**) and More Like This with Profile Summary trade-off Matching (**MLT TM$_{PS}$**).

Method 1. *The overlap between the UP and a product's profile is computed based on brute force matching. This method is termed More Like This with Brute Force trade-off Matching (**MLT TM$_{BF}$**).*

If $L1$ and $L2$ are a pair of trade-off lists, then the overlap score in brute force matching is given by the Equation below.

$$Overlap_{Brute}(L1, L2) = \frac{\sum\limits_{T1 \in L1} \sum\limits_{T2 \in L2} Match(T1, T2)}{|L1| * |L2|} \tag{4}$$

In MLT TM$_{BF}$, $L1$ and $L2$ stand for the user profile and local/global product profiles respectively. The overlap between a user's profile UP and some product profile P_{GP} or P_{LP} is measured by averaging the similarity of each trade-off in UP with each trade-off in P_{GP} or P_{LP}. Similarity estimation between trade-offs i.e. Match (T1, T2) is calculated using Eq. 3.

Method 2. *To compute the overlap between the user profile and the product profile, the profiles are summarized and then compared. This method is termed More Like This with Profile Summary trade-off Matching (**MLT TM$_{PS}$**).*

The intent behind MLT TM_{PS} is to simulate the behaviour of a shopkeeper who associates a tag with each customer such as *Mary may trade-off cost for compactness, Jane may trade-off zoom for price,* etc. A shopkeeper does this by summarizing the trade-offs the user has been making over time. Similarly products are summarized, one summary based on its local profile and one based on its global profile.

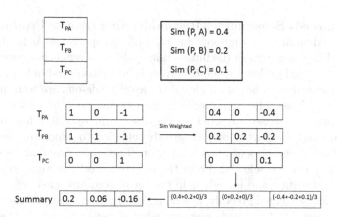

Fig. 2. Computing the summary of a profile - an example.

Figure 2 illustrates an example of summarizing a trade-off list. Suppose that the user has preferred product P over products A, B, C in some interaction cycle. Then the trade-off list TL includes T_{PA}, T_{PB} and T_{PC}. The influence a trade-off has on the profile summary of the product P is directly proportional to the similarity of the product to which it is compared against. We are interested in finding the trade-off summary TS for this trade-off list. TS is a vector of real values and TS_a is the value of TS corresponding to the attribute a. Let T_{PA_a} represent the trade-off for a specific attribute a and $Sim(P, A)$ represent the similarity between products P and A. For each attribute 'a' in the domain TS_a is computed using the Eq. 5. If a1, a2,... a_n are the attributes of the domain the profile summary of TS is as in Eq. 6

$$TS_a(TL) = \sum_{T_{AB_a} \in TL} T_{AB_a} * Sim(A, B) \tag{5}$$

$$TS(TL) :=< TS_{a_1}(TL), TS_{a_2}(TL), ...TS_{a_n}(TL) > \tag{6}$$

The overlap between two trade-off summaries $TS1$ and $TS2$ is computed using the Equation given below.

$$Overlap_{Summary}(TS1, TS2) = \frac{\sum\limits_{a \in Attributes} 1 - Dist(TS1_a, TS2_a)}{|Attributes|} \tag{7}$$

While creating summaries of each trade-off lists, the trade-off representation for each attribute is treated as a real value. The distance between a pair of trade-off summaries $TS1$ and $TS2$ with respect to a specific attribute a is given by the Equation below. abs in Eq. 8 represents the absolute value of the quantity.

$$Dist(TS1_a, TS2_a) = \frac{abs(TS1_a - TS2_a)}{2} \tag{8}$$

Bounded Greedy Selection for Recommending Diverse Products. The diversity based on similarity ignores the trade-offs comparisons. As in MLT AS [6] (see Sect. 2.1), we distinguish the interaction cycles into refine and refocus phase. The products based on local trade-off diversity are introduced only in the refine phase and the products based on global trade-off trade-offs are introduced only in the refocus phase. The user profile is used in conjunction with global/local profiles of products based on whether the user is in refocus/refine phase. We employ a method similar to bounded greedy selection to select diverse products both in the refine and refocus phases. The top B products based on its similarity to the given query are selected. From the selected products we greedily choose one product at a time and include it in the set of recommended products. Each time a product is selected greedily, it is done based on a quality measure. In Eq. 9, R stands for the set of products recommended so far $\{r_1, r_2, ... r_m\}$, Q stands for Query, C stands for the product that we consider to add in R. PF refers to local profile or global profile of the product based on whether the user is in refine or refocus phase. Overlap$_M$ could be either brute force or summary based scores defined in Eqs. 4 and 7 respectively.

$$Quality(Q, C, PF) = Overlap_M(UP, C_{PF}) + 1 - \frac{\sum\limits_{r \in R}(Overlap_M(C_{PF}, r_{PF}))}{|R|} \tag{9}$$

Recommendation Process. The recommendation flow is same for Methods 1 and 2 discussed above, except for the quality measures used for including trade-off based diverse products.

Step 0: Computing *product profiles*: For each product P in the domain, the local profile P_{LP} of the product is constructed by comparing the product with its m nearest neighbours. To construct the global profile P_{GP} of the product, we sample n products probabilistically. The probability with which a product gets picked is proportional to the distance from P. The product under consideration is compared against each of the global samples to get the global profile of the product. In summary based method the summary of P_{LP} and P_{GP} is computed. This is done as a part of pre-computation and is used in the recommendation process.

Step 1: The user gives her initial preference, which is the query Q.

Step 2: Initially, we select k most similar products to the query and recommend to the user.

Step 3: The user provides her preference feedback. We compare the preferred product with each of the $k-1$ recommended products to get the *UP*.

Step 4: If the preferred product is different from the product preferred in the previous iteration, the user is assessed to be in the refine phase. In refine phase, the recommendation set if filled with a mix of products based on similarity and local trade-off based diversity.

Step 5: If the preferred product is same as the product preferred in the previous iteration, we consider it as the refocus phase. In refocus phase, the recommendation set is filled with a mix of products based on similarity, global trade-off based diversity and distance based diversity.

Step 6: The product preferred by user becomes the new query.

Step 7: We go to step 3 and continue the cycle till the user is satisfied with one of the products in the recommended set.

3.3 A Approach Based on Similarity and Trade-offs

Hypothesis 1. *If a product **A** is desirable to a user then a product **B** will also be desirable to the user if it is similar to product **A** and makes similar trade-offs with a set of products as product **A** does*

In this method unlike the previous ones we do not attempt to create profiles for the products. We define a similarity function that takes trade-offs into consideration. Unlike MLT AS [6] we do not categorize the interaction cycles in the recommendation process into refine and refocus phase. We set a parameter α that measures the importance given to the trade-off based overlap score. $(1 - \alpha)$ is set as the importance given to distance based similarity. To find the product that offers similar trade-offs, we select top **B** similar products to the query as the candidates and we compare each candidate product with the products rejected in the previous interaction cycle and find the overlap with the trade-offs obtained by comparing the preferred product with the same set of rejected products. The overlap score is computed as given in Eq. 10, where T_{CX} represents the trade-off considering the candidate product C as superior to the rejected product X. Similarly T_{PX} represents the trade-off considering the preferred product P as superior to the rejected product X. We term these scores as the overlap scores.

$$Overlap_{Realtime}(C, P) = \frac{\sum_{X \in RejectedList}(Match(T_{CX}, T_{PX}))}{|RejectedList|} \quad (10)$$

The overlap score along with the similarity is combined to get the final score, the combined score is computed as given in Eq. 11. If k is the number of slots in the recommendation set, $\lceil k * \alpha \rceil$ slots is filled by the products based on Eq. 11. One half of the rest of $\lceil k * (1 - \alpha) \rceil$ slots in the recommendation set is used to recommend products that are trade-off wise diverse to the products already included in the recommendation set. The other half is filled by products based on distance-based diversity. The diverse products based on similarity and trade-offs is introduced in the similar fashion as the bounded greedy selection with the quality function as given in Eq. 12. Initially α is set to 0.5, when the user selects a product from the slot dedicated to trade-off based similarity or diversity the α value is boosted up else it is decreased. This method is termed More Like This with Real-Time trade-off Matching (**MLT TM$_{RT}$**)

$$TotalScore(C, P) = \alpha \times Overlap_{Realtime}(C, P) + (1 - \alpha) \times Sim(C, P) \quad (11)$$

$$Quality(Q, C, PF) = TotalScore(C, P) + 1 - (\frac{\sum_{r \in R}(Overlap_{Realtime}(C, r)}{|R|})$$

$$(12)$$

4   Experiments and Results

We test the effectiveness of our method on three datasets using leave one out methodology [3]. Datasets used for evaluation are Camera dataset [10] with 210 cameras, Cars dataset with 956 cars and PC dataset [5] with 120 computers. The Camera dataset has 6 numeric attributes and 4 nominal attributes. The Cars dataset has 5 numeric attributes and 3 nominal attributes. The PC dataset has 6 numeric attributes and 5 nominal attributes. In leave one out evaluation, one case is removed at random from the domain. We pretend that the product that is removed is the exact product that the user is searching for in the domain. We form three partial queries of sizes 1,3 and 5 by taking subsets of attributes of the product removed from the domain. These queries represent users with less, moderate and high knowledge about the product domain respectively. The product that is most similar to the removed product is set as the target that we would like to find in the recommended set of products. We start the recommendation process with the partial query as the initial query. We go on with the interaction cycles until the target product appears in the recommended set of products. In each interaction cycle, the preferred product is selected by picking a product that is most similar to the product that is removed from the domain. The number of interaction cycles taken by the system to achieve the target is used as a measure of comparison between various methods. This process is repeated for 1000 times. The average number of cycles required is used for comparison and is tabulated in Tables 4, 5 and 6.

The 1000 queries are split into 10 folds and the proposed methods are compared against MLT, wMLT [5] and MLT AS [6], the results that are statistically better than MLT AS are highlighted in bold (significance level $p < 0.05$, Paired t test). Among the three methods that we discussed, MLT TM$_{RT}$ has fared well

Table 4. Efficiency in Camera dataset (the lesser the average cycle length the better)

Query size	MLT	wMLT	MLT AS	MLT TM$_{BF}$	MLT TM$_{PS}$	MLT TM$_{RT}$
1	8.05	7.97	6.21	**6.09**	**5.87**	**5.70**
3	5.08	4.88	4.26	**4.00**	4.09	**3.88**
5	3.26	3.00	2.62	**2.48**	2.67	2.45

Table 5. Efficiency in Car dataset (the lesser the average cycle length the better)

Query size	MLT	wMLT	MLT AS	MLT TM$_{BF}$	MLT TM$_{PS}$	MLT TM$_{RT}$
1	24.83	23.67	13.91	13.78	13.83	**11.38**
3	16.74	13.94	9.67	9.39	9.78	**8.39**
5	10.03	8.93	7.07	**6.48**	6.75	**5.69**

Table 6. Efficiency in PC dataset (the lesser the average cycle length the better)

Query size	MLT	wMLT	MLT AS	MLT TM$_{BF}$	MLT TM$_{PS}$	MLT TM$_{RT}$
1	5.73	4.21	4.06	**3.95**	4.41	3.86
3	4.04	3.13	**3.05**	**2.98**	**3.17**	**2.95**
5	2.40	2.04	1.90	1.84	1.90	**1.78**

against MLT AS in all the datasets for all query sizes except in two cases where it is comparable to MLT AS. The highest performance improvement when compared to MLT AS is exhibited by MLT TM$_{RT}$ in Car dataset with a reduction in average cycle length by 18%, 13% and 19% for query sizes 1, 3 and 5 respectively.

MLT TM$_{BF}$ and MLT TM$_{PS}$ follows the same approach as MLT AS to identify if a user is in refine or refocus phase,i.e. they use the event of a user selecting the same product preferred in the previous iteration again to switch from refine to refocus phase. Identification of refine or refocus phase is crucial in MLT TM$_{BF}$ and MLT TM$_{PS}$ as it uses a product's local profile information in refine phase and global profile information in refocus phase. We would like to work on the better identification of refine and refocus phase in the future. MLT TM$_{RT}$ does not involve any product profiles that are sensitive to the identification of phases and thus have fared better than the rest.

5 Conclusion and Future Work

In this work we have introduced a novel way of representing trade-offs. We have introduced the notion of diversity based on trade-offs and proposed methods based on trade-offs for product recommendation. We have demonstrated the effectiveness of using the recommendation process empirically by evaluation in various real-world product domains. Currently, the proposed representation of trade-offs captures minimal information as to whether a trade-off has been made or not. We would like to explore options for representing trade-offs with their associated quantities as well in our future work.

References

1. Adomavicius, G., Tuzhilin, A.: Toward the next generation of recommender systems: a survey of the state-of-the-art and possible extensions. IEEE Trans. Knowl. Data Eng. **17**(6), 734–749 (2005)
2. Smyth, B., McClave, P.: Similarity vs. Diversity. In: Aha, D.W., Watson, I. (eds.) ICCBR 2001. LNCS (LNAI), vol. 2080, pp. 347–361. Springer, Heidelberg (2001). https://doi.org/10.1007/3-540-44593-5_25
3. Ginty, L.M., Smyth, B.: Evaluating preference-based feedback in recommender systems. In: O'Neill, M., Sutcliffe, R.F.E., Ryan, C., Eaton, M., Griffith, N.J.L. (eds.) AICS 2002. LNCS (LNAI), vol. 2464, pp. 209–214. Springer, Heidelberg (2002). https://doi.org/10.1007/3-540-45750-X_28
4. Keeney, R.L., Raiffa, H.: Decisions with Multiple Objectives: Preferences and Value Trade-offs. Cambridge University Press, Cambridge (1993)
5. Ginty, L.M., Smyth, B.: Comparison-based recommendation. In: Craw, S., Preece, A. (eds.) ECCBR 2002. LNCS (LNAI), vol. 2416, pp. 575–589. Springer, Heidelberg (2002). https://doi.org/10.1007/3-540-46119-1_42
6. McGinty, L., Smyth, B.: On the role of diversity in conversational recommender systems. In: Ashley, K.D., Bridge, D.G. (eds.) ICCBR 2003. LNCS (LNAI), vol. 2689, pp. 276–290. Springer, Heidelberg (2003). https://doi.org/10.1007/3-540-45006-8_23
7. McSherry, D.: Similarity and compromise. In: Ashley, K.D., Bridge, D.G. (eds.) ICCBR 2003. LNCS (LNAI), vol. 2689, pp. 291–305. Springer, Heidelberg (2003). https://doi.org/10.1007/3-540-45006-8_24
8. McSherry, D.: Balancing user satisfaction and cognitive load in coverage-optimised retrieval. Knowledge-Based Systems **17**(2–4), 113–119 (2004)
9. Mouli, S.C., Chakraborti, S.: Making the most of preference feedback by modeling feature dependencies. In: Proceedings of the 9th ACM Conference on Recommender Systems (2015)
10. myCBR. http://mycbr-project.net/download.html
11. R. Burke, K.H., Young, B.: Knowledge-based navigation of complex information spaces. In: Proceedings of the 13th National Conference on Artificial Intelligence, pp. 462–468 (1996)
12. Sekar, A., Chakraborti, S.: Towards bridging the gap between manufacturer and users to facilitate better recommendation. Florida Artificial Intelligence Research Society Conference (2018). https://aaai.org/ocs/index.php/FLAIRS/FLAIRS18/paper/view/17670

An Analysis of Case Representations for Marathon Race Prediction and Planning

Barry Smyth[✉] and Pádraig Cunningham

Insight Centre for Data Analytics School of Computer Science,
University College Dublin, Dublin, Ireland
{barry.smyth,padraig.cunningham}@ucd.ie

Abstract. We use case-based reasoning to help marathoners achieve a personal best for an upcoming race, by helping them to select an achievable goal-time and a suitable pacing plan. We evaluate several case representations and, using real-world race data, highlight their performance implications. Richer representations do not always deliver better prediction performance, but certain representational configurations do offer very significant practical benefits for runners, when it comes to predicting, and planning for, challenging goal-times during an upcoming race.

1 Introduction

Mobile and wearable technologies help capture data about our activities, habits, and lifestyles, often seducing us with the potential to live healthier and more productive lives [1]. Certainly the application of AI to personal health and healthcare is not new [2–5] but the always-on nature of smartphones and wearables creates an even greater opportunity for novel preventative, proactive, and personalised interventions [6–10]. Indeed, within the case-based reasoning community there has been a long history of applying case-based, data-driven methods to a wide range of healthcare problems [11]. Recently, the world of sports and fitness has similarly embraced this data-centric vision, as teams and athletes attempt to harness the power of data to optimise the business of sports and the training of athletes [12,13].

Mobile apps like Strava and RunKeeper record our daily activities (cycling, running etc.), but they remain largely silent when it comes to pro-actively assisting us as we train, recover, and compete. This offers some exciting opportunities for AI to support users with *personalized training plans* [14,15], *injury prevention advice, route/race/event recommendation, performance prediction and race planning* [16–18], among others.

Previously we proposed a novel, CBR approach to helping marathon runners to improve their race performance [19,20], by predicting a challenging but achievable PB (personal-best) finish-time, and by recommending a pacing plan (how fast to run during different sections of the race) to achieve this time. This is related to the general problem of race-time prediction, which plays an important role in many endurance sports. For example, Bartolucci and Murphy [18] use a

© Springer Nature Switzerland AG 2018
M. T. Cox et al. (Eds.): ICCBR 2018, LNAI 11156, pp. 369–384, 2018.
https://doi.org/10.1007/978-3-030-01081-2_25

finite mixture approach with partial race data to model the performance and strategy of runners in a 24-h ultra race, to identify clusters of runners who differ in their speed and propensity to stop; see also [21].

Briefly, our previous work described a CBR solution to finish-time prediction and race planning, by generating cases from simple pairs of past races for marathon runners (a recent non-PB race and a PB race) but with minimal feature engineering; the case features included only raw finish-times and paces for each of the 5 Km segments of the race. Despite this, the race predictions and pacing plans proved to be reasonably accurate, especially for faster runners. However, the error rate did increase steadily for slower runners who are arguably those who need better race advice and, as such, are likley to benefit disproportionately from this type of prediction and race planning system. For this reason, in this paper we seek to extend our earlier work [19,20] to address such representational shortcomings (simple cases and minimal feature engineering) in an effort to improve prediction accuracy for all runners. We do this by extending the basic case representation, to include additional races from a runner's race history and by evaluating certain types of *landmark* races, as high-level or abstract case features, to show how some past races can help prediction while others can be harmful. In fact we show that some enriched representations (involving more races) are not always beneficial, while others prove to be extremely effective. Furthermore, we also extend the evaluation of this approach by using race data from 25 major marathons across multiple years in 3 different cities.

2   Problem Statement

While our earlier work [19,20] has the advantage of being suitable for novice marathoners, because it required just one past race as basis for prediction, in this work we will target slightly more experienced marathoners, those with at least 2 previous races, depending on the representation used. We do this for two reasons: (1) novice marathoners are often focused on finishing the race, rather than achieving a PB; and (2) more experienced runners have a richer race history to exploit for prediction and planning.

In this work, as in the work of [19,20], we target two separate but related tasks: (1) the *prediction* of a suitable (achievable) goal-time (PB time) and (2) the *recommendation* of an appropriate pacing plan to achieve this goal-time.

2.1   Task 1: Predicting an Achievable PB Time

For a marathon runner, determining a challenging but achievable PB time is an important pre-race task. Choosing a time that is too conservative will leave the runner feeling unfulfilled at the finish-line, while an overly ambitious goal may sabatage their race, increasing the likelihood that they will 'hit the wall'. Thus, predicting a *best achievable* finish-time is non-trivial and getting it wrong can have a disastrous effect on race-day.

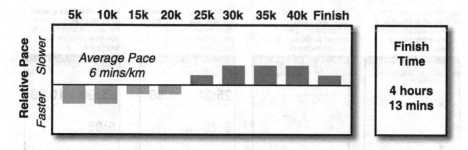

Fig. 1. An example marathon pacing profile showing the 5 Km segment paces for a 4 h 13 min finisher. The pacing bars indicate relative paces with those below the average pace line indicating faster pacing, and those above, slower pacing.

2.2   Task 2: Recommending Pacing Plans

Marathoners need to translate their goal-time into a pacing plan, for different segments of the race. For example, Fig. 1 shows a 5 km *pacing plan/profile* for one finisher who ran their first half *faster* than their second.

Many marathoners pay only limited attention to their pacing plan, often dividing up their race evenly based on their projected finish-time. While such a plan might suit a well-trained, high-performing runner, it is far less suitable for more recreational runners, whose pace during the race will be impacted by the changing terrain and increasing levels of fatigue as the race progresses. For this reason, we argue that many runners stand to benefit from a more *personalized* and *tailored* approach to pacing, one that matches their goal-time, personal fitness level, as well as the course conditions and terrain.

2.3   An Example User-Session

By way of context, Fig. 2 presents our app prototype, designed to provide PB advice and race planning. It shows the runner providing their race history (Fig. 2 (a)) to obtain their PB/goal-time prediction and race plan (Fig. 2 (b)); it is worth noting that historical race data may be harvested automatically from apps like Strava to save runners from tedious data entry tasks. Then, during the race itself the app provides real-time feedback by comparing the runner's current pace versus their goal-pace for that section of the course (Fig. 2 (c & d)). In this way the app supports the runner prior to and during the race, nudging the runner to speed-up or slow-down in order to maximise the likelihood that the runner's goal-time will be achieved.

3   Towards a Multi-Race Case Representation

In this section we describe how we extend the case representation to include multi-race histories instead of the single-race representation used previously in [19, 20].

(a) A PB prediction for the NYC Marathon based on a set of previous landmark races and their pacing profiles.

(b) The predicted PB time (and mean pace) is suggested along with a detailed pacing plan across the race segments.

(c) On race-day the runner's pacing is compared to the recommended pacing plan and adjustments suggested.

(d) The runner has speeded up too much at this stage in the race and is cautioned to slow-down to reach their target pace.

Fig. 2. Example screens from the PB app showing the prediction/recommendation process (a & b) and the race-day feedback (c & d).

3.1 Extending the Basic Case Representation

Our starting point is a marathon *race-record*, with a runner id, gender, city, date, finish-time, and the *5 km segment-times/paces*, as per Eq. 1; we refer to these as *basic* features. We use 5 Km segments because these data are usually provided by big city marathons. Segment paces are stored as *relative* paces, that is the relative difference between the segment pace and the mean race-pace (MRP), see Eq. 2. Thus, a relative pace of -0.1 means that the runner completed that segment 10% *faster* than their MRP; these segments are labeled as $rp5, rp10, \ldots,$ $rp35, rp40, rpFinal$ to indicate each of the 5 Km segment paces plus the pace for the *final* 2.2 km of the race.

$$m_i = (r, gender, city, date, time, rp5, \ldots, rp40, rpFinal) \qquad (1)$$

$$relPace(p, MRP) = \frac{p - MRP}{MRP} \qquad (2)$$

Consider a runner r with a history of races, $H(r)$ (Eq. 3). The work of [19,20] described one way to transform these race-records into *PB cases*: by identifying the fastest race as the runner's PB race and then by pairing each non-PB (nPB) race with this PB race; see Eqs. 4, 5, and 6.

In this way, a runner with three past races would result in two cases, both with the same PB race but a different non-PB race. This basic representation allows PB cases to be used as training instances in a CBR/ML setting, for example, by using the basic nPB features to predict PB finish-times and pacing profiles in $PB(r)$.

$$H(r) = \{m_1, \ldots, m_n\} \qquad (3)$$

$$PB(r) = arg \min_{i} H_i(r).time \tag{4}$$

$$nPB(r) = \{m_i \in H(r) : m_i \neq PB(r)\} \tag{5}$$

$$c_i(r) = \{nPB_i(r), PB(r)\} \tag{6}$$

3.2   Landmark Races as Abstract Case Features

Where the work of [19,20] stopped short, was any further consideration of richer case representations, such as by combining multiple races into a single case, rather than fragmenting extended race histories across multiple, simpler cases. Of course, from a representational perspective, extending single-races to variable length race histories is non-trivial.

Here we adopt a race representation based on a set of so-called *landmark races*. These are races chosen because they are likely to influence PB prediction and race planning. From a representational perspective these landmark races act as *abstract case features* — that is, they are higher-level features than *basic* finish-times and segment paces — for use during similarity assessment and case retrieval. For the purpose of this work, we identify the following landmark races from amongst a runner's nPB races:

- $MR(r)$, the *most recent* race in the runner's history.
- $LR(r)$, the *least recent* (first) race in the runner's history.
- $MV(r)$, the *most varied* race, with the highest coefficient of variation of pace.
- $LV(r)$, the *least varied* race with the lowest pacing variation.
- $PPB(r)$, the *previous PB* race.
- $PW(r)$, the *personal worst* race; the slowest race in the runner's history.
- $MnPB(r)$, a *pseudo race* based on the mean of the runner's non-PBs.

Each of these races relates to a particular type of race for a runner, some may be examples of *good* races, while others may correspond to races that are best forgotton. Either way, collectively, they present a more detailed picture of a runner's race history and performance progression. A key hypothesis in this work is that we might expect this richer representation to provide a better basis for prediction and planning.

It is worth emphasising that each landmark race (except $MnPB$) corresponds to a specific race-record in the runner's history, and as such they each contribute the usual set of basic features (year, finish-time, segment paces etc.) to a PB case. For example, Eq. 7 corresponds to a representation which includes a subset $(MR(r), LR(r), PPB(r), PW(r), MnPB(r))$ of these landmark races, as the *problem description* component, plus $PB(r)$, as the case *solution*. A different representation might include a different subset of landmark races. Of course some landmark races may correspond to the same race-record for a runner if, for example, the $PW(r)$ race is also the $MV(r)$ race. Note, in what follows we will typically refer to a given landmark race, such as $MR(r)$, as just MR, in order to simplify the presentation without loss of generality.

$$c(r) = \{[MR(r), LR(r), PPB(r), PW(r), MnPB(r)], PB(r)\} \qquad (7)$$

4   Case-Based Prediction and Race Planning

We treat the task of determining a challenging but achievable PB time as a prediction problem, using the PB cases as the cases in our case base For the purpose of this work, we are primarily interested in the impact of the different types of landmark races when used to extend basic case representations. To keep things straightforward, and to aid comparison to past work, we adopt the basic approach used in [19] (see Algorithm 1) and adapt it as follows to use our extended representations.

Given a query (q), that is a runner and their available landmark races, we filter the available cases (CB) based on the finish-times (of their most-recent, MR, race) and gender, so that we only consider cases for retrieval if their finish-times are within t minutes of the query finish-time.

Algorithm 1. Outline CBR Algorithm; adapted from [19].

Data: Given: q, query; CB, case base; k, number of cases to be retrieved; t, finish-time threshold.
Result: pb, predicted finish-time; pn, recommended pacing profile.
begin
$\quad C = \{c \in CB : Time(MR(q)) - t < Time(c) < Time(MR(q)) + t\}$
$\quad C = \{c \in C : c.gender == q.gender\}$
$\quad$ **if** $len \ (C) \geq k$ **then**
$\quad\quad R = sort_k(sim(q,c) \ \forall \ c \in C)$
$\quad\quad pb = predict(q, R)$
$\quad\quad pn = recommend(q, R)$
$\quad\quad return \ pb, pn$
$\quad$ **else**
$\quad\quad$ | $\ return \ None$
$\quad$ **end**
end

Next, we perform a standard, distance-weighted kNN retrieval over the filtered cases C. Since we will be using multi-race representations this involves comparing the basic features of each landmark race in q to the basic features of the corresponding landmark race in each case, using a standard Euclidean-based similarity metric. We select the top k most similar cases as the retrieved set, R.

Given a set of similar cases, R, we need to estimate the best achievable finish-time for q. Each case in R represents another runner who has gone on to achieve a personal best. The intuition is that since these PBs were achieved by runners with similar race histories to q, then a similar PB should be achievable by the query runner. In [19] a number of different prediction strategies were compared. The best performing based its predicted finish-time on the *weighted mean* of the PB finish-times of the retrieved cases, as in Eq. 8, and this is the approach adopted in this work.

$$PB_{mean}(q, C) = \frac{\sum_{\forall i \in 1..k} sim(q, C_i) \bullet Time(C_i(PB))}{k} \tag{8}$$

Likewise, in [19], a number of different race plan recommendation strategies were considered. The best peforming approach generated a new pacing plan based on the *mean* relative segment paces of the PB profiles from the k retrieved cases, and once again we will adopt this approach here.

In the section that follows we will evaluate this modified approach to race prediction and pacing planning, using our extended case representations, and comparing the results to those presented in [19, 20].

5   Evaluation Setup

The question to be answered in this paper is whether these enriched multi-race representations help or hinder our ability to make accurate PB predictions and recommend high quality race plans, and how any improvements in performance manifest when it comes to runners with different levels of ability or expectations?

5.1   Datasets

We use public race records from three marathon *majors*, the Berlin Marathon, the London Marathon, and New York City Marathon; see Table 1. From these data we can identify 170,000 runners who have completed at least 4 races (in a given city), which we used as the basis of our target dataset of PB cases. We set a minimum of 4 races to ensure that we have a sufficient set of races from which to identify landmark races; in theory our landmark races could be generated from a minimum of 2 races but this would result in abundant feature duplication across these abstract features.

Table 1. A summary of the evaluation dataset of marathon race records for Berlin, London, and New York, included the number of cases in each case base.

	Years	Runners/Yr	%Males	Time (F/M)	Cases
Berlin	'10–17	34,784	75	265/237	62,900
London	'11–17	36,737	62	286/253	20,471
New York	'06–16	44,046	62	280/253	89,594

5.2   Methodology

As already discussed, each PB case contains a PB part, using the features from the fastest race for the runner. This acts as the 'solution' to the problem we wish to solve. Each case also contains a 'problem' part. In [19,20] the problem part was limited to the features of a single race, which we refer to here as the *baseline* representation; we chose the most recent race (MR) for this baseline as per [20]. We wish to evaluate our approach using different landmark races in our case and so each representation includes this MR race plus one or more additional landmark races; in other words the problem description part of a case contains multiple landmark races and their basic features. In total there are 64 unique combinations of MR plus one or more of the 6 additional landmark races $(LR,$ $LV,$ $MV,$ $PPB,$ $PW,$ $MnPB)$ to act as problem descriptions.

To evaluate our CBR approach we use a standard 10-fold cross-validation methodology to generate and test our PB predictions and pacing recommendations. For each test instance/query, its problem part is used to generate a PB prediction, which is compared to the actual PB time of the test instance to compute a prediction error; thus we are using the past races of a runner to predict a future PB. Similarly, the recommended pacing plan is compared, segment by segment, to the actual pacing the runner ran during their actual PB race, to compute the similarity between the recommended and actual pacing. In what follows, we will compare the prediction error and pacing similarity results for different combinations of landmark races.

6   Prediction Error vs. Representation Richness

First we will consider how the different landmark races used in our representations influence the prediction error. Does including more landmark races produce better predictions than including fewer races, as we might expect? Are some landmark races more powerful predictors than others?

6.1   Do Richer Representations Make Better Representations?

To test whether richer representations (more landmark races) produce better predictions we compute the average prediction error for representations containing $1 \leq n \leq 7$ landmark races. There is only one representation involving a single landmark race (MR) and there is only one representation involving all 7 landmark races $(MR\_LR\_MnPB\_LV\_MV\_PW\_PPB)$. But there are multiple representations for other values of n. In theory we could have evaluated all combinations of the 7 landmark races, but fixing MR as the baseline made sense in order to compare our results to those reported in [19,20] more easily, and avoided a combinatorial explosion of representational choices.

The results are shown in Fig. 3 as the mean prediction error versus the number of landmark races in a given representation. On average, richer representations tend to enjoy better prediction accuracy (lower error rates), with a similar pattern of error rates evident across the three cities. It is worth noting how female

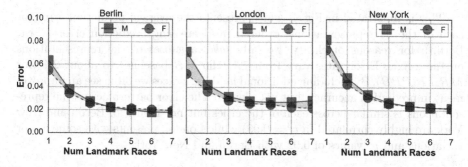

Fig. 3. The average prediction error for representations containing different numbers of landmark races for Berlin, London, and New York.

runners often enjoy slightly lower error rates, for a given representational size, than their male counterparts. This is consistent with the notion that women are more consistent (predictable) pacers than men; see for e.g. [22–24].

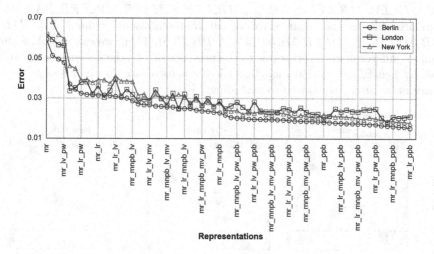

Fig. 4. The average PB prediction error for different representations among Berlin, London and New York runners.

6.2   An Analysis of Landmark Races

Although richer representations tend to produce more accurate predictions, this does not necessarily mean that a specific representation with n landmark races will *always* beat a representation containing $<n$ landmark races. For example, one of the best performing representation we have found is MR_LR_PPB, which contains just 3 landmark races.

This is illustrated in Fig. 4, which presents the average prediction error for each of the 64 representations, ordered by decreasing prediction error (w.r.t. Berlin); for reasons of clarity, we only *label* a subset of the representations on the x-axis. Error rates vary from 7% (the MR baseline) to about 2% (for MR_LR_PPB). By including additional landmark races we often see an improvement in prediction accuracy, but not always. The error pattern across the representations is similar across each of the cities but not identical. Berlin and New York are highly correlated (a $r^2 = 0.99$) while London presents with some minor variations and r^2 values of 0.92 with Berlin and New York.

6.3   Which Races Help the Most?

Clearly, not all landmark races are created equally. Or, alternatively, treating these landmark races as abstract features, some seem to be more useful (better predictors) than others. To explore this further, we compare the error rates for representations with a given landmark race, to those without it. For example, to evaluate the utility of LV (the race with the least pace variation) we calculate the mean error for all representations which include LV (MR_LV, MR_LV_MnPB,..., $MR\_LR\_LV\_MnPB\_MV\_PPB\_PW$), and compare this to the mean error of all representations without LV (MR, MR_MnPB,...,$MR\_LR\_MnPB\_MV\_PPB\_PW$). Then, we can calculate the relative difference in the error due to the presence of LV, the *benefit*, such that a *positive* benefit means that including LV tends to *reduce the error and improve predition accuracy* compared to excluding LV.

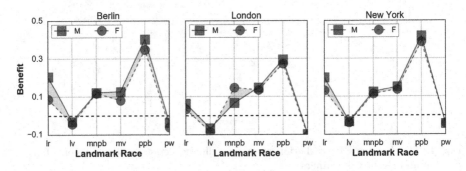

Fig. 5. The benefit for landmark races for Berlin, London, and New York.

Figure 5 presents the average benefit scores for each of the 6 additional landmark races (LR, LV, $MnPB$, MV, PPB, PW). The results are broadly similar, regardless of city, with some minor differences between male and female runners, but there are some striking differences in the benefits associated with particular landmark races. For example, the PPB landmark race (the runner's prior personal best race) stands out as the most useful to include in a case; PPB tends to improve the error by at least 30% (a benefit of 0.3) and sometimes by as much as 40%. That's perhaps not so surprising, because a runner's previous PB time is likely to provide a good basis for their future PB potential.

Conversely, landmark races such as LV (least varied) and PW (personal worst) do not appear to help improve prediction error; in fact they tend to disimprove it. This is probably because these types of races are unlikely to be representative of a runner's true ability; for example, a runner's worst race (PW) will typically be an outlier.

The negative LV benefit is more surprising and its explanation it less obvious, since the conventional wisdom asserts that well-trained and disciplined runners tend to pace their races evenly [25]. This might lead one to expect LV races to be examples of well-paced performances. However, while this conventional wisdom may hold for well-trained runners it does not mean that all evenly paced races are run by well trained, disciplined runners. Runners who are "taking it easy" on the day, or running a "tune-up" race, will often run a more evenly paced race, without pushing themselves particularly hard. Such a race is not representative of their true ability, and so it will not help when it comes to prediction.

In contrast the LR, $MnPB$, and MV races are helpful to a moderate degree, typically offering 5–20% improvements in prediction error. This is not surprising: LR (least recent) races provide some insight into how long a runner has been completing marathons, and their improvement trajectory over this time; $MnPB$ (the mean of the non-pb) races obviously provides a good sense of the typical race times for a runner; while MV (most varied pacing) races might be good examples of runners pushing themselves to their limits and, as such, provide a useful way to calibrate PB prediction.

6.4   Discussion

The results so far help to confirm the primary hypothesis of this work—that richer case representations can help to improve prediction accuracy—but at the same time we see that richer is not always better. Some landmark races serve as powerful abstract features for prediction, significantly improving error rates, while some others have a deleterious effect on prediction performance.

An important question that remains is how these prediction benefits are distributed across runners in practice. For example, our previous work [19,20] showed a deterioration in prediction accuracy among slower runners and runners achieving more ambitious PBs; the best predictions were available to faster runners and those achieving more modest PBs. In the next section we test whether this pattern persists for our extended case representations as we look at PB prediction and race plan recommendation for different types of runners.

7   Prediction and Recommendation in Practice

We present a side-by-side comparison between our baseline MR representation (similar to the approach used in [19,20]) and one of our best performing representations, MR_LR_PPB, to determine how both approaches perform in terms

of prediction error and pacing similarity. Once again we adopt the same approach as [19,20] by looking at runner ability (based on their finish-times) and
PB improvement levels.

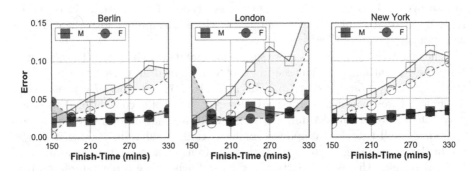

Fig. 6. The prediction error by finish-time for runners in Berlin, London, and New
York. The baseline (MR) results are shown with unfilled markers, and the high-
performing MR_LR_PPB results are shown with filled markers.

7.1 On Runner Ability

Figures 6 and 7 show the prediction error and pacing similarity for the baseline and best representations. Consistent with [19,20], the error for the baseline
tends to increase for slower runners, with males experiencing much higher error
rates than females. This means less accurate goal-time predictions for those (less
able) runners who are likely to need help the most. For instance, 270-min, male
finishers in London can expect an error rate of about 0.12. That is a potential
margin of more than 30 min for their PB.

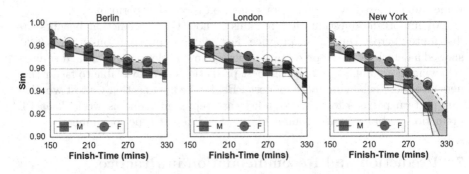

Fig. 7. The pacing similarity by finish-time for runners in Berlin, London, and New
York; the baseline MR results are indicated with unfilled markers.

The results for the best representation (MR_LR_PPB) offer a statistically significant improvement ($p < 0.01$) over the baseline, across all levels of ability for men and women. In fact using this approach the error rates remain more or less stable across all finish-times. Now our 270-min, male, London finisher can expect a PB prediction with an error rate of less than .03, a 4x improvement over the baseline. Moreover, the pacing plan similarity results in Fig. 7 indicate that this improved prediction accuracy is available without any material loss of pacing plan quality, compared to the baseline.

7.2   On the Degree of PB Improvement

Fig. 8 examines the relationship between prediction error and the degree of PB improvement. Some runners achieve a PB that is a large improvement on their current PB, while other PBs might be more modest. In [19,20] very small and very large PB improvements were associated with less accurate predictions. This pattern is evident in Fig. 8 for the baseline, but, once again, our best representation reduces this error across all levels of PB improvement; these differences are also statistically significant at $p < 0.01$. For example, for London runners, the baseline approach can predict PBs, which are a 15% speedup for runners, with an error rate of just under 0.1. In comparison, the MR_LR_PPB representation achieves an error rate of approximately 0.03, a 3x improvement, for the same speedup.

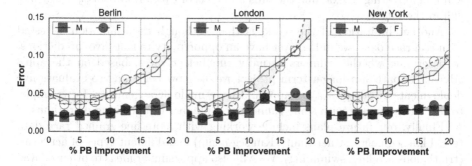

Fig. 8. The prediction error by degree of PB improvement for runners in Berlin, London, and New York; the baseline MR results are indicated with unfilled markers.

8   Conclusions and Future Work

This paper describes a novel application of CBR to support marathoners with targeted PB advice. Its main contribution is to extend our past work [19,20], by using richer case representations to demonstrate significant improvements in prediction performance, without compromising race-plan quality. We looked at the relative merits of different types of landmark races to serve as abstract case features, showing that richer representations do not always deliver better prediction performance, but some richer representations do.

As always, this work has its limitations. An evaluation focus on more experienced runners (>3 races) technically excludes novice, first-time marathoners, for instance. However, such runners are probably more concerned with finishing, and if anything it is the slightly more experienced runners who are likely to be more motivated to run a PB, and so more likely to use the proposed system. That being said, in the future we will examine whether it may be feasible to accommodate novice runners by substituting in more common, shorter races (half marathons, 10k's etc.) in place of 'missing' marathons.

Unlike our previous work [19,20], which evaluated performance based on a set of marathons from a single city, here we have extended the evaluation to multiple cities and more runners. That being said, each case base continues to be made up of cases from a single city. It is an interesting future research question to determine how prediction accuracy and race-plan quality might be impacted by using 'mixed' cases, made up of race histories spanning multiple different marathon courses. On the one hand this offers the potential to generate larger, richer case bases. On the other hand, performance in one city (on one marathon course) may not be a good predictor of performance in a different city. Perhaps, biasing predictions based on the *similarity* of different marathon courses will help; e.g. Berlin is more similar to London than it is to Boston. Either way, it will be interesting to examine the pros and cons of this form of *transfer learning* [26] in the future.

Another limitation of the work, is that, although the evaluation is tested with real race data, we did not yet have an opportunity to test 'live' predictions, to determine whether runners actually run better races, based on the app's advice. As part of a longer-term project we are now beginning to evaluate live deployments of our prototype app, and have made arrangements, for example, to test the approach with some runners of a number of upcoming marathons.

Finally, our future plans include working with more fine-grained race data (e.g. 1 km segments rather than 5 Km segments) and different types of activities (triathalons, cycling, swimming). We will also apply similar ideas to other related tasks, such as injury prevention, personalised training, recovery advice etc.

Acknowledgments. Supported by Science Foundation Ireland through the Insight Centre for Data Analytics under grant number SFI/12/RC/2289 and by Accenture Labs, Dublin.

References

1. Mayer-Schönberger, V., Cukier, K.: Big data: a revolution that will transform how we live, work, and think. Houghton Mifflin Harcourt, Boston (2013)
2. Peek, N., Combi, C., Marin, R., Bellazzi, R.: Thirty years of artificial intelligence in medicine (AIME) conferences: a review of research themes. Artif. Intell. Med. **65**(1), 61–73 (2015)

3. Buchanan, B.G., Shortliffe, E.H.: Rule Based Expert Systems: The Mycin Experiments of the Stanford Heuristic Programming Project (The Addison-Wesley Series in Artificial Intelligence). Addison-Wesley Longman Publishing Co., Inc., Boston (1984)
4. Wiesner, M., Pfeifer, D.: Health recommender systems: concepts, requirements, technical basics and challenges. Int. J. Environ. Res. Public Health 11(3), 2580–2607 (2014)
5. Wiesner, M., Pfeifer, D.: Adapting recommender systems to the requirements of personal health record systems. In: Proceedings of the 1st ACM International Health Informatics Symposium, IHI 2010, New York, NY, USA, pp. 410–414. ACM (2010)
6. Leijdekkers, P., Gay, V.: Improving user engagement by aggregating and analysing health and fitness data on a mobile App. In: Geissbühler, A., Demongeot, J., Mokhtari, M., Abdulrazak, B., Aloulou, H. (eds.) ICOST 2015. LNCS, vol. 9102, pp. 325–330. Springer, Cham (2015). https://doi.org/10.1007/978-3-319-19312-0_30
7. Möller, A., et al.: GymSkill: mobile exercise skill assessment to support personal health and fitness. In: 9th International Conference on Pervasive Computing, Pervasive: Video, CA, USA, San Francisco, p. 2011 (2011)
8. Hermens, H., op den Akker, H., Tabak, M., Wijsman, J., Vollenbroek-Hutten, M.: Personalized coaching systems to support healthy behavior in people with chronic conditions, vol. 24, no. 6, pp. 815–826 (2014). eemcs-eprint-25228
9. Ohlin, F., Olsson, C.M.: Intelligent computing in personal informatics: key design considerations. In: Proceedings of the 20th International Conference on Intelligent User Interfaces, IUI 2015, New York, NY, USA, pp. 263–274. ACM (2015)
10. Geleijnse, G., Nachtigall, P., van Kaam, P., Wijgergangs, L.: A personalized recipe advice system to promote healthful choices. In: Proceedings of the 16th International Conference on Intelligent User Interfaces, IUI 2011, New York, NY, USA, pp. 437–438. ACM (2011)
11. Bichindaritz, I., Montani, S., Portinale, L.: Special issue on case-based reasoning in the health sciences. Appl. Intell. 28(3), 207–209 (2008)
12. Lewis, M.: Moneyball: The Art of Winning an Unfair Game. WW Norton & Company, New York (2004)
13. Kelly, D., Coughlan, G.F., Green, B.S., Caulfield, B.: Automatic detection of collisions in elite level Rugby union using a wearable sensing device. Sports Eng. 15(2), 81–92 (2012)
14. Buttussi, F., Chittaro, L.: MOPET: a context-aware and user-adaptive wearable system for fitness training. Artif. Intell. Med. 42(2), 153–163 (2008)
15. Vales-Alonso, J., et al.: Ambient intelligence systems for personalized sport training. Sensors 10(3), 2359–2385 (2010)
16. de Oliveira, R., Oliver, N.: TripleBeat: enhancing exercise performance with persuasion. In: Proceedings of the 10th International Conference on Human Computer Interaction with Mobile Devices and Services, MobileHCI 2008, New York, NY, USA, pp. 255–264. ACM (2008)
17. Iyer, S.R., Sharda, R.: Prediction of athletes performance using neural networks: an application in cricket team selection. Expert Syst. Appl. 36(3), 5510–5522 (2009)
18. Bartolucci, F., Murphy, T.B.: A finite mixture latent trajectory model for modeling ultrarunners' behavior in a 24-hour race. J. Quant. Anal. Sport. 11(4), 193–203 (2015)

19. Smyth, B., Cunningham, P.: Running with cases: a CBR approach to running your best marathon. In: Case-Based Reasoning Research and Development - 25th International Conference, ICCBR 2017, Trondheim, Norway, 26–28 June 2017, Proceedings, pp. 360–374 (2017)
20. Smyth, B., Cunningham, P.: A novel recommender system for helping marathoners to achieve a new personal-best. In: Proceedings of the Eleventh ACM Conference on Recommender Systems, RecSys 2017, Como, Italy, 27–31 August 2017, pp. 116–120 (2017)
21. Vickers, A.J., Vertosick, E.A.: An empirical study of race times in recreational endurance runners. BMC Sport. Sci., Med. Rehabil. **8**(1), 26 (2016)
22. Deaner, R.O.: More males run fast: a stable sex difference in competitiveness in us distance runners. Evol. Hum. Behav. **27**(1), 63–84 (2006)
23. March, D.S., Vanderburgh, P.M., Titlebaum, P.J., Hoops, M.L.: Age, sex, and finish time as determinants of pacing in the marathon. J. Strength Cond. Res. **25**(2), 386–391 (2011)
24. Trubee, N.W.: The effects of age, sex, heat stress, and finish time on pacing in the marathon. Ph.D. thesis, University of Dayton (2011)
25. Abbiss, C.R., Laursen, P.B.: Describing and understanding pacing strategies during athletic competition. Sports Med. **38**(3), 239–252 (2008)
26. Pan, S.J., Yang, Q.: A survey on transfer learning. IEEE Trans. Knowl. Data Eng. **22**(10), 1345–1359 (2010)

Dynamic Case Bases
and the Asymmetrical Weighted
One-Mode Projection

Rotem Stram[1,2(✉)], Pascal Reuss[1,3], and Klaus-Dieter Althoff[1,3]

[1] Smart Data and Knowledge Services Group, German Research Center for Artificial Intelligence, Kaiserslautern, Germany
{rotem.stram,pascal.reuss,klaus-dieter.althoff}@dfki.de
[2] Department of Computer Science, Technical University of Kaiserslautern, Kaiserslautern, Germany
[3] Institute of Computer Science, Intelligent information Systems Lab, University of Hildesheim, Hildesheim, Germany

Abstract. Building a case base for a case-based reasoning (CBR) system is incomplete without similarity measures. For the attribute-value case structure similarity between values of an attribute should logically fit their relationship. Bipartite graphs have been shown to be a good representation of relationships between values of symbolic attributes and the diagnosis of the cases in a technical diagnosis CBR system, while using an asymmetrical weighted one-mode projection on the values to model their similarity.

However, the weighted one-mode projection assumes that the set of symbols is static, which is contradictory to the dynamic nature of case bases as defined by the retain phase of the CBR cycle. In this work we present two methods to update the similarity measure whenever new information is available and compare them. We show that even though updating the similarity measure to exactly reflect the case base had the new information been available a-priori produces better results, an imperfect update is a feasible, less time consuming temporary solution.

Keywords: Dynamic case bases · Bipartite graph
Weighted one-mode projection · Local similarity · Symbolic attributes

1 Introduction

The basic idea behind Case-Based Reasoning (CBR) is that similar problems have similar solutions. It is a paradigm for problem solving by using previously solved problems as the starting point for new solutions. The CBR cycle was formalyzed by Aamodt and Plaza in [1] and is also known as the four R cycle, named after its four steps: Retrieve, Reuse, Revise, and Retain.

The retrieve step of the cycle is one of its crucial parts, as it decides which past experiences the system uses as a basis for a new solution. It takes as input a

© Springer Nature Switzerland AG 2018
M. T. Cox et al. (Eds.): ICCBR 2018, LNAI 11156, pp. 385–398, 2018.
https://doi.org/10.1007/978-3-030-01081-2_26

case description representing a new problem, and outputs either the most similar case from the case base (past experience), or a list of n most similar cases. When considering a diagnosis system, where a solution is a member of a pre-defined set of possible diagnoses, there is usually almost no processing done on the retrieved cases, making the accuracy of this step even more crucial.

At the heart of the retrieval step is the similarity between two cases. There are two types of similarities in CBR, local and global. If we focus on the attribute-value case structure, local similarity is defined as the similarity between two values of a single attribute. Global similarity is then the similarity of two cases as a whole by aggregation of local similarity values.

For local similarities the type of the attribute defines the similarity function that is used. For numerical attributes, for instance, a distance measure such as Euclidean distance can be used. For strings the edit distance is a good solution [4], while the similarity of symbolic attributes is usually either modeled by experts, defined by taxonomies, or is a combination of both [2,10].

Recently, graph theory and network analysis methods have been introduced as tools to extract local similarity measures of symbolic attributes, most notably the weighted one-mode projection (WOMP) [15]. In this work from the technical diagnosis domain, textual problem description were transformed into keywords, and each keyword connected to the diagnosis of the case, effectively creating a bipartite graph (BPG) where the weight of each edge is the number of times each keyword appeared under each diagnosis. A novel method for asymmetrical weighted one-mode projection (aWOMP) was introduced, and used as a similarity measure between the keywords. This work, however, assumed that the set of keywords is fixed and did not address the possibility that the case-base will change over time. Here we will addresses the possible updates of the aWOMP as the case base is updated.

This work is structured as follows. In Sect. 2 we will give an introduction to aWOMP. Section 3 will discuss the update options of aWOMP and introduce two methods to update the similarity measure under different conditions. Section 4 will present the premise of our experimentation and their results. Section 5 will list works that are related to ours, while Sect. 6 will conclude this paper and offer possible directions for future work.

2   Asymmetrical Weighted One Mode Projection

One-mode projection (OMP) refers to an action performed on a bipartite graph (BPG) to transform it to another graph depicting the relationship of only some of the original nodes. A BPG, as can be seen in Fig. 1a, is a graph with two groups of nodes generally referred to as left (L) and right (R). Connections are only allowed between groups, but not within them. A OMP is a projection of the graph on either the L nodes or the R nodes, where two nodes are connected if they share a neighbor in the BPG (e.g. Fig. 1b).

In some cases a weighted OMP (WOMP) is needed, and even more so when the BPG itself is weighted. To this end, Stram et al. [15] introduced a novel

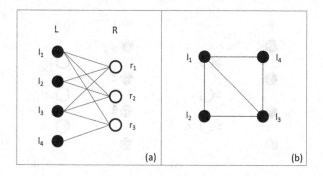

Fig. 1. a. A bipartite graph. b. The one-mode projection of the bipartite graph

WOMP method in their work from 2017 that produced asymmetrical weights in the resulting graph (aWOMP). This method was used as a local similarity measure of symbolic attributes in a Case-Based Reasoning (CBR) system, where they showed the superiority of aWOMP over other common methods.

The aWOMP relies on resource allocation of nodes in a bipartite graph, and is based on a method introduced by Zhou et al. [16]. It takes a weighted BPG as an input, and produces a new graph quantifying the relationship between nodes in a single group from the BPG by measuring the amount of resources node A allocated to all the neighbors N_i that it shares with node B, together with the resources that nodes N_i allocate to node B.

Let $G = (L, R, E)$ be a BPG where E is a set of edges (l_i, r_j, w_{ij}), where w_{ij} the weight between nodes $l_i \in L$ and $r_j \in R$, and $|L| = n$, $|R| = m$. Then the resources that node l_i accumulates is the sum of its adjacent edges:

$$W_i^L = \sum_{j=1}^{m} w_{ij} \tag{1}$$

The resources that node l_i allocates to node r_j is the weight of the edge between them normalized by the total amount of l_i's resources:

$$w_{ij}^{L \to R} = \frac{w_{ij}}{W_i^L} \tag{2}$$

Which leads to the resources that each node $r_j \in R$ accumulates:

$$W_j^R = \sum_{i=1}^{n} w_{ij}^{L \to R} \tag{3}$$

This process corresponds to the flow of resources seen in Fig. 2a. Now we switch directions and regard the flow from R to L:

$$w_{ij}^{R \to L} = \frac{w_{ij}^{L \to R}}{W_j^R} \tag{4}$$

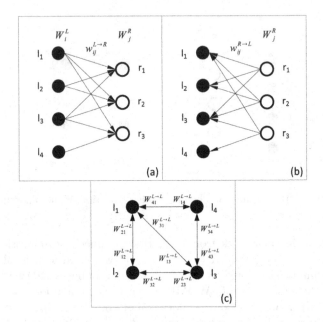

Fig. 2. a. Resource allocation from L to R. b. Resource allocation from R to L. c. Asymmetrically weighted one-mode projection

This is visualized in Fig. 2b. When we look at two nodes $l_a, l_b \in L$, the resources that flow between them are:

$$w_{ab}^{L \to L} = \sum_{j=1}^{m} p_{aj} \cdot p_{bj} \cdot (w_{aj}^{L \to R} + w_{Bj}^{R \to L}) \tag{5}$$

where $p_{ij} = 1$ if l_i and r_j are neighbors, and $p_{ij} = 0$ otherwise. We then normalize this weight:

$$W_{ab}^{L \to L} = \frac{w_{ab}^{L \to L}}{w_{bb}^{L \to L}} \tag{6}$$

The resulting weights are those used in the aWOMP graph as seen in Fig. 2c.

3   aWOMP and Dynamic Case Bases

The case base of a diagnostic CBR system is comprised of case description and diagnosis pairs. We focus on the attribute-value case description type, and so cases are comprised of a set of attribute values, where a value can on its own be a set of values. As an example take the system described by Reuss et al. [10] in the technical diagnosis of aircraft faults domain. Here, symbolic attributes were extracted from textual fault descriptions and divided into different attributes such as *fault*, *location*, and *time*. For a single case each attribute can hold several values. Focusing on a single attribute, each value representing a keyword is connected to the diagnosis of the case. In the BPG the keywords build the node set L and the diagnoses the node set R. The weight between a keyword and a diagnosis is the number of cases the keyword appeared in that had this diagnosis. If this keyword appears in several cases with different diagnoses then in the BPG it will be connected to several nodes from R.

In order to use the aWOMP as a local similarity measure, the BPG needs to be known beforehand, and the aWOMP is calculated offline. However, in real-world applications the environment is dynamic and new information is constantly added. In order to overcome this, the aWOMP should be updated whenever new information arises. New information in this context could be one of the follwoing:

- a new node in L
- a new node in R
- a new edge
- a different weight on an existing edge
- removing a node from L
- removing a node from R
- removing an edge

Removing nodes or edges from the graph is a result of removing cases from the case base in a process called *forgetting* [9]. Since *forgetting* is outside the scope of this work we will focus only on changes resulting from adding new cases to the case base. More specifically, we will focus on adding a new node to L, adding a new edge, and changing the weight of an existing edge. Adding a new node to R will not be described here for simplicity reasons, however it is straight forward since the new node will only have one edge when it is added.

In this section we will discuss two possible update method to the BPG so that the similarity measure remains up to date with the case base.

3.1   Perfect Update

A perfect update is an update to the aWOMP such that it is indistinguishable from an aWOMP that would have been calculated had we built the BPG with the new information in advance. There are two ways to obtain a perfect update of an aWOMP: either calculate the new aWOMP from scratch, or making local changes to the BPG only where it is relevant. Let's focus on two possible local changes to the BPG: adding a new node to L and changing the weight of an existing edge.

Adding a New Node to L. Assume that we have a BPG, and for each node $l_i \in L$ and $r_j \in R$ we know the values of W_i^L and W_j^R respectively. Adding a new node l_x to L, along with an edge to at least one $r_j \in R$ (e.g. Figure 3) would affect W_j^R (see Eq. 3) and thus ultimately $W_{ab}^{L \to L}$ (Eq. 6) for all l_a and l_b that share r_j as a neighbor.

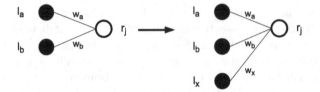

Fig. 3. Adding a new node to a bipartite graph

The required local changes are then:

$$W_{jnew}^{R} = W_j^R + \frac{w_x}{W_x^L} \tag{7}$$

and from here on every call to $W_{ab}^{L \to L}$ would give the correct weight.

Changing the Weight of an Existing Edge. Assuming again that for a given BPG and for each node $l_i \in L$ and $r_j \in R$ we know the values of W_i^L and W_j^R respectively (e.g. Fig. 4). We now change the weight of w_b. The effect here is much greater than adding a new node, due to its effect on all the neighbors of l_b, since the sum of all its resources, which is used in Eq. 2, is now different. Subsequently, W_j^R of all $r_j \in R$, r_j is a neighbor of l_b needs to be updated.

Fig. 4. Changing the weight of an existing edge in a bipartite graph

The following changes need to be made:

$$W_{bnew}^{L} = W_b^L - w_b + w_{bnew} \tag{8}$$

And then for each $r_j \in R$, r_j is a neighbor of l_b:

$$W_{jnew}^{R} = W_j^R - \frac{w_b}{W_b^L} + \frac{w_{bnew}^L}{W_{bnew}^L} \tag{9}$$

From here on every call to $W_{ab}^{L \to L}$ would give the correct weight. With these example, perfectly updating the aWOMP for the remaining scenarios can be easily extrapolated.

Discussion. Remaining in the CBR domain where aWOMP is used as a similarity measure, adding or removing a single case may result in a massive chain reaction of changes to the BPG, depending on the density of the graph. A case can be seen as a BPG on its own, where $|R| = 1$ containing the diagnosis of the case (see example in Fig. 5b). Adding this graph representation of the case to the case-base BPG (Fig. 5a) results in a new weight for the shared edges, and possible new nodes and edges.

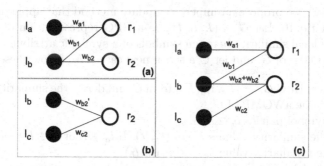

Fig. 5. a. An existing BPG representing a case base. b. A BPG representation of a new case. c. The new BPG resulting from adding the new case to the case base.

A change in the weight of just one edge adjacent to a node $l_i \in L$ would require an update to the resources l_i allocates to all its neighbors (see Eq. 2) and subsequently an update to the resources allocated to all of the neighbors of $r_j \in R$, r_j a neighbor of l_i. Now imagine the new case is comprised of several keywords. This makes the scalability of the perfect update only slightly more feasible than calculating the aWOMP from scratch, if at all, especially when the BPG is dense.

Dynamic real-time systems with large case bases and tens of thousands of keywords in just one attribute may not have the resources to perfectly update the aWOMP for every new case, requiring a temporary scalable solution that is feasible in the short run. A solution can be temporarily imperfect, allowing the BPG to be perfectly updated (or recalculated) in the background for future use.

3.2   Imperfect Update

In order to better understand the imperfect update of a weighted BPG we first define the relation $\leq^c$ between the similarity functions sim_1 and sim_2 under a context c. If the aWOMP of two BPGs is used as local similarity measures sim_1 and sim_2 between symbolic attributes of a case base domain d (the context), then $sim_1 \leq^d sim_2$ if sim_2 leads to better diagnosis accuracy than sim_1 for the same test set.

Let us assume that given a domain d, G_1 is a BPG representation of the case base CB_1, sim_1 the similarity measure, C a set of new cases, $CB_2 = CB_1 \cup C$ the case base after adding C, G_2 the BPG of CB_2 resulting from the perfect update of G_1, and sim_2 the similarity measure of G_2. We also assume that $sim_1 \leq^d sim_2$. An imperfect update of G_1 is a transformation of sim_1 into a new similarity measure sim_u that maintains the following inequality for some ranked results:

$$sim_1 \leq^d sim_u <^d sim_2 \tag{10}$$

In this work we propose an imperfect update method that approximates the inequality in Eq. 10. Let $G = (L, R, E)$ be a BPG representation of case base CB, sim the local similarity between symbols of a symbolic attribute as derived from the aWOMP of G, and let C a set of new cases. We follow these steps:

1. create a new BPG $G_c = (L_c, R_c, E_c)$ from C and derive the similarity measure sim_c from the aWOMP of C.
2. for each symbol pair $l_a, l_b \in L_c$
   (a) find the similarity value $s = sim(l_a, l_b)$. If $l_a \notin L$ or $l_b \notin L$ then $s = 0$.
   (b) find the similarity value $s_c = sim_c(l_a, l_b)$
   (c) $s_{new}(l_a, l_b) = s + (1 - s) * s_c$

For the case $l_a = l_b$ aWOMP ensures that $sim(l_a, l_b) = 1$, however even if the value is not in G then $sim_c(l_a, l_b) = 1$ and thanks to the equation in step 2c $s_{new}(l_a, l_b) = 1$. We expect that $sim \leq^d sim_{new} <^d sim_{perfect}$ where $sim_{perfect}$ the similarity measure of the perfectly updated BPG.

Discussion. The proposed imperfect update method provides a solution for local update of similarity between keywords that appeared in the new cases added to the case base. The advantage here is the quick update for only a subset of keywords instead of all keywords, meaning only those keywords that appeared in the new cases. This suggests that a simultaneous update for several cases at once would give better results than an update for one case at a time, meaning that batch updates would be more beneficial. On the other hand, this update requires calculating an aWOMP for the new cases, which is computationally intensive, especially considering that our goal is to avoid recomputing the aWOMP for the entire case base. This leads to the conclusion that the batches need to be small enough for the update to be worth while.

4   Experimental Results

The dataset used for testing in this work was taken from [15]. This dataset is based on IMDB[1] data and contains 8,000 movies with a list of descriptive keywords for each. The movies are tagged with one of the following genres: action, comedy, horror, and romance. The movies are divided equally between

---

[1] www.imdb.com.

the genres. This dataset is split into training and test set with 6,000 items (1,500 items per genre) and 2,000 items in the test set (500 items per genre). We keep each dataset balanced since accuracy is our chosen method of evaluation.

In order to test if the proposed imperfect update method is viable for our purpose we divide the training set further into two sets: one with 1,300 items per genre, which we called set 1300, and two repository sets with 100 items per genre each. From set 1300 we built a BPG where $L = keywords$ and $R = genres$ and a keyword is connected to a genre if it is listed under a movie that is part of the genre. The edge weights of the BPG is the number of times each keyword appeared under each genre.

We performed both an imperfect and a perfect update on set 1300 with the first repository, the result of which we call 1300 imperfect and 1400 respectively. This was done again on 1400 with the second repository, resulting in BPGs 1400 imperfect and 1500. It is clear that 1500 is equivalent to the BPG of the full training set. At the end of this process we had five similarity functions.

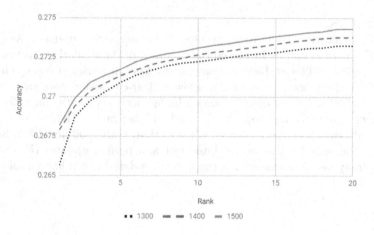

Fig. 6. The retrieval accuracy of the similarity functions derived from 1300 and the two perfect updates

From the test set we built five case bases, one for each similarity function, using the myCBR tool [3], where each case represents a movie and contains a single symbolic attribute with multiple values for the keywords. If a keyword or a link between two keywords did not exist in the aWOMP or the updates, the equality function was used (i.e. $sim(a, b) = 0$ if $a \neq b$ and $sim(a, b) = 1$ if $a = b$). To quantify how well each similarity function performed a retrieval test was done for each case from the test set. A case was deemed as correctly retrieved if it belonged to the same genre of the query case. Using this definition allows us to simulate a diagnostic problem with a dataset that is usually used for recommendation. The aggregated accuracy values were then calculated by retrieval rank (i.e. 1st rank is the case retrieved with the highest similarity value, the 20st rank the case retrieved with the 20st highest similarity value).

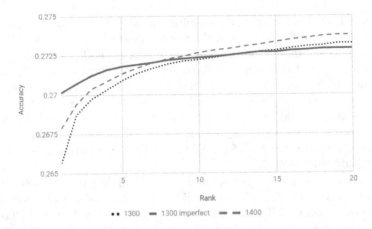

Fig. 7. The retrieval accuracy of the similarity functions derived from one imperfect and one perfect update of 1300

We first compare the accuracy results of the two perfect updates. As can be seen in Fig. 6, each update increased the accuracy of the similarity function. It is clear that $1300 < 1400 < 1500$ at least for the first 20 retrieved cases. The first imperfect update, however, does not allow a clear-cut assumption that $1300 < 1300\,imperfect < 1400$. Figure 7 shows a higher accuracy for the imperfect over the perfect update for the first 7 ranks, and a higher rank over 1300 for the first 13 rank, afterwards its performance is worse than both 1300 and 1400. Similar ratios can be seen for the second imperfect and perfect updates (Fig. 8), and here accuracy becomes worse than the perfect update in even lower ranks.

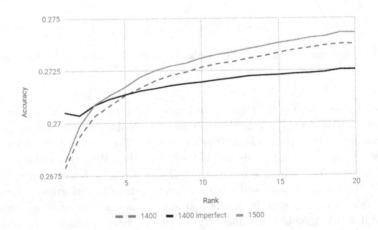

Fig. 8. The retrieval accuracy of the similarity functions derived from one imperfect and one perfect update of 1400

The questions arise, why does the imprefect update perform better in higher ranks than both perfect measures, and why does it perform worse in lower ranks? In order to answer these questions we first need to look into the properties of the evaluation method. Accuracy by rank can also be seen as accuracy for k-nearest neighbor, i.e. $k = $ rank. The imperfect update, in its nature, is local and therefore impacts only nodes in its vicinity. This creates a strong positive impact on lower k's, however this impact is diminished when increasing the scope of influence.

These results show that the proposed imperfect update method is not as reliable as perfect updates, however it is still usable as a temporary solution with the assumption that a recalibration with a perfect update is performed in the future.

Discussion. The question is asked, when should the perfect and imperfect updates be used? As stated before, adding new information to a dense BPG can cause a wave of changes across the graph, making the perfect update almost as computationally intensive as recalculating the aWOMP from scratch. In this scenario it would be more beneficial to use the imperfect update when new information becomes available, as it has been shown to be reliable *enough*, while a new aWOMP can be recalibrated either periodically or when a predefined number of new cases have been added to the case base. On the other hand, if the graph is sparse then a perfect update may be the best course of action.

5   Related Work

Several works combined complex network analysis (CNA) methods with CBR. Cunnigham et al. in [5] described a system that transforms textual case descriptions into graphs where terms are connected according to the sequence of their appearance in the text. The similarity measure on these cases was then defined as the maximum common subgraph. Although experiments showed promise, the time complexity of the similarity measure is polynomial, making its feasibility for real-world applications difficult.

Another notable work that combined CNA and CBR is Sizov's Text Reasoning Graph (TRG) [12,13]. Here detailed descriptions of how each case was solved are transformed into a graph representing causal relationships with textual entailments and paraphrase relations. In their first attempt this graph was built only for the solution of the case, while case similarity was based on the vector space model with TF-IDF weights. In their followup work the TRG was incorporated into the case description and the so-call longest common paraphrase was used as the similarity function. In order for this method to be applicable, the solution process needs to be available beforehand for each case, and this is unfortunately hard to obtain for most domains.

There has been some discussion on how symbolic attributes should be compared. A common way to define symbolic attribute similarity is by using a taxonomy [6]. Recently, Bach et al. [2] described a technical fault diagnosis system where fault descriptions were given in textual form. Keywords were extracted using NLP methods and a taxonomy was manually constructed by experts. Reuss et al. described a similar scenario in [10], where keywords were extracted from textual fault descriptions in the technical fault diagnosis domain. Again, taxonomies were manually defined by experts, however they were also automatically supplemented with further information from tools such as wordnet[2].

More complex automated similarity measure have also been discussed in the past. In 1995 Ricci et al. described a reinforcement method for learning a similarity function for symbolic attributes [11], and in 2003, Stahl et al. described an evolutionary algorithm for the same purpose [14]. Both these methods require an arduous learning phase with intensive time complexities. For a static case base and set of attribute values this can be feasibly done offline, however if a new case is added to the case base containing a new keyword retraining the similarity function is required.

Simply weighted one-mode projection (sWOMP) was used by Jimenes-Diaz in a CBR recommendation system for link prediction. The system recommended students with programming tasks based on previously solved task. A BPG was built between students and tasks and the sWOMP was derived on the tasks, where the weights between them were the number of common neighbors in the BPG. In a followup work, Gómez-Martin et al. [8] performed the sWOMP on the users, and a user was recommended a task they hadn't completed yet if a similar user completed it.

6   Conclusions and Future Work

In this work we discussed the aWOMP method in its role as a local similarity method in a diagnosis CBR system. In previous works the aWOMP was seen as a single-pass similarity measure of static symbolic attributes, however, real-world application are dynamic and ever-changing. We presented two update options for aWOMP, the perfect and the imperfect update, which can be used when new cases are added to the case base. The perfect update is equivalent to recalculating the aWOMP from scratch with the updated case base and is computationally intensive for dense BPGs, while the imperfect update allows for local changes on-the-fly that should be usable until a recalibration of the aWOMP is possible.

In our experimentation we showed that a perfect update of the BPG improves the retrieval accuracy, and this is consistent with the notion that more information allows for a better modeling of an environment. The proposed imperfect update method performed better than the perfect update for higher retrieval ranks, however it did not keep its superiority for lower ranks. In the future the imperfect update method can be refined in order to improve retrieval results.

As for the perfect update, in order to allow faster updates that make this solution feasible to be used over many changes to the case base, a map-reduce [7] type system could be used. In an initial architecture, for instance, one could use a sequence of mappers and reducers where the first mapper phase could

---

[2] wordnet.princeton.edu.

collect the resources of each keyword while the reducer calculates Eq. 1, and the second mapper would then accumulate the resources that nodes l_i allocate to their neighbors, with the reducer performing a sum function that would result in Eq. 3. Once we know the values of W_i^L and W_j^R, finding the aWOMP is straightforward.

References

1. Aamodt, A., Plaza, E.: Case-based reasoning: foundational issues, methodological variations and system approaches. AI Commun. **7**(1), 39–59 (1994)
2. Bach, K., Althoff, K.-D., Newo, R., Stahl, A.: A case-based reasoning approach for providing machine diagnosis from service reports. In: Ram, A., Wiratunga, N. (eds.) ICCBR 2011. LNCS (LNAI), vol. 6880, pp. 363–377. Springer, Heidelberg (2011). https://doi.org/10.1007/978-3-642-23291-6_27
3. Bach, K., Sauer, C., Althoff, K.D., Roth-Berghofer, T.: Knowledge modelling with the open source tool myCBR. In: CEUR Workshop Proceedings (2014)
4. Ceausu, V., Desprès, S.: A semantic case-based reasoning framework for text categorization. In: Aberer, K., Choi, K.-S., Noy, N., Allemang, D., Lee, K.-I., Nixon, L., Golbeck, J., Mika, P., Maynard, D., Mizoguchi, R., Schreiber, G., Cudré-Mauroux, P. (eds.) ASWC/ISWC -2007. LNCS, vol. 4825, pp. 736–749. Springer, Heidelberg (2007). https://doi.org/10.1007/978-3-540-76298-0_53
5. Cunningham, C., Weber, R., Proctor, J.M., Fowler, C., Murphy, M.: Investigating graphs in textual case-based reasoning. In: Funk, P., González Calero, P.A. (eds.) ECCBR 2004. LNCS (LNAI), vol. 3155, pp. 573–586. Springer, Heidelberg (2004). https://doi.org/10.1007/978-3-540-28631-8_42
6. Cunningham, P.: A taxonomy of similarity mechanisms for case-based reasoning. IEEE Trans. Knowl. Data Eng. **21**(11), 1532–1543 (2009)
7. Dean, J., Ghemawat, S.: Mapreduce: simplified data processing on large clusters. Commun. ACM **51**(1), 107–113 (2008)
8. Gómez-Martin, P.P., Gómez-Martin, M.A.: Case-based recommendation for online judges using learning itineraries. In: Case-Based Reasoning Research and Development: 25th International Conference, ICCBR (2017)
9. Markovitch, S., Scott, P.D.: The role of forgetting in learning. In: Machine Learning Proceedings (1988)
10. Reuss, P., Stram, R., Juckenack, C., Althoff, K.-D., Henkel, W., Fischer, D., Henning, F.: FEATURE-TAK - framework for extraction, analysis, and transformation of unstructured textual aircraft knowledge. In: Goel, A., Díaz-Agudo, M.B., Roth-Berghofer, T. (eds.) ICCBR 2016. LNCS (LNAI), vol. 9969, pp. 327–341. Springer, Cham (2016). https://doi.org/10.1007/978-3-319-47096-2_22
11. Ricci, F., Avesani, P.: Learning a local similarity metric for case-based reasoning. In: International Conference on Case-Based Reasoning, pp. 301–312 (1995)
12. Sizov, G., Öztürk, P., Aamodt, A.: Evidence-driven retrieval in textual CBR: bridging the gap between retrieval and reuse. In: Hüllermeier, E., Minor, M. (eds.) ICCBR 2015. LNCS (LNAI), vol. 9343, pp. 351–365. Springer, Cham (2015). https://doi.org/10.1007/978-3-319-24586-7_24
13. Sizov, G., Öztürk, P., Štyrák, J.: Acquisition and reuse of reasoning knowledge from textual cases for automated analysis. In: Lamontagne, L., Plaza, E. (eds.) ICCBR 2014. LNCS (LNAI), vol. 8765, pp. 465–479. Springer, Cham (2014). https://doi.org/10.1007/978-3-319-11209-1_33

14. Stahl, A., Gabel, T.: Using evolution programs to learn local similarity measures. In: Ashley, K.D., Bridge, D.G. (eds.) ICCBR 2003. LNCS (LNAI), vol. 2689, pp. 537–551. Springer, Heidelberg (2003). https://doi.org/10.1007/3-540-45006-8_41

15. Stram, R., Reuss, P., Althoff, K.-D.: Weighted one mode projection of a bipartite graph as a local similarity measure. In: Aha, D.W., Lieber, J. (eds.) ICCBR 2017. LNCS (LNAI), vol. 10339, pp. 375–389. Springer, Cham (2017). https://doi.org/10.1007/978-3-319-61030-6_26

16. Zhou, T., Ren, J., Medo, M., Zhang, T.C.: Bipartite network projection and personal recommendation. Phys. Rev. E **76**(4), 046115 (2007)

Novel Object Discovery Using Case-Based Reasoning and Convolutional Neural Networks

J. T. Turner[1], Michael W. Floyd[1(✉)], Kalyan Moy Gupta[1],
and David W. Aha[2]

[1] Knexus Research Corporation, Springfield, VA, USA
{j.turner,michael.floyd,
kalyan.gupta}@knexusresearch.com
[2] Navy Center for Applied Research in AI, Naval Research Laboratory,
Washington, DC Code 5514, USA
david.aha@nrl.navy.mil

Abstract. The development of Convolutional Neural Networks (CNNs) has resulted in significant improvements to object classification and detection in image data. One of their primary benefits is that they learn image features rather than relying on hand-crafted features, thereby reducing the amount of knowledge engineering that must be performed. However, another form of knowledge engineering bias exists in how objects are labelled in images, thereby limiting CNNs to classifying the set of object types that have been predefined by a domain expert. We describe a case-based method for detecting novel object types using a combination of an image's raw pixel values and detectable parts. Our approach works alongside existing CNN architectures, thereby leveraging the state-of-the-art performance of CNNs, and is able to detect novel classes using limited training instances. We evaluate our approach using an existing object detection dataset and provide evidence of our approach's ability to classify images even if the object in the image has not been previously encountered.

Keywords: Computer vision · Novel object discovery · Deep learning
Convolutional neural networks

1 Introduction

Computer Vision has seen rapid advancement in recent years as a result of Deep Learning (DL) techniques, especially for object classification tasks. DL algorithms are able to leverage large annotated image datasets for training, and achieve significant classification improvement over traditional vision approaches. Convolutional Neural Networks (CNNs) [1] have been a driving force behind these improvements as they are able to use an image's raw pixel values as inputs and learn higher-level features from the training data. Thus, they remove the need for manual feature engineering and extraction, and may learn more discriminative features than those that are hand-crafted by a domain expert. For example, during training a CNN may learn low-level image features like lines or curves, and combine those into increasingly complex features like shapes, wheels, or faces.

M. T. Cox et al. (Eds.): ICCBR 2018, LNAI 11156, pp. 399–414, 2018.
https://doi.org/10.1007/978-3-030-01081-2_27

Although CNNs greatly reduce the knowledge engineering required by removing the need for hand-crafted features, they do require knowledge about the types of objects that are present in the training images (i.e., an annotation of the object labels). This adds significant bias based on the types of objects that are used to annotate images. For example, an image of an office typically contains dozens of visible objects but may only have labels for a small subset of those (e.g., humans, computers, desks) and treat the others as unlabeled background (e.g., books, pencils, papers). Thus, the CNN is only able to learn to classify objects that the domain expert felt were important enough to annotate. Similarly, the level of granularity of annotations can impact what a CNN learns. For example, the CNN will learn differently depending on if an image of a dog is labelled as *"animal"*, *"dog"*, or as the specific dog breed. These issues can become more significant when you have large datasets containing thousands or millions of annotated images, since it reduces the likelihood that a consistent annotation methodology was used on all images (e.g., different annotators, human error, time-varying methods of annotation). The annotated object types in training images restrict the potential classifications that a CNN can make when deployed; if an object type is not annotated in the training data, the CNN will be unable to classify that object type. For example, if a CNN is trained with images of *airplanes*, *boats*, and *houses*, an image of a *dog* would either be classified as one of those three object classes or not classified at all (i.e., if the confidence was too low).

We propose a case-based approach for novel object detection that uses a combination of raw pixel values and detectable object part information to identify when input images differ noticeably from known object types. Our approach is intended to be used in combination with existing CNN vision approaches and leverage their state-of-the-art performance while addressing some of their limitations. More specifically, our approach makes the following contributions: (1) a method to detect novel object types without prior knowledge of those types; (2) a method to identify variations in images of objects of the same type; (3) an approach that can be used in combination with existing CNN architectures; and (4) an approach that can be used even with small datasets and a single example of each object type. We believe the ability to operate using a small dataset is important given the large dataset requirements that are typically required by existing Deep Learning systems.

The remainder of the paper outlines our case-based novel object detection approach. Section 2 provides background on Convolutional Neural Networks, with Sect. 3 describing our method for novel object detection and how we leverage CNNs for this task. Section 4 describes our empirical evaluation using an existing object detection dataset. In Sect. 5, we discuss related work in case-based Deep Learning, case-based Computer Vision, and novel object type detection. Section 6 discusses areas of future work and concluding remarks.

2 Background: Convolutional Neural Networks

The typical architecture of a Convolutional Neural Network has three primary building blocks: *convolutional layers*, *pooling layers*, and *fully-connected layers*. Convolutional layers are composed of *filters* that encode features that will be detected in the input. For example, consider a greyscale image of $n \times n$ pixels used as input to a convolutional layer composed of k filters, each of which are $m \times m$ ($m \leq n$). The filters encode feature patterns that will be identified in the input image. Each $m \times m$ filter is applied to each distinct (and possibly overlapping) $m \times m$ subregion of the input image, with the results stored in new $(n - m + 1) \times (n - m + 1)$ matrix[1], called a feature map. This can be thought of as the filter sweeping across the image, starting from the top left, and applying the filter to each subregion along a row before moving down to the row below (and ending in the bottom right). Each of the k filters are applied in this manner, resulting in k feature maps from the convolutional layer. Thus, the feature map for a particular filter represents the presence of that feature in the various subregions of the image. When a CNN is trained, the filters (i.e., the features to look for) are part of what is learned.

Pooling layers are used to reduce the dimensionality of a convolutional layer's output and for abstraction to avoid overfitting. For example, the convolutional layer in the previous example took an $n \times n$ input and produced a $k \times (n - m + 1) \times (n - m + 1)$ output (i.e., one feature map for each of the k filters). Depending on the values of k, n, and m, this could result in a larger output than the input. Pooling prevents the outputs from growing progressively larger, since in a typical CNN architecture you will have multiple convolutional layers in a series. A common form of pooling is *max pooling* that partitions the layer's input into a set of contiguous non-overlapping $p \times p$ subregions and selects the maximum value contained in each subregion. As was the case with convolutional layers, pooling layers produce k output matrices (i.e., one for each input feature map they receive). For example, if $p = \frac{n-m+1}{2}$, then each input matrix would be downsampled to a 2×2 matrix (i.e., containing the maximum value from the top-left, top-right, bottom-left, and bottom-right regions of the input).

A typical CNN architecture will contain multiple convolutional layers and pooling layers arranged in a series. The input to the first convolutional layer $conv_1$ will be the input image, and its output out_{conv_1} (i.e., the feature maps it produces) will be the input to the first pooling layer $pool_1$. The output of the first pooling layer out_{pool_1} is then used as input to the next convolutional layer $conv_2$, and this sequence of convolutional and pooling layer continues until the output from the n th pooling layer out_{pool_n}. Such an architecture results in early convolutional layers detecting relatively simple features whereas later layers detect increasingly complex features (i.e., patterns of lower-level features). After the final pooling layer, that layer's output out_{pool_n} is flattened from a set of matrices into a single one-dimensional feature vector. For example, if out_{pool_n} produced six 3×3 output matrices, the flattened output would be a feature vector containing 54 values ($6 \times 3 \times 3$).

The final building blocks in a CNN are the fully-connected layers. These layers are typically multilayer perceptrons (MLPs), and use the flattened feature vector output by the final pooling layer as input. For a classification task, the fully-connected layer will output the class label (or probability of each class label) of the input. During training,

---

[1] This example assumes a step size of 1, where the center on the filter is moved by 1 pixel at each step. However, in practice the step size can be set as a parameter.

the weights used by the MLP to produce the output classification are learned. At a high level, we can think of the convolutional and pooling layers as performing feature extraction on the input image, and the fully-connected layers use those extracted features to perform classification.

3   Case-Based Novel Object Detection

Convolutional Neutral Networks perform supervised machine learning, so their ability to classify the presence of objects in images is directly related to the labeled training data they have available; they cannot detect the correct object type if no annotated training data exists with a label for that object type. If a CNN outputs the confidence in each known class label (i.e., the output of the fully-connected layers), it could, at best, label an input image as *unknown* if none of the possible class labels were above a confidence threshold. For example, if a CNN was trained to classify *airplanes*, *boats*, and *houses*, an image of a *dog* would either be classified as one of the three known classes (i.e., if the CNN output a high confidence for one of the classes) or as *unknown* (i.e., if none of the classes had a high confidence). If several different novel objects are encountered, they would all be classified together into the generic *unknown* class, even if the objects were significantly different from each other. Returning to the example, images of *dogs*, *books*, *space stations*, and *humans* would all be classified together as *unknown*. One solution would be to retrain the CNN after each novel object type is detected. However, this is generally impractical as CNNs require both a large number of labeled training examples (i.e., more than a single training instance) and significant computational time to retrain the fully-connected layers.

We propose a case-based reasoning approach to detect the presence of novel object types and quickly learn from limited training data. Unlike CNNs, a CBR approach can learn using only a single training example and requires no training time. However, our approach does not propose to remove CNNs from the object classification process. Instead, our approach leverages the state-of-the-art performance of CNNs while providing capabilities that alleviate some of their limitations. For the remainder of this section we will largely present the CBR component in isolation, but will discuss how it can be integrated with existing CNN architectures at the end of this section.

Our CBR system encodes each image I_i as a case C_i. Each case is a triple containing the image's feature vector F_i, its set of observable parts P_i, and object label l_i:

$$C_i = \langle F_i, P_i, l_i \rangle$$

This representation assumes the availability of two functions: *features* and *parts*. The *features* function converts a raw image $I_i \in I$, where I is the set of all images, into a feature vector $F_i = \langle f_i^1, \ldots f_i^n \rangle \in F$, where F is the set of all feature vectors (*features*: $I \rightarrow F$), composed of n feature values. For the *features* function, we use the convolutional and pooling layers from a CNN to perform this conversion, since they convert a raw image into a flat feature vector. This is essentially a version of the CNN with the fully-connected layers removed such that the CNN is only used for feature extraction. The *parts* function extracts a set of observable parts $P_i = \{p_i^1, \ldots, p_i^{m_i}\} \subseteq P$, where P is the set of all object parts, from image I_i. The number of observable parts in an image m_i is not fixed, so the size and contents of P_i is image-specific. In this work, we consider object parts to be low-level components that make up larger objects. For example, the parts of a *dog* could include its *legs, tail, torso, tail, head,* and *ears*. Although the object parts provide more detail about an object, they are assumed to be generic such that the same parts can be part of numerous object types. Returning to the *dog* example, many mammals would share some or all of the same parts. However, even two instances of the same object may have different observable parts depending on what is visible in the image. In the *dog* example, the *dog's* tail may not be visible depending on where it is facing or its legs may not be visible if the bottom of its body is occluded by another object. The *parts* function requires a separate vision system that can identify these generic object parts from visible images. However, as we will discuss later, while our CBR approach can leverage parts information, it is not strictly necessary for case retrieval. For example, if no parts extraction was possible, each case could contain an empty set of parts ($P_i = \emptyset$) and rely only on the feature vector for retrieval. We assume each case has a single object label $l_i \in L$, where L is the set of all object labels. This assumes that each image will contain only a single object of interest. Such an assumption is valid for uncluttered images or, more realistically, when used as part of a Region-Based Convolutional Neural Network (R-CNN) [2]. R-CNNs use a *region proposal* stage to propose subregions of the input image and then classify those subregions individually. Thus, instead of the entire image being used as input to the CNN, each subregion is used as a distinct input to the CNN (i.e., the CNN is run multiple times) and each subregion is used to perform a single classification. In our work, the images stored in cases and used as input to the CBR system could be the image data from these subregions. Using this case representation, the feature vector and set of parts represent the *problem* and the object label is the *solution*.

When an input image is received, either a complete image or a proposed subregion from an R-CNN, object classification is performed using Algorithm 1. In addition to the input image I_{in}, the algorithm uses as input a case base CB, number of nearest neighbors k, feature vector similarity threshold λ_f, and parts similarity threshold λ_p. The algorithm starts by extracting the features and parts from the image (Lines 1 and 2). If the case base is empty (i.e., the CBR system has no training instances), a novel object label is generated using the *generateLabel* function (Line 5). We do not expect this function to generate an informative label based on knowledge of the image (e.g., *dog, cat, airplane, house*) but instead a unique label for the object type (e.g., *class1, class2, class3*). If the case base is not empty, the top k most similar cases are retrieved from the case base (Line 7). The similarity only considers the feature vector similarity (e.g., using a similarity function based on the Euclidean distance between feature vectors), so no parts information is considered. Cases are only added to the top k if their similarity is above the feature vector similarity threshold λ_f, so it is possible for fewer than k cases to be retrieved. In some situations, no cases will be retrieved if none of the cases are similar to the input image (Line 8). In such a situation, the input image is assumed to be of a novel object type so a new class label is created for it (Line 9).

The previous stages of the algorithm only considered the feature vectors when comparing the input image to cases. The remainder of the algorithm leverages the detectable parts information. The parts of the input image are compared to the parts of each of the top k nearest neighbors (Lines 12–15). The similarity function used (Line 13) is assumed to be a similarity function that calculates set similarity (e.g., Jaccard similarity). Similar to when comparing feature vector similarity, only cases with a parts similarity above the parts similarity threshold λ_p are retained (Line 14). If there were no cases above this threshold (Line 16), the input image is considered to be a novel object type so a novel label is generated (Line 17). Otherwise, the label from the most similar case (based on parts similarity, with feature vector similarity used as a tie-breaker) is used to label the input image (Line 19). Finally, a novel case is created and added to the case base (Line 20) and the object label is returned (Line 21).

Algorithm 1. Object classification using image features and parts

Function: $classify(I_{in}, CB, k, \lambda_f, \lambda_p)$ *returns* l_{in}

1   $F_{in} \leftarrow features(I_{in})$;
2   $P_{in} \leftarrow parts(I_{in})$;
3   $l_{in} = \emptyset$;
4   **if** $CB = \emptyset$ **then**
5     $l_{in} \leftarrow generateLabel()$;
6   **else**
7     $topK \leftarrow retrieveTopK(F_{in}, CB, k, \lambda_f)$;
8   **if** $topK = \emptyset$ **then**
9       $l_{in} \leftarrow generateLabel()$;
10   **else**
11       $nn = \emptyset; nnSim = -1$;
12   **foreach** $C_i \in topK$ **do**
13         $sim \leftarrow partSim(P_{in}, C_i.P_i)$;
14   **if** $sim > nnSim$ **and** $sim > \lambda_p$ **then**
15           $nn = C_i; nnSim = sim$;
16   **if** $nn = \emptyset$ **then**
17         $l_{in} \leftarrow generateLabel()$;
18   **else**
19         $l_{in} \leftarrow nn.l_i$;
20 $CB \leftarrow CB \cup \langle F_{in}, P_{in}, l_{in} \rangle$;
21 **return** l_{in};

An existing label is only returned when there is a case that is similar to both the input image's feature vector and its parts set. Thus, there are three situations where a novel object label, and therefore a new object class, are created: (1) when the case base is empty; (2) when none of the cases have similar feature similarity; and (3) when there is at least one case with similar features but none of those cases have similar parts. As we mentioned earlier, although parts information is used in the algorithm, it is not strictly necessary. Assuming no parts information is available, the parts set of the input image and all cases will be empty. If the parts similarity function is designed to return maximal similarity when comparing two empty sets, all of the top k cases will be above λ_p and have an equal similarity value. Thus, as long as the top k cases are iterated over in order of descending feature vector similarity (Lines 12–15), the case with the most similar feature vector similarity will be selected as the nearest neighbor and have its label returned.

One of the primary benefits of this algorithm is that it is able to learn using only a single training instance. Once a novel class has been detected (Lines 5, 9, or 17), it is immediately added to the case base and can be used to classify future input images. Similarly, this algorithm can be used even when no existing training data exists (i.e., an initially empty case base). For example, this algorithm could be used from a cold-start to perform object classification without any labeled data. At such a time when sufficient data was collected and annotated, and sufficient time was available, a Convolutional Neural Network could be trained. Once a CNN is trained, the CBR algorithm could run in parallel to the CNN. Assuming the fully trained CNN has superior performance classifying known object types, the CBR system could defer classification for known object types and only interject when a novel class is detected or an input image is most similar to an object class that the CNN has not been trained on (i.e., a previously detected novel class). Thus, the CBR system can be used in situations where it has advantages over the CNN, and defer in other situations.

4   Evaluation

In this section, we evaluate the claim that *our case-based reasoning system can be used to detect and learn from novel object types*. Our evaluation tests the following hypotheses:

H1:   Extracting a feature vector representation from images, using a CNN, provides sufficient information for a CBR algorithm to differentiate between object types

H2:   The addition of observable parts information improves object classification performance

H3:   Our CBR approach is able to detect novel object classes and learn from detected classes

H4:   Our CBR approach discovers finer-grained object classes than those provided by the dataset's human annotators

4.1   Data Set

The dataset we use for evaluation is the publicly available *PASCAL-Part Dataset* [3]. It is based on the dataset used for the *Visual Object Classes Challenge 2010*, a Computer Vision competition to recognize objects in realistic scenes. While the *Visual Object Classes Challenge 2010* dataset only contains the annotated object types visible in each image, the *PASCAL-Part Dataset* contains additional annotations for the object parts that are visible in the image. The dataset contains 20 object types: *aeroplane, bicycle, bird, boat, bottle, bus, car, cat, chair, cow, diningtable, dog, horse, motorbike, person, pottedplant, sheep, sofa, train,* and *tvmonitor.* Each object can have between 0 (*boat, chair, diningtable, sofa*) and 24 (*person*) object parts annotated. However, images of the same object type may have a different number of annotated parts due to object occlusion, object positioning, or annotator error. In addition to providing object part annotations, the *PASCAL-Part Dataset* has several properties that make it a suitable dataset for us to use. The images are realistic real-world images, so most images contain multiple objects (including objects from the 20 annotated object types as well as other unlabeled object types). The objects have varying locations, rotations, sizes, and scales. Additionally, images have different backgrounds (e.g., beach, indoors, forest) and lighting conditions. The annotated objects may be partially occluded, located partially outside the image, or incorrectly labeled by human annotators.

Our work is focused on detecting a single object type in each image, as we justified in the previous section, so we preprocessed the *PASCAL-Part Dataset* to extract only the images with a single annotated object. However, it should be noted that although each image only contains a single annotated object, many of them contain multiple visible objects. The additional object are either objects that are not of the 20 labelled object types, or objects that have been omitted due to annotator error. After preprocessing, 4737 images remained (from an initial dataset size of 10,103).

The *features* function used in Algorithm 1 is a Convolutional Neural Network using the ResNet [4] architecture (i.e., how the various layers are connected). The CNN was trained using the *ImageNet* dataset [5], a dataset containing hundreds of thousands of annotated images. This was performed to learn the filters (i.e., the image features) used by the convolutional layers of the CNN, and after training the fully-connected layers were removed. The output of the CNN is a feature vector of length 2048. Although *ImageNet* is a different dataset than the *PASCAL-Part Dataset*, pretraining a CNN on *ImageNet* learns many general-purpose image features (e.g., lines and shapes). Thus, it allows training a generic *features* function that can be used regardless of domain, and with significantly less time and computational effort than retraining the CNN for each new image dataset. However, it should be noted that due to the size and scope of *ImageNet*, there is likely some overlap with the objects contained in the *PASCAL-Part Dataset* (but none of the labels from *ImageNet* are used during our evaluation). The *parts* function in Algorithm 1 uses the ground-truth parts annotations provided by the dataset (i.e., assumes the presence of a perfect parts extractor). Although in real computer vision tasks the parts would need to be extracted using a separate vision system, we used the provided parts labels in order to remove error during our initial evaluations. Future work will examine how our CBR system's performance is influenced when parts are extracted using a more realistic *parts* function. Thus, each image in the preprocessed *PASCAL-Part Dataset* can be converted into our case representation using the *features* function, *parts* function, and object type annotation.

4.2   Classification Accuracy

Our initial set of experiments aims to evaluate the ability of our CBR algorithm to correctly classify the objects contained in images. More specifically, we examine the classification performance based on what information is used during case retrieval:

feature vector only, *parts only*, or *both feature vector and parts*. Essentially, these experiments look to confirm that CBR can reasonably discriminate between the various object types and that reasonable data is contained in cases.

In the experiments, we use a variation of Algorithm 1 that does not attempt to identify novel classes; the label from the nearest neighbor is used even if that neighbor is dissimilar. This is achieved by using a non-empty case base (avoiding Algorithm 1, Line 5), and setting $\lambda_f = \lambda_p = 0.0$ (avoiding Algorithm 1, Lines 9 and 17). The experiments used leave-one-out testing, such that each of the 4737 cases are used as input with the remaining 4736 cases used as the case base. The accuracy is measured as the percentage of input cases that have a retrieved object type that is identical to their true object type (i.e., the solution portion of the case). The three variants we test are:

- **Feature Vector Only**: We used $k = 15$ and an empty parts set for all images, thereby only basing similarity on the feature vectors. In practice, this is identical to using $k = 1$ since the case with the highest feature vector similarity will be selected given that there is no influence from parts similarity (i.e., all cases have empty parts sets). We used $k = 15$ to highlight that the various experiments were using similar parameter values.
- **Parts Only**: We used $k = 4736$ so that the entire case base was retrieved, regardless of feature vector similarity. All cases contained parts information. Thus, the most similar case is the case with the most similar parts.
- **Both Feature Vector and Parts**: We used $k = 15$ and all cases contained parts information. Thus, the most similar case is the case with the most similar set of parts from amongst its 15-nearest neighbors (based on feature vector similarity).

Using only a single component of the case for retrieval resulted in lower performance, with a classification accuracy of 80.14% when only the feature vector is used and 88.79% when only the parts are used. The best performance was achieved when both the feature vector and parts were used for retrieval, with a classification accuracy of 91.13%. These results demonstrate that using CBR with only the feature vector provides reasonable classification performance (giving support for **H1**) but that performance can be increased by using both the feature vector and parts information (giving support for **H2**).

4.3 Novel Class Detection

The results in the previous subsection demonstrate the ability of our approach to be used to classify known objects in images. However, the primary motivation of our work is to detect and learn from novel object types in images. In this experiment, we use Algorithm 1 such that is can detect novel object types (i.e., the case base may be initially empty, or either λ_f or λ_p are non-zero values). The experiment starts with an empty case base, and cases are randomly removed from the dataset and used as input to Algorithm 1. After each input, the algorithm stores a case in its case base using the object classification it made for the image (i.e., Algorithm 1, Line 20). Thus, 4737 total inputs are provided to the algorithm, and after the n th input the algorithm will have a case base of size n. The evaluation was designed to simulate how the CBR system would start with no knowledge (i.e., an empty case base) and incrementally learn based on its novel object detection capabilities. The parameters used are $k = 15$, $\lambda_f = 0.45$, $\lambda_p = 0.45$. The thresholds were selected to be relatively low such that they only exclude cases if they are significantly different than the input image. Similarly, the k value was selected such that a neighborhood of similar cases would be retrieved.

We use two metrics to evaluate the algorithm's performance: *Class Purity* and *Class Count Divergence*. *Class Purity* measures, after all 4737 input images have been classified and added to the case base, the percentage of images that are placed in a class where they share a true object type with the majority of other images in that class. Since our algorithm starts with no training data, all classes in the case base are novel classes learned by the algorithm. Thus, we compare whether images with the same algorithm-generated object type classification have the same ground-truth object type classification. For example, the algorithm would be performing well if all images of *dogs* were given the same novel object classification of *class10* (or any other class label, as long as all *dogs* were given the same label). This metric calculates values between 0 and 1 (inclusive), with higher values being better.

Class Count Divergence measures how close the number of detected object types is to the true number of objects types in the dataset. In our dataset, there are 20 true object labels. The motivation for using the metric is to penalize creating an unnecessarily large number of classes. For example, creating 4737 unique class labels would result in a perfect *Class Purity* score but each object label would be overfit to a single image. We use a curved function that has the maximal value when the number of predicted classes $class_{pred}$ is equal to the true number of classes $class_{true}$ and decreases as those values diverge:

$$ClassCountDivergence = \frac{1}{\left(\frac{class_{true}-class_{pred}}{500}\right)^2 + 1}$$

Similar to *Class Purity*, *Class Count Divergence* calculates values between 0 and 1 (inclusive), with higher values being better. The value 500 was selected for use in the *Class Count Divergence* based on the size of the dataset, such that the metric would be below 0.50 if the number of detected classes was larger than approximately 10% of the dataset size. Additionally, we report the *Overall Performance* of the algorithm as the harmonic mean of *Class Purity* and *Class Count Divergence*.

We repeated the experiment 25 times, and Table 1 shows a summary of the results. Based on the *Class Purity*, our approach does a reasonable job detecting novel object types and using those to classify images it encounters in the future. As a baseline, when input images are randomly assigned to 20 object types (i.e., no novel classes are learned), the *Class Purity* is 0.168. The majority of the mistakes made by the algorithm were to provide the same label to objects that are both physically similar and have similar parts. For example, many of the four-legged animals were given the same label, especially in situations where they were small or occluded. Overall, occlusion had a significant impact on performance since it often resulted in very little of the object being visible (i.e., $< 10\%$) and no parts information being available. Even for humans, it was difficult to know that these highly obscured objects were the objects of interest. In fact, it was often the situation that unlabeled objects (i.e., not among the 20 annotated labels) were the most prevalent objects in images. By examining the learned class labels, we found that our algorithm was learning based on these unlabeled object types. However, given that the *Class Purity* metric only considers the 20 annotated object types, the metric is unable to quantify how well the algorithm was able to learn object types that were not annotated in the dataset. Overall, these results provide support for **H3**.

Table 1. Results of novel object type detection over 25 experimental runs

Metric	Mean	Minimum	Maximum	Standard Deviation
Class Purity	0.676	0.572	0.738	0.052
Object Types	121.7	111	133	6.2
Class Count Divergence	0.960	0.951	0.968	0.005
Overall Performance	0.792	0.717	0.838	0.036

4.4 Number of Object Types

The results in Table 1 show that our algorithm is learning approximately six times as many object types as are labelled in the dataset. This is reasonable performance, considering that it would have created 4737 object types had each image been assigned its own label, but higher than anticipated. However, our qualitative examination of the classifications uncovered that the number of object types is not exclusively a result of algorithm error but primarily a result of learning finer-grained object types. For example, images annotated as *pottedplant* are largely divided by our algorithm into two distinct classes: one for images of *fully-grown plants* and one for *seedling plants*. To a human, there are clear and obvious distinctions between these two subsets of images, providing support that the algorithm learned a meaningful subdivision. Numerous other similar examples were found where the algorithm learned meaningful finer-grained object types, a selection of which include: *full-sized cars* vs. *go-karts* (both annotated as *car*), *people in water* vs. *babies* vs. *athletes* (all annotated as *person*), and *locomotives* vs. *subway trains* vs. *empty train tracks* (all annotated as *train*). However, although a significant number of the additional object types learned by our algorithm appear to be meaningful object types, it also learned less meaningful single-image object types. Although some of those singleton object types are uninteresting or redundant, it learned several interesting singleton object types based on unusual images in the dataset: a sheep standing in a bus shelter, a train car with a picture of a dinosaur painted on it, an alpaca (incorrectly annotated in the *PASCAL-Part Dataset* as *sheep*), and a Ferris wheel. However, there were also situations where our algorithm erroneously subdivided object types, or performed divisions that a human would not deem as necessary (i.e., too fine-grained). This qualitative analysis provides partial support for **H4**, but a more detailed analysis will be necessary to definitively prove that our algorithm is identifying meaningful object sub-types.

5 Related Work

Integrations of Deep Learning and CBR have seen increased interest recently, with many researchers exploring how the two approaches can benefit each other. In the domain of Human Activity Recognition (HAR), CNNs have been used for feature extraction [6]. This work differs from our own in that it uses accelerometer data rather than image data, but similarly finds that reasonable results can be achieved with instance-based algorithms when features are automatically learned and extracted using CNNs. Instance-based retrieval in the HAR domain has also been used to find similar existing data that can be used to train a classifier for a new user [7]. Their system also uses CNN-extracted features and, like our work, is motivated to allow learning under limited data availability. However, their work is focused on classifier personalization rather that novel class identification (e.g., they do not detect new types of activities that have not been seen before). They have also examined how Siamese Neural Networks can be used to learn similarity functions [8], and such an approach could potentially be used in our algorithm to improve retrieval. Deep Learning has been combined with CBR to generate novel recipes that are both surprising and plausible [9]. However, this differs from our own work in that their system creates novel items rather than discovering previously unknown items.

Case-based reasoning has been used for a variety of image processing and computer vision tasks [10]. One application area that has seen particular interest is medical CBR (e.g., [11–13]), primarily due to the prevalence of medical imagery in patient files and the need to retrieve similar images to aid in diagnosis. However, unlike our work, the majority of CBR approaches rely on hand-crafted features rather than learned features (e.g., [14–16]). Additionally, while CBR systems are often used for image retrieval and classification, to the best of our knowledge none are able to detect novel object types (or, more generally, novel classes in non-image systems). Some systems may be able to perform outlier detection (e.g., when no similar cases are retrieved) but do not attempt to learn novel object types from these outliers. For example, rather than attempt to generate a novel object label, a CBR system may present an input image to a domain expert for manual labelling. Although having human annotations is valuable, it is not always practical when a system is operating autonomously for long periods of time.

The most similar work to our own involves classifying webpages based on multimedia data (e.g., images) rather than only the contained text [17]. Like our approach, they use CNNs to perform feature extraction from images and use those features during case retrieval. The primary difference between their work and our own is that they only classify images into predefined classes, so no novel object discovery is performed. They do perform outlier detection, but that is to identify mislabeled or irrelevant images contained in a webpage rather than to detect novel webpage themes; outliers influence the case structure but do not modify the set of class labels.

As we mentioned previously, existing approaches to Computer Vision tend to focus on object classification (e.g., CNNs [1]) or detecting regions containing objects (e.g., R-CNNs [2]). These approaches rely on a predefined set of object types, with fewer works examining novel object discovery. Existing approaches for unsupervised object class discovery are similar to our own work in that they learn from images containing a single object type per image [18–20]. However, as we mentioned previously, the images we use in this work often contain multiple objects in each image but with only one of the objects labelled by human annotators. The primary difference between these approaches and our work is that they perform offline object detection using the entire dataset. Our approach is both online and incremental; novel object types are detected at run-time based on the content of input images. To the best of our knowledge, no other approaches exist to allow online and incremental unsupervised object discovery. As we discussed previously, existing computer vision systems can only identify that an input image is unlikely to be of a known object type. They do not provide online labels for these unknown objects or learn from them (i.e., how to classify future images of that object type). However, our approach can perform such labelling and learning, and can learn after retaining only a single case.

Our algorithm learns in an unsupervised manner when no expert-annotated training cases are provided to it (e.g., as in our evaluation that started with an empty case base). As such, it has many similarities to clustering since it is grouping input images by assigning them generated class labels. Many traditional clustering algorithms, like k-means [21], divide data into a fixed number of partitions, whereas our approach dynamically creates new object types as necessary. Hierarchal clustering methods, like single-linkage [22], are able to dynamically increase the number of clusters created but do not cluster incrementally; the entire dataset must be provided as a batch. Incremental clustering algorithms have been developed, such as incremental k-means [23], that allow data points to be added sequentially rather than as a batch. However, even incremental clustering algorithms rely on comparing each data point to a set of cluster centroids. Our approach compares data points (i.e., input images) to any existing case in the case base. This is important given the two-stage retrieval process we use. Since retrieval is based on both an image's feature vector representation and its observable parts, there can be a high degree of variability amongst cases of the same object type. For example, since the similarity thresholds used by our algorithm may be relatively low (e.g., 0.45 in our experiments), cases of the same object type may not have highly similar feature vector representations (i.e., a medium feature vector similarity but high parts similarity). Similarly, cases of the same object type may have high feature vector similarity but only medium parts similarity. If only cases representing class centroids were retrieved, an input image could appear dissimilar to all of the centroids (i.e., treated as a novel object type) but would have been similar to one or more of the non-centroid cases. Additionally, unlike clustering algorithms, our algorithm can be used for both classification and novel class discovery. Without any labeled data, it performs classification based on its generated object type labels. However, if some cases are provided using labelled training data (i.e., some supervised learning was performed) the algorithm can either generate novel class labels or perform classification based on existing object type labels.

6   Conclusions

This paper described a method for detecting novel object types in images using a combination of case-based reasoning and Convolutional Neural Networks. Our approach leverages the automated feature learning and extraction provided by CNNs while taking advantage of CBR's ability to perform incremental learning with relatively few training instances. A set of nearest neighbors are initially retrieved based solely on similarity between extracted image features, with subsequent retrieval based on the similarity between observable object parts. Although our approach leverages observable object parts during case retrieval, it can be used even if such information is unavailable. Additionally, since CBR is an instance-based learner, it does not abstract the object parts contained in images, thereby allowing them to be directly used during similarity calculation. If a CNN was to include object part information it would likely learn an abstraction of what parts exist in a class. For example, it would learn what parts are generally observable in images of *dogs*, possibly losing valuable information necessary to detect uncommon images, like a dog with most of its observable parts obscured by a costume it is wearing.

Our evaluation was performed using realistic images from the publicly available *PASCAL-Part Dataset*. The initial results demonstrated the ability of a CBR system to classify images using CNN-extracted feature vectors, and the performance improvement provided by including object parts information during retrieval. We also provided evidence of our algorithm's ability to be used to detect novel object types. Even when the algorithm had an empty initial case base and no background knowledge about object types, it was able to detect novel object types and use them to classify subsequent images. One important finding of these experiments was that the algorithm appeared to learn finer-grained object types than those provided by the human dataset annotators, based on an initial qualitative analysis.

Several areas of future work remain. First, while we briefly discussed how our approach could be used in parallel with a full CNN (i.e., including fully-connected layers), we have not provided a full methodology to integrate them. In this paper, we focused on learning without an existing dataset, so it would not be possible to train a CNN in such a situation. However, if a subset of existing object types are known and have sufficient data, a full CNN could be used to classify those known types while our approach could handle novel object type detection. Second, our approach learns a flat object type hierarchy. Future work will examine how novel object types can be compared to existing types to determine relationships (e.g., a *fully-grown plant* is similar to a *seedling plant*) or to provide explanations (e.g., "*I think this is different than a fully-grown plant because it doesn't have any leaves*"). Third, we used ground truth parts information, but future work will detect both parts and object types. Finally, we plan to integrate our work with existing R-CNN architectures to allow learning with images containing multiple annotated objects.

Acknowledgements. Thanks to the Office of Naval Research for supporting this work.

References

1. Krizhevsky, A., Sutskever, I., Hinton, G.E.: ImageNet classification with deep convolutional neural networks. In: Proceedings of the 26th Annual Conference on Neural Information Processing Systems, pp. 1106–1114, Lake Tahoe, USA (2012)
2. Girshick, R.B., Donahue, J., Darrell, T., Malik, J.: Rich feature hierarchies for accurate object detection and semantic segmentation. In: Proceedings of the IEEE Conference on Computer Vision and Pattern Recognition, pp. 580–587. IEEE Computer Society, Columbus (2014)
3. Chen, X., Mottaghi, R., Liu, X., Fidler, S., Urtasun, R., Yuille, A.: Detect what you can: Detecting and representing objects using holistic models and body parts. In: Proceedings of the IEEE Conference on Computer Vision and Pattern Recognition, pp. 1979–1986. IEEE Computer Society, Columbus (2014)
4. He, K., Zhang, X., Ren, S., Sun, J.: Deep residual learning for image recognition. In: Proceedings of the IEEE Conference on Computer Vision and Pattern Recognition, pp. 770–778. IEEE Computer Society, Las Vegas (2016)
5. Russakovsky, O., et al.: ImageNet large scale visual recognition challenge. Int. J. Comput. Vis. **115**(3), 211–252 (2015)
6. Sani, S., Wiratunga, N., Massie, S.: Learning deep features for kNN-based Human Activity Recognition. In: Proceedings of the International Conference on Case-Based Reasoning Workshops, pp. 95–103. CEUR Workshop Proceedings, Trondheim (2017)
7. Sani, S., Wiratunga, N., Massie, S., Cooper, K.: kNN sampling for personalised human activity recognition. In: Aha, D.W., Lieber, J. (eds.) ICCBR 2017. LNCS (LNAI), vol. 10339, pp. 330–344. Springer, Cham (2017). https://doi.org/10.1007/978-3-319-61030-6_23
8. Martin, K., Wiratunga, N., Sani, S., Massie, S., Clos, J.: A Convolutional siamese network for developing similarity knowledge in the SelfBACK dataset. In: Proceedings of the International Conference on Case-Based Reasoning Workshops, pp. 85–94. CEUR Workshop Proceedings, Trondheim (2017)
9. Grace, K., Maher, M.L., Wilson, D.C., Najjar, N.A.: Combining CBR and deep learning to generate surprising recipe designs. In: Goel, A., Díaz-Agudo, M.B., Roth-Berghofer, T. (eds.) ICCBR 2016. LNCS (LNAI), vol. 9969, pp. 154–169. Springer, Cham (2016). https://doi.org/10.1007/978-3-319-47096-2_11
10. Perner, P., Holt, A., Richter, M.: Image processing in case-based reasoning. Knowledge Engineering Review **20**(3), 311–314 (2005)
11. Macura, R.T., Macura, K.J.: *MacRad*: Radiology image resource with a case-based retrieval system. In: Veloso, M., Aamodt, A. (eds.) ICCBR 1995. LNCS, vol. 1010, pp. 43–54. Springer, Heidelberg (1995). https://doi.org/10.1007/3-540-60598-3_5
12. Haddad, M., Adlassnig, K.-P., Porenta, G.: Feasibility analysis of a case-based reasoning system for automated detection of coronary heart disease from myocardial scintigrams. Artif. Intell. Med. **9**(1), 61–78 (1997)
13. Allampalli-Nagaraj, G., Bichindaritz, I.: Automatic semantic indexing of medical images using a web ontology language for case-based image retrieval. Eng. Appl. Artif. Intell. **22**(1), 18–25 (2009)
14. Perner, P., Bühring, A.: Case-based object recognition. In: Funk, P., González Calero, P.A. (eds.) ECCBR 2004. LNCS (LNAI), vol. 3155, pp. 375–388. Springer, Heidelberg (2004). https://doi.org/10.1007/978-3-540-28631-8_28
15. Micarelli, A., Neri, A., Sansonetti, G.: A case-based approach to image recognition. In: Blanzieri, E., Portinale, L. (eds.) EWCBR 2000. LNCS, vol. 1898, pp. 443–454. Springer, Heidelberg (2000). https://doi.org/10.1007/3-540-44527-7_38

16. López-Sánchez, D., Corchado, J.M., González Arrieta, A.: A CBR system for efficient face recognition under partial occlusion. In: Aha, D.W., Lieber, J. (eds.) ICCBR 2017. LNCS (LNAI), vol. 10339, pp. 170–184. Springer, Cham (2017). https://doi.org/10.1007/978-3-319-61030-6_12

17. López-Sánchez, D., Corchado, J.M., González Arrieta, A.: A CBR system for image-based webpage classification: case representation with convolutional neural networks. In: Proceedings of the Thirtieth International Florida Artificial Intelligence Research Society Conference, pp. 483–488. AAAI Press, Marco Island (2017)

18. Tuytelaars, T., Lampert, C.H., Blaschko, M.B., Buntine, W.L.: Unsupervised object discovery: a comparison. Int. J. Comput. Vis. **88**(2), 284–302 (2010)

19. Zhu, J.-Y., Wu, J., Xu, Y., Chang, E., Tu, Z.: Unsupervised object class discovery via saliency-guided multiple class learning. IEEE Trans. Pattern Anal. Mach. Intell. **37**(4), 862–875 (2015)

20. Chen, X., Shrivastava, A., Gupta, A.: Enriching visual knowledge bases via object discovery and segmentation. In: Proceedings of the IEEE Conference on Computer Vision and Pattern Recognition, pp. 2035–2042. IEEE Computer Society, Columbus (2014)

21. MacQueen, J.: Some methods for classification and analysis of multivariate observations. In: Proceedings of the 5th Berkeley Symposium on Mathematical Statistics and Probability, pp. 281–297 (1967)

22. Hartigan, J.A.: Clustering Algorithms. Wiley, New York (1975)

23. Aaron, B., Tamir, D.E., Rishe, N.D., and Kandel, A.: Dynamic incremental k-means clustering. In: Proceedings of the International Conference on Computational Science and Computational Intelligence, pp. 308–313. IEEE Press, Las Vegas (2014)

Modelling Similarity for Comparing Physical Activity Profiles - A Data-Driven Approach

Deepika Verma[1]([✉]), Kerstin Bach[1], and Paul Jarle Mork[2]

[1] Department of Computer Science,
Norwegian University of Science and Technology, Trondheim, Norway
deepika.verma@ntnu.no
[2] Department of Public Health and Nursing,
Norwegian University of Science and Technology, Trondheim, Norway
http://www.idi.ntnu.no, http://www.ntnu.no/ism

Abstract. Objective measurements of physical behaviour are an interesting research field from the public health and computer science perspective. While for public health research, measurements with a high quality and feasible setup is important, the analysis of and reasoning about the data is what we will present in this work. Our focus in this work is the comprehensive representation of physical behaviour throughout consecutive days and allowing to find subgroups in the population with similar physical activity levels.

We have a unique data set of 4628 participants wearing tri-axial accelerometers for six days and will present a case-based reasoning (CBR) system that can find and compare similar activity profiles. In this work, we focus on creating a CBR model using myCBR and do initial experiments with the resulting system. We will introduce a data-driven approach for modelling local similarity measures. Eventually, in the experiments we will show that for the given data set, the CBR system outperforms a k-Nearest Neighbor regressor in finding most similar participants.

Keywords: Physical activity · Case-based reasoning
Local similarity modelling · k-Nearest Neighbor

1 Introduction

Physical inactivity and poor sleep are considered global health problems [16,25] that contribute substantially to poor health and premature mortality. It is estimated that physical inactivity is responsible for about 9% premature mortality [19], which is similar to the effect of smoking [31] and obesity [1].

CBR has become more popular over the last few years, especially in an area where continuous measurements become more and more available [9,23]. It offers a way for abstracting and transferring specific domain expert knowledge into a self-explanatory and user-friendly tool, which can be used to generate solutions

© Springer Nature Switzerland AG 2018
M. T. Cox et al. (Eds.): ICCBR 2018, LNAI 11156, pp. 415–430, 2018.
https://doi.org/10.1007/978-3-030-01081-2_28

for problems ranging from simple daily life tasks to complex issues (which otherwise necessitate expert help), with an appropriate reasoning behind them. Not only is it being applied for finding similar cases to provide solutions, but also for the classification of medical [8,33] and activity data [30]. In [30], the authors propose a CBR method to classify different physical activities of elderly based on their pulse rate.

In this paper, we focus on the knowledge engineering process of creating a CBR model and present a data-driven approach for modelling local similarity measures for physical activity data in the myCBR workbench [5,29]. We will show in our experiments that a CBR system comparing physical activity profiles is less erroneous than a k-Nearest Neighbour (k-NN) regressor model. In our experiments, both approaches are used to find groups of similar activity profiles and their performance is evaluated statistically. The second contribution of this paper is a method for modelling the local similarity measures utilizing data driven methods. We will showcase how a data set can lead to strong initial definitions for numerical value ranges and therewith easen and stratify the knowledge modelling process.

The remaining of this paper is divided into sections as follows: in Sect. 2, we discuss related work on reasoning about physical activity behaviour using various approaches within machine learning and artificial intelligence. In Sect. 3, we discuss the importance of objective measurements of physical activity behaviour from both public health and computer science perspective. Section 4 is dedicated to similarity modelling for the data set in myCBR. In Sect. 5, we present the experiments performed to evaluate the CBR model generated and compare it with that of k-NN model. Sections 6 and 7 are for discussion and conclusion respectively.

2   Related Work

The amalgamation of sensors, Internet of Things (IoT) and Artificial Intelligence (AI) provides a unique opportunity not only for health researchers, but also for AI researchers to perform objective measurements and utilize raw data recordings to generate physical activity profiles of a large number of participants and determine similar physical activity profile groups. With the help of AI techniques, it is possible to perform objective analysis of sensor data stream to not only identify different physical activities uniquely [4,7,32], but also find out groups of similar activity profiles. Finding and clustering similar physical activity profiles is crucial in facilitating the understanding of health and activity characteristics of a population and identifying different activity phenotypes[1]. In [21], the author proposed an ATLAS index to cluster and identify four activity phenotypes using NHANES[2] data set. Similarly, in [32], authors proposed a statistical machine learning model to identify different sleep and physical activity phenotypes. Further, the authors in [13] apply latent class analysis to identify

---

[1] https://www.biology-online.org/dictionary/Phenotype.

[2] https://wwwn.cdc.gov/nchs/nhanes/default.aspx.

five different activity phenotypes among young adults in a cohort study where data was collected using hip-worn accelerometers for seven days. Our long term goals and target data are similar to these studies, however the approach differs slightly.

Similar to the preference-based CBR framework presented by Hüllermeier and Schlegel [14], we are presenting a framework for modelling local similarity measures based on the data set available. Therewith we can tailor each similarity measure to the application domain. In the continuation of their work Abdel-Aziz, Strickert and Hüllermeier [2] show that the data distributions and distances in data sets can be used for learning similarity measures. While the authors focus on learning preferences, we show with the work presented here that the data-driven view can be carried over to general knowledge engineering tasks. Using a data-driven approach for automatic similarity learning and feature weighting has been presented by Gabel and Godehardt [11]. In their work they trained a neural network to induce local and global similarity measures. While we are not automatically assigning the similarity measures, we also use existing cases to derive them. In [28], the authors explore a case-based approach for recommending 5 km times for marathon runners in order to achieve their personal best. The approach they apply is similar to the one presented in this paper as they use timing profiles as basis for the similarity-based assessment. In a slightly different approach, Sani et al. [27] explore using k-NN for detecting physical activities from wrist worn sensors. In their work they show that applying k-NN for detecting movement patterns is very successful for creating personalized models. Even though the approaches differ, our work is similar in terms of comparing physical activity profiles with raw data coming for accelerometers.

3   Physical Activity Analysis for Public Health Application Scenarios

Regular physical activity is important for people of all age groups, including the elderly. It can significantly reduce the risk of various health problems such as stroke, diabetes, various types of cancer, depression, as well as hypertension and improve bone and muscle health[3]. Physical inactivity is one of the most important public health problems of this century and has a strong negative impact on the physical and mental well being of an individual. It is estimated that about 23% adults and 81% adolescents globally are physically inactive. The figures are alarmingly high for adolescents. Moreover, being physically active is not just about moving around in the house or walking at a slow pace, they must include some form of Moderate to Vigorous Physical Activity (MVPA) such as brisk walking, dancing, running, cycling, or moving/lifting heavy load.

Over the last few years, researchers in public health domain have moved rapidly from using self-reported subjective activity data to objectively measured activity data with the use of body-worn sensors [4,18,20]. Not only are the sensors a more viable option due to the simplicity of extracting and utilizing raw

---

[3] http://who.int/features/factfiles/physical_activity/en/.

data, but also eliminate the problem of bias due to self reporting [17,24], which has been a major concern among researchers as it leads to inaccuracy and uncertainty. Moreover, the accelerometers directly measure the subject's physiology motion status to indicate the motion pattern within a given time period, which is helpful in activity recognition and are much more energy efficient.

The physical activity data used for this work is primarily based on accelerometer data collected during the HUNT4[4]cohort study. The Nørd-Trøndelag Health Study (HUNT)[5] in Norway is one of the largest health studies of its kind. The study consists of a large amount of health data collected through questionnaires and clinical examinations during three intensive previous studies (HUNT1 1984-86, HUNT2 1995-97 and HUNT3 2006-08). In the ongoing study HUNT4 (2017-19), each participant is offered to participate in the objective measurements data collection. If accepted, they are fitted with two wearable tri-axial accelerometers, placed at their thigh and lower back, which are used to collect activity data for one week. The raw sensor data is then classified into 17 different physical activities using Support Vector Machines (for the synchronization of sensor data) and Random forest classifiers (for the prediction of activity classes). Afterwards, these activities are grouped into six main physical activities: lying, sitting, standing, walking, running, cycling, which is the basis data set for our work[6].

By determining the variation among participants in different activity clusters through similarity, it is possible to provide activity recommendations to less active profiles in order to make them more active. Every person has different activity characteristics and finding a group of activity profiles most similar to that person with respect to the duration of every activity is a challenging task and we aim to address this task using Case-Based Reasoning (CBR), because it offers the flexibility and transparency in its reasoning process.

4   Data-Driven Knowledge Modelling

In this section, we explain how we implement a CBR system that can be applied to find and compare similar activity profiles from objectively measured population data. We are using the local-global-principle [26] for creating similarity measures and thereby build a knowledge model that tailors the similarity measure for each attribute. Once the local similarity measures are defined, we continue to use weighted sum for defining the global similarity.

While the HUNT4 data set is unique in the world, the challenges for utilizing it for developing a CBR system are very common such as the identification of suitable data set context for the problem at hand, definition of initial similarity measures, representation of cases and determination of valuable cases for populating the casebase. In this work we will introduce a method for utilizing a given data set to model similarity measures. Further we will take into account the

---

[4] https://www.ntnu.no/hunt4/.

[5] https://www.ntnu.no/hunt/.

[6] Since the study is ongoing, we have used the data available by March, 12 2018.

effect of growing casebases and show a methodology that can help to visualize and understand how a CBR system learns.

This section is further divided into subsections as follows: First, we describe how we populate the casebase and generate cases in the developed case representation. Second, we describe our data-driven approach to model the local similarity measures for the numerical activity attributes. Once the model is in place, we then query the casebase and compare the most similar activity profiles retrieved.

4.1 Case Generation

Developing a case representation is the first part of the system development. Depending on the domain and the available data this can be a challenging process on its own [6,12,15]. For our application domain we utilize the pre-processed HUNT4 data. While HUNT4 collects a very comprehensive set of data, we are only focusing on the objective measurements. The sensor data is collected over a period of seven days per participant and the overall data collection in the cohort stretches over 18 months, starting from the autumn of 2017 until February 2019. It is an ongoing study and until March 2018, data for 17409 participants has been automatically classified and for each participant aggregated into the six main physical activities. In Table 1 we present the description of the six activity types used in our data set.

Table 1. Activity descriptions

Activity	Description
Lying	The person lies down
Sitting	When the person's buttocks is on the seat of the chair, bed or floor
Standing	Upright, feet supporting the person's body weigh
Walking	Locomotion towards a destination with one stride or more
Running	Locomotion towards a destination, with at least two steps where both feet leave the ground during each stride
Cycling	The person is riding bicycle

Each participant is fitted with two tri-axial accelerometers, AX3 Axivity[7], one on the thigh and second on lower back. The sensors are used to detect vibrations, movement and orientation changes in the three axes. The sampling frequency of the sensors is set at 50 Hz. After the participant has worn the sensors for seven days, they are returned to the HUNT research center where the raw data is downloaded, extracted and classified using Support Vector Machines and Random Forest algorithms. The resulting data set contains the H4ID (unique

---

[7] https://axivity.com/downloads/ax3.

ID for each HUNT4 participant), number of minutes of each different activity, the date and day of the week in a csv file.

When preparing the data for the CBR system, we further process it by removing the records where we assume the sensor was taken off or the prediction failed. Those are very long times of the same activities. Records are removed based on the following criteria:

- sum of all the activities for a single record exceeds 1440, which is the total minutes in a day
- records containing zero minutes for lying, sitting, standing and walking
- data set for one participant has less than seven days of data

Eventually, we chose to keep records where exactly six days of data per H4ID was present, while the rest of the records were removed. For each unique H4ID, the total minutes of each activity were summed up for six days. We experimented with different knowledge representations including mean, maximum and sum of duration of each activity per H4ID and found the sum representation to suit best since it captures the overall physical behaviour of the participants over the days as well as the variance of the similarity measure over its' entire range. At this point, after pre-processing, the data set contains 4628 rows, each record containing sum of each activity over six days for a single participant. Table 2 gives a brief account of the data set.

Table 2. Data set statistics

	Lying	Sitting	Standing	Walking	Running	Cycling
count	4628	4628	4628	4628	4628	4628
mean	3090.49	3322.82	1401.22	790.67	6.86	26.45
min	7.35	253.25	56.50	1.55	0	0
max	7513.80	7846.10	4247.10	2101.65	172.70	719.10

Cases are populated from the previously described data set by loading into the previously defined case representation using the myCBR tool. A single case in myCBR is represented as shown in Fig. 1, where *Participant* is the name of the concept which consists of six attributes namely *cycling, lying, running, sitting, standing and walking.*

4.2 Data-Driven Similarity Measures Development

The local-global-principle requires that both types of similarity measures, the local one on the attribute level and the global one on the conceptual need to be defined.

Modelling the local similarity measures for different attributes in myCBR can be challenging as researchers have to balance the input from the domain

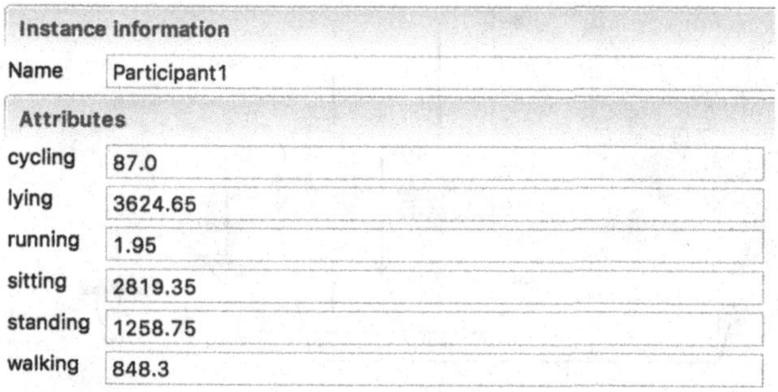

Instance information	
Name	Participant1
Attributes	
cycling	87.0
lying	3624.65
running	1.95
sitting	2819.35
standing	1258.75
walking	848.3

Fig. 1. Case representation in myCBR

experts and the available data. Having criteria which can lead the knowledge modelling process is helpful for both parties. We therefore suggest to make use of the existing data in this process. As we assume that the collected data set covers the scope of what type of problems (cases) we have seen before, this is a useful departure point. In the following, we would have a reality check with the domain experts that discusses whether the defined value ranges cover the domain well. While setting upper and lower limits is straight forward, assigning the similarity behaviour is not. Consecutively, we assume that numerical local similarity measures are distance functions and the question is how steep of a similarity decline should be chosen. We use polynomial functions to model similarity measure since they are more flexible and provide better convergence when using continuous numerical data. Therefore, we will focus on the polynomial function of the similarity measure and our goal is to determine their degree.

Taken this task in our application domain, we see an activity variation among different profiles, but also in the aggregation of activities over all profiles. We use box plots for visualizing the distributions and variations in our data set and transfer this into modelling local similarity measures.

Figure 2 shows an example of a numerical local similarity measure. In the example, it is the total amount of sitting during six days. From there we look into the Q_1 and Q_3 which indicated the majority spread for the data set. We decided to take these values as reference points for determining the decrease of similarity.

Hence, creating a box-plot of the data set will allow modelling each activity attribute since we only take the Inter Quartile Range (IQR) and the range (min to max) into account:

$$r_1 = IQR$$
$$r_2 = range$$

(1)

It represents the difference between upper (Q_3) and lower (Q_1) quartiles in the box-plot, that is $IQR = Q_3 - Q_1$.

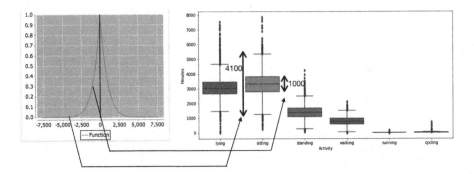

Fig. 2. Example for Data-driven Local Similarity Modelling: On the left there is a screen shot of a polynomial similarity function for a value range between 0 and 7500. With the arrows we depict how the box-plot for sitting relates to the decrease of similarity at a certain distance. $IQR * 1.5$ method has been used for the box plots.

We assume that all similarity functions are polynomial and adjust the polynomial degree of the similarity function such that

$$y(r_1) \approx 0.30$$
$$y(r_2) \approx 0 \tag{2}$$

We can observe in Fig. 2 how the similarity function varies after applying the methodology in Eqs. 1 and 2. The bigger the polynomial degree, the steeper the similarity function and more precise the attribute values in retrieved cases. The decline in the similarity function is steeper in the beginning until at r_1 it reaches close to $y(r_1)$ and then decreases gradually until at r_2 it is approximately close to $y(r_2)$. This way, the similarity function covers the entire attribute range as well as the similarity measure range [0,1]. While the choice of $y(r_1)$ and $y(r_2)$ depends on the domain-expert's knowledge and satisfaction with the outcome, we however experimented with different values and found these best suited for our application domain. We use this as the initial definition of similarity measures. If required, the function can of course be further customized if the relevant domain knowledge is available.

4.3   Comparing Physical Activity Profiles

Once the casebase and similarity measures are in place, the model can be used to find similar profiles. Figure 3 shows the result of one such query retrieval in myCBR. The figure shows that the retrieved cases are sorted by similarity value in descending order, that is, most similar case are displayed at the top while least similar are at the bottom. On the lower part of the screen shot the four most similar profiles are shown in a detailed view. The tool marks closer matches darker.

While the myCBR workbench indicates that we can do a similarity-based retrieval, it is hard to judge how the CBR system works with increasing casebase

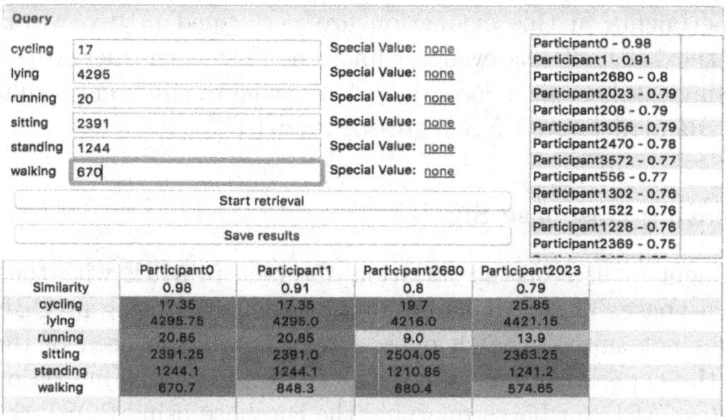

Fig. 3. A Query and its retrieval result in the myCBR workbench

or changing similarity measures. In the next section we will investigate how the casebase size and different retrieval methods perform in our application domain.

5 Evaluation of Increasing Casebase Sizes and Retrieval Methods

A performance evaluation of the CBR model has been conducted using holdout-repeat cross-validation in which 200 random cases were held out to be used for testing. Therewith for each run our casebase consisted of 4428 cases. A test set, comprising of ten randomly selected cases from the held out set of 200 cases, represents a single epoch in the experiments and performance is reported using Mean Relative Error (MRE) as a measure of precision. Each experiment is repeated five times and the results are averaged over all the epochs.

For each query instance q_i in the test set, the number of similar cases retrieved r from the casebase is 20. The relative error of each activity is the computed between q_i and r for one case at a time. The errors are averaged to obtain MRE of each activity for q_i. The process is repeated for every q_i in the test set, that is, for $i = [1, 10]$.

The MRE of the six activities are added to get the total relative error for each q_i. MRE is then calculated by averaging the relative errors for the entire queried test set.

The total relative error T for each queried instance is calculated as:

$$T = \sum_{i=1}^{6} MRE(A_i)$$

where A is the activity type as they were introduced in Sect. 4.1. MRE for the each test set is calculated as:

$$MRE = \frac{\sum_{i=1}^{10} T_i}{10}$$

The experiments in this evaluation are performed in two ways: First, by calculating the MRE of retrieved instances against each queried test instance with increasing casebase size. Second, by comparing the different results obtained using the CBR model and k-NN regressor model.

5.1   Increasing Casebase Size

This experiment focuses on the variation observed in MRE with the increasing size of the casebase. The CBR model was implemented using myCBR, however the tool does not support batch queries, which was the need of the hour for conducting the experiments for our work. To overcome this limitation, we used a myCBR Rest API[8] for batch querying the casebase using POST calls and the implementation was done in Python (version 3.6.3).

In this experiment, a test set is passed as a query using POST call when the casebase initially has 500 instances. Subsequently, MRE for that test set is calculated. 500 cases are then added to the casebase and the process is repeated until the casebase consists of the entire data set. The experiment is repeated five times, each with a different random test set. The average MRE of all the epochs for the given casebase size is shown in Fig. 4.

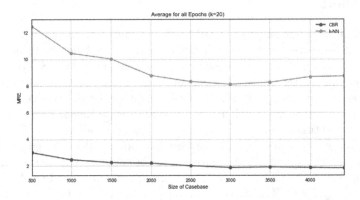

Fig. 4. MRE comparison between the CBR model and k-NN regressor model with increasing casebase sizes (MRE is calculated for $k = 20$ retrieved cases)

In order to have a comparison of the performance of the CBR model, the same experiment was conducted using k-NN regression model (with $k = 20$). The implementation of the k-NN regressor was done using Scikit learn [22] library (version 0.19.1) in Python (version 3.6.3). The results obtained with the k-NN model are presented along with the results of the CBR model in Fig. 4, where x-axis shows the size of the casebase (or size of data set for k-NN) and y-axis shows the MRE averaged over five epochs.

---

[8] https://github.com/kerstinbach/mycbr-rest-example.

It can be observed from the results that MRE decreases steadily with increase in size of the casebase in the CBR implementation. However, the same cannot be said for k-NN, as the results show uncertain response to the increase in size of the data set. Even after introducing the entire data set, no improvement is observed. This decline in performance in k-NN is caused by the presence of outliers in the test set. CBR is able to estimate closest similar cases with respect to every activity for outliers very well, whereas k-NN cannot estimate the nearest neighbors with respect to every activity when presented with outliers. For instance, if there is an instance in the test set which has some or all attributes with values either below 25% or above 75% of the data range for those attributes in the data set, it leads to the k-NN algorithm computing nearest neighbors which are closer to the non-outlier attributes but farther from the outlier attributes. Thus, resulting in higher MRE even with an increased size of the data set.

5.2 Selection of k

Selecting an appropriate value of k is crucial in determining the success or failure of a k-NN regressor model. To see how the error varies, we experimented with different values of k in the range [3,100]. Figure 5(b) shows the variation in MRE with the change in value of k. Here, x-axis shows the value of k and y-axis shows the MRE.

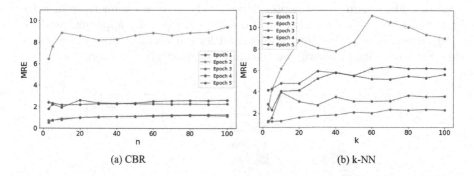

(a) CBR   (b) k-NN

Fig. 5. Number of closest cases: On the left is the graph depicting the variation in MRE with the number of most similar cases retrieved (n) in CBR implementation. On the right is the graph for k-NN model depicting the variation in MRE with different values of k.

Although the determination of the closest similar profile in the CBR model is independent of n (number of retrieved cases), it is interesting to see how the MRE changes by varying n progressively. This allows us to further compare and contrast the performance of CBR model with that of k-NN model. Figure 5(a) shows the variation of MRE with increasing value of n in myCBR, where the x-axis shows the value of n and y-axis shows the MRE. It is clear from the results that the value of k in k-NN (refer Fig. 5(b)) has a huge impact on the

MRE for each epoch. The implication of this graph is that with an increase in k, more neighboring cases are taken into consideration which are either less similar altogether or less similar with respect to a subset of activities, resulting in the sudden variation in errors. Whereas the CBR model has a relatively smoother response in creating the number of retrieved similar cases. It can be argued from the results that lower values of k would have been more suitable due to less MRE. However, our aim in this work is not to predict using k-NN, but to find a number of nearest neighbors of the queried profile, which is why we chose $k = 20$ for our experiments. As our data set is large, $k = 20$ is reasonably acceptable for this application domain. Also, from CBR perspective, considering more neighboring profiles helps in making improvements to the similarity measure to a greater extent than considering just one neighbor profile.

5.3   Composition of Error

As we are using activity data to find other similar profiles, it is important to know the error observed in the approximation of each activity in the similar profiles.

Figure 6 shows the MRE (in log) for each activity using both the approaches when introduced with the entire data set. The figure underlines that for inactive time (lying, sitting, standing) - which is the majority for the participants (see Table 2 and Fig. 2) - the k-NN approach produces less of an error. For moderate activities, like walking, both approaches are very close, while for rigorous activities, which we see only limited in the data set, the CBR approach produces much better results. This is very important for our overall aim of this work, as we eventually want to identify beneficial physical activity phenotypes.

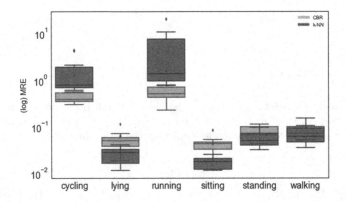

Fig. 6. MRE per activity for the entire data set by the k-NN regressor and the CBR model

This observation is undermined by Fig. 7, which shows the distribution of MRE for each of the activity calculated for both approaches after introducing the entire data set. It can be observed that in both k-NN and CBR, most of the error is attributed to the approximation of activity *running* (approx. 79% and 51% respectively). On the other hand, it is far lower in CBR, the result of which is relatively higher error composition of other activities as compared to those in k-NN. However, since these are compositional parts and convey only relative information, rather than concrete information, we must take into consideration the actual MRE, refer to Fig. 4, which is significantly lower in case of CBR.

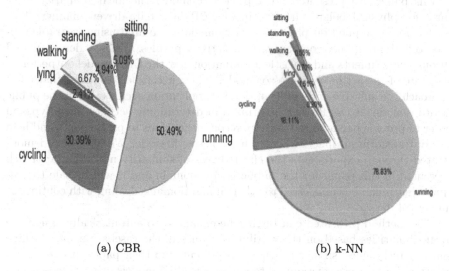

      (a) CBR   (b) k-NN

Fig. 7. Error Composition for the CBR (a) and k-NN (b) model

6   Discussion

The experimental results shown in Fig. 4 demonstrate that the CBR model performs well in finding similar physical activity profiles. While k-NN is able to well approximate four out of six physical activities when finding the nearest neighbours, however it fails miserably in finding with respect to the other two activities, which results in higher MRE. On the other hand, the CBR model is able to determine the most similar physical activity profiles with respect to every activity more closely, resulting in far lower MRE as compared to the k-NN model. Furthermore, k-NN is susceptible to outliers, which is the cause of increase in MRE even after introducing the entire data set. Whereas this is not an issue with the CBR model. In Fig. 5 we observe very minor increase in MRE with increasing number of retrieved instances using CBR model, whereas the variations are more pronounced when using the k-NN model. These experiments demonstrate that the similarity modelling approach presented is working successfully for our application domain. Consequently, the CBR model significantly outperforms the k-NN algorithm and is more robust in finding similar physical activity profiles in a population. CBR approach can be applied to find and cluster similar activity groups, which will further be helpful in determining activity phenotypes.

7 Conclusion and Future Work

In this paper, we presented an approach to model the local similarity measures for physical behaviour data in myCBR in a data-driven manner. This model can be applied on physical behaviour data acquired using wearable sensors to find, group and compare similar activity profiles. We have demonstrated through experiments and statistical evaluation how the CBR model outperforms the state-of-the-art k-NN regressor model. Thus, it can be concluded that CBR approach is a suitable and viable option for application such as this in the public health domain. It can further be utilized in determining activity phenotypes in order to provide personalized activity recommendations to participants and help slowly transform an inactive into a more active lifestyle. We have also demonstrated through experiments the effectiveness of similarity modelling approach presented in this paper for the public health domain and it will be safe to conclude that it can be transferred to other similar domains dealing with continuous numerical data.

The method presented can further be enhanced to automatically assign the local similarities based on the attributes' values in the casebase using machine learning techniques, similar to what [11] presented in their paper. It can significantly reduce the efforts required to create new CBR models using different data sets from scratch.

In the future, we aim to extend our research towards compositional data analysis [3] on the HUNT4 data and applying CBR on the resulting compositional data. Compositional data analysis has been applied by researchers [10] for estimating the effect of change in physical activity behaviour for daily activities. Whether a change in one type of behaviour is beneficial or harmful for health depends on the compensatory shifts in other behaviours. The compositional nature of the HUNT4 data has therefore important consequences for both the analytical approach undertaken and interpretation of effects on health outcomes. Utilizing CBR for compositional data analysis will facilitate (i) getting insights into the behavioural characteristics between similar profiles in a population, (ii) understanding the association and co-dependency among various behaviours in different profiles, and (iii) identifying physical behaviour phenotypes.

References

1. A, A., MH, F., MB, R.: Health effects of overweight and obesity in 195 countries over 25 years. New England Journal of Medicine 377(1), 13–27 (2017), pMID: 28604169

2. Abdel-Aziz, A., Strickert, M., Hüllermeier, E.: Learning solution similarity in preference-based CBR. In: Lamontagne, L., Plaza, E. (eds.) ICCBR 2014. LNCS (LNAI), vol. 8765, pp. 17–31. Springer, Cham (2014). https://doi.org/10.1007/978-3-319-11209-1_3

3. Aitchison, J., Egozcue, J.J.: Compositional data analysis: where are we and where should we be heading? Math. Geol. **37**(7), 829–850 (2005)

4. Arif, M., Kattan, A.: Physical activities monitoring using wearable acceleration sensors attached to the body. PLOS ONE **10**(7), 1–16 (2015)

5. Bach, K., Althoff, K.-D.: Developing case-based reasoning applications using myCBR 3. In: Agudo, B.D., Watson, I. (eds.) ICCBR 2012. LNCS (LNAI), vol. 7466, pp. 17–31. Springer, Heidelberg (2012). https://doi.org/10.1007/978-3-642-32986-9_4

6. Bergmann, R., Kolodner, J., Plaza, E.: Representation in case-based reasoning. Knowl. Eng. Rev. **20**(03), 209 (2005)

7. Bulling, A., Blanke, U., Schiele, B.: A tutorial on human activity recognition using body-worn inertial sensors. ACM Comput. Surv. **46**(3), 1–33 (2014)

8. Campillo-Gimenez, B., Jouini, W., Bayat, S., Cuggia, M.: Improving case-based reasoning systems by combining k-nearest neighbour algorithm with logistic regression in the prediction of patients' registration on the renal transplant waiting list. PLoS ONE **8**(9), e71991 (2013)

9. Canensi, L., Leonardi, G., Montani, S., Terenziani, P.: Multi-level interactive medical process mining. In: ten Teije, A., Popow, C., Holmes, J.H., Sacchi, L. (eds.) AIME 2017. LNCS (LNAI), vol. 10259, pp. 256–260. Springer, Cham (2017). https://doi.org/10.1007/978-3-319-59758-4_28

10. Dumuid, D., et al.: The compositional isotemporal substitution model: a method for estimating changes in a health outcome for reallocation of time between sleep, physical activity and sedentary behaviour. Stat. Methods Med. Res. (2017)

11. Gabel, T., Godehardt, E.: Top-down induction of similarity measures using similarity clouds. In: Hüllermeier, E., Minor, M. (eds.) ICCBR 2015. LNCS (LNAI), vol. 9343, pp. 149–164. Springer, Cham (2015). https://doi.org/10.1007/978-3-319-24586-7_11

12. El-Sappagh, H., El-Sappagh, S., Elmogy, M.: Case representation and indexing. In: Foundations of Soft Case-Based Reasoning, pp. 34–74 (2004)

13. Howie, E.K., Smith, A.L., Mcveigh, J.A., Straker, L.M.: Accelerometer-derived activity phenotypes in young adults: a latent class analysis. Int. J. Behav. Med. (2018)

14. Hüllermeier, E., Schlegel, P.: Preference-based CBR: first steps toward a methodological framework. In: Ram, A., Wiratunga, N. (eds.) ICCBR 2011. LNCS (LNAI), vol. 6880, pp. 77–91. Springer, Heidelberg (2011). https://doi.org/10.1007/978-3-642-23291-6_8

15. Khamparia, A., Pandey, B.: A novel method of case representation and retrieval in CBR for e-learning. Educ. Inf. Technol. **22**(1), 337–354 (2017)

16. Kohl, H.W., et al.: The pandemic of physical inactivity: global action for public health. Lancet **380**(9838), 294–305 (2012)

17. Lagersted-Olsen, J., et al.: Comparison of objectively measured and self-reported time spent sitting. Int. J. Sport. Med. **35**(06), 534–540 (2013)

18. Lee, I.M., Shiroma, E.J.: Using accelerometers to measure physical activity in large-scale epidemiological studies: issues and challenges. Br. J. Sport. Med. **48**(3), 197–201 (2013)

19. Lee, I.M., Shiroma, E.J., Lobelo, F., Puska, P., Blair, S.N., Katzmarzyk, P.T.: Effect of physical inactivity on major non-communicable diseases worldwide: an analysis of burden of disease and life expectancy. Lancet **380**(9838), 219–229 (2012)
20. Li, X.: Digital health: tracking physiomes and activity using wearable biosensors reveals useful health-related information. PLOS Biol. **15**(1), e2001402 (2017)
21. Marschollek, M.: A semi-quantitative method to denote generic physical activity phenotypes from long-term accelerometer data - the atlas index. PLoS ONE **8**(5), e63522 (2013)
22. Pedregosa, F., et al.: Scikit-learn: machine learning in Python. J. Mach. Learn. Res. **12**, 2825–2830 (2011)
23. Plis, K., Bunescu, R.C., Marling, C.R., Shubrook, J., Schwartz, F.: A machine learning approach to predicting blood glucose levels for diabetes management. In: AAAI Workshop: Modern Artificial Intelligence for Health Analytics (2014)
24. Prince, S.A., Adamo, K.B., Hamel, M., Hardt, J., Gorber, S.C., Tremblay, M.: A comparison of direct versus self-report measures for assessing physical activity in adults: a systematic review. Int. J. Behav. Nutr. Phys. Act. **5**(1), 56 (2008)
25. Raitakan, O.T., Porkka, K.V.K., Taimela, S., Telama, R., Räsänen, L., Vllkari, J.S.: Effects of persistent physical activity and inactivity on coronary risk factors in children and young adults the cardiovascular risk in young finns study. Am. J. Epidemiol. **140**(3), 195–205 (1994)
26. Richter, M.M.: The knowledge contained in similarity measures. In: Veloso, M.M., Aamodt, A. (eds.) Case-Based Reasoning Research and Development, Proceedings of the First International Conference, ICCBR 1995. LNCS, vol. 1010. Springer, Heidelberg (1995). https://doi.org/10.1007/3-540-60598-3
27. Sani, S., Wiratunga, N., Massie, S., Cooper, K.: kNN sampling for personalised human activity recognition. In: Aha, D.W., Lieber, J. (eds.) ICCBR 2017. LNCS (LNAI), vol. 10339, pp. 330–344. Springer, Cham (2017). https://doi.org/10.1007/978-3-319-61030-6_23
28. Smyth, B., Cunningham, P.: Running with cases: a CBR approach to running your best marathon. In: Aha, D.W., Lieber, J. (eds.) ICCBR 2017. LNCS (LNAI), vol. 10339, pp. 360–374. Springer, Cham (2017). https://doi.org/10.1007/978-3-319-61030-6_25
29. Stahl, A., Roth-Berghofer, T.R.: Rapid prototyping of CBR applications with the open source tool myCBR. In: Althoff, K.-D., Bergmann, R., Minor, M., Hanft, A. (eds.) ECCBR 2008. LNCS (LNAI), vol. 5239, pp. 615–629. Springer, Heidelberg (2008). https://doi.org/10.1007/978-3-540-85502-6_42
30. Uddin, M., Loutfi, A.: Physical activity identification using supervised machine learning and based on pulse rate. Int. J. Adv. Comput. Sci. Appl. **4**(7), 210–217 (2013)
31. Wen, C.P., Wu, X.: Stressing harms of physical inactivity to promote exercise. Lancet **380**(9838), 192–193 (2012)
32. Willetts, M., Hollowell, S., Aslett, L., Holmes, C., Doherty, A.: Statistical machine learning of sleep and physical activity phenotypes from sensor data in 96,220 uk biobank participants. BioRxiv (2018)
33. Yao, B., Li, S.: Anmm4cbr: a case-based reasoning method for gene expression data classification. Algorithms Mol. Biol. **5**(1), 14 (2010)

Investigating Textual Case-Based XAI

Rosina O. Weber[✉], Adam J. Johs, Jianfei Li, and Kent Huang

Information Science, Drexel University, Philadelphia, PA 19104, USA
{rw37,ajj37,jl3429,kh592}@drexel.edu

Abstract. This paper demonstrates how case-based reasoning (CBR) can be used for an explainable artificial intelligence (XAI) approach to justify solutions produced by an opaque learning method (i.e., *target method*), particularly in the context of unstructured textual data. Our general hypothesis is twofold: (1) There exists patterns in the relationship between problems and solutions and there should be data or a body of knowledge that describes how problems and solutions relate; and (2) the identification, manipulation, and learning of such patterns through case features can help create and reuse explanations for solutions produced by the target method. When the target method relies on neural network architectures (e.g., deep learning), the resulting latent space (i.e., word embeddings) becomes useful for finding patterns and semantic relatedness in textual data. In the proposed approach, case problems are input-output pairs from the target method, and case solutions are explanations. We exemplify our approach by explaining recommended citations from Citeomatic - a multi-layer neural-network architecture from the Allen Institute for Artificial Intelligence. Citation analysis is the body of knowledge that describes how query documents (i.e., inputs) relate to recommended citations (i.e., outputs). We build cases and similarity assessment to learn features that represent patterns between problems and solutions that can lead to the reuse of corresponding explanations. The illustrative implementation we present becomes an explanation-augmented citation recommender that targets human-computer trust.

Keywords: Case-Based reasoning · Textual Case-Based reasoning Explainable artificial intelligence · Semantic relatedness · Word embeddings Citation recommendation · Human-Computer trust

1 Introduction and Background

Case-based reasoning (CBR) is a suitable methodology to manage and learn from experiences, particularly amenable to generating explanations, integrating with other methods, and manipulating various sources of domain knowledge. Previous work in CBR has demonstrated multiple strategies for creating explanations [1, 2], and for dealing with textual sources [3]. The combination of said characteristics reveals the marked potential for use of CBR in producing explanations for opaque (i.e., black box) artificial intelligence (AI) methods, which is the focus of explainable AI (XAI) [4], particularly in textual contexts.

© Springer Nature Switzerland AG 2018
M. T. Cox et al. (Eds.): ICCBR 2018, LNAI 11156, pp. 431–447, 2018.
https://doi.org/10.1007/978-3-030-01081-2_29

Our work resembles that by Nugent and Cunningham [2] in being a generic case-based approach to explain solutions from black-box methods that acts as an intelligent agent and learns from observing the black-box behavior, and from its accessible data. Ours differs in that we start without a case base and focus on textual aspects. Also starting from the black-box method only (i.e., without a case base), Li et al. [5] propose to augment a deep learning classification architecture with a prototype layer and an autoencoder. The training favors prototypes that are similar to inputs. As a result, the decoder enables visualization of the prototypes that can be used as explanations for the learned classifications. This way, their method explains classifications based on how similar the prototypes are to inputs. Because an input-outcome class pair plays the role of a case problem and explanatory prototypes work as case solutions, the authors [5] describe this reasoning as case-based.

In contrast, our proposed approach separates the execution of the *target method*, i.e., the method whose solutions we want to explain, from reasoning with cases. We propose a case problem to be the input-output pair from the target method, and the case solution to be an explanation. For a given target method, designing the TCBR-XAI approach starts by considering the target method's input-output pair as the basis of each case. The first step is to identify explanation categories, which requires comprehension of the application domain and the users' goals to consider possible circumstances that would constitute anomalies and thus require explanations [6]. The second step is to extend cases with features that enable the retrieval of appropriate explanations (Fig. 1). Case extension learning seeks patterns that describe how input and output relate. The case extension module relies on external data and knowledge and can reach back to the target method for patterns. This is particularly important when the target method uses neural networks fed with textual instances, thus producing latent spaces like word embeddings that can be used to represent the behavior of words with respect to their context in the model of the data they were trained (e.g., [7]).

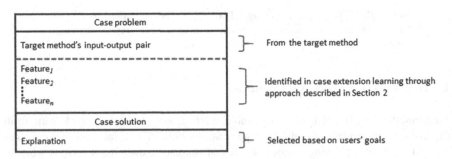

Fig. 1. Cases are designed from the target method's input-output pairs (first), explanations to meet users' goals (second), and case extension learning (third)

Once the approach is ready, operation requires an interface manager to manipulate inputs and outputs between users, target method, and the CBR module. When a user inputs a problem, it is sent to the target method, which produces an output. This input-output pair becomes the CBR new problem. The approach computes the values for extended case features and triggers Retrieve to search for the candidate case most suitable for Reuse. This retrieved case lends its classification—that is, an explanation, to the new problem that is appended to the solution presented to the user.

The value of XAI approaches has been widely illustrated. For example, [5] mentions how the Food and Drug Administration considers opaqueness of deep learning products a problem. Enabling explanations for powerful but opaque learning methods is crucial for acceptance. Hence, XAI plays a key role in the field of human-computer trust.

We illustrate the proposed approach using as target method the multi-layer neural-network architecture citation recommender - Citeomatic [8]. We conducted a study to investigate whether initially identified patterns in Citeomatic's input-output pairs can be used to learn a similarity measure that allows the reuse of explanations with reasonable accuracy.

In the illustrated application, the solution of each case is an explanation for the target method's recommended citation, aiming to justify why the user should include the recommended citation in her literature review. Citation recommendation is not typically idealized in support of literature reviews, but in combination with an explanation component, we expect to increase trust in such solutions. To the best of our knowledge, this is the first study investigating case-based explanations starting without a case base thus requiring case extension. We also believe this is the first use of explanations to make use of citation recommendation in support of conducting literature reviews.

In Sect. 2, we describe the proposed approach. Section 3 describes the use of the approach in support of literature reviews. Section 4 describes the steps of the study, results, and discussion. Section 5 discusses related works, we conclude in Sect. 6.

2 Proposed Textual Case-Based XAI Approach

This proposed method is inspired in the notion that explanations are needed when users are presented with facts that deviate from their view of the world [6]. We focus on explanations for the results of neural-network methods that typically execute some form of the classification task. Our premise is that the explanation for the discrepancy between the user's view of the world and the results of a target method can be found in the universe of relationships between the target method's input and output, including external data and knowledge that helps analyze how input and output relate.

In the proposed approach, we define a target method TM as one that processes input problems P into output solutions S. It is expected that at least P is textual. Each input-output pair P-S is the starting point of a case $c \in C$. Cases in C are represented through a sequence of attributes in A, where $A = \{P, S, F_f, E\}$, respectively, problems P and solutions S, multiple attributes F_f used to describe how input problems P and output solutions S relate, and an explanation $e \in E$, as case solution. Attributes F_f extend case description by representing relationships between TM's inputs and outputs.

The goal of this TCBR-XAI reasoner is to predict which outcome class each *P-S* pair belongs. Each explanation corresponds to a classification, i.e., to classify the class of a *P-S* relationship is how to select their corresponding explanation. This approach includes two steps described next.

2.1   Identifying Explanation Categories

The proposed case-based explanation method relies on cases that are instances of problem contexts that correspond to unique explanations. These problem contexts may fall within categories that correspond to each explanation. The source of explanations are users' goals [6] as they react to discrepancies between their expectation and the target method's solutions. Designing this case-based explanation method requires capturing users' goals and explanation categories, and matching them to create cases.

2.2   Case Extension Learning

Case extension learning refers to the identification of case features that can be used to represent relations between the target method's problem-solution pairs so they can be used to retrieve their corresponding explanations. This problem goes beyond traditional case acquisition because it requires domain knowledge and data that is external to recorded case problem-solution experiences.

The target method's *P-S* pairs and other representations produced by the target method are the main sources where to search for candidate features. Such features would represent patterns that may repeat when the same explanation applies. Multiple features may be acquired and they will be confirmed when learning from labeled instances determines their relevance. In this sense, case extension is a learning step. The requirements are the categories of explanations and *P-S* pairs labeled with their corresponding classifications associated with explanations.

Consider a system designed to prescribe workout routines where one of the explanations identified is working out in water is less strenuous to the joints. There is domain knowledge that associates this explanation with problems containing knee problems and solutions that contain swimming. Given a textual problem and solution descriptions that may discuss many other aspects, case extension learning must identify features in the P-S pairs that leads to the reuse of the explanation above. Ideally, it should include a feature that captures this knee problems-swimming relationship.

3   Explaining Citation Recommendations

The application problem we illustrate involves the use case of a user who seeks relevant works for a systematic literature review. A user who needs to conduct a literature review would expect to conduct a search and find a number of relevant papers that are humanly processable. This is not what happens in academic searches. Recent advances using neural networks and knowledge graphs have increased recall by expanding queries [9] but precision is still an issue. Works that target automation of literature reviews typically summarize relevant works based on citation sentences (e.g., [10–12]), but rely on existing academic search methods.

We interpret the vast volume of articles in response to academic search as an anomaly. Based on Leake's goals for users' explanations [6], we contend that, in the context of conducting systematic literature reviews, users need an explanation that can help them decide whether to include a specific recommended article in their literature review. Based on citation analysis, this explanation would indicate a citation category. For example, think of citations that pay homage to pioneers. Articles to be cited in that category will certainly be included in the literature review of a dissertation, but they may not necessarily be included in a small conference paper. Consequently, presenting the citation category would lead to an explanation for why a certain article is relevant, helping the user decide whether to include it.

Citation analysis [13–15] is one of the fields motivated by the concern that researchers may miss relevant related works in their reviews. Combining citation analysis and information retrieval, the field of citation recommendation (e.g., [8, 16]) proposed the crucial innovation of requiring more than just a few keywords as input. This improves the recall side of retrieval, decreasing the need for expansion. We selected Citeomatic [8] because it is the only citation recommender we found that also implements a step considering precision of retrieval is Citeomatic [8], which combines the scale of neural networks, semantic relatedness from word embeddings, pruning of less relevant works for precision, and requires at least an abstract input.

3.1   Identifying Categories

Given the preliminary nature of this work, we have not yet captured the possible spectrum of user goals when conducting literature reviews. The literature suggests categories of citations along multiple dimensions [15], including classifying them as meaningful or not [17]. Those categorizations inspired us, but none directly supported a user conducting literature reviews.

> *This publication shares important contents with your research.*
> *In my experience, this is an indispensable citation to include.*

Fig. 2. The explanation corresponding to a citation classified as *substantiation*

The citations recommended by Citeomatic achieved state of the art performance [8], so we assume they are all relevant. We adopted two categories that could lead the user to one of two goals, to include, or not include the citation. The categories are *substantiation* and *background*. A citation that falls in the *substantiation* category is more indispensable than a *background* citation. One way to interpret a *substantiation* citation is that the contents of the citing document include ideas that are discussed and potentially developed in the *substantiation* citation. An example is a citation that a reviewer suggests as missing the proper acknowledgement to the authors who contributed to an idea. In a *substantiation* citation, the citing document describes contents that appear in the recommended citation. When Citeomatic recommends a citation that our approach classifies as *substantiation*, the corresponding explanation presented to the user is in Fig. 2. Note this language is preliminary until user studies are performed.

A citation that falls in the *background* category also shares contents with the citing document (or Citeomatic would not have recommended it). The relevance of the *background* citations is marginal. Their contents are related to the citing document but the citing document does not include ideas that were developed in the *background* citation. This kind of citation may be included in extensive literature reviews that exhaustively survey a topic, but they are not indispensable. When Citeomatic recommends a citation that our approach classifies as *background*, the corresponding explanation presented to the user is in Fig. 3. These are the only two explanations offered in this implementation using Citeomatic as the target method.

> *This publication does not share substantial contents with your research. Although pertinent, its inclusion is not indispensable.*

Fig. 3. The explanation corresponding to a citation classified as *background*

3.2   Extending Cases

Extending cases for explaining recommended citations implies seeking representations that could capture the relations between query and cited paper that would justify their citation as either *substantiation* or *background*. The nature of these relations is unknown. Identifying features whose values will lead to reasonably accurate retrieval of explanations would serve both CBR and citation analysis domains. We chose to start from methods to assess semantic relatedness and descriptive features.

Table 1. Case description

Case role	Attributes	Example value	Description
Case problem	Query paper	Q05.txt	Query file name
	Cited paper	C0502.txt	Cited file name
Candidate extended features	W2V-based relatedness	0.133884853	Non-normalized value
	PVDM-based relatedness	0.027161114	
	Jaccard coefficient	0.041467305	
	Cited paper size	33,716	Number of bytes
	Publication type pair	0	Not the same type
	Citation position	2000	2nd out of 8 parts
Case solution	Classification (Explanation)	0	0 is substantiation

The list of candidate feature names, example values, and a brief description are in Table 1. These features and the methods used to obtain their values are described in the next section.

4 Experimental Design

The approach proposed in this paper is based on the premise that patterns that associate target method's inputs with outputs can be identified and used to learn a similarity measure that allows for reuse of explanations with reasonable accuracy. Accuracy in this study is given by the ratio of correct classifications to the total number of classifications, where a correct classification indicates the explanation that corresponds to the citation category.

To investigate the above premise, we start from a sample of 10 (*query*) papers. For each query paper, we select 10 papers recommended by Citeomatic. We check that those recommendations are papers that were indeed cited by the query papers, so the recommended papers we refer to as *cited* papers. The 10 query papers, plus 10 cited papers for each, amount to 110 papers. Each pair query-cited becomes a case, so there are 100 cases. For case extension learning, we label each of the 10 cited papers using the categories *substantiation* and *background*. These are the outcome classes for the cases, which correspond to one of two possible explanations. To extend cases, we identify six candidate features. We create local and global similarity functions, and run leave one out cross validation (LOOCV) to assess the average accuracy of the case base. Average accuracy, given in percentage, is the average of the case base accuracy obtained for 100 iterations when each of the cases is left out. We conduct an ablation study to assess the impact of each candidate feature in accurately classifying cases.

4.1 Data

To select the data for our study, we had some requirements. Citeomatic relies only on paper abstracts, but for analyzing the relationship between query and cited articles, we needed the full text of articles. There is evidence that an article's claims are not necessarily reported in the abstract [18], so there may be important language that is never included when only abstracts are used. The analysis we want to represent in extended case features aims to determine the citation category in which a citation in the query paper belongs. Citation analysis emphasizes that the location where a citation occurs is meaningful [15], thus we could not properly analyze citation relations with abstracts only. We needed a corpus large enough so we could try to build language models to benefit from measures of semantic relatedness. Given that Citeomatic targets computer science and neuroscience, we selected the ACL anthology network corpus [19]. We used the 2013 version, consisting of 23,594 scholarly publications in the field of computational linguistics. Most full-text papers in the ACL corpus are also in OpenCorpus[1] (openC), an important data source used in Citeomatic studies [8].

---

[1] https://github.com/allenai/citeomatic/blob/master/README.md.

To select the sample, we had to consider that based on the concepts of *substantiation* and *background* citation categories, the proportion of overlapping contents between query and cited articles may be relevant, so our data needs to cover examples when this occurs and when it does not occur so we can verify this. This led us to select at least some of the sample articles within a narrow domain of the field. The goal of 10 query articles with 10 citations was defined as the limit so humans could easily label them.

We elected the field of Sentiment Analysis to choose an initial (arbitrary) number of four widely cited seminal papers. We included only peer-reviewed workshop, conference papers, and journal articles, excluding books and presentations. We expanded this set from 4 to 100 by submitting these initial papers to Citeomatic and adding papers from recommended citations. From this pool of 100 papers, we manually selected 10 papers that had at least 10 actual citations that were both in ACL and in openC. This produced 110 papers, 10 queries and 100 cited. This is our base sample. Table 2 lists query and cited papers, their sizes and quantity.

Table 2. Volume and length of query and cited papers

Quantity	Document group	Average size in bytes
10	Whole query papers (WQ)	68,045
100	Cited papers (C)	36,044

4.2   Preprocessing

We downloaded the file with ACL papers already converted to text[2]. The quality is not ideal, there are words joined together, words with all letters repeated or separated by spaces, tables as meaningless text sequences, various unknown characters, etc.

The first step was to extract and name the files of the 10 sample articles. We could not locate five papers in the corpus likely due to their unsatisfactory quality. We resorted to manually converting those papers from PDF into text and adding them to the merged corpus. We started preprocessing with 22,396 papers, which included the 110 in the sample. The preprocessing steps were: 1. Removal of non-English words, using a library[3] that detects language and does not remove foreign language words, but removes noise. We only set the parameter *en* for English. 2. Removal of hyphens and paragraph marks so each article in the corpus is separated by one paragraph mark. Data, code, and raw results are available (See footnote 2).

4.3   Labels

Three members of our team manually labeled the 100 citations in the 10 query sample articles as either *substantiation* or *background* based on the definitions presented in the last section. We selected only one citation by query to create cases.

---

[2] https://github.com/Rosinaweber/iccbr2018.

[3] https://github.com/Mimino666/langdetect/blob/master/README.md.

4.4 Methods Used to Derive Candidate Extended Features

The two first candidate features, W2V-based relatedness [7 20] and PVDM[4]-based relatedness [21] require language models. The third feature is the Jaccard coefficient. The last three features are descriptive. We note that language models and metrics to assess semantic relatedness are not intended to assess similarity between cases, but to estimate relationships between a target method's inputs and outputs. These executions are also not meant to compare the performance of such models. For this reason, we adopted configurations and methods that seemed to be suited for the data and the techniques used, without making them uniform.

W2V-Based Relatedness. The first candidate feature computes the semantic related-ness between query and cited papers. Words that are highly semantically related are not synonyms, but they occur in the same contexts. For example, the words *natural* and *language* are highly semantically related. Word2vec (W2V) [7, 20] is a neural network that uses batches of text segments to predict the subsequent words in the text, using a corpus in a supervised fashion and benefiting from the ordering of words. W2V pro-duces a latent space of vectors with useful properties like the cosine of two word-vectors that represents how semantically related the two words are in the trained corpus. We used the cosine similarity as in Eq. 1 where the dot product of the vectors is divided by the product of their L2 norms:

$$\cos(Q, C) = \frac{Q \cdot C}{\|Q\|_2 \|C\|_2} \tag{1}$$

We used the Skip-gram version of the W2V algorithm [7] on the ACL data to obtain its language model through word embeddings for all 2,176,977 distinct vocabulary words. We removed stopwords with the English stopwords corpus from NLTK[5], points and commas. Before preprocessing, the ACL file contained approxi-mately 100 million words. The ACL raw data file size is of 611,933 KB.

We used Tensorflow[6] to run W2V with two configurations, namely, window of 5, embedding of 300, batch size 300, 100 negative samples, and 50 thousand iterations (W2V-5); and window of 21, same embeddings and negative samples, and 100 thousand iterations (W2V-21). To compute semantic relatedness between documents, we used the produced embedding vectors to represent each word in the query and cited files and computed the cosine of each pair. Lastly, we averaged the cosine of all vector pairs to estimate the semantic relatedness between query and cited files.

Another W2V configuration used was the popular pretrained model word2vec-google-news-300[7] [20] (W2V-Gnews). Because it was trained on 100 billion words and a vocabulary of 3 million words, this model is frequently used for reference. Despite the fact that this model was trained from news articles, it bears relevance due to

---

[4] PVDM stands for distributed memory model of paragraph vectors as per [21].

[5] https://www.nltk.org/data.html.

[6] https://www.tensorflow.org/.

[7] https://rare-technologies.com/new-download-api-for-pretrained-nlp-models-and-datasets-in-gensim/.

its well- validated quality. For this variant we used Gensim[8]. When using pretrained embeddings, it is faster and less prone to error to reuse supported libraries for estimating the semantic relatedness between the documents, so we used the Gensim library[9] for the word mover distance (WMD) metric [22]. WMD is a document similarity metric based on the Earth Mover's Distance transportation problem. The principle is to compute the cumulative distance that each word in a document has to *travel* [22] to match the position of the word in the document being compared. The WMD metric is computed over a word embedding space, and thus is suitable for using with pretrained word embeddings.

The last configuration of W2V used was a model trained with the openC data (W2V-openC), the same data used by Citeomatic [8]. Despite limiting the language model to abstracts only, the volume of over 39 million abstracts and the fact that this is the basis of Citeomatic makes this model appealing. The ACL raw data file size is of 9,596,523 KB. Because this data was also trained in Citeomatic with Gensim, we used the same configuration as Citeomatic: window 21, embedding 300, and 10 iterations.

PVDM-Based Relatedness. PVDM stands for the distributed memory version of the paragraph vector algorithm [21]. This algorithm attempts to combine the strengths of word vectors in paragraph vectors. The PVDM algorithm uses the same principle as W2V to predict the context of words with neural networks. It differs in that it concatenates entire paragraph vectors with word vectors to predict an output word [21].

We used the Gensim library (See footnote 6) of PVDM, also known as Doc2vec on the previously described ACL corpus. We used window 21 and embedding 300 in 5,000 iterations. To assess semantic relatedness, we again rely on a library created for this purpose, *similarity_unseen_docs*, which computes the cosine between two paragraph vectors, being one paragraph vector created for each document, i.e., query and cited.

Jaccard Coefficient. This metric takes the ratio of shared to non-shared tokens of a corpus. We used it to assess the coefficient for every query-cited document pair. We computed it by dividing the total of the tokens common to the two files by the sum of all tokens in both files, minus the total of shared tokens. This is the same as dividing the intersection between two files by their union.

Descriptive Features. Cited paper size is the number in bytes of the cited paper. There is one cited paper by case, so these values are all unique. Publication type pair is a binary value that represents whether query and cited paper in each case are of the same type, the possible types being journal article and conference paper. Citation position indicates the position in the query paper where the cited paper in each case is cited. We divided the query papers in eight parts, so the values can be one of eight. A value of 1000 indicates the citation is in the first eighth of the query document, whereas 8000 indicates it is in the last eighth.

---

[8] https://rare-technologies.com/category/gensim/.

[9] https://radimrehurek.com/gensim/similarities/docsim.html#gensim.similarities.docsim. WmdSimilarity.

4.5   Similarity, Weight Learning, and LOOCV

Similarity assessment was designed through aggregation of local similarity functions via weighted average. The result of the average of similarity functions weighted on learned weights produces a similarity score between each candidate case and a new case. The candidate case with highest similarity score is the nearest neighbor (NN) (k-NN with $k = 1$). Next, we describe local similarity functions, the weight learning method, and how we investigated other values of k.

Local Similarity Functions. The local similarity functions for W2V-based relatedness, PVDM-based relatedness, Jaccard coefficient and Cited paper size are linear, symmetric, and continuous. We compute the local similarity functions for these four attributes as follows. For attributes $a \in A$, a_{cc} refers to the value of the current attribute in the candidate case cc from the case base, a_{nc} refers to the value of the current attribute in the new case, and $range_a$ denotes the difference between the maximum and the minimum values of $a \in A$. The local similarity is computed with Eq. 2:

$$sim(a_{nc}, a_{cc}) = \left\| \left(\frac{a_{nc} - a_{cc}}{range_a} \right) - 1 \right\|$$ (2)

The attribute Citation position is discrete, so we create a table for each pair a_{nc}–a_{cc}, following Eq. (2). The attribute Publication type pair is symbolic and binary, being 1 when values are equal and 0 when different.

Weight Learning. We used the standard gradient descent (i.e., not stochastic) to learn weights based on the so-called *vanilla* implementation[10], which relies on a sigmoid activation function, partial derivatives, and least squares to compute error.

Number of Nearest Neighbors. We varied the value of k to reuse classifications. To avoid ties, we computed only odd numbers of neighbors, namely, $k = 1$, $k = 3$, and $k = 5$. When $k = 3$ and $k = 5$, we decide on the classification of the new case to be the mode of the set of classifications of the nearest neighbors.

Evaluation. Given the non-deterministic nature of gradient descent, we evaluated the performance of the similarity measure via LOOCV on the 100 cases. At each iteration, one case is removed to become the new problem, weights are learned via gradient descent, similarity is assessed, and the candidate case(s) with the highest score(s) lend (s) its(their) classification to the new case. If the predicted accuracy equals the actual accuracy for that case, then one positive unit is added to compute the total accuracy for the 100 cases, which gives the percental accuracy of the case base.

---

[10] https://www.pyimagesearch.com/2016/10/10/gradient-descent-with-python/.

4.6   Results

Different Numbers of Nearest Neighbors. Using the four different W2V configurations (i.e., W2V-5, W2V-21, W2V-Gnews, W2V-openC), we compared results obtained with k-nearest neighbors with $k = 1$, $k = 3$, and $k = 5$ along these seven configurations. We computed the correlation between results with $k = 1$ and $k = 3$, $k = 1$ and $k = 5$, then $k = 3$ and $k = 5$. Because all correlation values were 1.0 (when using single digits) we will present the final study using $k = 1$.

W2V Configurations. We compared the four different W2V configurations (i.e., W2V-5, W2V-21, W2V-Gnews, W2V-openC). First, we computed the correlation between the average accuracies to identify the lowest and highest results. We found that the main differences were between W2V-5 and W2V-Gnews. We compared those two sets of results and the average accuracies were higher when using W2V-Gnews. W2V-Gnews produced average accuracy 4.37% higher than W2V-5. We thus selected the values computed with the W2V-Gnews model to populate the W2V-based relatedness feature in the cases for the final study.

Table 3. Averages and standard deviations of 100 executions of LOOCV in 100 cases

Attribute removed	Average	Variation	St dev
None	69.03	100	2.10
W2V-based relatedness	68.81	0.00	2.35
PVDM-based relatedness	69.68	0.01	2.51
Jaccard coefficient	68.39	−0.01	2.44
Cited paper size	60.67	−0.12	2.34
Publication type pair	71.53	0.04	2.40
Citation position	73.43	0.06	2.20

Case Extension Learning. We confirm which candidate features we will keep for case extension with a feature ablation study, focusing on the six candidate features previously described. Table 3 shows average accuracies for the case base first with none feature removed, then with each of the six candidate features removed. Because the effect in accuracy is positive when features Publication type pair and Citation position are individually removed, they are excluded.

Table 4. Averages and standard deviations of 100 executions of LOOCV in 100 cases

Attribute removed	Average	Variation	St dev
None	68.75	100.00	1.48
W2V-based relatedness	68.55	0.00	1.75
PVDM-based relatedness	67.58	0.01	1.52
Jaccard coefficient	66.85	−0.01	1.63
Cited paper size	64.10	−0.12	3.25

Table 4 shows results for the four features in Table 4, which can retrieve explanations with an average accuracy of 68.75%. These features entail repeatable patterns in the relationship between the target method's inputs and outputs as they lead to reasonably accurate average accuracies when retrieving explanations.

The 0.01 increase when the PVDM-based semantic relatedness feature is removed (Table 4) is considered negligible because it becomes 0.0 when using single digits. Note that when the two features are removed (from Table 3 to Table 4) the average accuracy of the none removed decreased, indicating the effect on the remaining features when a feature or more are removed.

Discussion. The resulting average accuracy seems low but promising, and the low standard deviation shows consistency. Because this is a novel task, there are no alternative approaches for comparison.

Looking at the results in Table 4, we observe that the attribute whose absence penalized the accuracy the most was the Cited paper size (shaded in Table 4) that brought down the accuracy from 68.75% to 64.10%. Interestingly, its absence also increases standard deviation, suggesting this may indeed be an important feature.

The second attribute that penalized accuracy the most was not expected to be this influential, namely, the Jaccard coefficient. This was added to help distinguish a content-based similarity versus one at the surface level. This result says more about the low quality of the two first embedding-based similarities than of the quality of this one. This indicates that more effort needs to be put in the language models to learn embeddings. New features and/or data are needed to reach higher average accuracy.

The resulting average accuracy suggests that the selected features represent these classes of input-output relationships with noise. As we attempt to visualize the patterns revealed by these features, only the feature W2V-based relatedness shows clear distinct patterns for classes *substantiation* and *background*. Figure 4 illustrates how the values for W2V-based relatedness (left) for a sample of 25 cases in each class reveals a discernible pattern while the values for PVDM-based relatedness (right) for the same cases of the same classes are not discernible.

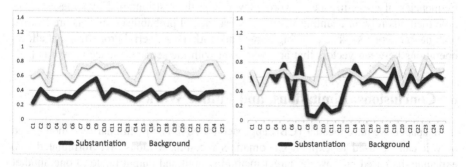

Fig. 4. The pattern of W2V-based relatedness (left) vs. PVDM-based relatedness (right) by class. W2V-based is discernable while PVDM-based is not

5 Related Work

We introduced this paper including background and motivating work. In Sect. 3, while presenting the problem context of our application, we discussed works related to citation analysis, citation recommendation, automation of literature reviews, and academic search. In this section, we limit our discussion to related works within CBR.

In addition to pioneering contributions in CBR, Schank [23] was of the first to propose case-based explanation, catalyzing the development of early, influential CBR systems capable of generating explanations (e.g., [6, 24]). Some initial work in case-based explanation saw interest in creativity aspects [24], whereas others sought CBR approaches for leveraging domain knowledge to produce contextual explanations [25].

Not constrained to a single tool, so to speak, Kofod-Petersen et al. [26] examined user goals concerning explanations, and the utility of the knowledge-intensive CBR CREEK framework in the context of the five explanation goals detailed by Sørmo et al. [1]: transparency, justification, relevance, conceptualization, and learning.

Roth-Berghofer [27] insightfully outlined key challenges of case-based explanation, elaborating as to what is afforded via each of the four CBR knowledge containers in terms of what can be explained naturally by each container; offering useful discussion as to the importance of human-computer trust regarding case-based explanation.

Also proposing a generic case-based approach to explain solutions of opaque methods, [2] use the target method as an oracle to learn a local case base to increase explanation quality. Most works create explanations as a *posthoc* analysis, which [5] argue against. A recent demonstration [28] however shows that noise in training data may interfere with explanations but not with classifications, showing that it is difficult to guarantee alignment even when explanation and classification are synced.

TCBR methods have usually relied on innovations from the fields of information retrieval, natural language processing, and text mining. Using information extraction [3], cosine similarity [29], and language models based on cooccurrence [30] have marked some of the stages in the TCBR literature. Not surprisingly, it is now the time to explore neural probabilistic language models (e.g., [7]). The principle is the same as in latent semantic analysis (LSA) [31] and its variants, to model a corpus based on the frequencies of cooccurrence of words, leveraging the distributional hypothesis. LSA-type methods rely on counting words, whereas neural probabilistic models are learned with neural networks. The resulting trained network has powerful properties that allows operations between vectors that are consistent with the semantic space of words [7].

6 Conclusions, Limitations, and Future Work

In this paper, we introduced a TCBR approach for XAI, and preliminarily demonstrated how it can be used to explain Citeomatic's recommendations. We formulated two explanations based on how the target method's input and output relate to one another based on external knowledge from citation analysis [15]. We described a study where we investigated six candidate attributes to describe the target method's input-output relationship. We conducted an ablation study to confirm the contribution of candidate features and only confirmed 4 out of the six features, illustrating how to implement the proposed approach.

Our goal to find features that could be used to retrieve explanations was achieved. The resulting average accuracy over 100 executions on 100 cases in which those features can propose explanations is 68.75%. This result manifests the competence of our approach in observing the target method behavior, capturing those observations as cases, and extending them with results of analyses done by combining domain knowledge from citation analysis, textual methods, and data accessible from the target method to offer explanations for the method's solutions. This result also demonstrates that case extension has indeed captured repeatable patterns in cases. There are no alternative means to compare this performance because the illustrated application is unprecedented. The value of this result is limited by the small number of 100 cases, and the only two categories of explanations.

These results suggest that new features should be investigated for improving this average accuracy. The better results for semantic relatedness in alignment with the labeled instances came from the embeddings pretrained with Google news and not from any of the data from scientific articles. These features may require more robust vocabularies in support of more predictive language models. With better average accuracies, close examination of the repeatable patterns in case extension features may shed light on citation categories and potentially on how to implement the proposed approach to other application problems.

The two other directions to explore are those from [2, 5]. Subsequently, we will explore more categories of explanations as we conduct user studies to assess their goals with respect to systematic literature reviews.

Acknowledgements. We would like to thank the anonymous reviewers who helped improve the quality of this work. We also would like to thank Meaghan Lutts for her help labeling citations.

References

1. Sørmo, F., Cassens, J., Aamodt, A.: Explanation in case-based reasoning: perspectives and goals. Artif. Intell. Rev. **24**(2), 109–143 (2005)
2. Nugent, C., Cunningham, P.: A case-based explanation system for black-box systems. Artif. Intell. Rev. **24**(2), 163–178 (2005)
3. Weber, R.O., Ashley, K.D., Brüninghaus, S.: Textual case-based reasoning. Knowl. Eng. Rev. **20**(3), 255–260 (2005)
4. Biran, O., Cotton, C.: Explanation and justification in machine learning: a survey. In: Aha, D.W., Darrell, T., Pazzani, M., Reid, D., Sammut, C., Stone, P. (eds.) Explainable AI: Papers from the IJCAI Workshop, pp. 8–13. Melbourne, Australia (2017)
5. Li, O., Liu, H., Chen, C., Rudin, C.: Deep learning for case-based reasoning through prototypes: a neural network that explains its predictions. In: AAAI Conference on Artificial Intelligence. https://www.aaai.org/ocs/index.php/AAAI/AAAI18/paper/view/17082/16552. Accessed 15 June 2018
6. Leake, D.B.: Evaluating explanations: a content theory. Lawrence Erlbaum Associates (1992). Reprint Psychology Press, New York (2014)
7. Mikolov, T., Sutskever, I., Chen, K., Corrado, G.S., Dean, J.: Distributed representations of words and phrases and their compositionality. In: Advances in Neural Information Processing Systems, pp. 3111–3119 (2013)

8. Bhagavatula, C., Feldman, S., Power, R., Ammar, W.: Content-based citation recommendation. In: NAACL: HLT (2018). http://aclweb.org/anthology/N18-1022. Accessed 15 June 2018

9. Xiong, C., Power, R., Callan, J.: Explicit semantic ranking for academic search via knowledge graph embedding. In: Proceedings of the 26th International Conference on World Wide Web, pp. 1271–1279. ACM (2017)

10. Nanba, H., Okumura, M.: Towards multi-paper summarization using reference information. In: Sixteenth International Joint Conference on Artificial Intelligence, pp. 926–931 (1999)

11. Qazvinian, V., et al.: Generating extractive summaries of scientific paradigms. J. Artif. Intell. Res. **46**, 165–201 (2013)

12. Tsafnat, G., Dunn, A., Glasziou, P., Coiera, E.: The automation of systematic reviews. BMJ **346**, f139 (2013)

13. Garfield, E.: Citation indexes for science. Science **122**, 108–111 (1955)

14. Small, H.: Co-citation in scientific literature-new measure of relationship between 2 documents. J. Am. Soc. Inf. Sci. **24**(4), 265–269 (1973)

15. Ding, Y., Zhang, G., Chambers, T., Song, M., Wang, X., Zhai, C.: Content-based citation analysis. The next generation of citation analysis. J. Assoc. Inf. Sci. Technol. **65**(9), 1820–1833 (2014)

16. Huang, W., Wu, Z., Chen, L., Mitra, P., Giles, C.L.: A neural probabilistic model for context based citation recommendation. In: AAAI, pp. 2404–2410. AAAI (2015)

17. Valenzuela, M., Ha, V., Etzioni, O.: Identifying meaningful citations. In: AAAI Workshop: Scholarly Big Data (2015)

18. Blake, C.: Beyond genes, proteins, and abstracts: Identifying scientific claims from full-text biomedical articles. J. Biomed. Inf. **43**(2), 173–189 (2010)

19. Radev, D.R., Muthukrishnan, P., Qazvinian, V., Abu-Jbara, A.: The ACL anthology network corpus. Lang. Resour. Eval. **47**(4), 919–944 (2013)

20. Mikolov, T., Chen, K., Corrado, G., Dean, J.: Efficient estimation of word representations in vector space (2013). https://arxiv.org/abs/1301.3781. Accessed 15 June 2018

21. Le, Q., Mikolov, T.: Distributed representations of sentences and documents. In: International Conference on Machine Learning, pp. 1188–1196 (2014)

22. Kusner, M., Sun, Y., Kolkin, N., Weinberger, K.: From word embeddings to document distances. In: International Conference on Machine Learning, pp. 957–966 (2015)

23. Schank, R.C.: Explanation Patterns– Understanding Mechanically and Creatively. Lawrence Erlbaum, New York (1986)

24. Schank, R.C., Leake, D.: Creativity and learning in a case-based explainer. Artif. Intell. **40** (1–3), 353–385 (1989)

25. Aamodt, A.: Explanation-driven case-based reasoning. In: Wess, S., Althoff, K.-D., Richter, Michael M. (eds.) EWCBR 1993. LNCS, vol. 837, pp. 274–288. Springer, Heidelberg (1994). https://doi.org/10.1007/3-540-58330-0_93

26. Kofod-Petersen, A., Cassens, J., Aamodt, A.: Explanatory capabilities in the CREEK knowledge-intensive case-based reasoner. Front. Artif. Intell. Appl. **173**, 28–35 (2008)

27. Roth-Berghofer, T.R.: Explanations and case-based reasoning: foundational issues. In: Funk, P., González Calero, P.A. (eds.) ECCBR 2004. LNCS (LNAI), vol. 3155, pp. 389–403. Springer, Heidelberg (2004). https://doi.org/10.1007/978-3-540-28631-8_29

28. Kindermans, P-J, et al.: The (un)reliability of saliency methods. In: 31st Conference on Neural Information Processing Systems (NIPS) (2017)

29. Wilson, D.C., Bradshaw, S.: CBR Textuality. Expert. Updat. **3**(1), 28–37 (2000)
30. Wiratunga, N., Koychev, I., Massie, S.: Feature selection and generalisation for retrieval of textual cases. In: Funk, P., González Calero, P.A. (eds.) ECCBR 2004. LNCS (LNAI), vol. 3155, pp. 806–820. Springer, Heidelberg (2004). https://doi.org/10.1007/978-3-540-28631-8_58
31. Dumais, S.T., Furnas, G.W., Landauer, T.K., Deerwester, S., Harshman, R.: Using latent semantic analysis to improve access to textual information. In: SIGCHI Conference on Human Factors in Computing Systems, pp. 281–285. ACM (1988)

Improving kNN for Human Activity Recognition with Privileged Learning Using Translation Models

Anjana Wijekoon[1](✉)(ID), Nirmalie Wiratunga[1](ID), Sadiq Sani[1](ID),
Stewart Massie[1](ID), and Kay Cooper[2](ID)

[1] School of Computing Science and Digital Media, Robert Gordon University,
Aberdeen AB10 7GJ, Scotland, U.K.
{a.wijekoon,n.wiratunga,s.sani,s.massie}@rgu.ac.uk
[2] School of Health Sciences, Robert Gordon University, Aberdeen AB10 7GJ,
Scotland, U.K.
k.cooper@rgu.ac.uk

Abstract. Multiple sensor modalities provide more accurate Human Activity Recognition (HAR) compared to using a single modality, yet the latter is preferred by consumers as it is more convenient and less intrusive. This presents a challenge to researchers, as a single modality is likely to pick up movement that is both relevant as well as extraneous to the human activity being tracked and lead to poorer performance. The goal of an optimal HAR solution is therefore to utilise the fewest sensors at deployment, while maintaining performance levels achievable using all available sensors. To this end, we introduce two translation approaches, capable of generating missing modalities from available modalities. These can be used to generate missing or "privileged" modalities at deployment to augment case representations and improve HAR. We evaluate the presented translators with k-NN classifiers on two HAR datasets and achieve up-to 5% performance improvements using representations augmented with privileged modalities. This suggests that non-intrusive modalities suited for deployment benefit from translation models that generates privileged modalities.

Keywords: Human Activity Recognition · Machine learning
Case representation · Privileged Learning

1 Introduction

Human Activity Recognition (HAR) involves the computational analysis of human movement. The types of movement which are recognised are directly dependent on the application requirements. Typically these applications relate to tracking or monitoring movements such as ambulatory activities (i.e. walking or jogging) [9,11], daily activities of living (i.e. gardening or cooking) [1] or exercises (i.e. muscle strength increasing exercises or stretching) [12]. In these

© Springer Nature Switzerland AG 2018
M. T. Cox et al. (Eds.): ICCBR 2018, LNAI 11156, pp. 448–463, 2018.
https://doi.org/10.1007/978-3-030-01081-2_30

situations we would expect to use sensing devices comprised of wearables (inertial sensors such as an accelerometer or a gyroscope) and ambient sensors in the environment (such as movement sensors in a home) to track user activity.

Reasoning with multi-modal sensor data is an active area of AI research [17] with applications fielded in a range of domains, including health and well-being, smart cities, robotics and interactive natural interfaces. For HAR having different modalities for sensing is advantageous as it provides contextually richer representations. However access to all sensor modalities at deployment can be restricted due to a variety of reasons. Economics in some situations will limit the number of available sensors; erroneous behaviour may cause loss of data temporarily or ease of use may restrict the number of sensors one may be willing to use. In short, considerations such as usability, ease of deployment and cost all suggest that access to data from all modalities is likely to be a privilege to be had at training, and not necessarily at deployment (test time). This poses an interesting question of how representations learnt using all modalities at train time can also be exploited at test time. Here instead of simply ignoring missing modalities at test time we explore how performance gains can be achieved by learning to estimate them.

In this paper we focus on HAR in the context of Privileged Learning (PL) [14]. Specifically we show how PL can be used to estimate missing parts of a representation when one or more modalities are absent at test time. The key idea is to learn a generative model that can use existing modalities to estimate representations for any missing modalities. An initial study on linear correlation between modalities has as expected revealed that a simpler technique such as a linear regression is ineffective at estimating missing modalities. Our solution borrows ideas from computational language translation [13], but instead of translating between language pairs, we translate between data generated by sensor modalities - from present to missing modalities. The main assumption here is that there is a non-linear correlation between modalities and that we can discover them from a parallel corpus of modality pairs using translators. Accordingly we make the following three contributions:

- formalise PL in the context of HAR by recognising how different modalities contribute towards improved classification;
- introduce novel translation methods that can learn a mapping between sensors to estimate missing modalities at deployment; and
- conduct a comparative study of the proposed algorithms on the SelfBACK[1] and PAMAP2[2] datasets to demonstrate their ability to achieve improved performance with fewer modalities at deployment.

This paper is organised as follows: in Sect. 2 we explore work related on HAR, PL and Sequence generation; in Sect. 3 we interpret Privileged Information (PI)

---

[1] The SelfBACK project is funded by European Union's H2020 research and innovation programme under grant agreement No. 689043. More details available: http://www. selfback.eu. The SelfBACK dataset associated with this paper is publicly accessible from https://github.com/selfback/activity-recognition.

[2] https://archive.ics.uci.edu/ml/datasets/PAMAP2+Physical+Activity+Monitoring.

in the domain of HAR and offer formalisations for our approaches. We detail the datasets, experiment design and evaluation techniques in Sect. 4; in Sect. 5 we present results and discuss outcomes; followed by conclusions and future improvements in Sect. 6.

2   Related Work

Significant research has been carried out on reasoning with sensors for HAR using machine learning techniques. While early work was focused on using a single sensor to perform HAR with hand crafted features [6], more recent advancements are largely due to the successes of deep learning. Much of the latest research has focussed on exploiting multiple sensors for HAR with deep learning models to achieve state of the art performance [8,16]. In [9] the authors explore the impact of different sensor placements on HAR performance and discuss the trade-off between convenience (wrist placement) versus accuracy (thigh placement). Ideally we want to optimise sensor placement convenience whilst minimising the negative impact this can have on accuracy.

Privileged Learning (PL) mimics how humans learn with a teacher. In a learning environment the teacher provides the student with explanations and additional information around the topic, but at test time the student must rely on what they have learned with no access to the teacher. This concept was introduced by [14] where they define an additional feature space, Privileged Information (PI) that guarantees 100% classification accuracy, but only available at training. We can draw parallels here in sensor placements; whereby sensors that lead to improved performance but not considered to be convenient placements are analogous to the teacher in PL. However unlike with PL, a privileged sensor placement can only promise positive improvements.

In this paper we explore how an additional PI space can be constructed for HAR. Typically PI can be viewed as an extra set of features describing the same problem. For example, using additional image masks to influence improved orthogonality in convolutional functions for image classification [2] or the use of skeleton information to improve depth sequence analysis [10]. In the latter paper, the authors demonstrate a system capable of learning to generate privileged (skeleton) information from training data (depth sequences) which can then be used to support classification at test time. Similarly, in our work we generate a PI feature space from existing sensors but use both feature spaces to improve HAR. However our translation model is a reusable standalone component which translates between sensor data compared to [10] where skeleton generation is continuously refined with classification.

Sequence to sequence (seq2seq), learning has been successfully applied in many domains, such as image/video captioning [15,18], language translation [3] and time-series forecasting [4] with Recurrent Neural Networks (RNNs). We also see Sequence generation with Deep Belief Networks (DBNs) and Deep Autoencoders applied successfully in audio and video reconstruction [5]. Learning to reconstruct missing sensor data is similar to sequence generation, but as we focus on a small window of time, there are less temporal dependencies to be learnt. The mapping between input and output data in an autoencoder is more relevant to our work. Unlike with autoencoders our input and output is not meant to be identical - instead they involve different sensor streams aligned in time. As such we focus more on learning a mapping between different sensor data to capitalise on their spatial dependencies.

3   HAR with Privileged Learning

Figure 1 illustrates how we create the casebase for HAR task from a sample of people wearing two modalities (i.e. wrist and thigh). We use a sliding window approach, with a window size of w, to decompose data streams from each modality. Accordingly the case representation, $C = \{X_1, X_2, X_3, ..., X_n, L\}$, captures all n modalities together with the activity class label L at each time window, where X_i is the i_{th} sensor modality.

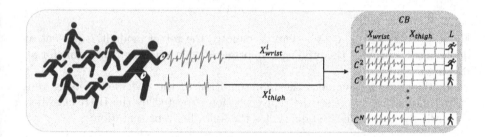

Fig. 1. HAR casebase creation

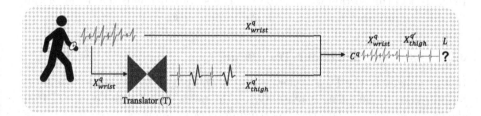

Fig. 2. Case creation at deployment

Unlike with Fig. 1, in Fig. 2 at deployment the user is wearing a single modality (a wrist sensor). We use a translator to estimate the missing modality, using the data that is present. Thereafter both the present modality X_i^q and the estimated modality $X_j^{q\prime}$ are used to form the query case C^q. Here $X_j^{q\prime}$ forms our privileged information and the translation model is simply a mapping between the input and output modalities. In our example (Fig. 2) the translation model can be learnt from a parallel corpus of wrist-to-thigh instances. We use cases from our casebase to learn the translation model, as each case contains all potential modalities. More generally, this mapping can be between any number of input and output modalities.

3.1   A Privileged Classification Model with Translators

In this section we formalise classification with privileged learning for HAR. We consider privileged information in HAR as a set modalities that is present at casebase creation but missing at deployment. The HAR classifier receives n number of modalities as input to predict an activity class. Given a query case $C^q = \{X_1, X_2, ..., X_m\}$, where m is the number of modalities present at deployment, we determine the missing modalities as $n - m$. We then use one or more translators, T, to generate those missing modalities.

$$\chi' = T(\chi)$$

where $\chi \subset X$ and $\chi' \subset X'$. Here X denotes the set of modalities present at deployment and X' is the privileged information generated by translators for all missing modalities.

In this way, we augment the representation of the query case, using generated modalities to create the representation expected by the HAR classifier. Accordingly, the augmented query has the following representation:

$$C'^q = \{X_1, X_2, ..., X_m, X'_{m+1}, X'_{m+2}, ..., X'_n\}$$

$$C'^q = \{X, X'\}$$

In the rest of this section we describe two translation methods that can generate the missing modalities, $n - m$, from the m modalities.

3.2   k-Nearest Neighbour Translator

In this approach, the PI is generated for a query case by exploiting similarity based retrieval and solution reuse. Given the query case C^q and a case C from the casebase, we calculate their paired difference as follows:

$$Distance_{(C^q, C)} = \sum_{i=0}^{m} \delta(X_i^q, X_i)$$

where δ calculates the distance between a pair of modalities.

The top, k, cases are retrieved and their solutions (i.e. PI) is reused to estimate the missing modalities values in C^q. More specifically, we reuse the values from the privileged information attributes X_i as taken from the k nearest neighbours and average over k to estimate the privileged attribute X'_i.

$$X'_i = \frac{1}{k} \sum_{j=1}^{k} X_i^j$$

We iterate over all privileged modalities to form an augmented representation, C'^q, for the query case. This k-Nearest Neighbour Translator will be referred to as T^{kNN}.

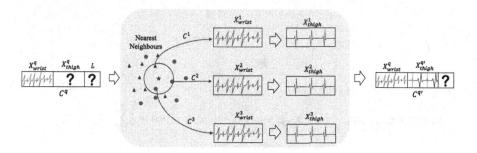

Fig. 3. An example wrist-to-thigh Nearest Neighbour Translator

Figure 3 illustrates an example T^{kNN} translator which retrieves the first 3 nearest neighbour cases from the casebase using the wrist modality attributes of the query case. The thigh attribute modalities of the retrieved cases are averaged to form an estimate thigh attribute for the query case. In this way an augmented representation is formed by combining the estimated thigh modality with the initial wrist modality.

3.3   Neural Translator

We use a fully connected neural network to generate privileged information; where it learns a neural mapping between its input and output layers. Here the input layer consists of features representing modalities that are present only at test time and the output estimates the missing modalities.

More specifically we have, $p * w$, input units where p is the number of input modalities and w is the window size and the output layer consists of units from a subset of missing modalities, $q * w$ where q is the number of output modalities. A single hidden layer is introduced to learn the feature mapping from input to the output units. We propose to use a narrow middle layer to force the network to learn the most significant features from the input when estimating its output. This also helps avoid learning arbitrary noisy features from the input.

Figure 4 illustrates an example Neural Translator training using a single input modality (i.e. wrist) to generate another single modality (i.e. thigh). For training

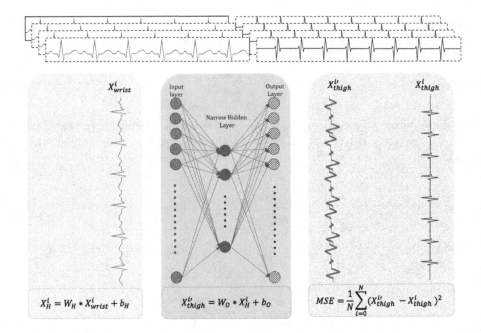

Fig. 4. An example wrist-to-thigh Neural Translator

we use a parallel corpus of wrist-thigh pairs where wrist is input, and thigh is the solution that is being estimated by the network. The figure also indicates the node activation and loss functions expressions used for model training.

Let X_H denote the hidden layer representation of the input X_{wrist} and calculated with weights W_H and biases b_H on the hidden layer. The network derives X'_{thigh} using the hidden layer representation X_H and weights W_O and biases b_O of the output layer. During training, given an input, the network learns to generate a representation of the output modalities that is as close to the actual values. This is enforced by using a loss function of Mean Squared Error (MSE) between predicted output and expected output, in Fig. 4, it is the difference between predicted thigh X'_{thigh} and actual thigh data, X_{thigh}.

When a query case C^q is presented at deployment, we use one or more Neural Translators to generate all missing modalities required to re-construct C'^q for classification. We refer to this Neural Translator as T^N. Formally the privileged information generated by T^N is:

$$\chi' = \theta(\chi)$$

Here θ denotes parameters of the trained neural translator.

4   Evaluation

We conduct a comparative study to explore the utility of translation models to augment representations for HAR. Accordingly we include the following algorithms:

- T^{kNN} (Sect. 3.2) for several k values (1, 3 and 5) with Euclidean Distance for δ; and
- T^N (Sect. 3.3) using the hyper parameters in Table 1 which were found to be empirically most effective.

Table 1. Hyper-parameters for Neural Translator

Hyper-parameter	Value
Number of hidden layers	1
Number of hidden units	96
Loss function	Mean squared error
Optimizer/Learning rate	Adam/0.01
Number of epochs	100

In the rest of this section we detail datasets, preprocessing and experiment designs.

4.1   Datasets

We use two HAR datasets in our experiments and their details appear in Table 2.

SelfBACK dataset was compiled with two tri-axial accelerometer data streams belonging to 6 activity classes performed by 34 individuals for approximately 3 min. Accelerometers were mounted on the right-hand wrist and thigh of the subject (thus forming 2 modalities). The data for three axes was recorded at 100 Hz for each modality with time stamp. The dataset was recorded simultaneously on two sensors but dispersed as two separate datasets for each modality. For this study we merge the two datasets aligning them by timestamps to create a dataset with 8 columns as follows: 1 for the time stamp, 3 (x, y, z) columns each for wrist and thigh and the label.

PAMAP2 is a Physical Activity Monitoring dataset which contains data from 3 inertial measurement units (IMUs) located on wrist, chest and ankle. 18 different physical activities were recorded by 9 subjects following a pre-defined protocol [7]. Due to class imbalance within subjects in the dataset we filter out

one subject and 9 activities with insufficient data. In addition we only selected
accelerometer data from IMUs. The refined dataset contained 8 subjects and
9 activity classes. Previous literature of PAMAP2 dataset provides benchmark
classification using all modalities [7]. But for the purpose of this research we
created classification models using individual sensor modality.

Table 2. Summary - Datasets

	SelfBACK	PAMAP2
Number of subjects	34	8
Number of activity classes	6	9
Accelerometer calibration	$\pm$ 8 g, 100 Hz	$\pm$ 16 g, 100 Hz
Sensor placements and notation	Wrist (W) and Thigh (T)	Wrist (W), Chest (C) and Ankle (A)
Window size	3 s	3 s
Number of instances	9889	4833
Case base	$\{C^1, C^2, C^3, ..., C^{9889}\}$	$\{C^1, C^2, C^3, ..., C^{4833}\}$
Case	$C^i = \{X_W^i, X_T^i, L^i\}$	$C^i = \{X_W^i, X_C^i, X_A^i, L^i\}$

4.2   Data Pre-processing

We perform three pre-processing steps on each dataset to create case bases for
our translators and classification.

1. We use a sliding window size of 3 seconds with no overlap to create instances
   for each subject.
2. We convert the three-dimensional (x, y, z) raw data into a single dimension
   Discrete Cosine Transform (DCT) instance. First we convert each axis data
   instance of 300 timestamps into a DCT feature array and then select the first
   60 DCT features. We append DCT features from all axes to form one array
   of length 180.
3. Finally we normalize all data instances.

We use DCT feature transformations as it has been proven to result in significant performance improvements over raw multi-dimensional features. DCTs
extract generic and robust features compared to other statistically crafted features and was also shown to have slightly better or comparable results to deep
feature embeddings [9]. Importantly for us, it simplifies the task of translators
when the mapping can be carried over a proven feature representation for input
and output data. Finally data normalisation ensures that the k-NN classifiers are
unaffected by scalar differences between different modalities across all datasets.

4.3   Experiment Design

We employed Leave-One-Person-Out (LOPO) cross validation with all our experiments of HAR, with a k-NN classifier where $k = 3$. We use accuracy on classification to study the contribution of translators to performance gains in HAR and compare results for with and without privileged information. In order to establish which modalities are more likely to be considered as privileged in a given dataset, we also studied their individual performance and the contribution they each provide when combined with other modalities.

With the neural translator we perform several experiments to identify the most effective hyper-parameters. We experiment with different hidden units and hidden layers in the neural translator to understand the impact on learning the mapping between sensors. While maintaining the number of hidden layers to one, Fig. 5 reports the results obtained for different hidden units for SelfBACK dataset. We can observe how performance increases with number of hidden units, but after 96 (which is closer to half of the size of input units) performance declines. This confirms claims we made in Sect. 3.3 on how a narrow hidden layer supports learning better mappings between sensors while discarding arbitrary noise.

Figure 6 presents performance results obtained with different hidden layers on the SelfBACK dataset. In the first four columns, we maintain a considerably narrow layer size compared to the input and output units, while increasing the number of layers. These four experiments do not show substantial performance gains from having additional layers. Later we increase number of layers and make them broader which saw a significant drop in performance. We can observe that, when the number of parameters of the network increases, the network tends to over-fit the training data and leads to poorer performance. Accordingly we use the best hyper parameters in Table 1 on all Neural Translator experiments.

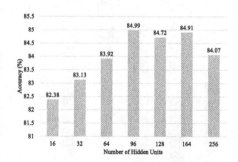

Fig. 5. T^N - hidden units

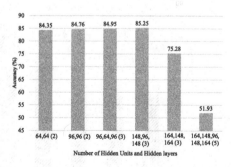

Fig. 6. T^N - hidden layers

We adopt the following naming convention, $f(X_i/X_j)$ to identify the different classifiers by the modalities that have been used for training, X_i, as well as to indicate which modalities (if any) are used as privileged information, X_j.

Here $X_j = \emptyset$ indicates the absence of modalities for privileged information. For example, the $f(T/\emptyset)$ denotes a classification model trained and tested with the single modality thigh data using no privilege information; similarly $f(W, C/\emptyset)$ is a classification model trained on two modalities, W (wrist) and C (chest), again with no privileged information. In contrast $f(W, C, A/A)$ suggests the use of 3 modalities for training with modality A (ankle) forming the privileged information which will be estimated by a translator. With translators we adopt the following naming convention $T(X_i/X_j)$; For instance $T^N(W, C/A)$ indicates a neural translator which generates A (ankle) as privilege information by translating from W & C (which are wrist and chest) data.

5   Results

In this section we will first identify PI for each dataset by comparing baseline results, next we present performance we obtained with k-Nearest Neighbour Translator, finally we present performance we obtained with our Neural Translator. We discuss results and their implications at each subsection.

5.1   Comparison of Baselines to Identify Privileged Information

For each dataset we create several baselines classifiers with no privileged information (see Fig. 7). This allows us to analyse individual performance on the HAR classification task and identify modality placements that are ideal for activity recognition.

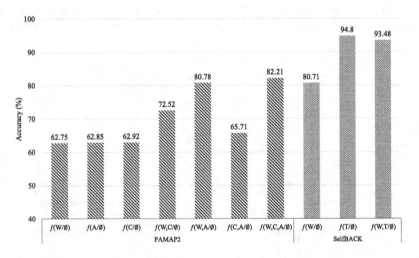

Fig. 7. Baseline classification results for SelfBACK and PAMAP2

In Fig. 7 there are results from 3 baselines created for the SelfBACK dataset. The best baselines are $f(W, T/\emptyset)$ and $f(T/\emptyset)$, with the inclusion of the wrist suggesting a slight decline in performance. With $f(W/\emptyset)$ using only the wrist, we see a considerable performance decline of almost 15% compared to the other two. These baseline results confirm that thigh is clearly a Privileged Information in the SelfBACK dataset.

The 7 baseline classifier accuracies for PAMAP2 dataset are also shown in Fig. 7. Here we can see that each of the 3 single modality classifiers have comparable performance but appear to have as much as a 10% performs degradation compared to the multi-modal baselines (e.g. $f(W, C, A/\emptyset)$). This might be explained by the similarities between some activity classes for example such as "Walking" and "Nordic Walking" which are harder to differentiate with a single sensor and would instead require multiple modalities.

Of the multi-modal classifiers on PAMPA2, $f(W, A/\emptyset)$ outperforms $f(W, C/\emptyset)$ and $f(C, A/\emptyset)$, furthermore, performance of $f(W, A/\emptyset)$ is notably close to the three-modality classifier $f(W, C, A/\emptyset)$. Surprisingly the two-modality classifiers $f(C, A/\emptyset)$ does not improve their single-modality performance substantially, but they both (Ankle and Chest) show improved performance when combined with wrist modality. Accordingly in this dataset we assess the use of both chest and ankle modalities as privileged information. We believe this is sensible especially when considering the intrusiveness of either of these wearables compared to an inertial sensor on the wrist.

5.2   Privilege Information Generation with the k-NN Translator

In general k-NN as a translator failed to provide any significant improvements over classification without privileged information on the SelfBACK dataset (see Table 3). We studied two classifiers with both using a translator to generate thigh; where one used only thigh data (first column) and the other uses both wrist and thigh (second column). However at most, we only observed a classification performance improvement of only 1.32% over the baseline classifier $f(W/\emptyset)$. Increasing the number of neighbours (from k values 1, 3 to 5) also had no significant impact apart from a marginal improvement (as little as 1%).

Table 3. T^{kNN} with SelfBACK and PAMAP2

	SelfBACK		PAMAP2		
	$f(T/T)$, $T^{kNN}(W/T)$	$f(W, T/T)$, $T^{kNN}(W/T)$	$f(W, A/A)$, $T^{kNN}(W/A)$	$f(W, C/C)$, $T^{kNN}(W/C)$	$f(W, C, A/A)$, $T^{kNN}(W, C/A)$
T^{1NN}	81.03	81.02	62.47	62.25	71.01
T^{3NN}	81.52	81.57	63.01	63.37	72.41
T^{5NN}	81.50	82.02	62.58	62.82	71.56

Unlike with SelfBACK, in PAMPA2 we used only multi-modalities to train the HAR classifier following the poor results observed in Fig. 7 with single modalities. However once again results here did not exhibit any substantial improvement or decline in performance compared to the baselines. In addition we observe no significant performance difference was to be had by increasing the neighbourhood sizes.

We believe the poor translation capability of the kNN method is primarily due to the inherent noise in some of the modalities. This is particularly the case with SelfBACK (as observed in Fig. 7) and therefore is not surprising that the translation mapping was also not able to recover from this noise already captured in the case representation from wrist. However with PAMPA2 we did not see any significant difference between any of the single modalities (Fig. 7) and as such do not believe that wrist is any nosier than, say chest for instance. Here we believe that the poor performance might be explained by the inability of the single modality to discriminate between the activity classes. These uncertainties are emphasised when selecting neighbours using single modality, thus end up not gaining any performance improvement from privileged information.

In general we expect that an incremental learner such as the neural translator will have a better opportunity to learn an improved mapping as it minimises the differences between estimated and actual privileged information during training. This alone helps to create an improved feature embedding compared to kNN.

5.3   Privilege Information Generation with the Neural Translator

Figure 8 shows classification results for the Neural Translator for both SelfBACK and PAMAP2 datasets. Here each bar shows the lower and upper bounds set by the baselines. For instance the upper bound is simply the baseline that uses the

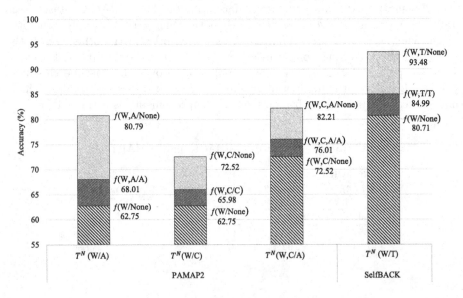

Fig. 8. T^N with PAMAP2 and SelfBACK

actual data instead of the estimated generated by a translator; whilst the lower bound is when the privileged modality is not used for HAR. Ideally we want the translator to improve upon the lower bound to get closer to the upper.

On PAMAP2 we experimented with three multi-modal Neural Translators. Translator $T^N(W/A)$ learns from wrist case attribute to generate ankle case attribute from CB_{PAMAP2}. Results suggests a 5.26% increment in accuracy between $f(W, A/A)$ and the corresponding baseline $f(W/\emptyset)$. Similarly both Translators $T^N(W/C)$ and $T^N(W, C/A)$ improves accuracy of their corresponding baselines $f(W/\emptyset)$ by 3.23% and $f(W, C/\emptyset)$ by 3.49% respectively.

The SelfBACK results appear in the last column of Fig. 8. Here we can see that the Neural Translator for SelfBACK has significantly improved the performance of the lower bound baselines $f(W/\emptyset)$ brining it closer to the upper bound set by $f(W, T/\emptyset)$ baseline (which is when all modalities are available without the need for translation). Specifically we observe that the $T^N(W/T)$ translator (wrist-to-thigh) achieves a 4.28% increment in accuracy using privileged information at deployment.

These results suggest that using a classifier trained with multiple modalities, with a single or subset of modalities in deployment, is not only possible but improves performance significantly. Unlike the k-NN Translator, the Neural Translator is less affected by the ambiguities of the source modalities. Instead, it learns relationships that help to map between source and target modalities. As a result the generated modalities improve performance of the HAR classifiers at deployment using the estimated knowledge.

6   Conclusions

We introduced two Translator approaches for privileged learning with HAR. Our results showed the Neural Translator to have significant performance improvements over the baselines which have no privilege learning. kNN translators were less effective in this domain, and we concluded that this was due to the inherent noise and class ambiguities in HAR which requires effective case representations. But unlike the neural translator, the kNN translator had no mechanisms to iteratively refine its representations.

Overall the neural translator had significantly outperformed the lower bounds set by the baseline classifiers on both datasets. However we believe there is further opportunity to improve on the translator generated representations allowing us to move closer to the upper bound or optimal performance observed when actual privileged information is used.

Accordingly in future work we will explore a number of directions in which to improve our Neural Translator, for instance exploring other network optimisation techniques, different data representations and also considering how ideas from case adaptation might be employed here in a neural setting. Another direction involves the creation of personalised translators that are better able to capture personal traits and individual differences when estimating missing modalities.

Finally this research has demonstrated that translation methods can help to minimise the number of sensors needed at deployment; which we argue is one of the key components of an optimal HAR solution.

References

1. Chavarriaga, R., et al.: The opportunity challenge: a benchmark database for on-body sensor-based activity recognition. Pattern Recognit. Lett. **34**(15), 2033–2042 (2013)
2. Chen, Y., Jin, X., Feng, J., Yan, S.: Training group orthogonal neural networks with privileged information. arXiv preprint arXiv:1701.06772 (2017)
3. Luong, M.T., Le, Q.V., Sutskever, I., Vinyals, O., Kaiser, L.: Multi-task sequence to sequence learning. arXiv preprint arXiv:1511.06114 (2015)
4. Ma, X., Tao, Z., Wang, Y., Yu, H., Wang, Y.: Long short-term memory neural network for traffic speed prediction using remote microwave sensor data. Transp. Res. Part C: Emerg. Technol. **54**, 187–197 (2015)
5. Ngiam, J., Khosla, A., Kim, M., Nam, J., Lee, H., Ng, A.Y.: Multimodal deep learning. In: Proceedings of the 28th International Conference on Machine Learning (ICML 2011), pp. 689–696 (2011)
6. Preece, S.J., Goulermas, J.Y., Kenney, L.P., Howard, D.: A comparison of feature extraction methods for the classification of dynamic activities from accelerometer data. IEEE Trans. Biomed. Eng. **56**(3), 871–879 (2009)
7. Reiss, A., Stricker, D.: Introducing a new benchmarked dataset for activity monitoring. In: 2012 16th International Symposium on Wearable Computers (ISWC), pp. 108–109. IEEE (2012)
8. Ronao, C.A., Cho, S.B.: Human activity recognition with smartphone sensors using deep learning neural networks. Expert. Syst. Appl. **59**, 235–244 (2016)
9. Sani, S., Massie, S., Wiratunga, N., Cooper, K.: Learning deep and shallow features for human activity recognition. In: Li, G., Ge, Y., Zhang, Z., Jin, Z., Blumenstein, M. (eds.) KSEM 2017. LNCS (LNAI), vol. 10412, pp. 469–482. Springer, Cham (2017). https://doi.org/10.1007/978-3-319-63558-3_40
10. Shi, Z., Kim, T.K.: Learning and refining of privileged information-based RNNs for action recognition from depth sequences. In: Proceedings of the IEEE Conference on Computer Vision and Pattern Recognition (CVPR) (2017)
11. Stisen, A., et al.: Smart devices are different: assessing and mitigatingmobile sensing heterogeneities for activity recognition. In: Proceedings of the 13th ACM Conference on Embedded Networked Sensor Systems, pp. 127–140. ACM (2015)
12. Sundholm, M., Cheng, J., Zhou, B., Sethi, A., Lukowicz, P.: Smart-mat: recognizing and counting gym exercises with low-cost resistive pressure sensing matrix. In: Proceedings of the 2014 ACM International Joint Conference on Pervasive and Ubiquitous Computing, pp. 373–382. ACM (2014)
13. Sutskever, I., Vinyals, O., Le, Q.V.: Sequence to sequence learning with neural networks. In: Advances in Neural Information Processing Systems, pp. 3104–3112 (2014)
14. Vapnik, V., Vashist, A.: A new learning paradigm: learning using privileged information. Neural Netw. **22**(5), 544–557 (2009)
15. Vinyals, O., Toshev, A., Bengio, S., Erhan, D.: Show and tell: a neural image caption generator. In: 2015 IEEE Conference on Computer Vision and Pattern Recognition (CVPR), pp. 3156–3164. IEEE (2015)

16. Yao, S., Hu, S., Zhao, Y., Zhang, A., Abdelzaher, T.: Deepsense: a unified deep learning framework for time-series mobile sensing data processing. In: Proceedings of the 26th International Conference on World Wide Web, pp. 351–360. International World Wide Web Conferences Steering Committee (2017)
17. Yin, W., Schütze, H., Xiang, B., Zhou, B.: Abcnn: attention-based convolutional neural network for modeling sentence pairs. arXiv preprint arXiv:1512.05193 (2015)
18. Yu, H., Wang, J., Huang, Z., Yang, Y., Xu, W.: Video paragraph captioning using hierarchical recurrent neural networks. In: Proceedings of the IEEE Conference on Computer Vision and Pattern Recognition, pp. 4584–4593 (2016)

Considering Nutrients During the Generation of Recipes by Process-Oriented Case-Based Reasoning

Christian Zeyen[(✉)], Maximilian Hoffmann, Gilbert Müller,
and Ralph Bergmann

Business Information Systems II, University of Trier, 54286 Trier, Germany
{zeyen,s4mnhoff,muellerg,bergmann}@uni-trier.de
http://www.wi2.uni-trier.de

Abstract. This paper investigates the generation of recipes in consideration of user-defined nutrient contents. For this purpose, we extend our previous case-based reasoning approach that already covers the formulation of user queries with various dietary practices. More precisely, this work augments the domain ontology with nutritional information and introduces a novel nutrition concept fulfillment into the retrieval and adaptation process. An experimental evaluation with real cooking recipes demonstrates the applicability of the approach and systematically investigates the influence of various adaptation methods on the query fulfillment with multiple constraints. It is shown, that all adaptation methods are able to optimize generated recipes according to certain nutritional constraints as well as ingredient and cooking step preferences and that the adaptation outperforms the sole retrieval of available recipes.

Keywords: Process-oriented case-based reasoning
Workflow adaptation · Recipe generation · Nutrient content

1 Introduction

A healthy and balanced diet is of high importance for many people. In some cases, allergies or intolerances require particularly a nutrition that is tailored to individual needs. Thus, numerous different dietary practices exist such as avoiding specific kinds of foods when following a lactose-free or vegetarian diet, preparing food in a certain way for a raw food diet, or reaching a certain amount of nutrients while being on a high-protein diet. Cooking portals make it convenient for amateur chefs to find desired recipes by providing diverse search capabilities such as a faceted search for different diets or local specialties. While many portals enable the adaptation of ingredient quantities for a desired number of servings, the vast majority is not able to customize available recipes according to more comprehensive user queries, e.g., by exchanging ingredients or adapting preparation steps in a recipe. Since 2008, the computer cooking contest (CCC)

© Springer Nature Switzerland AG 2018
M. T. Cox et al. (Eds.): ICCBR 2018, LNAI 11156, pp. 464–479, 2018.
https://doi.org/10.1007/978-3-030-01081-2_31

has been organized almost every year and provided varying cooking challenges some of which demanded the creation of recipes for certain dietary practices. In recent years, various applications emerged mainly utilizing case-based reasoning (CBR) [1] for the experience-based creation of recipes by retrieval and adaptation of available recipes. For example, JadaWeb [2,7] is a textual CBR system that provides desired and undesired ingredients as query capabilities and does also consider pre-defined diet restrictions such as vegetarian, nut-free, or non-alcoholic using the knowledge encoded in an ontology. The CookIIS system [6] provides similar capabilities and utilizes pre-defined lists of recommended and not recommended ingredients for certain diets such as vegetarian, gout, or low-cholesterol diets. Not recommended ingredients are used as filters during retrieval and the subsequent rule-based adaptation tries to insert recommended ingredients to further optimize the retrieved recipe. Taaable [4,5] is another textual CBR system that is able to substitute ingredients and adapt their quantities based on a semantic wiki and a domain ontology that captures dietary practices and nutritional information about ingredients and dishes. Our contribution to this contest is a process-oriented CBR (POCBR) [9] system named Cook-ingCAKE [12]. We represent recipes as cooking workflows in order to enable queries containing ingredients in conjunction with preparation instructions. In the process-oriented query language (POQL) [15] the user can specify desired and undesired ingredients and/or preparation steps as workflow fragments. Analogous to other approaches, the user may specify queries for recipes that comply with different dietary practices. For instance, vegetarian dishes can be requested by inserting meat as a restriction and a diet with raw food can be achieved by adding a generalized preparation step increase temperature as a restriction to the query. However, we are not aware of any approach that covers the specification of queries for dishes having a certain distribution of nutrients. Thus, in this paper, we propose an extension of the recipe generation that additionally considers nutrient contents.

The contribution of this paper is twofold. From an application-oriented point of view, we augment the case representation with ontological knowledge about nutrition, nutrients, and conversions of ingredient quantities. Furthermore, besides the POQL query, we introduce a second query component for the specification of desired nutrient contents. This also requires the extension of the retrieval and adaptation with a novel nutrient content fulfillment. Due to the additional query component, the creation of recipes becomes a multi-objective optimization problem and thus the system may not be able to maximize the fulfillment of both query parts at the same time. Hence, from a methodological perspective, we provide an experimental evaluation that systematically examines the influence of adaptation methods on the solution of this problem.

This paper is organized as follows: In Sect. 2 we briefly summarize relevant previous work in the field of POCBR. Subsequently, Sect. 3 describes our approach. The experimental evaluation is presented in Sect. 4 while Sect. 5 summarizes our findings and discusses future work.

2   Generating Recipes with Process-Oriented CBR

We now briefly give some background information about our previous work on the generation of recipes represented as workflows with POCBR.

2.1   Similarity-Based Workflow Retrieval

In POCBR, cases are often represented as processes or workflows that describe the logical or chronological order of tasks and the exchange of physical products or data to produce a certain outcome [17]. In cooking workflows, tasks represent preparation instructions and exchange ingredients in order to produce a certain dish. We represent workflows as semantically labeled directed graphs [3]. In the graph representation, nodes and edges have semantic descriptions consisting of pairs of attributes and values. Figure 1 gives an example of a simple cooking workflow for the preparation of a tomato cheese sandwich. Each task and data node has a *name* attribute used as the label. The values for this attribute are structured hierarchically in a data and task taxonomy in order to enable the assessment of the semantic similarity among them. The data nodes that represent real ingredients have an extended semantic description specifying their *unit* and *quantity*.

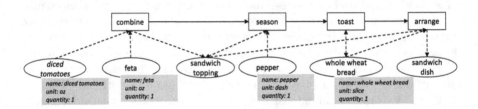

Fig. 1. Example of a cooking workflow

Queries in POCBR are used to describe the users' requirements for retrieving the most useful workflows. In previous work [15], we proposed a process-oriented query language (POQL) to specify such queries. One part of a POQL query $Q = (Q^+, Q^-)$ is a query workflow representing desired properties of a workflow. The other part consists of several restriction workflows each defining one undesired situation that should be avoided. Figure 2 illustrates such a POQL query. In this example, the query workflow specifies the desired properties toasted bread, tomato, and cheese. The first restriction workflow restricts the desired dish to be a raw food dish while the second restriction workflow favors vegetarian dishes. Comparing the query with the cooking workflow depicted above, one can see that all properties defined by the query are fulfilled in the workflow when considering the subsumption of concepts defined by the taxonomies. Please note that the POQL query in the example does not specify any quantities of ingredients, which are thus ignored during the retrieval and adaptation of workflows.

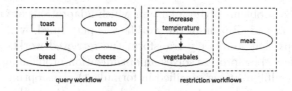

Fig. 2. Example of a POQL query

To compute the query fulfillment between a POQL query $Q = (Q^+, Q^-)$ and a workflow W we propose the following formula:

$$QF_{poql}(Q, W) = \frac{\text{sim}(Q^+, W) + \text{RS}(Q^-, W)}{2} \tag{1}$$

The similarity between a query workflow Q^+ and a workflow W is determined by a semantic similarity measure $\text{sim}(Q^+, W) \to [0, 1]$. We use a measure by Bergmann and Gil [3] that applies graph-matching combined with a heuristic search to find the best possible mapping between the nodes and edges of both workflows. Each mapping is rated with local similarity measures by comparing the semantic descriptions of mapped nodes and edges. Following the local-global principle, the overall similarity is computed by aggregating all the local similarity according to an aggregation function. The restriction workflows $q^- \in Q^-$ are compared with a workflow W using a restriction satisfaction function $\text{RS}(Q^-, W) \to [0, 1]$ that is also based on the semantic similarity measure:

$$\text{RS}(Q^-, W) = 1 - \frac{|\{q^- | q^- \in Q^- \wedge \text{sim}(q^-, W) = 1\}|}{|Q^-|} \tag{2}$$

A restriction component is not satisfied and thus reduces the overall restriction satisfaction if the similarity between both workflows is 1.0. Consequently, matching desired data items or tasks increase the query fulfillment while matching undesired data items or tasks reduce the query fulfillment between a POQL query and a workflow.

2.2 Automatic Workflow Adaptation

If the best matching workflow from the case base does not entirely fulfill the user query, we aim to adapted the workflow according to the restrictions and requirements specified in the query by adding missing desired ingredients/preparation steps and removing undesired ingredients/preparation steps. For this purpose, we proposed several automatic workflow adaptation methods which we now briefly describe (for a more detailed description of these methods we refer to our previous works [11–14]). Since such adaptation methods usually require a significant amount of domain-specific adaptation knowledge, we additionally developed new methods that allow automatic learning of the required knowledge from the workflow repository. Hence, we distinguish between a learning phase of adaptation knowledge and a problem solving phase in which adaptations are performed. In all approaches, the adaptation of the workflow is performed by chaining several adaptation steps that iteratively transform the retrieved workflow towards an adapted workflow. This process solves an optimization problem aiming to maximize the query fulfillment (as specified in formula 1). This optimization process is implemented as a heuristic search procedure with the goal of achieving an adapted workflow with the highest possible query fulfillment.

The *adaptation operator adaptation* [14] performs individual transformation steps which are denoted in a STRIPS-like manner. An operator consists of two workflow sub-graphs that we call *streamlets*: A DELETE-streamlet specifies a workflow fragment to be deleted from the workflow and an ADD-streamlet represents a workflow fragment to be added to the workflow. The overall adaptation is implemented as a search process that aims to incrementally modify the workflow with the goal of increasing the query fulfillment. The required workflow adaptation operators can be learned from the workflow repository by analyzing pairs of highly similar workflows (selected by using a similarity threshold). For each pair, the difference is determined and workflow operators are generated, whose ADD and DELETE-streamlets basically cover those differences.

The *workflow stream adaptation* [11] decomposes workflows into meaningful sub-workflows named workflow streams in the learning phase. Workflow streams represent valuable adaptation knowledge and can be exchanged during compositional adaptation. More precisely, a workflow stream can be replaced by a stream learned from another workflow that produces the same partial output but in a different manner, i.e., with other task or data items. Workflow streams can only be replaced, if their data nodes indicate that they represent the same kind of sub-workflow. This ensures that replacing an arbitrary stream does not violate the syntactic correctness of the workflow. This adaptation is also implemented as a search process that aims to increase the query fulfillment, but it replaces larger portions of a workflow than the *adaptation operator adaptation*.

The adaptation by *generalization and specialization* [13] first produces a generalized workflow that is structurally identical to the base workflow but its semantic descriptions of task and data items are generalized. The approach generalizes a workflow by considering a set of similar workflows as training samples and selects generalized semantic descriptions from the domain taxonomy as generalization hierarchy. The *generalization* produces a generalized workflow repository which is then used for workflow retrieval. The retrieved workflow is adapted by the *specialization* such that the query fulfillment is maximized.

The three approaches can be integrated to form a *combined adaptation approach* [12]. This integration involves the actual adaptation process as well as the learning phase. First of all, during the learning phase, adaptation operators and workflow streams can be learned not only from the available specific workflows, but also from workflows resulting from generalization. Thus, we first apply generalization to the workflows in the repository and then we learn adaptation operators and workflow streams from the generalized workflows. The adaptation process itself then uses the three adaptation methods in combination (see Fig. 3).

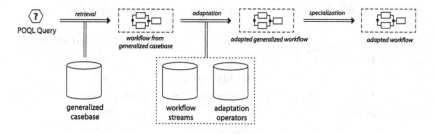

Fig. 3. Combined adaptation approach

First, similarity-based retrieval selects the best matching generalized workflow from the generalized case base. Then, the *workflow stream adaptation* replaces entire sub-workflows (e.g., the preparation of the *sandwich sauce*) by matching sub-workflows (e.g., other *sauces*) learned from other workflows. Next, the *adaptation operator adaptation* performs additional modifications on the workflows (e.g., the ingredient *tomato* is replaced by *mushrooms*). Finally, the *specialization* adapts workflows (if necessary) by replacing single generalized data items or tasks with more specific ones by means of the respective taxonomy (e.g. the generalized ingredient *meat* is replaced by *chicken*).

3   Generation of Recipes in Consideration of Nutrients

Generally speaking, there are three basic components in a diet providing food energy to humans: protein, fat, and carbohydrates. Unlike these macronutrients, the micronutrients such as vitamins and minerals are a group of essential nutrients that are present in relatively low amounts in foods. The National Academy of Sciences (NAS) provide comprehensive reports (see [8]) recommending reference values for nutrient intakes for U.S. and Canadian individuals. One aspect of the recommendations includes the *Acceptable Macronutrient Distribution Ranges* for healthy diets, which are expressed as a percentage of total energy intake (i.e. calories). Many online sources as well as literature in the health and fitness sector provide various recommendations for diets (e.g. to count macronutrients instead of calories) and do also propose numerous different ratios of nutrients as a percentage of the daily intake of calories. We follow these recommendations by considering the absolute amounts of desired nutrient contents during the generation of recipes and we take macronutrients as well as micronutrients into account. In order to enable the user to pose a query for a customized dish, we define a *nutrition concept* as follows:

Definition 1. *A nutrition concept* $N = \{(n_1, min_1, max_1), \ldots, (n_k, min_k, max_k)\}$ *is a set of* k *triplets each defining a nutrient* n_i *with a lower and upper limit* $(0 \leq min_i \leq max_i)$ *for the absolute amount in grams of the nutrient in a desired dish.*

Table 1. Example of nutrition concepts for a single meal

Nutrition concept (goal)	Nutrient	Desired amount [g]
Moderate (lose weight)	Protein	16.67
	Total lipid (fat)	9.26
	Carbohydrate, by difference	45.83
Major minerals (healthy diet)	Calcium	0.17
	Magnesium	0.06
Least fat (lose weight)	Total lipid (fat)	0.0

According to this definition, Table 1 exemplifies some nutrition concepts for different goals. The nutrient contents (except for the last concept *least fat*) are based on the recommendations by the NAS and the portion size of one serving of the available recipes. The last nutrition concept is not based on a recommendation and zero fat can be considered as an unrealistic goal. However, it can be suitable to obtain dishes with the least amount of fat. Since this concept defines a minimization problem w.r.t. the creation of a recipe, it is assumed that the need of adaptations for reaching this nutrient content is increased. Please note that, for the sake of simplicity, the example concepts only define the desired nutrient amount as a single value (i.e., $min = max$). However, retrieval and adaptation also support more elaborate queries according to Definition 1.

In the following, this section describes the extensions made to the existing domain ontology, the novel nutrition concept fulfillment, and the assessment of nutrient contents as prerequisites for the nutrient-aware generation of recipes.

3.1 Enriching the Case Representation and Domain Model

In order to consider nutrient contents, the domain ontology containing the taxonomic relations between ingredients is enriched with knowledge about nutrition concepts, nutrients, as well as quantity and unit conversions. We propose a knowledge model similar to the one presented by the *Taaable* project [4] but with the addition of global conversions that are broadly applicable and user-defined nutrition concepts as specified in Definition 1. Figure 4 illustrates the core components of our ontology. According to the definition of nutrition concepts, each concept specifies several nutrients with a minimum and maximum quantity. We implemented the nutrition concepts depicted in Table 1 in the ontology in order to make them available to users and to use them in the evaluation of the approach.

The ontology assigns nutrient information and measuring units to each non-abstract ingredient. The nutrient information consists of a name and an indication of quantity per 100 grams. The measuring units of ingredients state different kinds of kitchen measurements such as slices, cups, knife tips, or tablespoons. The ontology further defines ingredient-specific unit conversions to obtain gram equivalents (e.g. *4 tomato slices* $\cong$ *100g*) and it also includes global unit mappings and conversions (e.g. *1 tablespoon = 1 tbsp*, *1 tbsp = 3 tsp*, or *1 tbsp = 10g*). In the event where a given ingredient quantity in a (new) recipe cannot be converted into grams since there is no matching ingredient-specific conversion available, the global conversions ensure that either a unit can be mapped to another unit for which a ingredient-specific conversion exists or that a quantity can be directly converted into a gram equivalent. The global conversions are prioritized in order to prefer transformations between semantically similar notations over conversions of different measuring units. For instance, a global conversion such as *1 tbsp = 10g* has a very low priority and is only applied to an ingredient quantity (given in *tbsp*) in the event where no matching ingredient-specific or higher prioritized global conversion has been found.

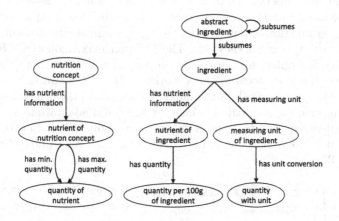

Fig. 4. Domain ontology with ingredients, nutrients, and nutrition concepts

For the nutrient-aware creation of recipes, the specific amounts of nutrients contained in each available dish must be considered. Hence, in a pre-processing step, the quantities of ingredients indicated in the recipes are converted into gram equivalents by means of the ontology. This computation differs for concrete and abstract ingredients. For concrete ingredients, the ontology provides unit conversions that are used to convert all ingredient quantities into gram equivalents. Subsequently, the nutrients contained in each ingredient and their masses are determined with the help of the ontology. Abstract ingredients (such as *meat*) are represented as inner nodes in the taxonomy and the ontology does not provide concrete nutrient information. In this event, all subsumed specific ingredients (e.g. *salami, ham, ...*) are determined and their amounts of nutrients are assessed. Then, the arithmetic mean of all the masses is calculated as an approximation for the nutrient contents of the abstract ingredient.

3.2 Nutrition Concept Query Fulfillment

Diets that require certain amounts of nutrients cannot be defined in POQL queries. Thus, we combine the existing query with a new nutrition concept query. In such a query, the user may specify an arbitrary number of nutrients according to Definition 1: $N = \{(n_1, min_1, max_1), \ldots, (n_k, min_k, max_k)\}$. In order to evaluate to which extent a given cooking workflow $W \in CB$ from the case base fulfills the desired nutrient distribution, we define a novel *nutrition concept query fulfillment* as a function $\mathrm{QF}_{nc}(N, W) \to [0, 1]$:

$$\mathrm{QF}_{nc}(N, W) = \sum_{s_i \in N} \frac{sim(s_i, W)}{|N|} \tag{3}$$

The similarity function $sim(s, W) \to [0, 1]$ (see formula 4) assesses a similarity score between a nutrient specification $s = (n, min, max)$ and a workflow W. Moreover, the function $amount(n, W) \to \mathbb{R}_0^+$ determines the absolute amount of the nutrient n in a workflow W. The function $maxAmount(n, CB) \to \mathbb{R}_0^+$ retrieves a cached value (for normalization purpose) of the nutrient's maximum amount that has ever occurred in a workflow $W \in CB$. Initially, the maximum amounts are set based on the nutrient contents in the original workflows. A maximum amount is updated, whenever successful adaptations increase the overall nutrient content to a novel highest maximum value. Consequently, if $amount(n, W) > maxAmount(n, CB)$ holds true then $maxAmount(n, CB) := amount(n, W)$.

$$sim(s, W) = \begin{cases} 1 - \frac{s.min - amount(s.n, W)}{\max(s.min, maxAmount(s.n, CB)) - s.max} & \text{if } amount(s.n, W) < s.min, \\ 1 - \frac{amount(s.n, W) - s.max}{\max(s.min, maxAmount(s.n, CB)) - s.max} & \text{else if } amount(s.n, W) > s.max, \\ 1 & \text{else.} \end{cases} \tag{4}$$

For the overall similarity computation, a combined query fulfillment $QF(Q, N, W)$ is computed that contains the conventional POQL query fulfillment $\mathrm{QF}_{poql}(Q, W)$ (see formula 1) as well as the novel *nutrition concept query fulfillment* $\mathrm{QF}_{nc}(N, W)$:

$$QF(Q, N, W) = \alpha \cdot \mathrm{QF}_{poql}(Q, W) + (1 - \alpha) \cdot \mathrm{QF}_{nc}(N, W) \tag{5}$$

Both criteria are weighted by a parameter $\alpha \in [0, 1]$. This combined query fulfillment measure replaces the conventional POQL query fulfillment. Thus, the retrieval process and subsequent adaptations now aim at optimizing recipes with regard to both criteria. However, this procedure results in a multi-objective optimization problem and thus the approach may not be able to maximize both query fulfillments at the same time. As described in Sect. 2, the best matching workflow w.r.t. the query is retrieved during the retrieval phase. In a linear retrieval, each workflow from the case base is evaluated concerning both query components: $\mathrm{QF}_{poql}(Q, W)$ is assessed by performing a heuristic search for the best possible mapping between the elements in the query and the workflow and $\mathrm{QF}_{nc}(N, W)$ is assessed by examining each nutrient content constraint. The best workflow is then used as a starting point for subsequent adaptations. In the combined adaptation approach, all adaptations are performed in a sequence while each adaptation step aims to maximize the combined query fulfillment analogous to the retrieval phase. For this purpose, the adaptations with workflow streams and the adaptation operators perform a heuristic search to find applicable adaptation steps that produce an adapted workflow with the highest possible query fulfillment. Subsequently, the adaptation by specialization specializes task and data items one by one in consideration of maximization of the query fulfillment. Since the constraint satisfaction is assessed implicitly by similarity scores, neither the retrieval nor the adaptation approaches have to be adjusted to new constraints. However, new types of constraints (e.g. desired percentage of nutrient content) require the definition of measures that are suitable to assess their satisfaction properly.

3.3   Generating Recipes with CookingCAKE

We implemented the approach as an extension to our CookingCAKE system [12], which is part of the CAKE framework[1]. CookingCAKE uses a case base of 70 cooking workflows that describe the preparation of sandwich recipes. The workflows are manually extracted from the cooking portal allrecipes.com and the *Taaable* project [5]. The semantic descriptions of data nodes (representing the ingredients) are extended with quantities and units in a semi-automatic process. During this process, all ingredient quantities are normalized to a single portion of a dish and unit terms are standardized. The domain ontology is enriched with data extracted from the *USDA Food Composition Databases*[2] of the United States Department of Agriculture, which have also been used by the *Taaable* project. In particular, these databases contain nutritional information such as name of the nutrient, measuring unit, and the amount per 100 grams of food for many thousands of foods. They also include food-specific weight indications and conversions in grams. In total, our domain ontology includes 33 nutrients for 154 ingredients.

Figure 5 illustrates the user interface[3] of the prototypical implementation.[4] In the upper third the user can state the first query part, i.e., desired ingredients and preparation steps as well as undesired ones. In the middle, arbitrary nutrition concepts can be created by specifying nutrients with minimum and maximum amounts as the second query part. At the bottom, the user can set a weight for the fulfillment of both query parts. However, a user may also define a query that consists of only one part.

Table 2 exemplifies two sandwich recipes that are created for a query with *croissant* as a desired ingredient and *least fat* as a nutrition concept. The first

---

[1] See cake.wi2.uni-trier.de.
[2] See https://ndb.nal.usda.gov/ndb/.
[3] Please note that this is a simplified user interface that does not allow the definition of workflow fragments. However, a full-featured interface is also available online.
[4] A running demo is available under cookingcake.wi2.uni-trier.de/diet.

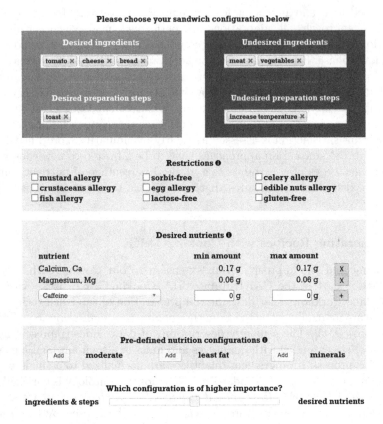

Fig. 5. The CookingCAKE user query interface

Table 2. Example of two sandwich recipes created for a query with *croissant* as a desired ingredient and *least fat* as a nutrition concept

	Generation with QF_{poql}	Generation with QF_{poql} and QF_{nc}
Ingredients	Croissant (0.5 slice)	Bread (1 piece)
	Spam (1.5oz)	Zucchini (0.25 piece)
	Emmental cheese (1 slice)	Red onion (0.25 piece)
	Italian dressing (1 tsp)	Yellow squash (0.25 cup)
	Banana (0.5 slice)	Red bell pepper (0.25 cup)
		Basil (4 leaf)
Nutrients	Total lipid (fat) (24g)	Total lipid (fat) (3g)
	. . .	. . .
QF_{poql}	1,0000	1,0000
QF_{nc}	0,9137	0,9879

sandwich is created using the conventional approach and the second one is created with the nutrient-aware approach. Comparing the POQL query fulfillment, one can see that both sandwiches fulfill the requirement although croissant is generalized to bread in the second sandwich. However, in the domain ontology, croissant is a child node of bread and thus the similarity measure rates the similarity with a score of 1.0. Regarding the nutrition concept fulfillment, the amount of fat is significantly reduced in the second dish.

4   Experimental Evaluation

We now present the evaluation of our approach, which is based on a previous evaluation [10] by Gilbert Müller. The evaluation shows that the adaptation methods summarized in Sect. 2.2 are capable of increasing the POQL query fulfillment significantly while maintaining the overall quality of the workflows at an adequate level. The evaluation also determines a ranking of adaptation algorithms w.r.t. the increase of the POQL query fulfillment. The combined adaptation has the largest leverage followed by the adaptation operators, the adaptation by generalization and specialization, and the workflow stream adaptation. We investigate the following hypotheses in this evaluation:

H1 The approach is able to consider nutrition concepts during the generation of cooking recipes.
H2 The adaptation methods outperform the sole retrieval in terms of the nutrition concept fulfillment.
H3 The ranking of the adaptation methods w.r.t. the increase of the nutrition concept fulfillment is identical to the order obtained w.r.t. the POQL query fulfillment.

4.1   Evaluation Setup

Based on the previous evaluation [10], we now extend the setup in this work. For the evaluation, we use 51 POQL queries for sandwich recipes, which were defined by nine amateur chefs. Based on the domain vocabulary, the users specified arbitrary queries using POQL as well as plain text, which was used for plausibility checks. Furthermore, each POQL query is combined with each of the nutrition concepts listed in Table 1 resulting in 153 queries in total.

With each of these queries, the experiments are performed using the setup as illustrated by Fig. 6. In a first experiment, the best-matching workflow W_R is retrieved from the repository without any adaptation. In a second test run, the retrieval is performed on the generalized workflow repository and a specialization is performed subsequently, resulting in an adapted workflow W_G. In the next two runs, the retrieval is based again on the original repository and the workflow stream adaptation or the adaptation operator adaptation is applied to the retrieved workflow, producing an adapted workflow W_S or W_O, respectively. In a last experiment, the retrieval is performed using the generalized repository.

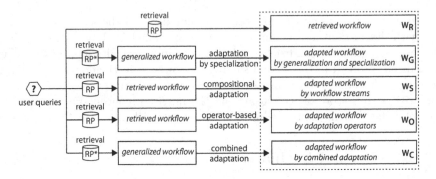

Fig. 6. Evaluation setup taken from [10]

Subsequently, a combined adaptation with workflow streams, adaptation operators, and specialization in that sequence is applied in order to obtain an adapted workflow W_C.

All the experiments described above are performed twice. In a first run, the recipes are generated using the conventional approach without the consideration of nutrition concepts. Consequently, only the POQL query fulfillment QF_{poql} is considered as the optimization criterion during retrieval and adaptation. In the other run, the nutrition concepts are taken into consideration and the combined, equally weighted query fulfillment $QF = 0.5 \cdot QF_{poql} + 0.5 \cdot QF_{nc}$ is used to control the creation process.

4.2 Evaluation Results

Table 3 summarizes the average results over all 153 queries. For each sample type obtained from the experiments (see Fig. 6), the average query fulfillments are listed for the workflows resulted from the generation while considering nutrition concepts. The difference to the query fulfillments obtained from the conventional generation are denoted in brackets. QF_{poql} denotes the POQL query fulfillment, QF_{nc} is the nutrition concept fulfillment, and the combined query fulfillment is stated by QF.

Table 3. Evaluation results: average values over all queries

Sample type	Query fulfillment (difference to conventional approach)		
	QF_{poql}	QF_{nc}	QF
W_R	0.8285 (−0.0155)	0.9610 (0.0534)	0.8948 (0.0190)
W_G	0.8639 (−0.0132)	0.9761 (0.0816)	0.9200 (0.0342)
W_S	0.8503 (−0.0122)	0.9667 (0.0754)	0.9085 (0.0316)
W_O	0.8906 (−0.0060)	0.9694 (0.0859)	0.9300 (0.0400)
W_C	0.9295 (−0.0035)	0.9831 (0.0867)	0.9563 (0.0416)

Comparing the average query fulfillments over all queries and samples between the nutrient-aware approach and the conventional approach, one can see that the nutrient-aware approach is able to increase the fulfillment of nutrition concepts about 8% points while QF_{poql} is slightly lower with an decrease of about 1% point. All differences in the table are statistically significant (except for the difference for the combined adaptation W_C w.r.t. QF_{poql}) as determined by a paired t-test ($p < 0.005$). Thus, hypothesis H1 can be confirmed.

Regarding hypothesis H2, we already investigated in previous work [10] the capability of the adaptation methods to optimize QF_{poql}. The ranking of the adaptation methods w.r.t. the increase QF_{poql} can be confirmed by this evaluation and the combined adaptation W_C does also outperform the other approaches. Especially the fulfillment of W_C is about 10% points higher than the fulfillment of W_R. Comparing QF_{nc} between W_C and W_R, it can be seen that the fulfillment is also increased about 2% points. The application of the sole adaptation methods does also produce adapted workflows (W_G, W_S, and W_O) that have a higher QF_{nc} than the retrieved workflow W_R. Consequently, hypothesis H2 is confirmed, too.

When looking closer at the nutrition concept query fulfillments produced by the different adaptation approaches, one can see that each adaptation method slightly increases the fulfillment and that the order assumed for this leverage in hypothesis H3 does hold true for the most part. As predicted, the combined adaptation has the highest potential to optimize the nutrient distribution as desired by the user. In this study, QF_{nc} is increased about 2.2% points. The adaptation by generalization and specialization reached the second highest increase with 1.5% points and outperforms (in contrast to QF_{poql}) the adaptation operators, which achieved an increase of about 0.8% points in average. The adaptation with workflow streams performed slightly worse with an increase of about 0.6% points. Based on the results, we assume hypothesis H3 at least to be partially confirmed.

The ranking observed can be explained by the function principle of the adaptation approaches. Concerning the generalization and specialization no structural changes are applied to the workflows. However, single ingredients can be replaced by semantically similar ones. The operator adaptation is suitable to perform more fine-grained adaptations than the workflow stream adaptation, since its workflow fragments are normally smaller. However, in both adaptations, it may happen that the substitution of workflow fragments also inserts or removes ingredients with nutrients that do not comply with a given nutrition concept.

5   Conclusions and Future Work

This paper presents a means for the consideration of nutrient contents during the creation of recipes. The definition of nutrition concept queries enables the user to specify desired dishes with certain minimum and maximum amounts of nutrients. The automatic generation of recipes provides customized solutions for the user by optimizing the recipes w.r.t. the combined query (consisting of the POQL and nutrient content component). Maximizing the combined query fulfillment is a multi-objective optimization problem that can be solved adequately by our approach. The experimental evaluation demonstrated that each adaptation method is able to optimize the workflows w.r.t. the POQL query while also optimizing the fulfillment of the nutrient contents. While the single adaptation methods only achieve a rather slight increase, the combined adaptation approach is able to significantly elevate the fulfillment of both query components. This result does also confirm the results obtained from a previous evaluation [16] that investigated the performance of the combined adaptation with a different combined query fulfillment consisting of the POQL query fulfillment and a complexity-aware query fulfillment. Consequently, we have shown that changing the underlying similarity measures for a newly composed query type ensures that retrieval and adaptation are able to handle multiple, potentially conflicting constraints by optimizing the overall query fulfillment. Thus, we assume that this framework will be applicable beyond recipe generation, which we would like to investigate in future work.

Regarding the cooking domain, future work could extend the definition of nutrition concepts to support other common specifications of nutrient contents such as the desired macronutrient distribution expressed as a percentage of the daily intake of calories. Furthermore, the adaptation of ingredient quantities should be integrated in the creation process of recipes. By this means, we assume that the nutrients can be better adapted according to the user query since in the current approach only fixed amounts of ingredients (normalized to produce a single serving of a dish) can be substituted by the adaptations. The current repository does only contain 70 cooking workflows. Hence, it is desirable to have some more recipes that comply with certain nutrient distributions and thus are particularly suitable for this approach.

Acknowledgments. This work was funded by the German Research Foundation (DFG), project number BE 1373/3-3.

References

1. Aamodt, A., Plaza, E.: Case-based reasoning: foundational issues, methodological variations, and system approaches. AI Communi. **7**(1), 39–59 (1994)
2. Ballesteros, M., Martın, R., Dıaz-Agudo, B.: JADAWeb: A CBR System for Cooking Recipes. In: Bichindaritz, I., Montani, S. (eds.) Case-Based Reasoning. Research and Development, ICCBR 2010. LNCS, vol. 6176, pp. 179–188. Springer (2010)
3. Bergmann, R., Gil, Y.: Similarity assessment and efficient retrieval of semantic workflows. Inf. Syst. **40**, 115–127 (2014)
4. Blansché, A., et al.: TAAABLE 3: adaptation of ingredient quantities and of textual preparations. In: Bichindaritz, I., Montani, S. (eds.) ICCBR 2010 Workshop Proceedings, pp. 189–198 (2010)

5. Cordier, A., Lieber, J., Molli, P., Nauer, E., Skaf-Molli, H., Toussaint, Y.: WIK-ITAAABLE: a semantic wiki as a blackboard for a textual case-base reasoning system. In: Lange, C., Schaffert, S., Skaf-Molli, H., Völkel, M. (eds.) 4th Semantic Wiki Workshop (SemWiki) at the 6th ESWC, CEUR Workshop Proceedings, vol. 464 (2009). CEUR-WS.org

6. Hanft, A., Newo, R., Bach, K., Ihle, N., Althoff, K.D.: CookIIS - A successful Recipe Advisor and Menu Creator. In: Mointani, S., Jain, L.C. (eds.) Successful Case-based Reasoning Applications - 1. Studies in Comput. Intell., vol. 305, pp. 187–222. Springer (2010)

7. Herrera, P.J., Iglesias, P., Romero, D., Rubio, I., D-Agudo, B.: JaDaCook: Java application developed and cooked over ontological knowledge. In: Schaaf, M. (ed.) The 9th ECCBR 2008, Workshop Proceedings, pp. 209–218 (2008)

8. Institute of Medicine: Dietary Reference Intakes for Energy, Carbohydrate, Fiber, Fat, Fatty Acids, Cholesterol, Protein, and Amino Acids. The National Academies Press, Washington, DC (2005)

9. Minor, M., Montani, S., Recio-Garcia, J.A.: Process-oriented case-based reasoning. Inf. Syst. 40, 103–105 (2014)

10. Müller, G.: Workflow Modeling Assistance by Case-based Reasoning. Ph.D. thesis, University of Trier (2018)

11. Müller, G., Bergmann, R.: Workflow streams: a means for compositional adaptation in process-oriented CBR. In: Lamontagne, L., Plaza, E. (eds.) ICCBR 2014. LNCS (LNAI), vol. 8765, pp. 315–329. Springer, Cham (2014). https://doi.org/10.1007/978-3-319-11209-1_23

12. Müller, G., Bergmann, R.: CookingCAKE: a framework for the adaptation of cooking recipes represented as workflows. In: Kendall-Morwick, J. (ed.) Workshop Proceedings from (ICCBR 2015), CEUR, vol. 1520, pp. 221–232 (2015). CEUR-WS.org

13. Müller, G., Bergmann, R.: Generalization of workflows in process-oriented case-based reasoning. In: Russell, I., Eberle, W. (eds.) Proceedings of FLAIRS 2015, pp. 391–396. AAAI Press (2015)

14. Müller, G., Bergmann, R.: Learning and applying adaptation operators in process-oriented case-based reasoning. In: Hüllermeier, E., Minor, M. (eds.) ICCBR 2015. LNCS (LNAI), vol. 9343, pp. 259–274. Springer, Cham (2015). https://doi.org/10.1007/978-3-319-24586-7_18

15. Müller, G., Bergmann, R.: POQL: a new query language for process-oriented case-based reasoning. In: Bergmann, R., Görg, S., Müller, G. (eds.) Proceedings of the LWA 2015, CEUR Workshop Proceedings, vol. 1458, pp. 247–255 (2015). CEUR-WS.org

16. Müller, G., Bergmann, R.: Complexity-aware generation of workflows by process-oriented case-based reasoning. In: Kern-Isberner, G., Fürnkranz, J., Thimm, M. (eds.) KI 2017. LNCS (LNAI), vol. 10505, pp. 207–221. Springer, Cham (2017). https://doi.org/10.1007/978-3-319-67190-1_16

17. Van Der Aalst, W.M.: Business process management: a comprehensive survey. ISRN Softw. Eng. 2013 (2013)

An Effective Method for Identifying Unknown Unknowns with Noisy Oracle

Bo Zheng[1], Xin Lin[1], Yanghua Xiao[2,3], Jing Yang[1(✉)], and Liang He[1]

[1] East China Normal University, Shanghai, China
bzheng@ica.stc.sh.cn, {xlin,jyang,lhe}@cs.ecnu.edu.cn
[2] School of Computer Science, Fudan University, Shanghai, China
shawyh@fudan.edu.cn
[3] Shanghai Institute of Intelligent Electronics and Systems, Shanghai, China

Abstract. Unknown Unknowns (UUs) are referred to the error predictions that with high confidence. The identifying of the UUs is important to understand the limitation of predictive models. Some proposed solutions are effective in such identifying. All of them assume there is a perfect Oracle to return the correct labels of the UUs. However, it is not practical since there is no perfect Oracle in real world. Even experts will make mistakes in UUs labelling. Such errors will lead to the terrible consequence since fake UUs will mislead the existing algorithms and reduce their performance. In this paper, we identify the impact of noisy Oracle and propose a UUs identifying algorithm that can be adapted to the setting of noisy Oracle. Experimental results demonstrate the effectiveness of our proposed method.

Keywords: Unknown Unknowns · Uncertainty AI · Model diagnosis
Active learning

1 Introduction

In recent years, machine learning and artificial intelligence (AI) have made great progress in a wide range of fields such as *Image Classification* [13], *Speech Recognition* [10], and *Go* [28]. When a predictive model, which is trained on a finite and biased dataset, is deployed to real world, there are some points which the model is highly confident about its predictions but wrong [1]. [2] referred to these high-confidence error predictions as **Unknown Unknowns** (UUs, and UU for Unknown Unknown). In the fields of AI safety and Uncertainty AI, UUs are catastrophic for some high-stakes tasks. For example, a medical diagnostic model makes the wrong prediction with high confidence on a potential patient, which leads to the patient being ignored by subsequent human inspection and causes the irreparable disaster. Therefore, it is important to identify these errors when the model is deployed to real world.

However, due to the model is highly confident about its predicted results, it is impossible to identify UUs effectively only by the model itself without additional annotation mechanism. As a human-based technology, crowdsourcing (e.g.,

M. T. Cox et al. (Eds.): ICCBR 2018, LNAI 11156, pp. 480–495, 2018.
https://doi.org/10.1007/978-3-030-01081-2_32

Amazon Mechanical Turk) can be exploited to help such identification. However, a large number of data points will incur much monetary and time cost in crowdsourcing. Therefore, how to identify more UUs under the limited budget is the key to this problem. [14] assumed that UUs are clustered in certain areas of the feature and confidence space, then they proposed a partition-based approach to identify UUs for any black-box classifiers. Their approach consists of two phases. First, they divide the test set into multiple partitions based on the feature similarity of instances and the confidence scores assigned by the predictive model. Second, they select the partition (arm) with the highest expected reward using their bandit algorithm and then sample the instances from the partition. Their paper demonstrated that the approach is effective in identifying UUs across various applications in the open world.

Fig. 1. The illustration that fake UUs will mislead the algorithm for identifying UUs. The algorithm samples the same number of instances in area 1 and 2. The algorithm discovered 6 UUs in area 1, and 5 UUs were discovered in area 2. Therefore, the algorithm will misestimate the probability of being a UU in area 1 is greater than that of in area 2, but the result is actually the opposite. (Color figure online)

However, their approach rely heavily on a highly reliable human-like Oracle (or perfect Oracle) which is impractical in real world. Even if the label comes from human experts, they may make mistakes for several reasons (e.g., distracted or fatigued when they annotate instances) [23]. At the same time the true UUs are rare in dataset, if we identify UUs with noisy Oracle, the **fake UUs** which are identified as UUs due to the wrong annotation of noisy Oracle will have a huge impact on our task. To illustrate this, Fig. 1 shows that the algorithm misestimate the probability of being a UU in two regions in limited steps, thus results in spending more query resources on area 2 rather than area 1. Meanwhile, fake UUs, which affect the understanding of the limitations of model, will reduce the ratio of true UUs in all identified UUs and account for a large ratio of all identified UUs. Therefore, we need to take into consideration fake UUs when we identify UUs with a noisy Oracle.

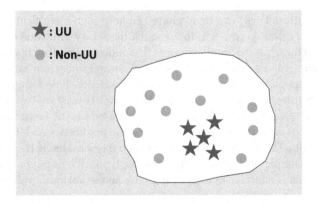

Fig. 2. The illustration that UUs are clustered together in the same partition. In the figure, the red stars represent UU and the blue circles represent non-UU.

Moreover, the partition-based approach has the limitation in identifying more UUs. After the exploration of each partition, the optimal policy in their approach will choose the partition with the highest concentration of UUs and use random sampling to discover UUs in the exploitation process. However, the instances in this partition should be clustered together such as shown in Fig. 2 rather than evenly distributed. Since the random sampling ignores such information, it may not achieve high performance in terms of the quantity of identified UUs. Therefore, if we want to identify more UUs under the limited budget, we should take advantage of the distribution of UUs in this partition.

In order to solve the above problems, in this paper, we extend the utility model proposed in [14] to adapt to noisy Oracle, and proposed a more effective method for identifying UUs. In our method, we remove the partition hypothesis and propose a dynamic nearest neighbour algorithm to estimate the probability that whether the instance is a UU with the limited information. Meanwhile, we use the epsilon-greedy strategy, which is commonly used in reinforcement learning [29], to solve the explore-exploit dilemma in the process of identifying UUs. The experiments demonstrated that our method is more effective in identifying UUs and is more robust to noisy Oracle than previous methods.

Overall, the main contributions of our work can be concluded as follows.

1. First, we identify the impact of noisy Oracle when discovering UUs that is, the fake UU caused by the wrong annotation will mislead the UUs identifying algorithm and make understanding the limitation of model difficult.
2. Second, we extend the existing utility model of identifying UUs to adapt to noisy Oracle.
3. Third, we propose a method for identifying UUs which is effective in identifying more UUs and more robust to noisy Oracle.
4. Fourth, our experimental results show that our method performs substantially better than previous methods.

The rest of this paper is organized as follows. In Sect. 2, we make a formulation of the task of identifying UUs and extend the existing utility objective to adapt to noisy Oracle. Then, we describe our effective method for identifying UUs in Sect. 3, including the harmfulness of noisy Oracle for the task. And in Sect. 4.3, we present experimental results compared with previous works. We discuss related works in Sect. 5. Finally, Sect. 6 is devoted to conclusions and future work.

2 Problem Formulation

2.1 Preliminaries

In a traditional predictive task, the model $\mathcal{M}$ trained on a limited number of training set D_{train}, and predicts the test set D_{test}. Let $y_i \in Y$ denote the true label of the instance x_i, y_i' denote the predicted label from $\mathcal{M}$, and $s_i \in [0,1]$ denote the confidence of prediction from $\mathcal{M}$. Following the definition of UUs from [14], the instance x is a UU only if the predicted label y' is wrong while its confidence score s is larger than a fixed threshold τ.

Same as previous works, we simplified the predictive task into binary classification (i.e., $Y = \{-1, 1\}$), and set the positive class as the critical class c where the *false positives* are costly and need to be identified [7]. Thus our search space D for identifying UUs constitutes all the samples in test set D_{test} that are predicted positive and their confidence scores are larger than a threshold τ (i.e., $D = \{x_i | x_i \in D_{test} \wedge y_i' = 1 \wedge s_i \geq \tau\}$). Meanwhile, we assume that the probability of a human-like Oracle O_α making mistakes (return the wrong label) is fixed to α for each instance.

Assumption 1. *UUs are clustered in certain locations in the feature space rather than randomly distributed* [14].

If the UUs are randomly distributed in the feature space, we cannot design a method that is better than random sampling. At the same time, a common cause for the emergence of UUs is due to the systematic bias in the training set, thus the UUs should be clustered in certain locations in the space.

2.2 Extended Utility Model with Noisy Oracle

To discover UUs under the limited budget, [14] proposed their utility function $u(\cdot)$ with a prefect Oracle:

$$u(x(t)) = \mathbb{1}_{\{O_\alpha(x(t)) \neq c\}} - \lambda \times cost(x(t)), \tag{1}$$

where $x(t)$ is the instance selected at t^{th} step, $O_\alpha(x(t))$ is the returned label from Oracle (in their study, the Oracle is perfect and the α is equal to 0), $\mathbb{1}_{\{O_\alpha(x(t)) \neq c\}}$ is an indicator function which returns 1 if $x(t)$ is a UU else 0, $cost(x(t))$ is the cost for asking Oracle to label $x(t)$ (set to 1 for simplicity), and λ is a trade-off parameter which is defined by user.

The above utility function tends to pick the instance with the maximum probability of being a UU to query for Oracle. However, there are fake UUs which are mislabelled from noisy Oracle, and we need to punish them in the utility function. Therefore, we extend their utility function as follows.

$$u(x(t), O_\alpha) = \mathbb{1}_{\{O_\alpha(x(t)) \neq c\}} - \lambda \times cost(x(t))$$
$$- \beta \times \mathbb{1}_{\{O_\alpha(x(t)) \neq c \wedge y(t) = c\}}, \tag{2}$$

where $y(t)$ is the true label of $x(t)$, $\mathbb{1}_{\{O_\alpha(x(t)) \neq c \wedge y(t) = c\}}$ is an indicator function which return 1 if $x(t)$ is a fake UU else 0, and β is a penalty term parameter.

Problem Statement: *Let B denote the limited number of queries to the noisy Oracle O_α, our objective is to find an optimal set S^* of B instances in search space D to maximize the cumulative utility. The formal equation is as follows.*

$$S^* = \arg\max_{S \subset D} \sum_{x \in S} u(x, O_\alpha). \tag{3}$$

3   Methodology

In this section, we first explain why noisy Oracle will have a huge impact on the task of identifying UUs, especially when the error rate α is about the same as the concentration of UUs. Then, we present our effective method for identifying UUs with noisy Oracle and corresponding empirical and theoretical analysis. To better illustrate the effectiveness of our method, we follow the assumptions from [14] that the model is black-box and we have no access to the training set.

3.1   Harmfulness of Noisy Oracle

Proposition 1. *If the probability of being a UU is equal to the error rate of noisy Oracle, the ratio of true UUs in all identified UUs is only 50%.*

Let p denote the probability of an instance which is chosen by an automatic method being a true UU, and assume that p and the error rate α are independent. Therefore, the conditional probability of an instance being a true UU given that the instance is an identified UU (referred to P for simplicity) is satisfied:

$$P = \frac{p \cdot (1 - \alpha)}{\alpha \cdot (1 - p) + p \cdot (1 - \alpha)}$$
$$= \frac{p - p \cdot \alpha}{\alpha + p - 2 \cdot \alpha \cdot p}$$
$$= 1 - \frac{1 - p}{\frac{p}{\alpha} + 1 - 2 \cdot p} \tag{4}$$
$$= \frac{1 - \alpha}{\frac{\alpha}{p} + 1 - 2 \cdot \alpha} \tag{5}$$
$$\text{s.t.} \quad 0 < p \leq 1$$
$$0 < \alpha \leq 1$$

According to the above equations, P will decrease with the increase of α (Eq. 4), and will increase with the increase of p (Eq. 5). This shows that when the error rate is large, or when the concentration of UU is low, the fake UUs will account for a large percentage of all identified UUs. Meanwhile because the probability of being a UU is small due to the UUs are rare in dataset, if α is equal to p, the ratio of true UUs in all identified UUs is only 50%. Therefore, we must consider the fake UUs of noisy Oracle when we identify UUs.

3.2   Our Effective Method

Our method draws inspiration from selective sampling in CBR [22] and k-NN confidence measures in Active Learning [12]. The biggest difference between our method and them is that our method aims to discover more UUs effectively under limited budget with noisy Oracle, but their approaches aim to pick the most informative instances to improve the performance of the model. According to the utility function (Eq. 2), we should select the instance with the maximum probability of being a UU. Meanwhile because we do not know the probability of being a UU for each instance, we need to explore the search space to prevent the algorithm from falling into the local optimum. Therefore, we use an epsilon-greedy strategy [29] in our method to solve this explore-exploit dilemma. Specifically, at the tth step in our method, we randomly select an unvisited instance with the probability of $\epsilon(t)$ (with uniform distributed), otherwise we select the instance with the maximum probability of being a UU.

In order to know which instance is most likely to be a UU with current information, we first select a visited instance $\hat{x}$ with the maximum probability of being a UU, and then sample an unvisited instance nearest to the instance $\hat{x}$ as our optimal choice. The intuition in our method is that if an instance x with the maximum probability of being a UU, the instance that is unvisited and nearest to x is most likely to be a UU. Therefore, as long as we estimate the probability for each discovered instance, we can exploit UUs near the instance with the maximum probability of being a UU. Since we don't know the true label of each instance in test set, we use a dynamic k-nearest neighbour approach to estimate the probability in our method. The details are as follows.

At the tth step, let D_t denote the current unvisited instance set, S_t denote the current queried instance set, and $\mathcal{N}(x, D_t)$ denote the nearest instance in D_t to x. The probability $\mathcal{P}_t(x)$ of the instance x being a UU in our estimation approach as follows.

$$\mathcal{P}_t(x) = \frac{\sum_{x' \in D_t(x)} \mathbb{1}_{\{O_\alpha(x') \neq c\}}}{|D_t(x)|}, \tag{6}$$

$$D_t(x) = \{x'' | x'' \in S_t \wedge d(x, x'') < d(x, \mathcal{N}(x, D_t))\}, \tag{7}$$

where $d(\cdot, \cdot)$ is a distance function, and we use the Euclidean distance in the feature space plus the absolute value of the difference in confidence as the distance between two instances. Meanwhile because the probability of UU near a

---

Algorithm 1. Our Method for Identifying UUs

Input: search space $D = \{x_1, x_2, \ldots, x_n\}$, limited number of queries B, confidence scores $\{s_1, s_2, \ldots, s_n\}$, explore sequence $\{\epsilon(1), \epsilon(2), \ldots, \epsilon(B)\}$, the critical class c, and noisy Oracle O_α

Output: the cumulative utility $\sum_{t=1}^{B} u(x(t), O_\alpha)$

1: $S_1 = \emptyset, D_1 = D$
2: **for** t from 1 to B **do**
3:     **if** $rand() \leq \epsilon(t)$ **or** no UUs in S_t **then**
4:        Select an instance $x(t)$ from D_t randomly
5:     **else**
6:        $\hat{x} = \underset{x \in S_t \wedge O_\alpha(x) \neq c}{\arg\max} \mathcal{P}(x)$
7:        $x(t) = \mathcal{N}(\hat{x}, D_t)$
8:        Query the Oracle O_α for its label
9:        $S_{t+1} = S_t \cup x(t)$
10:       $D_{t+1} = D_t \setminus x(t)$
11:       Update $\mathcal{P}(x)$ for each x in S_{t+1}.
12: **return** $\sum_{t=1}^{B} u(x(t), O_\alpha)$

UU is larger than the probability of UU near a non-UU, we only choose the identified UU with the maximum probability of being a UU to explore new UUs. Algorithm 1 gives the pseudo code for our method for identifying UUs.

3.3 Analysis of Our Method

In this subsection, we compare our method with the partition-based approach [14] to analyse the effectiveness of identifying more UUs and being more robust to noisy Oracle.

Identifying More UUs: Assuming that the partition-based approach has already known which partition with the largest concentration of UUs, and we assume that the probability of being a UU in this partition is $\hat{p} \in (0, 1)$. Meanwhile, there is a UU has been identified but the location in this partition is uncertain.

The partition-based approach is heavily dependent on the result of partitioning algorithm, if $\hat{p}$ is high, the approach will perform well on this dataset. On the contrary, our method does not have this dependency, and as long as the UUs are clustered together rather than evenly distributed our method will perform well. Especially if the UUs are all clustered together and away from other non-UUs (e.g., in Fig. 2), the probability of our method of discovering a new UU from an identified UU is **1.0** which is larger than $\hat{p}$ in this case. Furthermore, the subsequent experimental results (see Sect. 4.3) also show that our method is better than the partition-based approach in identifying more UUs.

Noise Robustness: Our method is robust against noisy Oracle due to two reasons. First, our method is better than the partition-based approach in identifying more UUs (i.e., with a greater probability of the selected instance being a UU) according to the previous analysis. Therefore, according to Eq. 5, the conditional probability of an instance being a true UU given that the instance is an identified UU in our method is larger than that in the partition-based approach. Second, the partition-based approach randomly sample instances in the same partition, thus we cannot tell which ones are true UUs and which ones are fake UUs. On the contrary, in our method, we make the probability estimation for each queried instance to be a UU, and the estimated probability of being a UU for the fake UU is lower than that for the true UU. Therefore, the system can be aware of that those identified UUs with low estimated probability are likely to be fake UUs.

4 Evaluation

In this section, we conduct experiments to verify the effectiveness of our method in identifying more UUs with a perfect Oracle and the robustness to a noisy Oracle.

4.1 Datasets

In our experiments, we choose four benchmark datasets processed by [3][1] including three text datasets and one image dataset:

- **Pang05**: This dataset is collected from [20]. It contains 10 K sentiment snippets (or sentences) expressing opinions on various movies. The expressing opinions including positive and negative sentiment and we set the positive sentiment as our critical class.
- **Pang04**: This dataset is collected from [19]. It contains 10 K subjective and objective snippets (or sentences) extracted from Rotten Tomatoes pages and IMDb plot summaries. We set the objective as our critical class.
- **McAuley15**: This dataset is collected from [16]. It contains 50 K reviews of book and electronics randomly sampling from Amazon reviews, and the objective is to classify whether a sentence has positive or negative sentiment. We set the positive sentiment as our critical class, and trained on the electronics reviews then test on the book reviews.
- **Kaggle13**[2]: This dataset contains 25 K cat and dog images from Kaggle. The objective is to classify whether an input image is a cat or a dog. We set dog as our critical class.

---

[1] http://aiweb.cs.washington.edu/ai/unkunk18/.
[2] https://www.kaggle.com/c/dogs-vs-cats/data.

For all datasets (except for McAuley15), the data is divided equally into a training set and a test set firstly. Then, to make the bias on Pang05 and Pang04, [3] use a decision tree to randomly remove part of the training set. And for Kaggle13, they remove all black cats from training set by asking crowd workers. Finally, the size of all test sets is limited by random sampling to 5000, and we construct search space on these fixed-size test sets.

4.2 Experimental Settings

In our experiments, in order for the original biased model to have high performance on the validation set, we use the distributed representation, which has been proven to be effective and is commonly used [17,30], as the features of text data and image data. Specifically, for text data, we use the pre-trained Word2Vec model [17] which is trained on Google News to represent the averaged distribution for each sentence. And for image data, we use the features obtained from the last max-pooling layer of a pre-trained AlexNet model [13] which is trained on ImageNet dataset. Meanwhile, we use logistic regression as the classifier for image dataset and random forest as the classifier for all text datasets.

All hyper-parameters in training process are set to the default parameters in sklearn[3]. Meanwhile, we set the trade-off parameter γ to 0.2 and the cost of each instance to 1. Notice that the values of these two parameters do not actually affect the process of the algorithm, and we set this up to align with previous work [14]. We set the penalty term parameter β to 3, and we will discuss it in more detail later. Meanwhile, we set the confidence threshold τ to 0.65[4] and set our explore sequence to:

$$\epsilon(t) = \begin{cases} 1.0 - \frac{2t}{B}, & t \leq \frac{B}{2}, \\ 0, & else, \end{cases} \tag{8}$$

where B is the limited steps and set to 500 for all datasets. This is done in order to try to discover UUs in different areas as far as possible, then go to exploit UUs near the discovered UUs. Meanwhile, we follow the setting from [26] and simulate noise by flipping label randomly (i.e., the noise rate α), which is beneficial to the quantitative analysis of experiments.

To demonstrate the effectiveness of identifying UUs, we compared our method with random sampling and the partition-based approach [14]. Since [14] did not release the code, we use the reproduced code by [3]. Specifically, for the partition-based approach used in our experiments, we first partition the input data by the confidence scores and then partition the features. The number of partitions is selected using the elbow method[5]. Second, through *Bandit for Unknown*

---

[3] http://scikit-learn.org/.

[4] Actually, τ is a parameter worth discussing, and different thresholds will construct different search spaces. However, we tried several candidate values such as 0.70 and 0.75 in our experiments, and the results basically consistent, so we use the value in previous works [3,14] without further discussion.

[5] https://en.wikipedia.org/wiki/Elbow_method_(clustering).

Unknowns (UUB) algorithm [14], we greedily sample the new instance from the partition with the maximum expected reward. Further, the results demonstrated for all methods are the average across 50 runs.

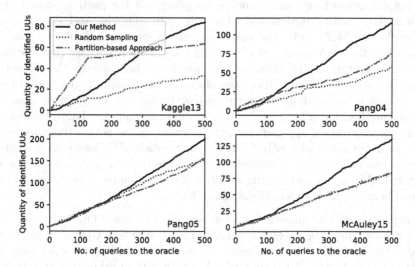

Fig. 3. A comparison of the quantity of identified UUs by different methods with a prefect Oracle. The result shows that our method outperforms the other two methods on all datasets.

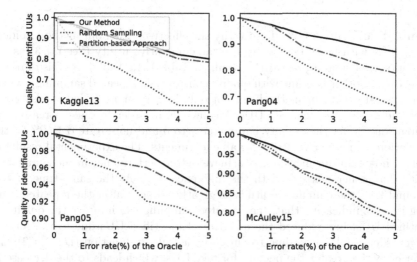

Fig. 4. A comparison of the quality of identified UUs by different methods at different error rate. The result shows that our method outperforms the other two methods on all datasets.

4.3   Discussion of Results

Quantity: We use the quantity of identified UUs to evaluate the ability of identifying more UUs for all methods. From the result shown in Fig. 3, we observe that our method outperforms than random sampling and the partition-based approach in the quantity of identified UUs with perfect Oracle. And also observed in Pang05 and McAuley15, the partition-based approach is similar to random sampling in the performance of identifying UUs. This is because that the partitioning algorithm in [14] does not well partition the space by the difference of concentration of UUs on these two datasets. In Kaggle13, the reason that our method is worse than the partition-based approach in the early stage is that our method has a large probability of random sampling. Later, the reason for the partition-based approach being significantly worse is that there are fewer instances in the partitions with the high concentration of UUs and the algorithm has exhausted all of them. The results also indicate that the partition-based approach is highly dependent on the result of its partitioning algorithm, and our method is more stable in identifying more UUs.

Quality: To test the robustness of our approach to noisy Oracle, we use the quality of identified UUs, which is equal to the ratio of true UUs in all identified UUs, as the evaluation metric. From the result shown in Fig. 4, we see that the quality of UUs identified in our method is higher than other two approaches, which shows that our method is more robust to noisy Oracle when we discovery UUs. Especially in the Pang04, when the error rate reaches 5%, the quality of identified UUs in our method is about 90%, while the quality of identified UUs in partition-based approach is only 80%, and that in random sampling is less than 70%.

Cumulative Utility: Overall, to verify the effectiveness of our method in identifying UUs with noisy Oracle, we use the cumulative utility (See Eq. 3) as the evaluation metric and present the result in Table 1. In Table 1, we also present result from another baseline with quality control (i.e., repeated sampling), which is to illustrate that our method can not only identify more UUs but also guarantee the quality of identified UUs. Meanwhile, in order to make a reasonable comparison, we fix the penalty parameter γ to 0 and noise rate α to 2% in the calculation of cumulative utility for all experiments. The experimental results in Table 1 show that our method can achieve better performance in the cumulative utility than other methods with the difference of β. At the same time, it can be found that the cumulative utility is greatly reduced after the repeated sampling is used, indicating that, the repeated sampling can improve the quality of identified UUs, but reduced the quantity of identified UUs due to the limited budget. Meanwhile, according to our extended utility function (i.e., Eq. 2), the larger of β, the greater the penalty for fake UUs, which leads to the decrease in cumulative utility.

Table 1. The comparison of the cumulative utility by different methods on four datasets with a noisy Oracle. The penalty parameter γ is fixed to 0 for simplicity, and the noise rate α is set to 2%.

Dataset	Number of Labellers	Number of Queries	Method	$\beta = 1$	$\beta = 2$	$\beta = 3$
Pang04	1	500	Random Sampling	57.2	45.2	33.3
			Partition-based Approach	69.6	61.2	52.8
			Our Method	**113.9**	**106.2**	**98.4**
	3	500/3	Random Sampling	16.1	11.1	6.1
			Partition-based Approach	25.8	23.8	21.7
			Our Method	44.7	42.2	39.7
Pang05	1	500	Random Sampling	149.9	143.0	136.0
			Partition-based Approach	151.2	146.0	140.8
			Our Method	**196.0**	**192.9**	**189.9**
	3	500/3	Random Sampling	51.0	48.0	45.1
			Partition-based Approach	49.1	48.8	48.6
			Our Method	65.6	63.5	61.5
McAuley15	1	500	Random Sampling	82.7	73.8	64.8
			Partition-based Approach	82.4	74.0	65.5
			Our Method	**125.3**	**117.0**	**108.7**
	3	500/3	Random Sampling	26.8	22.1	17.4
			Partition-based Approach	25.9	22.5	19.1
			Our Method	39.1	37.2	35.3
Kaggle13	1	500	Random Sampling	30.2	21.5	12.7
			Partition-based Approach	75.7	67.8	59.8
			Our Method	**80.2**	**71.5**	**62.8**
	3	500/3	Random Sampling	10.9	5.9	2.2
			Partition-based Approach	61.0	52.3	55.0
			Our Method	38.2	35.2	32.2

5   Related Work

5.1   Unknown Unknowns

Unknown Unknowns are cases where the model fails while being confident that it is correct to have been studied in [2]. They designed a crowdsourcing framework (Beat The Machine, BTM) in a game-like setting to leverage humans to identify them. The experiments demonstrate that their framework could discovery more UUs than some variant random sampling strategies. Meanwhile, they found that there is consistency and internal coherence in the identified UUs. However, the BTM is completely dependent on humans without assistance and is not realistic enough for automatic identifying UUs.

Therefore, [14] proposed a two-step framework, which is only requiring a human-like Oracle to annotate the instance for task, to discover UUs in the specified test set. Their framework is based on the assumption that UUs are clustered in certain space but not randomly. In their first step which is called *Descriptive Space Partitioning* (DSP), they induce a similarity preserving partition on test set. Then, they present a multi-armed bandit algorithm which is called *Bandit for Unknown Unknowns* (UUB) for discovering UUs in these partitions. They estimate the concentration of UUs in each partition by random sampling strategy. Later, [3] argued that it is not enough to identify more independent UUs to understand the machine learner's limitations. And they proposed a coverage-based utility model to maximize the coverage of identified UUs for test set. Their utility model is based on a custom coverage function, and they prove that the greedy strategy will find a cover within a constant factor of optimal if the positions of all UUs are known in advance. Their model selects the sample with the highest expected utility gain in each step and achieve better results in the objective of coverage than [14].

However, the approaches from [3,14] all rely on a highly reliable human-like Oracle which is impractical in real world. Meanwhile, the probability of each instance being UU is estimated by dividing the search space into multiple partitions and then sampling, which is a limitation for more accurate estimation of the probability of being a UU between different instances in the same partition. In this work, we follow the utility model proposed from [14] and extend the utility function to adapt to noisy Oracle. Meanwhile, we propose a more effective method for identifying UUs with noisy Oracle.

5.2   Other Related Work

Active Learning [12,23] is a common method for improving the generalization ability of model by labelling a limited number samples, including *Uncertainty sampling* [15], *Query by committee* [25], *Excepted model change* [24], *Expected error reduction* [32], and *Expected variance reduction* [31]. However, these query strategies focus on samples that the model is uncertain about, or prefer to the samples in dense regions of the space which is likely to modify the decision of model. Therefore, Active Learning approaches are tend to identify the error data with low confidence score, which are called *Known Unknowns* [2], and are not suitable for identifying UUs.

Repeated Labelling [11] (or other quality control mechanism) is the common approach for improving the data quality from crowdsourcing, which is also useful for modelling [26]. However, it will increase the cost of querying Oracle and reducing the number of queries, thus it is not suitable for the identifying UUs task. Meanwhile, our experimental results confirm that repeated labelling reduces the cumulative utility under the limited budget.

Outlier Detection (or *Anomaly Detection*) [5,6,9] is the commonly used identification of detecting the anomalous points in test set. However, these works assume that the training set distribution is known, thus conflict with our assumptions.

The main problem causing UUs is the different distribution between source domain and target domain. There is a variety of fields are relevant to this problem, such as *Domain Adaptation* [4,8], *Covariate Shift* [27], and *Transfer Learning* [18]. However, they also need access to the training set is the same as outlier detection.

6 Conclusions and Future Work

In this paper, we discuss the impact of noisy Oracle on identifying UUs, and extend the utility model proposed from [14] to adapt to noisy Oracle. At the same time, we present an effective method for identifying UUs which is also robust to noisy Oracle. The experimental results show that our method outperforms than other benchmarks in terms of quantity and quality of identified UUs. Meanwhile, the experimental results also show that the partition-based approach is highly dependent on the partitioning algorithm for identifying UUs, and the partition-based approach is not as stable as our method in our experiments.

Two considerations have been identified for future work. First, our method has effectively identified a lot of UUs for specified model, but how can we leverage them to understand the limitation of model? Some fancy frameworks [21] in explainable AI (XAI) have been proposed, and then how to combine the identified UUs with them so that researchers or users can better understand the model? Second, the identified UUs are valuable for further enhancement of the model's performance, how to leverage these error cases to improve the performance of the model is our another research work in future.

Acknowledgments. We thank all reviewers who provided the thoughtful and constructive comments on this paper. This research is funded by the National Key R&D Program of China (No. 2017YFC0803700), the National Natural Science Foundation of China (No. 61773167), the Shanghai Municipal Commission of Economy and Informatization (No. 170513), and the Open Research Fund of Shanghai Key Laboratory of Multidimensional Information Processing, East China Normal University. The computation is performed in the Supercomputer Center of ECNU.

References

1. Amodei, D., Olah, C., Steinhardt, J., Christiano, P., Schulman, J., Man, D.: Concrete problems in ai safety (2016)
2. Attenberg, J., Ipeirotis, P., Provost, F.: Beat the machine: challenging humans to find a predictive model's unknown unknowns. J. Data Inf. Qual. (JDIQ) **6**(1), 1 (2015)
3. Bansal, G., Weld, D.S.: A coverage-based utility model for identifying unknown unknowns. In: AAAI (2018)
4. Blitzer, J., Dredze, M., Pereira, F.: Biographies, bollywood, boom-boxes and blenders: domain adaptation for sentiment classification. In: ACL, pp. 187–205 (2007)
5. Chandola, V., Banerjee, A., Kumar, V.: Outlier detection: a survey. ACM Comput. Surv. (2007)
6. Chandola, V., Banerjee, A., Kumar, V.: Anomaly detection: a survey. ACM Comput. Surv. (CSUR) **41**(3), 15 (2009)
7. Elkan, C.: The foundations of cost-sensitive learning. In: IJCAI, vol. 17, pp. 973–978. Lawrence Erlbaum Associates Ltd. (2001)
8. Glorot, X., Bordes, A., Bengio, Y.: Domain adaptation for large-scale sentiment classification: a deep learning approach. In: ICML, pp. 513–520 (2011)
9. Han, J., Pei, J., Kamber, M.: Data Mining: Concepts and Techniques. Elsevier, Burlington (2011)
10. Hinton, G., et al.: Deep neural networks for acoustic modeling in speech recognition: the shared views of four research groups. IEEE Signal Process. Mag. **29**(6), 82–97 (2012)
11. Hsueh, P.Y., Melville, P., Sindhwani, V.: Data quality from crowdsourcing: a study of annotation selection criteria. In: NAACL HLT Workshop on Active Learning and NLP, pp. 27–35. Association for Computational Linguistics (2009)
12. Hu, R., Delany, S., MacNamee, B.: Sampling with confidence: using K-NN confidence measures in active learning. In: ICCBR, p. 50 (2009)
13. Krizhevsky, A., Sutskever, I., Hinton, G.E.: Imagenet classification with deep convolutional neural networks. In: NIPS, pp. 1097–1105 (2012)
14. Lakkaraju, H., Kamar, E., Caruana, R., Horvitz, E.: Identifying unknown unknowns in the open world: representations and policies for guided exploration. In: AAAI, pp. 2124–2132 (2017)
15. Lewis, D.D., Gale, W.A.: A sequential algorithm for training text classifiers. In: Croft, B.W., van Rijsbergen, C.J. (eds.) SIGIR, pp. 3–12. Springer, New York (1994). https://doi.org/10.1007/978-1-4471-2099-5_1
16. McAuley, J., Pandey, R., Leskovec, J.: Inferring networks of substitutable and complementary products. In: KDD, pp. 785–794. ACM (2015)
17. Mikolov, T., Chen, K., Corrado, G., Dean, J.: Efficient estimation of word representations in vector space. arXiv preprint arXiv:1301.3781 (2013)
18. Pan, S.J., Yang, Q.: A survey on transfer learning. TKDE **22**(10), 1345–1359 (2010)
19. Pang, B., Lee, L.: A sentimental education: sentiment analysis using subjectivity summarization based on minimum cuts. In: ACL, p. 271. Association for Computational Linguistics (2004)
20. Pang, B., Lee, L.: Seeing stars: exploiting class relationships for sentiment categorization with respect to rating scales. In: ACL, pp. 115–124. Association for Computational Linguistics (2005)

21. Ribeiro, M.T., Singh, S., Guestrin, C.: Why should i trust you? Explaining the predictions of any classifier. In: KDD, pp. 1135–1144. ACM (2016)
22. Sani, S., Wiratunga, N., Massie, S., Cooper, K.: kNN sampling for personalised human activity recognition. In: Aha, D.W., Lieber, J. (eds.) ICCBR 2017. LNCS (LNAI), vol. 10339, pp. 330–344. Springer, Cham (2017). https://doi.org/10.1007/978-3-319-61030-6_23
23. Settles, B.: Active learning literature survey. University of Wisconsin, Madison 52(55–66), 11 (2010)
24. Settles, B., Craven, M., Ray, S.: Multiple-instance active learning. In: NIPS, pp. 1289–1296 (2008)
25. Seung, H.S., Opper, M., Sompolinsky, H.: Query by committee. In: COLT, pp. 287–294. ACM (1992)
26. Sheng, V.S., Provost, F., Ipeirotis, P.G.: Get another label? Improving data quality and data mining using multiple, noisy labelers. In: KDD, pp. 614–622. ACM (2008)
27. Shimodaira, H.: Improving predictive inference under covariate shift by weighting the log-likelihood function. J. Stat. Plan. Inference 90(2), 227–244 (2000)
28. Silver, D., et al.: Mastering the game of go with deep neural networks and tree search. Nature 529(7587), 484 (2016)
29. Sutton, R.S., Barto, A.G.: Reinforcement Learning: An Introduction, vol. 1. MIT Press, Cambridge (1998)
30. Vinyals, O., Toshev, A., Bengio, S., Erhan, D.: Show and tell: lessons learned from the 2015 mscoco image captioning challenge. IEEE Trans. Pattern Anal. Mach. Intell. 39(4), 652–663 (2017)
31. Zhang, T., Oles, F.: The value of unlabeled data for classification problems. In: ICML, pp. 1191–1198. Citeseer (2000)
32. Zhu, X., Lafferty, J., Ghahramani, Z.: Combining active learning and semi-supervised learning using gaussian fields and harmonic functions. In: ICML 2003 Workshop on the Continuum From Labeled to Unlabeled Data in Machine Learning and Data Mining, vol. 3 (2003)

Special Track: Computational Analogy

On the Role of Similarity in Analogical Transfer

Fadi Badra[1]([⊠]), Karima Sedki[1], and Adrien Ugon[2]

[1] Université Paris 13, Sorbonne Université, Inserm, Laboratoire d'informatique médicale et d'ingénierie des connaissances en e-santé LIMICS, 75006 Paris, France
{badra,karima.sedki}@univ-paris13.fr
[2] ESIEE-Paris, Noisy-le-Grand, France
adrien.ugon@esiee.fr

Abstract. Analogical transfer consists in making the assumption that if two situations are alike in some respect, they may be alike in others. This article explores the links that exist between analogical transfer and the qualitative measurement of differences. The main idea is to formulate the similarity principle as a dependency between two measurements of difference. Analogical transfer is formulated as a similarity-based reasoning: it is plausible that equally different pairs in a certain dimension are also equally different in another dimension, at least for pairs that are not too (analogically) dissimilar.

Keywords: Analogical transfer · Qualitative modeling
Similarity measurement

1 Introduction

Case-based reasoning (CBR) can be seen as the application of an analogical inference to problem solving. Analogical reasoning is a cognitive process in which some structural pattern identified in a source conceptualization is transferred to a target domain (possibly the same domain) in order to learn a target conceptualization [10]. Three main subtasks are identified: retrieval, mapping, and transfer. The aim of the retrieval phase is to use some memory to identify to which source situation the new (target) situation can be compared with. The mapping phase produces a mapping from the retrieved source situation to the target situation. The transfer phase uses this mapping to makes some prediction on how to complete the description of the target situation. Analogies in which mapping is followed with a transfer of information or explanations are called predictive analogies in [10].

This article explores the links that exist between analogical transfer and the qualitative measurement of differences. The main idea is that the similarity principle can be formulated as a dependency between two measurements of difference: it is plausible that an equal difference observed on a certain dimension is accompagnied by an equal difference in some other dimension. We show

© Springer Nature Switzerland AG 2018
M. T. Cox et al. (Eds.): ICCBR 2018, LNAI 11156, pp. 499–514, 2018.
https://doi.org/10.1007/978-3-030-01081-2_33

that difference equality ("a and b are as different as c and d") and degrees of difference ("a and b are more different than c and d") can be measured by applying a scale on the set of pairs of situations. A scale is a homomorphism (*i.e.*, a structure-preserving mapping) between relational structures which is used in mathematical theories of measurement [28] to assign numbers to objects so that they can be compared. Such a scale groups into equivalence classes the pairs of equally different situations for the considered dimension. Taking a geometrical metaphor, such equivalence class can be seen as a "contour line", or a "line of equal differences" in the underlying qualitative similarity model. Analogical transfer is thus formulated as a similarity-based reasoning on such contour lines: if a contour line is included in another at a given point, then it may also be included at other points that are not too (analogically) dissimilar.

The paper is organized as follows. The next section discusses the role that differences play in analogical transfer through a review of the literature. Section 3 introduces qualitative similarity relations. In Sect. 4, differences are measured by defining scales on the set of pairs. Section 5 shows that in this framework, analogical dissimilarity corresponds to a difference between two scale values. Section 6 provides a formalization of the similarity principle, which is used in Sect. 7 to propose a qualitative formalization of analogical transfer. Section 8 concludes the paper.

2   The Use of Differences in Analogical Transfer

Analogical transfer is stated from a logical perspective in [6] as the following hypothetical rule of inference, referred to as the "analogical jump" (AJ):

$$\frac{P(s) \quad P(t) \quad Q(s)}{Q(t)} \tag{AJ}$$

The authors of [6] claim that a sufficient condition for the inference (AJ) to be justified should: (i) be weaker than a generalization rule $\forall x P(x) \Rightarrow Q(x)$ (otherwise the inference is simply deductive), (ii) on the contrary, be stronger than an enumerative induction that consists in applying the rule $P \Rightarrow Q$ to t only because it was seen to hold on one example s, (iii) be in proportion to the *amount* of similarity between sources and targets, but similarity degrees are highly subjective and context-dependent. One criteria that seems satisfying is when a functional dependency holds between P and Q. To be able to make an analogical jump, instance-based learning approaches apply a *similarity principle*, that states that the more similar two causes are, the more plausible it is that they have the same effect. In numerical settings, this property can be translated in the geometrical property that locally, a bounded similarity on problems results in a bounded similarity on solutions [14].

Analogical transfer can be used to transfer either *commonalities* between a target situation and the source situations retrieved from memory, or *differences*. Case-based adaptation can be seen as a more complex transfer of differences that is required when a simple copy of (parts of) a source case appears not to be sufficient to predict the description of the target situation.

Transferring Commonalities. The properties P and Q may represent commonalities. For example, Bob's car and John's car share the property P of being a 1982 Mustang GLX V6 hatchbacks, and Bob's car has the property Q of having a price of 3 500\$. The inference is that the price of John's car should also be around 3 500\$. Another example of predictive analogy that transfers a commonality is the k-Nearest Neighbor algorithm [20], an instance-based machine learning algorithm in which the class $cls(x_0)$ of a target instance x_0 is predicted from the class value $cls(x)$ of the k instances x that are most similar to x_0. The inference schema (AJ) is applied on a neighborhood $\mathcal{N}(x)$ of the retrieved instance x:

$$\frac{x \in \mathcal{N}(x) \quad cls(x) = c \quad x_0 \in \mathcal{N}(x)}{cls(x_0) = c}$$

Transferring Differences. In the analogical jump (AJ), P and Q may also represent differences. For example, in Fig. 1, adapted from [29], the pair (a, a') can be mapped to the pair (b, b') because b' differs from b in the same way that a' differs from a. Both pairs instanciate the two relational predicates $R_1 =$ "differs in profile shape from round to sharp" and $R_2 =$ "has the same eyebrow as". If we know that d' has a sharp profile (*i.e.*, $R_1(d, d')$ holds), then assuming d' is to d what a' is to a, applying the rule (AJ) enables to make the hypothesis that d' has the same eyebrow (curved) as d, *i.e.*, that $R_2(d, d')$ holds:

$$\frac{R_1(a, a') \quad R_2(a, a') \quad R_1(d, d')}{R_2(d, d')}$$

Another example of predictive analogy that transfers differences is the analogical proportion-based inference, used in analogical classification, which, as shown e.g., in [3], also consists in making an analogical jump.

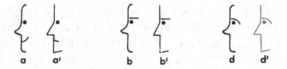

a   a'   b   b'   d   d'

Fig. 1. Six faces.

Transfer and Adaptation. Adaptation, *i.e.*, the cognitive ability to envision a target solution that is different from any previously encountered solution, is considered in cognitive psychology [21, 24], as one of the core components of analogical transfer. In the following example, taken from [21], students adapt solution procedures to solve new mathematical problems. They are asked to adapt the solution procedure of a mathematical problem (called the *garden problem* [22]), in which the goal is to calculate the number of plants that two people have in their garden. The solution procedure consists in (i) computing the least common multiple (LCM) of a set of numbers (the LCM of 10, 4, and 5, is 20), (ii) generate the first multiples of the obtained number (20, 40, 60, etc.), (iii) add a left over to each multiple (the left over is 2, so we obtain 22, 42, 62, etc.), and (iv) find the smallest candidate solution that is divisible by a given number (the smallest divisible by 6 is 42). Two other mathematical problems, the *marching band* problem and the *cookies problem*, are structurally very similar to the garden problem, but differ by the value given to three attributes: the goal (**g**), the set of divisors (**d**), and the left over (**l**). Fig. 2 represents the difference between these problems: garden denotes the description of the garden problem, band denotes the description of the marching band problem, and cookies denotes the description of the cookies problem. The cookies problem is solved by adapting the solution procedure of the garden problem. To do so, the student has to assess how to modify the solution procedure to account for the differences observed between the two problems. From the remembering of how the marching band problem has been previously solved by adapting the solution of the garden problem, most students were able to induce that a problem with the same structure as the garden problem may be solved by the same solution procedure, up to a substitution of attribute values. However, more complex differences between problems may require a deeper modification of the solution procedure, such as adding or removing steps. The authors give the example of the seashell problem, for which the number of multipliers is greater than the one of the garden problem. Adapting the solution of the garden problem to solve the seashell problem would require to add some reasoning steps to its solution procedure. Adaptation is recognized as being part of the case-based reasoning cycle. But surprisingly, a study of the CBR literature shows that the adaptation step is not included in the case-based analogical inference [23]. The adaptation step is always performed *after* the analogical inference (*i.e.*, retrieval, mapping, and transfer) has taken place, and only aims at modifying its result. Some adaptation methods such as critique-based adaptation [11], or conservative adaptation [16] are used to resolve inconsistencies in the reused source case, whereas others such as differential adaptation [9], case-based adaptation [4] or adaptation by reformulation [17] modify the reused source case in order to fit the requirements on the target case. This singular status of adaptation in CBR research with respect to analogical transfer appears even more striking since many adaptation strategies apply to themselves an analogical process, by reusing adaptation knowledge retrieved from memory, in form of adaptation rules [5], substitutions [18], or adaptation cases [4]. One of the reasons why adaptation is left out of the case-based analogical inference is that adaptation essentially consists in reasoning on the *differences* that exist between two cases and the case-based inference is currently unable to transfer such differences to the target case. While the importance of capturing and reusing case differences has long been acknowledged in adaptation research (see e.g.,[5,9,12,15,18]), the link between case differences and a theory of similarity remains unclear.

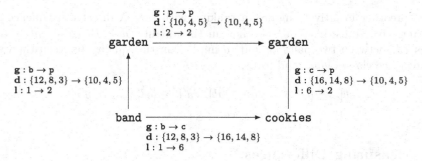

Fig. 2. The differences between the values of the three attributes goal (**g**), set of divisors (**d**), and left over (**l**) in the descriptions of some mathematical problems.

3   Qualitative Similarity Relations

A qualitative representation of similarity consists in dropping numerical values in similarity assessment, which is justified by the fact that actual values of distance between two cases are less significant than the ability to compare two distances. Let $\mathcal{U}$ be a finite, non-empty set, called the *universe*. An element of the square product $\mathcal{U} \times \mathcal{U}$ represents a pair of elements, and is denoted (a, b), or simply ab. Following [30], a *qualitative similarity relation* $\succ$ is defined as a strict weak order on $\mathcal{U} \times \mathcal{U}$. For two pairs $ab, cd \in \mathcal{U} \times \mathcal{U}$, a strict ordering $ab \succ cd$ for a similarity relation $\succ$ is interpreted as "a and b are more similar than c and d", and represents a strict inequality. A strict weak order is a binary relation with the following two properties, for $ab, cd, ef \in \mathcal{U} \times \mathcal{U}$: *asymetry* ($ab \succ cd \Rightarrow \neg (cd \succ ab)$), and *negative transitivity* ($\neg (ab \succ cd) \wedge \neg (cd \succ ef) \Rightarrow \neg (ab \succ ef)$). The axioms of asymetry and negative transitivity define a form of *rationality* of a similarity comparison [28]. If one states that a and b are more similar than c and d, then one can not state that c and d are more similar than a and b. Besides, if one *does not* think that a and b are more similar than c and d, *nor* that c and d are more similar than e and f, then it is reasonable to think also that a and b are *not* more similar than e and f. For a strict weak order $\succ$, let $\sim$ be a binary relation, called the *indifference* relation, defined as: $ab \sim cd \Leftrightarrow \neg (ab \succ cd) \wedge \neg (cd \succ ab)$. An element $ab \sim cd$ is interpreted as "a and b are as similar as c and d". The indifference relation $\sim$ is an equivalence relation: it is reflexive, transitive, and symmetric. Each equivalence relation defines a partition, which is a collection of non-empty disjoint subsets of a set whose union is the whole set. The subset of $\sim$ that contains a pair $ab \in \mathcal{U} \times \mathcal{U}$ is written $[ab]_\sim = \{uv \in \mathcal{U} \times \mathcal{U} \mid ab \sim uv\}$, and is called the equivalence class of ab. Defining a rational (*i.e.*, strict weak) similarity relation $\succ$ on a set of pairs $\mathcal{U} \times \mathcal{U}$ is equivalent to defining a total preorder $\succeq$ on $\mathcal{U} \times \mathcal{U}$. Because $\succ$ is strict weak, there holds that for any $ab, cd \in \mathcal{U} \times \mathcal{U}$, exactly one of $ab \succ cd$, $cd \succ ab$, or $ab \sim cd$ hold. As a result, the relation $\succeq$ defined as $ab \succeq cd$ iff $ab \succ cd$ or $ab \sim cd$ corresponds to the inverse of the complement of the strict weak relation $\succ$ ($ab \succeq cd$ when it is not the case that $ab \prec cd$), and the complement of a strict weak relation is a total preorder. A total preorder intuitively models a ranking with ties. A direct consequence of the negative transitivity of $\succ$ is that an (in)equality $ab \succeq cd$ (resp., $ab \succ cd$, $ab \sim cd$) between two pairs ab and cd implies an (in)equality between the two equivalence classes $[ab]_\sim$ and $[cd]_\sim$:

$$[ab]_\sim \succeq [cd]_\sim \Leftrightarrow \forall uv \in [ab]_\sim, u'v' \in [cd]_\sim, uv \succeq u'v'$$
$$\Leftrightarrow ab \succeq cd$$

4   Measuring Differences

To be able to measure differences on a particular dimension, a scale is defined on the set of pairs of elements of a set. Such a scale is called a variation[1].

Definition 1. *A variation is a scale* $\upsilon : (\mathcal{U} \times \mathcal{U}, \succeq) \longrightarrow (\mathcal{V}, \geq)$.

A scale is a homomorphism, *i.e.*, a mapping that preserves all relations and operations. Therefore, defining such a scale is a way to specify a similarity relation $\succeq$ on a particular dimension: for $a, b, c, d \in \mathcal{U}$, $\upsilon(ab) \sim \upsilon(cd) \Leftrightarrow ab \sim cd$ (two pairs are assigned the same value by the scale υ are equally different), and $\upsilon(ab) > \upsilon(cd) \Leftrightarrow ab \succ cd$ (a and b are more similar than c and d whenever the value assigned to ab is greater than the value assigned to cd). Variations can be used to describe a wide range of similarity relations, from the most specific one ($\upsilon(ab) = ab$) to the most general ($\upsilon(ab) = 1$). In this paper, we will restrict the discussion to variations that are constructed by scaling the set of pairs of values taken by a given feature[2]. A feature is a variable on the set $\mathcal{U}$, and can be modeled as a function $\varphi : \mathcal{U} \longrightarrow \mathcal{X}$. In the following, the term *feature* denotes either a binary variable ($\mathcal{X} = \{0, 1\}$), a nominal variable ($\mathcal{X}$ is an enumerated set, like $\{\mathtt{d}, \mathtt{m}, \mathtt{u}\}$), a quantity ($\mathcal{X}$ is a set of values on an ordinal, interval, or ratio scale), or a variable that takes its value in the powerset $\mathscr{P}(\mathcal{A})$ of a set $\mathcal{A}$. The term *feature space* denotes the set $\mathcal{X}$ of values taken by a feature.

Proposition 1. *Given a feature* $\varphi : \mathcal{U} \to \mathcal{X}$, *a scale* $o : \mathcal{X} \times \mathcal{X} \longrightarrow \mathcal{V}$, *and a strict weak order* $>$ *on* $\mathcal{V}$, *the function* $\upsilon_o^\varphi : \mathcal{U} \times \mathcal{U} \longrightarrow \mathcal{V}$ *defined by*

$$\upsilon_o^\varphi(ab) = o(\varphi(a), \varphi(b))$$

is a variation iff $ab \succ cd \Leftrightarrow \varphi(a)\varphi(b) \succ_{\mathcal{X} \times \mathcal{X}} \varphi(c)\varphi(d)$, *where* $\succ_{\mathcal{X} \times \mathcal{X}}$ *is the (strict weak) order induced on* $\mathcal{X} \times \mathcal{X}$ *by the scale* o *(i.e.,* $o(xy) > o(zt) \Leftrightarrow xy \succ_{\mathcal{X} \times \mathcal{X}} zt$*).*

---

[1] The term *variation* was introduced in [1] to denote a qualitative representation of differences between two or more states. In [1], (binary) variations were represented by functions whose domain is the set of pairs.

[2] The latter are a very common way to represent differences between two objects, although not the only one. Variations could for example represent complex rewriting rules, such as term reduction relations.

Proof. (Sketch) For two pairs ab and cd of $\mathcal{U} \times \mathcal{U}$, $\varphi(a)\varphi(b) \in \mathcal{X} \times \mathcal{X}$, and $\varphi(c)\varphi(d) \in \mathcal{X} \times \mathcal{X}$. The relation $>$ on $\mathcal{V}$ is strict weak, so exactly one of $\varphi(a)\varphi(b) \succ_{\mathcal{X} \times \mathcal{X}} \varphi(c)\varphi(d)$, $\varphi(a)\varphi(b) \prec_{\mathcal{X} \times \mathcal{X}} \varphi(c)\varphi(d)$, or $\varphi(a)\varphi(b) \sim_{\mathcal{X} \times \mathcal{X}} \varphi(c)\varphi(d)$ holds.

Table 1. Some examples of scales $\mathbf{o} : \mathcal{X} \times \mathcal{X} \longrightarrow \mathcal{V}$ defined on the square product of a feature space $\mathcal{X}$.

Feature space	Examples
All	$\neq(xy) = \begin{cases} 1 & \text{if } x \neq y \\ 0 & \text{if } x = y \end{cases}$ $\mathbf{1}(xy) = \begin{cases} 0 & \text{if } x = y = 1 \\ 1 & \text{otherwise} \end{cases}$ $Id(xy) = xy$
Ordinal	$\leq(xy) = \begin{cases} 1 & \text{if } x \leq y \\ 0 & \text{otherwise} \end{cases}$
Continuous	$-(xy) = y - x$ $Sign(xy) = \begin{cases} + & \text{if } x < y \\ \mathbf{o} & \text{if } x = y \\ - & \text{if } x > y \end{cases}$ $d_p(xy) = \|y - x\|_p$
Sets	$\Delta(XY) = |X \setminus Y| + |Y \setminus X|$ $AP(XY) = (X \setminus Y, Y \setminus X)$ $s(XY) = (X \setminus Y, X \cap Y, Y \setminus X)$

Examples. Table 1 gives some examples of scales $\mathbf{o}$ defined on the set $\mathcal{X} \times \mathcal{X}$. The variation $\upsilon_{\neq}^{\text{eyebrow}}$ can be defined from the nominal feature $\varphi = \text{eyebrow} : \mathcal{U} \longrightarrow \mathcal{X}$ and the scale $=: \mathcal{X} \times \mathcal{X} \longrightarrow \{0,1\}$ as follows:

$$\upsilon_{\neq}^{\text{eyebrow}}(ab) = \begin{cases} 1 & \text{if } \text{eyebrow}(a) \neq \text{eyebrow}(b) \\ 0 & \text{if } \text{eyebrow}(a) = \text{eyebrow}(b) \end{cases}$$

The indicator function $\mathbf{1}_P$ of the class "sharing the property P" can be defined from the feature $\varphi = P$ and the scale $\mathbf{1} : \mathcal{X} \times \mathcal{X} \longrightarrow \{0,1\}$ as follows:

$$\mathbf{1}_P(ab) = \upsilon_{\mathbf{1}}^{P}(ab) = \begin{cases} 0 & \text{if both } P(a) \text{ and } P(b) \text{ hold} \\ 1 & \text{otherwise} \end{cases}$$

The variation $\upsilon_{Id}^{\text{color}}(ab) = (\text{color}(a), \text{color}(b))$ can be defined from the nominal feature $\varphi = \text{color} : \mathcal{U} \longrightarrow \mathcal{X}$ with $\mathcal{X} = \{\mathsf{r}, \mathsf{g}, \mathsf{b}\}$, and the scale $Id(xy) = xy$. The variation $\upsilon_{d_1}^{\mathbf{age}}(xy) = |\mathbf{age}(y) - \mathbf{age}(x)|$ can be defined from the numerical feature $\varphi = \mathbf{age} : \mathcal{U} \longrightarrow \mathbb{N}$ and the scale $d_1 : \mathbb{N} \times \mathbb{N} \longrightarrow \mathbb{N}$ where d_1 is the Manhattan distance. This function returns a natural number representing the (absolute) difference in value of the property $\mathbf{age}$. Let $\varphi_1, \varphi_2, \ldots, \varphi_n$ be n numerical features, and $\mathbf{v}$ be the function such that $\mathbf{v}(a) = (\varphi_1(a), \varphi_2(a), \ldots, \varphi_n(a)) \in \mathbb{R}^n$ for $a \in \mathcal{U}$. The variation $\overrightarrow{ab} = \upsilon_-^{\mathbf{v}}(ab) = \mathbf{v}(b) - \mathbf{v}(a)$ gives the difference between two vectors. Let $\succeq_{a_-}$ be the restriction of $\succeq$ to $\{a\} \times \mathcal{U}$. An inequality $ab \succeq_{a_-} ac$ is interpreted as "b is at least as similar to a as c is to a". If the order $\succeq_{a_-}$ is a complete preorder on $\{a\} \times \mathcal{U}$, there exists a function $u : \{a\} \times \mathcal{U} \longrightarrow \mathbb{R}$, called a *utility function*, such that for all $b, c \in \mathcal{U}$, $ab \succ ac \Leftrightarrow u(ab) > u(ac)$. The utility function can be defined for example using a distance measure $\|.\|_p$ on $\mathcal{U}$ by taking $u = \upsilon_{d_p}^{\mathbf{v}}$ where $\upsilon_{d_p}^{\mathbf{v}}(ab) = \|\overrightarrow{ab}\|_p$ gives the distance between a and b. Consider the function $\varphi = a_\rightarrow : \mathcal{U} \longrightarrow \mathbb{N}^+$ that gives for each $p \in \mathcal{U}$ the size of the principal ideal $\downarrow ap = \{ab \in \{a\} \times \mathcal{U} \mid ap \succeq ab\}$. The variation $\upsilon_{d_1}^{a_\rightarrow}(bc) = |size(\downarrow ac) - size(\downarrow ab)|$ gives a numerical measure of distance between two elements b and c when a is chosen as a frame of reference. In particular, if $b = a$, $\upsilon_{d_1}^{a_\rightarrow}(ac) = |size(\downarrow ac) - 1|$ gives a distance from a to c in the sense of the nearest neighbors: $\upsilon_{d_1}^{a_\rightarrow}(ac) = k$ iff c is the $k-$Nearest Neighbor of a. The scale $AP(XY) = (X \setminus Y, Y \setminus X)$ represents the difference from a set X to a set Y by "what is lost" from X to Y and "what is gained" from X to Y. The scale $\Delta(XY) = |X \setminus Y| + |Y \setminus X|$ measures the symmetric difference between X and Y. If the n-tuples $X = (X_1, X_2, \ldots, X_n)$ and $Y = (Y_1, Y_2, \ldots, Y_n)$ are elements of a cartesian product $A_1 \times A_2 \times \ldots A_n$ (such that $\forall i, X_i \subseteq A_i$ and $Y_i \subseteq A_i$), the scale Δ is given by $\Delta(XY) = \sum_i (|X_i \setminus Y_i| + |Y_i \setminus X_i|)$. The function $s(X, Y) = (X \setminus Y, X \cap Y, Y \setminus X)$ corresponds to what Amos Tversky called a *matching function* in [29].

Measuring an Equality of Differences. An equality $\upsilon(ab) \sim_\upsilon \upsilon(cd)$ holds if d differs from c as b differs from a according to the scale υ. The equivalence class $[ab]_\upsilon = \{cd \in \mathcal{U} \times \mathcal{U} \mid \upsilon(ab) \sim_\upsilon \upsilon(cd)\}$ of a pair ab groups a set of pairs of $\mathcal{U} \times \mathcal{U}$ which are "equally different", *i.e.*, which differ from each other as much as b differs from a. Taking the geometric metaphor, such an equivalence class can be seen as a "contour line" of the underlying similarity model. If $\sim_\upsilon$ is the identity relation ($ab \sim_\upsilon cd \Leftrightarrow \upsilon(ab) = \upsilon(cd)$), then each value $\ell \in \mathcal{V}$ defines an equivalence class denoted by $(\upsilon : \ell) = \{ab \in \mathcal{U} \times \mathcal{U} \mid \upsilon(ab) = \ell\}$. Mapping a pair ab to a pair cd consists in finding a scale υ for which the two pairs belong to the same contour line for υ:

$$\text{Find } \upsilon \text{ such that } \upsilon(ab) \sim_\upsilon \upsilon(cd) \qquad \text{(Mapping)}$$

Sharing a difference defines a contour line. In Fig. 1, the pair aa' can be mapped to the pair bb' since $\upsilon_{\neq}^{\mathbf{eyebrow}}(aa') = \upsilon_{\neq}^{\mathbf{eyebrow}}(bb') = 0$, so they belong to the same equivalence class $(\upsilon_{\neq}^{\mathbf{eyebrow}} : 0)$ for the variation $\upsilon_{\neq}^{\mathbf{eyebrow}}$. Similarly, a contour line of the variation $\upsilon_-^{\mathbf{v}}$ groups in the same equivalence class the pairs ab and cd when their difference is represented by the same vector (*i.e.*, such that $\overrightarrow{ab} = \overrightarrow{cd}$). Sharing a commonality (like having a property P) also defines a contour line.

Let $s \in \mathcal{U}$ be an element that has a property P (*i.e.*, such that $P(s)$ holds). The variation 1_P can be used to map the pair ss to all pairs $st \in [ss]_{1_P} = (1_P : 0)$ (and thus s to t). An analogical proportion also defines a contour line. The analogical proportion $X : Y :: Z : T$ is defined [26] by $X \setminus Y = Z \setminus T$ and $Y \setminus X = T \setminus Z$, which means that the analogical proportion $X : Y :: Z : T$ holds for two pairs XY and ZT iff the two pairs take the same value for the variation $AP(XY) = (X \setminus Y, Y \setminus X)$. Similarly, in preference theory, the pairs of transactions satisfying the same conditional preference rules constitute a contour line. Suppose $\mathcal{U}$ denotes a set of objects called *transactions*. Let $\mathcal{I}$ be a set of distinct literals (called *items*), and $\varphi : \mathcal{U} \longrightarrow \mathscr{P}(\mathcal{I})$ the function that associates to each transaction a set of items. A transaction t is said to be preferred to u according to a conditional preference rule $\pi : i^+ \succ i^- \mid C$ iff $(i^+, C, i^-) \subseteq s(\varphi(t), \varphi(u))$ with $s(XY) = (X \setminus Y, X \cap Y, Y \setminus X)$ [7]. As a result, two transactions that take the same value for this variation satisfy the same conditional preference rules.

Measuring a Degree of Difference. An difference inequality $\upsilon(ab) \geq \upsilon(cd)$ holds if b differs from a more than d differs from c according to the scale υ. Inequalities order contour lines (since $ab \succeq cd \Leftrightarrow [ab]_\sim \succeq [cd]_\sim$). The relation $[ab]_\sim \succeq [cd]_\sim$ is noted $a : b \ll c : d$ in [27]. For example, in Fig. 1, two faces having the same eyebrow may be more similar than two faces having different eyebrows, *i.e.*, $0 \leq 1 \Leftrightarrow (\upsilon_{\neq}^{\text{eyebrow}} : 0) \succeq (\upsilon_{\neq}^{\text{eyebrow}} : 1)$. Similarly, by taking the usual order $\leq$ on $\mathbb{N}$, one can define a contour scale: $n \leq m \Leftrightarrow (\upsilon_{d_1}^{\text{age}} : n) \succeq (\upsilon_{d_1}^{\text{age}} : m)$. This scale expresses that "the lower the age difference, the more similar". By structuring the set $\mathscr{P}(\mathcal{A}) \times \mathscr{P}(\mathcal{A})$ with the (strict weak) inclusion relation $\subset$ defined by $(A, B) \subset (A', B')$ iff $A \subset A'$ and $B \subset B'$, a contour scale can be defined on analogical proportions: $\ell \subset k \Leftrightarrow (AP : \ell) \succ (AP : k)$. Such a scale formalizes that all things equal, the less properties are lost or gained when going from a set X to a set Y, the more similar X and Y are. For example, if $X = \{\mathsf{a}, \mathsf{b}\}$, $Y = \{\mathsf{b}, \mathsf{d}\}$, $Z = \{\mathsf{a}, \mathsf{c}\}$, and $T = \{\mathsf{c}\}$, then $ZT \succ XY$ since $AP(ZT) = \{\{\mathsf{a}\}, \{\}\} = \ell \subset AP(X, Y) = \{\{\mathsf{a}\}, \{\mathsf{d}\}\} = k$. According to Tversky, a matching function $s(X, Y) = (X \setminus Y, X \cap Y, Y \setminus X)$ should enforce a *monotony* property. This property is enforced if the scale $\geq$ on $\mathcal{V} = \mathscr{P}(\mathcal{A}) \times \mathscr{P}(\mathcal{A}) \times \mathscr{P}(\mathcal{A})$ is such that $s(ab) = (A, B, C) \geq s(cd) = (A', B', C')$ whenever $A \subseteq A'$, $B \supseteq B'$, and $C \subseteq C'$.

5   Analogical Dissimilarity

Analogical dissimilarity is a "difference between differences": it measures the difference between two scale values. Taking the geometric metaphor, analogical dissimilarity measures the "distance" between two contour lines (Fig. 3).

Analogical dissimilarity is given by a scale ad on $\mathcal{V}$, which is coherent with analogy, *i.e.*, $\mathsf{ad}(ab, cd) = 0 \Leftrightarrow ab \sim_\upsilon cd$. As a consequence, if $ab \sim_\upsilon a'b'$ and $cd \sim_\upsilon c'd'$, then $\mathsf{ad}(ab, cd) = \mathsf{ad}(a'b', c'd')$. If $\sim_\upsilon$ is the identity relation, the previous observation implies that $\mathsf{ad}(ab, cd)$ gives the same value for all $ab \in (\upsilon : \ell)$ and $cd \in (\upsilon : \ell')$ taken in two different contour lines. Therefore, we will write:

$$\mathsf{ad}(\ell, \ell') = \mathsf{ad}(ab, cd) \text{ for } ab \in (\upsilon : \ell) \text{ and } cd \in (\upsilon : \ell')$$

The analogical dissimilarity between two vectors [19] is their difference:

$$\mathsf{ad}(ab, cd) = \upsilon_{d_p}^{\overset{\vee}{\upsilon}}(ab, cd) = \|\overrightarrow{ab} - \overrightarrow{cd}\|_p$$

i.e., $$\mathsf{ad}(\overrightarrow{u}, \overrightarrow{v}) = \|\overrightarrow{v} - \overrightarrow{u}\|_p$$

The variation $\upsilon_{d_1}^{a\rightarrow}$ is such that $\upsilon_{d_1}^{a\rightarrow}(ac) = k$ iff c is the k-Nearest Neighbor of a. Analogical dissimilarity measures the difference between two values of this variation, and thus corresponds to a ranking difference:

$$\mathsf{ad}(ab, ac) = \upsilon_{d_1}^{\overset{\upsilon_{d_1}^{a\rightarrow}}{}}(ab, ac) \qquad \text{for } a, b, c \in \mathcal{U}$$

i.e., $$\mathsf{ad}(n, m) = |n - m| \qquad \text{for } n, m \in \mathbb{N}$$

If the feature $\varphi : \mathcal{U} \longrightarrow \mathscr{P}(\mathcal{A})$ associates to each element of $\mathcal{U}$ a subset of a set $\mathcal{A}$, the analogical dissimilarity between analogical proportions is given by a symmetric difference:

$$\mathsf{ad}(ab, cd) = \upsilon_{\Delta}^{\upsilon_{\mathcal{A}}^{\varphi P}}(ab, cd)$$
$$= |U \setminus W| + |W \setminus U| + |V \setminus Q| + |Q \setminus V|$$
$$\text{with } U = X \setminus Y, V = Y \setminus X, W = Z \setminus T, \text{ and } Q = T \setminus Z$$
$$\text{where } X = \varphi(a), Y = \varphi(b), Z = \varphi(c), \text{ and } T = \varphi(d)$$

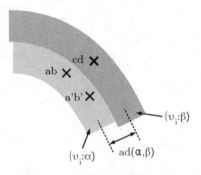

Fig. 3. Analogical dissimilarity ad measures the distance between two contour lines.

To illustrate, take $\mathcal{A} = \{\mathsf{a}, \mathsf{b}, \mathsf{c}, \mathsf{d}\}$, and $a, b, c, d \in \mathcal{U}$ such that $X = \varphi(a) = \{\mathsf{a}, \mathsf{b}\}$, $Y = \varphi(b) = \{\mathsf{c}\}$, $Z = \varphi(c) = \{\mathsf{b}, \mathsf{c}\}$, and $T = \varphi(d) = \{\mathsf{a}, \mathsf{c}, \mathsf{d}\}$ (Table 2). The scale AP gives $AP(XY) = UV$ with

$- U = X \setminus Y = \{\mathsf{a}, \mathsf{b}\}$ is what is lost from X to Y

Table 2. Four subsets X, Y, Z, and T.

	a	b	c	d
X	1	1	0	0
Y	0	0	1	0
Z	0	1	1	0
T	1	0	1	1

– $V = Y \setminus X = \{c\}$ is what is gained from X to Y

and $AP(ZT) = WQ$ with

– $W = Z \setminus T = \{b\}$ is what is lost from Z to T
– $Q = T \setminus Z = \{a, d\}$ is what is gained from Z to T

The analogical dissimilarity between ab and cd is $\mathsf{ad}(ab, cd) = 1 + 0 + 1 + 2 = 4$. If the feature $\varphi : \mathcal{U} \longrightarrow \mathscr{P}(\mathcal{I})$ associates to each transaction a set of items, the analogical dissimilarity between two pairs of transactions is given by the symmetric difference:

$$\mathsf{ad}(ab, cd) = \upsilon_{\Delta}^{\upsilon_s^{\varphi}}(ab, cd)$$
$$= |U \setminus W| + |W \setminus U| + |R \setminus S| + |S \setminus R|$$
$$+ |V \setminus Q| + |Q \setminus V|$$
$$\text{with } U = X \setminus Y, V = Y \setminus X, R = X \cap Y, S = Z \cap T,$$
$$W = Z \setminus T, \text{ and } Q = T \setminus Z$$
$$\text{where } X = \varphi(a), Y = \varphi(b), Z = \varphi(c), \text{ and } T = \varphi(d)$$

For example, if $\mathcal{I} = \{a, b, c, d\}$, and $a, b, c, d \in \mathcal{U}$ are defined as above by $X = \varphi(a) = \{a, b\}$, $Y = \varphi(b) = \{c\}$, $Z = \varphi(c) = \{b, c\}$, and $T = \varphi(d) = \{a, c, d\}$, then

– $R = X \cap Y = \varnothing$ is what is preserved X to Y
– $S = Z \cap T = \{c\}$ is what is preserved from Z to T

The analogical dissimilarity between ab and cd is $\mathsf{ad}(ab, cd) = 1 + 0 + 0 + 1 + 1 + 2 = 5$. Therefore, we can say that the distance between the two conditional preference rules $\pi_1 : i^+{}_1 \succ i^-{}_1 \mid C_1$ and $\pi_2 : i^+{}_2 \succ i^-{}_2 \mid C_2$ is

$$\mathsf{ad}(\pi_1, \pi_2) = \left| i^+{}_1 \, \Delta \, i^+{}_2 \right| + \left| i^-{}_1 \, \Delta \, i^-{}_2 \right| + |C_1 \, \Delta \, C_2|$$

For example, the distance between $\pi_1 : c \succ ab \mid \varnothing$ and $\pi_2 : ad \succ b \mid c$ is 5. Such measure could be useful e.g., to predict preferences in a transductive way [25].

6   The Similarity Principle

When more than one scale is considered, the contour lines of the different scales may intersect. The similarity principle, according to which an equal difference observed on a certain dimension is accompagnied by an equal difference in some other dimension, corresponds to an inclusion relation between two contour lines.

Let $\Upsilon = \{\upsilon_1, \upsilon_2, \ldots, \upsilon_n\}$ be a set of n variations with $\upsilon_i : \mathcal{U} \times \mathcal{U} \longrightarrow \mathcal{V}_i$, and $n \geq 2$. For $\upsilon_i, \upsilon_j \in \Upsilon$, the inclusion of two contour lines at a point ab is called a *co-variation* and is written $\upsilon_i \overset{ab}{\curvearrowright} \upsilon_j$. We say that the variation υ_i *co-varies* with the variation υ_j at ab. The notion of co-variation at a point $ab \in \mathcal{U} \times \mathcal{U}$ can be extended to a subset $S \subseteq \mathcal{U} \times \mathcal{U}$ by stating that:

$$\upsilon_i \overset{S}{\curvearrowright} \upsilon_j \text{ iff } \upsilon_i \overset{ab}{\curvearrowright} \upsilon_j \text{ for all } ab \in S$$

If each $\sim_{\upsilon_i}$ is the identity relation, then a co-variation is a functional dependency [2] between the two values $\ell = \upsilon_i(ab)$ and $k = \upsilon_j(ab)$, and the co-variation $\upsilon_i \overset{ab}{\curvearrowright} \upsilon_j$ can be written $(\upsilon_i : \ell) \overset{ab}{\curvearrowright} (\upsilon_j : k)$. For example, the co-variation $(\upsilon_{Id}^{\texttt{profile}} : (\texttt{round}, \texttt{sharp})) \overset{\{aa', bb'\}}{\curvearrowright} (\upsilon_{\neq}^{\texttt{eyebrow}} : 0)$ represents the fact that when the profile changes from round to sharp, the eyebrow stays the same.

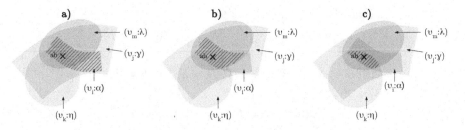

Fig. 4. The co-variation $(\upsilon_i : \alpha) \overset{ab}{\curvearrowright} (\upsilon_j : \gamma)$ can be interpreted with different semantics on the set $\Upsilon = \{\upsilon_i, \upsilon_j, \upsilon_k, \upsilon_m\}$. Hatched areas on the figure represent the resulting domains of validity of the co-variation. **(a)** Bayesian semantics: the co-variation is verified on the whole equivalence class $(\upsilon_i : \alpha)$ **(b)** Semi-bayesian semantics: the co-variation is verified only on a subset of the equivalence class where some other variations (here, υ_m) keep the same value **(c)** Ceteris paribus semantics: the co-variation is verified on the subset of the equivalence class where *all* other variations keep the same value.

Different semantics can be given to a co-variation, depending on how it is interpreted with respect to the inclusion of equivalence classes $[ab]_{\upsilon_i} \subseteq [ab]_{\upsilon_j}$. Such an inclusion of equivalence classes is known as the *similarity principle*, and states that the equivalence relations $\sim_{\upsilon_i}$ and $\sim_{\upsilon_j}$ are locally co-monotone, *i.e.*, for all $a, b, c, d \in \mathcal{U}$, $ab \sim_{\upsilon_i} cd \Rightarrow ab \sim_{\upsilon_j} cd$. This principle expresses that if a and b are as similar as c and d for υ_i, then a and b are also as similar as c and d for υ_j. Therefore, different semantics can be given to a co-variation depending on which subset $R \subseteq [ab]_{\upsilon_i}$ of the equivalence class $[ab]_{\upsilon_i}$ the similarity principle is to be verified (Fig. 4):

- *Bayesian semantics*: $R = [ab]_{\upsilon_i}$, *i.e.*, the co-variation is verified on the whole equivalence class;
- *Semi-bayesian semantics*: $R = \bigcap_{k \in \{i\} \cup D} [ab]_{\upsilon_k}$, *i.e.*, the co-variation is verified *all things equal*, but only in the subset of $[ab]_{\upsilon_i}$ where a set of variations υ_k with $k \in D$ take the same value [31];
- *Ceteris paribus semantics*: $R = \bigcap_{k \neq j} [ab]_{\upsilon_k}$, *i.e.*, the co-variation is verified *all things equal*, in the subset of $[ab]_{\upsilon_i}$ where all other variations take the same value.

7 Analogical Transfer

Performing an analogical transfer consists in taking the similarity principle as a local inference rule, in order to make the hypothesis that if a contour line $[ab]_{\upsilon_i}$ is included in a contour line $[ab]_{\upsilon_j}$ at a point ab, then $[ab]_{\upsilon_i}$ should also be included in $[ab]_{\upsilon_j}$ at (at least some of) other points cd of $[ab]_{\upsilon_i}$ (*i.e.*, in some points cd for which $\mathsf{ad}(ab, cd) = 0$), and even maybe at points that are not too dissimilar (*i.e.*, in some points cd for which $\mathsf{ad}(ab, cd) \leq k$):

$$\frac{\upsilon_i \overset{ab}{\curvearrowright} \upsilon_j,\ \mathsf{ad}(ab, cd) \leq k}{\upsilon_i \overset{cd}{\curvearrowright} \upsilon_j} \qquad \text{(Transfer)}$$

If each $\sim_{\upsilon_i}$ is the identity relation, then (Transfer) gives:

$$\frac{(\upsilon_i : \ell_0) \overset{ab}{\curvearrowright} (\upsilon_j : \gamma),\ cd \in (\upsilon_i : \ell)\ \text{such that}\ \mathsf{ad}(\ell_0, \ell) \leq k}{(\upsilon_i : \ell) \overset{cd}{\curvearrowright} (\upsilon_j : \gamma)}$$

The analogical "jump" (AJ) is a the expression of an analogical transfer where $\upsilon_i = \mathbf{1}_P$, and $\upsilon_j = \mathbf{1}_Q$:

$$\frac{(\mathbf{1}_P : 0) \overset{ss}{\curvearrowright} (\mathbf{1}_Q : 0),\ tt \in (\mathbf{1}_P : 0),\ \text{with}\ \mathsf{ad}(0, 0) = 0}{(\mathbf{1}_P : 0) \overset{tt}{\curvearrowright} (\mathbf{1}_Q : 0)}$$

By applying the co-variation $\mathbf{1}_P \overset{tt}{\curvearrowright} \mathbf{1}_Q$, the state of sharing the property Q is transferred to t. The co-variation is a functional dependency, which is consistent with the observation of [6] that a sufficient condition for an analogical jump (AJ) to be justified is that there exists a functional dependency holding between P and Q. Differences may also be used in the transfer. In Fig. 1, if we know that d' has a sharp profile, we can make the hypothesis that d' has the same eyebrow as d (curved), since d has a round profile and d' has a sharp profile:

$$\frac{(\upsilon_{Id}^{\text{profile}} : (\textbf{round}, \textbf{sharp})) \overset{\{\text{aa}', \text{bb}'\}}{\curvearrowright} (\upsilon_{\neq}^{\text{eyebrow}} : 0)}{\textbf{dd}' \in (\upsilon_{Id}^{\text{profile}} : (\textbf{round}, \textbf{sharp}))}$$
$$\frac{}{(\upsilon_{Id}^{\text{profile}} : (\textbf{round}, \textbf{sharp})) \overset{dd'}{\curvearrowright} (\upsilon_{\neq}^{\text{eyebrow}} : 0)}$$

A fortiori reasoning is a type of inference that exploits the co-monotony of two partial orders to estimate the value of an attribute. In [8], the authors give the following example: "If whiskey is stronger than beer, and buying beer is illegal under the age of 18, then we can plausibly derive that buying whiskey is illegal under the age of 18". This inference consists in applying the co-variation $(\upsilon_{\leq}^{\texttt{degree}} : 1) \overset{\texttt{bw}}{\curvearrowright} (\upsilon_{\leq}^{\texttt{legal\_age}} : 1)$, where **b** stands for beer, **w** stands for whiskey, and $\texttt{degree}$ and $\texttt{legal\_age}$ are two numerical features that associate to alcohols their degree and minimum legal age of consumption. Suppose now that we want to estimate the minimum legal age for cider (denoted by **c**). If we know that cider is less strong than beer ($\texttt{degree}(\texttt{c}) \leq \texttt{degree}(\texttt{b})$), then one can use analogical transfer to infer make the hypothesis that the minimum legal age for cider is less than the one for beer (18):

$$\frac{(\upsilon_{\leq}^{\texttt{degree}} : 1) \overset{\texttt{bw}}{\curvearrowright} (\upsilon_{\leq}^{\texttt{legal\_age}} : 1), \mathbf{cb} \in (\upsilon_{\leq}^{\texttt{degree}} : 1)}{(\upsilon_{\leq}^{\texttt{degree}} : 1) \overset{\texttt{cb}}{\curvearrowright} (\upsilon_{\leq}^{\texttt{legal\_age}} : 1)}$$

Analogical classifiers and instance-based-learning methods apply the similarity principle to the *nearest analogical neighbors* [13]. In instance-based learning, the relation "*belonging to the same class*" is transferred from an element x to an element x_0 whenever x_0 is found to be in the neighborhood of x. For example, in the k-Nearest Neighbor algorithm, $(\upsilon_{d_p}^{x \to} : n)$ is the equivalence relation that relates the pairs xy that are the nth most distant from x according to $\|.\|_p$, and $(\upsilon_{\neq}^{cls} : 0)$ is the equivalence relation that relates all elements that share the same class. The rule (Transfer) writes:

$$\frac{(\upsilon_{d_p}^{x \to} : 0) \overset{xx}{\curvearrowright} (\upsilon_{\neq}^{cls} : 0), xx_0 \in (\upsilon_{d_p}^{x \to} : n) \text{ with } \mathbf{ad}(0, n) \leq k}{(\upsilon_{d_p}^{x \to} : n) \overset{xx_0}{\curvearrowright} (\upsilon_{\neq}^{cls} : 0)}$$

8   Conclusion

There is an intimate link between the qualitative measurement of differences and computational analogy. Some essential notions of formal models of analogy, such as analogical equalities/inequalities, or analogical dissimilarity, and the related inferences (mapping and transfer) can be formulated as operations on ordinal similarity relations. The qualitative measurement of differences thus provides a bridge between qualitative models and analogical methods. One direct outcome is that it should allow to inject more psychologically grounded similarity measures in learning methods. A new light is also shed on analogical dissimilarity which, as an operation on a qualitative similarity relation, could be used to define decision criteria in transductive methods.

References

1. Badra, F.: Representing and learning variations. In: International Conference on Tools for Artificial Intelligence, pp. 950–957. IEEE, Vietri sul Mare (2015). https://doi.org/10.1109/ICTAI.2015.137

2. Badra, F.: Reasoning with co-variations. In: Artificial Intelligence: Methodology, Systems, and Applications - 17th International Conference, AIMSA, Varna, Bulgaria (2016). https://doi.org/10.1007/978-3-319-44748-3_20

3. Bounhas, M., Prade, H., Richard, G.: Analogy-based classifiers for nominal or numerical data. Int. J. Approx. Reason. **91**, 36–55 (2017). https://doi.org/10.1016/j.ijar.2017.08.010

4. Craw, S., Wiratunga, N., Rowe, R.C.: Learning adaptation knowledge to improve case-based reasoning. Artif. Intell. **170**(16–17), 1175–1192 (2006). https://doi.org/10.1016/j.artint.2006.09.001

5. D'Aquin, M., Badra, F., Lafrogne, S., Lieber, J., Napoli, A., Szathmary, L.: Case base mining for adaptation knowledge acquisition. In: IJCAI International Joint Conference on Artificial Intelligence, Hyderabad, India, pp. 750–755 (2007)

6. Davis, T.R., Russell, S.J.: A logical approach to reasoning by analogy. In: IJCAI International Joint Conference on Artificial Intelligence (1987)

7. De Amo, S., Diallo, M.S., Diop, C.T., Giacometti, A., Li, D., Soulet, A.: Contextual preference mining for user profile construction. Inf. Syst. **49**(April), 182–199 (2015). https://doi.org/10.1016/j.is.2014.11.009

8. Derrac, J., Schockaert, S.: Inducing semantic relations from conceptual spaces: a data-driven approach to plausible reasoning. Artif. Intell. **228**, 66–94 (2015). https://doi.org/10.1016/j.artint.2015.07.002

9. Fuchs, B., Lieber, J., Mille, A., Napoli, A.: Differential adaptation: an operational approach to adaptation for solving numerical problems with CBR. Knowl.-Based Syst. **68**, 103–114 (2014). https://doi.org/10.1016/j.knosys.2014.03.009

10. Gust, H., Krumnack, U., Kühnberger, K., Schwering, A.: Analogical reasoning: a core of cognition. KI - Künstliche Intelligenz **22**(1), 8–12 (2008)

11. Hammond, K.J.: CHEF: a model of case-based planning. In: AAAI Proceedings, pp. 267–271 (1986)

12. Hanney, K., Keane, M.T.: The adaptation knowledge bottleneck: howto ease it by learning from cases. In: International Conference on Case-Based Reasoning, vol. 1266, pp. 359–370 (1997)

13. Hug, N., Prade, H., Richard, G., Serrurier, M.: Analogical classifiers: a theoretical perspective. In: 22nd European Conference on Artificial Intelligence - ECAI, vol. 285, pp. 689–697 (2016). DOIurl10.3233/978-1-61499-672-9-689

14. Hüllermeier, E.: Possibilistic instance-based learning. Artif. Intell. **148**(1–2), 335–383 (2003). https://doi.org/10.1016/S0004-3702(03)00019-5

15. Jalali, V., Leake, D., Forouzandehmehr, N.: Learning and applying case adaptation rules for classification: an ensemble approach. In: IJCAI International Joint Conference on Artificial Intelligence, pp. 4874–4878 (2017)

16. Lieber, J.: Application of the revision theory to adaptation in case-based reasoning: the conservative adaptation. In: Weber, R.O., Richter, M.M. (eds.) ICCBR 2007. LNCS (LNAI), vol. 4626, pp. 239–253. Springer, Heidelberg (2007). https://doi.org/10.1007/978-3-540-74141-1_17

17. Lieber, J., Napoli, A.: Correct and complete retrieval for case-based problem-solving. In: ECAI, pp. 68–72 (1998)

18. McSherry, D.: Demand-driven discovery of adaptation knowledge. In: IJCAI, pp. 222–227 (1999)

19. Miclet, L., Bayoudh, S., Delhay, A.: Analogical dissimilarity: definition, algorithms and two experiments in machine learning. J. Artif. Intell. Res. **32**, 793–824 (2008)

20. Mitchell, T.M.: Machine Learning. Elsevier (1983)

21. Novick, L.R., Holyoak, K.J.: Mathematical problem solving by analogy. J. Exp. Psychol. Learn. Mem. Cogn. **17**(3), 398–415 (1991). https://doi.org/10.1037/0278-7393.17.3.398. http://www.ncbi.nlm.nih.gov/pubmed/1829473

22. Novick, L.R.: Analogical transfer, problem similarity, and expertise. J. Exp. Psychol. Learn. Mem. Cogn. **14**(3), 510–529 (1988)

23. Ontañón, S., Plaza, E.: On knowledge transfer in case-based inference. In: Agudo, B.D., Watson, I. (eds.) ICCBR 2012. LNCS (LNAI), vol. 7466, pp. 312–326. Springer, Heidelberg (2012). https://doi.org/10.1007/978-3-642-32986-9_24

24. Paritosh, P.K., Klenk, M.E.: Cognitive processes in quantitative estimation: analogical anchors and causal adjustment. In: Proceedings of the 28th Annual Conference of the Cognitive Science Society (CogSci-06) (2006). http://www.cs.northwestern.edu/~mek802/papers/knack-formatted.pdf

25. Pirlot, M., Prade, H., Richard, G.: Completing preferences by means of analogical proportions. Model. Decis. Artif. Intell. **4617**, 318–329 (2016). https://doi.org/10.1007/978-3-540-73729-2

26. Prade, H., Richard, G.: Reasoning with logical proportions. In: Principles of Knowledge Representation and Reasoning: Proceedings of the Twelfth International Conference, (KR), Toronto, Canada, pp. 545–555 (2010)

27. Prade, H., Richard, G.: Analogical inequalities. In: Antonucci, A., Cholvy, L., Papini, O. (eds.) ECSQARU 2017. LNCS (LNAI), vol. 10369, pp. 3–9. Springer, Cham (2017). https://doi.org/10.1007/978-3-319-61581-3_1

28. Robert, F.S.: Measurement Theory (1985)

29. Tversky, A.: Features of similarity. In: Readings in Cognitive Science: A Perspective from Psychology and Artificial Intelligence, pp. 290–302. Elsevier Inc., October 2013

30. Yao, Y.Y.: Qualitative similarity. In: Suzuki, Y., Ovaska, S., Furuhashi, T., Roy, R., Dote, Y. (eds.) Soft Computing in IndustrialApplications, pp. 339–348. Springer, London (2000). https://doi.org/10.1007/978-1-4471-0509-1_29

31. Žabkar, J., Bratko, I., Demšar, J.: Extracting qualitative relations from categorical data. Artif. Intell. **239**, 54–69 (2016). https://doi.org/10.1016/j.artint.2016.06.007

Predicting Preferences by Means of Analogical Proportions

Myriam Bounhas[1,2]([✉]), Marc Pirlot[3], and Henri Prade[4,5]

[1] LARODEC Laboratory, ISG de Tunis, 41 rue de la Liberté, 2000 Le Bardo, Tunisia
myriam_bounhas@yahoo.fr
[2] Emirates College of Technology, P.O. Box: 41009,
Abu Dhabi, United Arab Emirates
[3] Faculté Polytechnique, Université de Mons, Mons, Belgium
marc.pirlot@umons.ac.be
[4] IRIT – CNRS, 118, route de Narbonne, Toulouse, France
prade@irit.fr
[5] QCIS, University of Technology, Sydney, Australia

Abstract. It is assumed that preferences between two items, described in terms of criteria values belonging to a finite scale, are known for a limited number of pairs of items, which constitutes a case base. The problem is then to predict the preference between the items of a new pair. A new approach based on analogical proportions is presented. Analogical proportions are statements of the form "*a* is to *b* as *c* is to *d*". If the change between item-1 and item-2 is the same as the change between item-3 and item-4, and a similar statement holds for item'-1, item'-2, item'-3, item'-4, then one may plausibly assume that the preference between item-1 and item'-1 is to the preference between item-2 and item'-2 as the preference between item-3 and item'-3 is to the preference between item-4 and item'-4. This offers a basis for a plausible prediction of the fourth preference if the three others are known. This approach fits well with the postulates underlying weighted averages. Two algorithms are proposed that look for triples of preferences appropriate for a prediction. The first one only exploits the given set of examples. The second one completes this set with new preferences deducible from this set under a monotony assumption. This completion is limited to the generation of preferences that are useful for the requested prediction. The predicted preferences should fit with the assumption that known preferences agree with a unique unknown weighted average. The reported experiments suggest the effectiveness of the proposed approach.

1 Introduction

Analogical reasoning is reputed to be a valuable heuristic means for extrapolating plausible conclusions on the basis of comparisons. A simple form of this idea is implemented by case-based reasoning (CBR) [1], where conclusions known for stored cases are tentatively associated to similar cases. A more sophisticated option relies on the idea of analogical proportions. By analogical proportions,

© Springer Nature Switzerland AG 2018
M. T. Cox et al. (Eds.): ICCBR 2018, LNAI 11156, pp. 515–531, 2018.
https://doi.org/10.1007/978-3-030-01081-2_34

we mean statements of the form "a is to b as c is to d". We assume here that, a, b, c, d refer to four items described by their vector of features values for a considered set of features. The analogical proportion is to be understood as "a differs from b as c differs from d" and conversely "b differs from a as d differs from c". Then inference is based on triples of vectors (rather than taking vectors one by one as in case-based reasoning). The underlying idea is that if four items a, b, c, d are making an analogical proportion on describing features, an analogical proportion may hold as well on another mark pertaining to them, and then if this mark is known for a, b and c, one may compute it for d in such a way that the marks make an analogical proportion.

The notion of analogical proportions and their formalization has raised a trend of interest in the last two decades [14,16,18,20,21]. Moreover analogical proportion-based classifiers have been designed and experienced with success [3,4,15], first for Boolean and then for nominal and numerical attributes. In this case, the predicted mark is the label of the class. Although it is not intuitively obvious why analogical proportion-based inference may work well, one may notice that such a proportion enforces a parallel between four situations in such a way that the change between a and b is the same as the change between c and d. So this inference exploits co-variations.

One may wonder if what is working in classification may also be applied to preference prediction. The aim of this paper is to check whether analogical proportions may be a suitable tool for predicting preferences. This idea has been recently advocated in [17], but without providing any experimental evidence that may work. This paper further investigates this idea and provides an experimentation of this idea. The problem considered is no longer to predict a class for a new item, but a preference relation between two items on the basis of a set of examples made of known comparisons applying to pairs of items. This set of examples plays the role of a case base, where a case is just a pair of vectors describing the two items together with information saying what item is preferred. Cases stating preferences are not usual in CBR literature, although they are clearly cases of interest. Still this should not be confused with "preference-based CBR" [2] where preferences between competing solutions in the context of a problem are handled.[1]

Preference learning has become a popular artificial intelligence topic [7,9,10, 12]. Preference learning often relies on the assumption that data sets are massively available. Interestingly enough, analogical proportion-based inference may work with a rather small amount of examples, as we shall see. Preference-learning approaches often rely on the hypothesis that known preferences agree with a

---

[1] During the time we were finalizing this paper, we become aware of a very recent work [8], also aiming at predicting preferences on an analogical basis. Their approach exploits what is called "the horizontal reading" in [17], while here we investigate "the vertical reading" (also introduced in [17]). Moreover the focus of [8] is on learning to rank evaluated with a loss function, which is slightly different from the one here on predicting preferences and computing the error rate of predictions. A detailed comparison of the relative merits of the two approaches are beyond the scope of this paper, but will be the topic of a forthcoming study.

unique unknown aggregation function or with a conditional preference structure that has to be identified. Analogical proportion-based methods extrapolate predictions from known cases without looking for some underlying explanation model.

The paper is structured as follows. Section 2 recalls the necessary background on analogical proportions and their use in plausible inference mechanisms, while Sect. 3 restates important facts in multiple criteria decision that are relevant for applying analogical proportion-based inference to preference prediction. Section 4 presents two algorithms, one exploiting a set of given examples, one using an extension of this set relying on a monotony assumption of the preferences. Section 5 shows that promising results can be obtained, while Sect. 6 provides some lines for further research.

2   Background on Analogical Proportions

As already said, an analogical proportion is a statement of the form "a is to b as c is to d". It is denoted $a : b :: c : d$ usually. The name comes from a parallel, already made in Ancient Greek time, with geometric proportions that equate the ratio of two numbers a and b with the ratio of c and d, which may appear as a particular case of an analogical proportion. This is maybe why analogical proportions are supposed to obey the three following postulates (which correspond to properties of geometric proportions):

(1) $a : b :: a : b$ (reflexivity);
(2) $a : b :: c : d = c : d :: a : b$ (symmetry);
(3) $a : b :: c : d = a : c :: b : d$ (central permutation).

Let us assume that a, b, c and d take their values in a finite set U with at least two elements. Let $u, v \in U$. It follows immediately that (u, u, u, u), (u, u, v, v), and (u, v, u, v) are valid schemas for the analogical proportion. Other possible schemas with two distinct values are on the one hand (u, u, u, v), (u, u, v, u), (u, v, u, u), and (v, u, u, u), and on the other hand (u, v, v, u). They all disagree with the idea of proportion: indeed, e.g., it would be weird to claim that "u is to u as u is to v" if $v \neq u$, while "u is to v as v is to u" looks debatable as well, since the change from v to u is opposite to the one from u to v.

So the simplest model for analogical proportions, is to consider that the quaternary relation in U^4 is valid if and only if $a : b :: c : d$ is of the form (u, u, u, u), (u, u, v, v), or (u, v, u, v). In the case where U would be replaced by the set of real numbers, a more liberal model may be considered where $a : b :: c : d$ holds as soon as $a - b = c - d$ [19], and where more than two distinct values may appear in the 4-tuples that make an analogical proportion, e.g., $0 : 0.5 :: 0.5 : 1$, or $0.2 : 0.4 :: 0.6 : 0.8$. However, we shall not use this modeling in the following since we use a finite set U, encoded by numbers, but where the difference operation '$-$' is not a closed operation.

The above definition of an analogical proportion extends to vectors straight-forwardly. Let $a = (a_1, \cdots, a_n)$, $b = (b_1, \cdots, b_n)$, $c = (c_1, \cdots, c_n)$, $d = (d_1, \cdots, d_n)$, then

$$a : b :: c : d \text{ if and only if } \forall i, a_i : b_i :: c_i : d_i, i = 1, n.$$

Then analogical proportion-based inference [4,20] is usually defined by the following pattern of plausible inference

$$\frac{\forall i \in [[1,n]], a_i : b_i :: c_i : d_i}{m(a) : m(b) :: m(c) : m(d)}$$

where $m(x)$ denotes a mark associated with vector x, e.g., the label of the class of x, in a classification problem. More generally, $m(x)$ may be also a vector. Here m represents the sign of the preference relation (the value of m is in $\{\preceq, \succeq\}$). Then if $m(a)$, $m(b)$, $m(c)$ are already known, while $m(d)$ is unknown, we can infer a plausible value for $m(d)$ by solving the equation $m(a) : m(b) :: m(c) : ?$ whose solution is always unique, when it exists. However, note that $u : v : v : ?$ has no solution, since neither $u : v : v : v$ nor $u : v : v : u$ are valid analogical proportions.

In the following, the items we consider are made of preferences between two vectors of criteria values, of the form $a^1 \preceq a^2$, $b^1 \preceq b^2$, $c^1 \preceq c^2$ and $d^1 \preceq d^2$. Then an instance of the analogical proportion-based preference inference is now

$$\forall j \in [[1,n]], a^1_j : b^1_j :: c^1_j : d^1_j \text{ and } a^2_j : b^2_j :: c^2_j : d^2_j$$
$$\frac{a^1 \preceq a^2, b^1 \preceq b^2, c^1 \preceq c^2}{------------------}$$
$$d^1 \preceq d^2.$$

Two other instances, which involve the reversed preference relation $\succeq$, and which are in agreement with the valid patterns of analogical proportions, would correspond to following the analogical entailments *with the same first premise as above* that we do not repeat:

$$\frac{a^1 \preceq a^2, b^1 \preceq b^2, c^1 \succeq c^2}{-----------}$$
$$d^1 \succeq d^2.$$

and

$$\frac{a^1 \preceq a^2, b^1 \succeq b^2, c^1 \preceq c^2}{-----------}$$
$$d^1 \succeq d^2.$$

As we are going to see now, other concerns should be taken into account for a proper preference prediction mechanism. For that we need to first recall some results in multiple criteria analysis, and to make some observations.

3 Multiple Criteria-Based Preference and Analogical Proportions

In practice, the most largely used multiple criteria aggregation operators are weighted sums. Let $x = (x_1, \ldots, x_n)$ be a vector of evaluations representing a choice according to n criteria. The same finite scale $S = \{1, 2, \ldots, k\}$ is used for all criteria (the greater the value, the better it is). As pointed out in [17], an important property satisfied by many aggregation operators, in particular weighted sums, is that *contradictory tradeoffs are forbidden* (in fact, not showing contradictory tradeoffs is a property shared by many preference models, not only by weighted sums). This is expressed by the following postulate.

We *cannot have together* the four following preference statements: $\forall i, j$

$$A : x_{-i}\alpha \preceq y_{-i}\beta$$
and $\quad B : x_{-i}\gamma \succeq y_{-i}\delta$
and $\quad C : v_{-j}\alpha \succeq w_{-j}\beta$
and $\quad D : v_{-j}\gamma \prec w_{-j}\delta$

So the first three statements should entail

$$D' : v_{-j}\gamma \succeq w_{-j}\delta$$

where $\succeq$ denotes a preference relation ($x \succeq y$ is the same as $y \preceq x$) and x_{-i} denotes the n-1-dimensional vector made of the evaluations of x on all criteria except the ith one for which the Greek letter denotes the substituted value. This postulate ensures that the difference between γ and δ is at least as large as that between α and β, independently of the criterion on which this difference shows up. In other words, in context x_{-i} the values of α, β are not enough for reversing the preference, while γ, δ are sufficient; in context v_{-j} the values of α, β are now sufficient for getting the preference reversed, then it should be a fortiori the case with γ, δ in this new context.

This postulate is verified by preferences that can be represented by a weighted sum of utilities, i.e., in case there exist a real-valued function u defined on S and a set of n weights p_i summing up to 1, such that, $\forall x, y$, $x \succeq y$ if and only if

$$U(x) = \sum_{i=1}^{n} p_i u(x_i) \geq U(y) = \sum_{i=1}^{n} p_i u(y_i).$$

where $U(x)$ is the global utility of the choice associated with vector x.

The above pattern of inference is compatible with the analogical proportion-based patterns of the previous section. In fact, a violation of this pattern would lead to observe a *reversed* analogical proportion (of the form a is to b as b is to a) on the preference symbols, which is opposite to what analogical proportion expresses [18].

Besides, the problem considered in this paper is the following. Given a set E of preferences of the form $x^k \succeq y^k$ ($k = 1, \cdots, m$), representing what we know about the preferences of an agent about some pairs of choices, can we predict its preference between two other choices x and y? First, an idea is to make the assumption that the preferences of the agent obey a weighted sum aggregation scheme, whose weights are unknown. Then, we might think of finding a sampling of systems of weights summing to 1 that are compatible with the constraints induced by E. But, enumerating the vertices of the polytope defined by the system of inequations corresponding to the preferences in E is a NP hard problem that is not easy at all to handle in practice [13]. Indeed given a feasible system of linear inequalities, generating all vertices of the corresponding polyhedron is hard. Yet, in the case of bounded polyhedra (i.e., polytope) the complexity remains open. It is why we have chosen to explore another route in this study, based on the exploitation of a pattern avoiding contradictory trade-offs, and patterns expressing that preferences should go well with analogical proportions. This idea which may sound fancy at first glance is based on the empirical evidence that analogical proportion-based classifiers work well and the theoretical result that such classifiers make no error in the Boolean case when the labeling function is affine [6]. A result of the same nature might be conjectured when attributes are nominal rather the Boolean. In our case since the scale S is finite, criteria may be regarded as nominal attributes.

4 Analogy-Based Preference Prediction

As just said, we investigate how analogical proportions can help for predicting preference relations from a given set of such relations, while avoiding the generation of contradictory trade-offs. We call APP such a method, which is short for "Analogy-based Preference Prediction".

Let us consider a preference relation $\succeq$ over the universe set S^n (n is the number of criteria) and a set of preference examples $E = \{e_i : x^i \succeq y^i\}$ telling us that choice x^i is preferred to choice y^i. We may apply monotony on examples in the set E, in order to produce other new valid examples. Namely, if $(x^i \succeq y^i) \in E$ and if x', y' are such that $x' \succeq x^i$ and $y^i \succeq y'$ due to dominance, then $x' \succeq y'$ should hold as well. We denote $comp(E)$ this completion of set E by repeated application of monotony. Moreover the scale $S = \{1, 2, ..., k\}$. In the experiments we use $S = \{1, 2, 3, 4, 5\}$. Such a scale is usual in practice.

4.1 Methodology

Given a new item $D : X, Y$ whose preference is to be predicted, the basic principle of APP is to find the *good* triples (A, B, C) of examples in E (or if possible in $comp(E)$) that form with D either the non-contradictory trade-offs pattern (considered in first), or one of the three analogical proportion-based inference patterns. Such triples, when applicable, will help to guess the preference of D by applying a majority vote on the solutions provided by each of these triples.

Let us consider one of the basic patterns:

$$A : x_{-i}\alpha \succeq y_{-i}\beta$$

$$B : x_{-i}\gamma \preceq y_{-i}\delta$$

$$C : v_{-j}\alpha \succeq w_{-j}\beta$$

$$D : v_{-j}\gamma \;?\; w_{-j}\delta$$

where preference of D is unknown.

The APP can be described by this basic process:

- For a given D, search for good triples in E.
- In case no good triples could be found in E, search for such triples in $comp(E)$.
- Apply a majority vote on the candidate solutions of these good triples to predict the preference of D.

The process of searching for good triples can be summarized by the following 3 steps:

1. **Find good** C: In the basic pattern, we can see that the item C may be any example in the set E which is identical to D except on one criterion that is denoted by its index j. The intuitive idea of APP is to start by searching for the *best* examples $C \in E$ that fit the basic pattern considered. As j may be any index in the set of criteria, a loop on all possible criteria $j \in \{1, ..., n\}$ should be executed in order to find j. Once a candidate C is found, this helps to also fix parameters α, β, γ and δ for the *current* candidate triple. We save such parameters as $param = \{\alpha, \beta, \gamma, \delta, j\}$.

2. **Find good** A: Once parameters α and β are fixed for each example C, it is easy to find a good example $A \in E$ in which α and β appears on the same criterion, indexed by i. As in the case of C, a similar process is to be applied to find such examples A. This helps to fix a new parameter i and update the set of parameters to be $param = \{\alpha, \beta, \gamma, \delta, j, i\}$.

3. **Find good** B: As a result of the previous step, to each candidate pair (A, C) along with D corresponds a set of candidate parameters $param = \{\alpha, \beta, \gamma, \delta, j, i\}$. The last step is to find *all* good examples $B \in E$ to enclose the triple (A, B, C), i.e., those that fit exactly the pattern: $p : x_{-i}\gamma, y_{-i}\delta$ regardless of the sign of the preference relation.

The next step of the APP is to predict preference based on the selected good triples. Each candidate triple helps to predict an atomic preference solution for D by inference based on any of the previous patterns described in Sects. 2 and 3. A global preference solution is computed through a majority vote applied on *all* atomic solutions and finally assigned to D.

As expected, the proposed APP may fail in case no examples C (or A, or B) could be found in the set E especially when E has a limited size (only few examples of preferences between choices are available). To overcome this problem, we propose to expand the set E and search for examples e in $comp(E)$.

For any example $e \in E$ s.t.: $e : x_{-i}\alpha \succeq y_{-i}\beta$, one may produce a new valid preference example by *dominance* (monotony) defined as:

$$newe \in comp(E) \text{ iff } newe : newx_{-i}\alpha \succeq newy_{-i}\beta$$
$$\text{and } newx_{-i} \geq x_{-i} \text{ and } y_{-i} \geq newy_{-i} \quad (1)$$

For any relation e with opposite preference sign corresponds a $newe$ by reversing the operators.

4.2   Algorithms

Based on the previous ideas, we propose two different algorithms for predicting preferences in the following.

Let E be a training set of examples whose preference is known. Given a new preference relation $D \notin E$ whose preference is to be predicted, the first alternative is to look at all good triples $(A, B, C) \in E$ that provide a solution for the item D. It is important to note that in a pre-processing step, one may search for the appropriate pairs $(A, B) \in E$, s.t: $A : x_{-i}\alpha, y_{-i}\beta$ and $B : x_{-i}\alpha', y_{-i}\beta'$, i.e., A is identical as B except in one attribute. This step aims to filtering the high number of pairs and keeping only those that fit the previous patterns. This first option is described by Algorithm 1.

Algorithm 1. APP with restricted set

Input: a training set E of examples with known preferences
a new item $D \notin E$ whose preference is unknown.
$PredictedPref = false$
Preprocess: $S_{(A,B)} = FindPairs(E)$.
CandidateVote(p)=0, for each $p \in \{\preceq, \succeq\}$
for each $C \in E$ **do**
  if IsGood(C) **then**
    for each $(A, B) \in S_{(A,B)}$ **do**
      if IsGood(A) AND IsGood(B) **then**
        $p = Sol(A, B, C, D)$
        $CandidateVote(p)$++
      end if
    end for
  end if
end for
$maxi = max\{CandidateVote(p)\}$
if $maxi \neq 0$ AND $unique(maxi, CandidateVote(p))$ **then**
  $Preference(D) = argmax_p\{CandidateVote(p)\}$
  $PredictedPref = true$
end if
if $PredictedPref$ **then**
  return$Preference(D)$
else
  return $(not\ predicted)$
end if

In case Algorithm 1 fails to find good triples, the second alternative (described by Algorithm 2) aims at expanding the set of preference examples E by searching for good triples (A, B, C) in $comp(E)$. In this set, examples are produced by applying dominance (monotony) on elements found in E.

Note that the algorithms that we proposed in this paper are quite different from the one in [17], where only a brute force procedure for preference prediction is presented without giving any clue for implementation. Neither an evaluation process nor comparisons are provided. Moreover, the algorithm in [17] assumes that a completed set Comp(E) is first computed and used as input for prediction. Generating the whole set Comp(E) is computationally very expensive, while it may be useless. In this paper we search for useful elements in Comp(E) only in case no appropriate triples can be found in E. This clearly reduces the computational burden. We then describe a precise process for searching for appropriate triples and also present a way to evaluate the algorithm's performance (which is not done in [17]). In terms of complexity, due to the use of triples of items, our algorithms have a cubic complexity while the approach to find the set of weights compatible with the set E has at least a complexity $O(|E| * |E'|^n)$, where n is the number of weighted averages to be generated and E' is the new set generated from one of these weights.

Algorithm 2. APP with a completion set

Input: a training set E of examples with known preferences
a new item $D \notin E$ whose preference is unknown.
Preprocess: $S_{(A,B)} = FindPairs(E)$.
if Algo1(D,E)=*not predicted* **then**
  CandidateVote(p)=0, for each $p \in \{\preceq, \succeq\}$
  for each $C \in E$ **do**
    newC=comp(C)
    for each $(A, B) \in E \times E$ **do**
      if IsGood(A) AND IsGood(B) **then**
        $p = Sol(A, B, newC, D)$
        $CandidateVote(p)++$
      end if
    end for
    if CandidateVote(p)=0, for each $p \in \{\preceq, \succeq\}$ **then**
      for each $A \in E$ **do**
        newB=comp(B)
        if IsGood(A) AND IsGood(NewB) **then**
          $p = Sol(A, newB, newC, D)$
          $CandidateVote(p)++$
        end if
      end for
    end if
  end for
end if
$Preference(D) = argmax_p\{CandidateVote(p)\}$
return $Preference(D)$

5 Experiments

In order to evaluate the proposed APP algorithms, we have developed a set of experiments that we describe in the following. We finally compare these algorithms to a nearest neighbors method.

5.1 Datasets and Validation Protocol

The experimental study is based on three datasets, the two first ones are synthetic data generated from a chosen weighted average function. For each of these datasets, all possible combinations of the feature values over the scale S are considered. For each pair of vectors $(x, y) \in E^2$, the preference is determined, through computing weighted averages as follows: $x \succeq y$ if and only if $U(x) = \sum_{i=1}^{n} w_i x_i \geq U(y) = \sum_{i=1}^{n} w_i y_i$, where w_i is the weight associated to criterion i.

– **Dataset 1**: we consider only 3 criteria in each preference relation i.e., $n = 3$ and we test with 3 different options of this dataset. In each of them, examples are generated using a different weighted average function:
  - Weights1(noted w_1) with $0.6, 0.3, 0.1$ weights respectively for criteria 1, 2 and 3.
  - Weights2(w_2) with $0.5, 0.3, 0.2$ weights respectively for criteria 1, 2 and 3.
  - Weights3(w_3) with $0.7, 0.2, 0.1$ weights respectively for criteria 1, 2 and 3.
– **Dataset 2**: we expand each preference relation to support 5 criteria, i.e.: $n = 5$ and similar to dataset1, we tried different options of weights:
  - Weights1(w_1) with $0.4, 0.3, 0.1, 0.1, 0.1$ weights respectively for criteria 1, 2, 3, 4 and 5.
  - Weights2(w_2) with $0.3, 0.3, 0.2, 0.1, 0.1$ weights respectively for criteria 1, 2, 3, 4 and 5.
  - Weights3(w_3) with $0.6, 0.2, 0.1, 0.05, 0.05$ weights respectively for criteria 1, 2, 3, 4 and 5.

We may consider that 5 criteria is already a rather high number of criteria for the cognitive appraisal of an item by a human user in practice. For both datasets, each criterion is evaluated on a scale with 5 different values, i.e., $S = \{1, ..., 5\}$.

To check the applicability of APP algorithms, it is important to measure their efficiency on real data. For such data, two choices/options are provided to a human judge and ask him/her to pick one of them. To the best of our knowledge, there is no such a dataset that is available in this format [5]. For this purpose, we select the Food dataset from context aware recommender systems available in[2].

---

[2] https://github.com/trungngv/gpfm.

– The **Food dataset** used by [5] contains 4036 user preferences among 20 food menus picked by 212 users. In each of them a user is supposed to provide a numerical rating. Each item in this dataset is represented by three features that correspond to three different level of user hunger. Each of them could be in 3 possible situations. To test this dataset, we first pre-process it to generate the preferences in the format recommended by our model: We group all the input data by user and by foods. For any two inputs with different ratings, we generate a preference relation. Since we are only dealing with nominal values in this paper, we limit our study to 5 different foods.

Regarding the validation protocol, for each dataset we have investigated different sizes of E between 20 to 1000 examples. For each subset of data, we repeat the experiment 100 times to get stable results. In each experiment, a standard 10 fold cross-validation technique is applied. The prediction accuracies shown in next subsection for both algorithms are for the testing set and are the average over the 100 rounds.

5.2   Results

Figures 1 and 2 show prediction accuracies of APP algorithms respectively for Datasets 1 and 2 for different sizes of each dataset and different weights (see curves "Algo1_$w_i(E)$" and "Algo2_$w_i(E)$"; the other curves using $InterE$ data are explained at the end of Sect. 5.2).

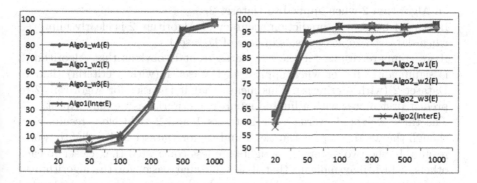

Fig. 1. Prediction accuracies for Dataset 1 with 3 criteria and different sizes of subsets of data.

If we compare results of Algorithm 1 and 2 in Figs. 1 and 2, we can draw the following conclusions:

– In case of Dataset 1, Algorithm 2 is largely better than Algorithm 1 for small sizes of the dataset (size < 500). Algorithm 1 and 2 provide close results for datasets with more than 500 examples even if Algorithm 2 is always better.

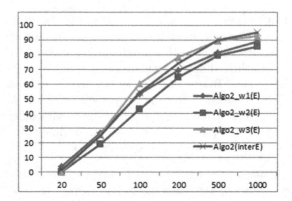

Fig. 2. Prediction accuracies for Dataset 2 with 5 criteria and different dataset sizes

- Algorithm 1 seems inefficient for prediction when only a small sample E of examples is given. Since we are only dealing with grades in a nominal way in this paper, many triples are rejected due to the 'yes-no' acceptance condition for appropriate triples. This may be relaxed and extended to deal with truly numerical values (which is a process under study).
- Algorithm 2 shows a very good prediction ability even with rather small samples (i.e., 50 preference examples). Due to monotony exploited by this algorithm, it is always possible to find appropriate triples in Comp(E).
- Since Algorithm 2 is clearly better than Algorithm 1, we limit our experiments on Algorithm 2 when applied to Dataset 2.
- In case of Dataset 2, prediction accuracy of Algorithm 2 is clearly improved when dataset size increases as in case of Dataset1.
- If we compare results for the two datasets, it is obvious that Algorithm 2 is significantly better when applied to Dataset 1 (with 3 criteria) than to Dataset 2 (with 5 criteria). This means that it is easier for Algorithm 2 to predict preferences with a limited number of criteria, as we may expect.
- The three weighted averages for Datasets 1 and 2 yield close results even though the weights w_1 for Dataset 1 and w_2 for Dataset 2 give slightly worse results. In the two latter, the weights are less contrasted (i.e., closer to each other), which may indicate that it is somewhat easier for the algorithm to predict preferences generated from a weighted average with more contrasted weights. Still the three weights sets yield very similar results for large dataset sizes.

The previous results show the effectiveness of Algorithm 2 as preference predictor which fits with a given weighted average used to produce the preference examples especially for small number of criteria.

It is worth pointing out that the predicted preferences have been evaluated as being valid, or not, on the basis of 3 weighted averages, the ones used for generating the dataset with its three versions. It is clear that a given set E of preference examples is compatible with a more large collections of weights.

Strictly speaking a prediction is valid if it is correct with respect to at least one of the collections of weights compatible with E. As already said, determining all the extreme points of the polytope of the weights compatible with E is quite tricky. So in the above reported experiments, we have compared the prediction to ones obtained by using the weighted averages used in the generation of the training set, and thus the reported accuracies are *lower bounds* of the true accuracies.

In the following, we aim at estimating the extent to which APP algorithms succeed to fit with a larger variety of weighted averages. For this purpose, we also experiment our algorithms on datasets obtained by applying the following procedure:

1. Select m different weighted averages $P_1, P_2, ...P_m$, all of them satisfying the same ranking for the importance of each criterion. We denote $E_1, E_2, ..., E_m$ respectively the corresponding sets of preference examples.
2. Find the *intersection* set of these preference sets denoted $InterE = E_1 \cap E_2 \cap ... \cap E_m$ containing only examples that *any* of all weighted averages $\in \{P_1, P_2, ...P_m\}$ can generate.
3. Apply APP Algorithms to predict preferences on subsets of $InterE$.

To test the previous idea, we use 5 different weighted averages ($m = 5$) keeping the same importance ranking for the criteria. Results of Algorithm 1 and 2 are given in Figs. 1 and 2 (See Algo1(InterE) and Algo2(InterE)). These results show that:

- Accuracy of Algorithm 2 is clearly improved when the set $InterE$ is used instead of the set E which is produced from *one* of the 5 weighted averages. This can be noticed for most dataset sizes especially large sizes of the data.
- For Algorithm1, a slight improvement is noticed when using the set $InterE$ especially for large dataset sizes exceeding 100 examples.

This confirms our intuition and shows that if preference examples agree with a variety of weighted averages, more predicted preferences can be considered as fitting with these examples.

5.3   Comparison with a Nearest Neighbor Method

In the following, we aim at comparing APP algorithms to a basic nearest-neighbor (NN) preference learning approach. That is why we implemented and tested a NN preference learning algorithm that we call $NNPL$. The basic principle of this algorithm is to predict any new preference example d in the same way as its *nearest − neighbor* preference example(s) belonging to the training set. For this purpose, we compute the distance of d to *all* training examples and we select those being sufficiently close. In case of ties, a majority vote is applied. Let us consider an example $d : u \ ? \ v$ to be predicted and $c : x^i \succeq y^i \in E$, we compute two distances to c defined as:

$$Dis1(c,d) = (\mid u - x^i \mid, \mid v - y^i \mid)$$

$$Dis2(c, d) = (\mid u - y^i \mid, \mid v - x^i \mid)$$

where $\mid a - b \mid$ is simply the Manhattan distance of vectors components.
We define:

$$NN(c, d) = \{c \in E \text{ s.t.}: Dis(c, d) \leq \theta\}$$

where $Dis(c, d) = Min(Dis1, Dis2)$.

We want to check if the preference d is predicted by APP in the same way as by NNPL. For this purpose, we computed the frequency of the cases where both APP and NNPL predict the correct preference for d (this case is denoted SS), the frequency of the cases where both algorithms predict an incorrect label (denoted FF), the frequency where APP prediction is correct and NNPL prediction is wrong (SF) and the frequency where APP prediction is wrong and NNPL prediction is correct (FS). For this experiment we exploit APP algorithms applied to Dataset 1 for which we only consider the cases where both APP and NNPL are able to provide a prediction (we only include examples that can be predicted by the two compared algorithms). Regarding the threshold θ, we tried 3 different values in $\{1, 2, 3\}$ and we report the results for the best one (θ is fixed to 2 in this experiment). Results are saved in Table 1.

Table 1. Frequency of success/fail of APP predictions that are predicted same/not same as the $NNPL$ approach

Dataset size	Algo1				Algo2			
	SS	FF	SF	FS	SS	FF	SF	FS
50	0.901	0	**0.099**	0	0.697	0.026	**0.2**	0.076
100	0.807	0.04	**0.113**	0.04	0.811	0.035	**0.134**	0.02
200	0.841	0.02	**0.081**	0.058	0.826	0.023	**0.106**	0.045
500	0.887	0.015	**0.056**	0.042	0.863	0.012	**0.069**	0.056
1000	0.92	0.011	**0.042**	0.027	0.911	0.013	**0.045**	0.031

In this table, we note that:

- For most cases, APP and NNPL agree and predict the same preference (the highest frequency can be seen in column SS).
- If we compare results in column SF and FS, we can see that the frequency of cases where APP provides the correct prediction, while $NNPL$ does not (column SF) is significantly better than the opposite case (column FS). This can be seen for all dataset sizes (except the smallest one). Especially for a size of 100 examples, more than 10% of the total correctly predicted examples are predicted differently from the NNPL.

Lastly, we also compare the prediction accuracy of APP algorithms to NNPL when applied to the Food dataset as representative of real data. Results of Food dataset, in Table 2, shows that:

Table 2. Classification accuracy of Algo 1 and 2 applied to Food dataset

Dataset	Algo1	Algo2	NNPL	[5]
Food	**73.31 ± 2.81**	**73.35 ± 2.63**	61.57 ± 3.58	61

- APP algorithms performs well when dealing with real dataset as in case of synthetic data.
- Algorithms 1 and 2 significantly outperform the probabilistic approach proposed by [5] applied to this dataset.
- Algorithms 1 and 2 also do better than the NNPL.

In fact, APP benefits from two basic differences if compared to the classic NNPL (i) using a large amount of *triple* voters for prediction while NNPL uses a simpler voting-based strategy that directly applies a vote on the nearest neighbor examples and (ii) using more complex calculation by comparing pairs of items instead of comparing simply two items. We note that the four items involved in each comparison are not necessarily closes as we shall see from the basic pattern described in Sect. 4.1. In this pattern, it is clear that D is neighbor to C (only one criteria is different) and B is neighbor to A but D is not necessarily neighbor to A or B. This increase in terms of complexity (which is cubic in case of APP) may explain the good results of APP if compared to NNPL having linear complexity.

6 Conclusion

The approach presented in the paper does not amount to inducing a general representation of the set of examples under the form of a particular class of aggregation functions or of a graphical preference representation, from which we could predict a preference relation between any pair of choices. We simply apply an analogical inference principle (or in the comparative study, a nearest neighbor principle) for making directly the prediction. This type of approach is successful in classification. The present study shows that it is applicable as well in preference learning. Still in classification, the classes have just to be mutually exclusive. Preferences are more structured in the sense that they are expected not to exhibit contradictory trade-offs and to be monotone, which has to be taken into account in the learning process. In our approach, our experiments have been on training sets generated by means of weighted sums, which is a quite standard aggregation function, and we have obtained good results for rather small subsets of examples. Still it is known that the representation of multiple-criteria preferences may require more general settings such as Choquet integrals [11] where the condition for avoiding contradictory trade-offs is weaker. Adapting the proposed approach to guess preferences generated by such more general settings is a topic for further research.

References

1. Aamodt, A., Plaza, E.: Case-based reasoning; foundational issues, methodological variations, and system approaches. AICom **7**(1), 39–59 (1994)
2. Abdel-Aziz, A., Hüllermeier, E.: Case base maintenance in preference-based CBR. In: Hüllermeier, E., Minor, M. (eds.) ICCBR 2015. LNCS (LNAI), vol. 9343, pp. 1–14. Springer, Cham (2015). https://doi.org/10.1007/978-3-319-24586-7_1
3. Bayoudh, S., Miclet, L., Delhay, A.: Learning by analogy: A classification rule for binary and nominal data. In: Proceedings International Joint Conference on Artificial Intelligence IJCAI07, pp. 678–683 (2007)
4. Bounhas, M., Prade, H., Richard, G.: Analogy-based classifiers for nominal or numerical data. Int. J. Approx. Reason. **91**, 36–55 (2017)
5. Chen, S., Joachims, T.: Predicting matchups and preferences in context. In: Proceedings of the 22nd ACM SIGKDD International Conference on Knowledge Discovery and Data Mining, KDD 2016, pp. 775–784. ACM, New York (2016)
6. Couceiro, M., Hug, N., Prade, H., Richard, G.: Analogy-preserving functions: a way to extend boolean samples. In: Proceedings 26th International Joint Conference on Artificial Intelligence, IJCAI 2017, Melbourne, Australia, 19–25 August 2017, pp. 1575–1581 (2017)
7. Domshlak, C., Hüllermeier, E., Kaci, S., Prade, H.: Preferences in AI: an overview. Artif. Intell. **175**(7–8), 1037–1052 (2011)
8. Fahandar, M.A., Hüllermeier, E.: Learning to rank based on analogical reasoning. In: Proceedings 32th National Conference on Artificial Intelligence (AAAI 2018), New Orleans, 2–7 February 2018
9. Fürnkranz, J., Hüllermeier, E. (eds.): Preference Learning. Springer, Heidelberg (2010). https://doi.org/10.1007/978-3-642-14125-6
10. Fürnkranz, J., Hüllermeier, E., Rudin, C., Slowinski, R., Sanner, S.: Preference learning (dagstuhl seminar 14101). Dagstuhl Rep. **4**(3), 1–27 (2014)
11. Grabisch, M., Labreuche, C.: A decade of application of the Choquet and Sugeno integrals in multi-criteria decision aid. Annals Oper. Res. **175**, 247–286 (2010)
12. Hüllermeier, E., Fürnkranz, J.: Editorial: preference learning and ranking. Mach. Learn. **93**(2–3), 185–189 (2013)
13. Khachiyan, L., Boros, E., Borys, K., Elbassioni, K., Gurvich, V.: Generating all vertices of a polyhedron is hard. Discret. Comput. Geom. **39**(1), 174–190 (2008)
14. Lepage, Y.: Analogy and formal languages. In: Proceedings FG/MOL 2001, pp. 373–378 (2001). http://www.slt.atr.co.jp/lepage/pdf/dhdryl.pdf.gz
15. Miclet, L., Bayoudh, S., Delhay, A.: Analogical dissimilarity: definition, algorithms and two experiments in machine learning. JAIR **32**, 793–824 (2008)
16. Miclet, L., Prade, H.: Handling analogical proportions in classical logic and fuzzy logics settings. In: Sossai, C., Chemello, G. (eds.) ECSQARU 2009. LNCS (LNAI), vol. 5590, pp. 638–650. Springer, Heidelberg (2009). https://doi.org/10.1007/978-3-642-02906-6_55
17. Pirlot, M., Prade, H., Richard, G.: Completing preferences by means of analogical proportions. In: Torra, V., Narukawa, Y., Navarro-Arribas, G., Yañez, C. (eds.) MDAI 2016. LNCS (LNAI), vol. 9880, pp. 135–147. Springer, Cham (2016). https://doi.org/10.1007/978-3-319-45656-0_12
18. Prade, H., Richard, G.: From analogical proportion to logical proportions. Logica Universalis **7**(4), 441–505 (2013)

19. Rumelhart, D.E., Abrahamson, A.A.: A model for analogical reasoning. Cognitive Psychol. 5, 1–28 (1973)
20. Stroppa, N., Yvon, F.: Analogical learning and formal proportions: Definitions and methodological issues. Technical report, June 2005
21. Yvon, F., Stroppa, N., Delhay, A., Miclet, L.: Solving analogical equations on words. Technical report, Ecole Nationale Supérieure des Télécommunications (2004)

A Fast Mapper as a Foundation for Forthcoming Conceptual Blending Experiments

João Gonçalves[✉], Pedro Martins, and Amílcar Cardoso

CISUC, Department of Informatics Engineering, University of Coimbra,
Coimbra, Portugal
{jcgonc,pjmm,amilcar}@dei.uc.pt

Abstract. Algorithms for finding analogies as mappings between pairs of concepts are fundamental to some implementations of Conceptual Blending (CB), a theory which has been suggested as explaining some cognitive processes behind the creativity phenomenon. When analogies are defined as sub-isomorphisms of semantic graphs, we find ourselves with a NP-complete problem. In this paper we propose and compare a new high performance stochastic mapper that efficiently handles semantic graphs containing millions of relations between concepts, while outputting in real-time analogy mappings ready for use by another algorithm, such as a computational system based on CB theory.

1 Introduction

In a paper titled *Analogy as the Core of Cognition* Hofstadter [14] stated that psychologists and cognitive scientists consider analogy as a sophisticated and cryptic mental tool used in problem-solving, especially artistic people [11]. Multiple authors [2,11,22] declare that analogy is a essential task in many creative processes. In our current main focus - Computational Creativity (CC) - researchers are typically concerned building algorithms for the creation of new ideas or the display of behaviours exhibiting creativity. From these we refer to a few which have influenced our work in [1,3,13,19,24]. Similar to other researchers in Computer Science we try to bring fruitful findings in cognitive science into implementing CC systems.

Simply stated, analogy is a method which relates ideas or pieces of thought. Analogy as a process can be easily observed when asking someone *"if a is to b then what is c to?"* Or the question *"the **composer** is to the **general** as the **drum** is to?"* [24] This question should develop in most people answers such as *cannon, bomb, tank,* etc. giving us a sense that analogy seems to be at the core of cognition [26]. Analogy emerges as a fundamental tool to associate the above two domains of knowledge - the composer and the general. It is not hard to think that this process can be taken further by combining (or *blending*) partially selected parts of information from the two domains into a new mental idea, for instance, that the composed is directing an orchestra of cannons and bombs

© Springer Nature Switzerland AG 2018
M. T. Cox et al. (Eds.): ICCBR 2018, LNAI 11156, pp. 532–547, 2018.
https://doi.org/10.1007/978-3-030-01081-2_35

emerging in a scenery of musical warfare. We are of the opinion that this text seems to possess some form of creativity [11]. In a nutshell, this is the idea behind CB, a cognitive theory which has been successfully applied in CC systems [3,19] including international projects such as CoInvent [20] and ConCreTe [27]. CB requires a mapping of concepts - an analogy - to be effective and is elaborated in the next section.

The contribution described in this paper flows from the current work of our research group in developing a computational system which in the future is expected to exhibit creativity. We previously reported [9] a CB module (named the Blender) based on a evolutionary algorithm which requires as an input a semantic graph and one or more analogies in the form of sets of concept pairs. These mappings are typically either produced manually (to validate a system) or produced by an existing computational analogy system such as the ones outlined in [6]. However, as far as we know we have not found an algorithm fast enough to extract in real-time mappings from giant non trivial semantic graphs available in the web, such as the Never-Ending Language Learning (NELL) project [17] and ConceptNet [21]. Our vision is that in a fully automated process the analogies should follow the frames pertinent to the blend (an instance of the blending space) being elaborated in the Blender module. In turn this requires a sort of feedback loop between the blender and the mapper (which creates suitable mappings) and therefore, a mapping module (the focus of this paper) capable of executing in real-time and concurrently with the blending module.

This paper is laid out as follows: we start with a short overview of CB and why it requires an analogy in the form of a mapping to work; it is followed by the description of a few computational analogy systems which were relevant for our work and CB in general; then we reveal our EEmapper and its inner workings; afterwards we compare it against an optimum mapper and jMapper and examine the results; finally, we outline further work to improve our mapper and conclude on our findings. Semantic graphs are given as relations in the form *(source, relation, target)*, an analogy is represented as a functional mapping between two sets of concepts and the size of a mapping corresponds to the number of one-to-one associations between concepts in the mapping set.

2   Conceptual Blending and the Importance of Analogies

Fauconnier and Turner [5] suggested CB as cognitive theory to explain processes of conceptual integration occurring in the human thought. Its potential to model mechanisms of concept invention has increasingly inspired research in CC in recent years [20,27] and also in our research group [3,9,19]. Initially, CB was proposed as a framework for conceptual metaphor theory, i.e., a cognitive explanation of the reasoning behind metaphors as a linguistic phenomenon. Later [8] it was adapted to include the projection of one information domain to another as a result of an analogy process with a partial recombination of concepts and relations characteristic of the blending process. The projection of concepts or analogy corresponds to a one to one mapping between concepts of different domains being one the source and the other the target. In graph theory, the analogy (or mapping) is defined as a structural alignment of concepts from different domains of knowledge and can be seen as a graph isomorphism between two semantic graphs or regions of a larger semantic graph. This way, CB includes the usage of analogy to blend elements from different thoughts and is equipped to explain the synthesis of new ideas and the everyday language [8].

An essential ingredient in the CB theory is the *mental space*, a partial and temporary structure of knowledge assembled for purposes of thought and action [5]. The CB process takes two *input spaces* and looks for a partial *mapping* between elements of both spaces that may be perceived as similar or analogous in some respect. A third mental space, called *generic*, encapsulates the conceptual structure shared by the input spaces, providing guidance to the next step of the process, where elements from each of the input spaces are *selectively projected* into a new mental space, called the *Blend Space*. Further stages of the process elaborate and complete the blend.

In the CC and Analogy fields the input spaces have been typically given in the form of semantic graphs, that is, graphs with directed edges representing relations between concepts. Mappings represent analogies and are defined as sets of ordered pairs of concepts, each concept usually coming from a different input space than the other concept in the pair. Mappings represent a one-to-one correspondence between concepts of different regions of the semantic space [18]. In this paper we term the computational systems which generate mappings as *mappers* and describe the ones we find crucial for our work below.

2.1 Structural Mapping Theory

In [7] Gentner conceived her Structure Mapping Theory (SMT) stating that in order to establish an analogy, two domains of knowledge defined by interconnected relations between concepts, are matched from one domain to the other. This matching is on its essence a structural alignment, or mapping, of one to one correspondences between concepts from both domains. First and foremost, particular crucial associations between the concepts from both domains are what will identify the analogy. However, more interesting results could materialize if the associations are fabricated using higher order relations, that is, relations between relations or some sort of abstract matching [8]. SMT gave rise to a robust algorithm - Structural Mapping Engine (SME) [4] - which probably is the most significant and earlier work in Computational Analogy [6].

2.2 Sapper

Sapper [25] is one of the first mappers offered as an alternative to Gentner's SME. Sapper was initially described as a model of memory for metaphor comprehension. Since then it has also been used as a dedicated mapping engine by itself [24] or as a foundation for developing further mappers [12,19]. Given two inputs in the form of semantic graphs representing the *Tenor* domain and the *Vehicle* domain (the components of a metaphor), Sapper lays out what the authors label as dormant bridges - one-to-one associations between concepts.

Sapper works as a spreading activation mechanism in the given input semantic graphs and thus, it is in a sense a hybrid algorithm integrating principles from symbolic computation with connectionist philosophies. Sapper works in batches of two phases exchanging information between a structural inference phase (mostly the Triangle and Square rules) and the opportunistic activation phase. Is in the second phase where the limits of the mapping are defined by checking how important the nearby pairs of concepts are.

The Triangle rule lays out a dormant bridge (equivalent to a association of two concepts) whenever those two concepts share a common concept with the same relation. For instance, if *dog, isa, animal* and *cat, isa, animal* the shared concept is *animal* through the *isa* relation. In this example Sapper associates both dog and cat concepts in the first phase. The Square rule builds on previously laid associations of concepts and if these also share the same relation with a third and a forth concepts, Sapper associates the latter two. Again, as an example if *dog* and *cat* are associated and the semantic network contains the two relations *cat, atlocation, crib* and *dog, atlocation, doghouse*, Sapper lays down a new association, in this case between the concepts *crib* and *doghouse*. When Sapper is complete it returns the largest mapping (in number of associations) containing the dormant bridges activated during its execution.

2.3   jMapper

In [19] Pereira developed in Prolog a mapper which found analogy mappings between concepts from two input spaces, using a structural alignment algorithm based on Sapper [24]. In [12] Pereira's mapper was re-implemented in Java with gains in efficiency and scalability, although maintaining the original idea. The authors state that jMapper reduces the search space and ranks the pairs of concept candidates in terms of potential similarity. This similarity is based on the number nearby relations shared between each concept and their nearby concepts. The mapper allows a similarity threshold to be set that avoids the exploration of portions of the search space. For instance, if a low threshold is set a region of the mapping which associates animals with plants could stop if their only relation in common is that they are a form of life. As such, jMapper prefers to explore concepts from the semantic graph that have more in common.

As stated above, jMapper has its roots on Sapper and looks for pairs of concepts that share the same relation to a third concept (the Triangle rule). From then on, it applies the Square rule to look for 1-to-1 correspondences. In the end, jMapper returns the largest mappings.

2.4   Optimum Mapper

This mapper was previously developed in our research group to investigate the complexity and feasibility of finding mappings in various semantic networks of diverse sizes [3]. As the name indicates, the algorithm is exhaustive and optimal, as it will create all sets of possible mappings in order to find the largest achievable analogy, that is, the mapping set with the greatest number of concept pairs. As the algorithm serves as a theoretical basis for the EEmapper we give a short summary next.

The algorithm begins in a root pair composed of two distinct concepts taken from the input spaces. Both concepts are not required to be related and thus contrasting the Triangle Rule in Sapper/jMapper. Then, the execution is performed in two stages. In the first stage, the algorithm finds a structural isomorphism in the global input space (combination of both input spaces), extracting two isomorphic sub-graphs. This isomorphism is edge based and reflects the same sequence of relations in the sub-graphs. We term the two input spaces *left* and *right*. Starting at the root pair, the isomorphic sub-graphs are extracted from the input spaces by executing two synchronized expansions of nearby concepts at increasingly depths, one from the left and the other from the right concepts defining the root pair. The expansion is done recursively in the form of a hybrid between a depth first expansion and a breadth first expansion, one expansion dedicated for the left sub-graph and the other to the right sub-graph. The left and right isomorphic sub-graphs define a mapping composed of a unique set of ordered pairs of concepts. Each concept of a pair comes from its respective left or right isomorphism and thus, from one of the input spaces. Any concept belonging to a pair is excluded from further expansions and future pairs.

While expanding, the algorithm stores additional associations between each matched relations and the corresponding concept which was reached through that relation. In reality, what is likely to happen is to occur a multitude of isomorphisms. In that case the algorithm will store various concept pairs relating any given concept to multiple matching concepts, as long as the same concepts where reached from a previous concept with the same relation. This is the basis to find an edge/relation based sub-graph isomorphism. The last stage corresponds to iterating all the isomorphisms found in the first stage and extracting the largest mapping in terms of concept pairs. It may happen that there are multiple mappings with the same size and in either case, all the equally largest mappings are outputted as analogies.

3   EEMapper

Our proposed algorithm for extracting mappings from semantic graphs is titled EEmapper and is based on evolutionary principles. Although there is quite a number of mappers in the literature, including the ones explained before, none is fully capable of handling semantic graphs in the order of millions of relations. Either the mappers do not halt at all or consume a vast amount of resources (memory included) and trigger software exceptions due to the combinatory explosion of possibilities they have to explore to output a mapping. There are also other problems such as the wait for a usable mapping. When a CB system depends on a mapping to do its elaboration and the mapping is not available, or if the mapping should change in a small part to allow the CB task to improve its results it is clear that the mapping engine must be fast enough to nourish the dependent tasks. In this case we have an optimisation issue inside of another optimisation problem and therefore the combined complexity must be lowered if we expect results in a useful time. Hence the purpose of this paper, a somewhat embryonic but highly fast mapper to find the largest mapping (in number of concept pairs - one to one associations of concepts). Although currently missing, in the future we expect this search to include a form of semantic quality or even of usefulness for a CB framework.

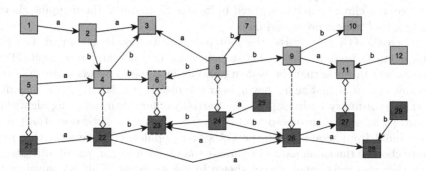

Fig. 1. Example of a mapping (analogy) between two domains of knowledge (green and red) of a larger semantic graph. Associations are shown with vertical dashed lines between concepts. Best viewed in colour. (Color figure online)

It is well known in Computer Science that finding the perfect answer to a problem (in our case the ideal mapping) may be impossible to reach. The only alternative then is to find an answer "good enough" to our problem and that is when we turn ourselves to stochastic algorithms. Both our CB framework [9] and our Domain Spotter [10] are based on a High Performance Genetic Algorithm (GA) and because of this, we have a good foundation for building the EEmapper. Our GA is prepared to handle multiple threads in parallel while minimising memory usage. The GA runs in multiple batches of three phases in parallel corresponding each batch to an epoch in the evolution of the population. The three phases are the population mutation and crossover (genetic operations phase), population selection for the next generation (k tournament selection) and fitness evaluation. Our EEmapper currently does not implement crossover and has a simple but fast mutation. Hence we consider it a system with evolutionary principles and not a fully GA, but this is expected to change in the future. Given the scope of this paper we do not describe the inner workings of a typical GA but only the required operations to implement the EEmapper. The mapper is founded on a partial but faster version of the isomorphism described in the optimum mapper.

Each chromosome is defined by what we name a *root pair* of two different concepts (vertices 6 and 23 in Fig. 1 representing a one to one association and the building blocks of the emerging mapping. Any association of concepts is possible, given the stochastic nature of the algorithm. In each epoch, EEmapper evolves hundreds or thousands of chromosomes, each representing a mapping. Hence the system not only outputs the best result but multiple mappings similar or resulting from a fluctuating population of chromosomes. Excluding speed optimizations in the algorithm (such as only running the fitness function whenever a chromosome changes) the fitness function reflects the execution of the stochastic sub-isomorphism finding algorithm, naturally applied to every chromosome of each generation. As in the Optimum Mapper, the score for each chromosome (and related mapping) is the number of concept pairs in the mapping. For instance, if a chromosome has stored in its genetic material the mapping shown in Fig. 1 its fitness score would be 6.

When the GA first starts, the root pairs are randomly generated, i.e., the mapper starts from an association such as *(dog, cat)* or from *(rock, light)*. This decision was taken so that the system could find mappings between disconnected domains even if at first sight they appear completely unrelated, as this may discover extraordinary findings [15]. The partial isomorphism matching algorithm executes whenever a chromosome changes (because of a genetic operation) or is reset (build from scratch or in the GA's first population). The algorithm randomly chooses the same path of relations (labels such as *isa, partof, atlocation*) in the left and right input spaces shown in the same Fig. This is equivalent to executing the full left and right expansion in the optimum mapper for later only choosing a single random mapping from that expansion, that is, one path from the root to a leaf in the deep first expansion of the semantic tree. Therefore, a mapping depends on the initial root pair and the (random) sequence of branches (associations of relations and thus concepts) generated by the Random Number Generator. In a sense, the defining of a root pair is equivalent to Sapper's Triangle rule and the mutation's random walk to Sapper's Square rule. However, contrary to Sapper, the EEmapper works without problems in disconnected input spaces. With the above described stochastic process executing in the mutation operator the search space is cut in a tiny fraction of the other mappers with the expected outcome of lowering the probability of finding the largest mapping.

The mutation mechanism does two types of operations. First, it randomly changes one or both of the concepts in its root pair to nearby connected concepts. This mechanism has a progressively smaller chance of randomly mutating a concept to a more distant neighbour. As an example, if a root pair is *dog, cat* a possible mutation is *canine, cat* or in Fig. 1 changing the root pair *6, 23* to *6, 24*. Second, the mutation re-executes a new partial isomorphism match from the existing or mutated root pair in the hope of shuffling the resulting mapping.

4   Comparative Evaluation

As an initial validation of our new mapper, we compared it against an optimal mapper we developed previously in our research group [3] and against an efficient implementation of Sapper - jMapper [12]. This comparison is as of this document done ingenuously in the form of the number of concept pairs present in the resulting mappings and naturally, the time required to obtain those mappings. We admit we are neglecting the semantic features of the mappings but as expressed in the Sect. 6, further study is expected in this aspect. The experiments were done with the following criteria in mind:

- for what size of the input spaces do the optimum mapper and jMapper fail to converge?
- for the time optimum mapper and jMapper took to execute what are the largest mappings obtained by EEmapper?
- if possible, how long does EEmapper require to reach similar results to the other mappers?

jMapper requires two input spaces with one requirement - the existence of common concepts in both input spaces to be used in the Triangle rule [24]. On the other hand, both our EEmapper and optimum mapper do not have this requirement. To use jMapper we decided to use our semantic graph splitter, titled Domain Spotter [10] to partition ConceptNet in various pairs of input spaces to be used in the experiments. The Spotter is based on the theory of Bisociation and extracts from a given semantic graph two apparently unrelated domains - the input spaces - ideally connected only through a single term [15] - the bridge node which is always present in both extracted input spaces.

The Domain Spotter runs as a Genetic Algorithm and aims to maximise the number of concepts present in both generated input spaces while minimising their intersection. It includes a penalisation parameter τ to control how hard is the separation (in concepts) of both input spaces. The higher the τ is, the higher the amount of concepts in the intersection between both extracted input spaces. In this case, jMapper will have a high amount of concepts available to apply its Triangle rule. The Spotter contains various parameters for fine-tuning the movement of the bridge vertex in the search space, with γ defining the nearby range where the bridge concept can move to.

To evaluate our EEmapper against the optimum mapper and jMapper we turned to ConceptNet v5, a known semantic network built from information collected by the Open Mind Common Sense project at the MIT. ConceptNet includes information extracted from data sources such as the Wikipedia and Wiktionary projects, a subset of DBPedia from the Leipzig University which contains information extracted from the infoboxes on Wikipedia articles and English facts from the word game Verbosity, formerly run by the GWAP project, an academic project at Carnegie Mellon University.

We agree with Baydin et al. [1] regarding noise in ConceptNet. We found biased relations against political subjects, gender issues, sexual or sexist remarks, incomplete or erroneous concepts, funny statements and incorrect relations such as the following: *cell_phone, isa, cat*; *montain_ion, isa, cat*; *food, isa, cat*; *prion,isa,prokaryote*; *woman, purposeof, cook*; etc.

We decided to clean ConceptNet from many of the above issues although many do yet remain. We did this not only for these experiments but expecting the future use of an optimized ConceptNet in further experiments on our research projects. Also removed where ambiguous concepts such as *this, that,* pronouns which do not define a clear subject, definite and indefinite articles, lengthy concepts as *thin_material_that_be_fold_entirely_around_object* and *large_bird_whimsically_think_of_as_wear_tuxedoes*, etc. Additionally, many incorrect relations were reversed, e.g., *person, isa, athlete* → *athlete, isa, person*.

From the pre-processed ConceptNet graph we chose the largest graph component which contains 1229508 concepts and 1791604 edges. To give an idea of the information present in the processed ConceptNet the number of relations of various types are displayed in Fig. 2 and the concepts T which are targets of *isa* relations are shown in Fig. 3.

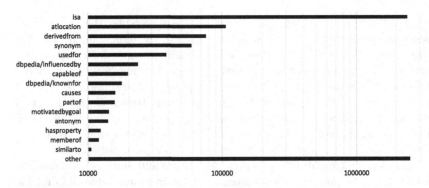

Fig. 2. A portion of the relations with the shown label and their number in the processed ConceptNet semantic graph. Notice the logarithmic scale.

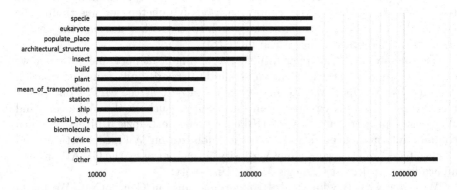

Fig. 3. The quantity of the source concepts of *isa* relations from a portion of the processed ConceptNet semantic graph. Notice the logarithmic scale.

The input space extracting algorithm, Domain Spotter, was run with a population of 256 chromosomes, a limit of 1024 epochs, binary tournament selection with the strongest chromosome having a winning probability of 85%. The bridge jumping parameter γ was set to 2. We varied the τ parameter and run the

Spotter multiple times in order to obtain pairs of input spaces with differing characteristics such as the shown in Table 1. This table is described as follows:

- The first column contains the τ parameter used in the Domain Spotter,
- the **bridge** column contains the required bridging concept which interconnects the two input spaces,
- the **degree** column shows the degree of the bridge node (number of incoming/outgoing relations),
- the **deep** column represents how many relations/edges is the farthest concept of each of the input spaces away from the bridge node,
- $\#s_0$ and $\#s_1$ are respectively the number of concepts present in input spaces 0 and 1,
- the **intersect** column contains the number of concepts intersecting both input spaces (and as such present in both of them),
- **concepts** shows the combined amount of concepts in both input spaces and is equal to $\#s_0 + \#s_1 - \#(s_0 \cap s_1) - 1$. The reduction by one is because of the bridge concept being present in each input space (thus twice in the sum of their cardinality) but only once in their intersection.

After obtaining the input space pairs using the Domain Spotter, we gave each pair to the three mappers (optimum, jMapper and EEmapper), executed each one seven times, recording the executing time and the resulting output mappings. The source code of the Optimum mapper and jMapper where changed to add a time-out and to return their best result until then, instead of using their original implementation of waiting forever and returning a result. This time-out and EEmapper's running time was limited to 3600 s.

Table 2 contains the cardinality (number of concept pairs) of the mappings obtained from the three mappers, including their standard deviation. Table 3 shows the time (in seconds) the optimum mapper and jMapper took to generate a mapping, except in the case of EEmapper this represents the average time the mapper needed to generate a mapping as big (in number of concept pairs) as the best mapping extracted by one of the other mappers. This is because EEmapper only stops its execution either when it reaches a limit of epochs or a time limit.

The two figures (Figs. 4a and b) compare the real-time cardinality of the mappings generated by all the mappers during their execution. Because we can not output both the optimum mapper and jMapper mappings in real-time, we terminate them after a time-out of 3600 s (one hour). Therefore their graphs are shown as a linearly interpolated lines between their start at $t = 0$ s and their termination at either $t = 3600$ s or when they complete.

All the experiments and mappers were executed on a Intel Xeon X3470 with 32 GB RAM, Windows 10 x64, Java JDK 9.0.4 and with JVM settings -Xms8g -Xmx24g. The EEmapper ran with 4 parallel threads to minimize cache inefficiency (pollution and misses) and the memory bottleneck, given the dispersive nature of the semantic graphs in computer memory [16,23].

Table 1. Input spaces extracted by the Domain Spotter from the processed ConceptNet knowledge base.

τ	Bridge	Degree	Deep	#s0	#s1	#intersect	Concepts
0.00	Exercise_physiology	2	4	4841	124	0	4964
0.01	Redwatch	2	3	13	17	0	29
0.01	Venography	2	4	42	21	0	62
0.10	Hiram_ohio	2	2	3	202368	0	202370
0.10	Horror_fiction	2	4	17919	19742	1594	36066
0.25	Redwatch	2	5	3379	40808	220	43966
0.25	Vascularity	2	4	412593	249954	8682	653864
0.25	Venography	2	6	52454	4349	701	56101

Table 2. The cardinality of the mappings for each experiment and mapper. The values shown in **bold** represent the largest mappings.

τ	Bridge	Optimum	jMapper	EEmapper
0.00	Exercise_physiology	14±0	1±0	**28.333±1.506**
0.01	Redwatch	**10±0**	0±0	6.000±0.000
0.01	Venography	**11±0**	0±0	6.000±0.000
0.10	Hiram_ohio	2±0	0±0	**5.833±1.329**
0.10	Horror_fiction	13±0	**3864±0**	1175.833±10.722
0.25	Redwatch	12±0	398±0	**1410.400±8.877**
0.25	Vascularity	2±0	0±0	**7318.600±35.529**
0.25	Venography	18±0	1174±0	**2277.600±8.019**

5   Discussion

The proposed EEmapper extracted the largest mappings for 5/8 of the experiments. Other than the experiments: $\tau = 0.1 \wedge$ bridge $=$ hiram_ohio, $\tau = 0.25 \wedge$ bridge $=$ vascularity, $\tau = 0.25 \wedge$ bridge $=$ venography, the mapper started outputting large mappings after thirty seconds of execution or less (Figs. 4a and b). In the last two mentioned experiments, including the case $\tau = 0.25 \wedge$ bridge $=$ redwatch, the EEmapper extracted from the input spaces mappings with far higher number of concept pairs when compared with the other mappers and in less than 1/6 of their time.

An example of a considerable large mapping is shown in Fig. 5.

In the experiment $\tau = 0.01 \wedge$ bridge $=$ redwatch, the optimum mapper was able to generate the largest mapping with EEmapper reaching 60% of the optimum mapping. In our opinion, this experiment matches the limit where the complexity of the problem at hand is simple enough that a stochastic solver is not justified for two reasons: (1) an exhaustive solver finds the optimum answer

Table 3. Time (in seconds) taken by each mapper in each experiment. The times in **bold** represent the time required to obtain the largest mapping.

τ	Bridge	Optimum	jMapper	EEmapper
0.00	Exercise_physiology	3644.666±85.5610.875	±0.247	**13.793±0.881**
0.01	Redwatch	**0.342±0.147**	0.000±0.000	3600.078±0.016
0.01	Venography	**3602.435±7.588**	0.000±0.000	33.037±0.016
0.10	Hiram_ohio	0.235±0.181	0.379±0.008	**207.844±15.870**
0.10	Horror_fiction	3631.042±54.753	**1836.532±63.679**	3602.374±1.277
0.25	Redwatch	3651.080±52.964	228.895±0.812	**34.667±1.562**
0.25	Vascularity	3633.345±91.153	3612.787±32.445	**425.866±54.790**
0.25	Venography	3615.587±17.392	837.980±12.292	**56.602±2.130**

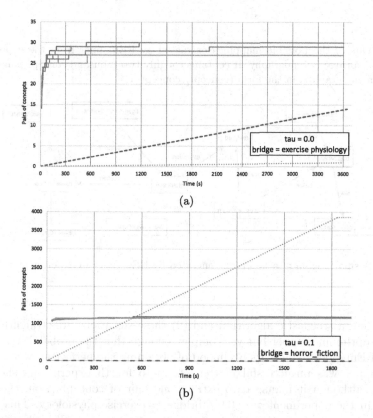

(a)

(b)

Fig. 4. Number of concept pairs being extracted during the mappers real-time execution for two experiments. The optimum mapper and jMapper are drawn as straight lines interpolating their starting and ending times. The mappers are represented with the following line strokes: red dashed - optimum mapper; green dotted - jMapper; remaining line strokes - EEmapper. (Color figure online)

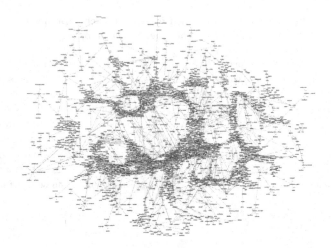

Fig. 5. One of the possible mappings extracted by EEmapper from the experiment $\tau = 0.25 \wedge$ bridge = venography. It contains roughly two thousand concept pairs. Each vertex in the graph is in the form $(\text{concept}_l, \text{concept}_r)$.

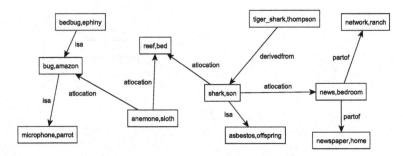

Fig. 6. A small region of a mapping generated by EEmapper in experiment $\tau = 0.1 \wedge$ bridge = horror_fiction.

faster than a stochastic algorithm and (2) these situations are straightforward for the optimum mapper but yet complex enough that the probabilistic nature of the EEmapper reduces its likelihood of obtaining the perfect answer.

jMapper was unsuccessful in the second to fourth experiments shown in Table 2, although it managed to extract one pair of concepts from the input spaces in the experiment $\tau = 0.0 \wedge$ bridge = exercise_physiology. This is due to the minimal intersection between the two input spaces (Table 1) with this intersection comprised of only the bridge concept. This minimal intersection restricts the usage of the Triangle rule, fundamental to Sapper and thus jMapper. This demonstrates that jMapper has difficulties finding analogies when the input spaces have little to no concepts in common.

In experiment $\tau = 0.1 \wedge$ bridge = horror_fiction jMapper managed to extract the largest mapping. Our hypothesis is that this experiment contains a large amount of concepts in the intersection of the two input spaces, favourable to Sapper's Triangle rule. This allowed jMapper to further trigger the Square rule and easily expand its mappings. We wonder if, were it given more execution time and computational resources, jMapper would also have extracted a large mapping in the experiment $\tau = 0.25 \wedge$ bridge = vascularity.

We find important to mention that the mapper is currently a stochastic mechanism without intricate mutation and crossover mechanisms typically expected from evolutionary algorithms and yet it obtained larger results when compared with the other mappers. This emphasises the complexity of the task at hand - extracting analogies from large semantic graphs - and the importance of not obtaining perfect results, but mappings "good enough" for their purpose. This is observed in 5/8 of the experiments except the three following: $\tau = 0.01 \wedge$ bridge = redwatch, $\tau = 0.01 \wedge$ bridge = venography, $\tau = 0.1 \wedge$ bridge = horror_fiction.

Lastly, given the main purpose of the proposed EEmapper - to be used in CB experiments - we find crucial that a first inspection of the mappings' semantic structure is made. Although we expect a deeper examination of this subject in a future paper, we illustrate in Fig. 6 a small region of a mapping generated in experiment $\tau = 0.1 \wedge$ bridge = horror_fiction. Part of the structure of the input spaces is present in the entire mapping, for instance *anemone, atlocation, reef* and *shark, atlocation, reef*.

Noise from ConcepNet is visible in relations such as *shark, isa, asbestos*. However, given this noise and the association of distantly related or even unrelated pairs of concepts in the mapping, we find promising the usage of our EEmapper in the next step of our research - its implementation in a CB framework. For example, who knows if the creative system elaborates a story of a *parrot* named *bug* who works as a *microphone* in the *amazon* rainforest.

6   Conclusions and Future Work

We have proposed a fast multi-threaded mapper for finding analogies in real-time. It was compared against an optimum mapper developed by us and against jMapper, based on Sapper. EEmapper was found to outperform the other mappers in large semantic graphs in the order of at least half a million of interconnected concepts. As far as we know, our mapper is the first of its kind to handle semantic graphs in this level of proportion and to scale beyond. The mapper is based on evolutionary principles and thus straightforward to adapt its fitness function should the mappings have to adhere to different criteria.

We find important to mention that the proposed mapper may appear somewhat elementary but we think that given the purpose of handling large semantic networks and future real-time interaction with a conceptual blending module, as a first step the mapper should be the fastest possible. Hence this requires a GA with a fast evolution, swift genetic operations and quick fitness evaluations because of existence of a blending module down the pipeline.

In the future we expect further development of our EEmapper in the form of refinements in its evolution algorithms, the addition of the genetic crossover operator and improvements in the mutation of mappings. Moreover, the mappings will undergo a semantic evaluation during their evolution within the EEmapper in order to be consistent with the CC System that we hope to realize in the future.

Acknowledgements. João Gonçalves is funded by Fundação para a Ciência e Tecnologia (FCT), Portugal, under the PhD grant SFRH/BD/133107/2017.

References

1. Baydin, A., de Mántaras, R.L., Ontañón, S.: Automated generation of cross-domain analogies via evolutionary computation. CoRR, abs/1204.2335 (2012)
2. Boden, M.: The Creative Mind: Myths and Mechanisms. Weidenfeld and Nicholson, London (1990)
3. Cunha, J.M., Gonçalves, J., Martins, P., Machado, P., Cardoso, A.: A pig, an angel and a cactus walk into a blender: A descriptive approach to visual blending. In Proceedings of the Eighth International Conference on Computational Creativity (ICCC 2017) (2017)
4. Falkenhainer, B., Forbus, K.D., Gentner, D.: The structure mapping engine: algorithm and examples. Artif. Intell. **41**, 1–63 (1989)
5. Fauconnier, G., Turner, M.: The Way We Think. Basic Books, New York (2002)
6. French, R.M.: The computational modeling of analogy-making. Trends Cogn. Sci. **6**(5), 200–205 (2002)
7. Gentner, D.: Structure-mapping: a theoretical framework for analogy. Cogn. Sci. **7**(2) (1983)
8. Gentner, D., Holyoak, K.J., Kokinov, B.N.: The Analogical Mind: Perspectives From Cognitive Science. Bradford Book, Cambridge (2001)
9. Gonçalves, J., Martins, P., Cardoso, A.: Blend city, blendville. In: Proceedings of the Eighth International Conference on Computational Creativity (ICCC 2017) (2017)
10. Gonçalves, J., Martins, P., Cruz, A., Cardoso, A.: Seeking divisions of domains on semantic networks by evolutionary bridging. In: The Twenty-Third International Conference on Case-Based Reasoning (ICCBR), Frankfurt, Germany. CEUR (2015)
11. Hall, C., Thomson, P.: Creativity in teaching: what can teachers learn from artists? Res. Pap. Educ. **32**(1), 106–120 (2017)
12. Hervás, R., Costa, R.P., Costa, H., Gervás, P., Pereira, F.C.: Enrichment of automatically generated texts using metaphor. In: Gelbukh, A., Kuri Morales, Á.F. (eds.) MICAI 2007. LNCS (LNAI), vol. 4827, pp. 944–954. Springer, Heidelberg (2007). https://doi.org/10.1007/978-3-540-76631-5_90
13. Hervás, R., Pereira, F.C., Gervás, P., Cardoso, A.: Cross-domain analogy in automated text generation. In: Proceedings 3rd Joint Workshop on Computational Creativity, ECAI 2006, Riva del Garda, Italy (2006)
14. Hofstadter, D.R.: Analogy as the core of cognition. In: The Analogical Mind: Perspectives from Cognitive Science, pp. 499–538 (2001)

15. Tobias Kötter, K.T., Berthold, M.R.: Domain bridging associations support creativity. In: Proceedings of the International Conference on Computational Creativity, pp. 200–204 (2010)
16. McCalpin, J.: Memory bandwidth and machine balance in high performance computers, pp. 19–25, December 1995
17. Mitchell, T., et al.: Never-ending learning. In: Proceedings of the Twenty-Ninth AAAI Conference on Artificial Intelligence (AAAI-15) (2015)
18. Pereira, F.C., Cardoso, A.: The horse-bird creature generation experiment. AISB J. **1**(3) (2003)
19. Pereira, F.C.: Creativity and AI: a conceptual blending approach. Ph.D. thesis, University of Coimbra, January 2005
20. Schorlemmer, M., et al.: COINVENT: towards a computational concept invention theory. In: Proceedings of the 5th International Conference on Computational Creativity, ICCC 2014, Ljubljana, Slovenia (2014)
21. Speer, R., Havasi, C.: Representing general relational knowledge in ConceptNet 5. In: LREC, pp. 3679–3686 (2012)
22. Stojanov, G., Indurkhya, B.: Perceptual similarity and analogy in creativity and cognitive development. In: Prade, H., Richard, G. (eds.) Computational Approaches to Analogical Reasoning: Current Trends. SCI, vol. 548, pp. 371–395. Springer, Heidelberg (2014). https://doi.org/10.1007/978-3-642-54516-0_15
23. Tramm, J.R., Siegel, A.R., et al.: Memory bottlenecks and memory contention in multi-core monte carlo transport codes. Ann. Nucl. Energy **82**, 195–202 (2015)
24. Veale, T., Keane, M.: The competence of sub-optimal structure mapping on hard analogies. In: Proceedings of the International Joint Conference on Artificial Intelligence, IJCAI-97 (1997)
25. Veale, T., O'Donoghue, D., Keane, M.: Computability as a limiting cognitive constraint: complexity concerns in metaphor comprehension about which cognitive linguists should be aware. In: Cultural, Psychological and Typological Issues in Cognitive Linguistics: Selected Papers of the Bi-Annual ICLA Meeting in Albuquerque, pp. 129–155, January 1995
26. Winston, P.H.: Learning and reasoning by analogy. Commun. ACM **23**(12), 689–703 (1980)
27. Žnidaršič, M., et al.: Computational creativity infrastructure for online software composition: a conceptual blending use case. In: Proceedings of the Seventh International Conference on Computational Creativity (ICCC 2016), Paris, France. Sony CSL (2016)

Production of Large Analogical Clusters from Smaller Example Seed Clusters Using Word Embeddings

Yuzhong Hong[(✉)] and Yves Lepage

Graduate School of IPS, Waseda University,
2-7 Hibikino, Wakamatsu-ku, Kitakyushu-shi, Fukuoka-ken 808-0135, Japan
eutronh@akane.waseda.jp, yves.lepage@waseda.jp

Abstract. We introduce a method to automatically produce large analogical clusters from smaller seed clusters of representative examples. The method is based on techniques of processing and solving analogical equations in word vector space models, i.e., word embeddings. In our experiments, we use standard data sets in English which cover different relations extending from derivational morphology (like adjective–adverb, positive–comparative forms of adjectives) or inflectional morphology (like present–past forms) to encyclopedic semantics (like country–capital relations). The analogical clusters produced by our method are shown to be of reasonably good quality, as shown by comparing human judgment against automatic NDCG@n scores. In total, they contain 8.5 times as many relevant word pairs as the seed clusters.

Keywords: Analogy · Analogical clusters · Word embeddings

1 Introduction

Analogy relates systems through structure-mapping [5,8,18] or connects words through relational or attributional similarity [16,17]. It can be applied to knowledge acquisition. For instance, in [3], a system is developed to help untrained volunteer contributors to extend a repository of commonsense knowledge by analogy. As another example, [19] used analogy as a principle to organize large knowledge bases.

Apart from applying analogy to knowledge bases, it is also promising to construct knowledge repositories which store the knowledge of analogy itself. [10] defines analogical clusters as sets of word pairs, any two pairs of which can form a valid analogy. As an illustration, Table 1 shows three analogical clusters. They correspond to the *string* : *string+ed* relation, the *present* : *past* relation and the *male* : *female* relation, respectively. From these three clusters, by picking any two word pairs, we can obtain analogies. For instance, *abcd* : *abcded* :: *he* : *heed*, *fly* : *flew* :: *walk* : *walked* and *king* : *queen* :: *man* : *woman* etc.

© Springer Nature Switzerland AG 2018
M. T. Cox et al. (Eds.): ICCBR 2018, LNAI 11156, pp. 548–562, 2018.
https://doi.org/10.1007/978-3-030-01081-2_36

Table 1. Example analogical clusters of three different types. Any two word pairs from each of these clusters form formal, morphological and semantic analogies, respectively.

formal	morphological	semantic
abcd : abcded	accept : accepted	actor : actress
he : heed	buy : bought	boy : girl
us : used	fly : flew	duke : duchess
we : weed	go : went	king : queen
work : worked	pack : packed	prince : princess
xyz : xyzed	walk : walked	man : woman
	work : worked	waiter : waitress
		widower : widow

Analogical clusters are used as test beds to assess the quality of word vector space models [6,13,15]. They are also used to build quasi-parallel corpora for under-resourced language pairs for machine translation [20]. In light of these applications, this paper presents an automatic method to produce analogical clusters by expanding small example seed clusters. The analogical clusters output by our method are constrained according to the following three axiomatic properties of analogy:

- exchange of the means: $A : B :: C : D \Leftrightarrow A : C :: B : D$;
- inverse of ratios: $A : B :: C : D \Leftrightarrow B : A :: D : C$;
- the salient features in A should appear either in B or C or both.

The whole process is based on word embeddings, as they have been shown to have the capability of capturing morphological and semantic analogies [13]. Figure 1 (next page) gives an overview of the method.

2 Related Work

2.1 Relation Extraction

Relation extraction is the task of labeling the relation between two labeled entities in a text segment, usually a sentence [1,7]. For example, the word pair (*dog, pup*) will be labeled as an *animal-young* relation in the sentence "*A homeless dog gave birth to a pup in the park.*".

Relation extraction techniques seem deployable for building analogical clusters. However, the reason that prevents us from using them are as follows.

Most semantic relations considered in relation extraction are more ontologically focused than linguistically focused, which makes it hard to form analogies. For example, *China* is located in *Asia* and *MIT* is located in *Massachusetts*. They are both *located_in* relations, but *China* : *Asia* :: *MIT* : *Massachusetts* is not a robust analogy because such salient features of *China* like being a "country" are neither to be found in *Asia* nor *MIT*.

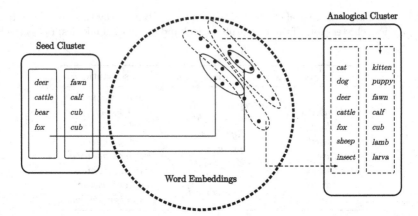

Fig. 1. Production of an analogical cluster from an example seed cluster by the proposed method. The seed cluster, as well as the produced analogical cluster, illustrates the relation *animal* : *young*. The method uses normalized word embeddings. Observe that the produced analogical cluster does not contain all the word pairs from the example seed cluster.

2.2   Formal Analogical Clusters Building

A method to build analogical clusters has been proposed in [10] for formal analogies (see *left* of Table 1). It is based on vector representations of words, but the feature values are limited to integer values for the method to work. The method groups word pairs by checking for equality of vector differences while traversing a tree structure obtained from the feature values.

As the goal of this paper is to produce analogical clusters which reflect morphological, semantic or even encyclopedic relations, not formal ones, we choose to base our method on word embedding models [14,15]. Word embedding models use continuous values for feature values, along dimensions automatically discovered during the process of building the word space. For this reason, more flexible and tolerant ways of checking for analogies in such continuous models are required. The next section discusses this point.

2.3   Analogy Test in Word Embeddings

Solving analogies, or solving analogical equations, is the task of finding a word D, given three words A, B and C, such that $A : B :: C : D$ is a valid analogy. Word embeddings have been shown to encapsulate analogical configurations between word vectors. Therefore, the task is commonly used as a benchmark to evaluate the quality of word embedding models [6,13,15], notwithstanding some doubts about its reliability [4,12]; this is referred to as the *analogy test*.

Several formulae for determining the solution of an analogical equation in vector space models have been proposed. They do so by selecting the word D with the highest score, hence the use of arg max, according to some formula supposed to characterize the analogical configuration in such vector spaces. The most used formulae respectively introduced in [4,11,13] are given below with their names.

$$3\text{CosAdd}(A, B, C) = \arg\max_{D \in V} \cos(v_D, v_C - v_A + v_B) \tag{1}$$

$$3\text{CosMul}(A, B, C) = \arg\max_{D \in V} \frac{\cos(v_D, v_C)\cos(v_D, v_B)}{\cos(v_D, v_A)} \tag{2}$$

$$\text{PairDirection}(A, B, C) = \arg\max_{D \in V} \cos(v_D - v_C, v_B - v_A) \tag{3}$$

$$\text{LRCos}(A, B, C) = \arg\max_{D \in V} P(D \in \text{Class}(B)) \times \cos(v_D, v_C) \tag{4}$$

In all these formulae, V is the vocabulary, v_X denotes the word vector of word X. For LRCos, $P(D \in \text{Class}(B))$ is the probability for word D to belong to the class of word B, obtained by training a logistic regression model.

3   Proposed Method

An analogy can be produced by solving an analogical equation $A : B :: C : D$ for D. The definition of analogical clusters states that each pair of words (C_j, D_j) in the cluster has the same relation. Consequently, it is possible to select a representative pair of words A and B, such that, for all j, the analogy $A : B :: C_j : D_j$ holds. Hence, given the representative pair of words A and B and a set of words $\{C_j\}$, it is possible to solve equations $A : B :: C_j : D$ and obtain a set of words $\{D_j\}$ which makes $\{(C_j, D_j)\}$ an analogical cluster.

This way of producing analogical clusters raises two questions:

1. How to determine the representative A and B?
2. How to guarantee that the word pairs in $\{(C_j, D_j)\}$ do form valid analogies, i.e., they satisfy the axiomatic properties of analogy?

Subsection 3.1 is dedicated in answering the first question and Subsects. 3.2 to 3.4 show how to satisfy each of the axiomatic properties of analogy.

3.1   Example Seed Clusters

To answer the first question, as A and B should be a representative word pair of a certain type of relation, the proposed method requires extra knowledge: this consists in a set of hand-crafted word pair instances for a given relation. Such sets do not have to be strictly analogical clusters. For example, the presence of *bear* : *cub* and *wolf* : *cub* prevents the seed cluster in Fig. 1 from being considered a valid analogical cluster according to [10], because no same word can appear on the same side of two different word pairs according to their definition. However, for our method, it is still possible to produce an analogical cluster out of such a set.

As these sets are clusters of word pairs and as they are used to produce analogical clusters, we call them *example seed clusters*. We denote each word pair in an example seed cluster by (A_i, B_i) with i ranging in some set of indices $\mathcal{I}$. Now, to answer the question of finding a representative word pair (A, B) of the set $\{(A_i, B_i), i \in \mathcal{I}\}$, rather than directly choosing a word pair from the example seed cluster itself, we independently choose the centroid of the vector representations of the set $\{A_i, i \in \mathcal{I}\}$ (resp. $\{B_i, i \in \mathcal{I}\}$) as A (resp. B). The decision to choose centroids rather than more intricate alternatives is motivated by simplicity. As a result, A and B are not necessarily actual words from the vocabulary: they are just vectors from the vector space which can be used directly in the analogy solving formulae presented in Sect. 2.3.

3.2   Word Clustering by Salient Feature

We now turn to determine a set of relevant word vectors $\{C_j\}$ which will belong to the analogical cluster built. Any of the A_i should be a good candidate to belong to the analogical cluster built. But any word vector C_j from the entire word space model cannot be selected to build an analogical cluster with any representative vector pair (A, B). This comes from the fact that, generally, when solving analogical equations $A : B :: C : D$ for D a solution D is always output by the word solving formulae (simply because of the use of arg max) even when the word C is not reasonable. Hence, $A : B :: C : D$ is not always guaranteed to be a valid analogy. Let us illustrate with A standing for *japan* and B for *japanese*. With C being *computer*, the analogy solving formula 3CosMul delivers the solution $D = computers$ with the word embeddings used in our experiments (Sect. 4.2). Obviously,   *japan : japanese :: computer : computers*   is not a valid analogy, neither formally, nor morphologically, nor semantically.

Our method to determine the set $\{C_j\}$ thus bases on the axiomatic properties of analogy mentioned in Sect. 1: for $A : B :: C_j : D_j$ to hold, the salient features of A should appear in either B or C_j or both. We select those C_j which satisfy this property from the vocabulary by imposing the constraint that, in the example seed cluster as well as in the analogical cluster built, the A_i and the C_j should belong to the same class.

We use an SVM classifier to determine the set $\{C_j\}$. To train the classifier, all A_i in the example seed cluster are used as positive examples; all B_i in the example seed cluster plus some words drawn at random from the entire vocabulary are used as negative examples.

3.3   Inverse of Ratios

The use of the axiomatic property of the inverse of ratios, $A : B :: C : D \Leftrightarrow B : A :: D : C$,   implies a symmetric work to select D_j. That is, in the above, we replace A_i with B_i, and C_j instead of D_j. Consequently a second SVM classifier is built with all B_i as positive examples and all A_i plus other random words as negative examples. This classifier will impose the constraint that all B_i and D_j belong to the same class. Indeed, this constraint is present in the LRCos analogy solving formula which takes into account the probability for word D to belong to the class of word B.

Consequently, for each representative vector pair (A, B), we build two classifiers and solve two sets of analogical equations. We then intersect these two sets of results to get a final set of word pairs $\{(C_j, D_j)\}$ which will constitute the analogical cluster output by the proposed method.

3.4 Ranking Mechanism

Although the definition of analogical clusters does not imply any sorting of the word pairs, a mechanism to sort the word pairs in $\{(C_j, D_j)\}$ is necessary for the analogical clusters output by the proposed method for two reasons. The first reason is that, as illustrated in Sect. 3.2, it is necessary to assess the validity of the analogies which can be formed from the analogical clusters built. The second reason is that the second axiomatic property of analogy, the exchange of the means, $A : B :: C : D \iff A : C :: B : D$, has not yet been taken into account.

Therefore, we define a score for each pair of words in the analogical cluster output by the proposed method as the product of the following four quantities.

- $P(C_j \in \text{Class}(\{A_i\}))$: the probability that word C_j is in $\text{Class}(\{A_i\})$, i.e., the class of all A_i.
- $P(D_j \in \text{Class}(\{B_i\}))$: the same as the previous one, replacing C_j with D_j and $\{A_i\}$ with $\{B_i\}$.
- $\cos(\boldsymbol{v}_{D_j} - \boldsymbol{v}_{C_j}, \boldsymbol{v}_B - \boldsymbol{v}_A)$: the similarity between the offset of the vectors of C_j and D_j and the offset of the representative vectors A and B.
- $\cos(\boldsymbol{v}_{D_j} - \boldsymbol{v}_B, \boldsymbol{v}_{C_j} - \boldsymbol{v}_A)$: the same as the previous one, replacing B with C_j.

The first two quantities are obtained by training SVMs using the same setting as the ones used in Sect. 3.2 except that their outputs are probabilistic rather than binary. Again, they reflect a similar idea as the one found in the analogy solving formula LRCos. The last two quantities are essentially the use of the analogy solving formula PairDirection applied twice (SCosAdd and 3CosMul already encapsulate the exchange of the means, while PairDirection does not). It is reasonable to estimate that the larger the product of the two cosine similarities is, the more valid the analogy is.

In our results, we rank the word pairs $\{(C_j, D_j)\}$ in decreasing order of scores.

4   Experiments and Results

4.1   Example Seed Cluster Data

We use BATS 3.0 [6] as our example seed clusters. There are four general categories relations:

- lexicographic semantics (e.g., binary antonymy);
- encyclopedic semantics (e.g., country - capital);
- derivational morphology (e.g., adjective - adverb obtained by suffixing -*ly*);
- inflectional morphology (e.g., singular - regular plural).

Each general category consists of ten different specific relations. There are 50 word pair instances for each specific relations. For example, the first three word pair instances of the country - language relation, which is an encyclopedic semantic relation, are *andorra* : *catalan*, *argentina* : *spanish* and *australia* : *english*. However, some relations like animal - young, contain entries like *wolf* : *cub/pup/ puppy/whelp*. In this experiment, only the first one of the multiple choices is adopted, i.e., only *wolf* : *cub* is kept.

4.2   Word Embeddings and Analogy Solving Formulae

The word embeddings used in the experiments are trained on pre-processed texts extracted from English Wikipedia dump (latest dump of Oct. 21st, 2017) with the word embedding model CBOW [14]. The number of vector dimensions is 300. Preprocessing consists of tokenizing, lowercasing, splitting into sentences and deleting punctuation and diacritics. Punctuation which is part of a word is not removed (e.g., *u.s.a.* is kept unchanged).

The analogy solving formulae we use for the experiments are CosAdd, CosMul and LRCos. We do not use PairDistance because it has been shown in [4] to exhibit lower performance than the other three ones.

4.3   Word Classification Using SVM

The SVM classifier for determining $\{C_j\}$ for each analogical cluster is trained using the 50 A_i in the corresponding seed cluster as positive examples and the corresponding 50 B_i in the seed cluster plus 150 random words from the vocabulary as negative examples. Training the SVM classifier for determining word $\{D_j\}$, on the contrary, uses the 50 B_i as positive examples and the 50 A_i plus 150 random words from the vocabulary as negative examples. Because words in word space models are located on a hyper-sphere and because we think of classes as groups of words located around a representative vector, we use an RBF kernel (by the way, the default kernel in many machine learning packages such as `scikit-learn`).

4.4   Metrics

As the evaluation of any ranking system, the first part is the evaluation of the relevancy of each word pair in the analogical clusters by humans. The scale of the relevancy is $\{0, 1, 2\}$, where 0 stands for irrelevant, 2 stands for relevant and 1 stands for partially relevant. We also use a widely used measure of ranking quality: Normalized Discounted Cumulative Gain at n (NDCG@n) for each cluster [2,9]. We compute the mean of NDCG@n over all clusters of each general category of relations to compare the system's overall performance across different general categories of relations. The NDCG@n score is computed as:

$$NDCG@n = \frac{DCG@n}{IDCG@n}$$

where

$$DCG@n = \sum_{i=1}^{n} (2^{rel(i)} - 1)/\log_2 (i + 1)$$

and IDCG@n is the DCG@n for the ideal ranking, where the relevancy of each entry in the result monotonically decreases. $rel(i)$ is the relevancy of the entry at position i. The DCG@n score is the weighted average of word pairs weighted by a factor depending on the position in the ranking: entries appearing earlier get a heavier weighted. The NDCG@n score is just the normalization of DCG@n by IDCG@n. The closer to 1.0 an NDCG@n score, the more consistent the actual ranking with an ideal ranking. We thus expect the NDCG score at each position to be as close to 1.0 as possible.

4.5   Results

Table 2 shows the number of word pairs in each analogical cluster. This number may vary because the training of the SVM classifier involves random negative examples. However, the variance could be ignored. Some analogical clusters are empty, i.e., no word pair is produced by the method for the corresponding relations. Our explanation for this undesirable phenomenon is that the kernel used in the experiments (RBF kernel) is suited for the classification at hand, like, typically, gradable antonyms. Different relations may require different kernels: experiments with other kernels such as linear kernel, polynomial kernel, etc. partially solved the problem for the relation under scrutiny, but produced empty clusters for other relations. From Table 2, it can also be observed that each seed cluster is not necessarily included in its corresponding output cluster. Essentially, this can be attributed to the fact that our method is not really designed to expand the seed clusters, but to find proper word pairs with the help of the information learned from them.

Table 2. Number of word pairs in each analogical cluster. Numbers in parentheses are the numbers of word pairs in common between each analogical cluster and its corresponding seed cluster. It cannot be more than the total number of word pair in each seed cluster, 50.

Relation type		3CosAdd	3CosMul	LRCos
Lexicographic semantics	hypernyms (animal)	1845 (1)	1562 (3)	95 (2)
	hypernyms (misc)	1604 (1)	1686 (1)	456 (1)
	hyponyms (misc)	0 (0)	0 (0)	0 (0)
	meronyms (substance)	1812 (2)	1694 (2)	344 (4)
	meronyms (member)	0 (0)	0 (0)	0 (0)
	meronyms (part)	3546 (1)	3809 (3)	1131 (4)
	synonyms (intensity)	0 (0)	0 (0)	0 (0)
	synonyms (exact)	13076 (9)	11944 (9)	5119 (10)
	antonyms (gradable)	0 (0)	0 (0)	0 (0)
	antonyms (binary)	3702 (11)	3899 (11)	1908 (9)
Encyclopedic semantics	country - capital	174 (36)	171 (36)	117 (34)
	country - language	117 (5)	132 (6)	105 (5)
	UK_city - county	530 (5)	504 (5)	28 (6)
	name - nationality	43 (1)	70 (1)	86 (2)
	name - occupation	82 (2)	94 (4)	90 (3)
	animal - young	1254 (2)	1047 (4)	100 (7)
	animal - sound	0 (0)	0 (0)	0 (0)
	animal - shelter	53 (0)	66 (0)	73 (1)
	things - color	40 (2)	63 (2)	21 (1)
	male - female	0 (0)	0 (0)	0 (0)
Derivational morphology	noun + less_reg	0 (0)	0 (0)	0 (0)
	un + adj_reg	783 (14)	1221 (19)	379 (18)
	adj + ly_reg	440 (20)	662 (24)	374 (29)
	over + adj_reg	91683 (1)	81184 (3)	982 (5)
	adj + ness_reg	0 (0)	0 (0)	0 (0)
	re + verb_reg	0 (0)	0 (0)	0 (0)
	verb + able_reg	1983 (0)	1756 (2)	853 (1)
	verb + er_irreg	185 (7)	237 (11)	406 (10)
	verb + tion_irreg	74542 (14)	43706 (24)	1208 (21)
	verb + ment_irreg	689 (15)	863 (25)	818 (24)
Inflectional morphology	noun - plural_reg	2924 (37)	3476 (39)	3250 (38)
	noun - plural_irreg	0 (0)	0 (0)	0 (0)
	adj - comparative	0 (0)	0 (0)	0 (0)
	adj - superlative	0 (0)	0 (0)	0 (0)
	verb_inf - 3pSg	1163 (49)	1147 (49)	828 (46)
	verb_inf - Ving	1448 (42)	1366 (41)	1078 (40)
	verb_inf - Ved	1337 (38)	1350 (42)	1158 (40)
	verb_Ving - 3pSg	1318 (26)	1357 (34)	753 (34)
	verb_Ving - Ved	1381 (31)	1938 (36)	1229 (37)
	verb_3pSg - Ved	1315 (42)	1284 (44)	668 (40)

Table 3. Content of the best analogical clusters obtained for lexicographic semantic relations on the *left* and encyclopedic semantic relations on the *right*. Each table lists the top 15 word pairs, 10 word pairs in the middle and the 5 word pairs at the end. Grayed-out lines indicate those word pairs which were judged as irrelevant (*darker gray*), or partially relevant (*lighter gray*) in human evaluation. The other ones were judged relevant.

hypernyms (misc)		country - language	
score ×10⁻³	word pair	score ×10⁻³	word pair
2.139	exotica : exotic	9.672	ireland : irish
2.086	carrots : vegetables	9.428	scotland : scottish
1.968	boat : boats	9.308	iceland : icelandic
1.951	trap : traps	9.184	slovenia : slovene
1.949	water. : water	9.064	lithuania : lithuanian
1.933	tent : tents	9.049	bangladesh : bengali
1.896	watchband : bean-to-bar	8.921	namibia : afrikaans
1.848	skylight : skylights	8.919	thailand : thai
1.841	clock : clocks	8.853	korea : korean
1.811	llama : alpaca	8.808	china : chinese
1.765	bushes : shrubs	8.752	mongolia : mongolian
1.738	secondhand : second-hand	8.729	latvia : latvian
1.696	machine : machines	8.728	kazakhstan : kazakh
1.682	cafe : restaurant	8.710	hungary : hungarian
1.668	underwear : clothing	8.604	england : english
⋮	⋮	⋮	⋮
0.356	diffuser : diffusers	6.894	abkhazia : abkhaz
0.356	enamelled : enameled	6.812	switzerland : swiss
0.355	flavourings : flavorings	6.811	regions : dialects
0.354	seatbelt : seatbelts	6.680	armenia : armenian
0.353	topman : topshop	6.653	tibet : tibetan
0.352	fufu : ugali	6.610	iran : iranian
0.351	doritos : cheetos	6.575	egypt : egyptian
0.351	churn : churns	6.534	pakistan : pakistani
0.349	mulch : mulches	6.429	italy : italian
0.348	thicker : thinner	6.421	philippines : filipino
⋮	⋮	⋮	⋮
-1.111	saunas : sauna	3.680	comoros : comorian
-1.113	showers : shower	3.570	cctld : xn-
-1.191	cameras : camera	3.553	andalusia : andalusian
-1.265	kits : kit	2.052	sahrawis : moroccans
-1.383	patches : patch	0.656	sahrawi : saharawi

Table 4. Same as Table 3 for derivational (*left*) and inflectional (*right*) morphological relations.

adj + ly_reg		verb inf - Ved	
score $\times 10^{-3}$	word pair	score $\times 10^{-3}$	word pair
6.376	*alleged : allegedly*	13.281	*pull : pulled*
5.986	*strategical : strategically*	12.370	*shoot : shot*
5.915	*operational : operationally*	12.060	*reunite : reunited*
5.653	*symbolic : symbolically*	12.053	*resume : resumed*
5.632	*occasional : occasionally*	11.949	*play : played*
5.587	*digital : digitally*	11.833	*recover : recovered*
5.552	*political : politically*	11.696	*spend : spent*
5.507	*impressive : impressively*	11.634	*catch : caught*
5.326	*seasonal : seasonally*	11.620	*join : joined*
5.241	*modest : modestly*	11.606	*wipe : wiped*
5.228	*sexual : sexually*	11.605	*publish : published*
5.193	*noticeable : noticeably*	11.280	*buy : bought*
5.102	*emotional : emotionally*	11.258	*save : saved*
5.033	*spiritual : spiritually*	11.221	*retire : retired*
5.030	*memorable : memorably*	11.211	*capture : captured*
⋮	⋮	⋮	⋮
1.959	*grandiosity : emotionalism*	7.959	*co-ordinate : co-ordinated*
1.953	*scalability : workloads*	7.957	*expound : expounded*
1.952	*probiotic : probiotics*	7.957	*abandon : abandoned*
1.951	*disorders : syndromes*	7.953	*degrade : degraded*
1.946	*policy : policies*	7.950	*unmask : unmasked*
1.921	*racism : bigotry*	7.942	*inform : informed*
1.920	*fetal : fetus*	7.941	*eject : ejecting*
1.914	*topics : subjects*	7.939	*fend : fended*
1.884	*impact : impacts*	7.934	*berate : berated*
1.881	*self-worth : self-esteem*	7.922	*rehearse : rehearsed*
⋮	⋮	⋮	⋮
-0.475	*constraints : limitations*	1.685	*regard : regards*
-0.553	*capabilities : capability*	0.465	*hinders : impedes*
-0.922	*efficacy : effectiveness*	0.330	*dedicates : devotes*
-0.957	*particularly : especially*	0.261	*assures : reassures*
-1.030	*risks : risk*	-0.133	*due : owing*

Figure 2 shows the mean NDCG@n across different general relation categories using different analogy solving techniques. This provides an overall evaluation of the performance in terms of relation categories and analogy solving formulae.

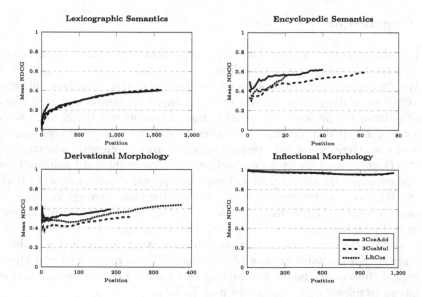

Fig. 2. Performance of the proposed method using 3 different analogy solving techniques on the four general categories of relations, evaluated by mean NDCG over all non-empty output clusters of each general category of relations. For each category, because the 10 clusters have different number of word pairs, the mean NDCG@n has to stop at the last position where all the clusters (empty clusters are ignored) have a word pair there. This explains why the curves exhibit different lengths.

As for categories of analogies, the proposed method delivers high performance for inflectional morphological relations as shown by NDCG values close to 1.0 at all positions. The performance decreases on encyclopedic semantic and derivational semantic relations with least values for lexicographical semantic relations.

As for analogy solving formulae, the performance of LRCos is not significantly better than 3CosAdd and 3CosMul, which is inconsistent with the significant gap between the performance of LRCos and that of the other two analogy solving formulae in analogy test [4]. It may be due to the fact that the advantage of LRCos in analogy tests comes from the use of a classification process, while 3CosAdd and 3CosMul do not make use of such a device. Because our proposed method for building analogical clusters makes use of such a classification process, independently of the analogy solving formula, LRCos loses its advantage and it thus does not appear significantly better than the other two formulae.

Tables 3 and 4 show examples of results obtained in our experiments for each general category using 3CosAdd as analogy solving technique.

5   Conclusion

We introduced a method to produce larger analogical clusters from smaller example seed clusters using word embeddings.

We applied our method to a widely used set of analogy relations, including four types of relations: encyclopedic or lexicographic semantics and derivational or inflectional morphology. Our results showed that overall the clusters are of arguably good quality despite the existence of some empty clusters and the method's relatively worse performance on lexicographic semantic relations.

Practically, removing irrelevant and partially irrelevant word pairs will help to produce larger analogical clusters than those provided in data sets like BATS 3.0 [6]. By merging the results produced using the three analogy formulae, we obtained a total of 17,198 distinct word pairs that were rated relevant for their category by human judgment. Compared with the original $4 \times 10 \times 50 = 2,000$ word pairs in the seed clusters, this number shows that our method was able to multiply by 8.5 the total number of word pairs. These scrutinized and filtered analogical clusters can be used in analogy test for word embeddings. Therefore, we intend to release such data in the near future.

There are of course limitations of the method and open questions. The corresponding future work to address them are as follows.

- The method cannot extract clusters for relations that are not exemplified by any seed cluster. The method could be largely improved if a mechanism to detect new relations could be designed and integrated into the current method.
- The method produces empty clusters for some relations, because of the type of kernel used in the SVM classifier. Study of the structure of the word vector space for specific relations seems necessary to select the best suited kernel.
- The method does not take into account the fact that some dimensions of a word vector may contribute less than other dimensions to specific relations. Weighting each dimension, and even better, learning how to weight dimensions from building the classifier, could help to obtain better representative vectors.
- The method is contingent on a strict and strong notion of analogy. Issues raised by one-to-many mappings (e.g., a language can be spoken by many countries; *cub* is the young of many animals), polysemous words, etc. are yet to be addressed[1] and will be addressed in the future work.

References

1. Bach, N., Badaskar, S.: A review of relation extraction. Lit. Rev. Lang. Stat. II 2 (2007)
2. Burges, C., et al.: Learning to rank using gradient descent. In: Proceedings of the 22nd International Conference on Machine Learning, ICML 2005, pp. 89–96. ACM, New York (2005). https://doi.org/10.1145/1102351.1102363

---

[1] We thank anonymous reviewers for pointing out these issues of our current method.

3. Chklovski, T.: Learner: a system for acquiring commonsense knowledge by analogy. In: Proceedings of the 2nd International Conference on Knowledge Capture, pp. 4–12. ACM (2003)
4. Drozd, A., Gladkova, A., Matsuoka, S.: Word embeddings, analogies, and machine learning: beyond king - man + woman = queen. In: Proceedings of COLING 2016, pp. 3519–3530 (2016)
5. Gentner, D.: Structure-mapping: a theoretical framework for analogy. Cogn. Sci. 7(2), 155–170 (1983)
6. Gladkova, A., Drozd, A., Matsuoka, S.: Analogy-based detection of morphological and semantic relations with word embeddings: what works and what doesn't. In: Proceedings of the NAACL Student Research Workshop, pp. 8–15 (2016)
7. Hendrickx, I., et al.: Semeval-2010 task 8: multi-way classification of semantic relations between pairs of nominals. In: Proceedings of the Workshop on Semantic Evaluations: Recent Achievements and Future Directions, DEW 2009, pp. 94–99. Association for Computational Linguistics, Stroudsburg (2009). http://dl.acm.org/citation.cfm?id=1621969.1621986
8. Holyoak, K.J., Holyoak, K.J., Thagard, P.: Mental Leaps: Analogy in Creative Thought. MIT Press, Cambridge (1996)
9. Järvelin, K., Kekäläinen, J.: Cumulated gain-based evaluation of IR techniques. ACM Trans. Inf. Syst. 20(4), 422–446 (2002). https://doi.org/10.1145/582415.582418
10. Lepage, Y.: Analogies between binary images: application to chinese characters. In: Prade, H., Richard, G. (eds.) Computational Approaches to Analogical Reasoning: Current Trends. SCI, vol. 548, pp. 25–57. Springer, Heidelberg (2014). https://doi.org/10.1007/978-3-642-54516-0_2
11. Levy, O., Goldberg, Y.: Linguistic regularities in sparse and explicit word representations. In: Proceedings of the Eighteenth Conference on Computational Natural Language Learning (CoNLL2014), pp. 171–180 (2014)
12. Linzen, T.: Issues in evaluating semantic spaces using word analogies. In: Proceedings of the 1st Workshop on Evaluating Vector-Space Representations for NLP, pp. 13–18. Association for Computational Linguistics (2016). https://doi.org/10.18653/v1/W16-2503. http://www.aclweb.org/anthology/W16-2503
13. Mikolov, T., Chen, K., Corrado, G., Dean, J.: Efficient estimation of word representations in vector space. arXiv preprint arXiv:1301.3781 (2013)
14. Mikolov, T., Sutskever, I., Chen, K., Corrado, G.S., Dean, J.: Distributed representations of words and phrases and their compositionality. In: Proceedings of Advances in Neural Information Processing Systems, pp. 3111–3119 (2013)
15. Pennington, J., Socher, R., Manning, C.: Glove: global vectors for word representation. In: Proceedings of the 2014 Conference on Empirical Methods in Natural Language Processing (EMNLP2014), pp. 1532–1543 (2014)
16. Turney, P.D.: Measuring semantic similarity by latent relational analysis. arXiv preprint arXiv:cs/0508053 (2005)
17. Turney, P.D.: A uniform approach to analogies, synonyms, antonyms, and associations. In: Proceedings of the 22nd International Conference on Computational Linguistics, vol. 1, pp. 905–912. Association for Computational Linguistics (2008)
18. Veale, T., Keane, M.T.: The competence of sub-optimal structure mapping on 'hard' analogies. The proceedings of IJCAI'97, the Int. In: Joint Conference on Artificial Intelligence, Nagoya, Japan. Morgan Kaufman, San Mateo California (1997)

19. Veale, T., Li, G.: Analogy as an organizational principle in the construction of large knowledge-bases. In: Prade, H., Richard, G. (eds.) Computational Approaches to Analogical Reasoning: Current Trends. SCI, vol. 548, pp. 83–101. Springer, Heidelberg (2014). https://doi.org/10.1007/978-3-642-54516-0_4
20. Wang, H., Yang, W., Lepage, Y.: Sentence generation by analogy: towards the construction of a quasi-parallel corpus for Chinese-Japanese. In: Proceedings of the 20th Annual Meeting of the Japanese Association for Natural Language Processing, Sapporo, pp. 900–903, March 2014

Case-Based Translation: First Steps from a Knowledge-Light Approach Based on Analogy to a Knowledge-Intensive One

Yves Lepage[1](✉) and Jean Lieber[2](✉)

[1] Waseda University, IPS, 2-7 Hibikino, Kitakyushu 808-0135, Japan
yves.lepage@waseda.jp
[2] Université de Lorraine, CNRS, Inria, LORIA, 54000 Nancy, France
jean.lieber@loria.fr

Abstract. This paper deals with case-based machine translation. It is based on a previous work using a proportional analogy on strings, i.e., a quaternary relation expressing that "String A is to string B as string C is to string D". The first contribution of this paper is the rewording of this work in terms of case-based reasoning: a case is a problem-solution pair (A, A') where A is a sentence in an origin language and A', its translation in the destination language. First, three cases (A, A'), (B, B'), (C, C') such that "A is to B as C is to the target problem D" are retrieved. Then, the analogical equation in the destination language "A' is to B' as C' is to x" is solved and $D' = x$ is a suggested translation of D. Although it does not involve any linguistic knowledge, this approach was effective and gave competitive results at the time it was proposed. The second contribution of this work aims at examining how this prior knowledge-light case-based machine translation approach could be improved by using additional pieces of knowledge associated with cases, domain knowledge, retrieval knowledge, and adaptation knowledge, and other principles or techniques from case-based reasoning and natural language processing.

Keywords: Analogy · Machine translation
Knowledge-light case-based reasoning
Knowledge-intensive case-based reasoning

1 Introduction

Right after the advent of computers, machine translation was the very first non-numerical application envisaged for these machines [40]. The first approach consisted in word-to-word translation, relying on large bilingual dictionaries that contained assembly instructions for insertion, deletion or movement of words relying on the inspection of close context. It was rapidly understood

---

The first author is supported by a JSPS Grant-In-Aid 18K11447: "Self-explainable and fast-to-train example-based machine translation using neural networks."

M. T. Cox et al. (Eds.): ICCBR 2018, LNAI 11156, pp. 563–579, 2018.
https://doi.org/10.1007/978-3-030-01081-2_37

that the focus should move from bilingual dictionaries to monolingual grammatical descriptions of languages and the design of parsers and generators, hence the so-called rule-based approach, in which translation itself took place in a transfer phase, working at a higher level of description [4].

1.1   Data-Oriented Approaches to Machine Translation

The idea of example-based machine translation was introduced for the first time in the seminal paper of Nagao [20]: translation should be performed by comparing a new sentence to be translated (the target problem) to existing examples of translations (a source problem and its solution, i.e., its translation). Although some research in example-based machine translation was started, it was rapidly overwhelmed by the stream of statistical machine translation (SMT), an approach that also entirely relies on the availability of aligned parallel corpora, i.e., sets of translated sentences. In the statistical approach to machine translation, several types of knowledge are extracted from aligned corpora: mainly dictionaries of corresponding short sequences of words with associated translation probabilities, probabilities for how they should be reordered, and probabilistic language models for the fluency in the destination language.

1.2   Availability of Data for Machine Translation

Statistical machine translation systems require aligned bilingual corpora to extract the above-mentioned knowledge. In 1988, the founders of the approach, IBM researchers [5], used the Hansard corpus of proceedings of the Canadian parliament for French-English. The need for such corpora intensified their production. In 2002, ATR officially announced a multilingual corpus with 160,000 sentences in Japanese, Chinese and English [33]. The European Parliament speeches corpus (Europarl) contained at least 400,000 sentences in combination with English for 23 other languages in its 3rd version in 2005 [14]. Evaluation campaigns then collected and released corpora of more that 1 million sentences (WMT 2006 et seq., IWLST 2014 et seq.). With the operational deployment of systems on the Web, large companies or institutions were able to collect very large corpora: Google is claiming 1 billion aligned sentences in French-English in 2016 [11,30]; the World Intellectual Property Organisation (WIPO) is also claiming hundreds of millions of aligned sentences extracted from patent families in various language pairs [43]; the DGT-Translation memory of the Directorate-General for Translation of the European Commission released 6.8 million translation units in March 2018 in addition to the several million units already released. Subtitles also constitute an invaluable resource of multilingual aligned data [17,34].

The statistical machine translation approach, which had been dominant in research approximately from 2005 to 2015, was in turn drowned under the tsunami of the neural network approach to machine translation (NMT). This last approach requires even larger amount of data than statistical machine translation systems (and also enormous computation time and power in comparison to statistical machine translation), but, for well-resourced languages, this is no more a problem. Indeed, very large amounts of data are available for such languages and part of such data is not even used during training. For instance, [30] reports that Google used only 15% of the total of the French-English data at their disposal for their neural machine translation system.

1.3 The Challenge of Less-Resourced Languages: An Opportunity for Case-Based Reasoning

As enough data is available for well-resourced languages or language-pairs, the consciousness about less-resourced languages is raising among researchers in the natural language processing community. There exist more than 6,000 languages in the world and only slightly more than 100 are available with Google Translate. The Linguistic Data Consortium is aware of the lack of data for the majority of the languages of the world and is starting to explore less expensive ways to collect data for such languages, e.g., through gamification [7]. Other techniques which are being proposed are in the vein of zero-shot translation, i.e., the possibility of mapping data across independently learnt neural network models [11].

Another possibility could well be the use of case-based reasoning, which is supposed to be a remedy when not so many examples are available. As explained above in Sect. 1.1, applying case-based reasoning to machine translation was indeed present in Nagao's proposal in 1984, however its first mention with its official name, or at least under the form of *memory-based reasoning,* is to be found in Kitano's description of massive parallel artificial intelligence later in 1993 [13]. It was then made explicit in 2003 [8].

1.4 Purpose of the Paper

The purpose of this paper is twofold. Its first objective is to reword example-based machine translation, in particular the approach described in [15], in terms of case-based reasoning, so as to open opportunities for CBR researchers to tackle machine translation for less-resourced language pairs. We will show that this particular approach to example-based machine translation corresponds indeed to a knowledge-light CBR approach using analogies.

The second objective is to open paths for improving this approach to example-based machine translation, as such rewording will open opportunities to CBR researchers to easily spot possible places where improvement can be brought. In particular, we see opportunities for CBR researchers to work on more elaborated description of cases, or introducing and representing domain knowledge, or knowledge dedicated to retrieval and adaptation.

These two objectives are addressed in Sects. 3 and 4. They are preceded by a section giving some preliminaries, Sect. 2.

2   Preliminaries: Definitions, Notations, Assumptions

2.1   On Case-Based Reasoning

A Reminder of the Main Notions. Case-based reasoning (CBR [26]) aims at solving a new problem—the *target problem*, denoted by tgt—with the help of cases, where a case represents a problem-solving episode. In this paper, a case is denoted by an ordered pair (pb, sol(pb)) where pb is a problem and sol(pb) is a solution of pb. However, it may occur that some additional pieces of information are associated with a case. The *case base* is a finite set of cases and constitutes an essential source of knowledge of the CBR system. A *source case* (srce, sol(srce)) is an element of the case base, srce is a *source problem*.

The *process model* of CBR consists usually in four steps: retrieval, adaptation, correction and memorization (also known as retrieve, reuse, revise and retain in the 4Rs model of [1]). Retrieval consists in selecting one or several source case(s). Adaptation uses this or these case(s) to propose a first solution sol(tgt) to tgt. This solution sol(tgt) is possibly corrected, e.g. by confrontation to a human expert. Finally, the newly formed case (tgt, sol(tgt)) is memorized in the case base if this is judged to be useful.

The *knowledge model* of CBR decomposes its knowledge base in four containers [25]. The first one is the case base, already mentioned. The *domain ontology* contains knowledge about the objects and properties used to represent the cases in the application domain. It can be considered as a representation of necessary conditions for a case to be licit. The *retrieval knowledge* is used during the retrieval step, the *adaptation knowledge*, during the adaptation step.

The First Approach to Example-Based Machine Translation. The seminal paper in example-based machine translation by Nagao in 1984 [20], was indeed "case-based reasoning comes early." In its introduction, the problem of translation is stated as follows: given a sentence in a language to be translated into another language, use another sentence in the same language that differs by only one word and for which the translation in the other language is known, change the word that differs in the other language to get the final translation. Given the above description of example-based machine translation, one can imagine a CBR process based on the use of a bilingual dictionary for managing several mismatches between the source and the target problems. This was the approach explored in [29]. An entry of such a dictionary is a pair (w^o, w^d) where w^o (resp., w^d) is a word in the origin language (resp., the destination language). It also contains the pair $(\varepsilon, \varepsilon)$: the empty string ε is considered as a particular word in both languages. The principle of this approach is as follows:

Retrieval: Find a case (srce, sol(srce)) that is similar to tgt in that a minimal number of words have to be substituted in srce to get tgt.

Adaptation: For each word substitution $w_s^o \rightsquigarrow w_t^o$ from srce to tgt in the origin language, the word substitution $w_s^d \rightsquigarrow w_t^d$ is built in the destination language, using the dictionary entries (w_s^o, w_s^d) and (w_t^o, w_t^d). Then, these substitutions are applied on sol(srce) to get sol(tgt).

For example, with French as origin language and English as destination language:

$$\texttt{tgt} = \textit{Amenez-moi à Pluton.}$$
$$\texttt{srce} = \textit{Amenez-moi à votre chef.}$$
$$\texttt{sol(srce)} = \textit{Take me to your leader.}$$

hence $\texttt{tgt} = \sigma^o(\texttt{srce})$ with $\sigma^o = \textit{chef} \rightsquigarrow \textit{Pluton} \circ \textit{votre} \rightsquigarrow \varepsilon$.

Given the entries $(\textit{Pluton}, \textit{Pluto}), (\textit{chef}, \textit{leader}), (\textit{votre}, \textit{your})$ and $(\varepsilon, \varepsilon)$

it comes $\sigma^d = \textit{leader} \rightsquigarrow \textit{Pluto} \circ \textit{your} \rightsquigarrow \varepsilon$

hence $\texttt{sol(tgt)} = \sigma^d(\texttt{sol(srce)}) = \textit{Take me to Pluto.}$ (correct translation)

Note that this approach is likely to propose a large number of incorrect translations among the proposed solutions, in particular because a single word in the origin language can be translated in different ways and no context is used here to select the appropriate word.

A more elaborate approach to example-based machine translation was proposed in [28] in which additional pieces of information are added to cases in the form of their dependency parses. Adaptation is constrained by the shape of the dependency trees, in that only sub-sequences of words which correspond to a sub-tree in dependency trees can be substituted for. It then becomes crucial to be able to align dependency sub-trees across languages and to perform fast approximate retrieval of sub-trees. The Kyoto EBMT system implemented such an approach [21].

2.2   On Strings and Texts

An *alphabet* $\mathcal{A}$ is a finite set. A *character* is an element of $\mathcal{A}$. A *string* of length $\ell \geq 0$ on $\mathcal{A}$ is a finite sequence $\alpha_1 \alpha_2 \dots \alpha_\ell$ of characters. The set of strings is denoted by $\mathcal{A}^*$. It contains the empty string ε. *Edit distances* on strings are distance functions on $\mathcal{A}^*$, defined as follows. An *edit operation* is a function from $\mathcal{A}^*$ to $\mathcal{A}^*$. Common edit operations are the following ones:

- *Deletions* consist in removing a character of a string. For example, the deletion of the 3rd character of the string *case* yields *cae*.
- *Insertions* consist in inserting a character into a string at a given position. For example, inserting *s* after position 4 of string *case* yields *cases*.
- *Substitutions* consist in replacing a character of a string with another character. For example, the substitution of *c* with *b* at the 1st position of *case* yields *base*. A substitution can be written as the composition of a deletion and an insertion. In the example: *case* $\mapsto$ *ase* $\mapsto$ *base*.
- *Swaps* consist in swapping two contiguous characters. For example, swapping *a* with *s* in *case* yields *csae*.
- *Shifts* are extension of swaps to non-necessarily contiguous sequences of characters. The length of the gap is usually taken into account to compute the weight of shifts. For example, shifting *se* with *ca* in *case* yields *seca*.
- Etc.

An *edit path* is a sequence $P = e_1 ; \ldots ; e_{p-1} ; e_p$ of edit operations e_i. Such a path *relates* a string S_1 to a string S_2 if $e_p(e_{p-1}(\ldots(e_1(S_1))\ldots)) = S_2$. Let `weight` be a function that associates to an edit operation e an integer `weight(e)` > 0. This function is extended on edit paths by `weight(`$e_1 ; e_2 ; \ldots ; e_p$`)` $= \sum_{i=1}^{p}$ `weight(`e_i`)`. Given a set of edit operations and a function `weight`, the edit distance from a string S_1 to a string S_2 is defined as

$$\text{dist}(S_1, S_2) = \min\{\text{weight}(P) \mid P : \text{path from } S_1 \text{ to } S_2\}$$

The Levenshtein distance is an edit distance that considers deletions, additions and substitutions only, each with a weight of 1. The LCS distance (longest common subsequence) is simpler in that it considers deletions and insertions only, with a weight of `weight(e)` $= 1$ for every operation (in this setting, substitutions have a weight of 2). The computation of the Levenshtein or the LCS distance is quadratic in the worst case [2] (proving that the Levenshtein distance can be computed in lesser time would imply $P = NP$ [39]). Better behaviours can be obtained for felicitous cases; for instance, the computation of the distance between two equal strings is of course linear in the length of the string by Ukkonen's algorithm [38].

It is worth noting that edit distances have been used in CBR on other structures, such as temporal sequences [27] or graphs [6,16].

3   A Knowledge-Light Approach to Case-Based Translation Using Analogies

In [15], an implementation of example-based machine translation was proposed and evaluated. The approach was effective: at that time, it delivered comparable results to nascent statistical methods. It worked only on the string level and did not involve any linguistic knowledge. The purpose of this section is to describe it anew, but this time, in terms of knowledge-light CBR. Before relating it to CBR, an analogical relation between strings is introduced.

3.1   Analogy Between Strings

A *proportional analogy* is a quaternary relation between four objects A, B, C and D denoted by $A : B :: C : D$. In all generality, we call *conformity* the operation denoted by the sign :: and *ratio* the operation denoted by the sign: An analogy should satisfy the following properties (for any objects A, B, C and D of the same type):

Reflexivity of conformity: $A : B :: A : B$;
Symmetry of conformity: if $A : B :: C : D$ then $C : D :: A : B$;
Exchange of the means: if $A : B :: C : D$ then $A : C :: B : D$.

An *analogical equation* is an expression of the form $A : B :: C : x$ where A, B and C are given objects and x is the unknow. Solving such an equation for x consists in finding the objects x satisfying this equation.

A proportional analogy between numbers is defined by $A : B :: C : D$ if $B - A = D - C$, i.e., conformity is equality and ratio is subtraction. A proportional analogy between n-tuples of numbers ($A = (a_1, a_2, \ldots, a_n)$) is defined by $A : B :: C : D$ if $a_i : b_i :: c_i : d_i$ for each $i \in \{1, 2, \ldots, n\}$. For instance, $(0, 2) : (3, 3) :: (1, 6) : (4, 7)$.

A proportional analogy between strings is defined as follows. First, let $\mathcal{A} = \{\alpha_1, \alpha_2, \ldots, \alpha_p\}$ be a predefined finite set of characters, i.e., an alphabet. For a given string $S \in \mathcal{A}^*$, where $\mathcal{A}^*$ is the set of all strings on $\mathcal{A}$, let $\pi(S) = (|S|_{\alpha_1}, |S|_{\alpha_2}, \ldots |S|_{\alpha_p})$ be the Parikh vector of string S, i.e., the vector of the number $|S|_{\alpha_i}$ of occurrences of each character α_i in S. Then, four strings A, B, C, D are in proportional analogy, i.e., $A : B :: C : D$, if $\pi(A) : \pi(B) :: \pi(C) : \pi(D)$ and $\mathtt{dist}(A, B) = \mathtt{dist}(C, D)$, with $\mathtt{dist}$ the LCS distance. If $A : B :: C : D$, it can be proven that $\mathtt{dist}(A, C) = \mathtt{dist}(B, D)$ also holds, thanks to the exchange of the means. For example, it can be easily checked that the following strings make a proportional analogy:

$$A = to\ reason \quad B = reasoning$$
$$C = to\ do \qquad\quad D = doing$$

In particular, $|B|_r - |A|_r = 1 - 1 = |D|_r - |C|_r = 0 - 0$, $|B|_n - |A|_n = 2 - 1 = |D|_n - |C|_n = 1 - 0$, $\mathtt{dist}(A, B) = \mathtt{dist}(C, D) = 6$, and $\mathtt{dist}(A, C) = \mathtt{dist}(B, D) = 6$.

Two words of caution: On integers, any analogical equation has exactly one solution ($D = B - A + C$ always exists). By contrast, on strings, it can have zero, one or multiple solutions. For example, $a : b :: ac : x$ has two solutions: bc or cb. Also, notice that, on strings, conformity is not transitive in the general case: $A : B :: C : D$ and $C : D :: E : F$ do not imply $A : B :: E : F$ in general.

3.2   Case Representation

In the domain of machine translation, a problem $\mathtt{pb}$ is given by a sentence in an "origin" language (e.g., French) and a solution of $\mathtt{pb}$ is a sentence $\mathtt{sol(pb)}$ in a "destination" language (e.g., English). A case is a pair $(\mathtt{pb}, \mathtt{sol(pb)})$, without additional information. Fig. 1 illustrates a case base containing such cases, i.e., pairs of translated sentences.

3.3   No Domain Knowledge Used

It is worth mentioning that this approach uses no domain knowledge (no linguistic knowledge about any of the two languages involved or about their relationships): the knowledge is contained only in the cases. This makes the approach independent of any language: only the case acquisition has to be carried out to apply it to a new pair of origin and destination languages.

srce	sol(srce)
As-tu sauté au plafond ?	*Did you hit the roof?*
Elle évite ce chien.	*She avoids this dog.*
Elle évite les chiens.	*She avoids dogs.*
Il veut faire ça.	*He wants to do that.*
Je peux faire du vélo aujourd'hui.	*I can ride my bicycle today.*
J'aime ce chat.	*I like this cat.*
J'ai sauté au plafond.	*I hit the roof.*

Fig. 1. A toy case base of translations from French into English.

3.4   Retrieval

Let `tgt` be the French sentence to be translated. In the running example, the following French sentence is chosen:

$$\mathtt{tgt} = Je\,veux\ faire\ du\ v\acute{e}lo.$$

Retrieval aims at finding one or several *triples* of source cases $((\mathtt{srce}_A, \mathtt{sol}(\mathtt{srce}_A)), (\mathtt{srce}_B, \mathtt{sol}(\mathtt{srce}_B)), (\mathtt{srce}_C, \mathtt{sol}(\mathtt{srce}_C)))$ such that $\mathtt{srce}_A : \mathtt{srce}_B :: \mathtt{srce}_C : \mathtt{tgt}$. With the running example, the source problems could be

$$\mathtt{srce}_A = Tu\ peux\ le\ faire\ aujourd'hui.$$
$$\mathtt{srce}_B = Tu\ veux\ le\ faire.$$
$$\mathtt{srce}_C = Je\ peux\ faire\ du\ v\acute{e}lo\ aujourd'hui.$$

If no such triple can be found, an alternative approach can be applied (see Sect. 3.6).

3.5   Adaptation

Given a target problem and a source case triple that has been retrieved, the adaptation is based on the following principle: if four sentences in the origin language are in proportional analogythen it is plausible that their translations in the destination language are also in proportional analogy. Based on this idea, the adaptation of the source case triple to solve the target problem consists in solving the following analogical equation:

$$\mathtt{sol}(\mathtt{srce}_A) : \mathtt{sol}(\mathtt{srce}_B) :: \mathtt{sol}(\mathtt{srce}_C) : x$$

In the running example, the English sentences translating the French sentences $\mathtt{srce}_A$, $\mathtt{srce}_B$ and $\mathtt{srce}_C$ are

$$\mathtt{sol}(\mathtt{srce}_A) = You\ can\ do\ it\ today.$$
$$\mathtt{sol}(\mathtt{srce}_B) = You\ want\ to\ do\ it.$$
$$\mathtt{sol}(\mathtt{srce}_C) = I\ can\ ride\ my\ bicycle\ today.$$

The equation is solvable and gives the following solution which is a correct translation of `tgt`:

$$\mathtt{sol(tgt)} = I \ want \ to \ ride \ my \ bicycle.$$

Since there may be several retrieved source case triples and, for each of them, several solutions to the analogical equation in the destination language, the approach may propose a set of solutions `sol(tgt)` (possibly repeated a number of times), not necessarily all correct. The translation examples in [15] suggest that the quality of the solutions should be correlated with their output frequency.

3.6 Recursive Application of the CBR Process

The main bottleneck of the above approach lies in the fact that the first step of retrieval is obviously prone to fail in the majority of cases, unless a more flexible definition of analogy between strings is provided. We will discuss more flexible approaches later (Sects. 4.1 and 4.5). With the purely symbolic approach described above in Sect. 3.1 for analogy between strings, there is statistically very little chance to find a source case triple of sentences which makes an analogy with a given target problem (the input sentence to translate), even in a dense data set consisting of very short sentences from similar restricted domains exhibiting a large number of commutations (like the BTEC corpus: *My tooth hurts.*, *My head hurts.*, *My head hurts badly.*, etc.). In [15] where a purely symbolic approach was adopted, a recursive application of the method was proposed to remedy this problem: instead of triples, pairs of cases ($\mathtt{srce}_A$, $\mathtt{srce}_B$) are retrieved. Solving $\mathtt{srce}_B : \mathtt{srce}_A :: \mathtt{tgt} : x$ for x yields $\mathtt{srce}_C$. When $\mathtt{srce}_C$ does not already belong to the case base, it is considered a new target on which to apply the CBR process recursively. This recursive application is different from [32] where recursive reasoning is applied to sub-components, hence on the hierarchical structure of the cases. Recursive CBR on sub-parts of sentences seems also a promising topic for translation. We think that all this opens new avenues to study: how to combine retrieval with a recursive application of the CBR process itself on entire cases or sub-parts of cases so as to lead to a solution of the target problem as fast as possible?

4   Towards a Knowledge-Intensive Approach to Case-Based Translation Using Analogies

The approach presented in the previous section is effective, though it only uses simple cases, the LCS edit distance and no other knowledge containers. The aim of this section is to examine how this approach can be improved thanks to a more flexible definition of analogies (Sect. 4.1), a richer case representation (Sect. 4.2), the use of domain knowledge (Sect. 4.3), and the modification of the following CBR steps using some additional knowledge: retrieval and adaptation (Sects. 4.4 and 4.5). Other techniques related to CBR or to natural language processing could be used as well to improve the system, such as case maintenance techniques or textual CBR techniques (see e.g. [31,41]).

4.1   Using More Flexible Analogies

Word vector representations may allow for a more flexible definition of analogies between sentences, considered as sequences of words. One of the recent breakthroughs in natural language processing is the use of (shallow) artificial neural networks for the fast computation of distributional semantic word vector representations (word embeddings) from large corpora [19,23,24]. This offers the possibility of solving semantic analogies, as illustrated by the hackneyed example $man : woman :: king : x$ leads to $x = queen$ [19], through the computation of semantic similarities between words. Vector representations of words had in fact already been proposed [35,37] to answer (SAT) questions using a model inspired by Gentner's structural mapping engine [10], called the Latent Relation Mapping Engine [36]. As for sentences, so-called soft alignment matrices give the word-to-word distance between each pair of words in two sentences. Figure 2 illustrates how it could be possible to use such representations to solve analogical equations between sentences. Some attempts have already been made either using soft alignment representations [12] or vector representations of sentences [18].

We think that this general problem is relevant for the CBR community as it falls within the topic of computational analogy: how to solve analogical equations between sentences in a truly semantic way?

4.2   Enriching the Case Representation

The approach of [15] shows that "raw cases", i.e. pairs of translated sentences only, can already be effective. However, additional pieces of information to a case can improve its re-usability through CBR. In particular, linguistic information can be used. For instance, parts of speech or morphological features like verb tenses (see an example in Sect. 4.3) or the fact that a sequence of characters constitutes a noun in singular form (example in Sect. 4.5), can be used.

This is related to the various steps of the CBR process and raises several issues. In particular, the following question is worth studying, from a case acquisition effort perspective: when is it more beneficial to (manually or automatically) acquire additional information on cases instead of acquiring new raw cases?

4.3   Taking into Account Domain Ontology

The domain ontology (or domain knowledge) is used for several purposes. First it expresses a vocabulary in which cases can be expressed. For example, in a cooking application (such as Taaable [9]), queries, cases and other knowledge units are expressed with terms like `citrus_fruit`, `lemon`, etc. Here, this would be the vocabulary used to represent features of the cases in an enriched representation.

Second it expresses *integrity constraints* about this vocabulary. In the cooking application, this could be for example $\varphi = $ `lemon` $\Rightarrow$ `citrus_fruit`.[1] Indeed, φ

---

[1] In this section, the ideas are illustrated in propositional logic, but could easily be expressed in other formalisms.

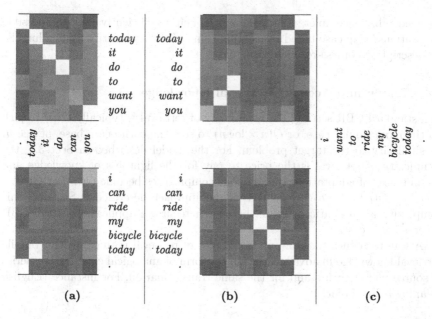

Fig. 2. Soft alignment matrices for analogies between sequences of words (example from Sect. 3.5). A cell in a matrix is the distance between the two corresponding words (arccos of the cosine of their vectors in the word embedding space), the closer the whiter. The two matrices in (**a**) are computed from three given sentences. How to compute the matrices in (**b**) from the matrices in (**a**) is an open problem. The solution of the analogy in (**c**) should be computed from the matrices in (**b**).

can be read as the integrity constraint "There is no recipe with lemon and without citrus fruit.", formally: "$\varphi \wedge$ lemon $\wedge \neg$citrus_fruit is insatisfiable." Back to the machine translation application, what could be such an integrity constraint and how could it be used to better solve translation problems? One possible answer is the use of linguistic knowledge about the destination language that will recognize that a sentence is not correct (because of a non existing word or because of an ungrammatical construction); this can be used to simply rank the possible solutions. For example, the sentence *I have gone.* should be preferred to *I have goed.*, if both are produced. Standard NLP techniques would, e.g., determine that future tense is used consistently in both languages, so that translation of future tense into future tense should be preferred. For example, the French sentence *Je me lèverai.* (future tense) could be translated into *I will get up.* and *I am going to get up.* According to this criterion, the first sentence could be preferred to the second one though, in fact, both translations are acceptable here. This is why the less preferred solution should be given a lower rank but not necessarily discarded.

What are the NLP techniques case-based translation using analogies can profit from when it is applied to less-resourced languages? E.g., when not enough data is available to build reliable N-gram language models, can linguistic knowledge like incomplete linguistic parsers help to efficiently rank the possible translations? Can case-based translation using analogies identify lacking linguistic descriptions of less-resourced languages?

4.4 Taking into Account Retrieval Knowledge

In a standard CBR setting, the complexity of retrieval is typically $O(n)$ to pick up the most similar case, or $O(n \times \log n)$ to sort the entire case base, of size n, by similarity to the target problem. For the model described in Sect. 3.4, the complexity of retrieval is the price to pay for the lightness of knowledge and the null cost of adaptation: the previous complexities become $O(n^3)$ or $O(n^3 \times \log n^3) = O(n^3 \times \log n)$. In the case of the approach described in Sect. 3.6, this complexity is quadratic or more, because a recursive application of the CBR process has a cost.

A way to reduce the computational cost of retrieval is to explicitly compile retrieval knowledge in advance, e.g., in the form of analogical clusters, i.e., series of source pairs which stand for the same transformation. For instance (English meaning below French):

> *Il peut faire ça aujourd'hui. : Il veut faire ça.*
> 'He can do that today.'   'He wants to do that.'
> *Je peux le faire aujourd'hui. : Je veux le faire.*
> 'I can do it today.'   'I want to do it.'
> *Tu peux la voir aujourd'hui ? : Tu veux la voir ?*
> 'Can you see her today?'   'Do you want to see her?'

This technique has never been applied to example-based machine translation, but it has been used for statistical machine translation to create new pairs of aligned sentences (in CBR terms, source problems and their solutions) so as to augment the training data (the case base in CBR terms) [42]. Analogical clusters identify well attested transformations, which should thus be reliable. It is then possible to choose to generate new source cases $\mathtt{srce}_C$ from such clusters only, by simultaneously solving all possible analogies formed by the set of the case pairs in a given cluster in conjunction with $\mathtt{tgt}$, as illustrated below (English meaning of $\mathtt{tgt}$ below: 'I want to ride a bicycle').

$\mathtt{srce}_B$	:	$\mathtt{srce}_A$	::	$\mathtt{tgt}$	: $\mathtt{srce}_C$
Il veut faire ça.		*Il peut faire ça aujourd'hui.*			
Je veux le faire.	:	*Je peux le faire aujourd'hui.*	::	*Je veux faire*	: x
Tu veux la voir ?		*Tu peux la voir aujourd'hui ?*		*du vélo.*	

> leads to $x =$ *Je peux faire du vélo aujourd'hui.*
> 'I can ride my bicycle today.'

During retrieval, computing the similarity of $\mathtt{tgt}$ to each sentence in the case base reduces the cost of retrieval to $O(n)$ or $O(\log n)$. The most similar cases can lead directly to the clusters they belong to using an inverse index. This avoids redundancy firstly in the retrieval of source case pairs, secondly in the generation of $srce_C$, and thirdly in adaptation, because the generation of the same $srce_C$ is factored once in comparison with several generations in the absence of clusters. This should thus considerably speed up the overall process.

As enriching not only the case base but also the retrieval knowledge should be an essential feature of a knowledge-intensive CBR approach, the question of managing the dynamic aspect of retrieval knowledge in the recursive application of the CBR process (Sect. 3.6) is a challenging question: when and how should new retrieval knowledge be compiled and added to profit from new cases of the type $(srce_C, sol(srce_C))$ that are added to the case base along the recursive application of the CBR process?

4.5   Using Adaptation Knowledge

The proportional analogy on strings defined in Sect. 3.1 is used for adapting three cases in order to solve a target problem. It covers a wide variety of situations. However, some situations that are recognized as analogies are not covered by it, hence the usefulness of defining specific edit operations or even specific edit distances for specific languages, constituting therefore new adaptation knowledge.

Let us exemplify with the case of marked plural forms of nouns in Indonesian or Malay. Marked plurals are expressed by repetition: the marked plural form of a noun w is w-w. For the sake of simplicity, let us express the case using English: the marked plural of cat (*several cats*) would be *cat-cat*. Therefore, in such languages, the analogy $A : B :: C : D$ between the following strings makes sense:

$$
\begin{aligned}
&A = I \; like \; this \; cat. \quad B = She \; likes \; cat\text{-}cat. \\
&C = I \; avoid \; this \; dog. \quad D = She \; avoids \; dog\text{-}dog.
\end{aligned}
\tag{1}
$$

The definition of proportional analogy of commutation presented in Sect. 3.1 does not cover this case, because, e.g., $|B|_t - |A|_t = 2 - 2 \neq |D|_t - |C|_t = 0 - 1$. In order to take this phenomenon into account, the idea is to define an edit distance $dist$ whose edit operations are the ones of the LCS distance, plus an edit operation $repeat\_noun$ that would replace a substring w that is recognized as a noun in singular form, with its marked plural form w-w (in a manner reminiscent of what was done for consonant spreading in Arabic in the framework of two-level morphology [3]) and its reverse edit operation, replacing w-w with w. Each of the above edit operations should be assigned a cost of 1. Another change to the proportional analogy of Sect. 3.1 is the fact that the number of occurrences $|S|_c$ of character c in string S is considered only for the strings obtained by removing the nouns w and w-w involved in the computation of the two new edit operations. With these changes the sentences in (1) are in analogy.

Another language-dependent procedure that can be integrated in the adaptation process is the use of correction techniques in the destination language. For example, for tgt = *As-tu mangé une orange ?*, a retrieved triple of source cases can be

$(\mathtt{srce}_A, \mathtt{sol}(\mathtt{srce}_A)) = (J'ai\ sauté\ au\ plafond., I\ hit\ the\ roof.)$

$(\mathtt{srce}_B, \mathtt{sol}(\mathtt{srce}_B)) = (J'ai\ mangé\ une\ orange., I\ ate\ an\ orange.)$

$(\mathtt{srce}_C, \mathtt{sol}(\mathtt{srce}_C)) = (As\text{-}tu\ sauté\ au\ plafond\ ?, Did\ you\ hit\ the\ roof?)$

This leads to the proposed solution $\mathtt{sol}(\mathtt{tgt}) = $ *Did you ate an orange?*, which is incorrect. A spell-checker, such as the ones used in some word processors, can be used to correct $\mathtt{sol}(\mathtt{tgt})$ in such a situation. It is noteworthy that domain knowledge can play a role in a correction process: linguistic knowledge can be used to examine what makes a sentence incorrect. If such an automatic correction process fails, a human user can correct the sentence, giving birth to a *correction case*: (*Did you ate an orange?, Did you eat an orange?*) in the example. Research in correcting SMT errors using, e.g., a NMT system trained on correction cases already exists [22]. Sets of correction cases are already available.[2] But basically, SMT and NMT systems are not traceable, which should be contrasted to case-based translation systems using analogies: used cases can easily be traced and the adaptation and correction knowledge is explicit.

This last topic is directly of interest to the CBR community: can we implement MT systems which are true explainable AI systems, i.e., systems where human-readable linguistic knowledge is easy to integrate and leads directly to visible improvement and where translation results can be intuitively explained?

5   Conclusion

The application aimed in this paper is machine translation (MT), especially MT for language pairs for which corpora of examples are small, relatively to the size of the corpora used in nowadays neural network approaches to MT. Indeed, it is our working hypothesis that case-based MT is competitive in such a context. This hypothesis is based on the prior work of [15] that is reformulated here in terms of case-based MT. This reformulation constitutes the first contribution of this paper. This approach is knowledge-light in the sense that the only language-dependent pieces of knowledge are the cases, which are raw cases, representing only the problem and the solution (the sentences in the origin and destination languages), without any additional information. This approach is based on the transfer of proportional analogies found in the origin language onto the destination language.

---

[2] E.g., https://www.matecat.com/. The authors of this paper are currently working on a slightly different scenario and are collecting such correction cases for use in a case-based correction system.

The second contribution of this work is a theoretical examination of the question: "How can this knowledge-light case-based MT approach be improved by incorporating some new pieces of knowledge and other principles, methods, and techniques from CBR or NLP?" Obviously, the answers given in this paper are at an embryonic stage. Therefore, future directions of work are obvious: implementing and testing the ideas presented and developing new ideas for knowledge-intensive case-based MT.

Our impression is that this issue of case-based MT, though little explored nowadays, deserves much research: there are certainly many ways to improve it and it is worth doing so with the aim of developing competitive MT systems that are not limited to pairs of languages with very large corpora. One way, still under investigation, is to continue this research through a contest, similar to the Computer Cooking Contest. Such contests already exist for MT, but they focus on very large corpora. The idea would be to organize such a contest on smaller corpora like the small ones offered by the Tatoeba project[3] and to use the off-the-shelf automatic evaluation techniques of the MT community.

References

1. Aamodt, A., Plaza, E.: Case-based reasoning: foundational issues, methodological variations, and system approaches. AI Commun. **7**(1), 39–59 (1994)
2. Backurs, A., Indyk, P.: Edit distance cannot be computed in strongly subquadratic time (unless SETH is false). In: STOC 2015, pp. 51–58. ACM (2015)
3. Beesley, K.R.: Consonant spreading in Arabic stems. In: COLING-ACL 1998, Montréal, vol. I, pp. 117–123 (1998)
4. Boitet, C.: Current state and future outlook of the research at GETA. In: MT Summit I, Hakone, pp. 26–35 (1987)
5. Brown, P., et al.: A statistical approach to machine translation. In: COLING 1988, pp. 71–76 (1988)
6. Bunke, H., Messmer, B.T.: Similarity measures for structured representations. In: Wess, S., Althoff, K.-D., Richter, M.M. (eds.) EWCBR 1993. LNCS, vol. 837, pp. 106–118. Springer, Heidelberg (1994). https://doi.org/10.1007/3-540-58330-0_80
7. Cieri, C.: Addressing the language resource gap through alternative incentives, workforces and workflows (invited keynote lecture). In: LTC 2017, Poznań (2017)
8. Collins, B., Somers, H.: EBMT seen as case-based reasoning. In: Carl, M., Way, A. (eds.) Recent Advances in Example-Based Machine Translation. Text, Speech and Language Technology, vol. 21, pp. 115–153. Springer, Dordrecht (2003). https://doi.org/10.1007/978-94-010-0181-6_4
9. Cordier, A., et al.: TAAABLE: a case-based system for personalized cooking. In: Montani, S., Jain, L.C. (eds.) Successful Case-Based Reasoning Applications-2. SCI, vol. 494, pp. 121–162. Springer, Heidelberg (2014). https://doi.org/10.1007/978-3-642-38736-4_7
10. Gentner, D.: Structure mapping: a theoretical model for analogy. Cogn. Sci. **7**(2), 155–170 (1983)
11. Johnson, M., et al.: Google's multilingual neural machine translation system: enabling zero-shot translation. CoRR (2016)

---

[3] https://tatoeba.org/.

12. Kaveeta, V., Lepage, Y.: Solving analogical equations between strings of symbols using neural networks. In: Computational Analogy Workshop at ICCBR-16, Atlanta, Georgia, pp. 67–76 (2016)
13. Kitano, H.: Challenges of massive parallelism. In: IJCAI 1993, vol. 1, pp. 813–834. Morgan Kaufmann Publishers Inc., San Francisco (1993)
14. Koehn, P.: Europarl: a parallel corpus for statistical machine translation. In: MT Summit X, Phuket, pp. 79–86 (2005)
15. Lepage, Y., Denoual, E.: Purest ever example-based machine translation: detailed presentation and assessment. Mach. Transl. **19**, 251–282 (2005)
16. Lieber, J., Napoli, A.: Using classification in case-based planning. In: Wahlster, W. (ed.) ECAI 1996, pp. 132–136. Wiley (1996)
17. Lison, P., Tiedemann, J.: OpenSubtitles2016: extracting large parallel corpora from movie and TV subtitles. In: LREC 2016, Paris, France (2016)
18. Ma, W., Suel, T.: Structural sentence similarity estimation for short texts. In: FLAIRS-29, pp. 232–237 (2016)
19. Mikolov, T., Chen, K., Corrado, G., Dean, J.: Efficient estimation of word representations in vector space. CoRR abs/1301.3781 (2013)
20. Nagao, M.: A framework of a mechanical translation between Japanese and English by analogy principle. Artif. Hum. Intell., 173–180 (1984)
21. Nakazawa, T., Kurohashi, S.: EBMT system of KYOTO team in patentMT task at NTCIR-9. In: NTCIR-9, Tokyo, Japan, pp. 657–660 (2011)
22. Pal, S., Naskar, S.K., Vela, M., van Genabith, J.: A neural network based approach to automatic post-editing. In: ACL 2016, pp. 281–286 (2016)
23. Pham, H., Luong, T., Manning, C.: Learning distributed representations for multilingual text sequences. In: 1st Workshop on Vector Space Modeling for NLP, Denver, Colorado, pp. 88–94 (2015)
24. Řehůřek, R.: Making sense of word2vec. Available online
25. Richter, M.: Knowledge containers (2003). Available online
26. Riesbeck, C.K., Schank, R.C.: Inside Case-Based Reasoning. Lawrence Erlbaum Associates Inc, Hillsdale (1989). Available online
27. Rougegrez-Loriette, S.: Prédiction de processus à partir de comportement observé: le système REBECAS. Ph.D. thesis, Université Paris 6 (1994)
28. Sadler, V., Vendelmans, R.: Pilot implementation of a bilingual knowledge bank. In: COLING-1990, Helsinki, vol. 3, pp. 449–451 (1990)
29. Sato, S.: Example-based machine translation. Ph.D. thesis, Kyoto University (1991)
30. Schuster, M.: The move to neural machine translation at Google (invited talk). In: IWSLT 2017 (2017)
31. Smyth, B., Keane, M.T.: Remembering to forget. In: IJCAI 1995, Montréal, vol. 1, pp. 377–382 (1995)
32. Stahl, A., Bergmann, R.: Applying recursive CBR for the customization of structured products in an electronic shop. In: Blanzieri, E., Portinale, L. (eds.) EWCBR 2000. LNCS, vol. 1898, pp. 297–308. Springer, Heidelberg (2000). https://doi.org/10.1007/3-540-44527-7_26
33. Takezawa, T., Sumita, E., Sugaya, F., Yamamoto, H., Yamamoto, S.: Toward a broad coverage bilingual corpus for speech translation of travel conversation in the real world. In: LREC 2002, Las Palmas, pp. 147–152 (2002)
34. Tiedemann, J.: News from OPUS - A collection of multilingual parallel corpora with tools and interfaces. In: RANLP-2009, vol. V, pp. 237–248. John Benjamins, Borovets (2009)

35. Turney, P., Pantel, P.: From frequency to meaning: vector space models of semantics. J. Artif. Intell. Res. **37**, 141–188 (2010)
36. Turney, P.D.: The latent relation mapping engine: algorithm and experiments. J. Artif. Int. Res. **33**(1), 615–655 (2008)
37. Turney, P.D., Littman, M.L.: Corpus-based learning of analogies and semantic relations. Mach. Learn. **60**(1–3), 251–278 (2005)
38. Ukkonen, E.: Algorithms for approximate string matching. Inf. Control **64**, 100–118 (1985)
39. Wagner, R.A., Fischer, M.J.: The string-to-string correction problem. J. Assoc. Comput. Mach. **21**(1), 168–173 (1974)
40. Weaver, W.: Translation. Technical report, The Rockfeller Foundation, New York (1949)
41. Weber, R.O., Ashley, K.D., Brüninghaus, S.: Textual case-based reasoning. Knowl. Eng. Rev. **20**(3), 255–260 (2005)
42. Yang, W., Shen, H., Lepage, Y.: Inflating a small parallel corpus into a large quasi-parallel corpus using monolingual data for Chinese-Japanese machine translation. J. Inf. Process. **25**, 88–99 (2017)
43. Ziemski, M., Junczys-Dowmunt, M., Pouliquen, B.: The United Nations Parallel Corpus v1.0. In: LREC 2016, Paris, France (2016)

Making the Best of Cases
by Approximation, Interpolation
and Extrapolation

Jean Lieber[1]($\boxtimes$), Emmanuel Nauer[1]($\boxtimes$), Henri Prade[2,3]($\boxtimes$), and
Gilles Richard[2]($\boxtimes$)

[1] Université de Lorraine, CNRS, Inria, LORIA, 54000 Nancy, France
Jean.Lieber@loria.fr
[2] IRIT, University of Toulouse, Toulouse, France
[3] QCIS, University of Technology, Sydney, Australia

Abstract. Case-based reasoning usually exploits source cases (consisting of a source problem and its solution) *individually*, on the basis of the similarity between the target problem and a particular source problem. This corresponds to approximation. Then the solution of the source case has to be adapted to the target. We advocate in this paper that it is also worthwhile to consider source cases by two, or by three. Handling cases by two allows for a form of interpolation, when the target problem is between two similar source problems. When cases come by three, it offers a basis for extrapolation. Namely the solution of the target problem is obtained, when possible, as the fourth term of an analogical proportion linking the three source cases with the target, where the analogical proportion handles both similarity and dissimilarity between cases. Experiments show that interpolation and extrapolation techniques are of interest for reusing cases, either in an independent or in a combined way.

Keywords: Analogy · Analogical proportion · Approximation
Interpolation · Extrapolation

1 Introduction

Case-based reasoning (CBR) [18] aims at solving a new problem—the *target problem*—thanks to a set of cases (the *case base*), where a case is a pair consisting of a problem and a solution of this problem. A *source case* is a case from the case base, consisting of a *source problem* and one of its solutions. The classical approach to CBR consists in (i) selecting source cases *similar* to the target problem and (ii) adapting them to solve it. In such a view, the target and the source are compared in terms of similarity, which is a (two-valued or gradual) *binary* relation, while information about the way they *differ* is not really considered in general.

In this paper, in addition to the binary relation of similarity (which is the basis of approximation), two other relations are considered: the *betweenness* and the *analogical proportion*, which in a way or another leave room to dissimilarity.

© Springer Nature Switzerland AG 2018
M. T. Cox et al. (Eds.): ICCBR 2018, LNAI 11156, pp. 580–596, 2018.
https://doi.org/10.1007/978-3-030-01081-2_38

Betweenness is a *ternary* relation stating that an object is "between" two other objects. It is used as an *interpolation* principle: if the target problem is between two source problems then it is plausible that a solution of it is between the solutions of these source problems. In a graded setting, this suggests that if the target problem is closer to one of two source problems, its solution should be closer as well to the solution to the corresponding source problem. In the Boolean setting, betweenness view may lead to several potential solutions, except if the solutions of the two source problems coincide.

Analogical proportion is a *quaternary* relation: four objects a, b, c and d are in analogical proportion if "a is to b as c is to d". A logical modeling of it [14,16] has pointed out that it expresses that "a differs from b as c differs from d (and vice-versa)", and that "what a and c have in common, b and d have it also". Thus, analogical proportion is a matter of both dissimilarity and similarity. The fact that we are no longer considering similarity only, enables us to escape the strict vicinity of known cases, and to perform a form of adaptation for free. More precisely, in a CBR perspective, we use it as an extrapolation principle: if the target problem and three source problems are in analogical proportion, the solutions of these four problems are (likely to be) in analogical proportion as well. Such an analogical jump enables us to extrapolate the solution of the target problem from the solutions of three distinct source problems. An illustration of this is given in [2] where in three distinct situations the recommended actions are respectively to (i) serve tea without milk without sugar, (ii) serve tea with milk without sugar, (iii) serve tea without milk with sugar, while in a fourth situation that makes an analogical proportion with the three others, the action to do would be (iv) "serve tea with milk with sugar".

The approach described in this paper combines the use of closeness, betweenness and analogical proportion for a knowledge-light approach to CBR. In fact, the only source of knowledge used in the inference lies in the case base: there is no domain knowledge nor adaptation knowledge and the similarity is based on some distance function.

Section 2 introduces the notions and notations used throughout the paper and the assumptions it is based on. Section 3 describes the approach for applying approximation, interpolation and extrapolation to CBR. Section 4 provides an evaluation in a Boolean setting. Section 5 presents a discussion and a comparison with related work, while Sect. 6 points out lines for future research.

2   Definitions, Notations and Assumptions

In this section, definitions are presented in a Boolean setting (objects are tuples of Boolean values).

2.1   Boolean Setting

Let $\mathbb{B} = \{0, 1\}$ be the set of Boolean values. The Boolean operators are denoted by the connector symbols of propositional logic: for $a, b \in \mathbb{B}$, $\neg a = 1 - a$,

$a \wedge b = \min(a, b)$, $a \vee b = \max(a, b)$, $a \oplus b = |b - a|$ ($\oplus$ is the exclusive or) and $a \equiv b = \neg(a \oplus b)$.

Let p be a positive integer. In the examples, an element of $\mathbb{B}^p$ is noted without parentheses and commas: $(0, 1, 0, 0, 1)$ is simply noted by 01001. The Hamming distance H on $\mathbb{B}^p$ is defined by $H(a, b) = \sum_{i=1}^{p} |b_i - a_i|$. For example, with $p = 5$, $H(01001, 11011) = 2$.

2.2   CBR

CBR aims at solving the target problem with the help of the case base. It consists most of the time (1) in selecting relevant source cases (retrieval), (2) in reusing these source cases in order to solve the target problem (adaptation). The other classical steps of CBR are not considered in this paper: they concern the validation-repair of the newly formed case and its potential adding to the case base.

Let $\mathcal{P}$ and $\mathcal{S}$ be two sets called the universe of problems and the universe of solutions: a *problem* $\mathbf{x}$ (resp., a *solution* $\mathbf{y}$) is by definition an element of $\mathcal{P}$ (resp., of $\mathcal{S}$). Here, $\mathcal{P} = \mathbb{B}^m$, where $m \geq 1$ is a constant. Similarly, $\mathcal{S} = \mathbb{B}^n$, $n \geq 1$. A binary relation on $\mathcal{P} \times \mathcal{S}$ denoted by $\rightsquigarrow$ and read "has for solution" is assumed to exist. Thus, "$\mathbf{y}$ solves $\mathbf{x}$" is denoted by $\mathbf{x} \rightsquigarrow \mathbf{y}$. A *case* is a pair $(\mathbf{x}, \mathbf{y}) \in \mathcal{P} \times \mathcal{S}$ such that $\mathbf{x} \rightsquigarrow \mathbf{y}$. The *case base* CB is a finite set of cases. A *source case* is an element of CB. The *target problem* is the problem to be solved. Note that $\rightsquigarrow$ is usually not completely known to the CBR system: such a system provides *plausible* solutions to problems, on the basis of what is known of $\rightsquigarrow$ from the case base.

In some situations, it is assumed that $\rightsquigarrow$ is functional. This assumption means that there exists a function $\mathbf{f} : \mathcal{P} \to \mathcal{S}$ such that $\mathbf{x} \rightsquigarrow \mathbf{y}$ iff $\mathbf{y} = \mathbf{f}(\mathbf{x})$, for any $\mathbf{x} \in \mathcal{P}$ and $\mathbf{y} \in \mathcal{S}$.

2.3   Betweenness

Let $\mathcal{U}$ be a set whose elements are represented by numerical features (including Boolean features). Let $a, b, c \in \mathcal{U}$; a is *between* b and c, denoted by $b−a−c$, if for every feature i, $((b_i \leq a_i \leq c_i)$ or $(c_i \leq a_i \leq b_i))$.[1] Let $\texttt{Between}(b, c) = \{a \in \mathcal{U} \mid b−a−c\}$, for $b, c \in \mathcal{U}$. For example, in $\mathcal{U} = \mathbb{B}^5$, $\texttt{Between}(01001, 11011) = \{01001, 11001, 01011, 11011\}$. For a logical view on betweenness, we refer to [22].

2.4   Analogical Proportion

Let $\mathcal{U}$ be a set. An analogical proportion on $\mathcal{U}$ is a quaternary relation between four elements a, b, c and d of $\mathcal{U}$, read "a is to b as c is to d" and denoted by $a{:}b{::}c{:}d$, having the following properties (see, e.g. [16]), for any $a, b, c, d \in \mathcal{U}$:

---

[1] When these values are Boolean, this can also be written $(b_i \wedge c_i \Rightarrow a_i) \wedge (a_i \Rightarrow b_i \vee c_i) = 1$.

reflexivity $a{:}b{::}a{:}b$,
symmetry if $a{:}b{::}c{:}d$ then $c{:}d{::}a{:}b$,
central permutation if $a{:}b{::}c{:}d$ then $a{:}c{::}b{:}d$.

In the Boolean setting, the analogical proportion considered is defined on $\mathbb{B}$ by

$$a{:}b{::}c{:}d \quad \text{if } (a \wedge \neg b \equiv c \wedge \neg d) \wedge (\neg a \wedge b \equiv \neg c \wedge d) = 1$$

that can be read "a differs from b as c differs from d" and "b differs from a as d differs from c". This can also be rewritten $b - a = d - c$, but mind that these differences belong to $\{-1, 0, 1\}$ ($-$ is not an operation that is closed in $\mathbb{B}$). Thus, the patterns $abcd$ such that $a{:}b{::}c{:}d$ are 0000, 1111, 0011, 1100, 0101 and 1010.

This analogical proportion can be extended on $\mathcal{U} = \mathbb{B}^p$ by

$$a{:}b{::}c{:}d \quad \text{if } a_i{:}b_i{::}c_i{:}d_i \text{ for each } i \in [1, p]$$

Given $a, b, c \in \mathcal{U}$, solving the *analogical equation* $a{:}b{::}c{:}y$ aims at finding the $y \in \mathcal{U}$ satisfying this relation. It may have no solution, e.g., when $a = 0$, $b = 1$ and $c = 1$. The equation $a{:}b{::}c{:}y$ in $\mathbb{B}$ has a solution iff $(a \equiv b) \vee (a \equiv c) = 1$ and, when this is the case, the solution is unique: $y = c \equiv (a \equiv b)$.

3 Reusing Cases by Approximation, Interpolation and Extrapolation

This section describes the three mentioned approaches: approximation, interpolation and extrapolation. For an integer $k \geq 1$, case retrieval can be done by considering ordered sets of k source cases. This principle is detailed in Sect. 3.2 and applied in Sects. 3.3, 3.4 and 3.5 respectively for $k = 1$, 2, and 3. The combination of these three approaches is discussed in Sect. 3.6. Let us start with an example.

3.1 A Basic Example

In order to support the intuition, we consider the following example where a suitable dish type (described via 3 two-valued attributes, i.e., $\mathcal{S} = \mathbb{B}^3$) has to be suggested to an individual (described via 8 two-valued attributes, i.e., $\mathcal{P} = \mathbb{B}^8$). The 8 attributes representing an individual $\mathbf{x}$ have the following semantics: $\mathbf{x}_1$: $\mathbf{x}$ suffers from gout, $\mathbf{x}_2$: $\mathbf{x}$ has diabetes, $\mathbf{x}_3$: $\mathbf{x}$ is allergic to nuts, $\mathbf{x}_4$: $\mathbf{x}$ does not eat mammal meat (beef, pork, etc.), $\mathbf{x}_5$: $\mathbf{x}$ needs to have a regular calcium supplement, $\mathbf{x}_6$: $\mathbf{x}$ needs to have a regular iron supplement, $\mathbf{x}_7$: $\mathbf{x}$ likes vegetables, and $\mathbf{x}_8$: $\mathbf{x}$ does not like dairy products. A dish type $\mathbf{y}$ is represented via 3 attributes: $\mathbf{y}_1$: $\mathbf{y}$ is a dish with sauce, $\mathbf{y}_2$: $\mathbf{y}$ is based on starchy food (e.g., a pasta dish), $\mathbf{y}_3$: $\mathbf{y}$ is a dish with fish. $\mathbf{x} \rightsquigarrow \mathbf{y}$ can be read as: $\mathbf{y}$ is a suitable dish type for $\mathbf{x}$. For a healthy individual 00010010 (with no specific requirement), all dishes are suitable. Therefore, $\rightsquigarrow$ is not functional in this application, as several types of dishes might be suitable for the same individual. The 3 approaches of case reuse developed in this paper can be applied to this application as follows (where $\mathbf{y}^j$ is a suitable class of dish for $\mathbf{x}^j$):

Approximation: If an individual x^{tgt} is not far from x^1, it is plausible that a suitable dish for x^{tgt} will not be far from a suitable dish y^1 for x^1.

Interpolation: If an individual x^{tgt} is between x^1 and x^2; it is plausible that a suitable dish for x^{tgt} will be between a suitable dish y^1 for x^1 and a suitable dish y^2 for x^2.

Extrapolation: If an individual x^{tgt} is as similar to x^3 as x^2 is similar to x^1, it is plausible that a suitable dish for x^{tgt} will be as similar to y^3 as y^2 is similar to y^1.

3.2   General Principle

Let $k \in \{1, 2, 3\}$: the approach presented here covers approximation ($k = 1$), interpolation ($k = 2$) and extrapolation ($k = 3$). Two ($k + 1$)-ary relations are considered: $\mathtt{Rel}_\mathcal{P}$ on $\mathcal{P}$ and $\mathtt{Rel}_\mathcal{S}$ on $\mathcal{S}$. Ideally, it would be assumed that these relations have the following properties, for $(x^1, \ldots, x^k, x^{k+1}) \in \mathcal{P}^{k+1}$ and $(y^1, \ldots, y^k, y^{k+1}) \in \mathcal{S}^{k+1}$, with the hypothesis that $\forall j \in [1; k + 1], x^j \rightsquigarrow y^j$:

$$\text{if } \mathtt{Rel}_\mathcal{P}\left(x^1, \ldots, x^k, x^{k+1}\right) \text{ then } \mathtt{Rel}_\mathcal{S}\left(y^1, \ldots, y^k, y^{k+1}\right)$$

However, this assumption is usually too strong: since the relation $\rightsquigarrow$ is only partially known to the CBR system, it seems odd to have such a certain relationship about $\rightsquigarrow$ given by the pair ($\mathtt{Rel}_\mathcal{P}, \mathtt{Rel}_\mathcal{S}$). So, only the following relaxed form of this property is assumed:

$$\text{if } \mathtt{Rel}_\mathcal{P}\left(x^1, \ldots, x^k, x^{k+1}\right) \text{ and } x^j \rightsquigarrow y^j \text{ for } j \in [1; k + 1]$$
$$\text{then it is plausible that } \mathtt{Rel}_\mathcal{S}\left(y^1, \ldots, y^k, y^{k+1}\right) \tag{1}$$

This property (1) can be used for CBR. Let x^{tgt} be the target problem. A *candidate* is an ordered set of k cases $((x^1, y^1), \ldots, (x^k, y^k)) \in \mathtt{CB}^k$ such that $\mathtt{Rel}_\mathcal{P}(x^1, \ldots, x^k, x^{tgt})$. Based on this notion, the following CBR steps can be specified:

retrieval: The set of candidates is computed.
adaptation: For a candidate $((x^1, y^1), \ldots, (x^k, y^k))$, it is plausible that the solution y^{tgt} of x^{tgt} satisfies $\mathtt{Rel}_\mathcal{S}(y^1, \ldots, y^k, y^{tgt})$.

Let $\mathtt{Candidates}$ be the set of candidates. When $\mathtt{Candidates} = \emptyset$, the approach fails. Let $\mathtt{potentialSols}$ be the multiset of $y \in \mathcal{S}$ such that $(x, y) \in \mathtt{Candidates}$. When there are several *distinct* solutions in this multiset, there is a need for a function to integrate these solutions into one. Let $\mathtt{integrate} : \mathtt{potentialSols} \mapsto y \in \mathcal{S}$ be such a function. The nature of this function can be different, depending on the solution space. When $\mathcal{S} = \mathbb{B}$ (or, more generally, a set of low cardinality) then $\mathtt{integrate}$ can be a simple vote. When $\mathcal{S} = \mathbb{B}^n$, the integration could be a component by component vote, for example:

$$\mathtt{integrate}(\{\{001, 001, 010, 111, 111\}\}) = 011$$

(with an arbitrary choice in case of ties).

3.3 Reusing Cases by Singletons: Approximation

When $k = 1$, candidates are singletons and source cases are considered individually in relation to the target problem. Usually $\text{Rel}_\mathcal{P}$ and $\text{Rel}_\mathcal{S}$ binary relations are related to the notion of similarity and denoted $x^1 \simeq x^2$ and $y^1 \simeq y^2$. When a distance dist is available on the universe, $\simeq$ is defined as $a \simeq b$ iff $\text{dist}(a, b) \leq \tau_{\text{dist}}$ where $\tau_{\text{dist}} > 0$ is a fixed threshold. Applying the general principle (1) leads to:

$$\text{if } x^1 \simeq x^2 \text{ and } x^j \rightsquigarrow y^j \text{ for } j \in \{1, 2\}$$
$$\text{then it is plausible that } y^1 \simeq y^2$$

i.e., similar problems have similar solutions, a principle often emphasized in CBR (see e.g., [9]).

---

function *approximation*(CB : *a set of cases*, x^{tgt} : *a problem*)
begin
     Candidates $\leftarrow \{(x, y) \in CB \mid x \simeq x^{tgt}\}$
     potentialSols $\leftarrow$ multiset of the y such that $(x, y) \in$ Candidates
     if *potentialSols* $= \emptyset$ **then**
         return *failure*   ▷ The approximation method fails.
     end
     $y^{tgt} \leftarrow$ integrate(potentialSols)
     return y^{tgt}
end

Fig. 1. The approximation method.

Back to our initial example, let us consider 2 individuals with close profiles (in terms of Hamming distance), e.g., $x^1 = 00010010$ and $x^2 = 00010011$. In that example, $H(x^1, x^2) = 1$ (x^2 does not like dairy product), and a dish type $y^2 = 011$ without sauce, at distance 1 of $y^1 = 111$ (a dish type suitable for x^1) will be suitable for x^2.

Figure 1 summarizes the approximation method with an algorithm.

3.4 Reusing Cases by Pairs: Interpolation

When $k = 2$, candidates are pairs, relations $\text{Rel}_\mathcal{P}$ and $\text{Rel}_\mathcal{S}$ are betweenness on $\mathcal{P}$ and on $\mathcal{S}$. The general principle (1) applied here leads to:

$$\text{if } x^1 - x^3 - x^2 \text{ and } x^j \rightsquigarrow y^j \text{ for } j \in \{1, 2, 3\}$$
$$\text{then it is plausible that } y^1 - y^3 - y^2$$

Applied to CBR, a retrieved pair $\{(x^1, y^1), (x^2, y^2)\} \in$ Candidates is such that $x^1 - x^{tgt} - x^2$ and then adaptation takes advantage of the inferred information

$y^1 - y^{tgt} - y^2$. A way to get a unique solution is to have $y^1 = y^2$, which entails $y^{tgt} = y^1$ as a candidate solution for x^{tgt}. If Candidates $= \emptyset$, the equality $y^1 = y^2$ can be relaxed in $\text{dist}(y^1, y^2) \leq \tau_{\text{dist}}$ (where dist is here a distance function on $\mathcal{S}$). In that case, uniqueness of y^{tgt} is not guaranteed anymore. By contrast, if Candidates is considered to be too large, it can be restricted by allowing only the pairs $\{(x^1, y^1), (x^2, y^2)\}$ such that $\text{dist}(x^1, x^2) \leq \tau_{\text{between}}$, where $\tau_{\text{between}} > 0$ is a given threshold.

function *interpolation*(CB : *a set of cases*, x^{tgt} : *a problem*)
begin

$$\text{Candidates} \leftarrow \left\{ \{(x^1, y^1), (x^2, y^2)\} \ \middle| \ \begin{array}{l} (x^1, y^1), (x^2, y^2) \in CB \\ \text{such that} \ \begin{vmatrix} y^1 = y^2 \\ x^1 - x^{tgt} - x^2 \end{vmatrix} \end{array} \right\}$$

$$\text{potentialSols} \leftarrow \left| \begin{array}{l} \text{multiset of the } y \text{ such that} \\ \{(x^1, y^1), (x^2, y^2)\} \in \text{Candidates and } y = y^1 = y^2 \end{array} \right.$$

if *potentialSols* $= \emptyset$ **then**
    return *failure*   ▷ The interpolation method fails.
end
$y^{tgt} \leftarrow \text{integrate}(\text{potentialSols})$
return y^{tgt}

end

Fig. 2. The interpolation method (for the situation in which the solutions of the retrieved cases are equal).

Back to our initial example, let $x^{tgt} = 11010010$, $(x^1, y^1) = (01110010, 001)$, and $(x^2, y^2) = (10010010, 001)$ (i.e. $H(x^1, x^2) = 3$): x^{tgt}, x^1 and x^2 differ only in the fact that the chosen individuals have/do not have gout/diabetes/allergy to nuts. $y^1 = y^2 = 001$ is the solution "dish without sauce, not based on starchy food, with fish". Since $x^1 - x^{tgt} - x^2$, a solution is $y^{tgt} \in \text{Between}(y^1, y^2) = \{y^1\}$, i.e., $y^{tgt} = y^1 = y^2$.

Figure 2 summarizes the interpolation method in an algorithm.

3.5   Reusing Cases by Triples: Extrapolation

When $k = 3$, candidates are triples. $\text{Rel}_{\mathcal{P}}$ and $\text{Rel}_{\mathcal{S}}$ are analogical proportions on $\mathcal{P}$ and on $\mathcal{S}$. The property (1) applied here leads to:

if $x^1 : x^2 :: x^3 : x^4$ and $x^j \rightsquigarrow y^j$ for $j \in \{1, 2, 3, 4\}$
then it is plausible that $y^1 : y^2 :: y^3 : y^4$

Applied to CBR, an element of Candidates is a triple $((x^1, y^1), (x^2, y^2), (x^3, y^3))$ of source cases such that (i) $x^1 : x^2 :: x^3 : x^{tgt}$ and (ii) the equation $y^1 : y^2 :: y^3 : y$ has a solution. Such a solution, unique in the Boolean setting, is considered as a plausible solution of x^{tgt}.

```
function extrapolation(CB : a set of cases, x^tgt : a problem)
begin
    Candidates ← {((x¹,y¹),(x²,y²),(x³,y³)) ∈ CB³ | x¹:x²::x³:x^tgt}
                        | multiset of the y such that
    potentialSols ← | ((x¹,y¹),(x²,y²),(x³,y³)) ∈ Candidates
                        | and y is a solution of y¹:y²::y³:y
    if potentialSols = ∅ then
        return failure                          ▷ The extrapolation method fails.
    end
    y^tgt ← integrate(potentialSols)
    return y^tgt
end
```

(a) A naive algorithm in $O(|CB|^3)$.

```
function compute_key_table(CB : a set of cases)
begin
    key_table ← empty hash table
    for (x¹, y¹) ∈ CB do
        for (x², y²) ∈ CB, (x², y²) ≠ (x¹, y¹) do
            key ← x² − x¹                        ▷ key ∈ {−1, 0, 1}^m
            value ← ((x¹, y¹), (x², y²))
            Add the pair (key, value) to key_table
                                ▷ without erasing other pairs with the same key!
        end
    end
    ▷ key_table associates to a key a set of case pairs.
end
```

```
function extrapolation(CB : a set of cases, x^tgt : a problem)
begin
    Candidates ← ∅
    for (x, y) ∈ CB, with x ≠ x^tgt do
        key ← x^tgt − x
        for ((x¹, y¹), (x², y²)) ∈ access(key, key_table), with x² ≠ x^tgt do
            ▷ By construction of key_table, x¹:x²::x:x^tgt holds.
            Candidates ← Candidates ∪ {((x¹,y¹),(x²,y²),(x,y))}
        end
    end
                        | multiset of the y such that
    potentialSols ← | ((x¹,y¹),(x²,y²),(x³,y³)) ∈ Candidates
                        | and y is a solution of y¹:y²::y³:y
    if potentialSols = ∅ then
        return failure                          ▷ The extrapolation method fails.
    end
    y^tgt ← integrate(potentialSols)
    return y^tgt
end
```

(b) A more efficient algorithm (with an offline function compute_key_table in $O(|CB|^2)$ and an online function extrapolation in $O(|CB|^2)$).

Fig. 3. The extrapolation method (in 2 versions: a simple one (a) and a more efficient one (b)).

Back to our example where we are searching for a suitable dish type y^{tgt} for an individual x^{tgt}:

x^1	$= 00001011$	y^1	$= 010$
x^2	$= 00100010$	y^2	$= 110$
x^3	$= 10001011$	y^3	$= 001$
x^{tgt}	$= 10100010$	y^{tgt}	$= ???$

The relation $x^1{:}x^2{::}x^3{:}x^{tgt}$ holds, and the equation $y^1{:}y^2{::}y^3{:}y$ has a unique solution $y^{tgt} = 101$. Our principle tells us that $y^{tgt} = 101$ is a suitable option for x^{tgt}. If we consider the intended meaning of the parameters, x^{tgt} has gout, no diabetes, is allergic to nut, is not refractory to meat, has no need for calcium nor iron supplement, likes vegs and dairy. The dish type $y^{tgt} = 101$ describing fish with sauce and no starchy food is suitable for this type of individual.

Figure 3(a) summarizes the extrapolation method in an algorithm and Fig. 3(b) presents a more efficient method described further.

3.6 Combining These Approaches

Now, we have three methods, approximation, interpolation and extrapolation, to solve a problem. These methods are plausible and incomplete: for a target problem x^{tgt}, each of them may fail either by providing an incorrect solution or by not providing any solution at all. A complete discussion of the options for combining these methods is out of the scope of this paper and constitutes a future work. However, this section discusses some ideas about the design of a good combination method.

function *combination*(CB : *a set of cases*, x^{tgt} : *a problem*)
begin

$(m_1, m_2, m_3) \leftarrow$ List of the three methods approximation, interpolation and extrapolation, ordered by decreasing preference

$y^{tgt} \leftarrow m_1(\text{CB}, x^{tgt})$
if $y^{tgt} \neq failure$ **then**
| **return** y^{tgt}
end
$y^{tgt} \leftarrow m_2(\text{CB}, x^{tgt})$
if $y^{tgt} \neq failure$ **then**
| **return** y^{tgt}
end
$y^{tgt} \leftarrow m_3(\text{CB}, x^{tgt})$
return y^{tgt}

end

Fig. 4. The combination method based on a preference relation on the set of methods {approximation, interpolation, extrapolation}.

A simple way to combine these methods is to use a preference relation between them: if the preferred method provides a solution, this is the solution returned, else the second preferred method is tried, and so on (this simple combination method is summarized in Fig. 4). This makes sense since a method may provide results unfrequently but with high plausibility and should be tried before a method providing frequent results with lower plausibility.

Now, given the three methods, how can such a preference relation be chosen? For this purpose, an analysis of the case base may help. In particular, for the extrapolation method, it has been shown that the functions f such that $x^1{:}x^2{::}x^3{:}x^4$ entails $f(x^1){:}f(x^2){::}f(x^3){:}f(x^4)$ for each $(x^1, x^2, x^3, x^4) \in \mathcal{P}^4$ are the affine functions [6].[2] Thus, if $\leadsto$ is functional ($\leadsto = f$) and f is affine, then the extrapolation method never gives an incorrect solution. If f is closed to an affine function, then this method gives good results (and should be highly ranked in the preference relation). A measure of closeness to affinity is the BLR test [3] that can be run on the case base.

Another approach to method combination consists in having a preference between methods depending on the target problem. For this purpose, an idea is to associate to the output of each method a score that is relative to the confidence of the method wrt its output: the preferred method is the one with the higher score. For example, the approximation method would have a high confidence if many source cases support the returned solution and few ones go against it. A similar principle can be applied for interpolation and extrapolation.

4 Evaluation

The objective of the evaluation is to study the behaviour of the three approaches, on various types of Boolean functions, in order to determinate which approach is the best and in which circumstancies. First experimental results are presented and a combination method based on the preference relation is proposed according to these results.

4.1 Experiment Setting

In the experiment, $\mathcal{P} = \mathbb{B}^8$ and $\mathcal{S} = \mathbb{B}^3$, as in the running example. $\leadsto$ is assumed to be functional: $\leadsto = f$.

The function f is randomly generated using the following generators that are based on the three main normal forms, with the purpose of having various types of functions:

CNF f is generated in a conjunctive normal form, i.e., $f(x)$ is a conjunction of n_{conj} disjunctions of literals, for example $f(x) = (x_1 \vee \neg x_7) \wedge (\neg x_3 \vee x_7 \vee x_8) \wedge x_4$. The value of n_{conj} is randomly chosen uniformly in $\{3, 4, 5\}$. Each disjunction is generated on the basis of two parameters, $p^+ > 0$ and $p^- > 0$, with $p^+ + p^- < 1$: each variable x_i occurs in the disjunct in a positive (resp. negative) literal with a probability p^+ (resp., p^-). In the experiment, the values $p^+ = p^- = 0.1$ were chosen.

---

[2] An affine function $f : \mathbb{B}^m \to \mathbb{B}$ has the form $f(x) = x_{i_1} \oplus \ldots \oplus x_{i_q} \oplus c$ where $\{i_1, \ldots, i_q\}$ is a subset of $[1, m]$ and $c \in \{0, 1\}$. An affine function $f : \mathbb{B}^m \to \mathbb{B}^n$ is of the form $f(x) = (f_1(x), \ldots, f_n(x))$ where $f_j : \mathbb{B}^m \to \mathbb{B}$ is an affine function.

DNF f is generated in a disjunctive normal form, i.e., it has the same form as for CNF except that the connectors $\wedge$ and $\vee$ are exchanged. The parameters n_{disj}, p^+ and p^- are set in the same way.

Pol is the same as DNF, except that the disjunctions ($\vee$) are replaced with exclusive or's ($\oplus$), thus giving a polynomial normal form. The only different parameter is $p^- = 0$ (only positive literals occur in the polynomial normal form).

The case base CB is generated randomly, with the values for its size: $|\text{CB}| \in \{16, 32, 64, 96, 128\}$, i.e. $|\text{CB}|$ is between $\frac{1}{16}$ and $\frac{1}{2}$ of $|\mathcal{P}| = 2^8 = 256$. Each source case $(\mathbf{x}, \mathbf{y})$ is generated as follows: $\mathbf{x}$ is randomly chosen in $\mathcal{P}$ with a uniform distribution and $\mathbf{y} = \mathbf{f}(\mathbf{x})$.

Each method may lead to several solutions. Let Y be the multiset of these solutions. The function **integrate** introduced at the end of Sect. 3.2 aims at associating to Y a unique element $\mathbf{y} \in \mathcal{S}$. Here, **integrate** consists in making a vote on each component: $\mathbf{y}_i = \text{argmax}_{\mathbf{y}_i \in Y_i} \texttt{multiplicity}(\mathbf{y}_i, Y_i)$, where Y_i is the multiset of the $\mathbf{y}_i$ for $\mathbf{y} \in$ Y.

Let ntp be the number of target problems posed to the system, na be the number of (correct or incorrect) answers (ntp $-$ na is the number of target problems for which the system fails to propose a solution), and sscapa be the sum of the similarities between the correct answer (according to the generated function f) and the predicted answer, where the similarity between two solutions $\mathbf{y}^1$ and $\mathbf{y}^2$ is computed by $1 - H(\mathbf{y}^1, \mathbf{y}^2)/n$ (with $n = 3$ since $\mathcal{S} = \mathbb{B}^n = \mathbb{B}^3$). For each method, the following scores are computed:

The precision prec is the average of the ratios $\dfrac{\texttt{sscapa}}{\texttt{na}}$.

The correct answer rate car is the average of the ratios $\dfrac{\texttt{sscapa}}{\texttt{ntp}}$.

The average is computed on 1 million problem solving for each function generator, requiring the generation of 1060 f for each of them. The average computing time of a CBR session (retrieval and adaptation for solving one problem) is about 0.8 ms (for $k = 1$), 19 ms (for $k = 2$) and 2 ms (for $k = 3$) on an current standard laptop.

The parameters for each method has been chosen as follows, after preliminary tests based on precision:

approximation: $\tau_{\text{dist}} = 1$ on $\mathcal{P}$;
interpolation: $\tau_{\text{dist}} = 0$ on $\mathcal{S}$ (i.e., $\mathbf{y}^1 = \mathbf{y}^2$), $\tau_{\text{between}} = 2$;
extrapolation: All the triples in analogy with $\mathbf{x}^{\text{tgt}}$ are considered.
combination: The chosen preference method is: interpolation preferred to approximation preferred to extrapolation for CNF and DNF, and extrapolation preferred to interpolation preferred to approximation for Pol.

For the sake of reproducibility, the code for this experiment is available at https://tinyurl.com/CBRTests, with the detailed results (generated functions and details of the evaluation).

A Note About Implementation. A naive algorithm for implementing each $k \in \{1, 2, 3\}$ method is in $O(|\text{CB}|^k)$ (cf. Figs. 1, 2 and 3(a)). However, this complexity can be reduced for interpolation to search Candidates by iterating only on pairs of cases $((\mathbf{x}^1, \mathbf{y}^1), (\mathbf{x}^2, \mathbf{y}^2)) \in \text{CB}^2$ such that $H(\mathbf{x}^1, \mathbf{x}^2) \leq \tau_{\text{dist}}$. For extrapolation, the complexity can be separated in an offline and on online part (cf. Fig. 3(b)). The offline part is in $O(|\text{CB}|^2)$ and generates a hashtable structure over keys representing the differences between $\mathbf{x}^1$ and $\mathbf{x}^2$ (considered as vectors in $\mathbb{R}^m$). For example, $\text{key}(01001, 11010) = (-1, 0, 0, -1, 0)$. The online part is in $O(|\text{CB}|^2)$ in the worst case (and frequently closer to $O(|\text{CB}|))^3$ and searches all the $(\mathbf{x}, \mathbf{y}) \in \text{CB}$ such that $\text{key}(\mathbf{x}, \mathbf{x}^{\text{tgt}}) = \text{key}(\mathbf{x}^1, \mathbf{x}^2)$, which is equivalent to $\mathbf{x}^1{:}\mathbf{x}^2{::}\mathbf{x}{:}\mathbf{x}^{\text{tgt}}$.

4.2   Results

Figure 5 pictures the detailed results given in Table 1.

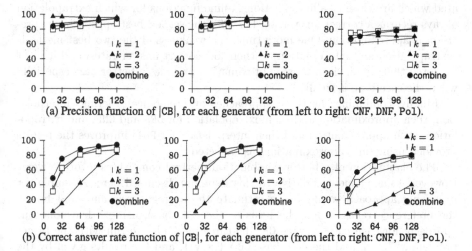

(a) Precision function of |CB|, for each generator (from left to right: CNF, DNF, Pol).

(b) Correct answer rate function of |CB|, for each generator (from left to right: CNF, DNF, Pol).

Fig. 5. Precision and correct answer rate function of the case base size for the three generators, for each method ($k = 1$, $k = 2$, $k = 3$ and "combine", i.e. combination of the three other methods).

The result precisions shows that, for CNF and DNF, interpolation gives better results than approximation and extrapolation, and also that approximation gives better results than extrapolation. However, when examining the results wrt the correct answer rate, interpolation has a low performance, especially when the

---

[3] The number of iterations in the for loop is $|\text{CB}| - 1$. In each iteration, the set access(key, key_table) contains at most $(|\text{CB}| - 1)$ elements, though in practice, this set contains in general a much smaller number of elements. So, the number of $O(1)$ operations of this online procedure in the worst case is not more than $(|\text{CB}| - 1) \times (|\text{CB}| - 1)$, hence a complexity in $O(|\text{CB}|^2)$.

Table 1. prec and car for $k \in \{1,2,3\}$ and combine (c.) for the different generators.

		|CB| = 16				|CB| = 32				|CB| = 64				|CB| = 96				|CB| = 128			
	$k =$	1	2	3	c.	1	2	3	c.	1	2	3	c.	1	2	3	c.	1	2	3	c.
CNF	prec	.87	**.97**	.80	.84	.88	**.97**	.81	.85	.90	**.96**	.84	.89	.93	**.96**	.86	.92	.95	**.96**	.88	.94
	car	.36	.04	.31	**.49**	.58	.15	.63	**.75**	.81	.42	.81	**.88**	.90	.67	.86	**.92**	**.94**	.83	.88	.94
DNF	prec	.87	**.97**	.80	.84	.88	**.97**	.81	.85	.90	**.96**	.84	.89	.93	**.96**	.87	.92	.95	**.96**	.88	.94
	car	.36	.04	.31	**.49**	.58	.15	.63	**.75**	.81	.43	.81	**.88**	.90	.67	.86	**.92**	**.94**	.83	.88	.94
POL	prec	.61	.72	**.75**	.67	.62	.72	**.75**	.70	.63	.71	**.77**	.75	.66	.71	**.79**	.78	.68	.70	**.81**	.80
	car	.25	.01	.18	**.34**	.41	.04	.44	**.57**	.57	.14	.66	**.73**	.64	.27	.75	**.78**	.68	.40	.79	**.80**

case base is small ($|CB| \in \{16, 32\}$), due to the difficulty to find two candidates for the betweenness relations.

The results are different for Pol, for which, extrapolation provides better results. This result can be explained by the functions that have been generated which are close to affine functions, affine functions for which extrapolation always returns a correct answer [6]. For DNF, the second best approach wrt precision is approximation. One more time, the weakness of the two best methods (extrapolation and interpolation) is their low correct answer rates, and it must be noted that, in all situations, approximation provides a better car, especially when the case base is small.

Finally, combining the three approaches by preference ordering (interpolation, then approximation and then extrapolation for DNF and CNF, and extrapolation, then approximation and then interpolation for Pol) improves the results provided using only approximation, as expected.

The elaboration of a better combination method constitutes a future work. However, some elements relative to this issue are discussed here. A simple yet promising approach would be to estimate the average precision—and hence, the preference relation—on the basis of the case base, using a leave-one out approach: for each case $(x, y) \in CB$, the three methods are run with the target problem $x^{tgt} = x$ and the case base $CB \setminus \{(x, y)\}$, and the results given by the three methods are compared with the known solution $y^{tgt} = y$, which enables us to compute the average precision for each method.

Another issue to be studied carefully is whether it is worth searching for a good combination method. Indeed, if all the methods are strongly correlated, their combination would not give much improvement. For this purpose, a preliminary test has been carried out that computes the covariance of the events "incorrect answer for method k" and "incorrect answer for method ℓ", with $k, \ell \in \{1, 2, 3\}$ and $k \neq \ell$: $\text{cov}_{k\ell} = P_{k\ell} - P_k P_\ell$ where $P_{k\ell}$ estimates the probability that the methods k and ℓ provide an incorrect answer, given that they both provide an answer, P_k estimates the probability that the method k provides incorrect answers, given that it provides an answer, and P_ℓ is defined similarly. The results on the generated data are: $\text{cov}_{12} = \text{cov}_{21} \simeq 0.90$, $\text{cov}_{23} = \text{cov}_{32} \simeq 0.41$, and $\text{cov}_{13} = \text{cov}_{31} \simeq 0.27$. This can be interpreted as follows. The high correlation between approximation and interpolation is mainly due to the tight bounds used in the experiments for interpolation. By contrast, extrapolation is *much less correlated* with the other methods. This suggests the complementarity of extrapolation, hence the worthiness of studying with more depth the combination issue.

5 Discussion and Related Work

An important issue raised in this paper is that the reuse of multiple cases ($k \geq 2$) does not necessarily rely on similarity (or not only): in the general situation, it relies on two ($k + 1$)-ary relations on $\mathcal{P}$ and $\mathcal{S}$, that may be non reducible to binary similarity relations. These relations structure the problem and solution spaces. Similar issues are addressed in other works of the CBR literature. For example, (simple or multiple) reuse may have profit of adaptation hierarchies on $\mathcal{P}$ and $\mathcal{S}$ [1,5,23]. Another example of relation used for multiple case retrieval and adaptation is the use of *diversity*: the retrieved cases should be diverse in order to better contribute to the solving of the target problem [13]. The main originality of this work is the use for CBR of betweenness and analogical proportion, two domain-independent relations that can be implemented in many formalisms (though it has been considered only in the Boolean setting here), e.g. on strings [12], and that enables to apply to CBR the principles of interpolation and extrapolation, in addition to the already frequently used principle of approximation.

The extrapolation approach based on analogical reasoning can be connected to the work of adaptation knowledge learning (AKL) in CBR, as explained hereafter. Most approaches to AKL consist in learning adaptation rules using as training set a set of source case pairs $((\mathbf{x}^i, \mathbf{y}^i), (\mathbf{x}^j, \mathbf{y}^j))$ [7,8,10]. A similar idea consists in considering one of such pairs as an *adaptation case* [11,15]. With $(\mathbf{x}^1, \mathbf{y}^1)$ a retrieved case, it can be adapted to solve $\mathbf{x}^{\mathsf{tgt}}$ if the difference from $\mathbf{x}^1$ to $\mathbf{x}^{\mathsf{tgt}}$ equals the difference from $\mathbf{x}^i$ to $\mathbf{x}^j$, which can be formalized using analogical proportion by $\mathbf{x}^i{:}\mathbf{x}^j{::}\mathbf{x}^1{:}\mathbf{x}^{\mathsf{tgt}}$. Then, the adaptation consists in applying on $\mathbf{y}^1$ the difference from $\mathbf{y}^i$ to $\mathbf{y}^j$, which amounts to solving the equation $\mathbf{y}^i{:}\mathbf{y}^j{::}\mathbf{y}^1{:}\mathbf{y}$. Therefore, one contribution of this work is the formalization of *case-based adaptation* in terms of analogical proportions on the problem and solution spaces.

The idea of applying analogical inference based on analogical proportions in CBR has been first advocated and outlined recently [17], based on the fact that such an approach has given good quality results in classification [4] in machine learning on real datasets. Interestingly enough, analogical proportions can be always found in such datasets, and the results obtained can be favorably compared to those yielded by nearest neighbor methods. The ideas of interpolative and extrapolative reasoning can be found in the setting of conceptual spaces furnished with qualitative knowledge [20] with an illustration in [19]. Similar ideas have been applied to the completion of bases made of if-then rules in relation with the idea of analogical proportion [22] and to the interpolation between default rules [21]. However, none of these papers mentions a CBR perspective.

6   Conclusion

Classical CBR exploits each known case individually, on the basis of its similarity with the target problem. In this paper, we have proposed to extend this paradigm by taking advantage of betweenness and analogical proportion relations for linking the current situation to pairs and triples of known cases. By doing that, we are no longer just proposing the known solution of a case problem as an approximate solution to the current problem, but we are also taking advantage of interpolation and extrapolation ideas that are respectively embedded in betweenness and analogical proportion relations.

We have also provided a first experimental study that shows the precision and the correct answer rate of the approximation, interpolation, and extrapolation approaches on various types of functions. Each approach has its own merits. Approximation is simple and is often very efficient. Interpolation provides the most precise results, but may fail to give an answer. Extrapolation is superior to the two other methods when the underlying function is affine or close to be, i.e., exhibits a form of simplicity. Moreover, the results of extrapolation are not much correlated with the results of the two other methods. Experiments also show that combining the approaches may be beneficial. Clearly, one should investigate less straightforward ways for combining the approaches. More experiments would be also of interest for varying more the parameters and for dealing with non functional dependencies between problems and solutions. Experiments have been made on a variety of artificial datasets, showing that the present implementation of extrapolation is especially of interest for datasets close to obey to an affine Boolean function, studying if another form of extrapolation would do better, or if such datasets are often encountered in practice, is a matter of further work.

There are still two other perspectives worth of consideration. First, it would be of interest to see how incorporating domain/retrieval/adaptation knowledge in the process. Lastly, relations $\mathtt{Rel}_{\mathcal{P}}$ and $\mathtt{Rel}_{\mathcal{S}}$ have been defined here on $\mathbb{B}^p$, but allowing for gradual relations and for nominal and numerical features in the description of problems and solutions would be an important improvement. Such a latter development should be feasible since extensions of analogical proportions have been satisfactorily experienced in classification for handling nominal and numerical features [4], and the idea of betweenness seems as well to be susceptible of natural extensions to these situations.

References

1. Bergmann, R., Wilke, W.: Building and refining abstract planning cases by change of representation language. J. Artif. Intell. Res. **3**, 53–118 (1995)
2. Billingsley, R., Prade, H., Richard, G., Williams, M.-A.: Towards analogy-based decision - a proposal. In: Christiansen, H., Jaudoin, H., Chountas, P., Andreasen, T., Legind Larsen, H. (eds.) FQAS 2017. LNCS (LNAI), vol. 10333, pp. 28–35. Springer, Cham (2017). https://doi.org/10.1007/978-3-319-59692-1_3
3. Blum, M., Luby, M., Rubinfeld, R.: Self-testing/correcting with applications to numerical problems. J. Comput. Syst. Sci. **47**(3), 549–595 (1993)

4. Bounhas, M., Prade, H., Richard, G.: Analogy-based classifiers for nominal or numerical data. Int. J. Approx. Reasoning **91**, 36–55 (2017)
5. Branting, L.K., Aha, D.W.: Stratified case-based reasoning: reusing hierarchical problem solving episodes. In: Proceedings of the 14th International Joint Conference on Artificial Intelligence (IJCAI 1995), vol. 1, pp. 384–390, August 1995
6. Couceiro, M., Hug, N., Prade, H., Richard, G.: Analogy-preserving functions: a way to extend Boolean samples. In: Proceedings of the 26th International Joint Conference on Artificial Intelligence (IJCAI 2017), pp. 1575–1581. Morgan Kaufmann, Inc. (2017)
7. Craw, S., Wiratunga, N., Rowe, R.C.: Learning adaptation knowledge to improve case-based reasoning. Artif. Intell. **170**(16–17), 1175–1192 (2006)
8. d'Aquin, M., Badra, F., Lafrogne, S., Lieber, J., Napoli, A., Szathmary, L.: Case base mining for adaptation knowledge acquisition. In: Veloso, M.M. (ed.) Proceedings of the 20th International Joint Conference on Artificial Intelligence (IJCAI 2007), pp. 750–755. Morgan Kaufmann, Inc. (2007)
9. Dubois, D., Hüllermeier, E., Prade, H.: Flexible control of case-based prediction in the framework of possibility theory. In: Blanzieri, E., Portinale, L. (eds.) EWCBR 2000. LNCS, vol. 1898, pp. 61–73. Springer, Heidelberg (2000). https://doi.org/10.1007/3-540-44527-7_7
10. Hanney, K., Keane, M.T.: Learning adaptation rules from a case-base. In: Smith, I., Faltings, B. (eds.) EWCBR 1996. LNCS, vol. 1168, pp. 179–192. Springer, Heidelberg (1996). https://doi.org/10.1007/BFb0020610
11. Jarmulak, J., Craw, S., Rowe, R.: Using case-base data to learn adaptation knowledge for design. In: Proceedings of the 17th International Joint Conference on Artificial Intelligence (IJCAI 2001), pp. 1011–1016. Morgan Kaufmann, Inc. (2001)
12. Lepage, Y., Denoual, É.: Purest ever example-based machine translation: detailed presentation and assessment. Mach. Transl. **19**, 251–282 (2005)
13. McSherry, D.: Diversity-conscious retrieval. In: Craw, S., Preece, A. (eds.) ECCBR 2002. LNCS (LNAI), vol. 2416, pp. 219–233. Springer, Heidelberg (2002). https://doi.org/10.1007/3-540-46119-1_17
14. Miclet, L., Prade, H.: Handling analogical proportions in classical logic and fuzzy logics settings. In: Sossai, C., Chemello, G. (eds.) ECSQARU 2009. LNCS (LNAI), vol. 5590, pp. 638–650. Springer, Heidelberg (2009). https://doi.org/10.1007/978-3-642-02906-6_55
15. Minor, M., Bergmann, R., Görg, S.: Case-based adaptation of workflows. Inf. Syst. **40**, 142–152 (2014)
16. Prade, H., Richard, G.: From analogical proportion to logical proportions. Logica Universalis **7**(4), 441–505 (2013)
17. Prade, H., Richard, G.: Analogical proportions and analogical reasoning - an introduction. In: Aha, D.W., Lieber, J. (eds.) ICCBR 2017. LNCS (LNAI), vol. 10339, pp. 16–32. Springer, Cham (2017). https://doi.org/10.1007/978-3-319-61030-6_2
18. Richter, M.M., Weber, R.O.: Case-Based Reasoning: A Textbook. Springer, Heidelberg (2013). https://doi.org/10.1007/978-3-642-40167-1
19. Schockaert, S., Prade, H.: Interpolation and extrapolation in conceptual spaces: a case study in the music domain. In: Rudolph, S., Gutierrez, C. (eds.) RR 2011. LNCS, vol. 6902, pp. 217–231. Springer, Heidelberg (2011). https://doi.org/10.1007/978-3-642-23580-1_16
20. Schockaert, S., Prade, H.: Interpolative and extrapolative reasoning in propositional theories using qualitative knowledge about conceptual spaces. Artif. Intell. **202**, 86–131 (2013)

21. Schockaert, S., Prade, H.: Interpolative reasoning with default rules. In: Rossi, F. (ed.) Proceedings of the 23rd International Joint Conference on Artificial Intelligence (IJCAI 2013), Beijing, 3–9 August 2013, pp. 1090–1096 (2013)
22. Schockaert, S., Prade, H.: Completing symbolic rule bases using betweenness and analogical proportion. In: Prade, H., Richard, G. (eds.) Computational Approaches to Analogical Reasoning: Current Trends. SCI, vol. 548, pp. 195–215. Springer, Heidelberg (2014). https://doi.org/10.1007/978-3-642-54516-0_8
23. Smyth, B.: Case-based design. Ph.D. thesis, Trinity College, University of Dublin (1996)

Opening the Parallelogram: Considerations on Non-Euclidean Analogies

Pierre-Alexandre Murena[1(✉)], Antoine Cornuéjols[2], and Jean-Louis Dessalles[1]

[1] Télécom ParisTech - Université Paris Saclay,
46 rue Barrault, 75013 Paris, France
murena@telecom-paristech.fr
[2] UMR MIA-Paris, AgroParisTech, INRA, Université Paris Saclay,
5 rue Claude Bernard, 75005 Paris, France
antoine.cornuejols@agroparistech.fr

Abstract. Analogical reasoning is a cognitively fundamental way of reasoning by comparing two pairs of elements. Several computational approaches are proposed to efficiently solve analogies: among them, a large number of practical methods rely on either a parallelogram representation of the analogy or, equivalently, a model of proportional analogy. In this paper, we propose to broaden this view by extending the parallelogram representation to differential manifolds, hence spaces where the notion of vectors does not exist. We show that, in this context, some classical properties of analogies do not hold any longer. We illustrate our considerations with two examples: analogies on a sphere and analogies on probability distribution manifold.

Keywords: Analogy · Non-Euclidean geometry

1 Introduction

Making analogies is considered by psychologists as a basic cognitive ability of human beings [8], yet it remains a challenging task for artificial intelligence. An analogy designates a situation where a parallel can be drawn between two distinct and *a priori* unrelated domains. Computational models of analogical reasoning have been developed either to map semantic domains [6], to solve analogical problems on character strings, either structured [10] or unstructured [12], or to characterize the quality of an analogy [5]. Apart from its major cognitive interpretation, analogy plays an important role in case-based reasoning (CBR) [1]: In order to solve a new case, CBR focuses on previously encountered cases and aims to adapt solutions to the new problem. This adaptation process can be interpreted as *one-domain* analogical reasoning (which means that the source and target domains are identical).

A classical representation of analogies between vectors is the *parallelogram model*, which states that the four elements of the analogy obey a regularity rule

© Springer Nature Switzerland AG 2018
M. T. Cox et al. (Eds.): ICCBR 2018, LNAI 11156, pp. 597–611, 2018.
https://doi.org/10.1007/978-3-030-01081-2_39

close to a parallelogram in the representation space. For instance, the analogy "Paris is to France what Stockholm is to Sweden" may be interpreted in the form of the equality "Paris - France + Sweden = Stockholm". The first occurrences of this representation date back to the earliest researches [17] and have been resurrected in the recent years throughout the neural networks representation skills, in particular in the Word2Vec paradigm [15], [14] or even in visual object categorization [11]. The idea can be summed up as follows: Considering the analogical equation $A : B :: C : x$ with variable x, we assume that each element can be represented as a point in a Euclidean space and that the solution x is defined as the vector $x = C + B - A$. This representation is consistent with the axioms of analogical proportion, as shown in Sect. 2.4 of [13].

In this paper, we address the question of what happens when this representation is not true. Our main point is to loosen the structure of the representation space and to consider analogies on *Riemannian manifolds* instead of analogies in Euclidean spaces. A manifold can be understood intuitively as a space which is almost a Euclidean space, in the sense that it is locally Euclidean. Because of their curvature, the notion of vector does not exist in differential manifolds, hence the parallelogram representation is not valid in them. A way to get around that is to consider the notions of *geodesic curve* and *parallel transport* in Riemannian manifolds which allow one to build parallelogram-like shapes. These notions will be explained with more details in Sect. 2.4. We will show that the parallelogram construction is a particular case of the proposed procedure for Euclidean manifolds, but that non-Euclidean structures do not verify the classical axioms of analogy with this setting.

The remainder of this article is organized as follows. In Sect. 2, we present the general problem of analogies in non-Euclidean spaces. The problem is introduced with the help of a trivial example (analogies on spheres), but a more general explanation follows. In particular, we discuss the link between a found analogical dissimilarity and manifold curvature. In Sect. 3, we propose an application of the proposed theory in the case of a very particular space: the space of normal distributions. We will illustrate the developed ideas through a couple of simulations which show the impact of curvature. Lastly, we propose a discussion on proportional analogy in differential manifolds.

2   Non-Euclidean Spaces and Non-commutative Analogies

2.1   Intuition: Analogies on the Sphere $\mathbb{S}^2$

In order to understand the ideas at play, we propose to consider the example of analogies on a sphere. We denote by $\mathbb{S}^2$ the sphere defined as the subset of $\mathbb{R}^3$ defined as $\mathbb{S}^2 = \{x | x_1^2 + x_2^2 + x_3^2 = 1\}$. The sphere can be shown to be a differential manifold, and is obviously not Euclidean.

We consider three points A, B and C on the sphere and we try to solve the analogical equation $A : B :: C : x$. In the context of this example, we will consider three specific points, but the conclusions we will draw would be the same for any 3 points which are "not aligned" (in the sense that the third point is not on the shortest path between the two others).

In order to solve this analogy, an intuitive idea would be to apply the same procedure as described by the parallelogram rule. On Earth, it is possible to use the parallelogram rule directly on a small scale: Since Earth is locally flat, we can consider the floor as a vector space and apply a parallelogram rule by walking from A to C by keeping in mind the direction to go to B from A.

The same procedure can be used when the three points are very distant. In mathematical terms, we can formulate this procedure as a three steps method:

1. **Direction finding:** Estimation of the direction d to reach B from A following a geodesic (i.e. a path of minimal length).
2. **Parallel transport:** The direction vector is transported along the geodesic from A to C.
3. **Geodesic shooting:** Point D is reached by following the transported direction d' from point C.

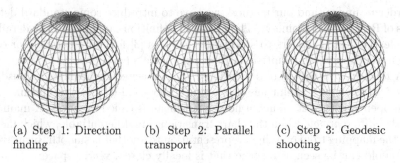

(a) Step 1: Direction finding

(b) Step 2: Parallel transport

(c) Step 3: Geodesic shooting

Fig. 1. Step by step resolution of the analogical equation $A : B :: C : x$ on the sphere $\mathbb{S}^2$. The solution found is $x = B$.

We consider for instance the case where B corresponds to the North pole and A and C are located on the equator. For simplicity purpose, we also suppose that the angle between the locations of A and C in the equator plane is $\pi/2$. The solution to this analogy is shown in Fig. 1.

The steps can be intuitively explained as follows. The first step consists in finding the shortest path from A to B: this path is characterized by the initial direction, which is mathematically encoded by a vector in the tangent space. The second step is of a different nature: The idea is to go along the shortest path from A to C while maintaining the initial direction vector "in the same direction" (the exact mathematical terminology will be precised in the next section). As an illustration of this, the second step can be seen as walking from A to C while maintaining one's nose parallel from one position to the other. The shortest path from A to C in our example is the equator and the initial direction is the vector pointing toward the North pole: Hence, step 2 is similar to walking from A to

C along the equator with the nose pointing toward the North pole at any time. The third step consists in following the transported initial direction the same time as done to join B from A in step 1.

Using this procedure, the solution of the analogical equation $A : B :: C : x$ is $x = B$. With the same procedure applied to the analogical equation $A : C :: B : x$, we obtain the solution $x = C$, which is in contradiction with the *exchange of the means* property of analogical proportion. However, we can easily verify that the other properties are verified:

- Symmetry of the 'as' relation: $C : B :: A : B$ and $B : C :: A : C$
- Determinism: the solution of $A : A :: B : x$ is $x = B$

In the following, we will call a **Non-commutative Analogy** an analogy which satisfies the symmetry of the 'as' relation and the determinism property, but not necessarily the exchange of the means. An analogical proportion is a more constrained case of a non-commutative analogy.

2.2   Reminder: Riemannian Geometry

In order to understand our method, we have to introduce some standard definitions of Riemannian geometry. The proposed definitions are not entirely detailed: we refer interested readers to standard references [3] for more details. For each notion, we propose an intuitive and less rigorous explanation.

A *topological manifold* of dimension d is a connected paracompact Hausdorff space for which every point has an open neighborhood U that is homeomorphic to an open subset of $\mathbb{R}^d$ (such a homeomorphism is called a *chart*). A manifold is called *differentiable* when the chart transitions are differentiable, which means that the mapping from one chart representation to another is smooth. Intuitively, a manifold can be seen as a space that is locally close a vector space.

A tangent vector ξ_x to a manifold $\mathcal{M}$ at point x can be defined as the equivalence class of differentiable curves γ such that $\gamma(0) = x$ modulo a first-order contact condition between curves. It can be interpreted as a "direction" from the point x (which only makes sense when $\mathcal{M}$ is a subset of a vector space). The set of all tangent vectors to $\mathcal{M}$ at x is denoted $T_x\mathcal{M}$ and called tangent space to $\mathcal{M}$ at x. The tangent space can be shown to have a vector space structure. When the tangent spaces $T_x\mathcal{M}$ are equipped with an inner-product g_x which varies smoothly from point to point, $\mathcal{M}$ is called a *Riemannian manifold*.

We define a connection ∇ as a mapping $C^\infty(T\mathcal{M}) \times C^\infty(T\mathcal{M}) \to C^\infty(T\mathcal{M})$ satisfying three properties that are not detailed here: A connection can be seen as a directional derivative of vector fields over the tangent space. It measures the way a tangent vector is modified when moving from one point to another in a given direction. A special connection, called the *Levi-Civita connection*, is defined as an intrinsic property of the Riemannian manifold which depends on its metric g only. This connection follows the "shape" of the manifold (here, the word shape is understood in its intuitive meaning).

These tools are used to define two notions that are fundamental in our interpretation of non-commutative analogies: parallel transport and geodesics. Let

$(\mathcal{M}, g)$ be a Riemannian manifold and let $\gamma : [0,1] \rightarrow \mathcal{M}$ be a smooth curve on $\mathcal{M}$. The curve γ is called a geodesic if $\nabla_{\dot\gamma}\dot\gamma = 0$ (which means that γ is auto-parallel, or keeps its tangent vector pointing "in the same direction" at any point). This definition of a geodesic can be shown to correspond to a minimum length curve between two points.

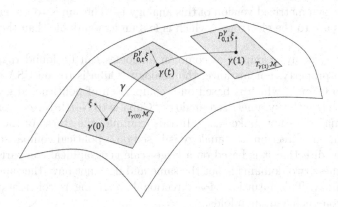

Fig. 2. Illustration of parallel transport on a differential manifolds. Vector ξ is transported along a curve γ. At any position t, we have $P^\gamma_{0,t}\xi \in T_{\gamma(t)}\mathcal{M}$.

A vector field X along γ is said to be parallel if $\nabla_{\dot\gamma}X = 0$. One can define the *parallel transport* as the application $P^\gamma_{t_0,t} : T_{\gamma(t_0)}\mathcal{M} \rightarrow T_{\gamma(t)}\mathcal{M}$ which maps any vector of the tangent space ξ at point $\gamma(t_0)$ to the corresponding value at $\gamma(t)$ for the parallel vector field X such that $X(\gamma(t_0)) = \xi$ (Fig. 2). Intuitively, the parallel transport along a curve keeps a tangent vector "pointing in the same direction".

2.3   Non-commutative Analogies

Following the ideas developed in Sect. 2.1, we propose the following definition for a non-commutative analogical proportion:

Definition 1. *A non-commutative analogy on a set X is a relation on X^4 such that, for every 4-uple $(A, B, C, D) \in X^4$, the following properties are observed:*

- *Symmetry of the 'as' relation: $R(A, B, C, D) \Leftrightarrow R(C, D, A, B)$*
- *Determinism: $R(A, B, A, x) \Rightarrow x = B$*

The second axiom (determinism) is slightly different from the original analogical proportion. For analogical proportion, two possible implications could be used to characterize determinism (the second characterization being the implication $R(A, A, B, x) \Rightarrow x = B$): One being true, the other is a consequence of the first. In non-commutative analogy, these two implications are not equivalent anymore.

Removing the exchange of the means from the definition of an analogy actually makes sense. The symmetry of the means operates in the cross-domain dimension of the analogy: Keeping this observation in mind, the symmetry of the means seems to be a natural property. In practice, it can be observed that the property is perceived as less natural in many examples. Consider for instance the well-known analogy "The sun is to the planets as the nucleus is to the electrons". The symmetrized version of this analogy is "The sun is to the nucleus as the planets are to the electrons", which is less understandable than the original analogy.

Moreover, many examples of common analogies can be found that do not satisfy this property. For instance, the analogy "Cuba is to the USA as North Korea is to China", which is based on a comparison of politics and geographic proximity, while the symmetrized analogy "Cuba is to North Korea as the USA are to China" does not make sense. In this example, the status of the terms is different: In one direction, the analogy is based on a political comparison, while in the other direction it is based on a large-scale geographical comparison. The nature of these two domains is not the same and does not have the same weight in the analogy. This intuition of a directional weighting is coherent with the model of non-euclidean manifolds.

2.4   Non-commutative Analogies on Riemannian Manifolds

Let $\mathcal{M}$ be a Riemannian manifold and $A, B, C, D \in \mathcal{M}$. We propose to find a geometric condition on the four points such that $A : B :: C : D$ defines a non-commutative analogy.

Definition 2. *The parallelogramoid algorithm $\mathcal{A}_p : \mathcal{M}^3 \mapsto \mathcal{M}$ is defined as follows. Consider $(A, B, C) \in \mathcal{M}^3$. Let $\gamma_1 : [0, 1] \to \mathcal{M}$ be a geodesic curve such that $\gamma_1(0) = A$ and $\gamma_1(1) = B$. Let $\xi \in T_A\mathcal{M}$ such that $\xi = \dot{\gamma}_1(0)$. Consider a geodesic curve $\gamma_2 : [0, 1] \to \mathcal{M}$ such that $\gamma_2(0) = A$ and $\gamma_2(1) = C$. Let γ_3 be the geodesic defined by $\gamma_3(0) = C$ and $\dot{\gamma}_3(0) = P_{0,1}^{\gamma_2}\xi$. Then $\mathcal{A}_p(A, B, C) = \gamma_3(1)$.*

Algorithm $\mathcal{A}_p$ corresponds to the procedure used in the case of a sphere. In general, the described procedure is not unique: The unicity of tangent vector ξ is not guaranteed. For instance, in the case of the sphere, if A and B correspond to the North and South poles, there exists an infinite number of such vectors ξ.

Theorem 1. *The relation $R(A, B, C, D) \vDash (\mathcal{A}_p(A, B, C) = D)$ defines a non-commutative analogy on $\mathcal{M}$.*

Proof. We would like to show that $C : D :: A : B$ (symmetry axiom) is correct with our construction. We use the tilde notation to describe the curves for this analogy. For instance, $\tilde{\gamma}_1$ is the geodesic from C to D, hence $\tilde{\gamma}_1 = \gamma_3$. Similarly, $\tilde{\gamma}_2 = -\gamma_2$, where $-\gamma$ designates the "opposite curve" (i.e. $\tilde{\gamma}_2(s) = \gamma(1-s)$). Since parallel transport is invertible, $\xi = P_{0,1}^{\tilde{\gamma}_2} P_{0,1}^{\gamma_2}\xi$. Thus, $\tilde{\gamma}_3$ is the geodesic curve such that $\tilde{\gamma}_3(0) = A$ and $\dot{\tilde{\gamma}}_3(0) = \xi$ and consequently $\tilde{\gamma}_3(1) = B$ (Fig. 3).

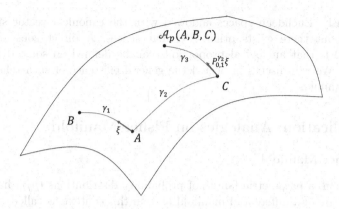

Fig. 3. Parallelogramoid procedure on a Riemannian manifold.

In general, the relation does not define a proportional analogy since symmetry of the means does not hold: $\mathcal{A}_p(A, B, C) \neq \mathcal{A}_p(A, C, B)$. We will show that we have equality only for a specific metric, called *flat metric*.

When $\mathcal{M} = \mathbb{R}^n$ endowed with the canonical inner-product, the proposed construction can be shown to be equivalent to the usual parallelogram rule, since a geodesic is defined as a straight line and parallel transport over a straight line is a simple translation of the original tangent vector. It can be shown that the converse is almost true: The manifolds for which $\mathcal{A}_p$ designs an analogical proportion have their *Ricci curvature* vanishing at any point.

Theorem 2. *The only Riemannian metrics g such that the relation defined by $R(A, B, C, D) \models (\mathcal{A}_p(A, B, C) = D)$ is an analogical proportion for any A, B and C are Ricci-flat.*

Proof. In this demonstration, we will consider the equivalent problem where we are given $A \in \mathcal{M}$ and $\xi_1, \xi_2 \in T_A\mathcal{M}$. With these notations, $B = \gamma_1(1)$ and $C = \gamma_2(1)$ where γ_1 is the geodesic drawn from A with initial vector ξ_1 and γ_2 is the geodesic drawn from A with initial vector ξ_2. Considering an infinitesimal parallelogramoid as defined in Definition 1.1 of [16], where δ is the distance between A and B, and ϵ the distance between A and C. Then the distance between C and $D = \mathcal{A}_p(A, B, C)$ is equal to

$$d = \delta \left(1 - \frac{\epsilon^2}{2} K(v, w) + \mathcal{O}(\epsilon^3 + \epsilon^2 \delta) \right)$$

where $K(v, w)$ is the sectional curvature in directions (v, w). In the case of analogical proportion, it can be verified that distance d must be equal to δ. Thus, we have necessarily $K(v, w) = 0$ and, by construction of Ricci curvature $Ric(v)$ as the average value of $K(v, w)$ when w runs over the unit sphere, we have the result.

Obviously, Euclidean spaces endowed with the canonical vector space are Ricci-flat, but there exists other Ricci-flat spaces. A direct consequence of Theorem 2 is that analogical proportions can be defined on some differential manifolds. We will discuss in Sect. 4 the general existence of such relations on general manifolds.

3   Application: Analogies on Fisher Manifold

3.1   Fisher Manifold

By definition, a parametric family of probability distributions $(p_\theta)_\theta$ has a natural structure of a differential manifold and, in this context, is called *statistical manifold*. Unless in general a manifold is not associated to a notion of distance or metric, *information geometry* states that there exists only one natural metric for statistical manifolds [4]. This metric, called *Fisher metric*, is defined as follows [7]:

$$g_{ab}(\theta) = \int p(x|\theta) \frac{\partial \log p(x|\theta)}{\partial \theta^a} \frac{\partial \log p(x|\theta)}{\partial \theta^b} dx \qquad (1)$$

It can be related to the variance of the relative difference between one distribution $p(x|\theta)$ and a neighbour $p(x|\theta + d\theta)$. For a more complete introduction to Fisher manifolds and more precise explanations on the nature of Fisher metric, we refer the reader to [2].

Among all possible statistical manifolds, we focus on the set of normal distributions, denoted by $\mathcal{N}(n)$. A complete description of the geometric nature of $\mathcal{N}(n)$ is given in [18]. As mentioned in this paper, a geodesic curve $(\mu(t), \Sigma(t))$ on $\mathcal{N}(n)$ is described by the following geodesic equation:

$$\begin{cases} \ddot{\Sigma} + \dot{\mu}\dot{\mu}^T - \dot{\Sigma}\Sigma^{-1}\dot{\Sigma} = 0 \\ \ddot{\mu} - \dot{\Sigma}\Sigma^{-1}\dot{\mu} = 0 \end{cases} \qquad (2)$$

In order to apply the parallelogrammoid algorithm and find non-commutative analogies on $\mathcal{N}(n)$, a fundamental issue has to be overcome. As explained in the reminder on Riemannian geometry, there exists two equivalent definitions of geodesic curves:

1. A geodesic can be interpreted as a curve of shortest length between two points. It is described by two points (A, B).
2. A geodesic can be interpreted as an auto-parallel curve, hence a curve generated by the parallel transport of its celerity. It is described by the initial state: the initial position $A \in \mathcal{M}$ and the initial celerity $\xi \in \mathcal{T}_A\mathcal{M}$.

These two definitions are equivalent but switching from the one to the other is a complex task in general. The second definition offers a simple computational model for geodesic shooting, since it corresponds to integrating a differential equation (Eq. 2 in our case), but using it to find a geodesic between two points requires to find initial celerity ξ.

In the scope of this paper, we consider the algorithm for minimal geodesic on $\mathcal{N}(n)$ proposed by [9]. The proposed algorithm is based on the simple idea to shoot a geodesic using initial celerity ξ using Eq. 2 and to update ξ based on the euclidean difference between the endpoint of the integrated curve and the actual expected endpoint. The algorithm is empirically shown to converge for lower dimensions ($n = 2$ or $n = 3$).

3.2   Experimental Results

We present the results of the parallelogrammoid procedures $\mathcal{A}_p(A, B, C)$ an $\mathcal{A}_p(A, C, B)$ obtained for various bidimensional multinormal distributions. We use the classical representation of the multivariate normal distributions by the isocontour of its covariance matrix, centered at the mean of the distribution. The results we display are presented as follows:

- In black: Intermediate points in the trajectories γ_1, γ_2 and γ_3.
- In blue: Normal distribution A.
- In green: Normal distribution B.
- In cyan: Normal distribution C.
- In red: Normal distribution $D_1 = \mathcal{A}_p(A, B, C)$.
- In magenta: Normal distribution $D_2 = \mathcal{A}_p(A, C, B)$.

Case 1: Fixed Covariance Matrix
For the first case, we fix $\mu_A = (0, 0)$, $\mu_B = (1, 1)$, $\mu_C = (0, 1)$ and $\Sigma_1 = \Sigma_B = \Sigma_C = \begin{pmatrix} 1 & 0 \\ 0 & .1 \end{pmatrix}$.

The space of normal distributions with fixed covariance matrix is euclidean, which implies that algorithm $\mathcal{A}_p$ is equivalent to the parallelogram rule under these conditions and that the defined relation is an analogical proportion. We observe on Fig. 4 that the trajectories of means in the space correspond to a parallelogram and that the two solutions are identical.

Case 2: Fixed Mean in Source Domain, Fixed Covariance from Source to Target
For the second case, we fix $\mu_A = \mu_B = (0, 0)$, $\mu_C = (0, 2)$ and, for covariance matrices, $\Sigma_A = \Sigma_C = \begin{pmatrix} 1 & 0 \\ 0 & .1 \end{pmatrix}$ and $\Sigma_B = \begin{pmatrix} .1 & 0 \\ 0 & 1 \end{pmatrix}$.

With these parameters, we observe that the two results are different (Fig. 5). The result of $\mathcal{A}_p(A, B, C)$ corresponds to the intuition that D will have the same mean as C and the same covariance change as B compared to A. However, for $\mathcal{A}_p(A, C, B)$, the results are non-intuitive: the mean of distribution D is different from the mean of C. It can be explained by the fact that the trajectory varies both in μ and Σ. The geometric properties of information require that these two dimensions are related together and that the change in μ depends on the change in Σ.

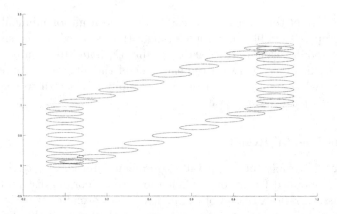

Fig. 4. Results for case 1 (fixed covariance matrix setting)

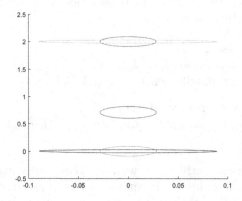

Fig. 5. Results for case 2 (fixed mean in source, fixed covariance from source to target)

Case 3: Symmetric Distributions

For the third case, we fix $\mu_A = (0,0), \mu_B = (1,0)$ and $\mu_C = (0,1)$, and, for covariance matrices, $\Sigma_B = \Sigma_C = \begin{pmatrix} 1 & -.5 \\ -.5 & .5 \end{pmatrix}$ and $\Sigma_A = \begin{pmatrix} 1 & .5 \\ .5 & .5 \end{pmatrix}$. We notice on Fig. 6 that the trajectory leads to a distributions with "flat" covariance matrix (with one large and one very small eigenvalue). No real intuitive interpretation can be given of the observed trajectory (which shows that information geometry cannot explain shape deformations, here ellipse deformations, as expected by human beings).

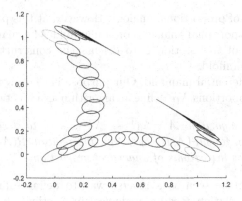

Fig. 6. Results for case 3 (symmetric)

Case 4: Slight Perturbation

For the third case, we fix $\mu_A = (0,0), \mu_B = (1,0)$ and $\mu_C = (0,1)$, and, for covariance matrices, $\Sigma_A = \begin{pmatrix} 1 & .5 \\ .5 & .5 \end{pmatrix}$, $\Sigma_B = \begin{pmatrix} 1 & -.5 \\ -.5 & .5 \end{pmatrix}$ and $\Sigma_C = \begin{pmatrix} 1 & .6 \\ .6 & .6 \end{pmatrix}$. Covariance matrix Σ_C is slightly different from Σ_1. If they were equal, the parallelogramoid would be closed. However, the slight modification introduces a perturbation large enough to make $\mathcal{A}_p(A, B, C) \neq \mathcal{A}_p(A, C, B)$ (Fig. 7). Such artifacts could introduce larger errors in case the distributions are not know with good precision (for instance if they were estimated from data).

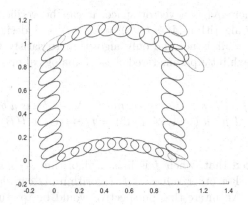

Fig. 7. Results for case 4 (slight perturbation)

4   Proportional Analogies on Manifolds

In previous sections, we have shown that the intuition of what an analogy can be in a differential manifold leads to a less constrained definition of analogies than the definition of proportional analogy. However, at this point of the paper, the existence of proportional analogies on a manifold $\mathcal{M}$ remains an open question. The purpose of this section is to discuss the construction of analogical proportions on a manifold.

Let $\mathcal{M}$ be a differential manifold. Our purpose is to design an algorithm to build analogical proportions. We define an algorithm as a function $\mathcal{A} : \mathcal{M}^3 \mapsto \mathcal{M}$.

Definition 3. *An algorithm $\mathcal{A} : \mathcal{M}^3 \mapsto \mathcal{M}$ is said to design an analogical proportion on $\mathcal{M}$ if, for all $(A, B, C) \in \mathcal{M}^3$, the relation $R(A, B, C, D) \models (D = \mathcal{A}(A, B, C))$ satisfies the axioms of analogical proportion.*

Definition 3 can be seen as a reverse way to define solutions of analogical equations. If a relation R is an analogical proportion over $\mathcal{M}$ designed by algorithm $\mathcal{A}$, then $x = \mathcal{A}(a, b, c)$ is the unique solution of equation $R(a, b, c, x)$ where x is the variable.

The following proposition offers an alternative characterization of proportion-designing algorithms based on global characteristics.

Proposition 1. *Algorithm $\mathcal{A}$ designs an analogical proportion if and only if the following three conditions hold true for any $(A, B, C) \in \mathcal{M}^3$:*

1. $\mathcal{A}(A, B, A) = B$ or $\mathcal{A}(A, A, B) = B$
2. $\mathcal{A}(A, B, C) = \mathcal{A}(A, C, B)$
3. $B = \mathcal{A}(C, \mathcal{A}(A, B, C), A)$.

Proof. The proof is a direct consequence of the axioms of analogical proportion.

In the case where $\mathcal{M}$ is a vector space, it can be verified easily that the parallelogram rule algorithm $\mathcal{A}(A, B, C) = C + B - A$ designs an analogical proportion. However, it is not the only algorithm to satisfy this property. In Proposition 2, we exhibit a parametered class of analogical proportion designing algorithms.

Proposition 2. *If $\mathcal{M}$ is a vector space and $f : \mathcal{M} \mapsto \mathcal{M}$ is a bijective mapping, then algorithm $\mathcal{A}_f$ defined by $\mathcal{A}_f(A, B, C) = f^{-1}(f(C) + f(B) - f(A))$ designs analogical proportion.*

It can be noticed that, when f is linear, algorithm $\mathcal{A}_f$ corresponds to the parallelogram rule. For other values of f, algorithm $\mathcal{A}_f$ can define proportions of another nature. An interesting perspective would be to study if these non-trivial proportions on a vector space can be related analogical proportions on a manifold.

The result of Proposition 2 can be generalized to any spaces:

Proposition 3. *Consider E and F two isomorphic sets with $f : E \mapsto F$ a corresponding isomorphism. If $\mathcal{A}_F : F^3 \mapsto F$ designs an analogical proportion on F then algorithm $\mathcal{A}_E : E^3 \mapsto E$ defined by $\mathcal{A}_E(a, b, c) = f^{-1}(\mathcal{A}_F(f(a), f(b), f(c)))$ designs an analogical proportion on E.*

Based on this result, it can be shown that analogical proportion defining algorithms exist on any manifold.

Theorem 3. *For any manifold $\mathcal{M}$, there exists an algorithm that defines analogical proportion on $\mathcal{M}$.*

Proof. Consider a finite atlas $\mathcal{A} = \{(U_\alpha, \psi_\alpha) | \alpha \in \{1, \ldots, m\}\}$. Such an atlas exists for m large enough. In this definition, U_α corresponds to a domain on $\mathcal{M}$ and $\psi_\alpha : U_\alpha \mapsto \mathcal{B}_n(0,1)$ is an homeomorphism from U_α onto the unitary ball $\mathcal{B}_n(0,1)$ on $\mathbb{R}^n$ (where n is the dimension of $\mathcal{M}$). If we denote $E_k = \{x \in \mathbb{R}^n | 2(k-1) < x_1 < 2(k+1)\}$, one can equivalently extend the mapping ψ_k to be homeomorphisms between U_k and E_k (Fig. 8).

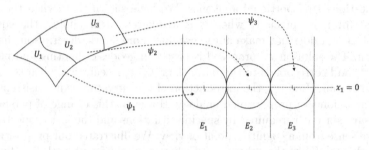

Fig. 8. Construction of a bijective mapping between n-dimensional manifold $\mathcal{M}$ and an open subset of $\mathbb{R}^n$. For simplicity purpose, the subsets U_k are presented as disjoint, which they are not.

We build a function $\psi : \mathcal{M} \mapsto \bigcap_{k=1}^m E_k$ as follows: If $x \in U_k \backslash \bigcap_{i>k} U_i$, then $\psi(x) = \psi_k(x) + e_k$ where e_k is the vector with first component equal to $2k$ and all other components equal to 0. This function defines a bijective mapping. Since $\bigcap_{k=1}^m E_k$ is an open subset of $\mathbb{R}^n$, there exists a bijection $\bigcap_{k=1}^m E_k \mapsto \mathbb{R}^n$. The theorem follows from Proposition 3 and the fact that $\mathbb{A}_{\mathbb{R}^n} \neq \emptyset$.

Theorem 3 is fundamental since it states the existence of analogical proportions on manifolds, which seems to invalidate the intuitions exposed with the parallelogrammoid method. However, the intuitive "validity" of the existing analogies (and in particular of the analogies produced by the proof) is not clear since they appear to be highly irregular since they are not continuous.

These observations point out a deficiency in the definition of analogical proportion, which comes from its main applicative domains. The definitions of analogical proportion were first designed for applications in character-string domains [12] and were discussed for applications in other non-continuous domains [13] such as analogies between finite sets. Among real continuous applications (hence applications which do not involve a discretization of the continuous space), most are based on parallelogram rule on a vector space. When defining analogical proportions on continuous spaces, a continuity property is also desirable, which is not induced by the definition of analogical proportion. Intuitively, this property makes sense: If two analogical problems are close, it is expected that their solutions will be close as well.

The question of the existence of analogical proportion defining algorithms that are also continuous (in the sense of a function $\mathcal{M}^3 \mapsto \mathcal{M}$) remains open at this step. It is impossible to adapt the proof of Theorem 3 in order to make the mapping continuous. More generally, the result cannot be directly adapted from Proposition 3.

5   Conclusion

In this paper, we proposed an extension of the well-known naive parallelogram representation of proportional analogies. We have shown that, when the space is curved (or more precisely when it is a differential manifold), the equality $D = C + B - A$ does not make any sense and more subtle descriptions have to be chosen. The solution we proposed is based on geodesic shooting and parallel transport, and corresponds to the parallelogram representation when the manifold is euclidean. However, the introduction of the curvature is inconsistent with one of the axioms of proportional analogy. However, this change of perspective is necessary since it is required by specific situations and the lost properties did not make sense from a cognitive point of view. We illustrated our proposition on two simple manifolds: the sphere and Fisher manifold for normal distributions. In the future, tests on more complex manifolds would be of interest, especially for analogies between objects which belong naturally to non-euclidean spaces. A study of feature relatedness in concept spaces and how such correlations induce a curve of the space is also directly connected to potential applications.

In addition, a work has to be done in the direction of finding relations of analogical proportions in manifolds. Until now, researches have focused mainly on more simple sets (boolean analogies, analogies between sets, character strings, or vectors) but some structures cannot be represented by simple objects and will require defining proportional analogies on manifolds, for instance shape spaces. We have shown the existence of analogical proportions in manifolds, but could not show the existence of *continuous* analogical proportions, which would be a fundamental property of a good intuitive proportion. The existence of continuous analogies remains an open question that will have to be solved in future researches.

Acknowledgments. This research is supported by the program Futur & Ruptures (Institut Mines Télécom).

References

1. Aamodt, A., Plaza, E.: Case-based reasoning: foundational issues, methodological variations, and system approaches. AI Commun. **7**(1), 39–59 (1994)
2. Amari, S.I.: Differential-Geometrical Methods in Statistics, vol. 28. Springer, New York (2012). https://doi.org/10.1007/978-1-4612-5056-2
3. Boothby, W.M.: An Introduction to Differentiable Manifolds and Riemannian Geometry, vol. 120. Academic Press, New York (1986)
4. Cencov, N.N.: Statistical Decision Rules and Optimal Inference, vol. 53. American Mathematical Soc., Providence (2000)
5. Cornuéjols, A., Ales-Bianchetti, J.: Analogy and induction: which (missing) link? In: Workshop "Advances in Analogy Research: Integration of Theory and Data from Cognitive, Computational and Neural Sciences". Sofia, Bulgaria (1998)
6. Falkenhainer, B., Forbus, K.D., Gentner, D.: The structure-mapping engine: algorithm and examples. Artif. Intell. **41**(1), 1–63 (1989)
7. Fisher, R.A.: Theory of statistical estimation. In: Mathematical Proceedings of the Cambridge Philosophical Society, vol. 22, pp. 700–725. Cambridge University Press, Cambridge (1925)
8. Goswami, U.: Analogical Reasoning in Children. Psychology Press, Hove (2013)
9. Han, M., Park, F.C.: DTI segmentation and fiber tracking using metrics on multivariate normal distributions. J. Math. Imaging Vis. **49**(2), 317–334 (2014)
10. Hofstadter, D., Mitchell, M.: The copycat project: a model of mental fluidity and analogy-making. In: Fluid Concepts and Creative Analogies, pp. 205–267. Basic Books Inc., New York (1995)
11. Hwang, S.J., Grauman, K., Sha, F.: Analogy-preserving semantic embedding for visual object categorization. In: Dasgupta, S., Mcallester, D. (eds.) Proceedings of the 30th International Conference on Machine Learning (ICML 2013), vol. 28, pp. 639–647. JMLR Workshop and Conference Proceedings, May 2013. http://jmlr.org/proceedings/papers/v28/juhwang13.pdf
12. Lepage, Y.: Solving analogies on words: an algorithm. In: Proceedings of the 17th international conference on Computational linguistics, vol. 1, pp. 728–734. Association for Computational Linguistics (1998)
13. Miclet, L., Bayoudh, S., Delhay, A.: Analogical dissimilarity: definition, algorithms and two experiments in machine learning. J. Artif. Intell. Res. **32**, 793–824 (2008). http://dblp.uni-trier.de/db/journals/jair/jair32.html#MicletBD08
14. Mikolov, T., Chen, K., Corrado, G., Dean, J.: Efficient estimation of word representations in vector space. CoRR abs/1301.3781 (2013). http://dblp.uni-trier.de/db/journals/corr/corr1301.html#abs-1301-3781
15. Mikolov, T., Yih, W.T., Zweig, G.: Linguistic regularities in continuous space word representations. In: HLT-NAACL, pp. 746–751 (2013)
16. Ollivier, Y.: A visual introduction to Riemannian curvatures and some discrete generalizations. In: Analysis and Geometry of Metric Measure Spaces: Lecture Notes of the 50th Séminaire de Mathématiques Supérieures (SMS), Montréal, pp. 197–219 (2011)
17. Rumelhart, D.E., Abrahamson, A.A.: A model for analogical reasoning. Cognit. Psychol. **5**(1), 1–28 (1973). http://www.sciencedirect.com/science/article/pii/0010028573900236
18. Skovgaard, L.T.: A Riemannian geometry of the multivariate normal model. Scand. J. Stat. **11**, 211–223 (1984)

Experiments in Learning to Solve Formal Analogical Equations

Rafik Rhouma and Philippe Langlais[(✉)]

RALI, Université de Montréal, DIRO, C.P. 6128, Succ Centre-Ville,
Montréal, Québec H3C3J7, Canada
felipe@iro.umontreal.ca
http://rali.iro.umontreal.ca

Abstract. Analogical learning is a lazy learning mechanism which maps input forms (e.g. strings) to output ones, thanks to analogies identified in a training material. It has proven effective in a number of Natural Language Processing (NLP) tasks such as machine translation. One challenge with this approach is the solving of so-called analogical equations. In this paper, we investigate how structured learning can be used for learning to solve formal analogical equations. We evaluate our learning procedure on several test sets and show that we can improve upon fair baselines.

Keywords: Natural language processing · Formal analogy
Solving analogical equation

1 Introduction

A *proportional analogy* (or analogy for short) — noted $[x : y :: z : t]$ — is a 4-uple of entities which reads "x is to y as z is to t", as in $[Paris : France :: Roma : Italy]$. In this work, we concentrate on *formal analogies*, that is, analogies at the formal or graphemic level, such as $[weak : weaker :: clean : cleaner]$.

Identifying proportional analogies is one core element of *analogical learning*, a learning strategy that can be explained as follows. Given a training set of pairs of input and output forms $\mathcal{D} \equiv \{(x, x')\}$, and an unknown input form u, analogical learning produces output entities u' by searching input elements in $\mathcal{D}$ that define with u an analogy $[x : y :: z : u]$. Those analogies are assumed to carry over the output space; that is, u' should be a solution of a so-called *analogical equation* $[x' : y' :: z' : ?]$, where x', y', z' are output forms corresponding in the training material to x, y and z respectively.

Let us illustrate those concepts by an example taken from [11] where the authors applied analogical learning to translate terms of the medical domain. Assume we have a training set of terms in Finnish along with their translation into English: $\mathcal{D} = \{(beeta\text{-}agonistit, adrenergic\ beta\text{-}agonists), (beetasalpaa\text{-}jat, adrenergic\ beta\text{-}antagonists), (alfa\text{-}agonistit, adrenergic\ alpha\text{-}agonists)\}$. We might translate the (unseen at training time) Finnish term *alfasalpaajat* into English by:

© Springer Nature Switzerland AG 2018
M. T. Cox et al. (Eds.): ICCBR 2018, LNAI 11156, pp. 612–626, 2018.
https://doi.org/10.1007/978-3-030-01081-2_40

1. identifying the input analogy:
   [*beeta-agonistit* : *beetasalpaajat* :: *alfa-agonistit* : *alfasalpaajat*]
2. projecting it into the equation:
   [*adrenergic beta-agonists* : *adrenergic beta-antagonists* ::
   adrenergic alpha-agonists : ?]
3. and solving it: *adrenergic alpha-antagonists* is one solution.

This learning paradigm has been tested in a number of NLP tasks, including grapheme-to-phoneme conversion [21], machine translation [10,13,15], transliteration [5,9], unsupervised morphology acquisition [19], as well as parsing [2,14]. It has also been used with some success to inflate training material, in tasks where we lack training data, as in [1] for hand-written character recognition and in machine translation [20].

One essential component of an analogical device is an algorithm for solving analogical equations. In [18], the authors observed that learning embeddings of words on large quantities of texts captures analogical regularities (both semantic and formal) that can be used for solving an analogical equation. One distinctive characteristic of the solvers we consider in this study is that they can produce forms never seen at training time, while the approach of [18] can only propose forms for which an embedding has been trained (by exploiting huge quantities of data). On the other hand, our solvers can only deal with formal analogies, which is a limitation.

There are several operational analogical solvers on forms. Notably, in [12], Lepage proposes an algorithm which aligns two by two (like an edit-distance alignment) the forms of an equation. Those alignments are in turn used to guide the production of a solution. In [19], the authors propose a definition of formal analogy which lends itself to a solver that may be implemented by a finite-state automaton. Both solvers have the advantage that no training is required for the solver to be deployed. On the other hand, they both produce several solutions, among which typically only one is valid.

In this paper, we study the averaged structured perceptron algorithm [3] for learning to solve analogical equations on forms. We present in Sect. 2, two very different state-of-the-art solvers we compare against. We describe in Sect. 3 the structured learning framework we deployed. We present in Sect. 4 two datasets we used for training and testing solvers. We report our results in Sect. 5 and conclude in Sect. 6.

2 Reference Solvers

2.1 Mikolov et al. (word2vec)

In [18], the authors discovered that the vector space induced by word2vec, a popular toolkit for computing word embeddings, has the interesting property of preserving analogies, that is, the difference of the vector representation of two words x and y in an analogy [x : y :: z: t] is a vector which is close to the

word2vec ($d = 300$)	unreadable *0.574*, illegible *0.496*, scrawled *0.496*, scribbled *0.496*, executor *0.475*
alea ($\rho = 10$)	undabloe *4*, undableo *3*, unabldoe *2*, undoeabl *2*, unodable *2*
alea ($\rho = 50$)	**undoable** *63* undabloe *45*, undaoble *27*, dunoable *27*, unadoble *22*
early (*beam* = 100)	**undoable** *510.9*, undaoble *488.9*, undabole *488.9*, undabloe *488.9*, unadbloe *488.94*

Fig. 1. 5-first solutions produced by different solvers to the equation [*reader : unreadable :: doer : ?*]. See the text for the details about the configurations. Note that word2vec ranks words in the vocabulary, while other solvers generate their solutions.

difference of the vectors associated to the other two words z and t. Therefore, their approach to solve an analogical equation consists in computing:

$$\hat{t} = \operatorname*{argmax}_{t \in V} \cos(t, z - x + y) \tag{1}$$

While this solver can handle both semantic and formal analogies, it can only produce solutions that have been seen at training time, which is of low interest in our case. It is also very slow to run since it requires to go over the full vocabulary of the application V in order to find the word with the best match. This would for instance hardly scale to a vocabulary composed of word sequences in a given language. Nevertheless, the ability of embedding methods to capture analogies, has received a lot of traction recently, leading to performances we can reproduce and compare against. We implemented Eq. 1, making use of embeddings trained by the authors[1]. See Fig. 1 for solutions produced by this solver.

2.2   Langlais et al. (alea)

In [22], the authors proposed a very different solver which relies on the following theorem:

Theorem 1. *t is a solution to [x : y :: z: ?]* ***iff*** *$t \in \{y \circ z\} \setminus x$*

where:

w ∘ **v** the *shuffle* of w and v, is the regular language of the forms obtained by selecting (without replacement) alternatively in w and v, sequences of characters in a left-to-right manner. For instance, both strings <u>unreadodableer</u> and <u>dunoreaderable</u> belong to <u>unreadable</u> ∘ *doer*.

w**v** the *complementary set* of w with respect to v, is the set of strings formed by removing from w, in a left-to-right manner, the symbols in v. For instance, *unodable* and *undoable* both belong to *unreadodableer* \\ *reader*.

---

[1] Over 3 million vectors of dimension 300 for words seen at least 5 times; trained with the skip-gram model on the large Google news corpus.

This theorem states that we can built a finite-state machine that recognizes the set of all the solutions of an analogical equation. However, building such an automaton may face combinatorial issues, which makes this approach practical for analogies involving short enough forms. The algorithm described in [11] that we implemented in this work consists in sampling randomly ρ elements of the shuffle language, then computing the complementary operation. This way, the automaton is never constructed, leading to a very time efficient algorithm. On the other hand, the solver may fail to deliver the correct solution if the number of shuffles considered (ρ) is to small. Since several combinations of shuffling and complementing operations may lead to the same solution, we can rank solutions in decreasing order of their frequency. See Fig. 1 for the solutions produced by two configurations of this solver.

3 Structured Learning

Given a function $g : \mathcal{I} \times \mathcal{O} \to \mathbb{R}$ which evaluates a fit between an object i in an input domain $\mathcal{I}$, to an object in a structured output domain $\mathcal{O}$, we seek to find:

$$\hat{t} = \underset{t \in \mathcal{O}}{\operatorname{argmax}}\, g(i, t) \tag{2}$$

In this work, input objects are triplets of strings $i \equiv (x, y, z)$ over an alphabet $\mathcal{A}$ and output objects are strings over this alphabet. We assume a linear model for $g = \langle \mathbf{w}, \Phi(i, t) \rangle$ parametrized by a feature vector $\mathbf{w}$ in $\mathbb{R}^K$ and a feature map $\Phi(i, t)$ decomposed into K binary feature fonctions $\phi_k : (i, t) \to \{0, 1\}$ controlled by the scalar $\mathbf{w}_k$. The vector $\mathbf{w}$ defines the parameters of the model we seek to adjust in order to maximise the quality of predictions made over a training set $\mathcal{D} = \{((x, y, z), t)\}$. In this work, we use variants of the averaged structured perceptron algorithm [3] for doing so, that we sketch hereafter.

3.1 Average Structured Perceptron

The standard version (standard) of the averaged structured perceptron algorithm is depicted in Fig. 2. The algorithm is based on the assumption that the inference (argmax) can be computed exactly, which is often impractical. In [6], the authors demonstrate that in cases of inexact search (our case), we should only make *valid updates*, that is, updates where the 1-best hypothesis has a higher model score than the correct sequence. There are several strategies for this. One solution (safe) consists in conducting the update after checking it is valid. While this variant is guaranteed to converge, it typically throws too many training examples. Another solution initially suggested in [4] consists in updating whenever the reference solution is not anymore attainable from the current search space, in which case the hypothesis with the largest score so far is being used for the update. This variant known as early update (early), has the drawback that only a fraction of an example is concerned by the update, leading to longer training times. Other alternatives are proposed in [6]; notably

$$\mathbf{w}, \mathbf{w}_a \leftarrow 0$$
$$e \leftarrow 0$$
repeat
$\quad e \leftarrow e + 1$
$\quad$ **for all** example $(i, t) \in D$ **do**
$\quad\quad \hat{t} = \text{argmax}_y\, \mathbf{w}^T \Phi(i, t)$
$\quad\quad$ **if** $\hat{t} \neq t$ **then**
$\quad\quad\quad \mathbf{w} \leftarrow \mathbf{w} + \Phi(i, t) - \Phi(i, \hat{t})$
$\quad\quad\quad \mathbf{w}_a \leftarrow \mathbf{w}_a + \mathbf{w}$
until converged
return $\mathbf{w}_a/e.|\mathcal{D}|$

Fig. 2. Standard averaged structured perceptron algorithm.

a variant (`late`) which selects the deepest node in the search space which is a valid update (the hypothesis with the largest prefix p). This way, the update is conducted on larger strings.

3.2   Search

In what follows, $x[i]$ stands for the ith symbol of string x,[2] $|x|$ is the length (the number of symbols) of x, $x[i:]$ designates the suffix of x starting at the ith symbol; and $x.y$ designates the concatenation of x with y.

For solving an equation $[x : y :: z: ?]$, our structured solver explores a search space in which a state is represented by a 5-uple $<s, i, j, k, p>$, meaning that $x[i:]$, $y[j:]$ and $z[k:]$ are yet to be visited, that p is the current prefix of a solution, and that s is the sequence of the shuffle being considered. The initial state of the search space is $<\epsilon, 0, 0, 0, \epsilon>$ (where ϵ designates the empty string) and goal states are of the form $<\epsilon, |x|, |y|, |z|, sol>$, where sol is a solution to the equation. There are three actions X, Y, and Z that can be applied to a given state and which are described in Fig. 3. It is worth noting that action X, the action which implements the complementation operation, is the only one which contributes to add symbols to the solution being generated. This is rather different from typical search spaces, where most actions do impact immediately the solution produced, as for instance in machine translation.

To further illustrate the singularity of the search procedure, let us consider nodes $n_1 = <uu, 0, 1, 1, \epsilon>$ that is generated from the initial one after two consumption operations took place (Y and Z, in whatever order), and node $n_2 = <undou, 0, 4, 1, \epsilon>$, that is reached after four Y and one Z operations. Three operations may expand n_1, that are illustrated in Fig. 4 (left part), while two expansions are possible from n_2 (right part). The X and Y operations are just reading one symbol in either y or z respectively, adding the read symbol to the shuffle. Since the y string has been entirely read in the n_2 configuration, only Z is considered. Because in both n_1 and n_2 the shuffle ends with u the symbol in $x[0]$, a complementary operation X is possible from both nodes. In the second

---

[2] The first valid index is 0.

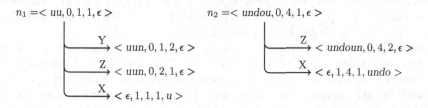

$< s, i, j, k, p >$

init: $< \epsilon, 0, 0, 0, \epsilon >$

goal: $< \epsilon, |x|, |y|, |z|, sol >$

$\xrightarrow{Y} < s.y[j], i, j+1, k, p >$ iff $j < |y|$

$\xrightarrow{Z} < s.z[k], i, j, k+1, p >$ iff $k < |z|$

$\xrightarrow{X} < \epsilon, i+1, j, k, p.p_s >$ iff $s \equiv p_s.x[i]$

Fig. 3. The three operations defining the search space of the structured learning solvers.

$n_1 = < uu, 0, 1, 1, \epsilon >$ $n_2 = < undou, 0, 4, 1, \epsilon >$

$\xrightarrow{Y} < uun, 0, 1, 2, \epsilon >$ $\xrightarrow{Z} < undoun, 0, 4, 2, \epsilon >$

$\xrightarrow{Z} < uun, 0, 2, 1, \epsilon >$ $\xrightarrow{X} < \epsilon, 1, 4, 1, undo >$

$\xrightarrow{X} < \epsilon, 1, 1, 1, u >$

Fig. 4. Expansions of two nodes belonging to the search space built to solve the equation [*unread : undo :: unreadable : ?*].

configuration, for instance, the shuffle is *undou*, which complementation with *u* leads to the sequence *undo* being generated in the prefix of the resulting node. Since X is the only operation that generates symbols of the solution, the search space is populated with a lot of nodes with an empty prefix (5 out of the 7 nodes in Fig. 4).

As often in problems of interest, the search space is too huge for a systematic exploration, and heuristics have to be applied in practice. First, the search space is organized as a graph, which avoids developing an hypothesis twice. This safely reduces the search space, without sacrificing optimality. For instance, the node resulting from n_2 in Fig. 4 after an X operation may also be generated from the initial state by applying in that order the sequence of operations: Z, Y, X, Y, Y, and Y. Second, we deploy a beam-search strategy to prune less promising hypotheses. Because of the specificity of the search space, the comparison of hypotheses that lead to the same prefix p is difficult, and we had to resort to a sophisticated beam policy (controlled by a metaparameter *beam*) which details are beyond the scope of this paper. But suffices it to say that in order to avoid filtering too many hypotheses, we have to resort to a third filtering strategy which consists in enforcing that at most η actions Y or Z happen before an action X occurs. The metaparameter η controls the number of hypotheses that can grow without generating a symbol of the solution. We experiment with values of this metaparameter in Sect. 5.

3.3 Features

As mentioned earlier, the feature map is defined by a number of binary feature functions that apply to any information available in a search node $<s, i, j, k, p>$

created while solving the equation $[x : y :: z: ?]$. In order to guide the search we rely on 3 families of features:

language model (14 features) because our solver produces a subset of permutations of the same form as a solution, ranking those solutions with a language model will favor hypotheses with a prefix that is likely in a given language. We compute the likelihood of a prefix p according to an n-gram language model trained on a large set of external data. Binary features check that the likelihood falls into specific predetermined range of probabilities. We also have features of the form $prob(p_i|p_{i-1} \ldots p_{i-n+1}) < \delta$ that fire whenever a symbol of p is predicted with less probability than δ. We also deploy similar features for the shuffle s under consideration.

edit-distance (20 features) A solution to a formal equation $[x : y :: z: ?]$ typically shares sequences of symbols of y and z. For instance in [*reader : unreadable :: doer : ?*], the solution *undoable* shares with *doer* the affix *do*. We compute the edit-distance between the prefix p and the forms y and z with the intuition that solutions that most resemble one of those strings are more likely to be good ones. Edit-distances are transformed into binary fonctions (binning into 10 intervals).

search-based (20k features) We compute features specific to the search space visited. We measure the percentage of consumption in each form x, y, and z. We also have features to capture the last operation taken, thus providing a first-order Markovian information. We also compute the total number of consecutive shuffling actions (Y or Z) taken so far. This feature might help the learning mechanism to favor a complementarity operation if too many shuffling operations took place. We also have features that record the value of each index (we have a binary feature for each possible value). On top of this, we also compute a number of binary features for capturing whether specific configurations of symbols have been observed in the search space visited when enforcing the production of the reference solution to an equation (forced-decoding). We compute the following features:

- a binary feature for each possible 3-tuple $(x[i], y[j], z[k])$,
- a binary feature for each bigram at the end of the shuffle s,
- a binary feature for each bigram at the end of the prefix p.

The description of those features is not intended for others to reproduce our experiments precisely, but instead to provide the intuition behind each feature family. We have not conducted a systematic analysis of the usefulness of each feature, but have noticed that removing one family of features leads invariably to a significant loss in performance.

4 Datasets

4.1 Word Equations

In [17], the authors designed a comprehensive task for evaluating the propension of word embeddings to preserve analogical relations. It contains

msr	# of analogies: 3664	word's avr. length: 6
JJ-JJR	[high : higher :: wild : wilder]	
JJR-JJ	[greater : greatest :: earlier : earliest]	
JJS-JJ	[low : lowest :: short : shortest]	
NN-NNPOS	[problem : problems :: program : programs]	
VB-VBP	[take : takes :: run : runs]	
VB-VBD	[prevent : prevented :: consider : considered]	
NNPOS-NN	[days : day :: citizens : citizen]	
VBZ-VBD	[believes : believed :: likes : liked]	

google		# of analogies: 4977	word's avr. length: 7
adjective-adverbe	ADJ-ADV	[amazing : amazingly :: serious : seriously]	
opposite	OPP	[certain : uncertain :: competitive : uncompetitive]	
comparative	COMP	[fast : faster :: bright : brighter]	
superlative	SUP	[warm : warmest :: strange : strangest]	
present-participle	PP	[code : coding :: dance : dancing]	
nationality-adverb	NAT	[Australia : Australian :: Croatia : Croatian]	
past-tense	PAST	[decreasing : decreased :: listening : listened]	
plural	PLUR	[eye : eyes :: donkey : donkeys]	
plural-verbs	PL-VB	[listen : listens :: eat : eats]	

Fig. 5. Main characteristics of the msr and the google datasets, and examples of formal analogies of each category.

19 544 analogies, categorized into 14 categories, including *capital-world* (*e.g.*, [*Dublin* : *Ireland* :: *Jakarta* : *Indonesia*]). Roughly 55% of those analogies are actually syntactic ones that capture various morphological phenomena in English (see Fig. 5). Many of those syntactic analogies, are actually not formal ones. For example, [*rare* : *rarely* :: *happy* : *happily*] is not formal according to the definition of Yvon et al. [22] we use in this study,[3] because of the commutation of y in *happy* into i in the adverbial form. Therefore, we removed non formal analogies to build a corpus of 4977 analogies named google hereafter. We also used the msr dataset of 8k syntactic analogies[4], 3664 of which being formal ones.

Examples of analogies of both datasets are reported in Fig. 5. Most analogies involve short word forms (6 to 7 characters on average) and are actually rather simple to solve (but see Sect. 5). We strengthen that because we filtered out all non formal analogies, we place ourselves in an optimistic scenario where the expected solution to an equation is reachable by our solvers, which only makes senses as a case study. We come back to this point later on.

---

[3] The definition immediately follows from Theorem 1.
[4] http://www.marekrei.com/blog/linguistic-regularities-word-representations/.

4.2   Phrasal Analogies

Identifying formal analogies on phrases is actually not the kind of task a human would be willing to do extensively and systematically. One might easily produce analogies such as [*She loves Paul* : *He loves Paul* :: *She likes Mark* : *He likes Mark*], but it would rapidly become a daunting task to collect representative analogies, that is, analogies that capture a rich set of linguistic phenomena (such as the fact that the 3rd person of a verb at the present tense should end with a *s* in the example). Therefore, we resorted to an automatic procedure to acquire analogies.

For this, we first trained a phrase-based machine translation (SMT) system on the English-Spanish Europarl corpus,[5] using the Moses toolkit [8]. We collected millions of phrase associations such as those in Fig. 6, and filtered in, those with a good association score ($prob \geq 0.1$). A subset of phrase pairs was elected as a reference $\mathcal{R}$, the remaining pairs being kept as a translation memory $\mathcal{M}$. Then, we applied an analogical learning translation device very similar to the one described in [13] for translating Spanish phrases of pairs $(u, u') \in \mathcal{R}$ into English. For a given form to translate, u, this system identifies $(x, x'), (y, y'), (z, z') \in \mathcal{M}$ such that $[x : y :: t: u]$, and solves equations $[x' : y' :: z': ?]$. Whenever a solution to such an equation produces u', we consider $[x' : y' :: z': u']$ a useful analogie. We could have identified analogies in the English part directly, but we would have ended up with many *spurious* analogies, that is, true formal analogies that are simply fortuitous as [*croyons* : *créons* :: *montroyal* : *montreal*]. The assumption here is that while a spurious source analogy might be identified, it is very unlikely that its projection into the target language (English) leads to an equation for which the reference translation is a solution.

```
a actualizar los acuerdos ||| to update the agreements ||| 1 0.00474847
a cambiar la base ||| to change the basis ||| 0.5 0.0035545
basado en el trabajo de ||| based on the efforts of ||| 1 2.02579e-05
```

Fig. 6. Phrases pairs collected by an SMT engine trained on the Spanish-English Europarl corpus. The format shows the source phrase (Spanish), the target phrase (English) and the first two scores estimating their likelihood of being in translation relation.

By applying this procedure, we collected many analogies: 10 000 of them where elected `simple` (we kept 1000 for training purposes, and the remaining ones for testing). For the remaining analogies, we solved with the `alea` solver the equations built by removing the forth form. We then split equations according to the rank of the reference translation (the forth term) among the ranked list of solutions proposed. We collected 400 analogies ranking in each of the following intervals : [1–5], [6–10], [11–20], [21–50] and [51–100], leading to a total of 2000 analogies (1000 for training, 1000 for testing). We qualify this dataset as `hard`

---

[5] http://statmt.org.

simple	phrase's avr. length: 16

▷   [*international investigation   :   international democracy   ::*
an international investigation : an international democracy]
▷   [*young girls   :   training of young girls   ::   young girls and   :*
training of young girls and]
▷   [*political situation is viable   :   political situation is still   ::*
the political situation is viable : the political situation is still]

hard	phrase's avr. length: 17

▷ [*adopted recently by   :   recently adopted by   ::   study published recently by   :*
study recently published by]
▷ [*competition and the   :   competition and against   ::   competition and of the   :*
of competition and against]
▷ [*their governments to   :   their governments are   ::   their governments and to   :*
and their governments are]

Fig. 7. Examples of phrasal analogies automatically identified.

in the sequel. As a matter of fact, 80% of analogies in the `simple` dataset have a degree[6] of 2 or 3, while this rate is only 20% for the `hard` dataset.

5   Experiments

5.1   Metrics

Each solver produced solutions to the equations we built by removing the last form of each analogy in the datasets presented in the previous section. We evaluated their *accuracy* at identifying this form in first position. Since some variants may fail to retrieve a solution (search failure), we also report — when pertinent — *silence* as the ratio of test equations for which no solution is being generated.

5.2   Word Equations

In this experiment, we take benefits of the analogies of the `google` and `msr` datasets. We trained on one corpus, and tested on the other. Because both `alea` and our structured solvers require a metaparameter (ρ or the beam size), we report in Fig. 8 the performance of different variants as a function of this metaparameter (that we varied from 1 to 20). We did not use the η metaparameter in this experiment, since equations involve short enough forms (6 characters on average), leading to search spaces manageable to visit entirely.

We observe that for both solvers, larger values of the metaparameter are preferable. For a value of 20, all solvers respond perfectly to all equations. Still, we observe that learning to solve equations leads to better accuracy overall, especially for low values of the metaparameter. That formal solvers produce the

---

[6] The degree of an analogy roughly correlates with the number of commutations among strings involved; the higher the degree, the harder it is to solve the analogy.

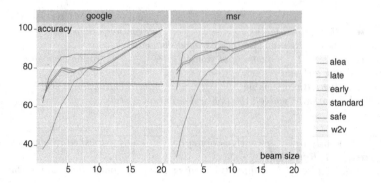

Fig. 8. Accuracy on `google` and `msr`, as a function of the beam size (or ρ for `alea`).

expected solution to all (formal) equations in the first place confirms that those equations are indeed very simple. Actually, most of them involve simple prefix-ation/suffixation operations (see Fig. 5). It is worth pointing that the `word2vec` solver is registering an accuracy of 78% and 71% on `msr` and `google` respectively. This is not a bad level of performance considering that the embeddings were not trained to capture such an information. But it also indicates that `alea` and the structured solvers are actually doing very well. Recall however, that we only con-sider formal equations here, which solutions are reachable by our solvers, while non formal ones are not. Last, we observe that solving the `msr` equations when training on the `google` analogies leads to slightly better results overall.

Figure 9 compares the accuracy of the `early` and the `word2vec` solvers on each category of equations for both datasets. The former solver systematically outperforms the latter, especially for a few categories such as NN-NNPOS in the `msr` dataset or ADJ-ADV in the `google` one. There are mainly two reasons for this. First, most nouns in English can be verbs as well, but each form of the vocabulary receives only one embedding, leading to some errors. Second, `word2vec` very often outputs terms that are semantically related to the solution expected. For instance, it produces the form *fantastic* to the equation [*cold* : *colder* :: *great* : *?*].

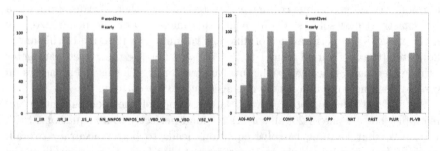

Fig. 9. Accuracy of the `word2vec` and the `early` solvers on formal analogies in the `msr` (left part) and the `google` (right part) datasets, detailed by categories of equations.

Table 1. Accuracy of different solvers on the full `google` and `msr` datasets. The last line is the best performance reported by the authors of [16].

	msr	google
word2vec	67%	63%
early+word2vec	72%	71%
Levy et al. 2015	72.9%	75.8%

To put those figures in perspective, we report in Table 1 the performance of a solver that would consider the output of the structured perceptron (the `early` variant) whenever we face an equation that has a formal solution, and the output of `word2vec` otherwise. Since in practice, we cannot know whether an equation admits a formal solution, this simulation only provides a point of comparison with other works that report the performance of embedding-based approaches on the full data sets. This is for instance the case of the work of [16] where Levy et al. compare many variants of distributional approaches, the best performing one recording a slightly better accuracy than our combination (third line of Table 1). That we compare to state-of-the-art results without much adjustments suggests that our structured solver is indeed very apt at solving formal equations.

5.3   Phrasal Equations

We trained variants of the structured perceptron using a beam size of 100, and a value of the metaparameter η of 7. Since a phrase has an average of 16 symbols, it roughly means that we enforce the solver to consume no more of 20% of the shuffle of y and z before a complementary operation (X) takes place. While we initially trained our solver on the training set the most similar to the test material, we also considered variants training of `hard` and testing on `simple`, or the reverse. Of course, we took care at construction time to ensure no overlap between training and test sets (see Sect. 4). Those configurations are compared to the `alea` solver where ρ was set to 1000, a conservative setting that leads the solver to always propose a solution. Results are presented in Table 2.

On the `simple` test set, only one configuration managed to outperform `alea`: equations are easier to solve than those of the `hard` test set, and the latter solver already achieves a decent job. Still the `early` variant managed to outperform `alea`, which is encouraging. It is also clear that it is far much preferable to train our models on `simple`. We observe that at best, we could solve correctly at rank 1 only 38% of the equations of the `simple` test set: obviously, solving equations on longer sequences is more challenging, than solving equations on words, as typically done in the literature. This is also consistent with [7] in which the authors trained a neural network for solving analogies, but reported a failure of their model to solve analogies involving long forms.

On the `hard` test set, the structured solvers deliver a much better accuracy than the `alea` solver ($\rho = 1000$) which accuracy plateaus at 18%. Expectedly, the

Table 2. Accuracy and silence rate (in parenthesis) of different configurations of structured solvers ($\eta = 7$) compared to the `alea` solver ($\rho = 1000$) on phrasal equations. Structured solvers have been trained on 10 epochs.

Test	simple		hard	
Train	simple	hard	simple	hard
standard	30.6 (7)	30.1 (10)	**19.6** (17)	**24.0** (56)
early	**38.4** (8)	27.6 (10)	**26.0** (6)	**22.9** (7)
late	26.9 (9)	20.3 (11)	**18.9** (9)	**20.1** (6.7)
safe	25.4 (8)	25.6 (13)	14.6 (18.7)	**21.0** (56)
alea	33 (0)		18 (0)	

accuracy of solvers on `hard` is much lower than the one measured on `simple`. We also observe that it is overall preferable to train our solvers on `hard`.

That the best configurations overall are recorded when training on data sets similar (in terms of difficulty) to the test material is disappointing, although we anticipated it. This means in practice that care must be taken to prepare an adequate training set. Understanding good practices for doing so is an open issue.

Figure 10 investigates the impact of the metaparameter η and the number of epochs used to train the solver. Four configurations for each variant we considered are evaluated on the `hard` test set. Training over 10 epochs (as done for the results reported in Table 2) is expectedly preferable to training only on one. Increasing the value of η seems to impact performance positively, but increases the size of the search space, leading to higher time response. It seems overall that `early` and `standard` are the best variants of the structured perceptron,

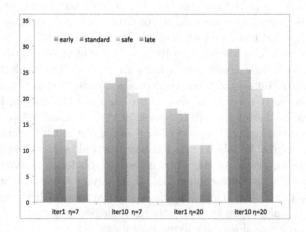

Fig. 10. Accuracy on the `hard` test set of different solvers after 1 and 10 epochs, and for 2 values of the metaparameter η.

at least on **hard**. The silence rate of the **standard** approach is very high and around 50%. This suggests that our pruning strategy eliminates from the search space hypotheses that should not, which is a problem. The silence rate of the **easy** variant is however much lower: 7% for $\eta = 7$, and 13% for $\eta = 20$. That it is higher for largest values of η simply suggests that there is an interplay between metaparameters that control the search.

6 Discussion

We have presented experiments for learning to solve an analogical equation thanks to structured learning. On formal word equations, our trained solvers achieve perfect performance, as does the **alea** solver of [11]. On phrase equations, the performance of our learning mechanism is lower, but still superior to the **alea** solver. Our approach requires example analogies for training. Therefore we proposed a methodology for acquiring those analogies from a parallel corpus, without supervision, but leveraging a parallel corpus and a statistical phrase-based translation model.

We are currently investigating the impact of training formal solvers on more epochs. We also plan to investigate more systematically the interplay between some metaparameters, as well as the usefulness of the all the features we considered in this work. Preliminary results indicate that better performance can be obtained with less features. Last, we must compare our approach to the one of [7]: while we do report higher results on equations involving long strings, an end-to-end comparison is required.

Acknowledgments. This work has been partly funded by the Natural Sciences and Engineering Research Council of Canada. We thank reviewers for their constructive comments.

References

1. Bayoudh, S., Mouchère, H., Miclet, L., Anquetil, E.: Learning a classifier with very few examples: analogy based and knowledge based generation of new examples for character recognition. In: Kok, J.N., Koronacki, J., Mantaras, R.L., Matwin, S., Mladenič, D., Skowron, A. (eds.) ECML 2007. LNCS (LNAI), vol. 4701, pp. 527–534. Springer, Heidelberg (2007). https://doi.org/10.1007/978-3-540-74958-5_49
2. Ben Hassena, A.: Apprentissage analogique par analogie de structures d'arbres. Ph.D. thesis, Univ. de Rennes I, France (2011)
3. Collins, M.: Discriminative training methods for hidden markov models: theory and experiments with perceptron algorithms. In: EMNLP, pp. 1–8 (2002)
4. Collins, M., Roark, B.: Incremental parsing with the perceptron algorithm. In: 42nd ACL (2004)
5. Dandapat, S., Morrissey, S., Naskar, S.K., Somers, H.: Mitigating problems in analogy-based EBMT with SMT and vice versa: a case study with named entity transliteration. In: PACLIC, Sendai, Japan (2010)
6. Huang, L., Fayong, S., Guo, Y.: Structured perceptron with inexact search. In: NAACL, pp. 142–151 (2012)

7. Kaveeta, V., Lepage, Y.: Solving analogical equations between strings of symbols using neural networks. In: Workshop on Computational Analogy at ICCBR 2016, pp. 67–76 (2016)

8. Koehn, P., et al.: Moses: open source toolkit for statistical machine translation. In: 45th ACL, pp. 177–180 (2007). Interactive Poster and Demonstration Sessions

9. Langlais, P.: Mapping source to target strings without alignment by analogical learning: a case study with transliteration. In: 51st ACL, pp. 684–689 (2013)

10. Langlais, P., Patry, A.: Translating unknown words by analogical learning. In: EMNLP, Prague, Czech Republic, pp. 877–886 (2007)

11. Langlais, P., Yvon, F., Zweigenbaum, P.: Improvements in analogical learning: application to translating multi-terms of the medical domain. In: 12th EACL, Athens, pp. 487–495 (2009)

12. Lepage, Y.: Solving analogies on words: an algorithm. In: COLING-ACL, Montreal, Canada, pp. 728–733 (1998)

13. Lepage, Y., Denoual, E.: Purest ever example-based machine translation: detailed presentation and assesment. Mach. Trans. **19**, 25–252 (2005)

14. Lepage, Y., Shin-ichi, A.: Saussurian analogy: a theoretical account and its application. In: 7th COLING, pp. 717–722 (1996)

15. Letard, V., Illouz, G., Rosset, S.: Reducing noise sensitivity of formal analogical reasoning applied to language transfer. In: Workshop on Computational Analogy at ICCBR 2016, pp. 87–97 (2016)

16. Levy, O., Goldberg, Y., Dagan, I.: Improving distributional similarity with lessons learned from word embeddings. Trans. Assoc. Comput. Linguist. **3**, 211–225 (2015)

17. Mikolov, T., Chen, K., Corrado, G., Dean, J.: Efficient estimation of word representations in vector space. CoRR abs/1301.3781 (2013)

18. Mikolov, T., Sutskever, I., Chen, K., Corrado, G., Dean, J.: Distributed representations of words and phrases and their compositionality. In: 26th NIPS, pp. 3111–3119 (2013)

19. Stroppa, N., Yvon, F.: An analogical learner for morphological analysis. In: 9th CONLL, Ann Arbor, USA, pp. 120–127 (2005)

20. Yang, W., Lepage, Y.: Inflating a small parallel corpus into a large quasi-parallel corpus using monolingual data for Chinese-Japanese machine translation. J. Inf. Process. (Information Processing Society of Japan) (2017)

21. Yvon, F.: Paradigmatic cascades: a linguistically sound model of pronunciation by analogy. In: 35th ACL, pp. 429–435 (1997)

22. Yvon, F., Stroppa, N., Delhay, A., Miclet, L.: Solving analogies on words. Technical report. D005, École Nationale Supérieure des Télécommuncations, Paris, France (2004)

Author Index

Printed in the United States
By Bookmasters